PERSPE

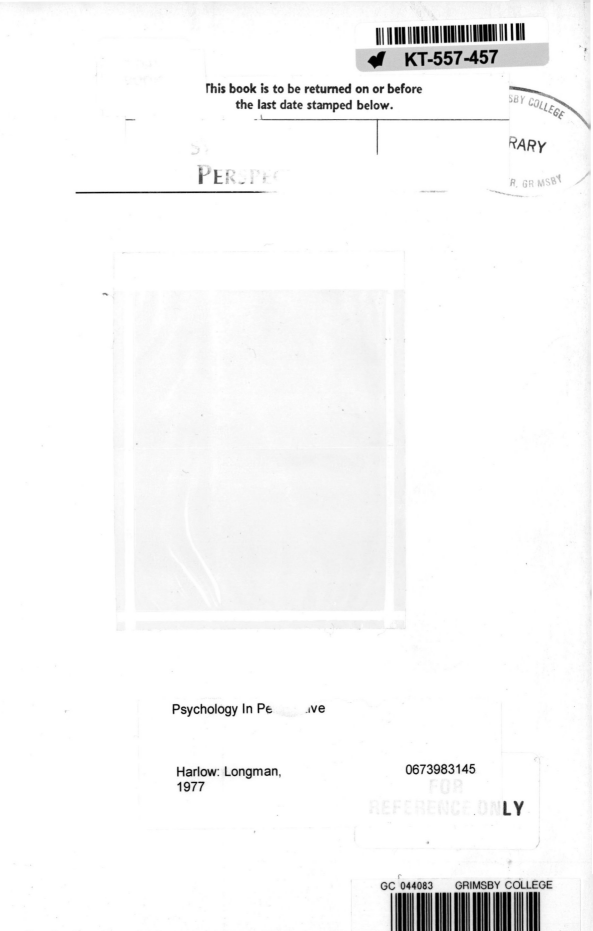

Psychology In Pe   ive

Harlow: Longman,   0673983145
1977

PSYCHOLOGY IN PERSPECTIVE

Second Edition

CAROL TAVRIS

CAROLE WADE
Dominican College of San Rafael

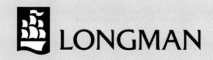 LONGMAN

An imprint of Addison Wesley Longman, Inc.

New York • Reading, Massachusetts • Menlo Park, California • Harlow, England
Don Mills, Ontario • Sydney • Mexico City • Madrid • Amsterdam

Acquisitions Editor: Rebecca Dudley
Developmental Editor: Melissa Mashburn
Project Editor: Donna DeBenedictis
Supplements Editor: Donna Campion
Text and Cover Designer: Alice Fernandes-Brown
Cover Illustration: John Odam
Text Art: Fineline Inc. and Jim Sullivan
Part-opening Art: Michael Beeler
Photo Researcher: Sandy Schneider
Electronic Production Manager: Alexandra Odulak
Desktop Technical Manager: Heather A. Peres
Manufacturing Manager: Hilda Koparanian
Electronic Page Makeup: Heather A. Peres
Printer and Binder: RR Donnelley & Sons Company
Cover Printer: The Lehigh Press, Inc.

For permission to use copyrighted material, grateful acknowledgment is made to the copyright holders on pp. C-1–C-2 which are hereby made part of this copyright page.

Library of Congress Cataloging-in-Publication Data

Tavris, Carol.
    Psychology in perspective / Carol Tavris, Carole Wade. — 2nd ed.
       p. cm.
    Includes bibliographical references and index.
    ISBN 0-673-98314-5
    1. Psychology.   I. Wade, Carole.   II. Title.
  BF121.T33 1996
   150–dc20   96-28865
                                               CIP

ISBN 0-673-98314-5

2345678910—DOW—999897

BRIEF CONTENTS

DETAILED CONTENTS

TO THE INSTRUCTOR

*P*ut any group of introductory psychology teachers together, and you will hear a litany of familiar complaints:

- ✦ "I have only 10 [or 14, or 15] weeks to cover 18 topics. It's impossible."
- ✦ "I've deleted four chapters from my reading assignments, but I feel guilty about it."
- ✦ "Introductory psychology is supposed to be a smorgasbord, but my students are overwhelmed by the dozens of dishes. The meal has become indigestible."
- ✦ "My students complain that there's no 'big picture' in psychology. How can we bring some sort of order to our courses?"

Nearly all the introductory books on the market—our own text, *Psychology*, included—take a topical approach to psychology: a chapter on the brain, a chapter on emotions, a chapter on child development, and so forth. There is certainly a place for such encyclopedias of psychology; we're quite fond of ours! Yet for many teachers this conventional organization has grown increasingly problematic. As findings in psychology have burgeoned, and the number of specialty areas has grown as well, textbooks have had to become longer and longer.

And so we thought it was time for a reconceptualization of the introductory course and a true alternative to the traditional, topic-by-topic way of teaching it. Many scientists and educators agree. Several years ago, the American Association for the Advancement of Science launched Project 2061, an effort to determine the best ways of increasing scientific literacy. To this end, they commissioned the National Council on Science and Technology Education to survey hundreds of scientists, engineers, and educators and draw up a report of their recommendations. The result, *Science for All Americans*, calls on instructors to aim for *depth* rather than *breadth* in their introductory courses; to "reduce the sheer amount of material covered"; "to present the scientific endeavor as a social enterprise that strongly influences—and is influenced by—human thought and action"; and "to foster scientific ways of thinking" (AAAS Project 2061, 1989; for the report from the social and behavioral sciences panel, see Appley & Maher, 1989).

TEACHING FOR DEPTH

Psychology in Perspective represents our effort to meet this challenge. Typically, courses and textbooks are constructed around the question, "What do I want students to know about my field?" With the question phrased that way, the answer has to be "Everything!" None of us likes the idea of "leaving something out," especially if the introductory course is the only one a student might ever take. In this book, however, we accept the premise of Project 2061 and ask a different question: "What should an educated citizen know about psychology?" With the question phrased that way, "Everything!" is no longer such a useful answer. For one thing, students can't remember everything. For another, specific findings change yearly, and in some areas (such as genetics and memory) faster than that. So we asked ourselves what kind of framework we could provide students that would help them evaluate the psychological findings and claims they will encounter when they leave the classroom. What, for example, should students know about genetics in particular, and biological approaches to behavior in general, that will help them assess someone's claim to have found "the" gene for aggression or homosexuality?

To teach for depth rather than breadth, and for ideas rather than facts alone, we have organized material not by topics or psychological specialties but by what we regard as the five major perspectives in the field: biological, cognitive, learning, sociocultural, and psychodynamic. Our objective is to provide a true introduction to how researchers in each perspective go about their business—the kinds of questions they ask, the methods they use, the assumptions they make, and their major findings. We have included many classic studies as well as groundbreaking new ones, but we do not attempt to be encyclopedic; we are trying to show students the different ways of "doing" psychology. We do not wish to imply that every perspective is monolithic; we discuss many conflicting views and debates within each field. But we also show that the perspectives do differ from one another in certain key assumptions researchers make about human behavior and human "nature," and in the methods they use to study them.

Writing a book for depth of concept rather than breadth of coverage means, we realize, that many instructors will find some of their favorite studies or even topics omitted entirely. Nevertheless, most of the topics of introductory psychology are in this book, although sometimes in an unfamiliar place. Therefore we encourage instructors to review the table of contents and look up topics in the index before becoming alarmed that their favorite subject is missing. For instance, subjects that would ordinarily be in a traditional child-development chapter have been broken up: Piaget and the development of reasoning abilities are in the cognitive perspective (Chapter 9); moral reasoning and the internalization of moral standards are topics we always thought appropriate for a cognitive social-learning analysis (Chapter 7); human attachment needs, starting with the infant's innate need for contact comfort and what John Bowlby called a "secure base," are in the biological perspective (Chapter 3). Similarly, although there is no chapter on psychotherapy, each evaluation includes a discussion of how that particular perspective has contributed to the treatment of mental disorder: the biological contribution to drug treatments (Chapter 5); learning theory's contribution to behavior therapy (Chapter 8); the contribution of cognitive findings to cognitive therapy (Chapter 11); the social and cultural contributions to family and systems therapies (Chapter 14); and of course the psychodynamic contribution to psychoanalysis and other depth therapies (Chapter 16, where we also assess the research on the effectiveness and limitations of all kinds of therapy). And disorders typically covered in an abnormal psychology chapter, such as depression, schizophrenia, anxiety, antisocial personality disorder, agoraphobia, and dissociative personality disorder ("multiple personality"), are discussed in various places in this text.

CONFRONTING THE CONTROVERSIES

Psychology in Perspective differs from traditional textbooks in yet another way. We want students to understand and appreciate the real debates and controversies within psychology—the ones psychologists talk about all the time but don't always discuss with their students. For example, the gap between research psychologists and certain psychotherapists is widening, as the split between the clinical and research constituencies of the American Psychological Association dramatically illustrates. Many researchers no longer even consider themselves "psychologists," preferring such labels as "cognitive scientist," "neuroscientist," and the like. This book candidly discusses this split—its origins, the reasons for it, and the consequences for the public (see especially Chapter 1 and Chapter 16, "Evaluating the Psychodynamic Perspective").

Further, each unit concludes with an **evaluation chapter,** in which we discuss what that perspective contributes to the understanding of behavior; its applications to public policy; its contributions to treating mental disorders; and some of the social and political issues it raises. These evaluation chapters are not summaries. They are a unique feature, to us the heart of the book. They represent our effort to tell students not only what psychology has contributed to human welfare, but also about the difficulties of applying research and the potential for misusing it. Each evaluation also cautions against the temptation to reduce behavior to only one level of explanation. Most people are familiar with the appeal of biological reductionism, but we also examine environmental reductionism ("With the right environment, anyone can become anything"), cognitive reductionism ("The mind can control everything"), sociocultural reductionism and relativism ("My culture or The System made me do it"), and psychodynamic reductionism ("Psychic reality is all that matters").

PUTTING THE PERSPECTIVES TOGETHER

In the final chapter, we offer an alternative to reductionism, showing how research from all five perspectives might be applied to understanding a complex issue of great interest to students: drug use and abuse. We know that many other issues lend themselves to a multi-perspective analysis and would make excellent assignments for term papers, including, just for starters, musical ability, emotional experience, sexual behavior, and eating habits.

Naturally, we recognize that many researchers in psychology travel across perspectives; for example, most psychologists who study emotion are well aware that emotion involves physiology, learning, cognition, culture, and unconscious processes. But, in practice, most psychologists do research from the vantage point of the perspective in which they were trained—biopsychologists study the physiology of emotion, social psychologists study the social construction and display of emotion, cognitive psychologists study how attributions create emotions, and so forth.

We learned quickly enough from some of our reviewers how attached psychologists can be to their favored perspective! One reviewer thought that we weren't making it clear enough that biology is the most important one because it underlies all the others. One thought that we should have begun with the sociocultural perspective because it influences all the others. One thought that we should have begun with learning because the laws of classical and operant conditioning are fundamental . . . well, you get the idea. And, reflecting the anomalous position of psychoanalysis in a field otherwise devoted to the scientific method, almost everyone had questions about our treatment of the psychodynamic perspective, ranging from why we treated it so kindly to why we treated it so harshly to why we included it at all. Of course, our goal is not to be "kind" or "harsh" but to show students *how researchers within each perspective see the world*—and then, in the evaluations, to examine the contributions, limitations, and outright misuses of that worldview.

WHAT'S NEW IN THE SECOND EDITION

In response to suggestions and reactions from reviewers and adopters of the first edition of *Psychology in Perspective,* we have made some constructive changes:

✦ **A NEW DESIGN, WITH THE ADDITION OF COLOR,** which makes the book more inviting and readable. We have also added more photographs, charts, and cartoons throughout the book, as many people requested—making sure that each illustration makes a pedagogical point and is not simply there as "filler."

✦ **MORE PEDAGOGICAL HELP FOR STUDENTS.** As before, we include a *running glossary,* which defines boldfaced terms on the pages where they occur for handy reference and study. But this time the chapter *summaries* and *key terms,* formerly in an appendix at the back of the book, follow at the end of each chapter, where students will find them more easily.

In addition, each chapter now contains several self-tests, called *What Do You Know?,* which encourage students to check their progress and to go back and review if necessary. These questions do more than just test for memorization of definitions; they tell students whether they comprehend the issues. We have varied the formats and included entertaining examples to motivate students to test themselves. Many of these self-tests also include critical-thinking items, identified by a symbol such as the one in the margin. These items invite the student to reflect on the implications of findings and consider how psychological principles might illuminate real-life issues. Although we offer some possible responses to such questions, most of them do not have a single correct answer, and students may have valid, well-reasoned answers that differ from our own.

✦ CHAPTER NUMBERS FOR THE PERSPECTIVE EVALUATIONS, which were previously unnumbered. This edition doesn't have more chapters than the first; it's just that all chapters are numbered this time!

✦ UPDATED RESEARCH. We have clarified our discussion of the growing new area of evolutionary psychology, for example, and expanded the discussion of genetics to include some of the latest findings in this burgeoning field (Chapter 3); added more findings from the exciting work on memory, particularly as they apply to the debate about children's testimony (Chapter 11) and repressed memories of sexual abuse (Chapter 16); added a discussion of humanistic psychology at the end of Chapter 15, as another approach to the "inner psychological life"; expanded our assessment of the effectiveness of all psychotherapies, as well as reasons for the scientist–practitioner gap (Chapter 16); and added new research on the nature and meanings of prejudice and efforts to reduce it (Chapter 14).

SUPPLEMENTS

Psychology in Perspective can be used on its own, or it can serve as a core book together with additional materials. Longman has provided a comprehensive supplements package coordinated by Donna Campion:

For the Instructor

✦ THE INSTRUCTOR'S RESOURCE MANUAL (ISBN 0-673-97811-7), written by Diane Addie of York University, anticipates concerns that teachers may have when organizing their course in terms of perspectives rather than topics. The Instructor's Resource Manual includes a sample course syllabus, chapter summaries and outlines, and, for each chapter, teaching suggestions, classroom activities, discussion questions, suggested readings, and listings of films/videos. This manual also contains twenty transparency masters.

✦ THE TEST BANK (ISBN 0-673-97815-X), prepared by William H. Calhoun of the University of Tennessee, Knoxville, contains approximately 2,000 multiple-choice, true-false, matching, short-answer, and essay questions. Each item is referenced by page, topic, and the skill it addresses (conceptual, factual, or applied). Answers are supplied.

✦ THE TESTMASTER COMPUTERIZED TESTING SYSTEM is a flexible, easy-to-master computerized test bank that includes all the test items in the Test Item File. The TestMaster Software allows you to edit existing questions and add your own items. Tests can be printed in several different formats and can include figures such as graphs and tables. TestMaster is available for IBM and IBM-compatible computers (ISBN 0-673-97816-8) and Macintosh computers (ISBN 0-673-97817-6).

✦ **TRANSPARENCIES, ELECTRONIC TRANSPARENCIES, VIDEOTAPES, LASERDISCS, AND OTHER ANCILLARY ITEMS** to enhance your classroom discussions and lectures are also available from Longman. Please contact your local sales representative for more information.

For the Student

✦ **THE STUDENT RESOURCE MANUAL** (ISBN 0-673-98420-6), written by Nancy Gussett of Baldwin-Wallace College, is designed to reinforce the text by providing students with a complete array of learning tools and study aids. It begins with a chapter on how to study, and it contains chapter summaries, fill-in-the-blank chapter outlines, practice tests, answer keys, learning objectives, key terms with definitions, and suggested readings, audiovisuals, and research projects.

✦ **THE SUPERSHELL COMPUTERIZED TUTORIAL,** an interactive program, was written by Carolyn Meyer of Lake Sumter Community College. It helps students learn major facts and concepts through drill, practice exercises, and diagnostic feedback. Supershell provides immediate correct answers and the page numbers in the text where the material is discussed. If a student misses a question, it will later reappear. A running score summarizing the student's performance appears on the screen throughout the session. This tutorial is available for IBM and IBM-compatible computers (ISBN 0-673-97813-3) as well as Macintosh computers (ISBN 0-673-97814-1). Supershell is available free to instructors or can be packaged with the book for students at a nominal cost.

ACKNOWLEDGMENTS

Our many reviewers—specialists, generalists, and phone survey respondents—were invaluable to the writing of both editions of *Psychology in Perspective*. Their advice, their attention to detail, and their approval of our departures from convention were enormously helpful both as moral support and as constructive criticism. We thank them all:

SPECIALIST REVIEWERS

Overall manuscript

> *Florence L. Denmark, Pace University*
> *Roy S. Malpass, University of Texas at El Paso*

Biological perspective

> *William Byne, The Albert Einstein College of Medicine*
> *Ruth Hubbard, Harvard University*
> *Richard F. Thompson, University of Southern California*

Learning perspective

Albert Bandura, Stanford University
Beverly I. Fagot, University of Oregon, Eugene

Cognitive perspective

Karen S. Kitchener, University of Denver
Keith E. Stanovich, The Ontario Institute for Studies in Education

Sociocultural perspective

Halford H. Fairchild, Pitzer College
Walter J. Lonner, Western Washington University
Steven R. López, University of California, Los Angeles

Psychodynamic perspective

Sarah Cirese, College of Marin
Gail Hornstein, Mount Holyoke College
Hans H. Strupp, Vanderbilt University

GENERALIST REVIEWERS

Emir Andrews, Memorial University of Newfoundland
James R. Antes, University of North Dakota
Susan L. Boatright-Horowitz, University of Rhode Island
Karen Christoff, University of Mississippi
Patricia G. Devine, University of Wisconsin, Madison
Thomas G. Fikes, University of Puget Sound
Anne L. Law, Rider University
Douglas Leber, University of Denver
Vira Lozano, College of the Sequoias
Vance Maloney, Taylor University
Linda Mealey, University of Queensland
Steven E. Meier, University of Idaho
Timothy E. Moore, Glendon College, York University
John B. Nezlek, College of William and Mary
Robert Patterson, Washington State University
Gordon Pitz, Southern Illinois University at Carbondale
Debra Ann Poole, Central Michigan University
Matthew J. Sharps, California State University, Fresno
Ray H. Starr, Jr., University of Maryland, Baltimore Campus
Steven A. Wygant, Brigham Young University

PHONE SURVEY RESPONDENTS

Patricia Barker, Schenectady County Community College
Steve R. Baumgardner, University of Wisconsin, Eau Claire

William H. Calhoun, University of Tennessee, Knoxville
Bonnie West Caruso, Los Angeles Valley College
Laura Craig-Bray, Merrimack College
Jacqueline Ernst, Manatee Community College
Karen E. Ford, Mesa State College
Mike Gardner, Los Angeles Valley College
Walter Griesinger, University of Cincinnati
Algea O. Harrison, Oakland University
Toby Klinger, Johnson County Community College
Kenneth McIntire, University of Wisconsin, Eau Claire
Richard Mascolo, El Camino College
Matthew Merrens, State Univesity of New York, Plattsburgh
Michael Nedelsky, Augustana College
Dennis R. Papini, Western Illinois University
Lawrence Shaffer, State University of New York, Plattsburgh
Debra Spear, South Dakota State University
Barbara Turpin, Southwest Missouri State University

The talented, creative editorial staff and production team who supported this project have become our friends as well as our colleagues. We offer special thanks to Melissa Mashburn, who shepherded both editions of this book from the start with such enthusiasm, good humor, hard work, and charm that we sometimes forgot she was working us to the bone; and heartfelt thanks as well to Rebecca Dudley, Donna Campion, Lisa Pinto, Priscilla McGeehon, and Mark Paluch, for the many sterling and imaginative contributions they made to this project. We owe special thanks to our indefatigable project editor, Donna DeBenedictis, who calmly, as the production hurricane swirls around her, gets everything done.

Our thanks to Design Manager Alice Fernandes-Brown for a great new design, giving the second edition a distinctive character and style that complements well the introduction of color and new pedagogical features. Her attention to detail clearly shows on every page. And warm thanks also to John Odam, for such a beautiful and inviting cover illustration.

Finally, we thank Ronan O'Casey and Howard Williams, who uncomplainingly supported us from start to finish, and who helped us meet our deadlines by providing ample amounts of coffee, food, humor, and love—the necessities of life.

This book has been a labor of love for us, and we hope that you will enjoy reading and using it. Because it is a departure from the conventional text, we particularly welcome your reactions, experiences using it, and suggestions for improvements or for teaching from it.

CAROL TAVRIS & CAROLE WADE

TO THE STUDENT

Our goal in writing this book is to encourage you to learn to think critically and imaginatively about a fabulous, complex subject: the human being. As you will see right away in Chapter 1, this is not going to be a book about psychobabble—all the psychological-sounding analysis you hear on talk shows or get from pop-psych books and self-appointed experts. We are going to give you the straight stuff about real psychology. We think it will surprise you.

This book is unconventional in another way, too. It is not only a book of answers; it is also, perhaps primarily, a book of questions. We have organized this text according to the five perspectives that psychologists use as they go about studying human beings: Some are mostly interested in biological contributions to behavior, others in environmental explanations, others in cultural influences, and so forth. In each section, we try to show you how psychologists in that perspective see the world, so that you will say, as they do, "Yes! Obviously, this approach makes the most sense!" But we do not stop there; we include a critical evaluation of the perspective—not only its contributions, but also its limitations and even misuses. The point of this assessment is not to cause you to throw up your hands and say, "Nothing is true! No one has the answers!" Rather, we want you to appreciate what some psychologists themselves do not—that all perspectives together are necessary to understand and appreciate the whole human being. We want you to learn to resist single, one-note explanations of anything.

We have done everything we can think of to make this subject as absorbing for you as it has always been for us. However, what you bring to this book is as important as what we have written. We can only be the pitchers; you're the ones at bat. The more actively you are involved with your own learning, the more successful the book and your course will be, and the more enjoyable, too.

In our years of teaching (and of having been students), we have found that certain study strategies can vastly improve learning. One key strategy is to make sure you are *reading actively,* not just nodding along saying "Hmmmm" to yourself. We have tried to write this book in a lively and interesting manner, but some of our own students said that they were occasionally deceived by the style—thinking they got the major points of a discussion when they actually had not. We therefore advise you to read a chapter through to get its overall content and message, but then reread it carefully, section by section. Instead of reading silently, *restate* what you have read in your own words at the end of each major section. Try to describe what you have learned to an interested friend or roommate—or perhaps a patient pet—and you will find out at once what you still don't understand. Some people find it helpful to write down the main points of each chapter on a piece of paper or on index cards, which can later be used in reviewing for exams.

To aid your learning, every chapter contains several self-tests, called *"What do You Know?"*, that permit you to test your understanding and retention of what you have just read and your ability to apply the material to examples. These quizzes are for your practical use and, we hope, for your enjoyment, too. When you can't answer a question, do not go on to the next section; pause right there, review what you have read, and try again. Some of these quizzes contain a *critical-thinking item,* denoted by a symbol such as the one in the margin. The answers we give for these items are only suggestions; feel free to come up with different ones. We think that if you take the time to respond thoughtfully to these special questions, you will learn more and become a more sophisticated user of psychology.

At the end of each chapter you will find two other important study aids: *summaries* of the highlights of the chapter and *key terms* (concepts and people) you need to know, including the pages on which they first appear. Either way, if you can define or identify each key term, the chances are good that you are mastering the material. The fact that we provide chapter summaries, by the way, doesn't mean you shouldn't write your own; some students find it very helpful to compare their summaries with ours.

There are some other features of this book you should know about. All important new terms are printed in **boldface** and are defined at the bottom of the pages on which they appear, which permits you to find them easily. A full *glossary* appears at the end of the book. Pronunciation guides are given for key terms and names that are often mispronounced.

You will notice that discussions of studies and theories are followed by one or more *citations* in parentheses, like this: (Smedley & Dooright, 1995). A citation tells the reader who the authors of the work are and when their paper or book was published. The full reference can then be looked up in the *bibliography* at the end of this book. Students often find citations useful, especially for locating material for term projects and reports.

At the back of the book you will also find an *author index* and a *subject index.* The author index lists the name of every author cited and the pages where the person's work is discussed. If you remember the name of a psychologist but you can't recall where he or she was mentioned, look up the name in the author index. The subject index provides a listing of all the major topics in the book. If you want to review material on, say, treatment of depression, which is discussed in various chapters, you can look up "depression" in the subject index.

We also recommend the *Student Resource Manual* which may be available at your bookstore. It will help you study and expand the information in this book, give you practice in taking tests, and help you review material for exams.

We have done our best to make your introduction to psychology a lively and provocative one. In the end, it is your efforts as much as ours that will determine whether you find psychology to be exciting or boring, and whether the field will matter in your own life. We welcome your ideas and reactions so that we will learn what works for you and what doesn't. In the meantime, welcome to psychology!

CAROL TAVRIS & CAROLE WADE

ABOUT THE AUTHORS

CAROL TAVRIS earned her Ph.D. in the interdisciplinary social psychology program at the University of Michigan, and ever since has sought to bring research from the many fields of psychology to the public. She is author of *The Mismeasure of Woman,* which won the 1992 Distinguished Media Contribution Award from the American Association for Applied and Preventive Psychology and the Heritage Publications Award from Division 35 of the American Psychological Association. Dr. Tavris is also the author of *Anger: The Misunderstood Emotion* and coauthor (with Carole Wade) of *Psychology; Critical and Creative Thinking: The Case of Love and War;* and *The Longest War: Sex Differences in Perspective.* She began her writing career at *Psychology Today* magazine and has gone on to write about psychological topics for a wide variety of magazines, journals, edited books, and newspapers, notably the *Los Angeles Times* and *The New York Times Book Review.* A highly regarded lecturer, she has given keynote addresses and workshops on, among other topics, critical thinking, anger, gender, and psychology and the media. She has taught in the psychology department at UCLA and at the Human Relations Center of the New School for Social Research in New York. Dr. Tavris is a Fellow of Divisions 1, 9, and 35 of the APA and a member of Division 8; a charter member and Fellow of the American Psychological Society; and a Fellow of the Committee for the Scientific Investigation of Claims of the Paranormal.

CAROLE WADE earned her Ph.D. in cognitive psychology at Stanford University. She began her academic career at the University of New Mexico (where she initiated a new course on gender roles); was professor of psychology for ten years at San Diego Mesa College; then taught at College of Marin; and currently teaches undergraduate courses in psychology at Dominican College of San Rafael. She is coauthor (with Carol Tavris) of *Psychology; Critical and Creative Thinking: The Case of Love and War;* and *The Longest War: Sex Differences in Perspective,* as well as coauthor (with Sarah Cirese) of *Human Sexuality.* A former associate editor of *Psychology Today*—where she met Dr. Tavris—Dr. Wade has a long-standing interest in making psychology accessible to students and the general public through lectures, workshops, general-interest articles, and the electronic media. For many years she has focused her efforts on the promotion of critical thinking skills. She is currently chair of the APA Board of Educational Affair's Task Force on Diversity Issues at the Pre-College and Undergraduate Levels of Education in Psychology. She is also a past chair of the APA's Public Information Committee and a past member of the APA's Committee on Undergraduate Education, and is active in APA's efforts to support undergraduate teaching. Dr. Wade is a Fellow of Divisions 1 and 2 and a member of Divisions 8, 9, and 35 of the APA, and is a charter member of the American Psychological Society.

PSYCHOLOGY IN PERSPECTIVE

PART I

INVITATION TO PSYCHOLOGY

The Blind Men and the Elephant

It was six men of Indostan
　　To learning much inclined,
Who went to see the elephant
　　(Though all of them were blind),
That each by observation
　　Might satisfy his mind.

The First approached the Elephant,
　　And, happening to fall
Against his broad and sturdy side,
　　At once began to bawl:
"God bless me! but the elephant
　　Is nothing but a wall!"

The Second, feeling of the tusk,
　　Cried, "Ho! what have we here
So very round and smooth and sharp?
　　To me 'tis mighty clear
This wonder of an Elephant
　　Is very like a spear!"

The Third approached the animal,
　　And, happening to take
The squirming trunk within his hands,
　　Thus boldly up and spake:
"I see," quoth he, "the elephant
　　Is very like a snake!"

The Fourth reached out his eager hand,
　　And felt about the knee:
"What most this wondrous beast is like
　　Is mighty plain," quoth he;

"'Tis clear enough the elephant
　　Is very like a tree."

The Fifth, who chanced to touch the ear,
　　Said, "E'en the blindest man
Can tell what this resembles most;
　　Deny the fact who can,
This marvel of an elephant
　　Is very like a fan!"

The Sixth no sooner had begun
　　About the beast to grope,
Than, seizing on the swinging tail
　　That fell within his scope,
"I see," quoth he, "the elephant
　　Is very like a rope!"

And so these men of Indostan
　　Disputed loud and long,
Each in his own opinion
　　Exceeding stiff and strong,
Though each was partly in the right,
　　And all were in the wrong!

So, oft in theologic wars
　　The disputants, I ween,
Rail on in utter ignorance
　　Of what each other mean,
And prate about an elephant
　　Not one of them has seen!

　　　　　　　　　　　　–John Godfrey Saxe

3

CHAPTER 1

Explaining Human Behavior

$\mathcal{W}$hat is psychology?

If you were to wander through the psychology section of your local bookstore (perhaps called "psychology and self-help" or "personal growth") you might come up with the following impressions:

- Psychology is all about psychotherapy and fixing yourself.

- Psychology is for helping people who suffer from syndromes and complexes, of which there seems to be one for every life experience—"The New Mother Syndrome," "The Superwoman Syndrome," "The Stress Syndrome," and, for men who fear commitment, "The 'Peter Pan' Syndrome" (which is hard on women who have a "Cinderella Complex").

- Psychology will help you cope with, or break away from, your parents, which you'll need to do because almost everyone has "toxic" parents and comes from a "dysfunctional" family. Those few parents who appear to be kind and loving are actually creating "emotional incest" by being too close to their children.

- Psychology is full of contradictory advice. You can find a book titled *Goodbye to Guilt* and also *What's So Bad About Guilt?* You can find *Getting the Love You Want* and also *Love Stinks.* You can *Learn to Love Again* as long as you don't join the *Women Who Love Too Much.* You can find books praising *The Art of Selfishness* and *The Art of Love.*

- Psychology can fix anything that ails you. It will tell you how to stop procrastinating, how to fix your relationships, how to make money, how to use your subconscious mind to cure your body, how to shape up your intuitive "right brain," how to recover from heartbreak, and how to think your way to a stress-free life.

The psychology that you are about to study bears very little relation to most of the titles you see in bookstores. It is more complex, more informative, and, we think, far more helpful. Psychologists take as their subject the entire spectrum of brave and cowardly, intelligent and foolish, beautiful and brutish things that human beings do. Their aim is to examine and explain how human beings—and other animals, too—learn, remember, solve problems, perceive, feel, and get along with others. Some psychologists study mental disorders, abnormal behavior, and personal problems, but not all of them do. Psychologists are just as likely to focus on experiences as universal and ordinary as rearing children, remembering a shopping list, daydreaming, gossiping, making love, and making a living.

Modern **psychology** is *the scientific study of behavior and mental processes and how they are affected by an organism's physical state, mental state, and external environment.* We realize that this definition of psychology is a little like defining a car as "a vehicle for transporting people from one place to another." Such a definition is accurate as far as it goes, but it doesn't tell you what a car looks like, how a car differs from a train or a bus, how a Ford differs from a Ferrari, or how a catalytic converter works. Similarly, to get a clear picture of what psychology is, you will need to know more about its methods, its findings, and its ways of interpreting information. The methods and approaches of psychology distinguish this field from other academic attempts to understand behavior— for example, through literature, philosophy, or history. And they distinguish psychology from the popular but nonscientific ideas that get media attention on such scholarly shows as *Geraldo* and *Oprah*.

PSEUDOSCIENCE AND PSYCHOBABBLE

The public's appetite for psychological information has created a huge market for what R. D. Rosen (1977) called "psychobabble"—pseudoscience and quackery covered by a veneer of psychological language. The particular examples that Rosen analyzed included various group encounters designed to transform a person's rotten life in one weekend; "primal scream therapy," in which people are supposed to link their current unhappiness to the trauma of being born (this therapy still exists); and "Theta," based on "rebirthing," in which people attempted to be "born anew" and thereby find peace, prosperity, and wisdom. Theta's leader asserted that "no one dies if they don't want to"—certainly the ultimate belief in mind over matter!

The particular programs and groups based on psychobabble change their names and leaders from year to year, but the common elements remain. All promise quick fixes for emotional problems. All rely on vaguely psychological and scientific-sounding language, such as "repression of feelings," "getting in touch with your real self," "reprogramming your brain," "identifying your unconscious talents," and so forth. Some forms of psychobabble combine Americans' trust in quick forms of self-help with their confi-

---

psychology The scientific study of behavior and mental processes and how they are affected by an organism's physical state, mental state, and external environment.

dence in technology. Thus all sorts of electrical gizmos have been marketed with the promise that they will get both halves of your brain working at their peak (Chance, 1989): the Graham Potentializer, the Tranquilite, the Floatarium, the Transcutaneous Electro-Neural Stimulator, the Brain SuperCharger, and the Whole Brain Wave Form Synchro-Energizer (we're not making these up). And of course there are dozens and dozens of so-called "subliminal" tapes that promise to make you happy, thin, rich, successful, healthy, and able to speak four languages, all while you sleep. (For the record, research shows that they don't deliver on any of these promises [Moore, 1995].) One ad we saw, with the banner headline "How to Use Your Mind to Do Anything You Choose," explained:

> The tapes are designed to overcome negativity and build self-esteem, which includes loving yourself. When you love yourself, it's easier to love others and easier for them to love you. . . . It normally takes about 30 days to overcome past negative programming and supplant it with positive programming.

Well, who wouldn't want to gain high self-esteem and love, all in 30 days? The promise of a simple answer to meet an obvious and universal human need—coated with what Rosen called "a light dusting of psychology"—is the sign of psychobabble.

Today, when so many pop-psych ideas have filtered into public consciousness, education, and even the law, people more than ever need to know the difference between psychobabble and serious psychology, and between unsupported *popular opinion* and documented *research evidence*. Here are a few examples of the gap between them:

Popular belief	Scientific evidence
Divorce is always horrible for children, *or* the bad effects of divorce soon wear off.	The effects of divorce depend on the parental relationship, age and sex of the children, whether the marriage was abusive or violent, and so on.
Abused children become abusers. Children of alcoholics become alcoholic.	The majority of these children do not.
Once an addict, always an addict.	Many addictions are outgrown when the person's circumstances change.
Almost all women "suffer" from "PMS."	Most women are no grumpier before menstruation than at any other time of the month, and their premenstrual moods are no different from men's moods all month long!
Memory works like a tape recorder, faithfully recording everything that happens to you from the moment of birth.	Memory works like a connect-the-dots puzzle; we fill in many details after the event. For physiological and psychological reasons, adults do not remember events that happened before about the age of three years.

Beliefs about psychological topics such as these are not neutral or trivial; people make major decisions based on them. For example, this letter appeared in the *Los*

Angeles Times: "As a child of alcoholic parents, I realized many years ago that I would not make a good mother since I did not have a proper role model. In the case of inheriting bad genes, I would not want to make a child of mine go through the nights of yelling and beatings that I experienced." Now, this woman may be right in deciding not to have children, for reasons we don't know. But if her decision is based only on the belief that without good parental role models a person is doomed to be a bad parent, or that "bad genes" will inevitably perpetuate a cycle of alcoholism and abusiveness, she is wrong.

This woman has uncritically accepted the popular notion that one key factor in a person's background can determine the person's destiny forever—in this case, that abuse inevitably breeds abuse. So prevalent is this idea that one judge denied a woman custody of her children solely because the woman had been abused as a child, even though she had never harmed her children in any way. But the supposed inevitability of the "cycle of abuse" is based mainly on *confirming cases*—cases of abused children who became abusive adults. A person knowledgeable about scientific psychology would want to ask about children who suffered abuse but did *not* grow up to mistreat their children, as well as about people who were not abused and then grew up to be abusive parents. Research psychologists would consider evidence for all four of the possibilities shown in the following table:

	Abused as a Child?	
	Yes	**No**
Abusive as a Parent? **Yes**	Abused children who become abusive parents	Nonabused children who become abusive parents
No	Abused children who do not become abusive parents	Nonabused children who do not become abusive parents

In fact, when you take all the existing evidence into account, you find that although being abused is definitely a risk factor for becoming an abusive parent, more than two-thirds of all abused children do *not* grow up to mistreat their own offspring (Kaufman & Zigler, 1987; Widom, 1989).

Perhaps the ultimate difference between psychobabble and scientific psychology is that psychobabble *confirms* our existing beliefs and prejudices—that's why it is so appealing—and psychology often *challenges* them. You don't have to be a psychologist to know that most people don't like to have their beliefs challenged. You rarely hear someone cheerfully say, "Oh, thank you for explaining to me why my lifelong philosophy of child raising is wrong! I'm so grateful for your facts!" The person usually says, "Oh, buzz off, and take your cockamamy ideas with you." (In Chapter 9 you'll learn why this is.)

Psychology has plenty of nonscientific competitors: palm readers, graphologists, fortune-tellers, numerologists, and, the most popular, astrologers. Are you having romantic problems? An astrologer may advise you to choose an Aries instead of an Aquarius as your next love. Are you unable to make decisions? A "past-lives channeler" may say it's because in a former life you were a twelfth-century peasant who had no decisions to make. These nonscientific systems of belief are testable in principle, although their followers often ignore the basic rules of evidence. One such rule is that you have to make predictions in advance of, not after, the fact. For instance, you don't get to survive an earthquake and *then* argue that the planets predicted your survival.

When put to the test, pseudoscientific predictions are rarely correct. Have you ever wondered why so many "psychics" are far from affluent? If they are psychic, why haven't they made fortunes in the stock market or the lottery? Whenever anyone has actually checked back on the predictions made by psychics at the start of the year, it always turns out that most of the predictions were dead wrong. For example, 1994 was supposed to be the year that

- ✦Charles Manson got a sex-change operation and was freed from prison (*Weekly World News*).

- ✦scientists "perfected a small four-cylinder car that can run on tap water" (*National Enquirer*).

- ✦Madonna married a Middle Eastern sheik and became a "totally traditional wife" (*Globe*).

- ✦Whoopi Goldberg gave up acting to join a convent (*National Enquirer*).

Moreover, no psychic has ever predicted anything that was truly a surprise, such as the assassination of Israeli Prime Minister Yitzhak Rabin or the (short-lived) marriage of Michael Jackson and Lisa Marie Presley. No psychic has ever found a missing child, identified a serial killer, or helped police solve any other crime solely by using "psychic powers"—in spite of frequent reports in the mass media that psychics do so all the time (Rowe, 1993). In a survey of 50 police departments in America's largest cities, no officer said that information from a psychic had ever been more helpful than information from a regular source, and many said that, in contrast, psychics merely "hamper an investigation and often cause distractions" and contribute nothing "other than offering false hope to survivors." One police chief summarized, "Psychic information has been volunteered many times, but has *never* been beneficial to a case" (Sweat & Durm, 1993). Whenever there is a tragedy in the news, self-proclaimed psychics turn up to offer their services, but don't be fooled. The U.S. Defense Department was. They wasted $20 million over two decades on "psychics" who were supposed to answer precise military questions, such as the location of Libyan dictator Mu'ammar Gadhafi in 1986. One psychic said, "I see sand. I see water. I see a mosque. . . ." Very helpful.

Astrologers do no better than psychics. In a review of many studies of predictions made by astrologers, Geoffrey Dean (1986/1987, 1987) found that their predictions had only chance-level accuracy. Their occasional on-target predictions were the result of shrewd guesses, vagueness (e.g., "A tragedy will hit the country this spring"), or inside information ("Movie star A will marry director B"). After studying the appeal of astrology in the face of its continued failure to confirm any of its premises or predictions, Geoffrey Dean concluded that astrology is "psychological chewing gum, satisfying but ultimately without real substance." The study of psychology, we believe, provides substance.

I see you being less gullible in the future.

CRITICAL AND CREATIVE THINKING

The purpose of psychology is to give us a completely different idea of the things we know best.

—Paul Valéry

One of the greatest benefits of studying psychology is that you learn not only how the brain works in general but also how to use yours in particular—by thinking critically. **Critical thinking** is the ability and willingness to assess claims and to make objective judgments on the basis of well-supported reasons. It is the ability to look for flaws in arguments and to resist claims that have no supporting evidence. Critical thinking, however, is not merely negative thinking. It also fosters the ability to be *creative and constructive*—to come up with various possible explanations for events, think of implications of research findings, and apply new knowledge to a broad range of social and personal problems. You can't separate critical thinking from creative thinking, for it is only when you question *what is* that you can begin to imagine *what can be*.

These days, most people know that you have to exercise the body to keep it in shape. But they assume that thinking doesn't take any effort at all and certainly no practice. You just do it, like breathing. But thinking does require practice. All around us we can see examples of flabby thinking, lazy thinking, emotional thinking, and non-

---

critical thinking The ability and willingness to assess claims and make objective judgments on the basis of well-supported reasons, to resist claims that have no supporting evidence, and to be creative and constructive in explaining events.

thinking. Sometimes people justify their mental laziness by proudly telling you they are "open-minded." "It's good to be open-minded," replies philosopher Jacob Needleman, "but not so open that your brains fall out."

One prevalent misreading of what it means to be open-minded is the idea that all opinions are created equal and that everybody's beliefs are as good as everybody else's. On matters of religious faith or personal preferences, that's true; if you prefer the look of a Ford Escort to the look of a Honda Civic, no one can argue with you. But if you say, "The Ford is a better car than a Honda," you have uttered a statement that is more than mere opinion. Now you have to support your belief with evidence of the car's reliability, track record, safety, and the like (Ruggiero, 1991). And if you say, "Fords are the best in the world, and Hondas do not exist; they are a conspiracy of the Japanese government," you forfeit the right to have your opinion taken seriously. Your opinion, if it ignores reality, is *not* equal to any other.

In the United States, the idea that there are two sides to every issue has added to the confusion between (a) beliefs based on matters of taste, preference, and wishful thinking, and (b) beliefs based on good reasoning and solid evidence. The "two sides" idea has been used by some college newspaper editors to explain why they accept advertisements for revisionist books claiming that the Holocaust never took place. But as Deborah Lipstadt, author of *Denying the Holocaust* (1993), observes, there are not two sides to the question of whether the Holocaust occurred; debating such a question is like debating whether the Roman Empire existed or whether there really was a French Revolution. The First Amendment states that Congress shall make no law abridging freedom of speech, but, notes Lipstadt (1994), "It says nothing about a paper's obligation to publish every absurd claim that comes its way," nor does it require that every opinion, no matter how half-baked, be given the same standing.

Critical thinking involves a set of skills that will help you distinguish arguments based on solidly grounded evidence from those that float along on delusion or wishful dreams. Patricia King and Karen Kitchener (1994) have studied what they call "reflective judgment" and we call critical thinking, and they find that people don't usually use such skills until they reach their mid-20s or until they have had many years of higher education—if then. (We will be discussing this research further in Chapter 9.) That does not mean, however, that people *can't* think critically. Even young children often do so, though they may not get much credit for it. We know one fourth-grader, who, when told that ancient Greece was the "cradle of democracy," replied, "But what about women and slaves, who couldn't vote and had no rights? Was Greece a democracy for them?" That's critical thinking. And it is also creative thinking, for once you question the assumption that Greece was a democracy for everyone, you can begin to imagine other interpretations of ancient Greek civilization.

Many educators, philosophers, and psychologists believe that contemporary education shortchanges students by not encouraging them to think critically and creatively. Too often, say these critics, teachers and students view the mind as a bin for storing "the right answers" or a sponge for "soaking up knowledge." The mind is neither a bin nor a sponge. Remembering, thinking, and understanding are all active processes. They require judgment, choice, and the weighing of evidence. Unfortunately, children who challenge prevailing opinion at home or in school are often called "rebellious" rather than "involved." As a result, say the critics, many high-school and college graduates cannot formulate a rational argument or see through misleading advertisements and propaganda that play on emotions. They do not know how to go about deciding whether to have children, make an investment, or support a political proposal. They do not know how to come up with imaginative solutions to their problems.

You can apply critical thinking to any subject you study or any problem you encounter. But critical thinking is particularly relevant to psychology for three reasons. First, the field itself includes the study of reasoning, problem solving, creativity, and curiosity, and so by its very nature, it fosters critical and creative thinking. Second, psychology also includes the study of *barriers* to clear thinking, such as the human propensity for rationalization, self-deception, and biases in perception. Third, the field of psychology generates many competing findings on topics of personal and social relevance—such as the nature of addiction and memory—and people need to be able to evaluate these findings and the resulting implications. Critical thinking can help you separate psychology from the psychobabble that clutters the airwaves and bookstores.

In part, learning to think critically means following the rules of logic. But there are several other guidelines involved (Ennis, 1986; Halpern, 1995; Paul, 1984; Ruggiero, 1991). Here are eight of the essential ones, which we emphasize throughout this book:

1 ASK QUESTIONS; BE WILLING TO WONDER. What is the one kind of question that most exasperates parents of young children? "Why is the sky blue, Mommy?" "Why doesn't the plane fall?" "Why don't pigs have wings?" Unfortunately, as children grow up, they tend to stop asking "why" questions. (Why do you think this is?)

Psychologist Bob Perloff (1992) has reflected on a few questions he'd like to have answered:

> Why are moths attracted to wool but indifferent to cotton? How is it that there exist minuscule organisms so small that they cannot be seen by the naked eye? And speaking about naked, why is it that there are so few nude beaches when many of us, truth to tell, like to look at naked bodies (except our own)? . . . Why is dust? Why is a rainbow arched? I used to feel foolish, even dumb, because I didn't know why or how the sun shines until I learned very recently that the astrophysicists themselves are in a quandary about this.

"The trigger mechanism for creative thinking is the disposition to be curious, to wonder, to inquire," writes Vincent Ruggiero (1988). "Asking 'What's wrong here?' and/or 'Why is this the way it is, and how did it come to be that way?' leads to the identification of problems and challenges." Some occupations actually teach their trainees to think this way. For instance, industrial engineers are taught to walk through a company and question everything, even procedures that have been used for years (Ruggiero, 1991). But other occupations prefer to give trainees "received wisdom" and discourage criticism.

2 **DEFINE THE PROBLEM.** Once you've raised a question, the next step is to identify the issues in clear and concrete terms. "What makes people happy?" is a fine question for midnight reveries, but it will not lead to answers unless you have specified what you mean by "happy." Does happiness require being in a constant state of euphoria all the time? How much of the time? Does it simply mean feeling a pleasant contentment with life? Does it mean the absence of serious problems or pain?

One difference between psychobabble and psychology has to do with how a question is formulated. A pop-psych proponent of hypnosis might ask, "How does hypnosis improve memory for events?" Notice that this question presupposes that hypnosis does reliably improve memory. But a critical thinker would ask a more neutral question, allowing for other results: "Does hypnosis affect memory, and if so, how?" In fact, hypnosis can increase memory *errors,* and many hypnotized people will make up details of an event that never happened (Dinges et al., 1992; Spanos et al., 1991).

3 **EXAMINE THE EVIDENCE.** Have you ever heard someone in the heat of argument exclaim, "I just know it's true, no matter what you say" or "That's my opinion; nothing's going to change it" or "If you don't understand my position, I can't explain it"? Have you ever made such statements yourself? Accepting a conclusion without evidence, or expecting others to do so, is a sure sign of uncritical thinking. It implies that all opinions are equal when they are not. A critical thinker asks, *What evidence supports or refutes this argument and its opposition? How reliable is the evidence?*

Some pop-psych ideas have been widely accepted on the basis of poor evidence or even no evidence at all. For example, many people believe that whenever they feel angry, it is psychologically and physically healthy to ventilate their anger at the first person, pet, or piece of furniture that gets in their way. Actually, studies across many different fields suggest that sometimes expressing anger is beneficial, but more often it is not. Often the venting of anger makes the angry person angrier, makes the target of the anger angry in return, lowers everybody's self-esteem, and fosters hostility and aggression (Tavris, 1989). Yet the belief that expressing anger is always healthy persists, despite the lack of evidence to support it. Can you think of some reasons why this might be so?

The reliance on **empirical** evidence—evidence gathered by careful observation, experimentation, and measurement—is the hallmark of the psychological method. Suppose that you want to know whether the passionate attraction you feel for your romantic companion will survive a summer's separation. A novelist might observe that "absence makes the heart grow fonder," and a poet might reply that the truth is closer to "out of sight, out of mind." A psychologist would want to determine the *conditions* under which absence might or might not make the heart grow fonder. One of those conditions is the degree of emotional attachment you feel for one another before you part. As lovers throughout history have learned and researchers have confirmed, absence often intensifies a bright flame but extinguishes a weak one (Brehm, 1992).

---

empirical Relying on or derived from observation, experimentation, or measurement.

4 Analyze assumptions and biases. Critical thinkers evaluate the assumptions and biases that underlie arguments. They ask how these assumptions and biases influence claims and conclusions in the books they read, the political speeches they hear, the news programs they watch, and the ads that bombard them every day. Here is an example: The manufacturer of a popular pain reliever advertises that hospitals prefer its product over all others. The natural assumption—the one the advertiser wants you to make—is that this product is better than all others. Actually, hospitals prefer the product because they get a bigger discount on it than on its competitors.

Critical thinkers also are aware of their own assumptions and are willing to question them. For example, many people are biased in favor of their parents' ways of doing things. When faced with difficult problems, they will reach for familiar solutions, saying, "If my dad voted Republican (or Democratic), then I should," or "I was brought up to believe that the best way to discipline children is to spank them." But critical thinking requires us to examine our biases when the evidence contradicts them. Everyone, of course, carries around a headful of assumptions about how the world works: Do people have free will, or are they constrained by biology and upbringing? Are government programs the solution to poverty, or would private programs do better? If we don't make our assumptions explicit, our ability to interpret evidence objectively can be seriously impaired.

5 Avoid emotional reasoning: "If I feel this way, it must be true." Emotion has a place in critical thinking. Passionate commitment to a view can motivate a person to think boldly without fear of what others will say, to defend an unpopular idea, and to seek evidence for creative new theories. Moreover, in the absence of the emotions of compassion and pity, logic and reason can lead to misguided or even destructive decisions and actions. Indeed, some of the most sadistic killers and military strategists in history have been bright, even brilliant, thinkers.

When "gut feelings" replace clear thinking, however, the results are equally dangerous. "Persecutions and wars and lynchings," observed Edward de Bono (1985), "are all a result of gut feeling." Because our feelings seem so right, it is hard to understand that people with opposing viewpoints feel just as strongly. But they usually do, which means that feelings alone are not a reliable guide to the truth.

You probably hold strong feelings about many topics, such as drugs, abortion, astrology, the causes of crime, racism, gender differences, welfare, and homosexuality. In order to make informed decisions about your personal life, how to vote, and what social policies to endorse, you will need to do more than rely on these feelings; you will also need to consider the evidence that applies to such issues. As you read about psychological research, you may find yourself quarreling with particular findings that you dislike. Disagreement with what you read is fine; it means that you are reading actively. All we ask is that you ask yourself *why* you are disagreeing—because the results cause you to question some assumption that you hold to be true, or because the evidence is unpersuasive?

6 Don't oversimplify. A critical thinker looks beyond the obvious, resists easy generalizations, and rejects either/or thinking. For example, when life serves up a miserable situation, should you deny your problems ("Everything's fine; let's go to the movies") or face them head-on? Either answer is simplistic. Sometimes denial can keep people from solving their problems, but at other times it helps them get through painful situations that can't be changed (Taylor, 1995).

A telltale sign of pop-psych and other simplistic ideas is that they are based on *arguing by anecdote*—generalizing from a personal experience or a few examples to everyone. One crime committed by a paroled ex-convict means that the whole parole program is bad; one friend who went through a weekend "Trek to Truth" experience, and who swears it changed his life, means that the program works for everybody. Anecdotal generalizations are the source of stereotyping as well: One dishonest welfare mother means that they are all dishonest; one encounter with an unconventional Californian means they are all flaky. And many people make themselves miserable by generalizing from a single unfortunate event to a whole pattern of defeat: "I did poorly on this test, and now I'll never get through college or have a job or kids or anything." A critical thinker wants more evidence than one or two stories before drawing such global generalizations.

7 CONSIDER OTHER INTERPRETATIONS. A critical thinker creatively formulates hypotheses that offer reasonable explanations of characteristics, behavior, and events. The ultimate goal is to find an explanation that accounts for the most evidence with the fewest assumptions. This is the principle of *Occam's razor*, named after the fourteenth-century philosopher William of Occam, who proposed it. For example, suppose that a fortune-teller offers to read your palm and predict your future. One of two things must be true (Steiner, 1989):

◆The fortune-teller can actually sort out the infinite number of interactions among people, animals, events, objects, and circumstances that could affect your life and can know for sure the outcome. Moreover, this particular fortune-teller is able to alter all the known laws of physics and defy the hundreds of studies showing that no one, under proper procedures for validating psychic predictions, has been able to read the future.

OR

◆The fortune-teller is faking it.

According to the maxim of Occam's razor, the second alternative is preferable because it requires the fewest assumptions.

But critical thinkers are also careful not to shut out alternative explanations too soon. They generate as many interpretations of the evidence as possible before settling on the most likely one. For example, suppose a news bulletin reports that people who are severely depressed are more likely than nondepressed people to develop cancer. Before you can conclude that depression causes cancer, what other explanations might be possible? Perhaps depressed people are more likely to smoke and drink too much, and it's those unhealthful habits that caused the cancer. Perhaps an undetected cancer, in its early stages, was responsible for the feelings of depression.

8 TOLERATE UNCERTAINTY. Ultimately, learning to think critically teaches us one of the hardest lessons of life: how to live with uncertainty. It is important to examine the evidence before drawing conclusions, yet sometimes there is little or no evidence to go on. Sometimes the evidence merely allows us to draw tentative conclusions. And sometimes the evidence seems good enough to permit strong conclusions . . . until, exasperatingly, new evidence throws our beliefs into disarray. Critical thinkers are willing to accept this state of uncertainty. They are not afraid to say, "I don't know" or "I'm not sure." This admission is not an evasion but a spur to further creative inquiry.

The desire for certainty often makes people uncomfortable when they go to experts for "the" answer and the experts cannot give it to them. Patients may demand of their doctors, "What do you mean you don't know what's wrong with me? Find out and fix it!" Students may demand of their professors, "What do you mean it's a controversial issue? Just tell me the answer!" Critical thinkers, however, know that the more important the question, the less likely it is to have a single simple answer.

Does this mean that there is no such thing as intellectual progress? Not at all. When a theory falls apart, a new and better theory may arise from its ashes, explaining more facts and solving more puzzles. This process of revision can be frustrating for those who want psychology and other sciences to hand them some absolute truths. But it is exciting for those who love the pursuit of understanding as much as the collection of facts.

The need to accept a certain amount of uncertainty does not mean that we must live without beliefs and convictions. "The fact that today's knowledge may be overturned or at least revised tomorrow," says Ruggiero (1988), "could lead us to the kind of skepticism that refuses to embrace any idea. That would be foolish because, in the practical sense, it is impossible to build a life on that view. Besides, it is not the embracing of an idea that causes problems—it is the refusal to relax that embrace when good sense dictates doing so. It is enough to form convictions with care and carry them lightly, being willing to reconsider them whenever new evidence calls them into question."

Of course, critical thinking cannot lead to definite answers to every question about life. Some beliefs, such as whether there is a God and what the nature of God might be, are ultimately matters of faith; they cannot be tested for accuracy. Moreover, critical thinking is a process, not a once-and-for-all accomplishment. No one ever becomes a perfect critical thinker, unaffected by emotional reasoning and wishful thinking in at least some areas of life. We are all less open-minded than we think, more reluctant to submit our own beliefs to honest analysis. That is why cleverness is not the same as critical thinking. Sharp debaters can learn to poke holes in the arguments of others, while twisting facts or conveniently ignoring arguments that might contradict their own position. True critical thinking, according to philosopher Richard Paul (1984), is "fair-mindedness brought into the heart of everyday life."

Critical thinking is not for people who expect things from psychology that it cannot deliver. Some people follow individual psychologists the way others follow religious leaders and gurus, hoping for enlightenment about the meaning of life. Others want psychology to relieve them of having to think critically and of having to take responsibility for their own actions. But knowing that your short temper is a result, in part, of your unhappy childhood doesn't give you a green light to yell at your family. The study of psychology does not require individuals or society to be legally or morally neutral about issues we wish to understand. A better understanding of the psychological origins of child beating may help us to reduce child abuse and treat offenders, but we can still hold child beaters accountable for their behavior.

WHAT DO YOU KNOW?

Amelia and Harold are arguing about the death penalty. "Look, I just feel strongly that it's barbaric, ineffective, and wrong," says Harold. "You're nuts," says Amelia, "I believe in an eye for an eye, and besides, I'm absolutely sure it's a deterrent to further crime." Which lapses of critical thinking might Amelia and Harold be committing?

ANSWERS:

Here are some problems in their style of argument; feel free to think of others. (1) They are reasoning by emotion ("I feel strongly about this, so I'm right and you're wrong."). (2) Their arguments are not based on evidence that supports or contradicts their arguments. What *do* studies show about the link between the death penalty and crime? Is the death penalty applied fairly to all who murder—that is, to rich and poor, men and women, blacks and whites? (3) They have not examined the assumptions and biases they bring to the discussion. (4) They may not be clearly defining the problem they are arguing about. What is the goal of the death penalty, for example? Is it to deter criminals, to satisfy the public desire for revenge, or to keep criminals from being paroled and returned to the streets?

PSYCHOLOGY PAST AND PRESENT

Until the nineteenth century, psychology was pretty much a hit-or-miss sort of business. It was not recognized as a separate field of study, and there were few formal rules on how it was to be conducted. Of course, most of the great thinkers of history, from Aristotle to Zoroaster, raised questions that today would be called psychological. They wanted to know how people take in information through their senses, use information to solve problems, and become motivated to act in brave or villainous ways. They wondered about the elusive nature of emotion, and whether it controls us or is something we can control. But unlike modern psychologists, scholars of the past did not rely heavily on empirical evidence. Their observations were often based on anecdotes or on descriptions of individual cases.

This does not mean that the forerunners of modern psychology were always wrong. Hippocrates, the ancient Greek physician known as the father of medicine, observed patients with head injuries and inferred that the brain must be the ultimate source of "our pleasures, joys, laughter, and jests as well as our sorrows, pains, griefs, and tears." And so it is. In the first century A.D., the Stoic philosophers observed that people do not become angry or sad or anxious because of actual events, but because of their explanations of those events. And so they do.

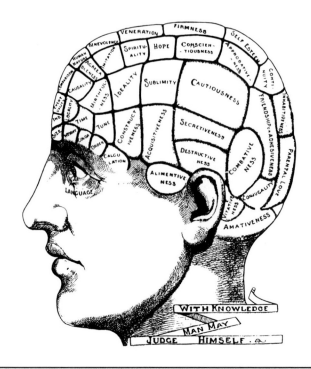

People have always proposed theories of human behavior, but they haven't always used empirical methods to test them. In the nineteenth century, phrenology—the idea that different brain areas accounted for specific traits, such as "stinginess" and "religiosity"—was wildly popular. Phrenologists thought that they could "read" these traits from bumps on the skull, and they drew up maps like this one to indicate where the traits supposedly were located in the brain. (Notice the tiny space for "self-esteem" at the top of the skull and the big chunk in the middle devoted to "cautiousness"!) Phrenology was sheer nonsense, but its underlying assumption of specialized brain parts has been confirmed by modern research.

But without empirical methods, the forerunners of psychology also committed some terrible blunders. Even Aristotle, one of the first great philosophers to advocate the use of empirical methods, did not always use them correctly himself. He thought that the brain could not possibly be responsible for sensation because the brain itself feels no pain, and he concluded that the brain was simply a radiator for cooling the blood. Aristotle was absolutely right that the brain is insensitive, but he was wrong about the brain being a radiator, and about many other things. For instance, he believed that small people have poor memories!

Although scientists in Europe and America had been doing research on psychological topics (such as sensation and perception) since the beginning of the nineteenth century, psychology as a formal science was officially born in the year 1879. In that year the first psychological laboratory was established in Leipzig, Germany, by Wilhelm Wundt (VILL-helm Voont; 1832–1920), who was trained in medicine and philosophy. Wundt was the first to announce, in 1873, that he intended to make psychology a science. One of Wundt's favorite research methods was *trained introspection,* in which specially trained people observed and analyzed their own mental experiences, under controlled conditions. This wasn't as easy as it sounds. Wundt's introspectors had to make 10,000 practice observations before they were allowed to participate in an actual study. Once trained, they might take as long as 20 minutes to report their inner experiences during a 1.5-second experiment. Wundt hoped that trained introspection would produce reliable, verifiable results. Ironically, although Wundt's goal was to make psychology an objective science, introspection was soon abandoned by other psychologists because it wasn't objective enough.

In America, Wundt's ideas had a great deal of influence, but they were opposed by the views of another early school of scientific psychology, called **functionalism,** which emphasized the function, or purpose, of behavior. One of its leaders was William James (1842–1910), an American philosopher, physician, and psychologist. Attempting to grasp the nature of the mind through introspection, wrote James (1890/1950), is "like seizing a spinning top to catch its motion, or trying to turn up the gas quickly enough to see how the darkness looks." (James was a wonderful writer who is still a joy to read, both for his ideas and his eloquence in expressing them.)

The functionalists were inspired in part by the evolutionary theories of Charles Darwin (1809–1882). Darwin had argued that a biologist's job is not merely to describe the brilliant plumage of a peacock or the drab markings of a lizard but also to figure out how these attributes enhance survival: Do they help the animal attract a mate or hide from its enemies? Similarly, functionalists wanted to know how various actions help a person or animal adapt to the environment. They looked for underlying causes and practical consequences of specific behaviors and mental strategies. They used many methods and broadened the field of psychology to include the study of children, animals, religious experiences, and what James called the "stream of consciousness"—a term still used because it so beautifully describes the way thoughts flow like a river, tumbling over each other in waves, sometimes placid, sometimes turbulent.

Psychology as a method of psychotherapy was born in Vienna, Austria. There, in 1900, a physician published a book titled *The Interpretation of Dreams.* The book was not exactly an overnight sensation. In fact, during the next eight years the publisher managed to sell only 600 copies. The author was Sigmund Freud (1856–1939), whose name today is as much a household word as Einstein's.

A neurologist by training, Freud originally hoped for a career as a medical researcher, but research did not pay well and family responsibilities forced him to go into private practice as a physician. As Freud listened to his patients' reports of depression, nervousness, and obsessive habits, he became convinced that many of their symptoms had mental, not bodily, causes. The patients' distress was due, he concluded, to conflicts, memories, and emotional traumas that occurred in early childhood. Freud's

---

functionalism An early psychological approach that stressed the function or purpose of behavior and consciousness.

ideas eventually evolved into a broad theory of personality, and both his theory and his methods of treating people with emotional problems became known as *psychoanalysis.*

From these early beginnings in philosophy, natural science, and medicine, psychology has grown into a complex field consisting of different specialties, perspectives, methods, and training. Psychology today is not a coherent entity, like a piece of furniture. A more appropriate metaphor is that modern psychology is like a large, sprawling family: The members share common great-grandparents, but some of the cousins have formed alliances, some are quarreling, and some are not speaking to one another.

The first thing the cousins are quarreling about is the very definition of the word *psychologist,* which has many different meanings and includes people in many different occupations (Gardner, 1992). When most people hear "psychologist" they conjure up Freud listening intently as a patient, who is lying comfortably on a couch, pours forth her or his troubles. Some psychologists do in fact fit this image (though chairs are more common than couches these days), but many others do not.

The professional activities of psychologists generally fall into three broad categories: (1) teaching and doing research in colleges and universities, (2) providing health or mental-health services, often referred to as *psychological practice,* and (3) conducting research and applying its findings in nonacademic settings such as business, sports, government, law, and the military. (Table 1.1 will give you an idea of the diverse things that psychologists do.) Many psychologists move flexibly across these areas. Some, for instance, do research *and* provide counseling services in a mental-

TABLE 1.1 ✦ What Is a "Psychologist"?

Psychologists have an advanced degree; many are psychotherapists (see clinical psychologists), but others do research, teach, work in business, or consult.

ACADEMIC/RESEARCH PSYCHOLOGISTS	CLINICAL PSYCHOLOGISTS	PSYCHOLOGISTS IN INDUSTRY, LAW, OR OTHER SETTINGS
Specialize in areas of pure or applied research, such as:	*May work in any of these settings, or some combination:*	*Do research or consult to institutions in the community on, e.g.:*
Social	Private practice	Sports
Developmental	Mental-health clinics	Consumer issues
Psychometric (testing)	or services	Advertising
Health	Hospitals	Environmental issues
Educational	Research	Public-policy analysis
Industrial/	Teaching	Survey research/opinion polls
organizational		Management, productivity,
Consumer		and other business issues
Physiological		
Perception and sensation		

health setting, such as a research hospital. Some work in universities *and* serve as professional consultants on legal cases or governmental policy decisions.

Psychological Research. Most of the psychologists who are academic researchers have doctoral degrees (a Ph.D. or an Ed.D., doctorate in education). Some, seeking knowledge for its own sake, work in **basic psychology,** doing "pure" research on specific problems. Others, concerned with the practical uses of knowledge, work in **applied psychology.** A psychologist doing basic research might ask, "How do children, adolescents, and adults differ in their approach to moral issues such as honesty?" An applied psychologist might ask, "How can knowledge about moral development be used to prevent teenage violence?" A psychologist in basic science might ask, "Can a chimpanzee or a gorilla learn to use sign language?" An applied psychologist might ask, "Can techniques used to teach language to a chimpanzee be used to help mentally impaired or disturbed children who do not speak?"

Psychologists doing basic and applied research have made important contributions in areas as diverse as health, education, marketing, management, consumer behavior, industrial design, worker productivity and satisfaction, and urban planning. Most of the findings you will be reading about in this book come from the efforts of research psychologists.

The Practice of Psychology. Psychological practitioners, whose goal is to understand and improve physical and mental health, work in general hospitals, mental hospitals, clinics, schools, counseling centers, and private practice. In the past two decades, the proportion of psychologists who are practitioners has greatly increased; today, they account for well over two-thirds of new psychology doctorates and members of the American Psychological Association (APA). Some practitioners are *counseling psychologists,* who help people with problems of everyday life, such as test anxiety or family conflicts. Some are *school psychologists,* who work with parents and students to improve students' performance and resolve their emotional difficulties. But the majority are *clinical psychologists,* who diagnose, treat, and study mental or emotional problems and disabilities. Clinical psychologists are trained to do psychotherapy with highly disturbed people, as well as with those who are simply troubled or unhappy or who want to learn to handle their problems better. Many clinical psychologists, in addition to their clinical practice, also teach and do research in colleges and universities.

In almost all states, a license to practice clinical psychology requires a doctorate. Most clinical psychologists have a Ph.D., some have an Ed.D., and a smaller but growing number have a relatively new degree called a Psy.D. (doctorate in psychology, pronounced "sy-dee"). Clinical psychologists typically do four or five years of graduate

---

basic psychology The study of psychological issues in order to seek knowledge for its own sake rather than for its practical application.

applied psychology The study of psychological issues that have direct practical significance; also, the application of psychological findings.

work in psychology, plus at least a year's internship. Clinical programs leading to a Ph.D. or an Ed.D. are designed to prepare a person both as a scientist and as a clinical practitioner; they require completion of a dissertation, a major scholarly research project. Programs leading to a Psy.D. focus on professional practice and do not usually require a dissertation. However, they do require the student to complete a research study, theoretical paper, or some other scholarly project.

Psychiatry is the medical specialty concerned with mental and emotional disorders. Psychiatrists are medical doctors (M.D.s) who have had three or four years of general medical training, a yearlong internship in general medicine, and a three-year residency in psychiatry. During the residency period, a psychiatrist learns to diagnose and treat psychiatric patients under the supervision of a more experienced physician. Some psychiatrists go on to do research on mental problems, such as depression or schizophrenia, rather than work with patients.

Although there are many similarities in what psychiatrists and clinical psychologists do, there are also important differences. Psychiatrists are more likely than psychologists to treat severe mental disorders. They tend to be more medically oriented because they have been trained to diagnose physical problems that can cause mental ones. In addition, psychiatrists can write prescriptions, and clinical psychologists cannot (at least not yet; many psychologists are currently pressing for prescription-writing privileges). Psychiatrists, however, are often not thoroughly trained in the theories and methods of modern psychology. These differences can affect approaches to treatment. For example, if a patient is depressed, a psychiatrist will often prescribe an antidepressant drug. A clinical psychologist is more likely to look for the psychological and social origins of depression.

A *psychoanalyst* is a person who practices one highly specific form of therapy, psychoanalysis. To call yourself a psychoanalyst, you must have an advanced degree, get specialized training at a recognized psychoanalytic institute, and undergo extensive psychoanalysis yourself.

When you hear in the news or read about someone who is described as "a psychotherapist in private practice," you should know that the word *psychotherapist* is simply a generic word for anyone who does any kind of therapy. The person could be a clinical psychologist, with a doctorate in that field. But he or she could also be a social worker, a counseling psychologist, or a Doctor of Anything But Psychology, who simply uses the label. Although the word *psychologist* is licensed and regulated everywhere, the word *psychotherapist* is not. That means that in most states, anyone can hang out a shingle saying "therapist," and plenty do. In *The Psychological Society,* Martin Gross (1978) listed a sampling of unlicensed therapies that included marathon therapy, encounter therapy, nude therapy, crisis therapy, electric sleep therapy, body-image therapy, deprivation therapy, expectation therapy, "art of living" therapy, and "do it now" therapy. As these have gone out of fashion, others have taken their place, such as

---

psychiatry The medical specialty concerned with mental disorders, maladjustment, and abnormal behavior.

TABLE 1.2 ✦ Types of Psychotherapists	
Psychotherapist	Anyone who does "psychotherapy"; may have anything from no degree to an advanced professional degree; the term is unregulated
Clinical psychologist	Has a Ph.D., Ed.D., or Psy.D.
Psychoanalyst	Has specific training in psychoanalysis beyond an advanced degree (M.D. or Ph.D.)
Psychiatrist	A medical doctor (M.D.) with a specialty in psychiatry
Other mental-health professionals: counselors; school psychologists; licensed social workers (LSWs); marriage, family, and child counselors (MFCCs)	Licensing requirements vary; generally has at least an M.A. (master of arts) in psychology or social work

aroma therapy and age-regression therapy. (For a summary of the types of psychotherapists and the training they receive, see Table 1.2.)

Many psychologists are worried about the flood of poorly trained psychotherapists across North America (Dawes, 1994). Some of these people have no credentials at all; many are entirely unschooled in research methods and the basic research findings of psychology; and many use therapy techniques that have not been tested and validated (we will return to this issue in Chapter 16). Some practitioners, too, are concerned about the lack of a uniform standard of professional education (Fox, 1994). In choosing a therapist, as in selecting the services of anyone who will have power to affect their lives and health, consumers need to use critical thinking and sound judgment.

Community Applications of Psychological Research. Psychologists in the third group are out in the community, working in just about any field you can think of. They consult with companies to improve worker satisfaction and productivity. They establish programs to improve race relations and reduce tensions between different ethnic communities. They advise commissions on how pollution and noise affect mental health. They do research for the military. They do rehabilitation training for people who are physically or mentally disabled. They educate judges and juries about the reliability of eyewitness testimony. They assist the police in emergencies involving hostages or disturbed persons. They conduct public-opinion surveys. They run suicide-prevention hotlines. They advise zoos on the care and training of animals. They help coaches improve the athletic performance of their teams. And on and on.

Partly because of this diversity of activities, and partly because the media and the public persist in equating "psychologist" with "therapist," some psychological scientists think it is time to come up with new labels to describe what they do. They want to distinguish themselves from psychotherapists and argue that it is time to yield the word *psychologist* to its popular meaning. Research psychologists, they say, should call themselves "cognitive scientists," "behavioral scientists," "neuroscientists," and so forth, depending on their area of study. This change in language is already underway and gathering steam. At present, however, the word *psychologist* still embraces all the cousins in the family.

What Do You Know?

A. 1. The forerunners of psychology depended heavily on (casual observation/ empirical methods).
    2. Credit for founding modern psychology is generally given to (William James/ Wilhelm Wundt).
    3. Early psychologists who emphasized how behavior helps an organism adapt to its environment were known as _____.

B. Can you match the specialties on the left with their defining credentials and approaches?

1. psychotherapist	a. Has M.D. or Ph.D. and training in an approach started by Freud
2. psychiatrist	
3. clinical psychologist	b. Has Ph.D., Psy.D., or Ed.D. and does research on, or psychotherapy for, mental-health problems
4. academic psychologist	
5. psychoanalyst	
	c. May have any credential or none
	d. Has advanced degree (usually a Ph.D.) and does applied or basic research
	e. Has M.D.; tends to take a medical approach to emotional problems

Answers:

A. 1. casual observation 2. Wundt 3. functionalists **B.** 1. c 2. e 3. b 4. d 5. a

The Perspectives of Psychology

Several people are discussing their problems with anger. A woman says, "I was *born* angry. I hissed at passersby when I was carried home from the hospital." A man attributes his bad temper to what he learned by observing his father: "My dad used to get drunk and blow up at us," he recalls, "and now I find myself doing just what he did." A teenage gang member explains why he attacked a stranger on the street: "I had no choice; the man dissed me. He showed me no respect." A woman confesses that she displaces her anger at her husband by yelling irrationally at her children, friends, and mother. "Then I feel so guilty about being angry," she says, "that I overeat or get migraines."

Finally, an observer looks at the whole group and says, "The trouble with all of you is that you're American—always blowing up at the slightest provocation, like selfish children who don't get their way. You have no sense of the consequences of your anger.

In my country, it would be a terrible loss of face to reveal anger. We are expected to behave like mature adults and remember how destructive anger can be."

All of these observations tell us something about anger, yet none gives us the whole story. The five comments offered by these five individuals correspond to the five leading psychological approaches to studying and explaining mental processes and behavior: biological, learning, cognitive, psychodynamic, and sociocultural. In terms of our critical-thinking guidelines, these five perspectives reflect different *questions* that psychologists ask about human behavior; different *assumptions* that they make about how the mind works; and, most of all, different *explanations* that they empha-size of why people do what they do.

You will be studying these five perspectives in more depth and detail as you read this book; here, we will introduce you briefly to each of them. To make their points of view more memorable to you at this early stage of your reading, we will show how each might approach the topic of anger.

The Biological Perspective

When they first start studying psychology, many people are surprised to find that psy-chologists are interested not only in actions and thoughts, but also in genes, hor-mones, and nerve cells. Yet the biological approach to psychology has been an impor-tant one from the very beginning. Wilhelm Wundt's best-known work was titled *Principles of Physiological Psychology,* and for good reason: He and most other early researchers expected their science to rest on a firm foundation of anatomy and physi-ology. Later, during the 1920s and 1930s, interest in mental processes and the brain flourished within *Gestalt psychology,* a movement that had begun in Germany in 1912. In German, *Gestalt* (Geh-SHTALT) means "pattern" or "configuration." The Gestalt psychologists studied how people interpret sensory information as patterns in order to acquire knowledge.

The premise behind the **biological perspective** is that all actions, feelings, and thoughts are associated with bodily events. Electrical impulses scurry along the intricate pathways of the nervous system. Hormones course through the bloodstream, sig-naling internal organs to slow down or speed up. Various chemi-cal substances flow across the tiny gaps that separate one micrscopic brain cell from another. *Biological psychologists* (sometimes called *behavioral neuroscientists, neuropsychologists,* or *psychobiologists*) want to know how these bodily events inter-act with events in the external environment to produce thoughts, memories, and behavior. They study how biology affects the individual's perceptions of reality, ability to learn, experience of emotion, temperaments, and vulnerability to emotional disor-der. And researchers in a popular new specialty, *evolutionary psychology,* have been

---

biological perspective An approach to behavior that emphasizes bodily events and changes associated with actions, feelings, and thoughts.

studying how our species' evolutionary past may help explain some of our present behaviors and psychological traits; we will focus on their contributions in Chapter 3.

In the past few decades, new techniques have made it possible to explore areas of an organism's "inner space" where no one has ventured before. One result has been a better understanding of how mind and body interact in illness and in health. This is the research focus of an interdisciplinary specialty called (cumbersomely) *psychoneuroimmunology,* or PNI for short: "psycho" for psychological processes such as emotions and perceptions, "neuro" for the nervous and endocrine systems, and "immunology" for the immune system. These researchers are learning that although bodily processes can affect one's moods and emotions, the converse is also true: Emotions, attitudes, and perceptions can influence the functioning of the immune system and thus a person's susceptibility to particular diseases (Andersen, Kiecolt-Glaser, & Glaser, 1994). Biological research has also renewed interest in the age-old debate over the relative contributions made by "nature" (genetic dispositions) and "nurture" (upbringing and environment) in the development of abilities and personality traits.

Many biological psychologists hope that their discoveries, along with those of biochemists and other scientists, will help solve some of the mysteries of mental and emotional problems. Researchers in the biological tradition would have a few questions about the woman at the start of this section who believes she was "born angry." What is going on in the bodies of people who are quick to become angry? Do they have a physical condition that might be affecting their behavior, such as an injury to the brain or a neurological disorder? Do they have a temperamental tendency to be easily aroused? Are drugs such as alcohol related to their emotions? Is there a biological factor—in genes, brain structure, or hormones—in violent behavior? Is being under physical stress related to anger?

People often think that the explanation for some puzzle of behavior must be *either* physiological or psychological, and they fail to appreciate how complex the interactions between body and mind really are. But the biological approach has a useful message for us all: We cannot know ourselves if we do not know our bodies.

The Learning Perspective

In 1913, a psychologist named John B. Watson (1878–1958) published a paper that rocked the young science of psychology. In "Psychology as the Behaviorist Views It," Watson argued that if psychology were ever to be an objective science, it would have to give up its preoccupation with the mind and consciousness. Psychologists, he said, should throw out introspection as a method of research and reject terms such as *mental state, mind,* or *emotion* in explanations of behavior. They should stick to what they can observe and measure directly: acts and events actually taking place in the environment.

In short, Watson said, they should give up mentalism for **behaviorism.** There's no point asking people what a pinprick feels like; a behaviorist would want to observe what happens if you stick someone's finger with a pin—tears, withdrawal of the hand, shouting curses, or whatever. Watson wrote approvingly of studies by the Russian physiologist Ivan Pavlov (1849–1936). Pavlov had shown that many kinds of automatic or involuntary behavior, such as salivating at the sight of food, were simply learned responses to specific events, or stimuli, in the environment. Like Pavlov, Watson believed that basic laws of learning could explain the behavior of human beings and animals.

Later, another psychologist, B. F. Skinner (1904–1990), extended the behavioral approach to voluntary acts, such as turning on a light switch, riding a bike, or getting dressed. Skinner showed that the consequences of an act powerfully affect the probability of its recurring: Acts that are followed by pleasant consequences are more likely to be repeated (a dog that is praised for heeling will continue to do so), and acts that are followed by unpleasant consequences are likely to cease.

At first, behaviorism excited not only psychologists but also sociologists and political scientists. Here, at last, was a way for the social sciences to be hardheaded and earn the respect of a skeptical world. And the behavioral approach broadened psychology by fostering the study of groups that could not be studied at all through introspection, including animals, infants, and mentally disturbed persons. Behaviorism soon became the predominant American school of experimental psychology and remained so until the early 1960s.

Critics of behaviorism have often accused its proponents of denying the existence of ideas and thoughts—of believing "that human beings do not think or ponder or worry, but instead only *think* that they do" (C. Sherif, 1979). This criticism, however, is misguided. In everyday conversation, behaviorists are as likely as anyone else to say that they think or feel this or that. They realize that they themselves are conscious! It's true that Watson wanted to eliminate thoughts, emotions, and visual images as topics of psychological study. Skinner, however, held that private events could be studied, so long as they were treated as types of behavior. Verbal reports, he said, could provide imperfect clues to these events. Where Skinner and other behaviorists parted company with nonbehaviorists was in their insistence that mental events could not *explain* behavior. For behaviorists, thoughts and feelings were simply behaviors to be explained. The prediction and modification of behavior depended on specifying the environmental conditions that maintained the behavior, not in describing people's thoughts or feelings. That is why behaviorists viewed discussions of the mind with suspicion.

Eventually, however, it became apparent to most psychologists that behavioral principles were not the only principles of learning. People also learn by observation, imitation, and insight; and they learn by thinking about what they see around them.

---

behaviorism An approach to psychology that emphasizes the study of objectively observable behavior and the role of the environment as a determinant of human and other animal behavior.

One outgrowth of behaviorism, **social-learning theory** (often called today *cognitive social-learning theory*), combines elements of classic behaviorism with research on thinking and consciousness. It emphasizes, for example, how people's plans, perceptions, and expectations influence their behavior. As Albert Bandura (1986), one leading proponent of this approach, has observed, "If actions were determined solely by external rewards and punishments, people would behave like weathervanes, constantly shifting direction to conform to whatever momentary influence happened to impinge on them." According to Bandura, the fact that people don't (always) act like weather vanes means that much of human learning is *self-regulated*—shaped by a person's thoughts, values, self-reflections, and intentions. Today, many psychologists feel comfortable combining elements of behaviorism with approaches that incorporate the study of thinking and consciousness.

Why, then, is the man in our anger discussion group imitating the explosive anger patterns of his father, even though he would like to break them? Researchers in the learning perspective would examine the consequences of both the man's and his father's angry outbursts. When they express anger, are they getting the attention and reactions they want from others? Researchers would also examine how the man learned to associate drinking alcohol with behaving abusively. Alcohol doesn't "liberate buried rage," they would say; rather, people learn that when they are drunk, they can get away with certain actions—actions they would be held accountable for if they were sober.

Because of its practical applications, the learning perspective has touched many people's lives. Behavioral techniques have helped people eliminate unreasonable fears, quit smoking, lose weight, toilet-train their toddlers, change destructive anger patterns, and acquire better study habits. Social-learning techniques have helped raise people's self-confidence, motivation, and achievement. The learning perspective's insistence on precision and objectivity has done much to advance psychology as a field.

The Cognitive Perspective

During the 1950s and 1960s, a new emphasis in psychology on the workings of the human mind gathered momentum from an unexpected source: The development of the computer encouraged scientists to study problem solving, informational "feedback," and other mental processes. The result was the rise of the **cognitive perspective** in psychology. (The word *cognitive* comes from the Latin for "to know.")

Cognitive psychologists argued that in order to understand how people use language, acquire moral codes, experience emotions, or behave in groups, psy-

---

social-learning theory (or cognitive social-learning theory) The theory that behavior is learned and maintained through observation and imitation of others, positive consequences, and cognitive processes such as plans and expectations.

cognitive perspective An approach to behavior that emphasizes mental processes in perception, memory, language, problem solving, and other areas of behavior.

chologists must know what is going on in people's heads. They must understand the origins and consequences of people's cognitions—that is, their thoughts, memories, beliefs, perceptions, explanations, and other mental processes. However, cognitive researchers did not wish to return to the old days of introspection. Instead, they developed new ways to infer mental processes from observable behavior. For example, by examining the kinds of errors people make when they try to recall words from a list, cognitive psychologists can draw conclusions about whether words are stored in memory in terms of sound or in terms of meaning.

One of the most important contributions of this perspective has been to show that people's explanations and perceptions affect what they do and feel. All of us are constantly seeking to make sense of the world around us and of our own physical and mental states. Our ideas may not always be realistic or sensible, but they continually influence our actions and choices. Consider the teenager who attacked a stranger because he believed that the stranger had insulted him. Although the teenager felt that his anger was inevitable and that he had no choice about reacting as he did, in fact his anger depended on his own *perception* that the stranger's behavior was a sign of disrespect. Perhaps there were other ways of interpreting the situation. Perhaps the stranger had no intention of being disrespectful. Perhaps the stranger was nearsighted and didn't even see the teenager. Researchers in the cognitive perspective would ask, How do our interpretations of events affect our emotions and reactions? What other interpretations are possible?

Hardly a topic in psychology has been unaffected by what is now often called the "cognitive revolution" (Gardner, 1985). Cognitive psychologists have studied how people explain their own behavior, understand a sentence, solve intellectual problems, reason, form opinions, and remember events. With new methods of investigation, they have been able to study phenomena that were once only the stuff of speculation, such as sleeping, dreaming, hypnosis, and drug-induced states of consciousness. They are designing computer programs that can perform complex cognitive tasks and predict how humans will perform, too. The cognitive approach is one of the strongest forces today in psychology, and it has inspired an explosion of research on the complex workings of the mind.

The Sociocultural Perspective

For the most part, the study of psychology has been the study of the individual—that is, the biological, cognitive, unconscious, or behavioral forces that affect an individual's behavior. During the 1930s and 1940s, some psychologists began to question this focus. They wanted to know how dictators such as Adolf Hitler could persuade people to commit the kinds of atrocities that led to the deaths of millions of people. They wondered why apparently nice people often hold hateful racial or ethnic stereotypes and whether such attitudes could be changed. They asked how cultural values and political systems affect everyday experience. The view that emerged from these questions is the **sociocultural perspective.**

---

sociocultural perspective An approach to behavior that emphasizes social and cultural influences on behavior.

Researchers working from this perspective have shown that most people tend to overlook how social contexts shape nearly everything that human beings do—perceiving the world, expressing joy, managing their households, rearing their children. All of us tend to underestimate the influence of the particular situation in which we happen to find ourselves. We are like fish that are unaware they live in water, so ubiquitous is water in their lives. Sociocultural psychologists study the water and how it affects everything that swims in it.

Psychologists who emphasize the social side of the sociocultural perspective study why, like Tweedledum and Tweedledee, we often conform to others—and fight those closest to us. They study why we obey authorities and blossom or wilt in relationships. They study how standards of masculinity and femininity influence the expression of emotion; how access to job opportunities affects a person's goals and ambitions; or how being in a group affects attitudes. They study how each of us is affected by other people—spouses, lovers, friends, bosses, parents, and strangers.

Psychologists working in this perspective also study features of the physical environment (such as room design, noise level, and temperature), the requirements of a specific job (such as whether the work requires an inflexible routine), and the aspects of a particular situation (such as which person in a relationship has more power) that are constantly affecting us. The right environment can help people cope better with disabilities, get along better with others, and become more creative. Poor working conditions can foster boredom and hostility.

Psychologists who emphasize the cultural side of this perspective study how cultures affect their members. In general, *culture* refers to a program of shared rules that govern the behavior of members of a community or society, and a set of values, beliefs, and attitudes shared by most members of that community. Sometimes the rules are explicit ("Every adult woman must cover her face and hair in public"), and sometimes they are nonverbal and implicit ("The correct nose-to-nose distance for talking to a friend is about 20 inches"). (Try it, and see whether that is your culture's rule for conversational distance.)

The cultures in which we grow up affect every aspect of human functioning, even something as basic as what we see. As cultural psychologist J. R. Kantor (1982) observed, a Hindu and a Christian will respond differently to the sight of a cow. Both have the perceptual ability to see a cow, but their reactions, emotions, and ideas about the cow will be profoundly different because the cow is sacred to one and not to the other. Similarly, people from Western cultures that emphasize individualism differ from people in Asian and Latino cultures that emphasize group loyalty and cooperation. Americans say, "The squeaky wheel gets the grease" (meaning, stand up and make noise to get what you want); the Japanese say, "The nail that stands up from the board gets pounded down" (meaning, don't be too noticeable; it's more important to fit in).

Researchers in the sociocultural perspective would agree with the observer of our anger group who noted that American culture encourages the ventilation of angry feelings. They would investigate how situation and culture affect the expression of anger. In what situations is it acceptable to express anger, and when is it unacceptable? What are the cultural messages about anger that are promoted by television, books, parents, and teachers? When groups or societies are small and close-knit, and when individuals must cooperate to survive, people tend to fear and avoid anger. In contrast, societies that value competition and freedom of individual expression often foster anger and aggression.

By placing the study of the individual human being in social, situational, and cultural context, the sociocultural perspective has made psychology a more fully representative and scientific endeavor.

The Psychodynamic Perspective

Psychodynamic psychology is the thumb on the hand of psychology—connected to the other fingers, but also set apart from them. This perspective is radically different from the others in its language, methods, and standards of acceptable evidence. Many research psychologists working from the biological, learning, cognitive, and sociocultural perspectives don't think it belongs in academic psychology at all. Whereas the other perspectives originated in scientific research, they argue, the psychodynamic perspective originated in Freudian psychoanalysis. It belongs, they say, with philosophy and literature rather than social science. But this perspective has had an important influence on mainstream psychology in various ways, and its assumptions are still widely held by many psychotherapists, which is why we include it and why we will candidly discuss the controversy about this approach.

The **psychodynamic perspective** emphasizes unconscious energy dynamics within the individual, such as inner forces, conflicts, or instinctual energy. Psychodynamic theories share an **intrapsychic** view of the individual, emphasizing the internal, hidden mechanisms of the psyche (mind)—such as the allegedly sexual symbolism of snakes, skyscrapers, and cigars. *Dynamics* is a term from physics that refers to the motion and balance of systems under the action of external or internal forces; for example, the science of thermodynamics studies the relationship between heat and mechanical energy. Freud borrowed from nineteenth-century physics the idea of the conservation of energy: Within any system, he thought, energy can be shifted or transformed, but the total amount of energy remains the same. Psychological energy—the energy it takes to carry out mental and emotional processes, such as thinking, dreaming, and worrying—was, to Freud, a form of physical energy.

---

psychodynamic perspective Psychological approaches, originating with Freud's theory of psychoanalysis, that emphasize unconscious energy dynamics within the individual, such as inner forces, conflicts, or the movement of instinctual energy.
intrapsychic Within the mind (psyche) or self.

Freud argued that conscious awareness is merely the tip of a mental iceberg. Beneath the visible tip, he said, lies the unconscious part of the mind, containing unrevealed wishes, ambitions, passions, guilty secrets, unspeakable yearnings, and conflicts between desire and duty. These unseen forces, Freud believed, have far more power over behavior than consciousness does, so the true study of psychology must probe beneath the surface. In effect, the psychoanalyst must be an archeologist of the mind.

Freud viewed aggression (and sexuality as well) as a basic instinct that lodges in the unconscious. Aggressive energy that is not channeled into productive activity, he believed, will inevitably be released or *displaced* in violent actions, ranging from anger to war. Think back to our group of angry people: The woman who said she "displaces" anger by yelling at her children and reveals her guilt in overeating and migraines is using psychodynamic language. Psychodynamic psychologists would want to know both why she feels guilty about being angry and what unconscious motives lead her to overeat and reveal her insecurities in physical symptoms such as headaches.

Freud's ideas inspired many of his followers to develop their own theories. Because they kept his fundamental belief in the importance of unconscious dynamics but broke away from certain specific ideas in psychoanalytic theory, we use the more general term *psychodynamic* to label this perspective rather than *psychoanalytic*. Although many psychodynamic assumptions are impossible to verify and will have to remain matters of philosophic dispute, others have generated lines of research. Some psychologists study the processes of rationalization, denial, and self-delusion, ideas that stemmed from Freud's theory that the conscious mind strives to protect itself from threatening information. Others are studying the nature and mechanisms of the unconscious—for example, how people can perceive something without being aware of it. Researchers today agree that thoughts and rational behavior can be distorted by guilt, anxiety, and shame. Prolonged emotional conflict may indeed play itself out in physical symptoms, immature habits, and self-defeating actions. Moreover, the psychodynamic perspective is the only one that tries to deal with the great existential human dilemmas, such as alienation in a lonely world and the universal fear of death. In these ways, psychodynamic theories have contributed to psychology and our understanding of human behavior.

Not all schools of psychology fall neatly into one of these five main perspectives. In the 1960s, for example, Abraham Maslow, Rollo May, and Carl Rogers rejected the traditional psychoanalytic emphasis on hostility and conflict as being too negative and pessimistic a view of human nature; and they also rejected the behavioral emphasis on rewards and punishments as being too mechanistic and "mindless" a view of human nature. It was time, they said, for a "third force" in psychology, which they called *humanistic psychology* (or *humanism*). Human behavior, they said, is not completely determined by either unconscious dynamics or the immediate situation. People are capable of free will and therefore have the potential to make more of themselves than psychoanalysis or behaviorism would predict. Maslow (1971) wrote, "When you select out for careful study very fine and healthy people, strong people, creative people, saintly people, sagacious people . . . then you get a very different view of mankind. You are asking how tall can people grow, what can a human being become?"

Although humanism is no longer a dominant school in psychology, it has had considerable influence inside and outside the field. (We will have more to say about this movement in Chapter 15.) Many psychologists across all perspectives embrace some humanistic ideas, although they regard humanism as a philosophy of life rather than a method or approach to psychology. Further, many of the topics the humanists raised, such as altruism and creativity, have been studied experimentally by scientific psychologists in other perspectives. But humanism has probably had its greatest influence in psychotherapy and in spiritual and self-help movements. Many of the descendants of the early humanists abandoned mainstream psychology in order to form popular "human-potential" movements; humanism is their philo-sophical parent.

Another movement that emerged in the 1970s was *feminist psychology.* Feminist psychologists threw an intellectual hand grenade into psychology, and the explosion is still reverberating. The grenade was the evidence of a pervasive bias in the research methods of psychology and in the very questions that researchers had been asking (Crawford & Marecek, 1989; Hare-Mustin & Marecek, 1990). Feminist psychologists documented the large number of studies that used only men as subjects—usually only young, white, middle-class men—and showed why it was often inappropriate to generalize to everyone else from such a narrow base. They showed that the researchers who did include women often described resulting gender differences as deficiencies in women rather than simply as, well, differences (Denmark et al., 1988).

The women and men who consider themselves feminist psychologists may identify with any of the five major perspectives, or draw on research from several approaches in analyzing gender relations and the reasons for the behavior of the two sexes. They have spurred the growth of research on topics traditionally ignored in psychology, such as menstruation, motherhood, the dynamics of power in close relationships, and the reasons for the changing definitions of masculinity and femininity. They have critically examined the male bias in psychotherapy, starting with Freud's own cases (Hare-Mustin, 1991). Finally, they have analyzed the social consequences of psychological findings, showing how research has often been used to justify the lower status of women and other disadvantaged groups.

Some critics, both outside and within this movement, are concerned that some feminist psychologists are replacing a male bias in research with a female bias—for example, by doing studies of women only and then drawing conclusions about gender differences, or by replacing the "women are inferior to men" stereotype with a "women are superior to men" stereotype (Tavris, 1992; Yoder & Kahn, 1993). They also worry that the overriding goal of feminist psychologists—promoting gender equality—sometimes leads them to embrace conclusions that are intuitively appealing but lack solid empirical support (M. Mednick, 1989; Peplau & Conrad, 1989; Stimpson, 1996). Feminist psychology, however, reminds all psychologists that research and psychotherapy are social processes, affected by all the influences and subjectivity that people bring to any enterprise. To improve psychology and the uses to which it is put, they say, we must become aware of our biases and attempt to correct them. This argument has inspired other movements in psychology that are striving to eliminate bias in studies of ethnic groups, gay men and lesbians, old people, disabled people, and the poor.

WHAT DO YOU KNOW?

A. Anxiety is a common problem. To see whether you understand the five major perspectives in psychology, try to match each possible explanation of anxiety on the left with a perspective on the right.

1. Anxious people often think about the future in distorted ways.
2. Anxiety is due to forbidden, unconscious desires.
3. Anxiety symptoms often bring hidden rewards, such as being excused from exams.
4. Excessive anxiety can be caused by a chemical imbalance, caffeine, or a sleep disorder.
5. A national emphasis on success and competition promotes anxiety about failure.

   a. behavioral
   b. psychodynamic
   c. sociocultural
   d. biological
   e. cognitive

B. Different assumptions about human behavior can lead to different conclusions. What assumption distinguishes cognitive psychology from behaviorism? What assumption distinguishes the psychodynamic perspective from the sociocultural perspective?

ANSWERS:

A. 1. e 2. b 3. a 4. d 5. c B. Cognitive psychologists assume that thoughts and feelings can explain behavior; behaviorists assume that thoughts and feelings are behaviors to be explained. Psychodynamic psychologists assume that behavior is driven largely by internal (intrapsychic) factors, such as unconscious drives; sociocultural psychologists assume that behavior is determined largely by social and cultural factors.

ABOUT THIS BOOK

The five perspectives that we have chosen for this book represent qualitatively different approaches to the psychological study of thought and action, and they have been the most enduring and productive in terms of research and application. We have not presented the five perspectives in order of importance. We might have started with the sociocultural view, because every baby is born into an existing cultural world that will influence his or her physical and mental development. But many students and instructors find it logical to start with biological influences on behavior and gradually move on to examine how a person thinks, what a person learns, and the environment the person lives in. We kept the psychodynamic perspective for last because it differs so significantly from the others.

We want to emphasize that no single one of these perspectives operates in isolation from the others. Moreover, individual psychologists who are studying a specific topic, such as memory or intelligence or depression, might well draw on findings and methods from several perspectives. The forces that govern our behavior are as intertwined as strands of ivy on a wall. (That message alone, if enough people believed it, would put an end to the pop-psych industry and its simple answers to complex matters.) Each perspective, by itself, is limited. Depression and alcoholism are not only or always a result of biochemical abnormalities. No one can "fulfill any potential," without regard to the limitations of their biology or the constraints of their environments. Tumors and diseases cannot be eliminated by the sheer force of holding positive, healthful thoughts. Generalizations about cultures permit us to overlook the human individuality that exists in every society as well as our commonalities across cultures.

At the end of each section—the one or two chapters that make up every perspective—we devote a chapter to evaluating the perspective as a whole. There we raise some of the important issues and questions we think the perspective generates, the limitations of the perspective, and some of the social and political implications of its findings. We will also discuss its relevance to what psychologists charmingly call "real life"—that is, ways in which findings from each perspective have been applied to psychotherapy and the treatment of mental disorder, the improvement of people's lives and relationships, or the resolution of a persistent social problem.

Although many psychologists acknowledge the importance of integrating the five perspectives, the reality is that most of them, like professionals in other fields, have become highly specialized. Someone who is trained to look for biological influences on behavior is unlikely to study, or even to think much about, the cultural influences on behavior, and vice versa. Like the blind men in the poem that begins this book, many psychologists tend to think that the part of the beast that they happen to study is the whole animal—or at least the most important part of it. That is why the differences among the perspectives of psychology have produced lively arguments, angry confrontations, and sometimes stony silences among their defenders.

Some social scientists hope for a unified approach that will one day bring all of psychology under one tent (Bevan, 1991; Gibson, 1994). Gregory Kimble (1994, 1996), for example, has proposed a unifying "frame of reference" for scientific psychology that involves general principles of behavior derived from biology, learning, cognition, and culture. "In the wealth of knowledge that has accumulated since [William] James," writes Kimble (1994), "it appears that there are patterns—something like the laws that Newton showed us—that are general enough to bring intellectual togetherness to psychology." We hope to show you some of those reliable patterns about human behavior in the following chapters.

But other psychologists have concluded that "intellectual togetherness" is a pipe dream. The diverse strands of psychological research can never be woven together into a coherent science, they maintain, and there is no point in trying to impose a false unity on them. Sigmund Koch (1992), for example, suggests we stop speaking of "the study of psychology," as if psychology were a single entity, and instead speak of "the psychological studies." Howard Gardner (1992) persuasively predicts that before long, there will be no field of psychology at all. The emerging disciplines of cognitive science and neuroscience, he believes, will absorb the biological, cognitive, and learning perspectives; a broad interdisciplinary field of cultural studies will absorb the sociocultural perspective; other subfields (such as clinical, survey research, industrial/organizational, and consumer psychology) will become applied disciplines; and psychodynamic and personality research will become allied with literature and the humanities.

We won't join in these predictions for the future of scientific psychology. But we do believe that the best way to understand any particular topic, let alone to formulate solutions for social problems, is to draw on the best features of the various perspectives and schools of thought. In the last chapter of this book, we will show how this might be done. There we will put all the perspectives together and try to describe the whole elephant.

If you are ready to share the excitement of studying psychological questions; if you love mysteries and want to know not only who did it but also why they did it; if you are willing to reconsider what you think you think . . . then you are ready to read on.

Bent Offerings *by Don Addis.*

✦ ✦ ✦

Summary

1. Modern psychology is the scientific study of behavior and mental processes and how they are affected by an organism's physical state, mental state, and external environment. Psychology's methods and approaches distinguish it from other academic disciplines, as well as from programs based on "psychobabble" and nonscientific approaches to human experience, such as psychic predictions and astrology.

2. An important benefit of studying psychology is the opportunity it provides for enhancing critical-thinking skills. *Critical thinking* enables a person to distinguish between beliefs based on matters of taste, preference, and wishful thinking and beliefs based on good reasoning and solid evidence. The critical thinker is curious and asks questions, defines problems clearly and accurately, examines the evidence, analyzes assumptions and biases, avoids emotional reasoning, avoids oversimplification, considers alternative interpretations, and tolerates uncertainty.

3. Until the nineteenth century, psychology was not recognized as a separate field of study, and there were few formal rules about how it was to be conducted. Generalizations about human behavior were often based on anecdotes or descriptions of individual cases. Psychology as a formal science was officially born in 1879, when Wilhelm Wundt established the first psychological laboratory, in Leipzig, Germany. Wundt's work relied heavily on *trained introspection,* which was soon abandoned by others as insufficiently objective.

4. An early school of psychology that opposed Wundt's ideas was known as *functionalism.* The functionalists were inspired in part by the evolutionary theories of Charles Darwin. They wanted to know how various actions help a person or animal adapt to the environment, and they looked for underlying causes, purposes, and practical consequences of specific behaviors and mental strategies.

5. Psychology as a method of psychotherapy was born in Vienna, Austria, with the work of Sigmund Freud. Freud's ideas eventually evolved into a broad theory of personality, and both his theory and his methods of treating people with emotional problems became known as *psychoanalysis.*

6. Today psychology is a complex field consisting of different schools, perspectives, methods, and approaches to training. Psychologists do research and teach in colleges and universities; provide health and mental-health services; and conduct research and apply findings in a variety of nonacademic settings. Many psychologists move flexibly across these areas.

7. The majority of psychological practitioners are *clinical psychologists.* In almost all states, a license to practice clinical psychology requires a doctorate. Not all people who call themselves psychotherapists are clinical psychologists; they may be psychiatrists (who have an M.D.), psychoanalysts (who have an M.D. or Ph.D. and specialized training in psychoanalysis), social workers, school or counseling psychologists, or marriage, family, and child counselors (MFCCs), for whom licensing requirements vary. In the United States and Canada, anyone may use the label "psychotherapist," which is an unregulated term. Many psychologists are concerned about an increasing number of poorly trained psychotherapists who lack credentials and have little understanding of research methods and findings.

8. Five points of view predominate today in psychology, distinguished by the questions they raise, the assumptions they make, and the explanations they offer. The *biological perspective* is concerned with how bodily events interact with events in the environment to produce perceptions, thoughts, emotions, memories, and behavior, and with the relative contributions of "nature" (genetic dispositions) and "nurture" (upbringing and environment) in the development of abilities and personality traits. The *learning perspective* emphasizes how the environment and a person's history affect behavior; within this perspective, behaviorists study learned

responses to events and the role of consequences in shaping behavior, and social-learning theorists combine elements of behaviorism with research on thinking, expectations, and intentions. The *cognitive perspective* emphasizes mental processes in perception, memory, language, emotion, problem solving, belief formation, and other aspects of thinking. The *sociocultural perspective* places the individual in situational and cultural context, emphasizing how social roles, situational demands, and cultural rules affect individual beliefs and behavior. The *psychodynamic perspective* emphasizes unconscious dynamics within the person, such as motives, conflicts, or instinctual energy; it differs greatly from the others in its language, methods, and standards of acceptable evidence.

9. Not all schools of psychology fall neatly into one of these five perspectives. *Humanistic psychology* emphasizes free will and human potential; although no longer a dominant school, it has had considerable influence on psychotherapy and on spiritual and self-help movements. *Feminist psychology* draws on research from all five perspectives in analyzing gender relations and gender differences, and it has challenged gender biases in research.

10. Because the forces that govern behavior are intertwined, each perspective, by itself, is limited. The strands of psychological research may never be woven together into a coherent and unified science, but the best way to formulate solutions for social and personal problems is to draw on the best features of each perspective.

Key Terms

psychology 6

psychobabble 6

critical thinking 10

empirical evidence 13

arguing by anecdote 15

Occam's razor 15

Wilhelm Wundt 18

trained introspection 19

functionalism 19

William James 19

Charles Darwin 19

Sigmund Freud 19

psychoanalysis 20

psychological practice 20

basic psychology 21

applied psychology 21

psychological practitioners:

    clinical psychologist 21

    psychiatrist 22

    psychoanalyst 22

    psychotherapist 22

Gestalt psychology 25

biological perspective 25

learning perspective 26

behaviorism 26

social-learning theory 28

cognitive perspective 28

sociocultural perspective 29

culture 30

psychodynamic perspective 31

intrapsychic 31

humanistic psychology 32

feminist psychology 33

CHAPTER 2

Studying Human Behavior

$\mathcal{S}$uppose that you are the parent of a nine-year-old boy who has been diagnosed as autistic. Your child lives in a silent world of his own, cut off from normal social inter-action. He rarely looks you in the eyes. He rocks back and forth for hours. Sometimes he does self-destructive things, such as biting through the skin on his fingers. He does not speak, and he cannot function in a public classroom.

Imagine your excitement, then, when you hear glowing reports on TV about a new technique, devised by an Australian teacher and now used by several American clinics, that seems to offer your child a way out of his mental prison. According to the proponents of this technique, when children who are autistic or mentally impaired are placed in front of a keyboard and an adult gently places a hand over the child's hand or forearm, children who have never used words before are able to peck out complete sentences. You find a clinic that will try such "facilitated communication" with your son. The fee is steep, but you are desperate.

The situation we have described is not hypothetical. In the past few years, thousands of desperate, hopeful parents have been drawn to the promise of facilitated communica-tion. Suddenly their children appear able to answer questions, convey their needs, and divulge their thoughts. Reportedly, some children, through their facilitators, have even mastered high-school-level math and reading; some have written poetry of astonishing beauty; and some have typed out secrets, such as sexual molestation by their fathers and mothers. Facilitated communication, say its boosters, is a miracle.

Or is it?

Psychological scientists have not been content with claims about the effectiveness of this method or persuaded by testimonials. Instead, they have put those claims and testimonials to the test in many controlled experiments involving hundreds of autistic children and adults (Jacobson & Mulick, 1994; Mulick, 1994). In one study, researchers arranged things so that the facilitator could not see a series of pictures presented to the child or hear the questions the child was being asked about the pictures; under these conditions, autistic children did not show any unexpected linguistic abilities (Eberlin et al., 1993). In another study, young and middle-aged autistic adults sometimes saw

Facilitated communication is thought by some to be a breakthrough for autistic people. But what does controlled research show?

the same picture as the facilitator and sometimes a different one; the only correct descriptions produced by the autistic subjects were for pictures shown to the facilitator (Wheeler et al., 1993). What happens in "facilitated communication" is exactly what happens when a medium guides a person's hand over a Ouija board to help the person receive "messages" from a "spirit": The person doing the "facilitating" is unconsciously nudging the other person's hand in the desired direction. Facilitated communication, on closer inspection, turns out to be *facilitator* communication.

This research is vitally important, because if parents waste their time and money on a treatment that doesn't work, they may never get the kind of help for their children that is actually helpful—and they may suffer terribly when their false hopes are finally demolished by reality. You can see, then, why research methods are so important to psychologists. These methods are the tools of the psychologist's trade. They offer a way to sort out conflicting views and to correct false ideas that may otherwise cause people enormous harm. They tell psychologists when to replace simplistic questions with more sophisticated and valuable ones. As we will see in this book, an innovative or clever research method can even reveal answers to questions about human behavior that once seemed impossible to study.

We know that students sometimes get impatient when they have to learn about research methods. "Why not cut right to the findings?" they wonder. But although scientists are the ones who *use* research methods, nonscientists also need to understand those methods if they want to be critical thinkers and sophisticated consumers of psychological (and other scientific) findings. You are constantly being bombarded by conflicting claims about matters that can affect your life—claims, for example, about how you should break bad habits, manage your emotions, dress for success, settle disputes, overcome shyness, improve your love life, or reduce stress. Not all studies on such matters are good ones, and some advice from self-styled "experts" is based on questionable evidence or no evidence at all.

When college students lack an adequate understanding of research methods, they tend to base their responses to research on how well the results happen to confirm their own expectations. If the results match their expectations, students usually feel confident about accepting them, even when the study's methods do not justify such confidence. But after students learn how to evaluate specific aspects of a study's design (such as how the participants were selected), they stop to consider the procedures used before drawing any conclusions (Forsyth, Arpey, & Stratton-Hess, 1992). We hope that when you hear and read about psychological issues, you, too, will consider how the information was obtained and how the results were interpreted, using guidelines in this chapter.

WHAT MAKES RESEARCH SCIENTIFIC?

When we refer to psychologists as scientists, we do not mean that they work with complicated gadgets and machines or wear white lab coats (although some do). The scientific enterprise has more to do with attitudes and procedures than with apparatus and apparel. Philosophers and scientists have written many fat books on the features that distinguish science from other ways of knowing. We can't go into all these features, but here are a few key characteristics of the ideal scientist:

1. **PRECISION.** Scientists usually start out with a **hypothesis,** a statement that attempts to describe or explain behavior. Initially, the hypothesis may be stated quite generally, as in "Misery loves company." But before any research can be done, the hypothesis must be put into more specific terms. For example, "Misery loves company" might be rephrased as, "People who are anxious about a threatening situation tend to seek out others who face the same threat."

   Some hypotheses are suggested by previous findings or casual observation. Others are derived from a general **theory,** an organized system of assumptions and principles that purports to explain certain phenomena and how they are related. A scientific theory is not just someone's personal hunch or opinion, as people imply when they say, "It's only a theory." Theories that come to be accepted within the scientific community are consistent with many different observations and empirical findings and are inconsistent with only a few (Stanovich, 1996).

---

hypothesis A statement that attempts to predict or account for a set of phenomena; scientific hypotheses specify relationships among events or variables and are supported or disconfirmed by empirical investigation.
theory An organized system of assumptions and principles that purports to explain a specified set of phenomena and their interrelationships.

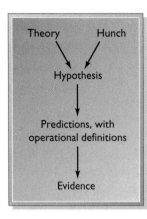

Theory   Hunch

Hypothesis

Predictions, with
operational definitions

Evidence

A hypothesis leads to explicit predictions about what will happen in a particular situation. In a prediction, vague terms such as "anxiety" or "threatening situation" are given **operational definitions** that specify how the behavior or situation is to be observed and measured. For example, a researcher might define *anxiety* as a score on an anxiety questionnaire and *threatening situation* as the threat of an electric shock. The prediction might be, "If you raise people's anxiety scores by telling them they are going to receive electric shocks, and then you give them the choice of waiting alone or with others in the same situation, they will be more likely to choose to wait with others than they would be if they were not anxious."

The prediction is then tested, using careful and systematic procedures. (In contrast, as we saw in Chapter 1, pseudoscientists often hide behind vague, empty terms and make predictions that are nearly meaningless.)

2. **SKEPTICISM.** Scientists do not accept ideas on faith or authority; their motto is "Show me!" Some of the greatest scientific advances have been made by those who dared to doubt what everyone else assumed to be true: that the sun revolves around the earth, that illness can be cured by applying leeches to the skin, that madness is a sign of demonic possession. In the world of the researcher, skepticism means accepting conclusions, both new and old, with caution. Caution, however, must be balanced by an openness to new ideas and evidence. Otherwise, the scientist may wind up as shortsighted as the famous physicist Lord Kelvin, who at the end of the nineteenth century reputedly declared with great confidence that radio had no future, X rays were a hoax, and "heavier-than-air flying machines" were impossible.

3. **RELIANCE ON EMPIRICAL EVIDENCE.** Unlike plays and poems, scientific theories and hypotheses are not judged by how aesthetically pleasing or entertaining they are. An idea may initially generate excitement simply because it is plausible, imaginative, or appealing. But no matter how true or right it may seem, eventually it must be backed by evidence if it is to be taken seriously. As Nobel Prize–winning scientist Peter Medawar (1979) wrote, "The intensity of the conviction that a hypothesis is true has no bearing on whether it is true or not." Further, as we noted in Chapter 1, the evidence for a scientific idea must be empirical—that is, based on careful and systematic observation. A collection of personal accounts or anecdotes, or an appeal to authority, will not do.

Consider again the problem of childhood autism. At one time, many clinicians thought this disorder was caused by a rejecting, cold "refrigerator mother." They were influenced in this belief by the writings of the eminent psychoanalyst Bruno Bettelheim. In his book *The Empty Fortress* (1967), Bettelheim's only evi-

---

operational definition A precise definition of a term in a hypothesis, which specifies the operations for observing and measuring the process or phenomenon being defined.

dence was case studies of three autistic children whose mothers had a history of psychological problems. He also alluded to 37 other cases but published no facts about them. Yet Bettelheim's authority was so great that many people accepted his claims in spite of his meager data. Then some researchers began to have doubts about Bettelheim's ideas. Instead of relying on subjective impressions, as Bettelheim had, they compared the parents of autistic children with parents who did not have an autistic child, using standardized tests of psychological adjustment and analyzing their data statistically. The results were clear: There were no differences between the two groups of parents in terms of personality traits, marital adjustment, or family life (DeMyer, 1975; Koegel et al., 1983). Because of Bettelheim's advice, thousands of parents had been wrongly led to believe that they were responsible for their children's disorder, suffering needless guilt and remorse. Today there is general agreement that autism stems from a neurological problem rather than from any psychological problems of the parents.

4. **WILLINGNESS TO MAKE "RISKY PREDICTIONS."** A scientist must state an idea in such a way that it can be refuted, or disproved by counterevidence. This principle, known as the **principle of falsifiability,** doesn't mean that the idea *will* be disproved, only that it *could* be if certain kinds of facts were to be discovered. Another way of saying this is that a scientist must predict not only what will happen, but also what will *not* happen. A willingness to make such "risky predictions" forces the scientist to take negative evidence seriously. Any researcher who refuses to go out on a limb and risk disconfirmation is not a true scientist.

This characteristic is a little tricky, so let's take an example. Some people think they can find subterranean water by holding a "dowsing" rod out in front of them and walking around until the rod bends down toward water hidden below. Some dowsers use special steel rods; others prefer such mundane objects as a straightened coat hanger or a forked branch. Dowsers believe that they are psychically tuned in to the presence of water and that this accounts for the rod's behavior; actually, it is due to involuntary movements of their own hands. (Unconscious hand movements again!) Illusionist and professional debunker James Randi (1982) has been challenging such claims for years by conducting controlled tests using scientific procedures to which the dowsers themselves agree. Randi is still offering a reward of thousands of dollars to any dowser who proves him wrong. He has never lost a cent; invariably the dowsers perform at levels no better than chance. Yet despite these failures, the dowsers rarely lose faith in their own abilities. Instead, they blame the alignment of the planets, or sunspots, or bad "vibes" from spectators. Thus it really doesn't matter at all how the dowsing demonstration turns out because the dowser has all the bases covered in advance.

Many critics of psychoanalysis find it guilty of a similar violation of the principle of falsifiability. If a person recalls some conflict in childhood that psychoana-

---

principle of falsifiability The principle that a scientific theory must make predictions that are specific enough to expose the theory to the possibility of disconfirmation; that is, the theory must predict not only what will happen, but also what will not happen.

lysts think is universal, the psychoanalysts say, "Aha, evidence for our theory!" If a person can't recall such a conflict, the psychoanalysts say it must have been repressed (forced into the unconscious mind so that it can't be remembered), or that the person is "in denial." Thus there is no evidence that can count against the theory, and no possible way to refute it, even if it is wrong. *Any theory that purports to explain everything that could conceivably happen is unscientific.*

If you keep your eyes open, you will find many violations of the principle of falsifiability around you. For example, research psychologists, the FBI, and police investigators have been unable to substantiate the supposedly murderous activities of satanic cults (Goodman et al., 1995; Hicks, 1991). But that doesn't keep some police officers and therapists from believing in the reality of the cults and their misdeeds. Those who believe such cults are widespread say they are not surprised by the lack of evidence because satanic cults cover up their activities by eating bodies or burying them. The FBI's failure to find the evidence is "proof," they say, that the FBI is part of a conspiracy to support the satanists. To believers, then, the lack of evidence of satanic cults is actually a sign of the cults' success. But think about that claim. If a lack of evidence can count as evidence, then what could possibly count as *counter*evidence?

5. **OPENNESS.** Scientists must be willing to tell others where they got their ideas, how they tested them, and what the results were. They must do this clearly and in detail so that other scientists can repeat, or *replicate*, their studies and verify the findings.

Replication is an important part of the scientific process because sometimes what seems to be a fabulous phenomenon turns out to be only a fluke. For example, many years ago, a team of researchers trained flatworms to cringe in response to a flashing light, and then they killed the worms, ground them into a mash, and fed the mash to a second set of worms. This cannibalistic diet, the researchers reported, sped up acquisition of the cringe response in the second group of worms (McConnell, 1962). As you can imagine, the findings caused tremendous excitement. If worms could learn faster by ingesting the "memory molecules" of their fellow worms, could memory pills be far behind? Students joked about grinding up professors; professors joked about doing brain transplants in students. But alas, the results proved difficult to replicate, and talk of memory pills eventually faded away.

Do psychologists and other scientists always live up to the lofty standards expected of them? Of course not. Being human, they may put too much trust in their personal experiences. They may deceive themselves. They may permit ambition to interfere with openness. They may fail to put their theories fully to the test: It is always easier to be skeptical about someone else's ideas than about your own pet theory. Even Albert Einstein sometimes resisted data that might have disconfirmed his own ideas.

Commitment to one's theories is not in itself a bad thing. Passion is the fuel of progress. It motivates researchers to think boldly, defend unpopular ideas, and do the exhaustive testing that is often required to support an idea. But passion can also cloud perceptions and in some sad cases has even led to deception and fraud. That is why science must be a communal activity. Scientists are expected to share their evidence and procedures with others. They are expected to submit their results to professional journals, which send the findings to experts in the field for comment before publishing them. Through this process, called *peer review,* scientists demonstrate that their position is well supported. The scientific community—in our case, the psychological community—acts as a jury, scrutinizing and sifting the evidence, approving some viewpoints and relegating others to the scientific scrap heap. This public process is not perfect, but it does give science a built-in system of checks and balances. Individuals are not necessarily objective, honest, or even rational, but science forces them to justify their claims.

WHAT DO YOU KNOW?

Test your understanding of science by identifying which of its rules was violated in each of the following cases.

1. For years, writer Norman Cousins told how he had cured himself of a rare and life-threatening disease through a combination of humor and vitamins. His book about his experience, *Anatomy of an Illness,* became a huge best-seller.
2. Alfred Russel Wallace hit upon the theory of evolution at about the same time that Charles Darwin did. Later he became fascinated by attempts to communicate with the dead. To prove that such communication was possible, he had mediums conduct séances. He trusted these mediums and was persuaded by their demonstrations.
3. Benjamin Rush, a physician and signer of the Declaration of Independence, believed that illnesses accompanied by fever should be treated by bloodletting. During an outbreak of yellow fever, many patients whom he treated in this manner died. Yet Rush did not lose faith in his approach; he attributed each case of improvement to his treatment and each death to the severity of the disease (Stanovich, 1996).

ANSWERS:

1. Cousins offered only a personal account and ignored disconfirming evidence. **2.** Wallace was gullible rather than skeptical. **3.** Rush violated the principle of falsifiability: He interpreted a patient's survival as support for his treatment and explained a death by saying that the person had been too ill for the treatment to work. Thus there was no possible counterevidence that could refute the theory (which, by the way, was dead wrong—the "treatment" was actually as dangerous as the disease).

DESCRIPTIVE RESEARCH

Psychologists use several different methods in their research, depending on the kinds of questions they want to answer. These methods are not mutually exclusive. Just as a police detective may use a magnifying glass *and* a fingerprint duster *and* interviews of suspects to figure out "who done it," psychological sleuths may draw on different techniques at different stages of an ongoing investigation.

Many psychological methods are descriptive in nature. **Descriptive methods** allow a researcher to describe and predict behavior but not necessarily to choose one explanation over other, competing ones. Some of these methods are used primarily by clinicians to describe and understand the behavior of individuals. Others are used primarily by researchers to compare groups of people and arrive at generalizations about behavior. And some methods can be used in either way. In this section we will discuss the most common descriptive methods. As you read, you might want to list each method's advantages and disadvantages on a piece of paper. When you finish this and the next two sections, check your list against the one in the table on page 64.

Case Studies

A **case study** (or *case history*) is a detailed description of a particular individual. It may be based on careful observation or formal psychological testing. It may include information about the person's childhood, dreams, fantasies, experiences, relationships, and hopes—anything that will provide insight into the person's behavior. Case studies are most commonly used by clinicians, but they are sometimes used by academic researchers as well. They are especially valuable in the investigation of a new topic. Many language researchers, for example, have started out by keeping detailed diaries on the language development of their own children. A case study can be a rich source of hypotheses for future research.

Case studies illustrate psychological principles in a way that abstract generalizations and cold statistics never can. They also produce a more detailed picture of an individual than other methods do. Often, however, case studies depend on people's memories of the past, and such memories may be both selective and inaccurate. Also, it is often hard to know how to choose one interpretation of a case over another. Most important, the case-study method has limited usefulness for psychologists who want to generalize about human behavior, because a person who is the subject of a case study may be unlike most other people about whom the researcher would like to draw conclusions. (One of Bruno Bettelheim's errors, you will recall, was to assume that the mothers he observed were representative of all parents of autistic children.)

Still, case studies can be enlightening when practical or ethical considerations prevent information from being gathered in other ways, or when unusual circumstances shed light on a general issue. Biological psychologists, for example, have studied cases of patients with brain damage for clues about how the brain is organized. They have learned that brain damage can have extremely specific effects, depending on the exact location of the damage. Some patients can recognize manufactured items, such as photographs, tools, or books, but not natural objects, such as rocks or trees. Others can recognize most natural objects but cannot distinguish among animals, or fruits, or

---

descriptive methods Methods that yield descriptions of behavior but not necessarily causal explanations.
case study A detailed description of a particular individual being studied or treated.

vegetables (Damasio, 1990). In one study (Cubelli, 1991), two patients were unable to write down correctly the vowels in words but had no trouble writing the consonants!

Ironically, then, unusual cases can sometimes shed light on a general question about human functioning. Most case studies, however, are sources, rather than tests, of hypotheses. You should be extremely cautious about pop-psych books and TV programs that present only testimonials and vivid case histories as evidence.

Observational Studies

In **observational studies,** the researcher systematically observes and records behavior without interfering in any way with the people (or animals) being observed. Unlike case studies, observational studies usually involve many different subjects. Often an observational study is the first step in a program of research; it is helpful to have a good description of behavior before you try to explain it.

The primary purpose of *naturalistic observation* is to describe behavior as it occurs in the natural environment. Ethologists such as Jane Goodall and the late Dian Fossey have used this method to study apes and other animals in the wild. Psychologists use naturalistic observation wherever people happen to be—at home, on playgrounds or streets, in bars, in schoolrooms, or in offices. In this kind of research, it is important to *count, rate,* or *measure* behavior in a systematic way. These procedures help to minimize the tendency of most observers to notice only what they expect or want to see. Careful record keeping ensures accuracy and allows different observers to cross-check their observations to be sure the observations are reliable, or consistent, from person to person. In some studies using naturalistic observation, researchers have concealed themselves entirely, so that the people they are observing will behave naturally. When such precautions are taken, this method gives us a glimpse of people as they really are, in their normal social contexts. However, it does not tell us what *causes* their behavior.

Sometimes it is preferable or necessary to make observations in the laboratory rather than in real-world settings. In *laboratory observation,* the psychologist has more control. He or she can use sophisticated equipment, determine how many people will be observed at once, maintain a clear line of vision while observing, and so forth. Suppose, for example, that you wanted to know how infants of different ages respond when left in the company of a stranger. You could observe children at a nursery school, but most would probably already be toddlers and would know the nursery-school personnel. You could visit private homes, but that might be slow and inconvenient. A solution would be to have parents and their infants come to your laboratory, observe them playing together for a while through a one-way window, then have a stranger enter the room and, a few minutes later, have the parent leave. You could record signs of distress, interactions with the stranger, and other behavior. If you used this procedure, you

---

observational study A study in which the researcher carefully and systematically observes and records behavior without interfering with the behavior; it may involve either naturalistic observation or laboratory observation.

would find that very young infants carry on cheerfully with whatever they are doing when the parent leaves. However, by the age of about eight months, children often burst into tears or show other signs of what child psychologists call "separation anxiety" (Ainsworth, 1979).

One shortcoming of laboratory observation, however, is that the presence of researchers and special equipment may cause subjects to behave differently than they would in their usual surroundings. Another is that laboratory observations, like naturalistic observations, are more useful for describing behavior than for explaining it. When we observe infants protesting whenever a parent leaves the room, we cannot be sure *why* they are protesting. Is it because they have become attached to their parents and want them nearby, or have they learned from experience that crying brings attention and affection? It is hard to answer such questions on the basis of observational studies alone.

Tests

Psychological tests are procedures used for measuring and evaluating personality traits, emotional states, aptitudes, interests, abilities, and values. Typically such tests require people to answer a series of written or oral questions. The answers may then be totaled to yield a single numerical score (or a set of scores) that reveals something about the person. *Objective tests,* also called "inventories," measure beliefs, feelings, or behaviors of which an individual is aware. In contrast, *projective tests* are designed to tap unconscious feelings or motives (see Chapter 16).

At one time or another, most people have probably taken a psychological test, such as an intelligence test, achievement test, or vocational-aptitude test. You may have taken other kinds of tests when applying for a job, joining the military, or starting psychotherapy. Hundreds of such tests are used in industry, education, research, and the helping professions. Some are given to individuals, others to large groups. These "assessment instruments" help clarify differences among individuals, as well as differences in the reactions of the same individual on different occasions or at different stages of life. They may be used to promote self-understanding, evaluate treatments and programs, or, in scientific research, draw generalizations about human behavior.

Well-constructed psychological tests are a great improvement over simple self-evaluation because many people have a distorted view of their own abilities and traits. For example, most people have a bias to see themselves as "better than average," even when they are not (Myers, 1980). Tests are also usually superior to the informal judgments of others that we all make. W. Grant Dahlstrom (1993) notes that in evaluating others, people tend to commit certain basic errors in thinking. For example, if they see one negative trait in someone, they may assume the presence of others as well—a bias known as the "negative halo" effect. Dahlstrom recalls that when he was a trainee in

---

psychological tests Procedures used to measure and evaluate personality traits, emotional states, aptitudes, interests, abilities, and values.

the inpatient psychiatric unit of a large hospital, a 15-year-old girl, "Mary," was admitted on referral from her family doctor. Mary was poorly dressed, unattractive, disheveled, and uncommunicative. The psychiatrist who admitted her decided that she was also schizophrenic and mentally retarded; he mockingly called her an example of "poor protoplasm." But when Dahlstrom gave Mary a series of psychological tests, he found that she was neither schizophrenic nor mentally impaired; she was depressed because she lived with an emotionally abusive father. Because of the negative halo effect, the psychiatrist had misjudged Mary's mental condition. Eventually, with therapy and support, Mary's emotional state improved, and when Dahlstrom last heard of her, she was working as the associate director of a local art institute.

One test of a good test is whether it is **standardized**—that is, whether there are uniform procedures for giving and scoring it. It would hardly be fair to give some people detailed instructions and plenty of time and others only vague instructions and limited time. Those who administer the test must know exactly how to explain the tasks involved, how much time to allow, and what materials to use. Scoring is usually done by referring to **norms,** or established standards of performance. The usual procedure for developing norms is to give the test to a large group of people who resemble those for whom the test is intended. Norms tell users of the test which scores can be considered high, low, or average.

Test construction, administration, and interpretation require specialized training. For one thing, the test must be **reliable**—that is, it must produce consistent results from one time and place to the next. A vocational-interest test is not reliable if it tells Tom he would make a wonderful engineer but a poor journalist, but then gives different results when Tom takes the test again a week later. Psychologists evaluate a test's reliability in several ways. For example, they may measure *test–retest reliability* by giving the test twice to the same group of people, then comparing the two sets of scores statistically. If the test is reliable, individuals' scores will be similar from one session to another. This method has a drawback, however: People tend to do better the second time they take a test, after they have become familiar with the strategies required and the actual test items used. A solution is to compute *alternate-forms reliability,* by giving different versions of the same test to the same group on two separate occasions. The items on the two forms are similar in format but not identical in content. With this method, performance cannot improve because of familiarity with the items, although people may still do somewhat better the second time because they have learned the general strategies and procedures expected of them.

In order to be useful, a test must also be **valid;** that is, it must measure what it sets out to measure. A creativity test is not valid if what it actually measures is verbal sophistication. If the items are broadly representative of the trait in question, the test is said to have *content validity.* Suppose you constructed a test to measure employees' job

---

standardize In test construction, to develop uniform procedures for giving and scoring a test.
norms In test construction, established standards of performance.
reliability In test construction, the consistency, from one time and place to another, of scores derived from a test.
validity The ability of a test to measure what it was designed to measure.

satisfaction. If your test tapped a broad sampling of relevant beliefs and behaviors (e.g., "Do you feel you have reached a dead end at work?" "Are you bored with your assignments?"), it would have content validity. If the test asked only how workers felt about their salary level, it would lack content validity and would be of little use; after all, highly paid people are not always satisfied with their jobs, nor are people who earn low wages always dissatisfied.

Most tests are also judged on *criterion validity,* the ability to predict other, independent measures, or criteria, of the trait in question. A test can have criterion validity and thus be useful even when some individual items don't *look* valid or sensible to the test-taker. The criterion for a scholastic aptitude test might be college grades; the criterion for a test of shyness might be behavior in social situations. To find out whether your job-satisfaction test had criterion validity, you might return a year later to see whether it correctly predicted absenteeism, resignations, or requests for job transfers.

Unfortunately, teachers, parents, and employers do not always stop to question a test's validity, especially when test results are summarized in a single number, such as an IQ score or a job applicant's ranking. Enthralled by the test score, they may simply assume that the test measures what they think it does. Robert Sternberg (1988) has noted that this assumption is especially common with mental tests, even though, he argues, such tests actually tap only a limited set of abilities important for intelligent behavior. "There is an allure to exact-sounding numbers," says Sternberg. "An IQ of 119, an SAT score of 580, a mental abilities score in the 74th percentile—all sound very precise. . . . But the appearance of precision is no substitute for the fact of validity."

Research on validity and reliability has found that even some widely used tests fail to measure up. Witness the rise and fall of the modern polygraph machine, also known as the "lie detector." The invention of the polygraph was based on the belief that a person who is guilty and fearful will reveal guilt in physiological symptoms—increased heart rate, respiration, and electrical conductivity of the skin—as the person responds with untruthful answers to questions. The lie-detector test had great appeal, because governments, employers, spouses, and spies all want guaranteed ways of detecting the truth. Until recently, many companies required that job applicants take lie-detector tests as part of a screening procedure. Some employers routinely used the devices to interrogate employees suspected of drug abuse or theft. The U.S. Senate Labor Committee estimated that by 1988, some 2 million tests were being given every year.

But when psychologists subjected the polygraph test to scientific evaluation, they found that the test's results are not sufficiently valid. The reason is that no physiological responses are peculiar to lying. Machines cannot tell whether you are feeling guilty, angry, nervous, thrilled, or revved up from an exciting day. Innocent people may react to a word such as *bank* not because they robbed one but because they recently bounced a check. The machine will nevertheless record a "lie." The opposite error is also common. Some accomplished liars can deceive without flinching, and others learn to "beat the machine" by tensing muscles or thinking about an exciting experience during neutral questions (Lykken, 1981).

The polygraph test is not sufficiently reliable, either. The people who administer the test often make errors in reading the results. They do not reliably agree with one another's judgments, and, worst of all, they are more likely to accuse the innocent of lying than to let the guilty off the hook (Gale, 1988; Kleinmuntz & Szucko, 1984). Because of the polygraph's problems with validity and reliability, the American Psychological Association (APA) opposes the use of lie detectors and has urged a total ban on their use. The U.S. Congress has not gone along with that recommendation, but in 1988, it did forbid the routine use of lie detectors in screening job applicants or randomly testing employees. As one shocked senator said, "Some 320,000 honest Americans are branded as liars every single year."

Criticisms and reevaluations of psychological tests keep psychological assessment honest and scientifically rigorous. In contrast, the pseudoscientific psychological tests frequently found in magazines usually have not been evaluated for validity or reliability. These questionnaires often have inviting headlines such as "What's Your Power Motivation?" or "Are You Self-Destructive?" or "The Seven Types of Lover." But these tests are only lists of questions that someone thought sounded good.

Surveys

Psychological tests usually generate information about people indirectly. In contrast, **surveys** are questionnaires and interviews that gather information by asking people *directly* about their experiences, attitudes, or opinions. Most people are familiar with surveys in the form of national opinion polls, such as the Gallup poll. Surveys have been done on many topics, from consumer preferences to sexual preferences.

Surveys produce bushels of data, but they are not easy to do well. The biggest hurdle is getting a **sample,** or group of subjects, that is **representative** of the larger population that the researcher wishes to describe. Suppose you want to know about drug use among college sophomores. You can't question every college sophomore in the country because that is not practical; instead, you must choose a sample. Special selection procedures can be used to ensure that this sample will contain the same proportion of women, men, blacks, whites, poor people, rich people, Catholics, Jews, and so on as in the general population of college sophomores.

A sample's size is less critical than its representativeness; a small but representative sample may yield extremely accurate results, whereas a survey or poll that fails to use proper sampling methods may yield questionable results no matter how large the sample. A radio station that asks its listeners to vote yes or no by telephone on a controversial question is hardly conducting a scientific poll. Only those who feel strongly about an issue *and* who happen to be listening to that particular station are likely to call in, and those who feel strongly may be likely to take a particular side. A psychologist or statistician would say that the poll suffers from a **volunteer bias:** Those who volunteer probably differ from those who stay silent.

---

surveys Questionnaires and interviews that ask people directly about their experiences, attitudes, or opinions.

sample A group of subjects selected from a population for study in order to estimate characteristics of the population.

representative sample A sample that matches the population in question on important characteristics, such as age and sex.

volunteer bias A shortcoming of findings derived from a sample of volunteers instead of a representative sample.

Many magazines—*Redbook, Cosmopolitan, Playboy, The Ladies' Home Journal*—have done highly publicized surveys on the sexual habits and attitudes of their readers, but these surveys, too, are vulnerable to the volunteer bias. Readers motivated to respond to such a survey may be more (or possibly less) sexually active, on the average, than those who do not respond. In addition, people who read magazines regularly tend to be younger, more educated, and more affluent than the population as a whole, and these characteristics may affect the results. When you read about a survey (or any other kind of study), always ask what sorts of people participated. A biased, nonrepresentative sample does not necessarily mean that a survey is worthless or uninteresting, but it does mean that the results may not hold for other groups.

Another problem with surveys is that people sometimes lie. This is especially likely when the survey is about a touchy topic. ("What? Me do that disgusting/dishonest/fattening thing? Never!") The likelihood of lying is reduced when respondents are guaranteed anonymity. Also, there are some ways to check for lying—for example, by asking a question several times in different ways. But not all surveys use these techniques, and even when people do not intentionally lie, they may misremember the past or misinterpret the survey questions (Tanur, 1992).

When you read the results of a survey or an opinion poll, it is important to notice how the questions were phrased. Political pollsters often design questions to produce the results they want; a Republican might ask people whether they support "increasing the amount spent on Medicare at a slower rate," whereas a Democrat might ask whether people favor "cuts in the projected growth of Medicare." The two phrases mean the same thing, but people are likely to react more negatively when the word "cuts" is used (Kolbert, 1995). Moreover, ambiguous phrases mean different things to different people. In 1992, a national survey asked people this question: "As you know, the term Holocaust usually refers to the killing of millions of Jews in Nazi death camps during World War II. Does it seem possible or does it seem impossible to you that the Nazi extermination of the Jews never happened?" Not only does the question contain a double negative, which is confusing, but some people might take "extermination" to mean *total* annihilation, in which case the answer "possible" is appropriate. In response to this question, 22 percent of Americans surveyed expressed doubts about the Holocaust. But when a follow-up survey asked a much clearer question—"Do you doubt that the Holocaust actually happened, or not?"—the number of doubters fell to 9 percent (*Skeptic* magazine, 1994).

If surveys are conducted and interpreted carefully, they can be very informative. But there is one final problem, rarely discussed, that you should know about. Sometimes surveys not only reflect people's attitudes and behavior but also *influence* them. People often wish to be like "everyone else," so when they learn from a survey that they hold a minority view on some social or political issue, they may become apathetic, concluding that "There's no point trying to do anything." Or they may do things they consider wrong, or alter their beliefs, because "everybody" (according to the surveys) is doing something or feels a certain way, and they don't want to be different. Sociologist Elisabeth Noelle-Neumann (1984) argues that this tendency to tailor opinions and values unconsciously to fit prevailing trends makes "public opinion" a potent form of social control. She describes a German election in which two parties were neck and neck until polls gave one party a slight edge. "And then, right at the end, people jumped on the bandwagon," she writes. "As if caught in a current, 3–4 percent of the votes were swept in the direction of the general expectation of who was going to win."

Actually, not only surveys, but any type of study, can influence the way people regard their own behavior. How will you react if you come across findings in this book that show your opinions and habits to be in the minority?

Single Slices by Kohlsaat.

WHAT DO YOU KNOW?

A. Which descriptive method would be most appropriate for studying each of the following topics? (All of these topics, by the way, have been the focus of study.)

1. Ways in which the games of boys differ from those of girls
2. Changes in attitudes toward nuclear disarmament after a television movie about nuclear holocaust
3. The math skills of U.S. versus Japanese children
4. Physiological changes that occur when people watch violent movies
5. The development of a male infant who was reared as a female after his penis was accidentally burned off during a supposedly routine circumcision involving electrocauterization

a. case study
b. naturalistic observation
c. laboratory observation
d. survey
e. test

B. Professor Flummox gives his new test of Aptitude for Studying Psychology to his psychology students at the start of the year. At the end of the year, he finds that those who did well on the test averaged only a C in the course. The test lacks

_____ .

C. Over a period of 55 years, an 80-year-old British woman sniffed large amounts of cocaine, which she obtained legally under British regulations for the treatment of addicts. Yet the woman appeared to show no negative effects, other than drug dependence (Brown & Middlefell, 1989). What does this case tell us about the dangers or safety of cocaine?

ANSWERS:

single case.

cocaine purchased on the street. Critical thinking requires that we resist generalizing from a

extremely harmful for others. Also, the cocaine she received may have been less potent than

much. Snorting cocaine may be relatively harmless for some people, such as this woman, but

A. 1. b 2. d 3. e 4. c 5. a **B.** validity (more specifically, criterion validity) **C.** Not

Correlational Research

In descriptive research, psychologists often want to know whether two or more phenomena are related and, if so, how strongly. To obtain this information, they do **correlational studies.** If a researcher surveys college students to find out how many hours a week they spend watching television, the study is not correlational. However, if the researcher looks for a relationship between hours in front of the television set and grade-point average, then it is.

The word **correlation** is often used as a synonym for relationship. Technically, however, a correlation is a numerical measure of the *strength* of the relationship between two things. The "things" may be events, scores, or anything else that can be recorded and tallied. In psychological studies, such things are called **variables** because they can vary in quantifiable ways. Height, weight, age, income, IQ scores, number of items recalled on a memory test, number of smiles in a given time period—anything that can be measured, rated, or scored can serve as a variable.

Correlations always occur between *sets* of observations. Sometimes the sets come from one individual. Suppose you measured both a person's temperature and the person's alertness several times during the day. To check for a relationship between temperature and alertness, you would need several measurements, or values, for each variable. Of course, your results would hold only for that individual. In psychological research, sets of correlated observations usually come from many individuals or are used to compare groups of people. For example, in research on the origins of intelli-

---

correlational study A descriptive study that looks for a consistent relationship between two phenomena.

correlation A measure of how strongly two variables are related to one another; it is expressed statistically by the *coefficient of correlation,* which can range in value from −1.00 to +1.00.

variables Characteristics of behavior or experience that can be measured or described by a numeric scale; variables are manipulated and assessed in scientific studies.

gence, psychologists look for a relationship between the IQ scores of parents and children. To do this, the researchers must gather scores from a set of parents and from the children of these parents. You cannot compute a correlation if you know the IQs of only one particular parent–child pair. To say that a relationship exists, you need more than one pair of values to compare.

A **positive correlation** means that high values of one variable are associated with high values of the other, and that low values of one variable are associated with low values of the other. Height and weight are positively correlated, for example; so are IQ scores and school grades. Rarely is a correlation perfect, however. Some tall people weigh less than some short ones; some people with average IQs are superstars in the classroom, and some with high IQs get poor grades.

The graph in Figure 2.1 shows a positive correlation obtained in one study between men's educational levels and their annual incomes. Each dot represents a man. You can find each man's educational level by drawing a horizontal line from his dot to the vertical axis. You can find his income by drawing a vertical line from his dot to the horizontal axis.

A **negative correlation** means that high values of one variable are associated with *low* values of the other. Figure 2.2 (next page) shows a negative correlation between average income and the incidence of dental disease for groups of 100 families. Each dot represents one group. In general, the higher the income, the fewer the dental problems. In the automobile business, the older the car, the lower the price, except for antiques and models favored by collectors. As for human beings, in general, the older adults are, the fewer miles they can run, the fewer crimes they are likely to commit, and the fewer hairs they have on their heads. See whether you can think of some other variables that are negatively correlated. Remember, though, a negative correlation means that a certain kind of relationship exists. If there is *no* relationship between two variables, we say they are *uncorrelated*. Shoe sizes and IQ scores are uncorrelated.

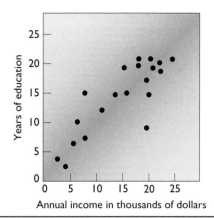

Figure 2.1   *A graph of a positive correlation between education and income in a group of men. (From Wright, 1976)*

positive correlation An association between increases in one variable and increases in another.
negative correlation An association between increases in one variable and decreases in another.

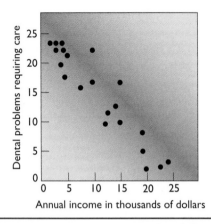

Figure 2.2 *A graph of a negative correlation between dental disease and average income in groups of families. (From Wright, 1976)*

The statistic used to express a correlation is called the *coefficient of correlation.* This number conveys both the size of the correlation and its direction. A perfect positive correlation has a coefficient of +1.00. A perfect negative correlation has a coefficient of −1.00. If you hear that the correlation between two variables is + .80, it means that the two are very strongly related. If you hear that the correlation is −.80, the relationship is just as strong, but it is negative. When there is no association between two variables, the coefficient is zero or close to zero.

Correlations allow researchers, using statistical techniques, to make general predictions about one variable if they know how it is related to another one. But because correlations are rarely perfect, predictions about a particular *individual* may be inaccurate. If you know that a person is well educated, you might predict, in the absence of any other information, that the person is fairly well off, because education and income are positively correlated. You would not be able to say exactly how much the person earned, but you would probably guess that the person's income was relatively high. You could be wrong, though, because the correlation is far from perfect. Some people with doctorates earn low salaries, and some people with only a grade-school education make fortunes.

Correlational studies in the social sciences are common and are often reported in the news. But beware: Correlations can be misleading. The important thing to remember is that *a correlation does not show causation.* It is easy to assume that if A predicts B, A must be causing B—that is, making B happen—but that is not necessarily so. The number of storks nesting in certain European villages is reportedly correlated (positively) with the number of human births in those villages. In other words, knowing when the storks nest allows you to predict when more births than usual will occur. But clearly that doesn't mean that storks bring babies or that babies attract storks. Human births seem to be somewhat more frequent at certain times of the year (you might want to speculate on the reasons), and the peaks just happen to coincide with the storks' nesting periods.

The coincidental nature of the correlation between nesting storks and human births may seem obvious, but in other cases, unwarranted conclusions about causation are more tempting. For example, television watching is positively correlated with children's aggressiveness. Therefore, many people assume that television watching (A) causes aggressiveness (B):

On the other hand, perhaps it is the case that being highly aggressive (B) causes children to watch more television (A):

However, there is yet another possibility. It could be that growing up in a violent household (C) causes children both to be aggressive *and* to watch television:

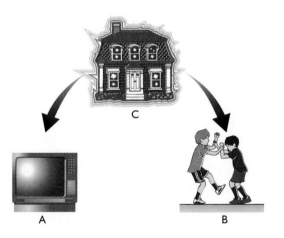

Psychologists are still debating which of these causal relationships is the strongest; actually, there is evidence for all three (APA Commission on Violence and Youth, 1993; Eron, 1982; Eron & Huesmann, 1987; Oskamp, 1988).

The moral of the story: When two variables are associated, one variable may or may not be causing the other.

WHAT DO YOU KNOW?

A. Are you clear about correlations? Indicate whether each of the following findings is a positive correlation or a negative correlation.

1. The higher a child's score on an intelligence test, the less physical force her mother is likely to use in disciplining her.
2. The higher a male monkey's level of the hormone testosterone, the more aggressive he is likely to be.
3. The older people are, the less frequently they tend to have sexual intercourse.
4. The hotter the weather, the more crimes against persons (such as muggings) tend to occur.

B. Now see whether you can generate two or three alternative explanations for each of the above findings.

ANSWERS:

A. 1. negative correlation 2. positive correlation 3. negative correlation 4. positive correlation B. 1. Physical force may impair a child's intellectual growth; brighter children may elicit less physical discipline from their parents; or brighter mothers may have brighter children and may also tend to use less physical force. 2. The hormone may cause aggressiveness, or acting aggressively may stimulate hormone production. 3. Older people may have less interest in sex than younger people, may have less energy, or may think they are supposed to have less interest in sex and behave accordingly; older people may also have trouble finding sexual partners. 4. Hot temperatures may make people edgy and cause them to commit crimes; potential victims may be more plentiful in warm weather because more people stroll outside and go out at night; criminals may find it more comfortable to be out committing their crimes in warm weather than in cold. (Our explanations for these correlations are not the only ones possible.)

EXPERIMENTAL RESEARCH

Researchers often propose explanations of behavior on the basis of descriptive studies, but to actually track down the causes of behavior, they rely heavily on the experimental method. An **experiment** allows the researcher to control the situation being studied. Instead of being a passive recorder of what is going on, the researcher actively does something that he or she thinks will affect the subjects' behavior and then observes what happens as a result. These procedures allow the experimenter to draw conclusions about cause and effect.

Basic Experimental Design

Suppose you are a psychologist and you come across reports that cigarette smoking improves performance on simple reaction-time tasks. You do not question these findings, but you have a hunch that nicotine may have the opposite effect on more complex

experiment A controlled test of a hypothesis in which the researcher manipulates one variable to discover its effect on another.

or demanding kinds of behavior, such as driving. You know that on the average, smokers have more car accidents than nonsmokers, even when differences in alcohol consumption, age, and other factors are taken into account (DiFranza et al., 1986). But this relationship doesn't prove that smoking *causes* accidents. Smokers may simply be greater risk-takers than nonsmokers, whether the risk is lung cancer or trying to beat a red light. Or perhaps the distraction of falling cigarette ashes or of fumbling for matches explains the relationship, rather than smoking itself. So you decide to do an experiment. In a laboratory, you ask smokers to "drive," using a computerized driving simulator equipped with a stick shift and a gas pedal. The object, you tell them, is to maximize the distance covered by driving as fast as possible on a winding road while avoiding rear-end collisions. At your request, some of the subjects smoke a cigarette immediately before climbing into the driver's seat. Others do not. You are interested in comparing how many collisions the two groups have. The basic design of this experiment is shown in Figure 2.3, which you may want to refer back to as you read the next few pages.

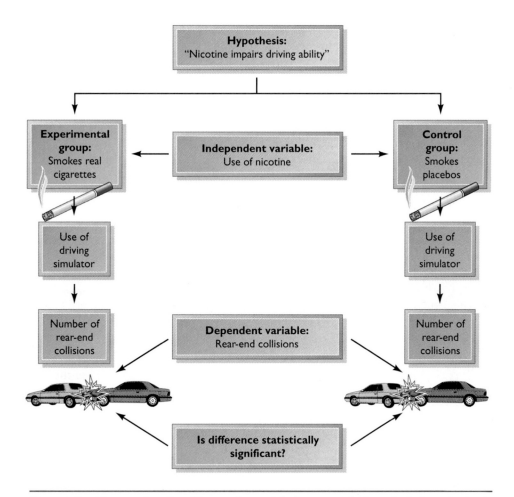

Figure 2.3 *The text describes this experimental design to test the hypothesis that nicotine in cigarettes impairs driving skills.*

The aspect of an experimental situation manipulated or varied by the researcher is known as the **independent variable.** The reaction of the subjects—the behavior that the researcher tries to predict—is called the **dependent variable.** Every experiment has at least one independent and one dependent variable. In our example, the independent variable is nicotine use: one cigarette versus none. The dependent variable is the number of rear-end collisions.

Ideally, everything about the experimental situation *except* the independent variable is held constant—that is, kept the same for all subjects. You would not have some people use a stick shift and others an automatic, unless shift type were an independent variable. Similarly, you would not have some people go through the experiment alone and others perform in front of an audience. Holding everything but the independent variable constant ensures that whatever happens is due to the researcher's manipulation and nothing else. It allows you to rule out other interpretations.

Understandably, students often have trouble keeping independent and dependent variables straight. You might think of it this way: The dependent variable—the outcome of the study—*depends* on the independent variable. When psychologists set up an experiment, they think, "If I do (such and such), the subjects in my study will do (such and such)." The first "such and such" represents the independent variable; the second represents the dependent variable:

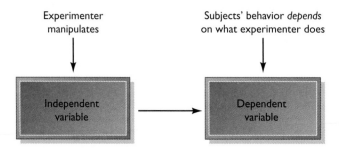

Most variables may be either independent or dependent, depending on what the experimenter is manipulating and trying to predict. If you want to know whether eating chocolate makes people nervous, then the amount of chocolate eaten is the independent variable. If you want to know whether feeling nervous makes people eat chocolate, then the amount of chocolate eaten is the dependent variable.

What Do You Know?

Name the independent and dependent variables in studies designed to answer the following questions:

1. Whether sleeping after learning a poem improves memory for the poem
2. Whether the presence of other people affects a person's willingness to help someone in distress

---

independent variable A variable that an experimenter manipulates.
dependent variable A variable that an experimenter predicts will be affected by manipulations of the independent variable.

3. Whether people get agitated from listening to heavy-metal music
4. Whether drinking caffeinated coffee makes people more talkative

Answers:

(you think up some ways to do experiments that might answer these questions?) decaffeinated) is the independent variable; talkativeness is the dependent variable. (Now, can dent variable; agitation is the dependent variable.   **4.** Coffee drinking (caffeinated versus to help others is the dependent variable.   **3.** Exposure to heavy-metal music is the independent variable.   **2.** The presence of other people is the independent variable; willingness dependent variable.   **1.** Opportunity to sleep after learning is the independent variable; memory for the poem is the

The Control Condition

Experiments usually require both an experimental condition and a comparison, or **control condition.** In the control condition, subjects are treated exactly like those in the experimental condition, except that they are not exposed to the same treatment, or manipulation of the independent variable. Without a control condition, you can't be sure that the behavior you are interested in would not have occurred anyway, even without your manipulation. In some studies, the same subjects can be used in both the control and the experimental conditions; they are said to serve as their own controls. In other studies, subjects are assigned to either an *experimental group* or a *control group.*

In the nicotine experiment, the people who smoke before driving make up the experimental group, and those who refrain from smoking make up the control group. We want these two groups to be roughly the same in terms of average driving skill. It wouldn't do to start out with a bunch of reckless roadrunners in the experimental group and a bunch of tired tortoises in the control group. We probably also want the two groups to be similar in average intelligence, education, smoking history, and other characteristics so that none of these variables will affect our results. To accomplish this, we must use **random assignment** to place people in the groups. We might randomly give each person a number, then put all those with even numbers in the experimental group and all those with odd numbers in the control group. At the beginning of the study, each subject will have the same probability as any other subject of being assigned to a given group. If we have enough subjects in our study, individual differences among them are likely to be roughly balanced in the two groups. However, for some characteristics, such as whether subjects are male or female, we may decide not to depend on random assignment. Instead, we may deliberately assign an equal number of people from each category to each group.

---

control condition In an experiment, a comparison condition in which subjects are not exposed to the same treatment or manipulation of the independent variable as in the experimental condition.
random assignment A procedure for assigning people to experimental and control groups in which each individual has the same probability as any other of being assigned to a given group.

Sometimes, researchers use several different experimental or control groups. For example, in our nicotine study, we might want to examine the effects of different levels of nicotine by having people smoke one, two, or three cigarettes before "driving," and then comparing each of these experimental groups to one another and to a control group of nonsmokers as well. For now, however, let's focus just on experimental subjects who smoked one cigarette.

We now have two groups. We also have a problem. In order to smoke, the experimental subjects must light up and inhale. These acts might set off certain expectations—of feeling relaxed, getting nervous, feeling confident, or whatever. These expectations, in turn, might affect driving performance. It would be better to have the control group do everything the experimental group does *except* use nicotine. Therefore, let's change the experimental design a bit. Instead of having the control subjects refrain from smoking, we will give them a **placebo,** or fake treatment. Placebos, which are used frequently in drug research, often take the form of pills or injections containing no active ingredients. Assume that it's possible in the nicotine study to use phony cigarettes that taste and smell like the real thing but contain no active ingredients. Our control subjects will not know their cigarettes are fake and will have no way of distinguishing them from real ones. Now if they have substantially fewer collisions than the experimental group, we will feel safe in concluding that nicotine increases the probability of an auto accident. (Placebos, by the way, sometimes produce effects that are as strong or nearly as strong as those of a real treatment. Thus, phony injections are often surprisingly effective in eliminating pain. Such placebo effects are a puzzle awaiting scientific solution.)

Experimenter Effects

Because expectations can influence the results of a study, subjects should not know whether they are in an experimental or a control group. When this is so (as it usually is), the experiment is said to be a **single-blind study.** But subjects are not the only ones who bring expectations to the laboratory; so do researchers. Their expectations and their hopes for a positive result may cause them to inadvertently influence the participants' responses through facial expressions, posture, tone of voice, or some other cue.

Many years ago, Robert Rosenthal (1966) demonstrated how powerful such **experimenter effects** can be. He had students teach rats to run a maze. Half the students were told that their rats had been bred to be "maze bright," and half were told that their rats had been bred to be "maze dull." In reality, there were no genetic differences between the two groups of rats, yet during the experiment, the supposedly

---

placebo An inactive substance or fake treatment used as a control in an experiment or given by a medical practitioner to a patient.

single-blind study An experiment in which subjects do not know whether they are in an experimental or a control group.

experimenter effects Unintended changes in subjects' behavior due to cues inadvertently given by the experimenter.

brainy rats actually did learn the maze more quickly, apparently because of the way the students treated them. If an experimenter's expectations can affect a rodent's behavior, reasoned Rosenthal, surely they can affect a human being's. He went on to demonstrate this point in many other studies (Rosenthal, 1994). In one, he learned that the cues an experimenter may give subjects can be as subtle as the smile on the Mona Lisa; in fact, the cue may *be* a smile. Rosenthal found that male researchers were far more likely to smile at female subjects than at males. Because one smile tends to invite another, such behavior on the part of the experimenter could easily ruin a study on friendliness or cooperation.

One solution to the problem of experimenter effects is to do a **double-blind study.** In such a study, the person running the experiment, the one having actual contact with the subjects, does not know which subjects are in which groups until the data have been gathered. Double-blind procedures are standard in drug research. Different doses of a drug are coded in some way, and the person administering the drug is kept in the dark about the code's meaning until after the data have been collected. To run our nicotine study in a double-blind fashion, we would keep the person dispensing the cigarettes from knowing which ones were real and which were placebos. In psychological research, double-blind studies are often more difficult to design than those that are merely single-blind. The goal, however, is always to control everything possible in an experiment.

Because experiments allow conclusions about cause and effect, they have long been the method of choice in psychology. However, like all methods, the experiment has its limitations. Sometimes procedures used for the convenience of the researchers can alter the results of a study. Consider a problem that has occurred in research with animals. A few years ago, a review found that most research with rats, mice, or hamsters has been conducted during the day, with the lights on. But these rodents are nocturnal; that is, they are normally active at night and sleep during the day. As the authors noted, "The field of psychology has been frequently criticized for being extensively based on studies of white male rats. . . . Perhaps that indictment should be revised to read '*sleepy* white male rats'!" (Brodie-Scott & Hobbs, 1992).

When the subjects are human beings, the laboratory encourages a certain kind of relationship with the researcher, one in which the researcher determines what the questions are and which behaviors will be recorded, and the participants try to do as they are told. In their desire to cooperate, advance scientific knowledge, or present themselves in a positive light, participants may act in ways that they ordinarily would not (Kilhstrom, 1995). Thus, research psychologists confront a problem: The more control they exercise over a situation, the more unlike real life it may be. For this reason, many psychologists are calling for more field research, the careful study of behavior in natural contexts, as well as careful evaluation of how participants in experiments perceive their situation and the role they are to play in it.

---

double-blind study An experiment in which neither the subjects nor the individuals running the study know which subjects are in the control group(s) and which in the experimental group(s) until after the results are tallied.

Now that we have come to the end of our discussion of research methods, how did you do on your list of their advantages and disadvantages? You can find out by comparing your list with the one in Table 2.1.

TABLE 2.1 ✦ Research Methods in Psychology: Their Advantages and Disadvantages

METHOD	ADVANTAGES	DISADVANTAGES
Case history	Good source of hypotheses. Provides in-depth information on individuals. Unusual cases can shed light on situations/problems that are unethical or impractical to study in other ways.	Individual may not be representative or typical. Difficult to know which subjective interpretation is best.
Naturalistic observation	Allows description of behavior as it occurs in the natural environment. Often useful in first stages of research program.	Allows researcher little or no control of the situation. Observations may be biased. Does not allow firm conclusions on cause and effect.
Laboratory observation	Allows more control than naturalistic observation. Allows use of sophisticated equipment.	Allows researcher only limited control of the situation. Observations may be biased. Does not allow firm conclusions on cause and effect. Behavior in the laboratory may differ from behavior in the natural environment.
Test	Yields information on personality traits, emotional states, aptitudes, abilities.	Difficult to construct tests that are valid and reliable.
Survey	Provides large amount of information on large numbers of people.	If sample is nonrepresentative or biased, it may be impossible to generalize from the results. Responses may be inaccurate or untrue.
Correlational study	Shows whether two or more variables are related. Allows general predictions.	Does not permit identification of cause and effect.
Experiment	Allows researcher to control the situation. Permits researcher to identify cause and effect.	Situation is artificial, and results may not generalize well to the real world. Sometimes difficult to avoid experimenter effects.

WHAT DO YOU KNOW?

A. What's wrong with these two studies?

1. A kidney specialist and a psychiatrist treated mentally disordered patients by filtering their blood through a dialysis machine, normally used with kidney patients. They reported several cases of dramatic improvement, which they attributed to the removal of an unknown toxin (Wagemaker & Cade, 1978).

2. A sex researcher surveyed women on their feelings about men and love. She sent out 100,000 lengthy questionnaires to women's groups and got back 4,500 replies (a 4.5 percent return). On the basis of these replies, she reported that 84 percent of women are dissatisfied with their relationships, 98 percent want more communication, and 70 percent of those married five years or more have had extramarital affairs (Hite, 1987).

B. Suppose you hear that a researcher reported a dramatic improvement in the functioning of Alzheimer's patients who took an experimental drug. As a critical thinker, what questions would you want to ask about this study? Try to come up with as many questions as you can.

ANSWERS:

A. 1. The dialysis study had no control group and was not double-blind. Patients' expectations that the "blood-cleansing" equipment would wash their madness out of them might have influenced the results, and so might the researchers' expectations. In later studies, using double-blind procedures, control subjects had their blood circulated through the machine, but the blood was not actually filtered. Little improvement occurred in either the experimental or the control condition, and the real treatment was no better than the fake treatment (Carpenter et al., 1983). **2.** Because of the way the sample was recruited and the low return rate, the findings may be flawed by a volunteer bias. Although the study produced information on the feelings of many women, figures and percentages from the study are not necessarily valid for the general population. **B.** Some possible questions: How many people were studied? Was there a control group? If so, did the control subjects receive placebos? How were patients assigned to the experimental and control groups? Were double-blind procedures used? How was "improved functioning" measured? How long did the effects last? Did the effects make any difference in the everyday lives of the patients or their families? Were there any negative effects? Has the experiment been replicated by other researchers?

WHY PSYCHOLOGISTS USE STATISTICS

If you are a psychologist who has just done an observational study, a survey, or an experiment, your work has only just begun. Once you have some results in hand, you must do three things with them: (1) describe them, (2) assess how reliable and meaningful they are, and (3) figure out how to explain them.

Descriptive Statistics: What's So?

Let's say that 30 people in the nicotine experiment smoked real cigarettes and 30 smoked placebos. We have recorded the number of collisions each person had on the driving simulator. Now we have 60 numbers. What can we do with them?

The first step is to summarize the data. The world does not want to hear how many collisions each person had. It wants to know what happened in the nicotine group as a whole, compared with what happened in the control group. To provide this information, we need numbers that sum up our data. Such numbers are known as **descriptive statistics** and are often depicted in graphs and charts.

A good way to summarize the data is to compute group averages. The most commonly used type of average is the *arithmetic mean.* It is calculated by adding up all the individual scores and dividing the result by the number of scores. We can compute a mean for the nicotine group by adding up the 30 collision scores and dividing the sum by 30. Then we can do the same for the control group. Now our 60 numbers have been boiled down to 2. For the sake of our example, let's assume that the nicotine group had an average of 10 collisions, while the control group's average was only 7.

We must be careful, however, about how we interpret these averages. An arithmetic mean does not necessarily tell us what is "typical"; it merely summarizes a mass of data. It is possible that no one in our nicotine group actually had 10 collisions. Perhaps half the people in the group were motoring maniacs and had 15 collisions, whereas the others were more cautious and had only 5. Perhaps almost all the subjects had 9, 10, or 11 collisions. Perhaps accidents were evenly distributed between 0 and 15.

The mean does not tell you about such variation in subjects' responses. For that, there are other statistics. One, the *range,* gives the difference between the lowest and the highest scores in a distribution of scores. If the lowest number of collisions in the nicotine group was 5 and the highest was 15, the range would be 10. Another, the **variance,** is more informative; it tells you how clustered or spread out the individual scores are around the mean. The more spread out they are, the less "typical" the mean is. But unfortunately, when research is reported in newspapers or on the nightly news, you usually hear only about the mean. There are other kinds of descriptive statistics as well, including the coefficient of correlation, which we covered earlier.

Inferential Statistics: So What?

At this point in our nicotine study, we have one group with an average of 10 collisions and another with an average of 7. Should we break out the champagne? Try to get on TV? Call our mothers?

Better hold off. Descriptive statistics do not tell us whether the outcome is anything to write home about. Perhaps if one group had an average of 15 collisions and the other an average of 1 we could get excited. But rarely does a psychological study hit you between the eyes with a sensationally clear result. In most cases, there is some pos-

---

descriptive statistics Statistics that organize and summarize research data.
variance A measure of the dispersion of scores around the mean.

sibility that the difference between the two groups was due simply to chance. Perhaps the people in the nicotine group just happened to be a little more accident-prone during the study, and their behavior had nothing to do with the nicotine. It would be surprising if the two groups had *exactly* the same number of collisions.

To find out how significant the data are, the psychologist uses **inferential statistics.** These statistics permit a researcher to draw *inferences* (conclusions based on evidence) about the findings. There are many inferential statistics to choose from, depending on the kind of study and what the researcher wants to know. Like descriptive statistics, inferential statistics involve the application of mathematical formulas to the data.

Inferential statistics do not merely describe or summarize the data. *They tell the researcher how likely it is that the result of the study occurred by chance.* More precisely, they reveal the probability of obtaining an effect as large as (or larger than) the one observed if manipulating the independent variable actually has no reliable effect on the behavior in question. In our nicotine study, these statistics will tell us how likely it is that the difference between the nicotine group and the placebo group occurred by chance. It is impossible to rule out chance entirely. However, if the likelihood that the result occurred by chance is extremely low, we say that the result is **statistically significant.** This means that the probability that the difference is real is overwhelming—not certain, mind you, but overwhelming. By convention, psychologists consider a result significant if it would be expected by chance 5 or fewer times in 100 repetitions of the study. Another way of saying this is that the result is significant at the .05, or "point oh five," level. If the difference could be expected to occur by chance in 6 out of 100 studies, we would have to say that the results failed to support the hypothesis—that the difference we obtained might well have occurred merely by chance—although we might still want to do further research to be sure.

Inferential statistics are necessary because a result that seems unlikely may not really be so unlikely after all. For example, how probable do you think it is that in a room of 25 people, at least 2 will have the same birthday? Most people think it is very unlikely, but in fact the odds are better than even. Even if there are only 10 people in the room, the chances are still 1 in 9. Among U.S. presidents, 2 had the same birthday (Warren Harding and James Polk) and 3 died on the fourth of July (John Adams, the second president; Thomas Jefferson, the third; and James Monroe, the fifth). Surprising? No. Such "coincidences" are not statistically striking at all.

Statistically significant results allow psychologists to make many general predictions about human behavior. These predictions are usually stated as probabilities ("On average, we can expect 60 percent of all students to do X, Y, or Z"). However, they do not tell us with certainty what a particular individual will do in a situation. Probabilistic results are typical of all the sciences. Medical research, for example, can tell us that the odds are high that someone who smokes will get lung cancer, but because many variables interact to produce any particular case of cancer, research can't tell us for sure whether Aunt Bessie, a two-pack-a-day smoker, will come down with the disease.

---

inferential statistics Statistical tests that allow researchers to assess how likely it is that their results occurred merely by chance.

statistically significant A term used to refer to a result that is extremely unlikely to have occurred by chance.

Indeed, highly specific predictions about individuals may, in principle, be impossible. New work by mathematicians on chaos theory suggests that even a slight, barely noticeable event can have profound but unpredictable effects on the behavior of a complex system—and a human being is certainly a complex system (Barton, 1994). Suppose you can't get into a class you really want because it's closed, so instead you take the only class available, one in introductory astronomy. As a result, ten years later you're working for NASA, something you never would have imagined in your wildest dreams. But chaos theory also tells us that *general* patterns do exist in natural phenomena and in human behavior, and these patterns can be identified.

By the way, a nicotine study similar to our hypothetical example, but with somewhat different and more complicated procedures, has actually been done (Spilich, June, & Renner, 1992). Smokers who lit up before driving got a little farther on the simulated road, but they also had significantly more rear-end collisions on average (10.7) than temporarily abstaining smokers (5.2) or nonsmokers (3.1). After hearing about this research, the head of Federal Express banned smoking on the job among all of the company's 12,000 drivers (George J. Spilich, personal communication).

WHAT DO YOU KNOW?

Check your understanding of the descriptive/inferential distinction by placing a check in the appropriate column for each phrase:

	Descriptive statistics	Inferential statistics
1. Summarize the data	_____	_____
2. Give likelihood of data occurring by chance	_____	_____
3. Include the mean	_____	_____
4. Give measure of statistical significance	_____	_____
5. Tell you whether to call your mother	_____	_____

ANSWERS:

1. descriptive 2. inferential 3. descriptive 4. inferential 5. inferential

---

Interpreting the Results

The last step in any study is to figure out what the findings mean. Trying to understand behavior from uninterpreted findings is like trying to become fluent in Welsh by reading a Welsh–English dictionary. Just as you need the grammar of Welsh to tell you how the words fit together, the psychologist needs hypotheses and theories to explain how the facts that emerge from research fit together.

Sometimes it is hard to choose between competing explanations. Does nicotine disrupt driving by impairing coordination, by increasing a driver's vulnerability to distraction, by interfering with the processing of information, or by clouding judgment or distorting the perception of danger? In general, the best explanation is the one that accounts for the greatest number of existing findings and makes the most accurate predictions about new ones.

Often the explanation for a finding will need to take into account many different factors. We saw in Chapter 1, for example, that being abused as a child does not inevitably turn a person into an abusive parent. Many influences—including life stresses, exposure to violence on television, and the nature of the abuse—interact in complicated ways to determine the kind of parent a person becomes (Widom, 1989). Fortunately, with special statistical procedures, psychologists can often analyze how much each variable contributes to a result and how the variables interact.

In interpreting any particular study, we must also be careful not to go too far beyond the facts. There may be several explanations that fit those facts equally well, which means that more research will be needed to determine the best explanation. Rarely does one study prove anything, in psychology or any other field. That is why you should be suspicious of headlines that announce a "Major Scientific Breakthrough!!!" Scientific progress usually occurs gradually, not in one fell swoop.

Sometimes the best interpretation of a finding does not emerge until a hypothesis has been tested in different ways. Although the methods we have described tend to be appropriate for different questions (see Table 2.2 on the next page), different methods can also complement one another. That is, one method can be used to confirm, disconfirm, or extend the results obtained with another. If the findings of studies using various methods converge, there is greater reason to be confident about them. On the other hand, if they conflict, researchers will know that they must modify their hypotheses or do more research.

As an example, when psychologists compare the mental test scores of young and old people, they usually find that younger people outscore older ones. This type of research, in which groups are compared at a given time, is called **cross-sectional.** Other researchers, however, have used **longitudinal studies** to investigate mental abilities across the life span. In a longitudinal study, the same people are followed over a period of time and reassessed at periodic intervals. In contrast to cross-sectional studies, longitudinal studies find that as people age, they often continue to perform as well as they ever did on many types of mental tests. A general decline in ability does not usually occur until the seventh or eighth decade of life, if at all (Baltes, Dittman-Kohli, & Dixon, 1984; Schaie, 1993). Why do results from the two types of studies conflict? Apparently, cross-sectional studies measure generational differences; younger generations tend to outperform older ones on many tests, perhaps because they are better educated or more famil-

---

cross-sectional study A study in which subjects of different ages are compared at a given time.
longitudinal study A study in which subjects are followed and periodically reassessed over a period of time.

TABLE 2.2 ✦ Psychological Research Methods Contrasted

Psychologists may use different methods to answer different questions about a topic. To illustrate, this table shows some ways in which the methods described in this chapter can be used to study different questions about aggression. The methods listed are not necessarily mutually exclusive. That is, sometimes two or more methods can be used to investigate the same question. As discussed in the text, findings based on one method may extend, support, or disconfirm findings based on another.

METHOD	PURPOSE	EXAMPLE
Case history	To understand the development of aggressive behavior in a particular individual; to formulate research hypotheses about the origins of aggressiveness.	Developmental history of a serial killer.
Naturalistic observation	To describe the nature of aggressive acts in early childhood.	Observation, tally, and description of hitting, kicking, etc. during free-play periods in a preschool.
Laboratory observation	To find out whether aggressiveness in pairs of same-sex and opposite-sex children differs in frequency or intensity.	Observation through a one-way window of same-sex and opposite-sex pairs of preschoolers. Pairs must negotiate who gets to play with an attractive toy that has been promised to each child.
Test	To compare the personality traits of aggressive and nonaggressive persons.	Administration of personality tests to violent and nonviolent prisoners.
Survey	To find out how common domestic violence is in the United States.	Questionnaire asking anonymous respondents (in a sample representative of the U.S. population) about the occurrence of slapping, hitting, etc. in their homes.
Correlational study	To examine the relationship between aggressiveness and television viewing.	Administration to college students of a paper-and-pencil test of aggressiveness and a questionnaire on number of hours spent watching TV weekly; computation of correlation coefficient.
Experiment	To find out whether high air temperatures elicit aggressive behavior.	Arrangement for individuals to "shock" a "learner" (actually a confederate of the experimenter) while seated in a room heated to either 72°F or 85°F.

iar with the types of items used on the tests. Without longitudinal studies, we might falsely conclude that mental ability inevitably declines with age.

Sometimes psychologists agree on the reliability and meaning of a finding, but not on its ultimate significance for theory or practice. Statistical significance alone does not provide the answer because statistical significance does not always imply real-world importance. A result may be statistically significant at the "point oh five level" but at the same time be small and of little consequence in everyday life. Other criticisms, beyond the scope of this book, have also been leveled against traditional tests of significance (Falk & Greenbaum, 1995; G. Loftus, 1993). Because of these problems, many psychologists now use other kinds of statistics to estimate how much of the variance among the scores in a study was accounted for by the independent variable. Often this *effect size* turns out to be small, even when the results were statistically significant.

One useful new technique, called **meta-analysis,** statistically combines and analyzes data from many studies, instead of assessing each study's results separately. Meta-analysis tells the researcher how much of the variation in scores across *all* the studies examined can be explained by a particular variable. For example, one recent meta-analysis of nearly 50 years of research on gender differences found that differences on some spatial-visual tasks are substantial, with males doing better on the average (Voyer, Voyer, & Bryden, 1995). In contrast, other meta-analyses have shown that some stereotypical gender differences—notably in verbal ability, math ability, and aggressiveness—are reliable but surprisingly small, with gender accounting for only 1 to 5 percent of the variance in scores (Eagly & Carli, 1981; Feingold, 1988; Hyde, 1981, 1984; Hyde, Fennema, & Lamon, 1990; Hyde & Linn, 1988). In plain English, this means that knowing whether a person is male or female doesn't tell you much about the person's performance in these three areas.

You can see this visually in Figure 2.4 (from Sapolsky, 1987, based on data from Benbow & Stanley, 1983). Seventh-grade boys do better, on the average, than seventh-grade girls on the math section of the SAT. But the difference, although reliable, is tiny,

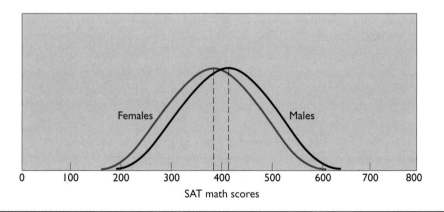

Figure 2.4   *As this graph illustrates, group differences that are statistically significant are sometimes small and are not very useful for predicting behavior.*

---

meta-analysis A statistical procedure for combining and analyzing data from many studies; it determines how much of the variance in scores across all studies can be explained by a particular variable.

and male and female scores greatly overlap. Therefore it is impossible to predict whether a particular boy will outperform a particular girl.

Critics of meta-analysis argue that this method is like combining apples and oranges; the blend is interesting, but it is bland—and it obliterates the distinctive flavors of the original ingredients. For example, research on verbal abilities has often relied on studies of high-school students. But students who don't read well are more likely to drop out of high school, and these dropouts are more likely to be male than female. Thus a meta-analysis may fail to identify an overall female advantage on verbal tests (Halpern, 1989). Similarly, a meta-analysis that combines studies of all math skills will miss a male advantage on problems of spatial visualization (McGuinness, 1993). Meta-analyses that turn up no overall sex differences in cognitive abilities are appealing to many people but ultimately unhelpful, critics believe, because such analyses gloss over differences that educators and parents should know about if they want *all* children to do well. Nevertheless, on topics that have generated dozens and even hundreds of studies, meta-analysis has been the most promising way of finding patterns in results, as long as its limitations are taken into account.

EVALUATING RESEARCH METHODS: SCIENCE UNDER SCRUTINY

Rigorous research methods are the very heart of science, so it is not surprising that psychologists spend considerable time discussing and debating their procedures for collecting, evaluating, and presenting data. In recent years, such debates have gone far beyond such matters as when to use questionnaires versus interviews, or how best to analyze the results.

The Misuse of Psychological Tests

Some of these disputes involve the use of psychological tests for inappropriate purposes. Anthropologist F. Allan Hanson (1993) has argued that tests are a harmful invasion of people's privacy, "instruments of the evolving system of dominating institutions that act to curtail individual freedom and dignity." For example, tests of aptitude and intelligence, he believes, destroy motivation and produce self-fulfilling prophecies. And they glorify a person's hypothetical "potential" over the person's actual performance; thus, we have the curious phenomenon of employers' asking to see a college graduate's SAT scores even when the person's actual grades in college are readily available.

Moreover, Hanson and others fear, tests that attempt to assess a person's character or future actions are too often used to keep people in line, fearful for their reputations, jobs, and livelihoods. When employers were denied the legal right to use the lie-detector test routinely (because, as we noted, the test has poor reliability and validity), they did not abandon the assumption that it is possible to identify people who lie. Many employers are now trying new methods of "lie detection," trying to identify people who, if hired, *might* in the future cheat, steal, or use drugs. One trend is the development of "integrity tests" that supposedly measure whether a prospective employee will steal on the job. Millions of people take these tests each year, yet questions remain about their reliability and validity (Saxe, 1991). Testing experts are concerned about the fact that many people who fail are not actually dishonest (Camera & Schneider, 1994). Imagine that on entering college you had to take a test that would supposedly reveal whether you were likely to cheat. How would you feel about it? How reliable does a test need to be before its widespread use can be justified? Is it acceptable if it misidentifies "only" one innocent person in ten? a hundred? a thousand?

Defenders of testing respond to such criticisms by noting that tests are only tools and that all tools can be misused. They observe that there is a difference between using tests carefully for specific research purposes or for the diagnosis of mental problems and using them routinely, mindlessly, or malevolently to get innocent people to confess, to try to predict who will commit future crimes, or to invade the privacy of employees. It seems clear, however, that anyone who takes a test of any kind should do so in an informed way, understanding why the test is being given and the uses to which it will be put.

Ethics in Research

Another set of issues has to do with the ethics of psychological research. One major concern has been the use of deception. Many studies, particularly in social psychology, require that researchers deceive their subjects about the purpose of the research until the study is completed. If participants in a study knew in advance why it was being done, the results might not be valid: If they knew that the study concerned the willingness to help others, they might try to be a Good Samaritan; if they knew that the study was measuring verbal ability, they might become as talkative as a sportscaster at the Super Bowl. The obvious solution is for researchers to disguise the purpose of their studies, or, to put it more bluntly, to lie.

But what if the deception causes the subjects to suffer anxiety or embarrassment? What if the participants are misled into thinking they will have to deliver electric shock to another person? What if they are going to be insulted or humiliated so that the researcher can study their reactions? Because of growing concern during the past few decades about the morality of deceptive procedures, the APA's ethical guidelines now require (a) that researchers who plan to use deception show an oversight committee that the deception is necessary and justified by the study's potential scientific, educational, or applied value and (b) that the researchers explore possible alternatives that do not require deception. Investigators must also protect participants from physical and mental discomfort or harm, and if any risk exists, participants must be warned in advance and given an opportunity to decline to participate.

A second ethical issue has to do with the use of animals in research. Animals are used in about 7 or 8 percent of psychological studies, and 95 percent of the animals are rodents (American Psychological Association, 1984), but psychologists also occasionally use pigeons, cats, monkeys, apes, and other species. Most studies involve no harm or discomfort to the animals (such as research on mating in hamsters) but some do (such as studies in which infant monkeys are reared apart from their mothers and as a consequence develop abnormal behaviors). Some studies even require the animal's death, as when rats brought up in deprived or enriched environments are sacrificed so that their brains can be examined for specific effects.

Animal studies have had many practical benefits for animals themselves. For example, using behavioral principles, farmers have been able to reduce crop destruction by birds and deer without resorting to their traditional method—shooting the animals. Animal studies have also led to numerous improvements in human health and well-being. Findings from these studies have helped psychologists and other researchers develop methods for treating enuresis (bed-wetting); teach retarded children to communicate; combat life-threatening malnutrition caused by chronic vomiting in infants; rehabilitate patients with neurological disorders and sensory impairment; develop better ways to reduce chronic pain; train animal companions for the disabled; and understand the mechanisms underlying memory loss and senility—to name only a few benefits (Feeney, 1987; Greenough, 1991; N. Miller, 1985).

In recent years, however, animal research has provoked angry disputes over the welfare of animals and even over whether to do any animal research at all. Some people on both sides have taken extreme positions. In one survey, 85 percent of committed animal-rights activists (versus 17 percent of a more representative comparison group) endorsed the statement, "If it were up to me, I would eliminate all research using animals" (Plous, 1991). For their part, some psychologists have refused to acknowledge that confinement in laboratories can be psychologically and physically harmful for some species. Unfortunately, the controversy has often degenerated into vicious name-calling or worse: Some animal-rights activists have vandalized laboratories and threatened and harassed researchers and their families, and some scientists have unfairly branded all animal-rights and animal-welfare activists as terrorists.

On the positive side, this conflict has motivated many researchers to find ways to improve the treatment of animals that are needed in research. The APA's ethical code has always contained provisions governing the humane treatment of animals, and in the past decade, more comprehensive guidelines have been formulated. New federal laws have also been passed to strengthen regulations governing the housing and care of research animals. Every experiment involving vertebrates must now be reviewed by a committee composed of representatives from the research institution and the community.

Most scientists, however, oppose proposals to ban or greatly reduce animal research. The APA and other scientific organizations believe that legislation to protect animals is desirable but must not jeopardize research that increases scientific understanding and improves human welfare. The difficult task—one that promises to be with us for many years—is to balance the many benefits of animal research with an acknowledgment of past abuses and a compassionate attitude toward species other than our own.

The Meaning of Knowledge

The continuing arguments over ethical issues show that methods in psychology can arouse as much disagreement as findings do. Conflict exists not only about how to do research, but also about what research in general can and cannot reveal. Indeed, heated exchanges are raging in all the sciences and humanities about the very meaning of knowledge itself.

For the past three centuries, the answer seemed clear enough. Knowledge was the discovery of some reality existing "out there," and the way to find it was to be objective, value-free, and detached. The purpose of a theory was to map or reflect this reality. A clear line was assumed to exist between the knower, on one side, and the phenomenon under study, on the other—and the knower wasn't supposed to cross that line.

Today, many scholars are questioning these fundamental assumptions. Adherents of *postmodernism* argue that detached objectivity, long considered the cornerstone of Western science, is a myth. In the postmodern view, the observer's values, judgments, and status in society inevitably affect how events are studied, how they are explained, and even how they take place. Scholars and researchers, in this view, are not exempt from subjectivity. Because they do their work at a particular time and in a particular culture, they bring with them shared assumptions and worldviews that influence what they count as an important fact, what parts of reality they notice, and how they determine standards of excellence. If you have encountered arguments about which books should be counted as "classics"—the familiar greats of Western literature or modern works by women and non-European writers—you have already observed a postmodern conflict.

In the social sciences, a postmodern theory called **social constructionism** holds that knowledge is not so much discovered as it is *created* or invented (Gergen, 1985; Guba, 1990; Hare-Mustin & Marecek, 1990; Rosaldo, 1989). Our understanding of things does not merely mirror what's "out there"; it organizes and orders it. Consider the concept of race. Many people speak of "blacks" or "Asians" or "whites" as if the boundaries between these groups were self-evident based on physical differences. But there are many ways to define *race*. Some societies base their definitions on ancestry, not on any obvious physical attribute such as skin color; a person can look white but be considered black if he or she has a single black ancestor. Indeed, as recently as 1970, Louisiana laws held that anyone with as little as one thirty-second "Negro blood" was black (Jones, 1991). South Africa has used ancestry to differentiate blacks from "coloreds" (people of mixed ancestry) for political and legal purposes. But in South America, where people come in all shades and many combinations of European, Indian, and African ancestry, this kind of classification does not exist. Besides, why should skin color or hair type be the primary basis for distinguishing races? As physiologist Jared Diamond (1994) observes, "There are many different, equally valid procedures for defining races, and those different procedures yield very different classifications." You could, for example, make distinctions based on gene frequencies for sickle-cell anemia, on types of fingerprints, on amount of body hair or shape of buttocks, or on body shape. One classification would group Italians, Greeks, and most African blacks into one race and the Xhosas of South Africa and Swedes into another.

Racial labels obscure the fact that few if any of us are "pure" anything, a fact that is causing all sorts of problems for the U.S. Census Bureau, which valiantly keeps trying to construct new terms. Racial labels also vastly exaggerate the differences between

---

social constructionism The view that there are no universal truths about human nature because people construct reality differently, depending on their culture, the historical moment, and the power arrangements within their society.

groups; there is far more genetic and physical variation *within* groups than between them (Betancourt & López, 1993; Jones, 1991; Zuckerman, 1990a). Of course, behavior can be profoundly affected by the way people label and identify themselves and others, as we will see in our discussion of the sociocultural perspective. And racism—hatred or intolerance toward others because of their race, however it is defined—is a lamentably real human problem. But both in society at large and within the discipline of psychology, there are no agreed-on definitions of race itself (Yee et al., 1993). Because the concept of race falsely implies the existence of physically unique and separate groups and is problematic from a scientific point of view, in this book, we will be avoiding the term *race* whenever possible. Instead, we will use the term *ethnic group* to refer to people who share a common culture, religion, or language.

Social-constructionist views are causing much debate and reflection throughout all fields of study. In psychology, social-constructionist debates about science are especially challenging. Psychologists have always had the goal of understanding the behavior and mental processes of human beings. Now they are being asked to analyze their own behavior as psychologists and to examine how their own values, gender, place in society, and cultural experiences affect their definitions, procedures, interpretations, and conclusions. Many welcome this challenge, drawing on a rich assortment of research methods and findings to aid them.

Nevertheless, many people, including many psychologists, react to postmodern views with alarm. They fear that these criticisms imply that we can never know the truth about anything and so we might as well give up on science, uniform standards of criticism, and the effort to apply objective methods. They fear that a legitimate critique of the limitations of research is turning into an attack on *all* traditional principles and methods of research, which in effect is throwing out the baby (rigorous standards and useful findings) with the bathwater (bias and narrow-mindedness) (Gross & Levitt, 1994; Peplau & Conrad, 1989; Smith, 1994). They worry too that postmodern philosophy is leading to extreme cultural relativism in moral and ethical judgments; if the truth is subjective, then why not conclude that "anything goes"?

This is a serious and interesting debate that is not going to be resolved soon, and that is why we have raised it here. Our own position, which guides our approach in this book, falls somewhere between extreme traditionalism and extreme postmodernism. We think that understanding how knowledge is constructed by scholars and researchers is essential to the study of psychology, as we will try to show in the evaluation of each perspective. New ways of looking at knowledge and of doing research have the potential to expand and enrich our understanding of behavior (Gergen, 1994). But for us, as for all scientific psychologists, some things will remain the same: an insistence on standards of evidence, a reliance on verifiable results, and an emphasis on critical thinking. That is why we hope that as you read the following chapters, you will resist the temptation to skip descriptions of how studies were done. If the assumptions and methods of a study are faulty, so are the results and the conclusions based on them. Ultimately, what we know about human behavior is inseparable from how we know it.

✦ ✦ ✦

Summary

1. Research methods provide a way for psychologists to separate well-supported conclusions from unfounded belief. An understanding of these methods can help people think critically about psychological issues and become astute consumers of psychological and other scientific findings.

2. The ideal scientist states hypotheses and predictions precisely; is skeptical of claims that rest solely on faith or authority; relies on empirical methods; is willing to comply with the *principle of falsifiability* and to make "risky predictions"; and is open about methods and results so that findings can be replicated. In contrast, pseudoscientists often hide behind vague and empty terms, make predictions that are nearly meaningless, and violate the principle of falsifiability.

3. *Descriptive methods* allow a researcher to describe and predict behavior but not necessarily to choose one explanation over others. Such methods include case studies, observational studies, psychological tests, surveys, and correlational methods. Some descriptive methods are used both by clinicians and by researchers.

4. *Case studies* are detailed descriptions of individuals. They are often used by clinicians, and in research, they can be valuable in exploring new topics and addressing questions that would otherwise be difficult or impossible to study. But because the person under study may not be representative of people in general, case studies are typically sources rather than tests of hypotheses.

5. *In observational studies,* the researcher carefully and systematically observes and records behavior without interfering in any way with the behavior. *Naturalistic observation* is used to obtain descriptions of how subjects behave in their natural environments. *Laboratory observation* allows more control and the use of special equipment; behavior in the laboratory, however, may differ in certain ways from behavior in natural contexts.

6. *Psychological tests* are used to measure and evaluate personality traits, emotional states, aptitudes, interests, abilities, and values. Tests that are *valid* and *reliable* are an improvement over simple self-evaluation and are also usually superior to informal judgments of others. But teachers, parents, and employers do not always stop to question a test's validity, especially when results are summarized in a single number. Some widely used tests, such as those involving the polygraph machine, have inadequate reliability and validity.

7. *Surveys* are questionnaires or interviews that ask people directly about their experiences, attitudes, and opinions. Precautions must be taken to obtain a sample that is *representative* of the larger population that the researcher wishes to describe and that yields results that are not skewed by a *volunteer bias*. Findings can be affected by the fact that respondents sometimes lie, misremember, or misinterpret the questions. Surveys not only reflect people's attitudes and behavior but also influence them.

8. In descriptive research, studies that look for relationships between phenomena are known as *correlational*. A *correlation* is a measure of the strength of a positive or

negative relationship between two variables. A correlation does *not* show a causal relationship between the variables.

9. *Experiments* allow researchers to control the situation being studied, to manipulate an *independent variable,* and to assess the effects of this manipulation on a *dependent variable.* Experimental studies usually require a comparison or *control* condition. In some studies, control subjects receive a *placebo. Single-blind* and *double-blind* procedures can be used to prevent the expectations of the subject or the experimenter from affecting the results. Because experiments allow conclusions about cause and effect, they have long been the method of choice in psychology. However, like laboratory observations, experiments create a special situation that may call forth behavior not typical in other environments.

10. Psychologists use *descriptive statistics,* such as the mean, range, and variance, to summarize their data. They use *inferential statistics* to find out how likely it is that the results of a study occurred merely by chance. The results are said to be *statistically significant* if this likelihood is very low. Statistically significant results allow psychologists to make many predictions about human behavior, but, as in all sciences, probabilistic results do not tell us with certainty what a particular individual will do in a situation.

11. It can be hard to choose among competing interpretations of a specific finding. Often, explanations must take into account many different factors, and care must be taken to avoid going beyond the facts. Sometimes the best interpretation does not emerge until a hypothesis has been tested in several different ways—for example, by using both *cross-sectional* and *longitudinal* studies.

12. Statistical significance does not always imply real-world importance because the proportion of the variance among scores that is accounted for by a particular variable may be small. The technique of *meta-analysis* reveals how much of the variation in scores across many different studies can be explained by a particular variable. Meta-analysis is useful for finding patterns in results, so long as some limitations of this method are kept in mind.

13. Psychologists spend considerable time discussing and debating their procedures for collecting, evaluating, and presenting data. One issue concerns the appropriate and inappropriate uses of psychological tests. Another concerns the ethics of psychological research, particularly the ethics of using deception and of using animals as subjects.

14. Some fundamental assumptions about the meaning of knowledge are currently under scrutiny. Adherents of *postmodernism* argue that an observer's values, judgments, and status in society inevitably affect which events are studied, how they are studied, and how they are explained. One postmodern theory, *social constructionism,* holds that knowledge is not so much discovered as it is created or invented. Some scholars are alarmed by postmodernism, fearing that a legitimate critique of the limitations of research is turning into an attack on all traditional methods. However, these new ideas, if combined with a traditional insistence on critical thinking and standards of evidence, have the potential for expanding and enriching our understanding of human behavior.

Key Terms

hypothesis *41*

theory *41*

operational definition *42*

principle of falsifiability *43*

"risky predictions" *43*

replicate *44*

descriptive methods *46*

case study *46*

observational studies *47*

naturalistic observation *47*

laboratory observation *47*

psychological tests *48*

standardization *49*

norms (in testing) *49*

reliable test *49*

   test–retest reliability *49*

   alternate-forms reliability *49*

valid test *49*

   content validity *49*

   criterion validity *50*

surveys *51*

sample *51*

representative sample *51*

volunteer bias *51*

correlational studies *54*

correlation *54*

variable *54*

positive correlation *55*

negative correlation *55*

coefficient of correlation *56*

experiment *58*

independent variable *60*

dependent variable *60*

control condition *61*

experimental/control groups *61*

random assignment *61*

placebo *62*

single-blind study *62*

experimenter effects *62*

double-blind study *63*

descriptive statistics *66*

arithmetic mean *66*

range *66*

variance *66*

inferential statistics *67*

statistical significance *67*

cross-sectional study *69*

longitudinal study *69*

meta-analysis *71*

postmodernism *75*

social constructionism *75*

PART II
THE BIOLOGICAL
PERSPECTIVE

One rainy afternoon a young woman named Sheila Allen went to a community hospital, asking for psychiatric help. Sheila Allen had virtually no strength left. She couldn't walk; she could barely sit up. For years, she had been going to doctors, getting sicker and sicker. The doctors didn't take her physical complaints seriously, and finally she agreed to enter the "kook hospital." Her diagnosis upon admission was "bizarre behavior, with looseness of thought associations and severe depression associated with suicidal thoughts."

Sheila Allen was lucky. At the hospital, she met a neurologist who suspected—correctly—that she had an uncommon disease called myasthenia gravis, which weakens the muscles. Fortunately, there is a treatment for this illness, and Sheila Allen recovered (Roueché, 1984). But others whose physical conditions have been mistaken for psychological ones have not been so lucky. The great composer George Gershwin, for example, spent years in psychoanalysis, complaining of headaches and depression. His analysts thought his problem was hatred for his mother and lack of regard for his father, when the real problem was a brain tumor that ultimately killed him. Similarly, songwriter Woody Guthrie ("This Land Is Your Land") was, for many years, mislabeled as an alcoholic, when his real affliction was Huntington's disease, a fatal genetic condition that usually strikes people in middle age, causing involuntary spasms and twisting movements of the body, facial grimacing, memory lapses, impulsive behavior, and sometimes paranoia, depression, and other psychological symptoms.

For psychologists who take a biological perspective on human behavior, such cases contain an important lesson: As physical creatures, we are all influenced in psychological ways by the workings of our bodies, and especially our brains. Therefore, in this view, to understand human beings—their temperaments, emotions, memories, perceptions, and mental disorders—we must understand the actions of genes, hormones, neurotransmitters, sensory organs, and neurons.

This section explores behavior from the biological psychologist's perspective. In Chapter 3, we will consider how knowledge about genes can help account for who we are and what we can become. In Chapter 4, we will look at how behavior is affected by the structure, biochemistry, and circuitry of the human nervous system.

CHAPTER 3

The Genetics of Behavior

*T*hink of all the ways that human beings are alike. Everywhere, no matter what their backgrounds or where they live, people love, work, argue, dance, sing, complain, and gossip. They rear families, celebrate marriages, and mourn losses. They reminisce about the past and plan for the future. They help their friends and fight with their enemies. They smile with amusement, frown with displeasure, and glare in anger. Where do all these commonalities come from?

Think of all the ways that human beings differ. Some of us are extroverts, always ready to throw a party, make a new friend, or speak up in a crowd; others are shy and introverted, preferring the safe and familiar. Some are trailblazers, ambitious and enterprising; others are placid, content with the way things are. Some take to book learning like a cat to catnip; others don't do so well in school but have lots of street smarts and practical know-how. Some are overwhelmed by even the most petty of problems; others, faced with severe difficulties, remain calm and resilient. Where do all these differences come from?

For many years, psychologists trying to answer these questions tended to fall into two camps. On one side were the *nativists,* who emphasized genes and inborn characteristics, or nature; on the other side were the *empiricists,* who focused on learning and experience, or nurture. E. L. Thorndike (1903), one of the leading psychologists of the early 1900s, staked out the nativist position when he claimed that "In the actual race of life . . . the chief determining factor is heredity." But his contemporary, behaviorist John B. Watson (1925), insisted that experience could write virtually any message on the blank slate of human nature: "Give me a dozen healthy infants, well-formed, and my own specified world to bring them up in and I'll guarantee to take any one at random and train him to become any type of specialist I might select—doctor, lawyer, artist, merchant-chief and yes, even beggar-man and thief, regardless of his talents, penchants, tendencies, abilities, vocations, and race of his ancestors."

In this chapter, we focus on the nature side of the debate and the findings of two related fields within the biological perspective. Researchers in **behavioral genetics** study the contribution of heredity to individual differences in personality, mental ability, and other human characteristics. Researchers in **evolutionary psychology** emphasize the evolutionary mechanisms that might help explain commonalities in language learning, attention, perception, memory, sexual behavior, reasoning, decision making, emotion, and many other aspects of human psychology (Barkow, Cosmides, & Tooby, 1992). Evolutionary psychology, which has emerged in the past few years as an increasingly important force in psychology, overlaps with *sociobiology*, an interdisciplinary field that looks for evolutionary explanations of social behavior in animals, including human beings. However, in the evaluation of the biological perspective, we will see that there are important differences between sociobiologists and evolutionary psychologists.

In the past, exchanges between the two sides in the nature–nurture debate sometimes sounded like a boxing match: "In this corner, we have Heredity, and in this corner, we have Environment. Okay, you guys, come out fighting." Today, no one argues in terms of nature *or* nurture; all scientists understand that heredity and environment interact to produce not only our psychological traits but even most of our physical ones.

Body weight is a good example. At one time, most psychologists thought that being fat was a sign of emotional disturbance. If you were overweight, it was because you hated your mother, feared intimacy, or were trying to fill an emotional hole in your psyche by loading up on rich desserts. But when researchers put this idea to the test, they found no support for it. On average, they found, fat people are no more and no less emotionally disturbed than average-weight people (Stunkard, 1980). Even more surprising, studies showed that *heaviness is not always caused by overeating* (C. Bouchard et al., 1990). Some heavy people do eat enormous quantities of food, but so do some very thin people. Some thin people eat very little, but so do some obese people. In one study that carefully monitored everything that subjects were eating, two 260-pound women maintained their weights while consuming only 1,000 calories a day (Wooley, Wooley, & Dyrenforth, 1979). In another study, in which volunteers were required to gorge themselves for months, it was as hard for slender people to gain weight as it is for most heavy people to lose weight. The minute the study was over, the slender people lost weight as fast as dieters gain it back (Sims, 1974).

One theory that integrates such findings argues that a biological mechanism keeps a person's body weight at a genetically influenced **set point**—the weight the person

---

behavioral genetics An interdisciplinary field of study concerned with the genetic bases of behavior and personality.

evolutionary psychology A field of psychology emphasizing evolutionary mechanisms that may help explain human commonalities in cognition, development, emotion, social practices, and other areas of behavior.

set point According to one theory, the genetically influenced weight range for an individual, thought to be maintained by a biological mechanism that regulates food intake, fat reserves, and metabolism.

stays at when not trying consciously to gain or lose (Lissner et al., 1991). According to this theory, everyone has a genetically programmed *basal metabolism rate,* the rate at which the body burns calories for energy, and a fixed number of *fat cells,* which store fat for energy. The fat cells can change in size but not in number. A complex interaction of metabolism, fat cells, and hormones keeps people at the weight their bodies are designed to be. When a heavy person diets, the body's metabolism slows down to conserve energy (and fat reserves). When a thin person overeats, metabolism speeds up, burning energy. Set-point theory, which has been supported by dozens of studies of animals and humans beings, explains why most people who go on restricted diets eventually gain their weight back; they are returning to their set-point weight.

Studies of twins and adopted children confirm that weight differences among people, and also the distribution of weight and general body shape, can be explained to some extent by genetic differences (Allison et al., 1994). Recently, enormous progress has been made in identifying the genes involved in some types of obesity. One team of researchers isolated a genetic variation in mice that causes animals with the variation to become obese (Zhang et al., 1994). The usual form of the gene, called "obese," or *ob* for short, causes fat cells to secrete a hormonelike protein, which the researchers called *leptin* (from the Greek *leptos,* "slender"). Leptin travels through the blood to the brain, and varying levels of the substance signal how large or small the body's fat cells are, so that the brain can regulate appetite and metabolism to maintain the animal's or person's set point. Several research teams have found that injecting leptin into mice reduces the animals' appetites, speeds up their metabolisms, and makes them more active; as a result, the animals shed weight, even if they were not overweight to begin with (e.g., Halaas et al., 1995).

Researchers initially thought that human obesity, too, occurred when the variant form of the *ob* gene caused fat cells to make less leptin or perhaps none at all, and that leptin injections might help obese people. It now seems, however, that leptin is much *higher* than average in most obese people, and that their obesity occurs not because they don't make leptin but because they are insensitive to it (Considine et al., 1996; Maffei et al., 1995). This insensitivity seems to be due to yet another genetic mutation, one that produces receptor cells in the brain that fail to respond normally to leptin's signals (Chua et al., 1996). As a result, the person stays hungry and keeps eating even when the body has enough stored fat to meet current energy demands.

Several other genes and body chemicals, too, are involved in appetite and weight regulation. According to evolutionary psychologists, genes that predispose individuals to obesity probably exist in our species because, in the past, starvation was all too often a real possibility, and a tendency to store calories in the form of fat provided a definite survival advantage.

Heredity is not the whole story, however: A person's habits also affect weight. Despite steady increases in the number of Americans trying to lose weight, the prevalence of obesity has jumped dramatically in the past few decades (Kuczmarski et al., 1994). The reasons no doubt have less to do with obesity genes than with the increased abundance of high-fat foods, the habit of eating high-calorie food on the run rather than leisurely meals, the rise in energy-saving (fat-conserving!) devices, the popularity of television over active hobbies, and increasingly sedentary lifestyles (Brownell & Rodin, 1994b). If you consume the high-fat junk-food diet that so many North Americans love, and if you eat such food in the large quantities that most Europeans and Asians find excessive, you are likely to be heavier than if you eat a low-fat diet in moderate portions. It may not be only a matter of calories: Research with mice suggests that a high-fat diet actually changes an individual's set point for body weight by somehow increasing the body's resistance to leptin (Frederich et al., 1995). On the other hand, regular moderate exercise, which boosts the body's metabolic rate and may lower its set point, can help a person lose weight and keep it off, especially when exercise is combined with a healthy diet (Wadden et al., 1990).

Still, even if you make daily trips to the gym and eat a healthy diet, you may never look like the current cultural ideal, which is biologically impossible for many people. The research on weight contains lessons from the biological perspective that apply to many other areas of behavior: Within a given environment, genes and other biological factors place limits on how much a person can change. Throughout life, these factors interact with environmental ones to shape—sometimes quite literally—who we are.

What's in a Gene?

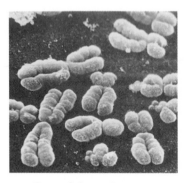

Let's look more closely at what genes are and how they operate. **Genes,** the basic units of heredity, are located on **chromosomes,** rod-shaped structures found in every cell of the body. (The chromosomes in this photo have been magnified almost 55,000 times.) Each sperm cell and each egg cell (ovum) possesses 23 chromosomes, so when a sperm and an egg unite at conception, the fertilized egg, and all the body cells that eventually develop from it (except for sperm cells and ova), contain 46 chromosomes—23 pairs.

One of these chromosome pairs usually determines a person's anatomical sex; it consists of an "X" chromosome from the mother's egg and either an "X" or a "Y" chromosome from the father's sperm. Because all eggs carry only an X, whereas sperm can carry either an X or a Y, it is the father's sperm that determines the offspring's sex. If the father contributes an X, the offspring is female (XX); if the father contributes a Y,

---

genes The functional units of heredity; they are composed of DNA and specify the structure of proteins.
chromosomes Rod-shaped structures within every body cell that carry the genes.

the offspring is male (XY). (When Henry VIII blamed Anne Boleyn for bearing a daughter instead of a son, he was following a long tradition—still alive in some societies—of assuming that the mother determines a child's sex. Had he known then what we know now about genetics, his unfortunate queen might have kept her crown and her head!) The only exceptions to the genetic rules governing anatomical sex are children born with hormonal or chromosomal anomalies that cause their anatomy to conflict with their genetic sex (that is, their sex chromosomes).

Chromosomes consist of threadlike strands of **DNA (deoxyribonucleic acid)** molecules, and genes consist of small segments of this DNA. Each human chromosome contains thousands of different genes, each with a fixed location; collectively, the 100,000 or so human genes are referred to as the human **genome.** Within each gene, four basic elements of DNA (called *bases*), identified by the letters A, T, C, and G, and numbering in the thousands or even tens of thousands, are arranged in a particular order: for example, ACGTCTCTATA. . . . This sequence comprises a chemical code that helps determine the synthesis of a particular protein by specifying the sequence of amino acids that are the protein's building blocks. In turn, proteins directly or indirectly affect virtually all of the structural and biochemical characteristics of the organism.

In the simplest type of inheritance, first described in the late nineteenth century by the Austrian monk Gregor Mendel, a single pair of genes is responsible for the expression of a particular trait. In many cases, one member of the pair is said to be *dominant* and the other *recessive,* which means that if an individual has one gene of each type, he or she will show the trait corresponding to the dominant gene. The ability to curl one's tongue lengthwise, for example, follows this pattern. If both of your parents contribute a gene for this ability (call it *A*), you will have it, too, and if both parents contribute the other form of the gene, the one associated with lack of the ability (call it *a*), you, too, will lack the ability. However, if one parent contributes an *A* and the other contributes an *a,* you will be able to curl your tongue, because the gene for the ability is dominant. You can still pass your "inability gene" on to your offspring, but it will not affect your own ability to curl your tongue.

Most human traits, even such seemingly straightforward ones as height and eye color, depend on more than one gene pair, which complicates matters enormously and makes tracking down the genetic contributions to a trait extremely difficult. Identifying even a single gene is daunting; biologist Joseph Levine and geneticist David Suzuki (1993) have compared the task to searching for a person when all you know is that the person lives somewhere on earth. There are about 3 *billion* units of DNA (all those As, Ts, Cs, and Gs) in the complete set of human chromosomes. So to locate a gene, you cannot just peer through a microscope. Instead, researchers must clone (produce

---

DNA (deoxyribonucleic acid) The chromosomal molecule that transfers genetic characteristics by way of coded instructions for the structure of proteins.
genome The full set of genes in each cell of an organism (with the exception of sperm and egg cells).

copies of) several different stretches of DNA on a chromosome, then use indirect methods to locate a given gene.

One method, which is being used to search for the genes associated with physical and mental conditions, involves doing **linkage studies.** These studies take advantage of the tendency of some genes lying close together on a chromosome to be inherited together across generations. The researchers start out by looking for *markers,* DNA segments that vary considerably among individuals and whose locations on the chromosomes are already known. They then look for patterns of inheritance of these markers in large families in which a particular condition is common. If a marker tends to exist in individuals who have the condition and not in those who don't, then the variant of the gene involved in the condition is apt to be located nearby on the chromosome, and the researchers have some idea where to search for it. The linkage method was used, for example, to locate the gene that causes Huntington's disease, the neurological disorder that killed Woody Guthrie (Huntington's Disease Collaborative Research Group, 1993). Although only one gene was involved, the search took a decade of painstaking work.

Scientists commonly refer to "the" human genome, but each of us, with the exception of identical twins, is a unique genetic mosaic, one that never existed before and never will again. Our uniqueness is due to the way inheritance operates. When the body cells that produce sperm cells and egg cells divide, one member of each original chromosome pair goes to one new cell and the other member goes to the other new cell. That is why sperm cells and egg cells contain only 23 *unpaired* chromosomes.

Chance alone decides which member of each chromosome pair goes to a particular sperm or egg. When you work out the mathematics, you find that each sperm- or egg-producing cell has the potential to produce more than 8 million different chromosome combinations in each new sperm or egg. But the actual diversity is far greater because genes can spontaneously change, or *mutate,* during formation of a sperm or an egg, due to an error in the copying of the original DNA sequence, and also because small segments of genetic material are apt to *cross over* (exchange places) between members of a chromosome pair before the final division.

The upshot is that each of us is the potential parent (given the time and energy) of billions of genetically different offspring. And because it takes two to make a baby, and each parent contributes one of billions of possible combinations to each child, the potential number of genetic combinations from any given set of parents is staggering. Thus, siblings, who share, on average, half their genes, can be unlike each other in many ways. And children, who share, on the average, half their genes with each parent, can be quite unlike their parents—in purely *genetic* terms.

---

linkage studies Studies that look for patterns of inheritance of genetic markers in large families in which a particular condition is common; the markers consist of DNA segments that vary considerably among individuals and that have known locations on the chromosomes.

OUR HUMAN HERITAGE

Just as genes guarantee human diversity, so they also guarantee some fundamental similarities. These similarities can be traced to our evolutionary history. British geneticist Steve Jones (1994) writes, "Genetics is the key to the past. Every human gene must have an ancestor. . . . Each gene is a message from our forebears and together they contain the whole story of human evolution."

Evolution is basically a change in the gene frequencies within a population over many generations. As particular genes become more or less common in the population, so do genetically influenced characteristics. Why do these frequencies change? For one thing, although parents pass on their genes to their offspring, new genetic variations keep arising as genes spontaneously mutate and recombine. According to the principle of **natural selection,** first formulated by British naturalist Charles Darwin in *On the Origin of Species* (1859/1964), the fate of these genetic variations depends on the environment. (Darwin didn't know about genes, which hadn't yet been discovered, but he did know that characteristics must somehow be transmitted from one generation to the next.) If, in a particular environment, individuals with a genetically influenced trait tend to be more successful in finding food, surviving the elements, fending off enemies, attracting sexual partners, and staying alive until they can reproduce, their genes will become more and more common in the population; over many generations, these genes may spread throughout the species. In contrast, individuals whose traits are not as adaptive in the struggle for survival will not be as reproductively fit: They will tend to die before reproducing, so their genes (and traits) will become less and less common and may eventually become extinct. There is debate about how gradually or abruptly such changes occur and whether competition for survival is always the primary mechanism of change (Gould & Eldredge, 1977), but scientists agree on the basic processes of evolution, and evolutionary principles guide all of the biological sciences.

Scientists who study evolution often start with some observed phenomenon (such as why the male peacock has such fabulous feathers) and then try to explain it in evolutionary terms after the fact (his preening display gets the attention of the female). But some evolutionary psychologists are taking a different tack. They begin by asking what sorts of challenges human beings might have faced in their prehistoric past—having to decide which foods were safe to eat, for example, or needing to size up a stranger's intentions quickly. They then draw inferences about the behavioral tendencies and psychological mechanisms that might have been selected because they helped our forebears solve these survival problems and enhanced their reproductive fitness. No assumption is made

---

evolution A change in gene frequencies within a population over many generations; a mechanism by which genetically influenced characteristics of a population change.

natural selection The evolutionary process in which individuals with genetically influenced traits that are adaptive in a particular environment tend to survive and to reproduce in greater numbers than do other individuals; as a result, their traits become more common in the population over time.

about whether the behavior is adaptive or intelligent in the *present* environment. They then design empirical studies or look for cross-cultural evidence to see whether their inferences are correct. Their guiding assumption is that the human mind is not a general-purpose computer but instead evolved as a collection of specialized and independent "modules" to handle specific survival problems (Buss, 1995; Cosmides, Tooby, & Barkow, 1992; Mealey, 1996). Culture and experience can affect which mechanisms get triggered, but everyone is born with the "wiring" for all of the mechanisms.

Critics of evolutionary psychology worry about the tendency of its advocates to assume that *every* behavior has biological, adaptive origins. They argue that the idea of mental modules is no improvement over instinct theory, the once popular notion in psychology that virtually every human activity and capacity, from cleanliness to cruelty, is innate. Evolutionary psychologists, however, contend that by drawing on different kinds of evidence they can distinguish behavior that has a biological origin from behavior that does not. As Steven Pinker (1994) explains,

> Using biological anthropology, we can look for evidence that the problem is one that our ancestors had to solve in the environments in which they evolved—so language and face recognition are at least candidates for innate modules, but reading and driving are not. Using data from psychology and ethnography, we can test the following prediction: when children solve problems for which they have mental modules, they should look like geniuses, knowing things they have not been taught; when they solve problems that their minds are not equipped for, it should be a long hard slog. Finally, if a module for some problem is real, neuroscience should discover that the brain tissue computing the problem has some kind of physiological cohesiveness, such as constituting a circuit or subsystem.

Because of our common evolutionary history, many abilities, tendencies, and characteristics are universal in human beings, and either are present at birth or develop as the child matures, given certain experiences. These traits include not just the obvious ones, such as being able to stand on two legs or to grasp objects with the forefinger and thumb, but less obvious ones as well. For example, babies are born with a number of *reflexes*—simple, automatic responses to specific stimuli. They will turn their heads toward a touch on the cheek or corner of the mouth and search for something to suck on, a handy "rooting" reflex that allows them to find the breast or bottle. They suck vigorously on a nipple, finger, or pacifier placed in their mouths. They grasp tightly a finger pressed on their palms. They follow a moving light with their eyes and turn toward a familiar sound, such as the mother's voice or the thump-thump of a heartbeat (both of which they heard in the womb). Many of these reflexes eventually disappear, but others, such as the knee-jerk, eye-blink, and sneeze reflexes, remain.

An attraction to novelty also seems to be part of our evolutionary heritage, and that of many other species. If a rat has eaten, it will prefer to explore an unfamiliar wing of a maze rather than the familiar wing where food is. Human babies, too, reveal a surprising interest in looking at and listening to the unfamiliar—which, of course, includes most of the world. A baby will even stop nursing if someone new enters his or her range of vision.

In recent years, researchers have taken advantage of the baby's tendency to look longer at novel than at familiar stimuli to devise ingenious ways of studying the innate bases of other kinds of behavior. For example, Elizabeth Spelke and her colleagues (1992) have found that infants as young as four months seem to understand some basic principles of physics! Babies look longer at a ball if it seems to roll through a solid barrier, or leap between two platforms, or hang in midair, than they do when an action obeys the laws of physics. Spelke believes that babies are programmed with a "core knowledge" about how the world works.

Possible event

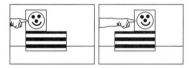

Impossible event

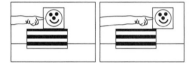

Similarly, Renée Baillargeon (1994) has found that infants as young as 2½ to 3½ months understand some of the physical properties of objects. One method she uses is to show infants a gloved hand pushing a colorful box from left to right along a striped platform. The box is pushed either until its edge reaches the end of the platform (a possible event) or until only a bit of its bottom surface rests on the platform with the rest extending beyond the platform (an impossible event). Babies look longer at the impossible event. Although researchers disagree about what precisely this means, Baillargeon infers that babies "are aware that objects continue to exist when masked by other objects, that objects cannot remain stable without support, that objects move along spatially continuous paths, and that objects cannot move through the space occupied by other objects."

Among all birds and mammals, the desire to explore and manipulate objects is also innate. Primates especially like to "monkey" with things, taking them apart and scrutinizing the pieces, apparently for the sheer pleasure of it (Harlow, Harlow, & Meyer, 1950). And from the first, human babies explore and manipulate their small worlds. They grasp whatever is put into their tiny hands, they shake rattles, they bang pots. For human beings, the natural impulse to handle interesting objects can be overwhelming, which may be one reason why the command "don't touch" is so often ignored by children, museum-goers, and shoppers.

Many species, including our own, also seem to have an inborn motive to play, to fool around, and to imitate others. Think of kittens and lion cubs, puppies and pandas, and all young primates, who will play with and pounce on one another all day until hunger or naptime calls. Some psychologists argue that play and exploration are biologically adaptive because they help members of a species find food and other necessities of life and learn to cope with their environments. Indeed, the young of many species enjoy *practice play*, behavior that will later be used for serious purposes when they are adults (Vandenberg, 1985). A kitten, for example, will stalk and attack a ball of yarn. In human beings, play has many purposes, including teaching children how to get along with others and giving them a chance to practice their motor and linguistic skills (Pellegrini & Galda, 1993).

> ### What Do You Know?
>
> How evolved is your understanding of genetics and evolution?
>
> 1. The basic units of heredity are called (a) chromosomes, (b) Xs and Ys, (c) genes, (d) DNA molecules.
> 2. Each of us is a unique genetic mosaic. What three processes during the formation of sperm and eggs explain this uniqueness?
> 3. Which is the *best* statement of the principle of natural selection? (a) Over time, the environment naturally selects some traits over others. (b) Particular genetic variations become more common over time if they are adaptive in a particular environment. (c) A species constantly improves as parents pass along their best traits to their offspring.
> 4. The guiding principle of evolutionary psychology is that the human mind evolved as (a) a collection of specialized modules to handle specific survival problems; (b) a general-purpose computer that adapts to any situation; (c) a collection of specific instincts for every human activity or capacity.
>
> **Answers:**
>
> 1. c 2. The random nature of chromosome-pair division, spontaneous genetic mutations, and crossover of genetic material between members of a chromosome pair before the final division. 3. b 4. a

The Genetics of Similarity

We turn now to a few other important characteristics and abilities that are a legacy of our evolutionary past: perceptual abilities, emotional expressions, a need for attachment and sociability, and a capacity for language. In Chapter 5, we will also discuss the application of evolutionary psychology to courtship and mating behavior.

The Origins of Perception

Virgil, age 50, had been almost totally blind since early childhood. Thick cataracts limited his vision to patches of light and dark, and doctors thought he might also have a hereditary disease that damages the retinas, the areas at the back of the eyes that contain the receptors for vision. Virgil was well adjusted to his disability; he read braille, enjoyed listening to sports events on the radio, and supported himself as a massage therapist at the local YMCA. Then something happened that changed Virgil's life: At the urging of his fiancée, he agreed to undergo cataract surgery on the chance that it might restore his sight.

Virgil's right eye was to be operated on first. As the big day approached, his family was filled with anticipation and hope. Perhaps, after so many years of living in darkness, Virgil would finally be able to see again. The operation was performed, and the following day the bandages were removed. Virgil's fiancée and family expected him to open his eyes, look around, and cry out "At last! I can see!" But to their surprise, he did not. It was obvious that Virgil could see *something,* but he seemed bewildered, and it soon became apparent that he had no idea *what* he was seeing. Neurologist and essayist Oliver Sacks (1993), reporting on Virgil's reactions, writes, "There was light, there was movement, there was color, all mixed up, all meaningless, a blur. Then out of the blur came a voice that said, 'Well?' Then, and only then . . . did he finally realize that this chaos of light and shadow was a face—and, indeed, the face of his surgeon. . . . His retina and optic nerve were active, transmitting impulses, but his brain could make no sense of them."

Virgil, like other people who have had their vision restored late in life, was never able to adjust completely to his new world. He continued to be confused about the shapes of many objects unless he could touch them. He might see an animal's paw, nose, tail, and ears yet fail to recognize that he was looking at a cat. He had to be led through his own house, and if he deviated at all from his usual route, he became disoriented. Eventually, perhaps because of continuing physical problems, Virgil lost most of the sight he had regained and once again became blind. But now he accepted his blindness as a gift, a release from the baffling and overwhelming world of sight.

Virgil's experience tells us that it is one thing for the visual receptors in the eyes to detect and respond to changes in physical energy in the environment, a process called **sensation,** and quite another for the brain to interpret and organize this information, a process called **perception.** Sensation produces an immediate awareness of sound, color, form, and other building blocks of consciousness, but it takes perceptual processes to assemble those building blocks into meaningful patterns. Our sense of vision merely produces a two-dimensional image on the back of the eye, but we *perceive* the world in three dimensions and *perceive* where one object begins and another ends. Virgil's problems were with perception.

Psychologists are interested in cases like Virgil's for the clues they might offer in solving an old problem: What aspects of sensation and perception does heredity prepare us for? What happens when babies first open their eyes? Do they see the world the way adults do? Do they hear the same sounds that adults do, smell the same smells, taste the same tastes? Are their strategies for organizing the world innate, wired into their brains from the beginning? Or is an infant's world, as William James once suggested, only a "blooming, buzzing confusion," waiting to be organized by experience and learning?

Unfortunately, fascinating though cases like Virgil's may be, they have drawbacks from a scientific standpoint. Blind people who regain their sight have relied all their lives on their sense of touch, and this reliance could interfere with their ability to make sense of the visual world after their sight is restored. Also, some patients, such as Virgil, have had retinal damage that could explain some of their postoperative visual problems. So to find out what happens when the usual perceptual experiences of early life

---

sensation The detection or direct experience of physical energy in the external or internal environment due to stimulation of receptors in the sense organs.

perception The process by which the brain organizes and interprets sensory information.

fail to occur, researchers prefer to study animals whose sensory and perceptual systems are similar to our own, such as cats.

What they find is that without certain experiences during critical periods of development, perception develops abnormally. Researchers studying vision, for example, have discovered that when newborn animals are reared in total darkness for a period of weeks or months, or are fitted with translucent goggles that permit only diffuse light to get through, or are allowed to see only one visual pattern and no others, visual development is impaired. In one famous study, kittens were exposed to either vertical or horizontal black and white stripes. Special collars kept them from seeing anything else, even their own bodies. After several months, the kittens exposed only to vertical stripes seemed blind to all horizontal contours; they bumped into horizontal obstacles placed in their way and ran to play with a bar that an experimenter held vertically but not to a bar held horizontally. In contrast, those exposed only to horizontal stripes bumped into vertical obstacles and ran to play with horizontal bars but not vertical ones (Blakemore & Cooper, 1970).

However, these findings don't necessarily mean that cats are blind to horizontal and vertical lines *at birth*. A biological psychologist would point out that normal experience may merely ensure the survival of skills already present at birth in rudimentary form. Physiological studies suggest that this second interpretation is the correct one, at least in the case of the perception of lines.

In all mammals, complex features of the visual world are processed by special *feature-detector cells* in a part of the brain called the visual cortex (Hubel & Wiesel, 1962, 1968). Laboratory studies show that many of these cells respond maximally to moving or stationary lines that are oriented in a particular direction and located in a particular part of the visual field. One type of cell might respond most often to a horizontal line in the lower right part of the visual field, another to a diagonal line at a specific angle in the upper left part of the visual field. In the real world, such features make up the boundaries and edges of objects. (In primates, other cells respond maximally to much more complex patterns, such as spirals, bull's-eyes, and star shapes.)

It turns out that the brains of newborn kittens are equipped with exactly the same kinds of feature-detector cells that adult cats have. When kittens are kept from seeing lines of a particular orientation, such as horizontal or vertical ones, cells sensitive to those orientations deteriorate or change, and perception suffers (Hirsch & Spinelli, 1970; Mitchell, 1980). Moreover, there seems to be a critical period in cats, during the first three months after birth, when exposure to verticality and horizontality is crucial. If a kitten doesn't get this exposure, its vision will continue to be abnormal even after many years of living in a normal environment.

From studies such as these, psychologists have concluded that human infants are probably born with an ability to detect and discriminate the edges and angles of objects. Direct observations of infants and their reactions to different sensory stimuli show that they have other visual talents as well. They can discriminate different sizes and colors very early, possibly at birth. They can distinguish contrasts, shadows, and complex patterns after only a few weeks. Even depth perception occurs early and may be present from the beginning.

Figure 3.1 *Studies done with the visual cliff have shown that even very young infants have depth perception.*

Testing an infant's perception of depth requires considerable ingenuity. One clever procedure that was used for decades was to place infants on a device called a *visual cliff* (Gibson & Walk, 1960). The "cliff" is a pane of glass covering a shallow surface and a deep one (see Figure 3.1). Both surfaces are covered by a checkerboard pattern. The infant is placed on a board in the middle, and the child's mother tries to coax the baby across either the shallow or the deep side. Babies as young as six months of age will crawl to their mothers across the shallow side but will refuse to crawl out over the "cliff." Their hesitation shows that they have depth perception.

Of course, by age six months, a baby has had quite a bit of experience with the world. But infants younger than six months, even though they are unable to crawl, can also be tested on the visual cliff. At only two months of age, babies show a drop in heart rate when placed on the deep side of the cliff, but no change when they are placed on the shallow side. A slowed heart rate is usually a sign of increased attention. Thus, although these infants may not be frightened the way an older infant would be, it seems they can notice the difference in depth (Banks, 1984). By age five months, infants can even coordinate visual information with auditory cues to judge distance: They are more likely to look at a video of an advancing or a retreating train when increasing or fading engine noises "match" what they are seeing than when there is a conflict (Pickens, 1994).

This is not to say that newborns perceive the world exactly as adults do. Their neurological connections are not completely formed, so their senses are not as acute as those of an adult. But the world of a newborn is far from the blooming, buzzing confusion that William James took it to be. Besides their visual skills, infants bring into the world many other sensory and perceptual abilities. They will startle to a loud noise and turn their heads toward its source, showing that they perceive sound as being localized in space. They can distinguish a person's voice from other kinds of sounds. They react strongly to certain smells, such as those of garlic and vinegar, but less strongly to others, such as those of licorice and alcohol, showing that they can discriminate among odors. They can distinguish salty from sweet. They show a distinct preference for sweet tastes and wrinkle up their noses at bitter ones.

All of these inborn sensory and perceptual abilities evolved to help us survive. It is enormously useful to be able to notice the edge of a cliff—or a crib, or a staircase. Our sense of smell allows us to sniff out danger by smelling smoke, spoiled food, and many poison gases, and our sense of hearing helps us detect the rustle of a snake in the grass and the voice of a friend in a crowd. A sweet tooth and an aversion to bitter tastes may have evolved because sweet tastes generally belong to substances that are healthful, such as fruits, whereas bitter substances are often poisonous.

Even pain, which causes so much misery, is an indispensable part of our evolutionary heritage, for it alerts us to illness and injury. In rare cases, people have been born without a sense of pain. Although free of the hurts and aches that plague the rest of us, they lead difficult lives. Because they feel none of pain's warnings, they burn, bruise, and cut themselves more than other people do. One young woman developed inflamed joints because she failed to turn over in her sleep or to shift her weight while standing—acts that people with normal pain sensation perform automatically. At the age of only 29 she died from massive infections, due in part to skin and bone injuries (Melzack, 1973).

Because other species have different needs, their bodies are attuned to different aspects of physical reality than ours are. Bees are blind to red, but they can see ultraviolet light, which merely gives humans a sunburn. Flowers that appear to us to be a single color must look patterned to a bee, because different parts of flowers reflect ultraviolet light to a different extent. Other animals have sensory systems that have no equivalent at all in human beings. Some snakes have an organ, in a pit on the head, that detects infrared rays. This organ permits them to sense heat given off by the bodies of their prey. The slightest change in temperature sends a message racing to the snake's brain. There the message is combined with information from the eyes, so that the snake actually sees an infrared pattern—and locates its prey with deadly accuracy, even in the dark (Newman & Hartline, 1982). We can't do that, just as we can't hear the high-frequency sound waves that dogs, bats, and porpoises can hear. Our sensory windows on the world are partly shuttered. Things appear to us as they do not only because of *their* nature but also because of *ours*.

The Face of Emotion

In his classic book *The Expression of the Emotions in Man and Animals* (1872/1965), Charles Darwin argued that certain human facial expressions of emotion—the smile, the frown, the grimace, the glare—are as biologically ordained as the purr of a contented cat or the snarl of a threatened wolf. Such expressions may have evolved because they allowed our forebears to tell the difference immediately between a friendly stranger and a hostile one.

Modern psychologists have supported Darwin's idea by studying the recognition of emotional expressions across diverse cultures. In a research program that has spanned a quarter of a century, Paul Ekman and his colleagues have gathered evidence for the universality of seven basic facial expressions of emotion: anger, happiness, fear, surprise, disgust, sadness, and contempt (Ekman, 1994; Ekman & Heider, 1988; Ekman et al., 1987). In every culture they have studied—in Brazil, Chile, Estonia, Germany, Greece, Hong Kong, Italy, Japan, New Guinea, Scotland, Sumatra, Turkey, and the United States—a large majority has recognized the emotional expressions portrayed by people in other cultures. Even most members of isolated tribes that have never watched a movie or read *People* magazine, such as the Foré of New Guinea or the Minangkabau of West Sumatra, can recognize the emotions expressed in pictures of people who are entirely foreign to them. (Sometimes, however, a large minority disagrees with the majority, suggesting that custom and learning also affect the display and recognition of emotions.)

Psychologists have also found that some emotional expressions resembling those of adults are present from birth, most notably those for pleasure, anger, surprise, disgust, and possibly fear and sadness—pretty much the same ones that are universal across cultures (Campos et al., 1984). These expressions help us communicate our intentions and "read" those of others. Such communication begins in infancy; a baby's expressions of misery, angry frustration, happiness, and disgust are apparent to most parents (Izard, 1994b; Stenberg & Campos, 1990). And babies, in turn, react to the facial expressions of their parents. American, German, Greek, Japanese, Trobriand Island, and Yanomamo mothers all "infect" their babies with happy moods by displaying happy expressions (Keating, 1994). Recall the visual cliff that we described in the previous section. It turns out that if the cliff is ambiguous and does not automatically evoke fear, and if the baby's mother is on the far side of the cliff and warns the baby against crossing by assuming an expression of fear or anger, the baby will not cross. If, however, the mother smiles at the baby warmly, the baby will cross to her, even though the baby is aware of the "cliff" (Sorce et al., 1985). Clearly, a baby's ability to recognize facial expressions of emotion has survival value.

Attachment and Sociability

Unlike a tadpole or a tarantula, a human infant cannot live without care and attention from its own kind. Human development, from infancy to old age, depends on learning from others. Without other people, we languish—if not physically, then emotionally—and it seems probable that without affiliation and cooperation, human societies could never have survived.

In developmental psychology, *attachment* refers to the deep emotional tie that children and their primary caregivers feel toward each other. In all primate infants, attachment begins with and requires touch, or *contact comfort.* Margaret and Harry Harlow first demonstrated this need by raising infant rhesus monkeys with two kinds of artificial mothers (Harlow, 1958; Harlow & Harlow, 1966). The first mother was a

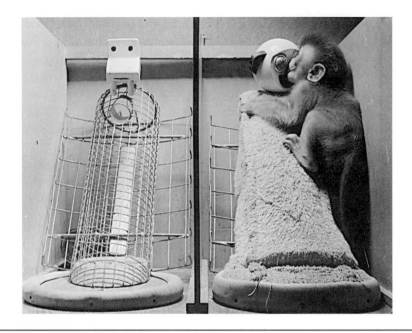

Figure 3.2   *In primates, the need for cuddling is as innate as the need for food. In Margaret and Harry Harlow's studies, infant rhesus monkeys got milk from a bare wire "mother," but preferred clinging to a terry "mother" when they weren't feeding or when they were afraid.*

forbidding construction of wires and warming lights, with a milk bottle attached. The second was also constructed of wire but was covered in foam rubber and cuddly terry cloth. At the time, psychologists thought that babies become attached to their parents because a parent provides food and warmth. But these baby monkeys ran to the terry-cloth "mother" when they were frightened or startled, and cuddling up to it calmed them down (see Figure 3.2.)

Human infants, too, initially become attached to their mothers or other caregivers because of the contact comfort the adults provide. For infants, cuddling is nearly as important as food. British psychiatrist John Bowlby (1969, 1973) discovered this fact years ago when he observed infants being reared in orphanages. When babies were given adequate food, water, and warmth but were deprived of being touched and held, they showed retarded emotional and physical development. (Emotional and physical symptoms also occur in adults in our society who are "undertouched," such as the sick and the aged.) According to Bowlby, infant attachment has an adaptive purpose: It provides a *secure base* from which the child can explore the environment, a haven of safety to which the child can return when he or she is afraid. A sense of security, said Bowlby, allows children to develop cognitive skills. A sense of safety allows them to develop trust. Bowlby's observations have been replicated by other researchers many times. When infants are consistently deprived of social contact, affection, and cuddling, the emotional, behavioral, and cognitive effects can be disastrous and long-lasting

(Bowlby, 1988; Jacobsen, Edelstein, & Hofmann, 1994; Speltz, Greenberg, & Deklyen, 1990).

The most famous method for studying a child's degree of attachment, called the *strange situation,* was devised by Mary Ainsworth (1973, 1979; Ainsworth et al., 1978). A mother brings her baby into an unfamiliar room containing lots of toys. After a while, a stranger comes in and attempts to play with the child. The mother leaves the baby with the stranger. She then returns, plays with the child, and the stranger leaves. Finally, the mother leaves the baby alone for three minutes and returns. In each case, observers carefully note how the baby behaves—with the mother, with the stranger, and when the baby is alone.

Ainsworth and her associates divided children into three categories, on the basis of the children's reactions to the strange situation. Some babies are *securely attached:* They cry or protest if the parent leaves the room; they welcome her back and then play happily again; they are clearly more attached to the mother than to the stranger. But other babies are insecurely attached. They may be detached or *avoidant,* not seeming to care when the mother leaves the room, making little effort to seek contact with her on her return, and treating the stranger about the same as the mother; or they may be *anxious* or *ambivalent,* resisting contact with the mother at reunion but protesting loudly if she leaves. Insecurely attached children may cry to be picked up and then demand to be put down. Some behave as if they are angry with the mother and resist her efforts to give comfort.

Many studies have demonstrated the powerful and persisting effects of these early attachment styles, and in particular the importance of secure attachment. In a longitudinal study that followed babies from 12 to 18 months of age until they were 21 years old, the researchers found that these early attachment styles remained remarkably stable (Waters et al., 1995). Insecurely or anxiously attached infants—those who lack what Bowlby called "a secure base"—often grow into children who have problems in social and cognitive functioning and who have a greater number of behavior problems in home and school (Posada, Lord, & Waters, 1995; Speltz, Greenberg, & Deklyen, 1990). And they may grow into adults who are anxious or avoidant in their own close relationships (Shaver, 1994).

Newborns not only need to touch and be touched, but they are also ready to be sociable in other ways as well. For one thing, they are primed to respond to human faces. Babies who are only nine *minutes* old will turn their heads to watch a drawing of a face if it moves in front of them, but they will not turn if the "face" consists of scrambled features or is just the outline of a face (Goren, Sarty, & Wu, 1975; Johnson et al., 1991). And babies who are only 45 hours old already prefer to look at their mother's face rather than the face of an unfamiliar woman (Field et al., 1984). A preference for faces over other stimuli in the environment may have survival value because it helps babies recognize where their next meal is likely to come from.

By the age of four to six weeks, babies are smiling regularly, especially in response to faces, even when they haven't yet the foggiest notion of whom they are smiling at. Babies also have rudimentary "conversations" with the people who tend them. Like many social exchanges, the first "conversation" a baby has with its mother or primary caregiver often takes place over a good meal. During breast or bottle feeding, babies and their mothers (or dads, or grandparents, or nannies) often play little games with each other, exchanging signals in a rhythmic pattern of sucks and pauses. During the pauses, the adult often jiggles the baby, who then starts to suck again. Like a spoken conversation, their exchange involves taking turns and waiting for a response: suck, pause, jiggle, pause, suck, pause, jiggle, pause (Kaye, 1977).

This early rhythmic dialogue illustrates a crucial aspect of all human exchanges: *synchrony,* the adjustment of one person's nonverbal behavior to coordinate with another's (Bernieri et al., 1994; Condon, 1982). People unconsciously adjust their rhythms of speech, their gestures, and their expressions to be "in sync" with each other, and these adjustments, which seem to be essential in establishing rapport between people, begin at birth. Newborn infants will synchronize their behavior and attention to adult speech but not to other sounds, such as street noise or tapping (Beebe et al., 1982). A mother and child tend to move in concert, moving at the same pace and rhythm, and coordinating their movements like well-matched dance partners. Their little dance will soon develop into a full-blown dialogue.

What Do You Know?

1. Research with animals and human infants suggests that the ability to discriminate edges and angles of objects is (a) innate, and develops regardless of experience; (b) innate, but depends on experience for survival and development; (c) learned only after maturation of the nervous system, many months after birth.
2. What two kinds of research support Darwin's notion that certain facial expressions of emotion are part of our biological heritage?
3. What findings support the idea that human infants are primed to be sociable?
4. According to Bowlby and others, attachment provides children with a _____ _____ from which they can explore the world. When the innate need for secure attachment is thwarted, children may develop an _____ or an _____ style of attachment.

Answers:

1. b 2. Cross-cultural research on facial expressions of emotion and research on the facial expressions of newborns. 3. Infants seek out and require contact comfort; develop best when they have secure attachments to their caregivers; show a preference for looking at human faces; smile regularly, especially at faces; and synchronize their behavior with that of a caregiver. 4. secure base; avoidant; anxious/ambivalent

The Capacity for Language

Try to read this sentence aloud:

Kamaunawezakusomamanenohayawewenimtuwamaanasana.

Can you tell where one word begins and another ends? Unless you happen to know Swahili, the syllables of this sentence probably sound like gibberish.*

Well, to a baby learning its native tongue, *every* sentence must, at first, be gibberish. How, then, does an infant pick out discrete syllables and words from the jumble of sounds in its environment, much less figure out what those words mean? Is there something about a human baby's brain that is special, something that allows the baby to "tune in" to language and discover how it works? Darwin thought so: Language, he wrote, "is not a true instinct, for every language has to be learned. It differs, however, widely from all other arts, for man has an instinctive tendency to speak" (Darwin, 1874). Modern research is supporting Darwin's view.

To understand this issue, we must first appreciate that a **language** is not just any old communication system; it is a system for combining elements that are in themselves meaningless into utterances that convey meaning. The elements are usually sounds, but not always. In North America, many hearing-impaired people use as their primary form of communication American Sign Language (ASL), which is based on gesture rather than sound, and in other countries, deaf people have developed other gestural languages.

Whether spoken or signed, language allows us to express and comprehend an infinite number of novel utterances, created on the spot. We seem to be the only species that does this naturally. Other primates use a variety of grunts and screeches to warn one another of danger, attract attention, and express emotions, but the sounds are not combined to produce original sentences (at least, as far as we can tell). Bongo may make a distinctive sound when he encounters food, but he cannot say, "The bananas in the next grove are a lot riper than the ones we ate last week and sure beat our usual diet of termites."

Except for a few fixed phrases ("How are you?" "Get a life"), most of the utterances we produce or hear over a lifetime are new. Thus you will find few, if any, sentences in this book that you have read, heard, or spoken before in exactly the same form. Yet you can understand what you are reading, and you can produce new sentences of your own. According to most *psycholinguists* (researchers who study the psychology of language), you do this by applying a large but finite set of rules that make up the grammar of your language. Rules of *syntax* tell you which strings of sounds (or gestural signs) form acceptable utterances and which do not. Most people cannot actually state the syntactic rules of their grammar ("Adjectives usually precede the noun they describe"), yet they are able to apply them, without even thinking about it. No native speaker of English would say, "He threw the ball big."

For adults, mastering the rules of a new language can be an intimidating task. But during the preschool years, children acquire new words at an amazingly rapid rate—about nine a day, for a total of more than 14,000 new words. They absorb these words

---

language A system that combines meaningless elements such as sounds or gestures into structured utterances that convey meaning.

Kama unaweza kusoma maneno haya, wewe ni mtu wa maana sana, in Swahili means "If you can read these words, you are a remarkable person."

as they encounter them in conversation, typically after hearing only one or two uses of a word in context (Rice, 1989). In only a few short years, a child is able to string all those new words together into sentences that make sense and, most impressive of all, produce and understand an infinite number of new word combinations.

Where do these dazzling abilities come from? Until the middle of this century, many psychologists assumed that children learned to speak simply by imitating adults and paying attention when adults corrected their mistakes. Then along came linguist Noam Chomsky (1957, 1980), who argued that language was far too complex to be learned bit by bit, as one might learn a list of U.S. presidents or the rules of algebra. Chomsky observed that children not only can figure out which sounds form words but also can take the *surface structure* of a sentence—the way the sentence is actually spoken—and apply rules of syntax to infer an underlying *deep structure* that contains meaning. For example, although "Mary kissed John" and "John was kissed by Mary" have different surface structures, a five-year-old knows that the two sentences have essentially the same deep structure, in which Mary is the actor and John the recipient of the action. The human brain, said Chomsky, must therefore contain a *language acquisition device,* a mental module that allows young children to develop language if they are exposed to an adequate sampling of speech. Just as a bird is designed to fly, human beings are designed to use language.

Chomsky and others have presented several arguments to support this position, including the following (Crain, 1991; Pinker, 1994):

1. Children everywhere seem to go through similar stages of linguistic development, whether they are learning Polish, English, or Chinese (Bloom, 1970; Brown & Fraser, 1964; Brown & Hanlon, 1970; Slobin, 1970). For example, children first form negatives simply by adding *no* or *not* at the beginning or end of a sentence ("No get dirty"); and at a later stage, they will often use double negatives ("He don't want no milk"; "Nobody don't like me"), even when their language does not allow such constructions (Klima & Bellugi, 1966; McNeill, 1966). Such facts fit the theory that children are born with a sort of "universal grammar," which is another way of saying that the human brain is disposed to notice the features common to all languages (nouns, verbs, phrase structures, and so forth), as well as the variations that can occur. In this view, it is the universal grammar that enables a child to hear the sentence "John likes fish," infer its deep structure, and come up with the similar sentence "Mary eats apples." And it is the same universal grammar that allows the child to know that "John likes fish" is different from "John might fish," because otherwise the child would say "John might apples" (Pinker, 1994).

2. Children combine words in ways that adults never would and so could not simply be imitating. They reduce a parent's sentences ("Let's go to the store") to their own two-word version ("Go store") and make errors an adult would not ("The alligator goed kerplunk," "Daddy taked me," "Hey, Horton heared a Who") (Ervin-Tripp, 1964; Marcus et al., 1992). Such errors are not random, however; they show that the child has grasped a grammatical rule (add the

t or *d* sound to make a verb past tense, as in *walked* and *hugged*) and is simply overgeneralizing it (*taked, goed*). Helen Bee (1997) reports the following charming conversation between a six-year-old and a three-year-old, who were arguing about the relative dangers of forgetting to feed pet goldfish or feeding them too much:

Six-year-old: It's worse to forget to feed them.

Three-year-old: No, it's badder to feed them too much.

Six-year-old: You don't say badder, you say worser.

Three-year-old: But it's baddest to give them too much food.

Six-year-old: No it's not. It's worsest to forget to feed them.

These children had learned a rule for comparisons (*-er* and *-est* endings) but had not yet learned all the exceptions. Such errors, which are called *overregularizations,* are really quite "smart" because they show that children are actively seeking regular, predictable rules of language.

3. **ADULTS DO NOT CONSISTENTLY CORRECT THEIR CHILDREN'S SYNTAX.** Learning explanations of language acquisition assume that children are rewarded for saying the right words and punished for making errors. But parents don't stop to correct every error in their children's speech, so long as they can understand what the child is trying to say (Brown, Cazden, & Bellugi, 1969). Indeed, parents often *reward* children for incorrect statements! The two-year-old who says "Want milk!" is likely to get it; most parents would not wait for a more grammatical (or polite) request. Yet, by the tender age of three, as Steven Pinker (1994) writes, the child has become "a grammatical genius—master of most constructions, obeying rules far more often than flouting them, respecting language universals, erring in sensible, adultlike ways, and avoiding many kinds of error altogether."

4. **EVEN CHILDREN WHO ARE PROFOUNDLY RETARDED ACQUIRE LANGUAGE.** Indeed, they typically show a facility for language that exceeds by far their abilities in other areas (Bellugi et al., 1992; Smith, Tsimpli, & Ouhalla, 1993).

Chomsky's ideas so revolutionized thinking about language and human nature that some linguists now refer to the publication of his ideas as The Event (Rymer, 1993). Chomsky completely changed the questions researchers asked about language development, and even the terms they use (language "acquisition" replaced language "learning"). Since then, there have been some efforts to revive the learning approach, using computer models that mimic aspects of language acquisition by finding patterns in linguistic input, without assuming any prior mental rules of grammar (Rumelhart & McClelland, 1987). And research now shows that in addition to the many similarities in the speech of children learning different languages, there are also many dissimilarities (Slobin, 1985, 1991). However, most psycholinguists accept Chomsky's argument that the human faculty for language is biologically based. Although Chomsky himself has avoided the evolutionary implications, others argue that language evolved in our species because it permitted our forebears to convey precise information about time, space, objects, and events, and to negotiate alliances that were necessary for survival (Pinker, 1994).

The next logical step might be to identify the specific brain modules and genes that contribute to our ability to acquire language. One clue comes from a fascinating Canadian study of a large three-generation family with a rare genetic disorder that prevents normal language acquisition (Gopnik, 1991; Matthews, 1994). Family members who are affected with this disorder have normal intelligence and perceptual abilities, but they cannot infer specific kinds of grammatical rules, including those for changing tenses or constructing plurals—rules that normal children learn easily and unconsciously. For example, they can learn the distinction between *mice* and *mouse* but cannot learn the general rule about adding an *s, z,* or *ez* sound to make a noun plural, as in *bikes* (*s*), *gloves* (*z*), and *kisses* (*ez*). Instead, they must learn each plural as a separate item, and they make many errors. Yet their other grammatical abilities are unimpaired. The pattern of inheritance seen in this study and others suggests that the disorder may be due to a single dominant gene (Gopnik, 1994).

But remember: In any complex behavior, nature and nurture interact. Studies find that even though parents may not go around correcting their children's speech all day, neither do they ignore their children's errors. For example, they are more likely to repeat verbatim a child's well-formed sentence than a sentence with errors ("That's a horse, mommy!" "Yes, that's a horse"). But when the child makes a mistake or produces a clumsy sentence, parents almost invariably respond by recasting it or expanding its elements ("Monkey climbing!" "Yes, the monkey is climbing the tree") (Bohannon & Stanowicz, 1988). In turn, children are more likely to imitate adult recasts and expansions, suggesting that they are learning from them (Bohannon & Symons, 1988). They also imitate their parents' accents, inflections, and tones of voice, and they will repeat some words that the parent tries to teach ("This is a ball, Erwin." "Baw"). Children may have a capacity to acquire language from mere exposure to it, but many parents help things along.

Language therefore depends on both biological readiness and social experience. Children who are abandoned and abused, and who are not exposed to language for years, rarely speak normally. One such case involved a 13-year-old girl whose parents had locked her up in one small room since age 1½. During the day, they usually kept her strapped in a child's potty seat. At night, they confined her to a straitjacket-like sleeping bag. The mother, a battered wife who lived in terror of her severely disturbed husband, barely cared for her daughter. Although the child may have been able to hear some speech through the walls of her room, there was no television or radio in the home, and no one spoke a word to her. If she made the slightest sound, her father beat her with a large piece of wood.

Genie, as researchers later called her, hardly seemed human when she was finally set free. She did not know how to chew or to stand erect, and she was not toilet trained. She slobbered uncontrollably, masturbated in public, and spat on anything that was handy, including herself and other people. When she was first observed by psychologists, her only sounds were high-pitched whimpers. She understood only a few words, most of them probably learned shortly after her release. Yet Genie was alert and curious. After her rescue, she developed physically, learned some rules of social conduct, and established relationships with others. Gradually, she began to use words and to understand short sentences. Eventually, she was able to use language to convey her needs, describe her moods, and even tell lies. However, her grammar and her pronunciation of words remained abnormal even after several years. She could not use pronouns correctly, ask questions, produce proper negative sentences, or use all the little word endings that communicate tense, conjunction, number, and possession (Curtiss, 1977, 1982; Rymer, 1993).

Such sad evidence, and other similar cases, suggest that there may be a critical period for normal language development, possibly the years between ages one and five or six years, or possibly the entire first decade of life (Curtiss, 1977; Pinker, 1994; Tartter, 1986). During these years, children do not necessarily need to hear *speech*—deaf children's acquisition of sign language parallels the development of spoken language—but they do need close relationships and practice in conversation. You will recall that if cats miss seeing vertical or horizontal lines during a critical period in infancy, they will lose forever their ability to see such lines. In the same way, the human brain may lose the capacity for syntax if a child is not exposed to language during a critical period early in life.

Genes, we have seen, contribute to many of the qualities that make us human: our pleasure in exploring and examining our environment; specific ways of seeing, tasting, smelling, and hearing the world; a need to touch and to be with others; a capacity for

The capacity for language is innate, but its full expression depends on exposure to conversation early in life—either speech or, as in the case of this deaf child, sign language.

the complexities of language. It is clear that when the seventeenth-century English philosopher John Locke wrote that the human mind at birth is a *tabula rasa*, a blank slate, he was mistaken. The tabula isn't rasa at all.

WHAT DO YOU KNOW?

How full of information is your mental tabula right now?

1. The most important distinction between human language and other communication systems is that language (a) allows for the generation of an infinite number of new utterances; (b) is spoken; (c) is learned only after explicit training; (d) directly expresses a linguistic deep structure.
2. Name four arguments for the existence of an innate "universal grammar."

ANSWERS:

1. a   2. Children everywhere seem to go through similar stages of linguistic development; children combine words in ways that adults never would; adults do not consistently correct their children's syntax; and even profoundly retarded children acquire language.

THE GENETICS OF DIFFERENCE

We turn now to the second great issue in the nature–nurture debate: the origins of the differences among us. We will begin with a critical discussion of what heritability means and how it can be estimated. Then we will examine behavioral-genetic explanations of intelligence and personality.

The Heritability Hunt

Suppose you want to measure flute-playing ability in a large group of music students. You have some independent raters assign each student a score, from 1 to 20, and when you plot the scores, you see that they vary considerably. Some people are what you might call melodically disadvantaged and should forget about a career in music; others are flute geniuses, practically ready for Carnegie Hall; and the rest fall somewhere in between. What causes the variation in this group of students? Why are some so musically talented and others so inept? Are these differences primarily genetic, or are they the result of experience and motivation?

The methods used by behavioral geneticists to study such questions typically yield a statistical estimate of the *proportion of the total variance* in a trait that is attributable to *genetic variation within a group*. This estimate is known as the trait's **heritability.** Because the heritability of a trait is expressed as a proportion, the maximum value it

---

heritability A statistical estimate of the proportion of the total variance in some trait within a group that is attributable to genetic differences among individuals within the group.

can have is 1.0. Height is highly heritable; that is, within a group of equally well-nourished individuals, most of the variation among individuals will be accounted for by their genetic differences. In contrast, table manners have low heritability because most variation among individuals is accounted for by differences in upbringing. Our guess is that flute-playing ability falls somewhere in the middle.

Many people hold completely mistaken ideas about heritability. You can't understand the nature–nurture issue without understanding this concept, and especially the following important facts:

1. **"HERITABLE" DOES NOT MEAN THE SAME THING AS "GENETIC."** The reason is that heritability applies only to traits and abilities that vary in a population. Many genetic abilities, such as breathing, are crucial for life and therefore do not vary; if you are alive, you breathe. Such traits are 100 percent genetic, but their calculated heritability would be zero because there is no variation to explain. (Of course, a tendency to develop a breathing disorder, such as asthma, can be partly heritable.)

2. **AN ESTIMATE OF HERITABILITY APPLIES ONLY TO A PARTICULAR GROUP LIVING IN A PARTICULAR ENVIRONMENT, AND ESTIMATES MAY DIFFER FOR DIFFERENT GROUPS.** Suppose that all the children in Oz County are affluent, eat plenty of high-quality food, have kind and attentive parents, and go to the same top-notch schools. The intellectual differences among them will probably be due largely to their genetic differences because their environments are similar and are optimal for intellectual development. In contrast, the children in Normal County are rich, poor, and in between. Some have healthy diets; others live on fatty foods and cupcakes. Some attend good schools; others go to inadequate ones. Some have doting parents, and some have unloving and neglectful ones. Because these children's intellectual differences might be due in part to their environmental differences, estimates of the heritability of intelligence will be lower in this group.

3. **HERITABILITY ESTIMATES DO NOT APPLY TO INDIVIDUALS, ONLY TO VARIATIONS WITHIN A GROUP.** No one can determine the impact of heredity on any *particular* individual's intellectual or emotional makeup. Journalistic accounts of behavioral-genetics research often overlook this fact. In a *Time* article on the heritability of intelligence (January 12, 1987), we once found this passage: "How much of any individual's personality is due to heredity? The . . . answer: about half." That statement is extremely misleading. As we saw earlier, each individual is a unique genetic mosaic. Each individual also has a unique history in terms of family relationships, intellectual training, and motivation. For these reasons, no one can say whether your genius at, say, flute playing is a result of inherited musical talent, living all your life in a family of devoted flute players, a private obsession that you acquired at age six when you saw the opera *The Magic Flute,* or a combination of all three. For one person, genes may make a tremendous difference in some aptitude or disposition; for another, the environment may be far more important.

4. **EVEN HIGHLY HERITABLE TRAITS CAN BE MODIFIED BY THE ENVIRONMENT.** Although height is highly heritable, malnourished children may not grow to be as tall as they would have with sufficient food. Conversely, if children eat a supernutritious diet, they may grow to be taller than anyone thought they could. The same

principle applies to psychological traits, although some writers have failed to realize this. Some biological determinists, for example, have argued that because IQ is highly heritable, IQ and school achievement cannot be boosted much. But even if the first part of the statement is true, the second part does not necessarily follow.

5. GENES TURN "ON" AND "OFF" OVER A LIFETIME. Although some of these changes in activation are "preprogrammed," factors such as stress and nutrition can also probably cause specific genes to be activated or deactivated (McClearn, 1993). As a result, the relative contribution of these genes to a particular behavior may wax and wane.

There is no way for scientists to estimate the heritability of a trait or behavior directly, so they must infer it by studying people whose degree of genetic similarity is known. The simplest approach might seem to be a comparison of blood relatives within families. Everyone knows of families that are famous for some talent or trait. But anecdotes and isolated examples can always be answered with counterexamples. There were seven generations of musical Bachs, but Mendelssohn's father was a banker, Chopin's a bookkeeper, and Schubert's a schoolmaster, and their mothers were not known to have musical talent (Lewontin, 1982). Results from controlled studies of families are also inconclusive, for close relatives usually share environments, as well as genes. If Carlo's parents and siblings all love lasagna, that doesn't mean that a taste for lasagna is heritable. The same applies if everyone in Carlo's family has a high IQ, is mentally ill, or is moody.

There are two ways out of this bind. One is to study adopted children (e.g., Loehlin, Horn, & Willerman, 1996; Plomin & DeFries, 1985). Such children share half their genes with each birth parent, but not their environment. On the other hand, they share an environment with their adoptive parents and adoptive siblings, but not their genes. Researchers can compare correlations between the children's traits and those of their biological and adoptive relatives and can use the results to estimate heritability.

The other approach is to compare **identical (monozygotic) twins** and **fraternal (dizygotic) twins.** Identical twins are created when a fertilized egg divides into two parts that then develop into two separate embryos. Because the twins come from the same fertilized egg, they share all their genes, barring genetic mutations or other accidents. (They may be slightly different at birth, however, because of birth complications, differences in the blood supply to the two fetuses, or other chance factors.) In contrast, fraternal twins develop when a woman's ovaries release two eggs instead of one, and each egg is fertilized by a different sperm. Fraternal twins are wombmates but

---

identical (monozygotic) twins Twins that develop when a fertilized egg divides into two parts that become separate embryos.
fraternal (dizygotic) twins Twins that develop from two separate eggs fertilized by different sperm; they are no more alike genetically than are any other pair of siblings.

are no more alike genetically than any other two siblings, and may be of different sexes. By comparing groups of same-sex fraternal twins with groups of identical twins, psychologists can try to estimate heritability. The assumption is that if identical twins are more alike than fraternal twins, the increased similarity must be genetic.

Perhaps, however, environments shared by identical twins differ from those shared by fraternal twins. People may treat identical twins, well, identically, or they may go to the other extreme by emphasizing the twins' differences (although no one has ever shown that such practices actually affect the traits of twins). To avoid this problem, investigators have studied identical twins who were separated early in life and reared apart. (Until recently, adoption policies and attitudes toward illegitimacy permitted such separations to occur.) In theory, separated identical twins share all their genes but not their environments. Any similarities between them should be primarily genetic and should permit a direct estimate of heritability.

In an important project begun in 1979, an interdisciplinary team at the University of Minnesota has tested and interviewed hundreds of identical and fraternal twins reared apart (Bouchard, 1984, 1995, 1996; Bouchard et al., 1990, 1991; Tellegen et al., 1988). Subjects have undergone comprehensive psychological and medical monitoring and have answered thousands of written questions. Information is now available on many sets of reunited twins and also on many twins reared together. Let's see what this project and other behavioral-genetics research can tell us about the origins of intelligence and personality.

Drawing by Chas. Addams; © 1981 The New Yorker Magazine, Inc.

Separated at birth, the Mallifert twins meet accidentally.

WHAT DO YOU KNOW?

1. Diane hears that basket-weaving ability is highly heritable and concludes that her low performance must be due mostly to genes. What's wrong with her reasoning?
2. Bertram hears that some mental ability is highly heritable and concludes that schools should stop trying to improve the skills of children who seem to lack the ability. What's wrong with his reasoning?
3. Carpentry skills seem to run in Andy's family. Why shouldn't Andy conclude that his talent is genetic?

ANSWERS:

1. Heritability applies only to differences among individuals within a group, not to particular individuals.   2. A trait may be highly heritable *and* susceptible to modification and improvement.   3. Family members share environments as well as genes.

Heritability and Intelligence

In heritability studies, the usual measure of intellectual functioning is an **intelligence quotient,** or **IQ** score. The term "IQ" is a holdover from the early days of psychological testing, when intelligence tests were given only to children. A child's *mental age* (MA)—the child's level of intellectual development relative to other children's—was divided by the child's chronological age (CA) and multiplied by 100 to yield an *intelligence quotient* (IQ). Thus a child of eight who performed like the average six-year-old would have a mental age of six and an IQ of 75 (6, divided by 8, times 100); and a child of eight who scored like an average ten-year-old would have a mental age of ten and an IQ of 125 (10, divided by 8, times 100). All average children, regardless of age, would have an IQ of 100 because MA and CA would be the same. (In actual calculations, months were used, not years, to yield a more precise figure.)

This method of figuring IQ had a serious flaw. At one age, scores might cluster tightly around the average, whereas at another age, they might be somewhat more dispersed. As a result, the IQ score necessary to be in the top 10 or 20 or 30 percent of one's age group varied, depending on one's age. Because of this problem, and because the IQ formula did not make much sense for adults, today's intelligence tests are scored differently. Usually the average is arbitrarily set at 100, and test scores—still informally referred to as "IQs"—are computed from tables. A score still reflects how a person compares with others, either children of a particular age or adults in general. At

---

intelligence quotient (IQ) A measure of intelligence originally computed by dividing a person's mental age by his or her chronological age and multiplying the result by 100; it is now derived from norms provided for standardized intelligence tests.

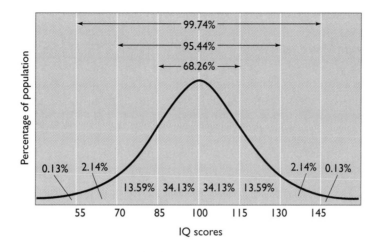

Figure 3.3   *In a large population, IQ scores will tend to be distributed on a normal (bell-shaped) curve. On most tests, about 68 percent of all people are expected to score between 85 and 115; about 95 percent will score between 70 and 130; and about 99.7 percent will score between 55 and 145.*

all ages, the distribution of scores in a large population approximates a normal (bell-shaped) curve, with scores near the average (mean) most common and very high or very low scores rare (see Figure 3.3).

IQ tests have many critics, and, in fact, the entire concept of intelligence is controversial. Some psychologists believe that intelligence is a single quality that can be summed up by a single number; others cite evidence that intelligence comes in many varieties, as we will see in Chapter 11, which evaluates the cognitive perspective. Moreover, nearly all aspects of intelligence are affected by culture, and the IQ test itself has many intrinsic biases, as we will see in Chapter 14, which evaluates the sociocultural perspective. But most heritability estimates are based on white people living in middle-class environments. Keep in mind, then, that heritability studies are estimating only the heritability of those mental skills that contribute to IQ test scores, not necessarily all aspects of mental performance; and that the tests are likely to be more valid for some groups than for others.

Variations Within Groups. Despite these important qualifications, it is clear that variations in IQ test scores are partly heritable. On the average, behavioral-genetics studies of children and adolescents estimate heritability to be about .50; that is, about half of the variance in IQ scores is explainable by genetic differences (Chipuer, Rovine, & Plomin, 1990; Plomin, 1989). And studies of adults tend to get higher estimates—in the .70 to .80 range (Bouchard, 1995; McGue et al., 1993). Although heritability estimates range widely across different studies, depending on the methods used—from as low as .10 to almost .90—the scores of identical twins are always more highly correlated than those of fraternal twins. In fact, the scores of identical twins reared *apart* are more highly correlated than those of fraternal twins reared *together*. In adoption studies, the scores of adopted children are more highly correlated with those of their birth parents than with those of their adoptive parents, and by adolescence, the scores of adopted children correlate only weakly, if at all, with those of their biologically unrelated siblings (Plomin, 1988; Scarr & Weinberg, 1994). By adulthood, the correlation is zero (Bouchard, in press; Scarr, 1993).

These are dramatic findings, but they do not mean that genes are the whole story. As Robert Plomin (1989), a leading behavioral geneticist, has observed, "The wave of acceptance of genetic influence on behavior is growing into a tidal wave that threatens to engulf the second message of this research: These same data provide the best available evidence for the importance of environmental influences."

Indeed, adoption studies show how environment can have a large impact even when heritability is fairly high. As we have noted, the IQ scores of adopted children correlate more highly with their birth parents' scores than with those of their adoptive parents. That is, if Johnny scores high relative to other adopted children, his birth parents are likely to score high relative to other adults who have put their children up for adoption. This fact supports the heritability of intelligence as measured by IQ tests. However, in *absolute* terms, Johnny's IQ may differ considerably from the scores of his birth parents. Indeed, on the average, adopted children have IQs that are 10 to 20 points higher than those of their birth parents—a huge difference (Scarr & Weinberg, 1977). Most psychologists believe that this difference exists because adoptive families are generally smaller, wealthier, and better educated than other families, and these environmental factors are associated with high IQs in children.

In other chapters, we will explore more fully the environmental influences on a child's mental abilities and brain development, including interactions with parents, mental stimulation, nutrition, and exposure to toxins. The point to understand here is that heredity may provide the range of a child's intellectual potential, but many other factors affect where in that range the child will actually fall.

Variations Between Groups. So far, we have considered intellectual differences only *within* a group of individuals. For many years, researchers have also wondered about the origins of differences *between* groups. Unfortunately, the history of this issue has been marred by ethnic, class, and gender prejudice. Too often, in the words of Stephen Jay Gould (1981), interpretations of research have been bent to support the belief that some groups are destined by "the harsh dictates of nature" to be subordinate to others.

Early in this century, for example, H. H. Goddard (1917), a leading educator, gave IQ tests to a group of immigrants at Ellis Island. Many of these immigrants knew little or no English, and many could neither read nor write their own language. Yet no sooner did they get off the boat after a long and tiring journey than they found themselves taking an IQ test. The results: 83 percent of the Jews, 80 percent of the Hungarians, 79 percent of the Italians, and 87 percent of the Russians scored as "feeble-minded," with a mental age lower than 12 years. (Note that Goddard singled the Jews out regardless of their nationality.) Goddard concluded that low intelligence and poor character were inherited and that "undesirables" should be prevented from having children.

This idea has continued to resurface ever since. In 1994, a heated debate erupted after publication of *The Bell Curve: Intelligence and Class Structure in American Life,* by the late psychologist Richard Herrnstein and conservative political scientist Charles Murray. In the book, Herrnstein and Murray argue that (a) intelligence is a single quality that is largely heritable; (b) because low-IQ people are having more children than high-IQ people, the nation's intelligence level is declining (the same argument that Goddard made years ago); (c) the United States may soon be divided into a huge low-IQ underclass and a "cognitive meritocracy" of wealthy, well-educated, high-IQ people; and (d) educational programs can do little to raise IQs. For many people, these authors wrote, there is nothing they can learn that will repay the cost of teaching, and resources spent on such people would be better spent on the gifted. Because African-American children score, on average, some 10 to 15 points lower on IQ tests than do white children, the implication of *The Bell Curve* is that the gap between the average white and the average black IQ can never be closed.

Psychologists who think that group differences in IQ are genetic agree with this conclusion, while maintaining that this is not a racist issue but a legitimate matter for scientific inquiry (Jensen, 1969, 1981; Rushton, 1993). Nevertheless, genetic explanations of intelligence are music to the ears of people who consider whites to be inherently superior to blacks (but who usually ignore the fact that Asians, on the average, score higher on IQ tests than whites do). Racists often cite such theories to justify their own hatreds, and politicians have used them to argue for cuts in programs that would benefit blacks and other minorities. For example, in the 1970s, Patrick Buchanan, then an aide to President Richard Nixon, wrote a memo in which he cited an *Atlantic Monthly* article by Herrnstein to bolster his argument that compensatory education programs for blacks and poor people might be a waste of money (reported in Levine & Suzuki, 1993). It is vital, therefore, that we all know how to evaluate genetic theories of group differences. What are the facts?

One fatal flaw in genetic theories of black–white differences is their use of heritability estimates based mainly on white middle-class samples to estimate the role heredity plays in *group* differences. This problem sounds pretty technical, but it is not really difficult to understand, so stay with us.

Consider, first, not people but tomatoes. (This "thought experiment," illustrated in Figure 3.4 on the next page, is based on Lewontin, 1970.) Suppose you have a bag of tomato seeds that vary genetically; all things being equal, some will produce tomatoes that are puny and tasteless, and some will produce tomatoes that are plump and delicious. Now you take a bunch of these seeds in your left hand and another bunch from the same bag in your right. Though one seed differs genetically from another, there is no *average* difference between the seeds in your left hand and those in your right hand. You plant the left hand's seeds in pot A, with some soil that you have doctored with nitrogen and other nutrients, and you plant the right hand's seeds in pot B, with soil from which you have extracted nutrients. When the tomatoes grow, they will vary in

(a) Rich soil   (b) Poor soil

Figure 3.4 *In the hypothetical tomato plant experiment described in the text, even if the differences among plants within each pot were due entirely to genetic differences, the average difference between pots could be environmental. The same principle applies to individual and group differences among human beings.*

size *within* each pot, purely because of genetic differences. But there will also be an average difference between pot A and pot B. This difference *between* pots is due entirely to the different soils—even though the *within*-pot heritability is 100 percent.

The principle is the same for people as it is for tomatoes. As we have seen, intellectual differences *within* groups are at least partly genetic. But that does not mean that differences *between* groups are genetic. Blacks and whites do not grow up, on the average, in the same kinds of environment. Because of a long legacy of discrimination and de facto segregation, black children (as well as Latino and other minority children) often receive far fewer nutrients—literally, in terms of food, and figuratively, in terms of education, encouragement by society, and intellectual opportunities.

Critics of *The Bell Curve* have made this very point in attacking the scholarship, methods, and assumptions of the book (Gould, 1994; Holt, 1994; Lane, 1994; Steele, 1994). They also note, as we have in this chapter, that high heritability does not mean that a trait is unmodifiable. Remedial efforts in the past have often been a matter of too little, too late; but early, intensive intervention that provides mental stimulation for children starting in infancy can raise IQ scores as much as 30 percent (Campbell &

Ramey, 1995). Such efforts, say the critics, should be expanded, not cut back. However, as Stephen Jay Gould (1994) observes, *The Bell Curve* appeared at a moment in American history when taxpayers were in the mood to slash social programs. At such times, people are more likely to accept uncritically the message that the beneficiaries of these programs cannot be helped anyway.

One sure way to settle the question of inherent racial differences would be to gather IQ information on blacks and whites reared in exactly the same circumstances. This task is nearly impossible at present in the United States, where racism affects the lives of even affluent, successful African-Americans (Cose, 1994; Staples, 1994). However, the handful of studies that have overcome past methodological problems fail to reveal any genetic differences between blacks and whites in whatever it is that IQ tests measure. For example, children fathered by black and white American soldiers in Germany after World War II and reared in similar German communities by similar families did not differ significantly in IQ (Eyferth, 1961). Moreover, degree of African ancestry (which can be roughly estimated from skin color, blood analysis, and genealogy) is not related to measured intelligence, as a genetic theory of black–white differences would predict (Scarr et al., 1977).

Researchers have been trying to pin down more precisely just how environmental and cultural factors affect the intellectual development of children. In Chapter 14, we will examine some of these factors and see how the educational system often prevents minority children's strengths from being recognized and developed.

Genes and Personality

A mother we know was describing her two children. "My daughter has always been emotionally intense and a little testy," she said, "but my son is the opposite, placid and good-natured. They came out of the womb that way." But is it possible to be born touchy or easygoing? What aspects of personality might have an inherited component? And if some of them do, does that mean that people are stuck with those traits forever?

Psychologists who take a biological perspective try to answer these questions in two ways: by studying temperaments in children and by doing heritability studies on adult personality traits. Their hope is that eventually, geneticists will be able to isolate the actual genes underlying these traits. Two separate research teams have announced the first candidate: a gene responsible for brain-cell receptors (molecular gateways) for the transmission of dopamine, a brain chemical that we will be discussing in Chapter 4. One version of the gene occurs more often in people who score high on tests of novelty-seeking than in other people (Benjamin et al., 1996; Ebstein et al., 1996). You will undoubtedly be hearing more findings like this one in the years to come.

Heredity and Temperament. **Temperaments** are relatively stable, characteristic styles of responding to the environment, which appear in infancy or early childhood, and which have some genetic basis (Kagan, 1994). If personality has some genetic

---

temperaments Characteristic styles of responding to the environment, which are present in infancy and are assumed to be innate.

basis, temperaments ought to emerge early in life and affect subsequent development. This is, in fact, the case. Even in the first weeks after birth, infants differ in activity level, mood, responsiveness, and attention span. Some are irritable and cranky. Others are placid and sweet-natured. Some cuddle up in any adult's arms and snuggle. Others squirm and fidget, as if they can't stand being held. Babies differ in activity level (wriggling and kicking), smiling and laughing, fussing and showing signs of distress, soothability (the time it takes for a baby to calm down after distress), emotionality and expressiveness, cooing and burbling in reaction to people or things, and amount of crying (Field, 1989; Kagan, 1994; Thomas & Chess, 1982).

Jerome Kagan and his colleagues have been studying the physiological correlates of two specific temperamental styles, which they call "inhibited" and "uninhibited." (These temperaments are extremes; most children fall somewhere in between.) Inhibited and uninhibited temperaments are detectable in infancy and, in the absence of intervention, they tend to remain stable throughout childhood (Kagan & Snidman, 1991). Inhibited children are shy and timid; they react negatively to novel situations, such as being introduced to a group of unfamiliar children. In contrast, uninhibited children are talkative, spontaneous, and bold. Kagan's group has found that during mildly stressful mental tasks, shy, socially inhibited five-year-olds are more likely than uninhibited children to show signs of activity in the sympathetic nervous system, the part of the nervous system generally responsible for physiological arousal. These signs include an increased heart rate, dilation of the pupils, characteristic patterns of brain activity, and high levels of norepinephrine and cortisol, hormones associated with physiological arousal during stress. In white children (most of the children studied have been white), inhibition is associated to some extent with having blue eyes and allergies, or having close relatives with these characteristics (Kagan et al., 1991).

Interestingly, Stephen Suomi (1987, 1991) has found exactly the same physiological attributes in shy, anxious infant rhesus monkeys (except for the blue eyes). Suomi calls the inhibited monkeys "uptight" and the uninhibited ones "laid back." Starting early in life, uptight monkeys, like Kagan's inhibited children, respond with anxiety to novelty and challenge. Like Kagan's human subjects, Suomi's monkeys have high heart rates and elevated levels of cortisol, and they are more likely to have allergic reactions starting in infancy. When uptight rhesus monkeys grow up, they usually continue to be anxious when challenged. They act traumatized, even though they have experienced no traumas. In stressful situations, they tend, as humans do, to turn to alcohol (which the researchers make available), and they drink more alcohol than other monkeys do (Higley et al., 1991).

Heredity and Traits. Another way to study the genetic basis of personality is to estimate the heritability of adult personality traits by doing behavioral-genetics studies. A **trait** is any characteristic that is assumed to describe a person—as shy, brave, reliable, friendly, hostile, serious, sullen, and so on—across many situations. Each of us is a constantly shifting kaleidoscope of qualities, moods, tendencies, and preferences, and no one psychological test can possibly summarize a person's entire personality. But a

---

trait A descriptive characteristic of an individual, assumed to be stable across situations and time.

variety of tests and assessment methods do provide information about such aspects of personality as needs, values, interests, and typical ways of responding to situations. Using these tests, psychologists have identified many fascinating traits, from "sensation seeking" (the enjoyment of risk) to "erotophobia" (the fear of sex).

Several decades ago, Raymond B. Cattell advanced the study of personality traits by applying a statistical method called **factor analysis.** This procedure identifies clusters of correlated test items that seem to be measuring some common, underlying quality. Performing a factor analysis on traits is like adding water to flour: It causes the material to clump up into little balls. Using questionnaires, life descriptions, and observations, Cattell (1965, 1973) measured dozens of traits in hundreds of people, including humor, music preferences, intelligence, creativity, leadership, and emotional disorder. His method of conducting large-scale research and carefully describing the connections among traits had a major influence on research in personality.

Cattell maintained that 16 factors are necessary to describe the complexities of personality, and some psychologists still agree with him. But others believe, on the basis of longitudinal studies and factor analysis, that personality encompasses five "robust factors," sometimes called the "Big Five." These factors are stable over a person's lifetime and have been identified in diverse cultures, including Chinese, Japanese, Filipino, Hawaiian, and Australian samples (Costa & McCrae, 1994; Digman, 1990; Goldberg, 1990, 1993; Zuckerman, Kuhlman, & Camac, 1988):

1. **INTROVERSION VERSUS EXTROVERSION** describes the extent to which people are outgoing or shy. It includes such traits as being talkative or silent, sociable or reclusive, adventurous or cautious, eager to be in the limelight or inclined to stay in the shadows.
2. **NEUROTICISM,** or emotional instability, includes such traits as anxiety and inability to control impulses, a tendency to have unrealistic ideas, and general emotional instability and negativity. Neurotic individuals are complainers and defeatists. They complain about different things at different ages, but they are always ready to see the sour side of life and none of its sweetness. They frequently feel worried, bitter, and tense, even in the absence of any major problems.
3. **AGREEABLENESS** describes the extent to which people are good-natured or irritable, gentle or headstrong, cooperative or abrasive, not jealous or jealous. It reflects the capacity for friendly relationships or the tendency to have hostile ones.
4. **CONSCIENTIOUSNESS** describes the degree to which people are responsible or undependable, persevering or likely to quit easily, steadfast or fickle, tidy or careless, scrupulous or unscrupulous.
5. **OPENNESS TO EXPERIENCE,** which in some personality measures is called *imagination,* describes the extent to which people are original, imaginative, questioning, artistic, and capable of divergent (creative) thinking—or are conforming, unimaginative, and predictable.

---

factor analysis A statistical method for analyzing the intercorrelations among different measures or test scores; clusters of measures or scores that are highly correlated are assumed to measure the same underlying trait, ability, or aptitude (factor).

Not everyone subscribes to the Big Five model. Hans Eysenck (1994) argues that there are only the "Giant Three"—psychoticism (the extent to which a person lacks empathy and is disposed to crime and mental illness), extroversion, and neuroticism. Others argue for four basic traits (Cloninger, Svrakic, & Przybeck, 1993), or for a set called the "Big Nine" (Bouchard, in press). Some theorists agree that there are five factors but disagree on what exactly they are (Saucier, 1994; Zuckerman et al., 1993).

But, however they divide up the pie of personality, behavioral geneticists are finding that many of these traits are not only stable but also highly heritable. Twin studies find that whether the trait in question is one of the Big Five, altruism, aggression, or even religious attitudes, heritability is typically between .40 and .60 (Bouchard et al., 1990; Loehlin, 1988; Pedersen et al., 1988; Tellegen et al., 1988; Waller et al., 1990). This means that within a group of people, 40 to 60 percent of the variance in such traits is usually attributable to genetic differences. Some researchers have even reported high heritability estimates for such specific behaviors as getting divorced (McGue & Lykken, 1992) and watching a lot of television in childhood (Plomin et al., 1990)!

These findings are surprising; how can religious attitudes, divorce, and TV watching be heritable? Our prehistoric ancestors didn't have marriage, let alone divorce, and they certainly didn't watch TV. What are the personality traits or temperaments underlying these behaviors? Even more startling is the finding that the only environmental contribution to personality differences comes from experiences not shared with family members, such as having had a particular teacher in the fourth grade or having won the lead in the school play. Study after study has found that *shared environment and parental child-rearing practices seem to have no significant effect on adult personality traits* (Bouchard, in press; Loehlin, 1992; Plomin & Daniels, 1987).

Understandably, scientists doing this kind of research are excited about their findings. They believe the evidence for the heritability of personality traits represents an overwhelming attack on the conventional wisdom that child-rearing practices are central to personality development. "Our retrospective study showed only meager associations between parent–child relations and adult personality," write Robert McCrae and Paul Costa (1988). "It will doubtless seem incredible to many readers that variables such as social class, educational opportunities, religious training, and parental love and discipline have no substantial influence on adult personality, but imagine for a moment that it is correct. What will it mean for research in developmental psychology? How will clinical psychology and theories of therapy be changed?"

Good questions! What would these findings, if true, mean for education, for raising children, for the treatment of personality and relationship problems? McCrae and Costa (1988) believe that these findings are too threatening for most psychologists to accept because they challenge the optimistic view that human nature can be improved by altering experiences.

But before we can conclude that differences in personality are based almost entirely on differences in heredity, we need to consider, once more, the complexities of measuring heritability. Heritability gives us the *relative* impact of genetics and the environment on behavior. To estimate heritability, you need sensitive measures for gauging both the genetic similarity or dissimilarity of individuals *and* the similarities or differences in their environments. Measures of environmental influences on behavior are still crude, often relying on vague, grab-bag categories such as "social class" or "religious training," and they probably fail to detect some important environmental influences. Underestimating the influence of the environment inevitably means overestimating the influence of heritability.

Another problem is that most separated twins have grown up in fairly similar environments. When subjects in heritability studies share similar environments—in terms of opportunities, stimulation, affluence, and experiences—there may be too few environmental differences among them to explain their personality differences; heritability estimates will be inflated, and the impact of the environment will be underestimated.

Moreover, even children at the extremes of some trait often change as they grow older, and such change seems to depend on how parents and others respond to the child. In his work with monkeys, Stephen Suomi (1989) has shown that a highly inhibited infant is likely to overcome its timidity if it is reared by an extremely nurturant foster mother. In human beings, the "fit" between a child's and the parents' temperaments is critical (Thomas & Chess, 1980). Not only do parents affect the baby, but the baby also affects the parents. Imagine a high-strung parent with a child who is difficult and sometimes slow to respond to affection. The parent may begin to feel desperate, angry, or rejected. Over time, the parent may withdraw from the child or use excessive punishment, which in turn makes the child even more difficult to live with. In contrast, a more easygoing parent may have a calming effect on a difficult child or may persist in showing affection even when the child holds back, causing the child to become more responsive.

So . . . how confining is our biology? The answer depends on which qualities we're talking about. Some qualities are flexible and can change significantly; others are less so. Behavioral-genetics research shows that there are limits to our ability to change our temperaments and fundamental traits: Despite the claims of pop-psych books that promise you a total personality transformation in a month, the biological perspective teaches that some things about you probably can't be changed in 30 years, let alone 30 days.

WHAT DO YOU KNOW?

1. Estimates of the heritability of intelligence (a) put heritability at about .90, (b) show heritability to be low at all ages, (c) average about .50 for children and adolescents.
2. *True or false:* If a trait is highly heritable within a group, then between-group differences in the trait must also be due mainly to heredity.
3. The available evidence (does/does not) show that ethnic differences in average IQ scores are due to genetic differences.
4. What two broad lines of research support the hypothesis that personality differences are due in part to genetic differences?
5. Which of the following traits are *not* among the five "robust factors" in personality? (a) introversion, (b) agreeableness, (c) psychoticism, (d) openness to experience, (e) intelligence, (f) neuroticism, (g) conscientiousness
6. A newspaper headline announces, "Couch Potatoes Born, Not Made: Kids' TV habits may be hereditary." Why is this headline misleading? What lapses in critical thinking does it reveal? What other explanations of the finding are possible? What aspects of TV watching could have a hereditary component?

IN PRAISE OF HUMAN VARIATION

This chapter opened with two simple questions: What makes us alike as human beings, and why do we differ? Here is the pop-psych answer to these questions:

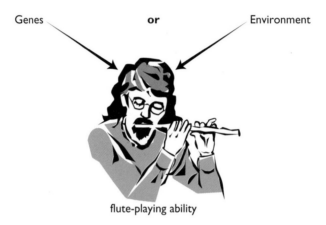

And here is the more complicated view that emerges from the study of human development:

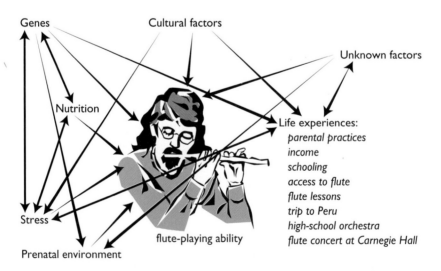

As we have seen, heredity and environment always interact to produce the unique mixture of qualities that make up a human being. Yet even this answer is much too simple, because each of us is, in a sense, *more* than the sum of the individual influences on us. Once these influences become a part of us, they blend and become indistinguishable. A geneticist, a neurobiologist, and a psychologist offer this analogy. Think, they say, of the baking of a cake: "The taste of the product is the result of a complex interaction of components—such as butter, sugar, and flour—exposed for various periods to elevated temperatures; it is not dissociable into such-or-such a percent of flour, such-or-such of butter, etc., although each and every component . . . has its contribution to make to the final product" (Lewontin, Rose, & Kamin, 1984). The "cake" that is a person is never done. Each moment, a slightly different self interacts with a slightly different environment. We can no more speak of genes, or of the environment, *causing* personality or intelligence than we can speak of butter, sugar, or flour individually *causing* the taste of a cake. Yet we do speak that way. Why? Perhaps out of a desire to make things seem clearer than they are, or, sometimes, to justify prejudices about culture, ethnicity, gender, or class.

Nature, however, loves diversity. Biologists agree that the fitness of any species depends on this diversity. If all members of a species had exactly the same strengths and weaknesses, the species could not survive changes in the physical or social environment. With diversity, at least some members have a good chance of survival. When we understand the world from the biological perspective, we realize that each of us has something valuable to contribute, whether it is artistic talent, academic ability, creativity, social skill, athletic prowess, a sense of humor, mechanical aptitude, practical wisdom, a social conscience, or the energy to get things done. The challenge, for any society, is to promote the potential of each of its members.

✦ ✦ ✦

Summary

1. From the perspective of *evolutionary psychologists* and *behavioral geneticists,* a key to understanding the qualities that unite human beings as a species and the qualities that differentiate them as individuals can be found in genes. Yet all scientists also understand that heredity and environment interact to produce not only psychological traits but also most physical ones.

2. Genetic research is transforming theories of behavior that were once solely psychological. For example, research on the *set-point theory* of weight gain has altered ideas about why some people are heavy and others thin, and why dieting so often fails.

3. *Genes,* the basic units of heredity, are located on *chromosomes,* which consist of strands of *DNA.* Within each gene, the sequence of four basic elements constitutes a chemical code that helps determine the synthesis of a particular protein by specifying the sequence of amino acids that are the protein's building blocks. In turn, proteins directly or indirectly affect virtually all of the structural and biochemical characteristics of the organism.

4. In the simplest type of inheritance, a single pair of genes is responsible for the expression of a trait. In many cases, one member of the pair is *dominant* and the other *recessive.* Most human traits, however, depend on more than one gene pair, which makes tracking down the genetic contributions to a trait extremely difficult. One method for doing so involves the use of *linkage studies.*

5. The way in which heredity operates ensures that each individual (with the exception of identical twins) will be a unique genetic mosaic. Each sperm- or egg-producing cell has the potential to produce millions of different chromosome combinations in each new sperm or egg, and mutations and crossover of segments of genetic material produce even greater genetic diversity. Thus, two people who are genetically related can be very different in purely genetic terms.

6. The guiding assumption in evolutionary psychology is that the mind is not a general-purpose computer but instead evolved as a collection of specialized and independent mental modules to handle specific survival problems. Many fundamental human similarities can be traced to the evolutionary workings of *natural selection*—for example, reflexes, an attraction to novelty, a motive to explore and manipulate objects, and a motive to play and to imitate others.

7. Basic sensory and perceptual processes, such as depth perception and the ability to detect and discriminate the edges and angles of objects, appear to be innate. Without certain experiences during critical periods early in life, perception develops abnormally, but such experiences may simply ensure the survival of skills already present in at least rudimentary form. Because other species have different survival needs, they are often perceptually attuned to different aspects of physical reality than humans are.

8. Several emotional expressions are part of the human evolutionary heritage: those for anger, happiness, fear, surprise, disgust, sadness, and contempt. From birth onward, emotional expressions help people communicate with one another and "read" the intentions of others.

9. Attachment and sociability are also necessary for human survival. Attachment probably begins with and requires touch, or *contact comfort*. Infant attachment provides a *secure base* from which the child can explore the environment, a haven of safety to which the child can return when afraid. Insecurely attached children may become *avoidant*, or *anxious* and *ambivalent*; these styles of attachment are associated with later social, cognitive, and behavioral problems, and with problems in close relationships in adulthood. Infants not only need attachment, but they are also primed to respond to human faces, and they develop a rhythmic synchrony with their caregivers.

10. Human beings are the only species that uses language naturally, to express and comprehend an infinite number of novel utterances. Noam Chomsky argued that the ability to take the *surface structure* of an utterance and apply rules of *syntax* to infer its underlying *deep structure* must depend on an innate faculty for language, a universal grammar; many others have supported this view and have explored its evolutionary implications. However, parental practices, such as repeating correct sentences verbatim and recasting incorrect ones, appear to aid in language acquisition. Case studies of children deprived of exposure to language suggest that a *critical period* exists for acquiring a first language.

11. *Behavioral geneticists* study differences among individuals, often by using studies of twins and adopted children to estimate the *heritability* of traits and abilities— the extent to which differences in traits or abilities within a group of individuals

are accounted for by genetic differences. Heritability estimates do not apply to specific individuals or to differences between groups; they apply only to differences within a particular group living in a particular environment. Further, even a highly heritable trait may be susceptible to environmental modification.

12. Heritability estimates for intelligence (as measured by IQ tests, which have come under fire by critics) vary widely, but these estimates average about .50 for children and adolescents and .70 to .80 for adults. Whatever their heritability, mental abilities can be greatly affected by environment.

13. Research on group differences in IQ has focused on average black–white differences. Genetic explanations have often mistakenly used heritability estimates derived from one group to estimate the genetic contribution to intergroup differences—an invalid procedure. The available evidence fails to support genetic explanations of these differences.

14. Psychologists explore the possible contribution of heredity to personality by studying *temperaments* in children and doing behavioral-genetics research on adult personality traits. Temperaments emerge early in life and can affect subsequent development. Temperamental differences in shyness and inhibition, found in children and monkeys, may be due to variations in the responsiveness of the sympathetic nervous system to change, stress, and novelty. Research suggests that there are five stable "robust factors" in adult personality: extroversion, neuroticism, agreeableness, conscientiousness, and openness to experience. For these and many other traits, heritability is typically around .50. In many studies, the only environmental contribution to personality differences comes from experiences that are *not* shared among family members.

15. There are limitations to behavioral-genetics studies, and common errors arise when interpreting their results: Measures of environmental influences on behavior are still crude, and so the impact of these influences may be underestimated; subjects in heritability studies often share similiar environments, which could inflate heritability estimates; and many people confuse heritability with immutability.

16. Neither nature nor nurture can explain people's similarities or differences. Genetic and environmental influences blend and become indistinguishable in the development of any individual.

Key Terms

nativists versus empiricists *83*

behavioral genetics *84*

evolutionary psychology *84*

set-point theory *84*

leptin *85*

genes *86*

chromosomes *86*

DNA (deoxyribonucleic acid) *87*

genome *87*

bases *87*

dominant/recessive genes *88*

linkage studies *88*

markers *88*

mutate *88*

evolution *89*

natural selection *89*

Charles Darwin *89*

reflexes *90*

sensation *93*

perception *93*

feature-detector cells *94*

visual cliff *95*

attachment *97*

contact comfort *97*

strange situation *99*

secure, avoidant, and anxious/
  ambivalent attachment *99*

synchrony *100*

language *101*

psycholinguists *101*

syntax *101*

surface structure/deep structure *102*

language acquisition device *102*

universal grammar *102*

overregularizations *103*

heritability *106*

identical (monozygotic) twins *108*

fraternal (dizygotic) twins *108*

intelligence quotient (IQ) *110*

temperaments *115*

trait *116*

factor analysis *117*

"Big Five" personality traits *117*

CHAPTER 4

Neurons, Hormones, and Neurotransmitters

*C*hristina, a young British woman, had a mysterious inflammation that permanently damaged the nerve fibers involved in kinesthesis—the sense that tells us where the parts of our body are and which parts are moving. Christina's brain no longer received signals from pain and pressure receptors in her muscles, joints, and tendons. At first, she was as floppy as a rag doll; she could not sit up, walk, or stand. Then, slowly, she learned to do these things, relying on visual cues and sheer willpower. But her movements remained unnatural, and Christina now experienced herself as strangely disembodied. "I feel my body is blind and deaf to itself," she said, "[that] it has no sense of itself. . . . It's like something's been scooped right out of me, right at the centre."

Emily D., a former English teacher and poet, had a tumor in an area on the right side of the brain that processes the expressive qualities of speech, such as rhythm, inflection, and intonation. Although Emily D. could understand words and sentences perfectly well, she could not tell whether a speaker was indignant, cheerful, or dejected unless she carefully analyzed the person's facial expressions and gestures, and, unfortunately, fading vision limited her ability to do so. Emily D.'s brain damage had left her entirely deaf to the emotional nuances of speech, the variations of tone and cadence that can move a listener to laughter, tears, or outrage. But she had one skill that many people lack. Because she could not be swayed by histrionics or tone of voice, she could easily spot a liar.

Dr. P., a cultured and charming musician of great repute, suffered damage in a part of the brain that handles visualization, probably because of a tumor or disease. Although his vision remained sharp and his abstract reasoning keen, he could no longer recognize people or objects, or even dream in visual images. He would pat the heads of water hydrants and parking meters, thinking them to be children, or chat with pieces of furniture and wonder why they didn't reply. He could spot a pin on the floor but did not know his own face in the mirror. Once, when looking around for his hat, he thought his wife's head was the hat and tried to lift it off. Neurologist Oliver Sacks, who studied Dr. P., came to call him "the man who mistook his wife for a hat" (Sacks, 1985).

These dramatic cases, reported by Sacks, show us that the brain is the bedrock of behavior. **Neuropsychologists,** along with neuroscientists from other disciplines, explore that bedrock, searching for the basis of behavior in the brain and the rest of the nervous system. Their goal is to discover the biological events that underlie consciousness, perception, memory, emotion, reasoning, stress, and cognitive clarity or confusion.

At this very moment, your own brain, assisted by other parts of your nervous system, is busily taking in these words. Whether you are excited, curious, or bored, your brain is registering some sort of emotional reaction to the material. As you continue reading, your brain will (we hope) store away much of the information in this chapter for future use. Later on, your brain may enable you to smell a flower, climb the stairs, greet a friend, solve a personal problem, or chuckle at a joke. But the brain's most startling accomplishment, by far, is its knowledge that it is doing all these things. This self-awareness makes brain research different from the study of anything else in the universe. Scientists must use the cells, biochemistry, and circuitry of their own brains to understand the cells, biochemistry, and circuitry of brains in general.

Because the brain is the site of consciousness, people disagree vehemently about what language to use in describing it. One reviewer who read this chapter before publication took issue with the way we wrote the preceding paragraph. How, he wanted to know, could we talk about "your" brain doing this or that; after all, if the brain is where consciousness happens, where is the "you" that is "using" that brain? Another reviewer had exactly the opposite complaint; she objected when we wrote that the brain interprets events, stores information, or registers emotions because she felt we were depersonalizing human beings and implying that brain mechanisms completely explain behavior. "I think people do these things," she wrote, "not brains. Brains are not actors." You can see our problem. After much discussion, we finally decided to stick with everyday constructions such as "We use our brains," but we want you to know that we are simply resorting to a convenient linguistic shorthand, without assuming the existence of an independent brain "operator" doing the using. On the other hand, we also do not want to imply that brain mechanisms are all you need to understand about behavior. At the end of this chapter, we will return to the fascinating issue of where "you" are, if not in your brain.

William Shakespeare had an opinion on this matter; he once called the brain "the soul's frail dwelling house." Actually, though, the brain is more like the main room in a house filled with many alcoves and passageways—the "house" being the nervous system as a whole. Before we can understand the windows, walls, and furniture of this house, we need to become acquainted with the overall floor plan. It's a pretty technical

---

neuropsychology The field of psychology concerned with the neural and biochemical bases of behavior and mental processes.

floor plan, which means that you will be learning many new terms, but you will need to know these terms in order to understand how psychologists with a biological perspective go about explaining psychological topics. Later, we will illustrate their approach by showing how biology is illuminating the mysterious world of sleep and dreams.

THE NERVOUS SYSTEM: A BASIC BLUEPRINT

The function of a nervous system is to gather and process information, produce responses to stimuli, and coordinate the workings of different cells. Even the lowly jellyfish and the humble worm have the beginnings of such a system. In very simple organisms that do little more than move, eat, and eliminate wastes, the "system" may be no more than one or two nerve cells. In human beings, who do such complex things as dance, cook, and take psychology courses, the nervous system contains billions of cells. For purposes of description, scientists divide this intricate network into two main parts, the central nervous system and the peripheral nervous system (see Figure 4.1 on the next page).

The **central nervous system (CNS)** receives, processes, interprets, and stores incoming sensory information—information about tastes, sounds, smells, color, pressure on the skin, the state of internal organs, and so forth. It also sends out messages destined for muscles, glands, and internal organs. It is usually conceptualized as having two components: the brain, which we will consider in detail later, and the spinal cord. But the spinal cord is actually an extension of the brain. It runs from the base of the brain down the center of the back, protected by a column of bones (the spinal column), and it acts as a sort of bridge between the brain and the parts of the body below the neck. It also handles some reflexes, such as the one that causes you automatically to pull your hand away from a hot iron.

The **peripheral nervous system (PNS)** handles the central nervous system's input and output. It contains all portions of the nervous system outside the brain and spinal cord, right down to nerves in the tips of the fingers and toes. If your brain could not collect information about the world by means of a peripheral nervous system, it would be like a radio without a receiver. In the peripheral nervous system, *sensory nerves* carry messages from special receptors in the skin, muscles, and other internal and external sense organs to the spinal cord, which sends them along to the brain. These nerves put us in touch with both the outside world and the activities of our own bodies. *Motor nerves* carry messages from the central nervous system to muscles, glands,

---

central nervous system (CNS) The portion of the nervous system consisting of the brain and spinal cord.
peripheral nervous system (PNS) All portions of the nervous system outside the brain and spinal cord; it includes sensory and motor nerves.

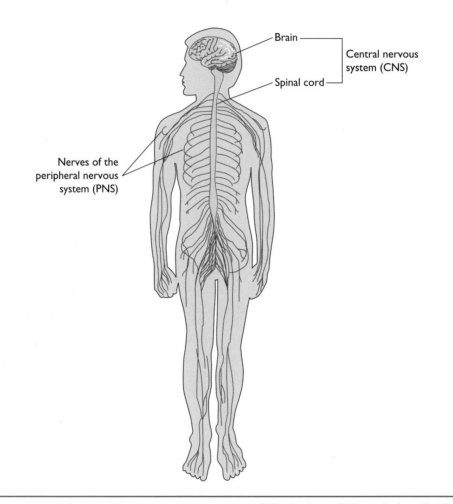

Figure 4.1 *The central nervous system consists of the brain and the spinal cord. The peripheral nervous system consists of 43 pairs of nerves that transmit information to and from the central nervous system.*

and internal organs. They enable us to move our bodies, and they cause glands to contract and to secrete various substances, including chemical messengers called *hormones*.

Scientists further divide the peripheral nervous system into two parts: the somatic (bodily) nervous system and the autonomic (self-governing) nervous system. The **somatic nervous system** consists of nerves that are connected to sensory receptors and to the skeletal muscles that permit voluntary action. When you sense the world

---

somatic nervous system The subdivision of the peripheral nervous system that connects to sensory receptors and skeletal muscles; sometimes called the *skeletal nervous system*.

around you, or when you turn off a light or write your name, your somatic system is active. The **autonomic nervous system** regulates the functioning of blood vessels, glands, and internal (visceral) organs such as the bladder, stomach, and heart. When you happen upon the secret object of your desire and your heart starts to pound, your hands get sweaty, and your cheeks feel hot, you can blame your autonomic nervous system.

The autonomic nervous system works more or less automatically, without a person's conscious control. We say more or less because some people can learn to heighten or suppress their autonomic responses intentionally. In India, some yogis can slow their heartbeats and metabolisms so dramatically that they can survive in a sealed booth long after most of us would have died of suffocation. And in the 1960s and 1970s, Neal Miller and his colleagues showed that you don't have to be a yogi to control visceral responses; many other people can as well, using a technique called *biofeedback* (Miller, 1978). In biofeedback, monitoring devices track the bodily process in question and deliver a signal, such as a light or a tone, whenever a person makes the desired response. The person may either use a specified method to produce the desired response or simply try in whatever way to increase the frequency of the signal. Using biofeedback, some people have learned to control such autonomic responses as blood pressure, blood flow, heart rate, and skin temperature. Some clinicians are therefore using biofeedback training to treat high blood pressure, asthma, and migraine headaches, although there is great controversy about success rates and about what, exactly, is being controlled—the actual autonomic responses, or responses that can be voluntarily produced, such as breathing, which then in turn affect the autonomic system.

The autonomic nervous system is itself divided into two parts: the **sympathetic nervous system** and the **parasympathetic nervous system.** These two parts work together, but in opposing ways, to adjust the body's responses to changing circumstances. To simplify, the sympathetic system acts like the accelerator of a car, mobilizing the body for action and an output of energy. It makes you blush, sweat, and breathe more deeply, and it pushes up your heart rate and blood pressure. When you are in a situation that requires the body to fight, flee, or cope, the sympathetic nervous system whirls into action. The parasympathetic system is more like a brake. It doesn't stop the body, but it does tend to slow things down or to keep them running smoothly. It enables the body to conserve and store energy. If you have to jump out of the way of a speeding motorcyclist, sympathetic nerves increase your heart rate. Afterward, parasympathetic nerves slow it down again and help keep its rhythm regular. Both systems are involved in emotion and stress.

---

autonomic nervous system The subdivision of the peripheral nervous system that regulates the internal organs and glands.

sympathetic nervous system The subdivision of the autonomic nervous system that mobilizes bodily resources and increases the output of energy during emotion and stress.

parasympathetic nervous system The subdivision of the autonomic nervous system that operates during relaxed states and that conserves energy.

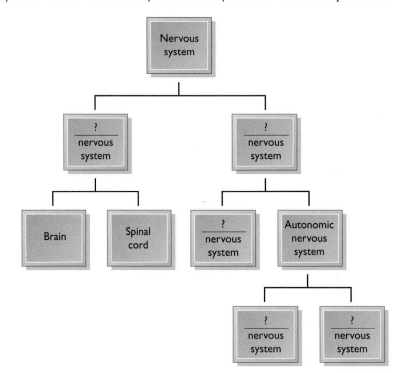

WHAT DO YOU KNOW?

Pause now to test your knowledge by mentally filling in the missing parts of the nervous system "house." Then see if you can briefly describe what each part does.

ANSWERS:

Check your answers against Figure 4.3 on page 132. If you had difficulty, or you could label the parts but forgot what they do, review the preceding section, and try again.

COMMUNICATION IN THE NERVOUS SYSTEM

The blueprint we have just described provides only a general idea of the nervous system's structure. Now let's turn to the details.

The nervous system is made up in part of **neurons,** or *nerve cells.* These neurons are held in place by **glial cells** (from the Greek for "glue"). Glial cells, which greatly outnumber neurons, also provide the neurons with nutrients, insulate the neurons, and remove cellular debris when the neurons die. Many neuroscientists suspect that glial cells carry

---

neuron A cell that conducts electrochemical signals; the basic unit of the nervous system. Also called a *nerve cell.*
glial cells Cells that hold neurons in place, insulate neurons, and provide neurons with nutrients.

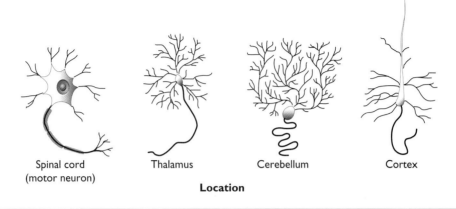

Spinal cord
(motor neuron)

Thalamus

Cerebellum

Cortex

Location

Figure 4.2 *Neurons vary in size and shape, depending on location and function. More than 200 types of neurons have been identified in mammals.*

electrical or chemical signals between parts of the nervous system, and that they some-how influence the activity of neighboring neurons (Cornell-Bell et al., 1990; Murphy, 1993; Nedergaard, 1994). It is the neurons, however, that are the communication special-ists, transmitting signals to, from, or within the central nervous system.

Although neurons are often called the building blocks of the nervous system, they look nothing like blocks; they are more like snowflakes, exquisitely delicate, differing from one another greatly in size and shape (see Figure 4.2). In the giraffe, a neuron that runs from the spinal cord down the animal's hind leg may be nine feet long! In the human brain, neurons are microscopic. No one is sure how many neurons the human brain contains, but a typical estimate is 100 billion, about the same number as there are stars in our galaxy—and some estimates go much higher.

The Structure of the Neuron

As you can see in Figure 4.4 on page 133, a neuron has three main parts: *dendrites,* a *cell body,* and an *axon.* The **dendrites** look like the branches of a tree; indeed, the word *den-drite* means "little tree" in Greek. Dendrites act like antennas, receiving messages from as many as 10,000 other nerve cells and transmitting them toward the cell body. The **cell body,** which is shaped roughly like a sphere or a pyramid, contains the biochemical machinery for keeping the neuron alive. It also determines whether the neuron should "fire"—that is, transmit a message to other neurons—based on the number of inputs from other neurons. The **axon** (from the Greek for "axle") is like the tree's trunk, though more slender. It transmits messages away from the cell body to other neurons or to mus-

dendrites A neuron's branches that receive information from other neurons and transmit it toward the cell body.
cell body The part of the neuron that keeps it alive and that determines whether it will fire.
axon A neuron's extending fiber that conducts impulses away from the cell body and transmits them to other neurons.

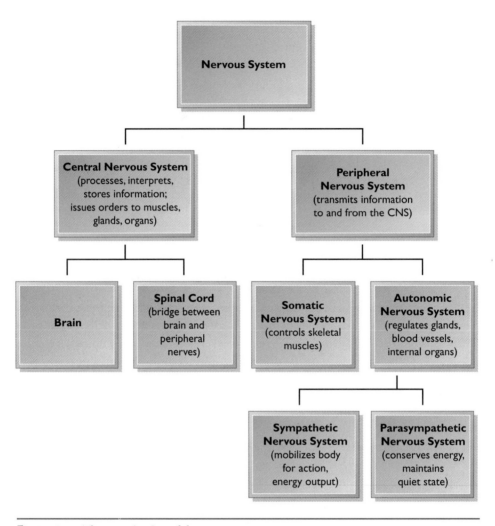

Figure 4.3 *The organization of the nervous system.*

cle or gland cells. Axons commonly divide at the end into branches, called *axon termi-nals.* In adult human beings, axons vary from only four one-thousandths of an inch to a few feet in length. Dendrites and axons give each neuron a double role: As one researcher put it, a neuron is first a catcher, then a batter (Gazzaniga, 1988).

In the peripheral nervous system, the fibers of individual neurons (axons and sometimes dendrites) are collected together in bundles called **nerves,** rather like the lines in a telephone cable. (In the central nervous system, similar bundles of neuron fibers are called *tracts.*) The human body has 43 pairs of peripheral nerves, one nerve from each pair on the left side of the body and the other on the right. Most of these nerves enter or leave the spinal cord, but the 12 pairs in the head, the *cranial nerves,* connect directly to the brain.

---

nerve A bundle of nerve fibers (axons and sometimes dendrites) in the peripheral nervous system.

Many axons, especially the larger ones, are insulated by a layer of fatty material called the **myelin sheath,** which is derived from glial cells. One purpose of this covering is to prevent signals in adjacent cells from interfering with each other. Another is to speed up the conduction of neural impulses. The myelin sheath is divided into segments that make the axon look a little like a string of link sausages (see Figure 4.4). Beneath the myelin sheath, conduction of an impulse is impossible, in part because conduction involves the passage of certain ions (charged particles) across the cell's membrane (enclosing cover) and into the cell, and in myelinated parts of the axon, there is no way for these ions to enter. Instead, when a neural impulse travels down the

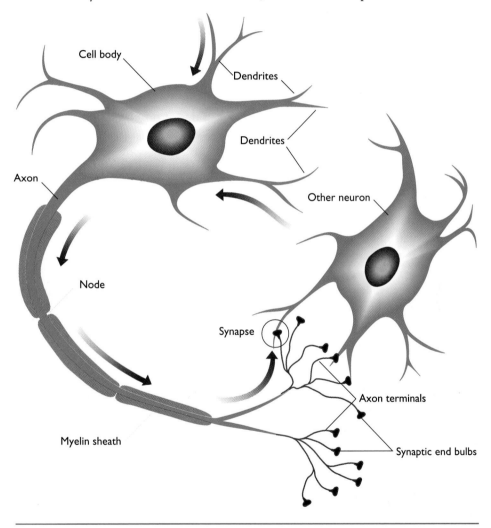

Figure 4.4 *Incoming neural impulses are received by the dendrites of a neuron and transmitted to the cell body. Outgoing signals pass along the axon to terminal branches. The arrows show the direction in which impulses travel.*

myelin sheath A fatty insulation that may surround the axon of a nerve cell; many axons have such insulation.

axon, it "hops" from one (node) break between two "sausages" to the next break. This arrangement allows the impulse to travel faster than it could if it moved along the entire axon. Nerve impulses travel more slowly in babies than in children and adults because when babies are born, their myelin sheaths are not yet fully developed. In individuals with multiple sclerosis, loss of myelin causes erratic nerve signals, leading to loss of sensation, weakness or paralysis, lack of coordination, or vision problems.

Until a decade ago, neuroscientists thought that neurons in the human central nervous system could neither reproduce nor regenerate to any significant degree. They assumed that if these cells were injured or damaged, there was nothing anyone could do about it. But animal studies have challenged these assumptions. In one study, researchers got severed axons in the spinal cords of rats to regrow by blocking the effects of nerve-growth-inhibiting substances found in the myelin sheath (Schnell & Schwab, 1990). In another study, researchers induced severed optic nerves in hamsters to regenerate by laying down a trail of transplanted nervous tissue from the animals' legs (Keirstead et al., 1989). What's more, Canadian neuroscientists have discovered that undifferentiated "precursor" cells from the brains of mice, when immersed in a growth-promoting protein in the laboratory, will produce new neurons, which then continue to divide and multiply (Reynolds & Weiss, 1992). One of the researchers, Samuel Weiss, said that this result was hard to believe at first: "It challenged everything I had read, everything I had learned when I was a student" (quoted in Barinaga, 1992). Since then, similar precursor cells have been discovered in human brains, and they, too, give rise to new neurons when bathed in growth-promoting protein in the laboratory (Kirschenbaum et al., 1994).

So far, these findings have not had any practical results; no one has been able to get severed nerve fibers to regrow in large quantities and then re-establish lost connections, nor has anyone used neurons grown from precursor cells for therapeutic purposes. But each year brings ever more astonishing findings about neurons. Eventually, many of these results may not only alter our understanding of the nervous system but may also lead to new treatments for neurological damage and brain diseases—treatments that promise to be among the most stunning contributions of the biological perspective.

How Neurons Communicate

Individual neurons do not form a continuous chain, with each neuron directly touching one other, end to end. If they did, the number of connections would be inadequate for the vast amount of information the nervous system must handle. Instead, neurons are separated by a minuscule space called the *synaptic cleft*, where the axon terminal of one neuron nearly touches a dendrite or the cell body of another. The entire site—the axon terminal, the cleft, and the membrane of the receiving dendrite or cell body—is called a **synapse.** Because a neuron's axon may have hundreds or even thousands of terminals, a single neuron may have synaptic connections with a great many others. As

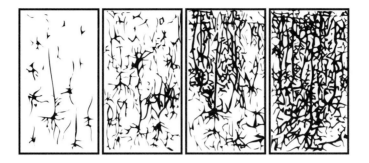

Figure 4.5   *At birth, neurons in the infant's brain are widely spaced, but they begin to form connections immediately. These drawings show the marked increased in the size and number of neurons from birth (far left) to age 15 months (far right).*

a result, the number of communication links in the nervous system runs into the trillions or perhaps even the quadrillions.

Although we seem to be born with nearly all the neurons we will ever have, many synapses have not yet formed at birth. Research with animals shows that axons and dendrites continue to grow as a result of both physical maturation and experience with the world, and tiny projections on dendrites called *spines* increase both in size and number. Figure 4.5 shows the marked increase in the size and number of neurons in a baby's first 15 months after birth.

Throughout life, new learning results in the establishment of new synaptic connections in the brain, with stimulating environments producing the greatest changes (Greenough & Anderson, 1991; Greenough & Black, 1992). Moreover, whenever we store information for the long term (days, weeks, or years), certain synaptic pathways are thought to become more excitable, in a process called **long-term potentiation.** This process, which involves a complex chain of biochemical changes, causes the receiving neurons in these pathways to become more responsive to the signals coming from the transmitting neurons. Conversely, over time, unused synaptic connections are lost as cells or their branches die and are not replaced (Camel, Withers, & Greenough, 1986). Thus, the brain's circuits are not fixed and immutable; they are continually changing in response to information, challenges, and changes in the environment.

Scientists refer to the brain's remarkable flexibility as *plasticity*. In people with brain damage, this plasticity can sometimes produce dramatic recoveries. Individuals

synapse   The site where transmission of a nerve impulse from one nerve cell to another occurs; it includes the axon terminal, the synaptic cleft, and receptor sites in the membrane of the receiving cell.
long-term potentiation   A long-lasting increase in the strength of synaptic responsiveness, thought to be a biological mechanism of memory.

who cannot recall simple words after a stroke may regain normal speech within a matter of months. Patients who cannot move an arm after a head injury may regain use of it after physical therapy. A few individuals have even survived and functioned well after such a drastic surgical procedure as the removal of half of the upper part of the brain! Some sorts of new connections must be responsible for such plasticity, but researchers still do not know why some people recover from damage to the brain, whereas others, with similar damage, are permanently disabled.

Neurons speak to one another, or in some cases to muscles or glands, in an electrical and chemical language. When a nerve cell is stimulated, a change in electrical potential between the inside and the outside of the cell causes a wave of electrical voltage—an *action potential*—to travel down the cell's axon, somewhat as fire travels along the fuse of a firecracker. When this impulse reaches the axon terminal's buttonlike tip (the *synaptic end bulb*), it must get its message across the synaptic cleft to another cell. At this point, *synaptic vesicles,* tiny sacs in the end bulb, open and release a few thousand molecules of a chemical substance called a **neurotransmitter,** or *transmitter* for short. Like sailors carrying a message from one island to another, these molecules then diffuse across the synaptic cleft (see Figure 4.6).

When they reach the other side, the transmitter molecules bind briefly with *receptor sites,* special molecules in the membrane of the receiving neuron, fitting these sites much as a key fits into a lock. This produces changes in the membrane of the receiving cell. The result is a brief change in electrical potential, caused largely by the momentary inflow of positively charged sodium ions across the membrane. The ultimate effect of this change is either *excitatory* (a voltage shift in a positive direction) or *inhibitory* (a voltage shift in a negative direction), depending on which receptor sites have been activated. If the effect is excitatory, the probability increases that the receiving neuron will fire; if it is inhibitory, the opposite is true. Inhibition in the nervous system is extremely important. Without it, we could not sleep or coordinate our movements. Excitation of the nervous system would be overwhelming, producing convulsions.

What any given neuron actually does at any given moment depends on the net effect of all the neurons that are sending messages to it. Only when the cell's voltage reaches a certain threshold will it fire. Thousands of messages, both excitatory and inhibitory, may be coming into the cell. Essentially, the neuron must average them. But how it does this, and how it "decides" whether to fire, is still a puzzle. The message that reaches a final destination depends on the rate at which individual neurons are firing, how many are firing, what types of neurons are firing, and where the neurons are located. It does *not* depend on how strongly the neurons are firing, however, because a neuron always either fires or it doesn't. In other words, the firing of a neuron, like the turning on of a light switch, is an *all-or-none* event.

---

neurotransmitter A chemical substance that is released by a transmitting neuron at the synapse and that alters the activity of a receiving neuron.

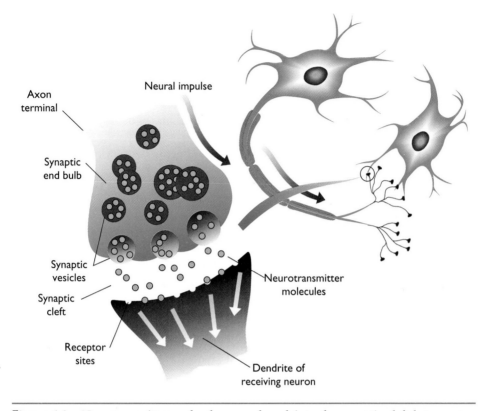

Figure 4.6 *Neurotransmitter molecules are released into the synaptic cleft between two neurons from vesicles (chambers) in the transmitting neuron's axon terminal. After crossing the cleft, the molecules bind to receptor sites on the receiving neuron. As a result, the electrical state of the receiving neuron changes, and the neuron becomes either more or less likely to fire an impulse, depending on the type of transmitter substance.*

Chemical Messengers in the Nervous System

It takes a lot of nerve to make up the nervous system "house," but that house would remain forever dark and lifeless without chemical couriers such as the neurotransmitters. We now look more closely at neurotransmitters, and at two other types of chemical messengers: endorphins and hormones.

Neurotransmitters: Versatile Couriers. As we have seen, neurotransmitters make it possible for one neuron to excite or inhibit another. Dozens of different substances are known or suspected to be transmitters, and the number keeps growing. Each neurotransmitter binds only to specific types of receptor sites. This means that if some of those "sailors" we mentioned (the transmitter molecules) get a little off course and reach the wrong "islands" (receiving neurons), their messages will not be heard (no binding will occur). The existence of different neurotransmitters and receptor sites ensures that messages go where they are supposed to go.

Neurotransmitters exist not only in the brain but also in the spinal cord, the peripheral nerves, and certain glands. Through their effects on specific nerve circuits, these substances can affect mood, memory, and well-being. The nature of the effect depends on the level of the neurotransmitter and its location. Here are a few of the better understood neurotransmitters and some of their known or suspected effects.

- ◆**Serotonin** affects neurons involved in sleep, appetite, sensory perception, temperature regulation, pain suppression, and mood.

- ◆**Dopamine** affects neurons involved in voluntary movement, learning, memory, and emotion.

- ◆**Acetylcholine** affects neurons involved in muscle action, cognitive functioning, memory, and emotion.

- ◆**Norepinephrine** affects neurons involved in increased heart rate and the slowing of intestinal activity during stress, and neurons involved in learning, memory, dreaming, waking from sleep, and emotion.

- ◆**GABA** (gamma-aminobutyric acid) functions as the major inhibitory neurotransmitter in the brain.

- ◆**Glutamate** functions as an important excitatory neurotransmitter in the brain. The long-term potentiation in memory that we mentioned earlier occurs because of an increase in the release of glutamate by transmitting neurons and changes in the receptors of receiving neurons that make them more responsive to glutamate (Bliss & Collingridge, 1993).

Harmful effects can occur when neurotransmitters are in either too great or too short supply. Low levels of norepinephrine and serotonin have been associated with severe depression. Abnormal GABA levels have been implicated in sleep and eating disorders and in convulsive disorders, including epilepsy (Bekenstein & Lothman, 1993). Elevated levels of serotonin, along with other biochemical and brain abnormalities, have been implicated in childhood autism, the disorder described at the beginning of Chapter 2 (du Verglas, Banks, & Guyer, 1988).

Deficiencies in a number of neurotransmitters have also been implicated in *Alzheimer's disease*, a devastating condition, most common in the elderly, that leads to memory loss, personality changes, and eventual disintegration of all physical and mental abilities. In Alzheimer's patients, many of the brain cells responsible for producing acetylcholine have been destroyed, and this deficit may help account for memory loss. Also, in the early stages of the disease, serotonin receptors normally present in certain layers of brain cells nearly disappear (Cross, 1990). This deficit could be related to the increased aggressiveness and moodiness often observed in Alzheimer's patients—although such reactions could also simply be understandable psychological responses to having the disease.

The degeneration of brain cells that produce and use another neurotransmitter, dopamine, appears to cause the symptoms of *Parkinson's disease,* a condition characterized by tremors, muscular spasms, and increasing muscular rigidity. Patients with advanced Parkinson's may "freeze" for minutes or even hours. Injections of dopamine do not help, because dopamine molecules cannot cross the *blood–brain barrier,* a system of densely packed capillary and glial cells whose function is to prevent potentially harmful substances from entering the brain. Symptoms can be lessened by the administration of levodopa (L-dopa), which is a *precursor* (building block) of dopamine, but patients must take larger and larger doses to achieve the desired results; after a while, adverse effects of the high doses, including depression, confusion, and even episodes of psychosis, may be worse than the disease itself.

During the past few years, surgeons have pioneered a dramatic new approach to treating Parkinson's disease and potentially other diseases as well. They have grafted dopamine-producing brain tissue from aborted fetuses into the brains of Parkinson's patients and also the brains of patients who developed symptoms similar to those of Parkinson's after having used a botched "designer drug" that killed their dopamine-producing cells (e.g., Freed et al., 1993; Lindvall et al., 1994; Widner et al., 1993). Not all patients have improved, but some who were virtually helpless before the operation can now move freely and even dress and feed themselves. Animal research suggests that transplants might also be able to help people with Huntington's disease, which involves the degeneration of neurons that make acetylcholine and GABA (Giordano et al., 1990; Sanberg et al., 1993). Although the long-term risks and benefits of brain tissue transplants are not yet known, and although the technique is not yet feasible on a large scale, this work has generated a lot of excitement.

Endorphins: The Brain's Natural Opiates. Another intriguing group of chemical messengers is known collectively as *endogenous opioid peptides,* or more popularly as **endorphins.** Endorphins have effects similar to those of natural opiates; that is, they reduce pain and promote pleasure. They are also thought to play a role in appetite, sexual activity, blood pressure, mood, learning, and memory. Some endorphins function as neurotransmitters, but most act primarily as **neuromodulators,** which increase or decrease the actions of specific neurotransmitters.

Endorphins were identified two and a half decades ago. Candace Pert and Solomon Snyder (1973) were doing research on morphine, a pain-relieving and mood-elevating opiate that derives from heroin, which is made from poppies. They found that morphine works by binding to certain receptor sites in the brain. This seemed odd. As Snyder later recalled, "We doubted that animals had evolved opiate receptors just to deal with certain properties of the poppy plant" (quoted in Radetsky,

---

endorphins Chemical substances in the nervous system that are similar in structure and action to opiates; they are involved in pain reduction, pleasure, and memory, and are known technically as *endogenous opioid peptides.*
neuromodulators Chemical substances in the nervous system that increase or decrease the action of specific neurotransmitters.

1991). Pert and Snyder reasoned that if opiate receptors exist, then the body must produce its own internally generated, or *endogenous,* morphinelike substances, which they named "endorphins." Soon they and other researchers confirmed this hypothesis.

Endorphin levels seem to shoot up when an animal or person is either afraid or under stress. This is no accident; by making pain bearable in such situations, endorphins give a species an evolutionary advantage (Levinthal, 1988). When an organism is threatened, it needs to do something fast. Pain, however, can interfere with action: A mouse that pauses to lick a wounded paw may become a cat's dinner; a soldier who is overcome by an injury may never get off the battlefield. Of course, the body's built-in system of counteracting pain is only partly successful, especially when painful stimulation is prolonged. Researchers are now searching for ways to stimulate endorphin production or to administer endorphins directly in order to alleviate chronic pain.

Other research, using animals, has demonstrated a link between endorphins and the pleasures of social contact. In one series of studies, Jaak Panksepp and his colleagues (1980) gave low doses of morphine or endorphins to young puppies, guinea pigs, and chicks. After the injections, the animals showed much less distress than usual when separated from their mothers. (In all other respects, they behaved normally.) The injections seemed to provide a biochemical replacement for the mother, or, more precisely, for the endorphin surge presumed to occur during contact with her. Conversely, when young guinea pigs and chicks received a chemical that *blocks* the effects of opiates, crying increased. These findings suggest that endorphin-stimulated euphoria may be a child's initial motive for seeking affection and cuddling—that in effect, a child attached to a parent is a child addicted to love.

Hormones: Long-Distance Messengers. **Hormones,** which make up the third class of chemical messengers, are substances that are produced in one part of the body but affect another. Hormones originate primarily in **endocrine glands** and are released directly into the bloodstream. (Figure 4.7 shows parts of the endocrine system that have known or suspected important effects on behavior or emotion.) The bloodstream then carries the hormones to organs and cells that may be far from their point of origin. Some endocrine glands are activated by nervous-system impulses. Conversely, hormones affect the way the nervous system functions. The parts of the nervous and endocrine systems that interact are often referred to as the *neuroendocrine system.* Hormones have dozens of functions, from promoting bodily growth to aiding digestion to regulating metabolism.

Note that neurotransmitters and hormones are not always chemically distinct. The two classifications are like clubs that admit some of the same members. A particular chemical, such as norepinephrine, may belong to more than one classification, depending on where it is located and what function it is performing. Nature has been efficient, giving some substances more than one task to perform.

---

hormones Chemical substances, secreted by organs called glands, that affect the functioning of other organs.
endocrine glands Internal organs that produce hormones and release them into the bloodstream.

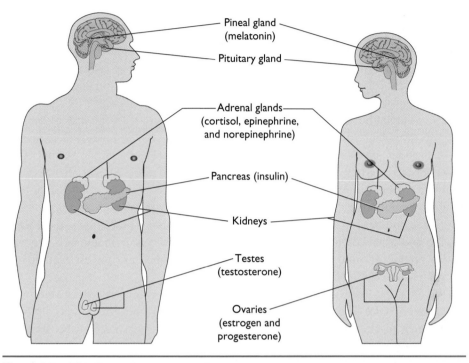

Figure 4.7   *This figure shows parts or the endocrine system that are of particular interest to psychologists.*

The following hormones, among others, are of particular interest to psychologists:

1. **Adrenal hormones,** which are produced by the *adrenal glands* (organs that are perched right above the kidneys), are involved in emotion and responses to stress. Each adrenal gland is composed of an outer layer, or *cortex,* and an inner core, or *medulla.* The outer part produces *cortisol,* which increases blood-sugar levels and boosts energy. The inner part produces *epinephrine* and *norepinephrine.* (Most scientists prefer these last two terms to their older names, adrenaline and noradrenaline, although the older terms are still in use.) When adrenal hormones are released in your body, they activate the sympathetic nervous system, which in turn increases your arousal level and prepares you for action. During arousal, the pupils dilate, widening to allow in more light; the heart beats faster; breathing speeds up; blood-sugar levels rise, providing the body with more energy; and digestion slows down, so that blood flow can be diverted from the stomach and intestines to the muscles and surface of the skin. This is why, when you are excited, scared, furious, or wildly in love, you may not want to eat.

adrenal hormones Hormones produced by the adrenal glands that are involved in emotion and stress; they include cortisol, epinephrine, and norepinephrine.

The adrenal glands produce epinephrine and norepinephrine in response to many challenges in the environment. These hormones will surge if you are laughing at a funny movie, playing a video game, worrying about an exam, cheering at a rock concert, or responding to an insult. They will also rise in response to non-emotional conditions, such as heat, cold, pain, injury, burns, and physical exercise; in response to some drugs; and in response to stress and pressure.

Adrenal hormones released during stress also appear to enhance memory. If you give people a drug that blocks the adrenal glands' response, they remember less about emotional stories they heard than control subjects do (Cahill et al., 1994). Conversely, if you administer epinephrine to animals right after learning, their memory improves (McGaugh, 1990). This effect occurs, however, only when the hormones are at moderate levels. If the dosages are too high, memory suffers. These findings suggest that a moderate level of arousal is best when you are learning and when you need to concentrate and encode events in memory. If you want to remember information well, you should probably aim for an arousal level somewhere between "hyper" and "laid back."

The link between emotional arousal and memory makes good evolutionary sense: Arousal tells the brain that an event or piece of information is important enough to attend to and store for future use. The exact mechanisms involved, however, remain unclear. One especially fascinating possibility involves, of all things, sugar. Epinephrine causes the level of glucose (a sugar) to rise in the bloodstream. Although epinephrine does not seem to enter the brain from the bloodstream readily, glucose does. Once in the brain, glucose may enhance memory either directly or by altering the effects of neurotransmitters (Gold, 1987). This "sweet memories" effect occurs both in aged rats and mice and in elderly human beings. In one study, healthy older people fasted overnight, drank a glass of lemonade sweetened with either glucose or saccharin, and then took two memory tests. The saccharine-laced drink had no effect on their performance, but drinking lemonade with glucose greatly boosted their ability to recall a taped passage 5 or 40 minutes after hearing it, and it enhanced their long-term ability to recall words from a list (Manning, Hall, & Gold, 1990). A similar study found that glucose improved the ability of Alzheimer's patients to recognize words, prose passages, and faces (Manning, Ragozzino, & Gold, 1993).

2. **Melatonin,** which is secreted by the *pineal body,* a small gland deep within the brain, appears to regulate daily biological rhythms. A **biological rhythm** is a periodic fluctuation in a biological system; it may or may not have psychological consequences. We've got dozens of such rhythms: A biological clock in our brains governs the waxing and waning of hormone levels, urine volume, blood pressure,

---

melatonin A hormone secreted by the pineal gland that is involved in the regulation of daily (circadian) biological rhythms.

biological rhythm A periodic, more or less regular fluctuation in a biological system; it may or may not have psychological implications.

and even the responsiveness of brain cells to stimulation. Biological rhythms are typically synchronized with external events, such as changes in clock time and daylight. But many rhythms will continue to occur (though perhaps with a somewhat different average length) even in the absence of all external time cues; they are endogenous.

Some biological rhythms, such as the female menstrual cycle, recur less frequently than once a day. Other rhythms—involving everything from stomach contractions to alertness to dreaming and daydreaming—recur more frequently than once a day, often following a roughly 90-minute schedule when social customs do not intervene. And still others, called **circadian rhythms,** recur approximately every 24 hours. Circadian rhythms, which are also found in plants, animals, and insects, reflect the adaptation of organisms to the many changes associated with the rotation of the earth on its axis, such as changes in light, air pressure, temperature, and wind. The best-known circadian rhythm is the sleep–wake cycle, but there are hundreds of others. For example, body temperature, which most people assume to be stable, fluctuates about 1 degree Centigrade each day, peaking, on average, in the late afternoon and hitting a low point, or trough, in the wee hours of the morning.

The biological clock or pacemaker that controls circadian rhythms is located in a part of the brain called the *hypothalamus* (which we will be describing later in this chapter). Melatonin, which is responsive to changes in light and dark, seems to keep the clock in phase with the light–dark cycle (Lewy et al., 1992; Reppert et al., 1988). Animal studies suggest that information about light and dark reaches the pineal gland via a neural pathway that leads from the back of the eyes through the hypothalamus and on to the pineal gland. In several cases, melatonin treatments have been used to synchronize the disturbed sleep–wake cycle of blind people whose sleep problems apparently stemmed from their inability to sense light and dark (Arendt, Aldhous, & Wright, 1988; Tzischinsky et al., 1992). Recently, physicians have started to recommend melatonin supplements for people who suffer from chronic insomnia, especially for older people, whose melatonin levels usually decline.

3. **Sex hormones,** which are secreted by tissue located within the gonads—testes in men, ovaries in women—include three main types, all occurring in both sexes but in differing amounts and proportions after puberty. *Androgens* (the most important of which is *testosterone*) are masculinizing hormones, produced mainly in the testes but also in the ovaries and the adrenal cortex. Androgens set in motion the physical changes males experience at puberty—for example, a deepened voice and facial and chest hair—and cause pubic and underarm hair to develop in females.

---

circadian rhythm A biological rhythm that recurs approximately every 24 hours.
sex hormones Hormones that regulate the development and functioning of reproductive and sex organs and that stimulate the development of male and female sexual characteristics; they include androgens (such as testosterone), estrogens, and progesterone.

Testosterone also influences sexual arousal in both sexes. *Estrogens* are feminizing hormones produced primarily in the ovaries but also in the testes and the adrenal cortex. They bring on the physical changes females experience at puberty, such as breast development and the onset of menstruation, and they influence the course of the menstrual cycle. *Progesterone* contributes to the growth and maintenance of the uterine lining in preparation for a fertilized egg, among other functions; it is produced mainly in the ovaries but also in the testes and the adrenal cortex.

There is much debate about the role of sex hormones in behavior unrelated to sex and reproduction. In the next chapter, we will examine the popular belief that fluctuating sex hormones make women, but not men, "emotional."

WHAT DO YOU KNOW?

A. Each of the following definitions is followed by a pair of words. Which word best fits the definition?

1. Basic building blocks of the nervous system (*nerves/neurons*)
2. Cell parts that receive nerve impulses (*axons/dendrites*)
3. Site of communication between neurons (*synapse/myelin sheath*)
4. Opiate-like substance in the brain (*dopamine/endorphin*)
5. Chemicals that make it possible for neurons to communicate (*neurotransmitters/hormones*)
6. Hormone closely associated with emotional excitement (*epinephrine/estrogen*)

B. Imagine that you are depressed, and you hear about a treatment for depression that affects the levels of several neurotransmitters thought to be involved in the disorder. Based on what you have learned about neurotransmitters, what questions would you want to ask before deciding whether to try the treatment?

ANSWERS:

A. 1. neurons **2.** dendrites **3.** synapse **4.** endorphin **5.** neurotransmitters **6.** epinephrine **B.** You might want to ask, among other things, about side effects (each neurotransmitter has several functions, all of which might be affected by the treatment); about evidence that the treatment works; and about whether there is any reason to believe that your own neurotransmitter levels are abnormal or whether there may be other reasons for your depression.

THE BRAIN

We come now to the main room of the nervous system "house," the brain. "It's amazing," neurologist Robert Collins once wrote, "to think that the body feeds the brain sugar and amino acids, and what comes out is poetry and pirouettes." Amazing, indeed. Certainly a disembodied brain is not very exciting to look at. Stored in a formaldehyde-filled container, it is a putty-colored, wrinkled glob of tissue that looks a little like a walnut whose growth has gotten out of hand. It takes an act of imagination to envision this modest-looking organ writing *Hamlet,* discovering radium, or inventing the paper clip.

Mapping the Brain

In a living person, of course, the brain is encased in a thick protective vault of bone. How, then, can scientists study it? One approach is to study patients who have had a part of the brain damaged or removed because of disease or injury. Another, called the *lesion method,* involves damaging or removing sections of brain in animals, then observing the effects.

The brain can also be probed by using devices called *electrodes.* Some electrodes are coin-shaped and are simply pasted or taped on the scalp. They detect the electrical activity of millions of neurons in particular regions of the brain and are widely used in research and medical diagnosis. The electrodes are connected by wires to a machine that translates the electrical energy from the brain into wavy lines on a moving piece of paper or visual patterns on a screen. That is why electrical patterns in the brain are known as "brain waves." Different wave patterns are associated with sleep, relaxation, and mental concentration.

A brain-wave recording is called an **electroencephalogram (EEG).** A standard EEG is useful, but not very precise, because it reflects the activities of many cells at once. "Listening" to the brain with an EEG machine is like standing outside a sports stadium: You know when something is happening, but you can't be sure what it is or who is doing it. Fortunately, computer technology can be combined with EEG technology to get a clearer picture of brain activity patterns associated with specific events and mental processes. To analyze such patterns, or *evoked potentials,* researchers use a computer to suppress all the background "noise" being produced by the brain, leaving only the pattern of the electrical response to the event.

For even more precise information, researchers use *needle electrodes,* very thin wires or hollow glass tubes that can be inserted into the brain, either directly in an exposed brain or through tiny holes in the skull. Only the skull and the membranes covering the brain need to be anesthetized; the brain itself, which processes all sensation and feeling, paradoxically feels nothing when touched. Therefore, a human patient or an animal can be awake and not feel pain during the procedure. Needle electrodes can be used both to record electrical activity from the brain and to stimulate the brain with weak electrical currents. Stimulating a given area often results in a specific sensation or movement. *Microelectrodes* are so fine that they can be inserted into single cells.

---

electroencephalogram (EEG) A recording of neural activity detected by electrodes.

Since the mid-1970s, even more amazing doors to the brain have opened. The most widely used method, the **PET scan (positron-emission tomography),** goes beyond anatomy to record biochemical changes in the brain as they are happening. One type of PET scan takes advantage of the fact that nerve cells convert glucose, the body's main fuel, into energy. A researcher can inject a patient with a glucoselike substance that contains a harmless radioactive element. This substance accumulates in brain areas that are particularly active and are consuming glucose rapidly. The substance emits radiation, which is a telltale sign of activity, like cookie crumbs on a child's face. The radiation is detected by a scanning device, and the result is a computer-processed picture of biochemical activity on a display screen, with different colors indicating different activity levels. The PET scan in Figure 4.8 shows, in black and white, an average healthy brain.

PET scans, which were originally designed to diagnose physical abnormalities, have produced evidence that certain brain areas in people with emotional disorders are either unusually quiet or unusually active. But PET technology can also show which parts of the brain are active during ordinary activities and emotions. It lets researchers see which areas are busiest when a person hears a song, recalls a sad memory, works on a math problem, or shifts attention from one task to another.

Another technique, **MRI (magnetic resonance imaging),** allows the exploration of "inner space" without injecting chemicals. Powerful magnetic fields and radio frequencies are used to produce vibrations in the nuclei of atoms making up body organs, and these vibrations are then picked up as signals by special receivers. A com-

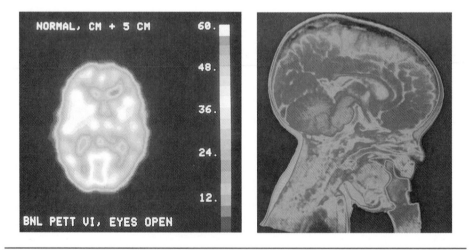

Figure 4.8 *On the left is a PET scan of a healthy brain. On the right is a magnetic resonance image (MRI) of a child's brain—and the bottle he was drinking while it was taken.*

PET scan (positron-emission tomography) A method for analyzing biochemical activity in the brain, using injections of a glucoselike substance containing a radioactive element.
MRI (magnetic resonance imaging) A method for studying body and brain tissue, using magnetic fields and special radio receivers.

puter analyzes the signals, taking into account their strength and duration, and converts them into a high-contrast picture. Like the PET scan, MRI is used both for diagnosing disease and for studying normal brains. The magnetic resonance image in Figure 4.8 shows a child's brain, and the bottle given to him to quiet him during the seven minutes it took to obtain the image.

Conventional MRI is too slow to map activity over time, but recent breakthroughs in computer hardware and software have led to faster techniques that can capture brain changes during specific mental activities, such as thinking of a word or looking at a scene (Rosen et al., 1993). Fast or "functional" MRI works indirectly; it detects blood flow by picking up magnetic signals from blood that has given up its oxygen to active brain cells.

Still newer techniques, although not yet widely used for psychological research, are becoming available with each passing year. Some of them convert still pictures or repeated EEG readings into a moving picture that shows changes in neuronal activity on a three-dimensional image of the brain! No longer can the brain hide from researchers behind the fortress of the skull. It is now possible to get a clear visual image of our most enigmatic organ without so much as lifting a scalpel.

A Tour Through the Brain

Let's take a little tour through the brain, starting at the lower part, just above the spine. In general, the more reflexive or automatic a behavior is, the more likely it is to be controlled by the lower areas, and the more complex a behavior, the more likely it is to involve areas that are higher up (although some lower areas also appear to be involved in some "higher" cognitive functions). Figure 4.9 on the next page, a cross section, shows the brain as though it were split in half; the view is of the inside surface of the right half. We will be describing the labeled structures as we take our tour.

Lower Areas. We begin at the base of the skull with the **brain stem,** which began to evolve some 500 million years ago in segmented worms. The brain stem looks like a stalk rising out of the spinal cord. Pathways to and from upper areas of the brain pass through its two main structures, the **medulla** and the **pons.** The pons is involved in (among other things) sleeping, waking, and dreaming. The medulla is responsible for bodily functions that do not have to be consciously willed, such as breathing and heart rate. Hanging has long been used as a method of execution because when it breaks the neck, nervous pathways from the medulla are severed, stopping respiration.

Extending upward from the core of the brain stem is the **reticular activating system (RAS).** This dense network of neurons, which has connections with many higher

---

brain stem The part of the brain at the top of the spinal cord; it is responsible for automatic functions such as heartbeat and respiration.

medulla A structure in the brain stem responsible for certain automatic functions, such as breathing and heart rate.

pons A structure in the brain stem involved in, among other things, sleeping, waking, and dreaming.

reticular activating system (RAS) A dense network of neurons found in the core of the brain stem; it arouses the cortex and screens incoming information.

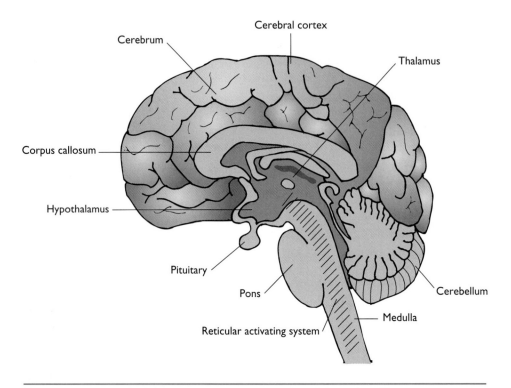

Figure 4.9 *This view of the brain is of the inside surface of the right half and shows the parts discussed in the text.*

areas of the brain, screens incoming information and arouses the higher centers when something happens that demands their attention. Without the RAS, we could not be alert or perhaps even conscious.

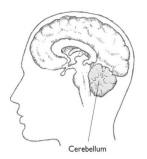

The Cerebellum. Toward the back part of the brain is a structure about the size of a small fist. It is the **cerebellum,** or "lesser brain," which contributes to a sense of balance and coordinates the muscles so that movement is smooth and precise. If your cerebellum were damaged, you would probably become exceedingly clumsy and uncoordinated; you might have trouble using a pencil, threading a needle, or riding a bicycle. The cerebellum is also involved in remembering some kinds of skills, and in the learning and storage of some simple responses. For example, in studies with rabbits, the animals could not learn to blink reflexively in response to a tone if parts of their cerebellums were destroyed or drugged (Thompson, 1986; Krupa, Thompson, & Thompson, 1993).

---

cerebellum A brain structure that regulates movement and balance and that is involved in the learning of certain kinds of simple responses.

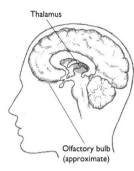

Thalamus

Olfactory bulb
(approximate)

The Thalamus. Above the brain stem, in the brain's interior, is the **thalamus,** the busy traffic officer of the brain. As sensory messages come into the brain, the thalamus directs them to higher centers. For example, the sight of a sunset sends signals that the thalamus directs to a vision area, and the sound of an oboe sends signals that are sent on to an auditory area. The only sense that completely bypasses the thalamus is the sense of smell, which has its own private switching station, the *olfactory bulb.* The olfactory bulb lies near areas that control emotion. Perhaps that is why particular odors—the smell of fresh laundry, gardenias, a steak sizzling on the grill—often rekindle memories of important personal experiences.

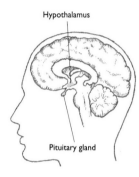

Hypothalamus

Pituitary gland

The Hypothalamus and the Pituitary Gland. Beneath the thalamus sits a structure called the **hypothalamus** (*hypo* means "under"). It is involved in drives associated with the survival of both the individual and the species—hunger, thirst, emotion, sex, and reproduction. It regulates body temperature by triggering sweating or shivering, and it controls the complex operations of the autonomic nervous system. As we have seen, it also contains the neurological "superclock" that regulates the body's circadian rhythms.

Hanging down from the hypothalamus, connected to it by a short stalk, is a cherry-sized endocrine gland called the **pituitary gland.** The pituitary is often called the body's "master gland" because the hormones it secretes affect many other endocrine glands. The master, however, is really only a supervisor. The true boss is the hypothalamus, which sends chemicals to the pituitary that tell it when to "talk" to the various endocrine glands. The pituitary, in turn, sends hormonal messages out to the glands.

The Limbic System. The hypothalamus has many connections to a set of loosely interconnected structures that form a sort of border on the underside of the brain's "cauliflower." Together, these structures make up the **limbic system** of the brain, shown in Figure 4.10. (*Limbic* comes from the Latin for "border.") Some anatomists include the hypothalamus and parts of the thalamus in the limbic system. The limbic system is heavily involved in emotions, such as rage and fear, that we share with other animals.

---

thalamus The brain structure that relays sensory messages to the cerebral cortex.
hypothalamus A brain structure involved in emotions and drives vital to survival, such as fear, hunger, thirst, and reproduction; it regulates the autonomic nervous system.
pituitary gland A small endocrine gland at the base of the brain that releases many hormones and regulates other endocrine glands.
limbic system A group of brain areas involved in emotional reactions and motivated behavior.

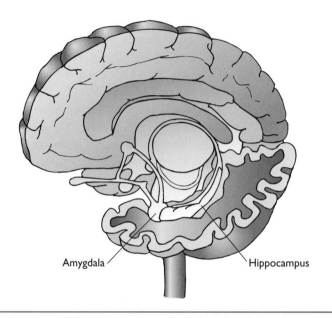

Figure 4.10 *Structures of the limbic system, shaded in this illustration, play an important role in memory and emotion.*

Many years ago, James Olds and Peter Milner reported the existence of "pleasure centers" in the limbic system (Olds, 1975; Olds & Milner, 1954). They found that rats could be trained to press a lever in order to get a buzz of electricity delivered through tiny electrodes to their limbic systems. Some rats would press the bar thousands of times an hour, for 15 to 20 hours at a time, until they collapsed from exhaustion. When they revived, they went right back to the bar. When forced to make a choice, the little hedonists opted for electrical stimulation over such temptations as water, food, and even an attractive rat of the other sex that was making provocative gestures. (You may be either relieved or disappointed to know that human beings do not act like rats in this regard. Patients who volunteered to have their pleasure areas stimulated as a treatment for depression said that the experience was merely "pleasant" [Sem-Jacobsen, 1959].) Today, researchers believe that brain stimulation activates neural pathways rather than discrete "centers," and that changes in neurotransmitter or neuromodulator levels are involved. Several lines of research have focused on the possible role of endorphins; the limbic system contains some of the highest concentrations of endorphins and endorphin receptors in the brain.

One part of the limbic system that especially concerns psychologists is the **amygdala,** which appears to be responsible for evaluating sensory information and quickly

---

amygdala A brain structure involved in the arousal and regulation of emotion and the initial emotional response to sensory information.

determining its emotional importance. It also contributes to the initial decision to approach or withdraw from a person or situation. According to studies by neuroscientist Joseph LeDoux (1989), pathways in the limbic system prompt the amygdala to trigger an emotional response to incoming sensory information, which may then be "overridden" by a more accurate appraisal from the cerebral cortex. (This is why you jump with fear when you suddenly feel a hand on your back in a dark alley, and why your fear evaporates when the cortex registers that the hand belongs to a friend.) If you damage a rat's amygdala, the animal "forgets" to be afraid when it should be; and people with damage to the amygdala often have difficulty recognizing fear in themselves or others (Damasio, 1994). The amygdala also plays an important role in mediating anxiety and depression; PET scans find that depressed and anxious patients show increased neural activity in this structure (Schulkin, 1994).

Another important limbic structure, the **hippocampus,** has a shape that must have reminded someone of a seahorse, for that is what its name means. The hippocampus is larger in human beings than in any other species. One of its tasks seems to be to compare sensory messages with what the brain has learned to expect about the world. When expectations are met, the hippocampus tells the reticular activating system, the brain's arousal center, to "cool it." It wouldn't do to be highly aroused in response to *everything*. What if neural alarm bells went off every time a car went by, a bird chirped, or you felt your saliva trickling down the back of your throat?

The hippocampus has also been called the "gateway to memory" because, along with other brain areas, it enables us to store *declarative memories,* memories of facts and events—the kind of information you need to identify a flower, tell a story, or recall a vacation trip. (We will discuss such memories further in Chapter 10.) The information then goes on to be stored in the cortex, which we will be discussing shortly; but without the hippocampus, the information would never get to its ultimate destination.

We know about this function of the hippocampus in part from research on brain-damaged patients with severe memory problems. The case of one man, known to researchers as H. M., is thought to be the most intensely studied in the annals of medicine, and it is still being studied today (Corkin, 1984; Milner, 1970; Ogden & Corkin, 1991). In 1953, when H. M. was 27, surgeons removed most of his hippocampus, along with part of the amygdala, in a last-ditch effort to relieve the patient's severe and life-threatening epilepsy. The operation did, in fact, achieve its goal: Afterward, the young man's seizures were milder and could be managed with medication. His memory, however, had been affected dramatically. Although H. M. continued to recall most events that had occurred before the operation, he could no longer remember new experiences for much longer than 15 minutes. These declarative memories vanished like water down the drain. With sufficient practice, H. M. could acquire new skills, such as solving a puzzle or playing tennis (psychologists call these *procedural memories*), but he could not remember learning these skills. Nor could he learn new words, songs, stories, or faces. H. M.'s doctors had to reintroduce themselves every time they

---

hippocampus A brain structure involved in the storage of new information in memory.

saw him. He would read the same issue of a magazine over and over again without realizing it. He could not recall the day of the week, the year, or even his last meal.

Today, many years later, H. M. will occasionally recall an unusually emotional event, such as the assassination of someone named Kennedy. He sometimes remembers that both his parents are dead, and he knows he has memory problems. But, according to Suzanne Corkin, who has studied H. M. extensively, these "islands of remembering" are the exceptions in a vast sea of forgetfulness. He still does not know the scientists who have studied him for decades. Although he is now in his seventies, he thinks he is much younger. This good-natured man can no longer recognize a photograph of his own face; he is stuck in a time warp from the past.

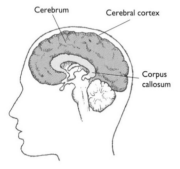

Cerebrum   Cerebral cortex

Corpus callosum

The Cerebrum and the Cerebral Cortex. Above the limbic system is the cauliflower-shaped **cerebrum,** where the higher forms of thinking take place. The complexity of the human brain's circuitry far exceeds that of any computer in existence, and much of its most complicated wiring is packed into this structure. Compared with many other creatures, we humans may be ungainly, feeble, and thin-skinned, but our well-developed cerebrum enables us to overcome these limitations and creatively control our environment (and, some would say, to mess it up).

The cerebrum is divided into two separate halves, or **cerebral hemispheres,** connected by a large band of fibers called the **corpus callosum.** In general, the right hemisphere is in charge of the left side of the body, and the left hemisphere is in charge of the right side of the body. As we will see shortly, the two sides also have somewhat different tasks and talents, a phenomenon known as **lateralization.**

The cerebrum is covered by several thin layers of densely packed cells known collectively as the **cerebral cortex.** Cell bodies in the cortex, as in many other parts of the brain, produce a grayish tissue—hence the term *gray matter.* In other parts of the brain (and the rest of the nervous system), long, myelin-covered axons prevail, providing the brain's *white matter.* Although the cortex is only about three millimeters thick, it contains almost three-fourths of all the cells in the human brain. In only one square *inch* of the cortex, there are around 10,000 miles of synaptically connected nerve cells. In the entire cortex, there are enough connections to stretch from the earth to the moon and back again, and then back to the moon (Davis, 1984).

---

cerebrum The largest brain structure, consisting of the upper part of the brain; it is in charge of most sensory, motor, and cognitive processes; from the Latin for "brain."

cerebral hemispheres The two halves of the cerebrum.

corpus callosum The bundle of nerve fibers connecting the two cerebral hemispheres.

lateralization Specialization of the two cerebral hemispheres for particular psychological operations.

cerebral cortex A collection of several thin layers of cells covering the cerebrum; it is largely responsible for higher mental functions; *cortex* is Latin for "bark" or "rind."

The cortex has many deep crevasses and wrinkles. These folds and fissures in the brain's surface enable it to contain its billions of neurons without requiring us to have the heads of giants. In other mammals, which have fewer neurons, the cortex is less crumpled; in rats, it is quite smooth. On each cerebral hemisphere, especially deep fissures divide the cortex into four distinct regions, or lobes (see Figure 4.11):

◆ The *occipital lobes* (from the Latin for "in back of the head") are at the lower back part of the brain. Among other things, they contain the *visual cortex,* where visual signals are processed. Damage to the visual cortex can cause impaired visual recognition or blindness.

◆ The *parietal lobes* (from the Latin for "pertaining to walls") are at the top of the brain. They contain the *somatosensory cortex,* which receives information about pressure, pain, touch, and temperature from all over the body. This sensory information tells you what the movable parts of your body are doing at every moment. The areas of the somatosensory cortex that receive signals from the hands and the face are disproportionately large because these body parts are particularly sensitive.

◆ The *temporal lobes* (from the Latin for "pertaining to the temples") are at the sides of the brain, just above the ears, behind the temples. They are involved in memory, perception, emotion, and language comprehension, and they contain the *auditory cortex,* which processes sounds.

◆ The *frontal lobes,* as their name indicates, are located toward the front of the brain, just under the skull in the area of the forehead. They contain the *motor cortex,* which issues orders to the 600 muscles of the body that produce voluntary movement. They also seem to be responsible for the ability to make plans, think creatively, and take initiative.

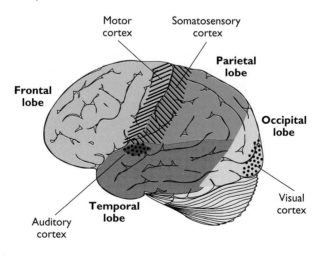

Figure 4.11   *In this drawing, crosshatched areas show regions specialized for movement and bodily sensation, and dotted areas show regions specialized for vision and hearing.*

When a surgeon probes these four pairs of lobes with an electrode, different things tend to happen. If current is applied to the somatosensory cortex in the parietal lobes, the patient may feel tingling in the skin or a sense of being gently touched. If the visual cortex in the occipital lobes is stimulated, the person may report a flash of light or swirls of color. However, there is considerable overlap in what the lobes do. And in most areas of the cortex, nothing happens as a result of electrical stimulation. These "silent" areas, which are sometimes called the *association cortex,* appear to be responsible for higher mental processes.

The silent areas of the cortex are finally beginning to reveal their secrets. Psychologists are especially interested in learning about the forwardmost part of the frontal lobes, the *prefrontal cortex.* This area barely exists in mice and rats and takes up only 3.5 percent of the cerebral cortex in cats, about 7 percent in dogs, and 17 percent in chimpanzees. In human beings, in contrast, it accounts for fully 29 percent of the cortex (Pines, 1983).

Scientists have long known that the frontal lobes, and the prefrontal cortex in particular, must have something to do with personality. The first clue appeared in 1848, when a bizarre accident drove an inch-thick, three-and-a-half foot long iron rod clear through the head of a young railroad worker named Phineas Gage. The rod (which is still on display at Harvard University, along with Gage's skull) entered beneath the left eye and exited through the top of the head, destroying much of the prefrontal cortex (H. Damasio et al., 1994). Miraculously, Gage survived this trauma. What's more, he retained the ability to speak, think, and remember. But his friends complained that he was "no longer Gage." In a sort of Jekyll-and-Hyde transformation, Gage had changed from a mild-mannered, friendly, efficient worker into a foul-mouthed, ill-tempered, undependable lout who could not hold a steady job or stick to a plan. His employers were forced to let him go, and he was reduced to exhibiting himself as a circus attraction.

This sad case and other cases of frontal-lobe damage suggest that parts of the frontal lobes are involved in social judgment, rational decision making, and the ability to set goals and to make and carry through plans—or what is commonly called "will." As neurologist Antonio Damasio (1994) writes, "Gage's unintentional message was that observing social convention, behaving ethically, and, in general, making decisions advantageous to one's survival and progress, require both knowledge of rules and strategies *and* the integrity of specific brain systems." Interestingly, the mental deficits that characterize damage to these areas are accompanied by a flattening out of emotion and feeling, which suggests that normal emotions are necessary for everyday reasoning and decision making. Without these emotions, we cannot learn from our successes and failures or recognize our errors and resolve to correct them.

The frontal lobes also govern the ability to do a series of tasks in the proper sequence and to stop doing them at the proper time. The pioneering Soviet psychologist A. R. Luria (1980) studied many cases in which damage to the frontal lobes disrupted these abilities. One man observed by Luria kept trying to light a match after it was already lit. Another planed a piece of wood in the hospital carpentry shop until it was gone, and then went on to plane the workbench!

Some researchers believe that damage to the prefrontal cortex, caused by birth complications or child abuse, might help account for some cases of criminally violent behavior (Raine, Brennan, & Mednick, 1994). A PET-scan study found that accused murderers had less brain activity in this area than did control subjects who were matched for age and sex (Raine, Buchsbaum, et al., 1994). These results, if verified by other researchers, will raise troubling legal questions: Should violent individuals who have damage in the prefrontal cortex be held responsible for their acts? And what treatment or punishment should they receive?

In the next section, we will continue our discussion of the cerebrum by considering two issues that have long intrigued brain researchers: the different tasks performed by the two cerebral hemispheres and the location of memories in the cerebral cortex. But first, it's time to see how your own brain is working.

WHAT DO YOU KNOW?

Match each of the descriptions on the left with one of the terms on the right.

1. Filters out irrelevant information
2. Known as the "gateway to memory"
3. Controls the autonomic nervous system; involved in drives associated with survival
4. Consists of two hemispheres
5. Wrinkled outer covering of the brain
6. Site of the motor cortex; associated with planning, thinking creatively, taking initiative

a. reticular activating system
b. cerebrum
c. hippocampus
d. cerebral cortex
e. frontal lobes
f. hypothalamus

ANSWERS:

1.a 2.c 3.f 4.b 5.d 6.e

Split Brains: A House Divided

We have seen that the cerebrum is divided into two hemispheres that control opposite sides of the body. In a normal brain, the two hemispheres communicate with each other across the corpus callosum, the bundle of fibers that connects them. Whatever happens in one side of the brain is instantly signaled to the other.

What would happen, though, if the communication lines were cut? An early clue appeared in a case study published in 1908. A mentally disturbed woman repeatedly tried to choke herself with her left hand. She would try with her right hand to pull the left hand away from her throat, but she claimed that the left hand was beyond her control. She also did other destructive things, like throwing pillows around and tearing her sheets—but only with her left hand. A neurologist suspected that the woman's corpus callosum had been damaged, with the result that the two sides of the brain could no longer communicate. When the woman died, an autopsy showed that he was right (Geschwind, in J. Miller, 1983).

This case suggested that the two sides of the brain can experience different emotions. What would happen if they were completely out of touch? Would they think different thoughts and store different memories? In 1953, Ronald E. Myers and Roger W. Sperry took the first step toward answering this question by severing the corpus callosum in cats. They also cut parts of the nerves leading from the eyes to the brain. Normally, each eye transmits messages to both sides of the brain. After this procedure, a cat's left eye sent information only to the left hemisphere and its right eye sent information only to the right hemisphere.

At first, the cats did not seem to be affected much by this drastic operation. But Myers and Sperry showed that something profound had happened. They trained the cats to perform tasks with one eye blindfolded. For example, a cat might have to push a panel with a square on it to get food but ignore a panel with a circle. Then the researchers switched the blindfold to the cat's other eye and tested the animal again. Now the cats behaved as if they had never learned the trick. Apparently, one side of the brain didn't know what the other side was doing. It was as if the animals had two minds in one body. Later studies confirmed this result with other species, including monkeys (Sperry, 1964).

In all the animal studies, ordinary behavior, such as eating and walking, remained normal. Encouraged by this finding, a team of surgeons led by Joseph Bogen decided in the early 1960s to try cutting the corpus callosum in patients with debilitating epilepsy. Epilepsy, a neurological disorder that has many causes and takes many forms, often causes seizures. Usually, the seizures are brief, mild, and controllable by drugs, but occasionally they are unrelenting and uncontrollable. In severe forms of the disease, disorganized electrical activity spreads from an injured area to other parts of the brain. The surgeons reasoned that cutting the connection between the two halves of the brain might stop the spread of electrical activity from one side to the other. The operation was a last resort.

The results of this *split-brain surgery* generally proved successful. Seizures were reduced and sometimes disappeared completely. As an added bonus, these patients gave scientists a chance to find out what each half of the brain can do when it is quite literally cut off from the other. It was already known that the two hemispheres are not mirror images of each other. In most people, language is largely handled by the left hemisphere: speech production in an area of the left frontal lobe known as *Broca's area,* and meaning and language comprehension in an area of the left temporal lobe known as *Wernicke's area.* (The two areas are named after the scientists who first described them.) Thus a person who suffers brain damage because of a stroke—a blockage in or rupture of a blood vessel in the brain—is much more likely to have language problems if the damage is in the left side than if it is in the right. How would splitting the brain affect language and other abilities?

In their daily lives, "split-brain" patients did not seem much affected by the fact that the two sides of their brains were incommunicado. Their personalities and general intelligence remained intact; they could walk, talk, and in general lead normal lives. Apparently, connections in the undivided brain stem kept body movements normal. But in a series of ingenious studies, Sperry and his colleagues (and later other researchers) showed that perception and memory had been profoundly affected, just as they had been in earlier animal research. In 1981, Sperry won a Nobel Prize for this work.

To understand this research, you must know how nerves connect the eyes to the brain. (The human patients, unlike Myers and Sperry's cats, did not have these nerves cut.) If you look straight ahead, everything in the left side of the scene before you—the "visual field"—goes to the right half of your brain, and everything in the right side of the scene goes to the left half of your brain. This is true for *both* eyes (see Figure 4.12).

The procedure was to present information only to one or the other side of the subjects' brains. In one early study (Levy, Trevarthen, & Sperry, 1972), the researchers took photographs of different faces, cut them in two, and pasted different halves

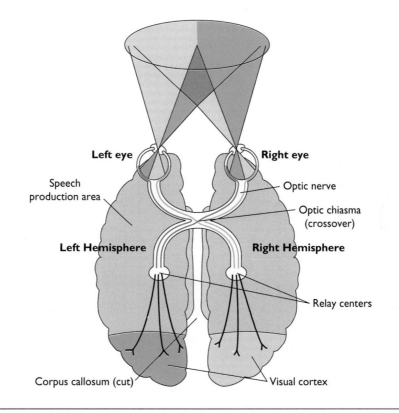

Figure 4.12 *Each hemisphere of the brain receives information from the eyes about the opposite side of the visual field. If you stare directly at the corner of a room, everything to the left of the juncture is represented in your right cerebral hemisphere and everything to the right is represented in your left cerebral hemisphere. This is so because half the axons in each optic nerve cross over (at the optic chiasma) to the opposite side of the brain. Normally, each hemisphere immediately shares its information with the other one. However, in split-brain patients, severing of the corpus callosum blocks such communication.*

together. The reconstructed photographs were then presented on slides. The person was told to stare at a dot on the middle of the screen, so that half the image fell to the left of this point and half to the right. Each image was flashed so quickly that there was no time for the person to move his or her eyes. When the subjects were asked to *say* what they had seen, they named the person in the right part of the image. But when they were asked to *point* with their left hands to the face they had seen, they chose the person in the left side of the image (see Figure 4.13). Further, they claimed they had noticed nothing unusual about the original photographs! Each side of the brain saw a different half-image and automatically filled in the missing part. Neither side knew what the other side had seen.

Why did the patients name one side of the picture but point to the other? Speech centers are in the left hemisphere. When the person responded with speech, it was the left side of the brain doing the talking. When the person pointed with the left hand, which is controlled by the right side of the brain, the right brain was giving *its* version of what the person had seen.

In another study, the researchers presented slides of ordinary objects, and then suddenly flashed a slide of a nude woman. Both sides of the brain were amused, but because only the left side has speech, the two sides responded differently. When the picture was flashed to her left hemisphere, one woman laughed and identified the pic-

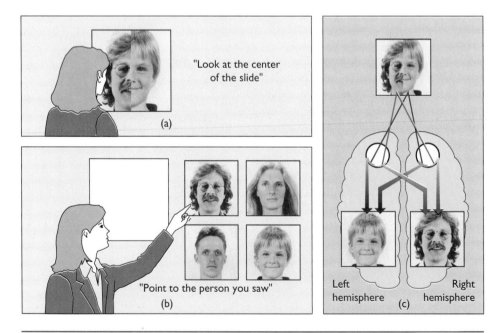

Figure 4.13 *When split-brain patients were shown composite photographs and then asked to pick out the face they had seen from a series of intact photographs, they said they had seen the face on the right side of the composite—yet they pointed with their left hands to the face that had been on the left. Because the two hemispheres of the brain could not communicate, the verbal left hemisphere was aware of only the right half of the picture and the relatively mute right hemisphere was aware of only the left half.*

ture as a nude. When it was flashed to her right hemisphere, she said nothing but began to chuckle. Asked what she was laughing at, she said, "I don't know . . . nothing . . . oh—that funny machine." The right hemisphere could not describe what it had seen, but it reacted emotionally, just the same (Gazzaniga, 1967).

Several dozen people have undergone the split-brain operation since the mid-1960s, and research on left–right differences has also been done with people whose brains are intact. Electrodes and PET scans have been used to gauge activity in the left and right sides of the brain while people perform different tasks. The results confirm that nearly all right-handed people and a majority of left-handers process language mainly in the left hemisphere. The left side is also more active during some logical, symbolic, and sequential tasks, such as solving math problems and understanding technical material. Because of its cognitive "talents," many researchers refer to the left hemisphere as *dominant.* They believe that the left side usually exerts control over the right hemisphere. One well-known split-brain researcher, Michael Gazzaniga (1983), has argued that without help from the left side, the right side's mental skills would probably be "vastly inferior to the cognitive skills of a chimpanzee." He also believes that the left hemisphere is constantly trying to explain actions and emotions generated by brain parts whose workings are nonverbal and outside of awareness.

You can see in split-brain patients how the left brain concocts such explanations. In one classic example, a picture of a chicken claw was flashed to a patient's left hemisphere, a picture of a snow scene to his right. The task was to point to a related image for each picture from an array, with a chicken the correct choice for the claw and a shovel for the snow scene. The patient chose the shovel with his left hand and the chicken with his right. When asked to explain why, he responded (with his left hemisphere) that the chicken claw went with the chicken, and the shovel was for cleaning out the chicken shed. The left brain had seen the left hand's response but did not know about the snow scene, so it interpreted the response by using the information it did have (Gazzaniga, 1988).

Other researchers, including Sperry (1982), have rushed to the right hemisphere's defense. The right side, they point out, is no dummy. It is superior in problems requiring spatial-visual ability, the ability you use to read a map or follow a dress pattern, and it excels in facial recognition and the ability to read facial expressions. (Dr. P. and Emily D., described at the beginning of this chapter, both had damage in the right hemisphere.) It is active during the creation and appreciation of art and music. It recognizes nonverbal sounds, such as a dog's barking. The right brain also has some language ability. Typically, it can read a word briefly flashed to it and can understand an experimenter's instructions. In a few split-brain patients, language ability has been quite well developed. Research with other brain-damaged people finds that the right brain actually outperforms the left at understanding familiar idioms and metaphors, such as "turning over a new leaf" (Van Lancker & Kempler, 1987).

Some brain researchers have credited the right hemisphere with having a cognitive style that is intuitive and holistic, in which things are seen as wholes, in contrast to the left hemisphere's more rational and analytic mode. However, many researchers are concerned about popular interpretations of such conclusions. Books and programs that promise to "beef up your brain," they observe, tend to oversimplify and exaggerate hemispheric differences. Most studies find these differences to be relative, not absolute—a matter of degree. Moreover, the "intuitive, holistic" right hemisphere, which is often praised in popular writings, is not always a hero. For example, regions of the right hemisphere seem to be specialized for the processing of negative emotions such as fear, anger, and depression, whereas regions of the left hemisphere are specialized for positive emotions such as happiness (Davidson et al., 1990; Fox & Davidson, 1988). Most important, in most real-life activities, the two hemispheres cooperate naturally as partners, with each making a valuable contribution (Kinsbourne, 1982; Levy, 1985). As Sperry (1982) himself once noted, "The left–right dichotomy . . . is an idea with which it is very easy to run wild."

In Search of Memory

Earlier, we saw that when we remember something for the long term, synaptic pathways become more excitable. We also saw that although the hippocampus is involved in the *formation* of declarative memories, those memories are *stored* in the cortex. But where, precisely, is any given memory located in the brain? Is the memory in just one location, or is it divided into many locations? Which circuits contain information about your first date, your best friend's face, or how to use a computer?

Most neuroscientists believe that the neural changes associated with individual memories must be *localized,* confined to specific areas of the brain. One reason is that brain damage can have extremely specific effects on perception and memory, depending on exactly where the damage is. In one study, for example, two female stroke patients both had problems with verbs. One woman could read or speak verbs but had trouble writing them; the other could do only the reverse. The first woman had no trouble writing down the word *crack* after hearing the sentence "There's a crack in the mirror" (in which *crack* is a noun), but she could not write the word after hearing "Don't crack the nuts in here" (in which *crack* is a verb). The other woman could write *crack* as both a noun and a verb but couldn't speak it as a verb (Caramazza & Hillis, 1991). In another study (Cubelli, 1991), two brain-damaged patients were unable to write down the vowels in words but had no trouble writing the consonants. As we noted in Chapter 2, researchers have also studied patients who can recognize manufactured items, such as photographs, tools, or books, but not natural objects, or who can recognize most natural objects but cannot distinguish among different animals, or fruits, or vegetables (Damasio, 1990).

In part because of such findings, localization remains the guiding principle of modern brain theories. However, there is a minority view, which holds that perceived, learned, or remembered information is *distributed* across large areas of the brain (John et al., 1986; Pribram, 1971, 1982). One of the first to make this argument was Karl Lashley, who many years ago set out to find where specific memories were stored in the rat's brain. His search turned out to be as frustrating as looking for a grain of sugar in a pile of sand. Lashley trained rats to run a complicated maze in order to find food, then destroyed a part of each rat's cortex (without killing the rat). Destroying any section of the cortex led to some impairment in the rat's ability to find the food, though the size of the area damaged was more important than where the damage was located.

Yet even when Lashley removed more than 90 percent of a rat's visual cortex, the animal could still make its way through the maze. After a quarter century, Lashley (1950) finally gave up searching for specific memory traces. He jokingly remarked that perhaps "learning just is not possible." More seriously, he concluded that every part of the cortex must somehow influence every other part.

These two views—that memories are localized and that memories are distributed—can be reconciled by recognizing that the typical memory consists of many bits and pieces of information, often gathered from more than one sense: sounds, images, locations, facts. Lashley's rats probably used several types of cues, each stored in a different place in the brain and each capable of helping the rat find its way even when the rest of the cues were unavailable because parts of the cortex had been removed. Similarly, when you recall meeting a man yesterday, you remember his greeting, his tone of voice, how he looked, and where he was. Different collections of neurons in the brain probably handle these pieces of information; many such collections, distributed across wide areas of the brain, participate in representing the entire event (Squire, 1987). The role of the hippocampus and adjacent structures may be to somehow "bind together" the diverse aspects of a memory at the time it is formed, so that even though these aspects are stored in separate cortical sites, the memory can be retrieved as one coherent entity (Squire & Zola-Morgan, 1991).

With each passing month, there are new discoveries about the circuits that are active during specific activities, thoughts, and memories. Each new finding nudges the neuroscientist's dream of describing behavior in physical terms a bit closer to reality. However, many mysteries remain. There is still much to be discovered about how the brain stores information, how distributed circuits link up with one another, and how a student is able to locate and retrieve information at the drop of a multiple-choice question.

What Do You Know?

1. Keeping in mind that both sides of the brain are involved in most activities, see whether you can identify which of the following is most closely associated with the left hemisphere: (a) enjoying a musical recording, (b) wiggling the left big toe, (c) giving a speech in class, (d) balancing a checkbook, (e) recognizing a long-lost friend

2. Modern research on the location of memories suggests that the information in a memory is both _____ and _____.

3. Over the past two decades, thousands of people have taken courses and bought tapes that promise to turn them into right-brained types. What characteristics of human thought might explain the eagerness of some people to glorify "right-brainedness" and disparage "left-brainedness" (or vice versa)?

Answers:

1. c, d   2. localized, distributed   3. One possible answer: Human beings like to make sense of the world, and one easy way to do that is to divide humanity into opposing categories. This kind of either–or thinking can lead to the conclusion that "fixing up" one of the categories (e.g., making left-brain types more right-brained) will make individuals happier and the world a better place. If only it were that simple!

THE BIOLOGY OF SLEEP AND DREAMS

Let us see now how biological psychologists draw on findings about the brain and nervous system to investigate a mystery that has always fascinated human beings: the puzzling nature of sleep and dreams.

Earlier, we saw that many bodily processes wax and wane in a predictable way. Perhaps the most perplexing of these biological rhythms is the one governing sleep and wakefulness. Human beings and most animals curl up and go to sleep at least once every 24 hours. The reason remains something of a puzzle. After all, sleeping puts an organism at risk: Muscles that are usually ready to respond to danger relax, and senses grow dull. As the late British psychologist Christopher Evans (1984) noted, "The behavior patterns involved in sleep are glaringly, almost insanely, at odds with common sense." Then why is sleep such a profound necessity?

Why We Sleep

One likely function of sleep is to provide a "time out" period, so that the body can restore depleted reserves of energy, eliminate waste products from muscles, repair cells, strengthen the immune system, or recover physical abilities lost during the day. The idea that sleep is for physical rest and recuperation accords with the undeniable fact that at the end of the day we feel tired and crave sleep. Though most people can function fairly normally after a day or two of sleeplessness, sleep deprivation that lasts for four days or longer is quite uncomfortable. In animals, forced sleeplessness leads to infections and eventually death (Rechtschaffen et al., 1983), and the same may be true for people. There is a case on record of a man who, at the age of 52, abruptly began to lose sleep. After sinking deeper and deeper into an exhausted stupor, he developed a lung infection and died. An autopsy showed he had lost almost all of the large neurons in two areas of the thalamus that have been linked to sleep and hormonal circadian rhythms (Lugaresi et al., 1986).

Nonetheless, when people go many days without any sleep, they do not then require an equal period of time to catch up; one night's rest usually eliminates all symptoms of fatigue (Dement, 1978). Moreover, the amount of time we sleep does not necessarily correspond to how active we have been; even after a relaxing day on the beach, we usually go to sleep at night as quickly as usual. For these reasons, simple rest or energy restoration cannot be the sole purpose of sleep.

Many researchers believe that sleep must have as much to do with brain function as with bodily restoration. Even though most people still function pretty well after losing a single night's sleep, mental flexibility, originality, and other aspects of creative thinking may suffer (Horne, 1988). Chronic sleepiness can impair performance on tasks requiring vigilance or divided attention, and it can lead to automotive and industrial accidents (Dement, 1992; Roehrs et al., 1990). Laboratory studies and observations of people participating in "wake-athons" have shown that after several days of sleep loss, people become irritable and begin to have hallucinations and delusions (Dement, 1978; Luce & Segal, 1966).

The brain, then, needs periodic rest. Researchers are trying to find out how sleep may contribute to the regulation of brain metabolism, the maintenance of normal nerve-cell activity, and the replenishment of neurotransmitters. It is clear, however, that during sleep, the brain is not simply resting. On the contrary, most of the brain remains quite active, as we are about to see.

The Realms of Sleep

Until the early 1950s, little was known about sleep. Then a breakthrough occurred in the laboratory of physiologist Nathaniel Kleitman, who at the time was the only person in the world who had spent an entire career studying sleep. Kleitman had given one of his graduate students, Eugene Aserinsky, the tedious task of finding out if the slow, rolling eye movements that characterize the onset of sleep continue throughout the night. To both men's surprise, eye movements did indeed occur, but they were rapid, not slow (Aserinsky & Kleitman, 1955). Using the electroencephalograph to measure the brain's electrical activity, these researchers, along with another of Kleitman's students, William Dement, were able to correlate the rapid eye movements of sleepers with changes in the sleepers' brain-wave patterns (Dement, 1992). Adult volunteers were soon spending their nights sleeping in laboratories while scientists observed them and measured changes in their brain activity, muscle tension, breathing, and other physiological responses.

As a result of this research, today we know that sleep is not an unbroken state of rest. In adults, periods of **rapid eye movement (REM)** alternate with periods of fewer eye movements, or *non-REM* (NREM), in a cycle that recurs, on the average, every 90 minutes or so. The REM periods last from a few minutes to as long as an hour, averaging about 20 minutes in length. Whenever they begin, the pattern of electrical activity from the sleeper's brain changes to resemble that of alert wakefulness. Non-REM periods are themselves divided into shorter, distinct stages, each one associated with a particular brain-wave pattern (see Figure 4.14).

When you first climb into bed, close your eyes, and relax, your brain emits bursts of **alpha waves.** On an EEG recording, alpha waves have a regular rhythm, high amplitude (height), and a low frequency of 8 to 12 cycles per second. Alpha activity is associated with relaxing or not concentrating on anything in particular. Gradually, these waves slow down even further, and you drift into the Land of Nod, passing through four stages, each deeper than the previous one.

---

rapid eye movement (REM) sleep Sleep periods characterized by eye movements, loss of muscle tone, and dreaming.
alpha waves Relatively large, slow brain waves characteristic of relaxed wakefulness.

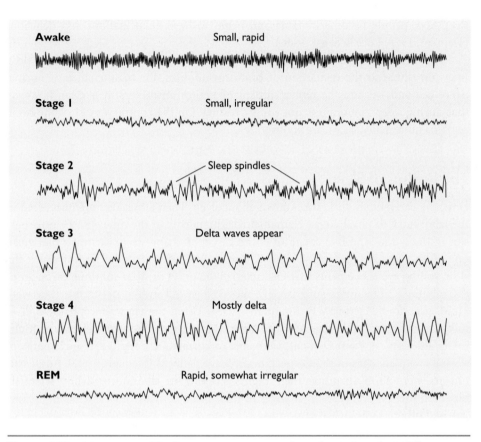

Figure 4.14 *Most types of brain waves are present throughout sleep, but different ones predominate at different stages.*

1. **STAGE 1.** Your brain waves become small and irregular, indicating activity with low voltage and mixed frequencies. You feel yourself drifting on the edge of consciousness, in a state of light sleep. If awakened, you may recall fantasies or a few visual images.
2. **STAGE 2.** Your brain emits occasional short bursts of rapid, high-peaking waves called *sleep spindles.* Minor noises probably won't disturb you.
3. **STAGE 3.** In addition to the waves characteristic of Stage 2, your brain occasionally emits very slow waves of about 1 to 3 cycles per second, with very high peaks. These **delta waves** are a sure sign that you will be hard to arouse. Your breathing and pulse have slowed down, your temperature has dropped, and your muscles are relaxed.

---

delta waves Slow, regular brain waves characteristic of Stage 3 and Stage 4 sleep.

4. **STAGE 4.** Delta waves have now largely taken over, and you are in deep sleep. It will probably take vigorous shaking or a loud noise to awaken you, and you won't be very happy about it. Oddly enough, though, if you talk or walk in your sleep, this is when you are likely to do so.

This sequence of four stages takes about 30 to 45 minutes. Then it reverses, and you move back up the ladder from Stage 4 to 3 to 2 to 1. At that point, about 70 to 90 minutes after the onset of sleep, something peculiar happens. Stage 1 does not turn into drowsy wakefulness, as you might expect. Instead, your brain begins to emit long bursts of very rapid, somewhat irregular waves, similar to those produced during Stage 1. Your heart rate increases, your blood pressure rises, and your breathing becomes faster and more irregular. There may be small twitches in the face and fingers. In men, the penis becomes somewhat erect, as vascular tissue relaxes and blood fills the genital area faster than it exits. In women, the clitoris enlarges, and vaginal lubrication increases. At the same time, most of your skeletal muscles go as limp as a rag doll, preventing your aroused brain from producing physical movement. Though you are supposedly in a "light" stage of sleep, you may be hard to awaken. You have entered the realm of REM.

Because the brain is extremely active while the body is almost devoid of muscle tone, REM sleep has also been called "paradoxical sleep." It is during these periods that you are most likely to dream (Aserinsky & Kleitman, 1955; Dement, 1955). Even people who claim they never dream at all will report dreams if awakened in a sleep laboratory during REM sleep. Dreaming is also sometimes reported during non-REM sleep, but less often, and the images are less vivid and more realistic than those reported during REM sleep.

The study of REM has opened a window on the world of dreams. We now know, for example, that dreams do not take place in an instant, as people used to think, but in "real time." When volunteers are awakened five minutes after REM starts, they report shorter dreams than when they are awakened after 15 minutes (Dement & Kleitman, 1957). If you dream that you are singing all the verses to "A Hundred Bottles of Beer on the Wall," your dream will probably last as long as it would take you to sing the song. Most dreams take several minutes, and some last much longer.

REM and non-REM sleep continue to alternate throughout the night, with the REM periods tending to get longer and closer together as the hours pass. An early REM period may last only a few minutes, whereas a later one may go on for 20 or 30 minutes and sometimes for as long as an hour—which is why people are likely to be dreaming when the alarm goes off in the morning. In the later part of sleep, Stages 3 and 4 become very short or disappear. But the cycles are far from regular. An individual may bounce directly from Stage 4 back to Stage 2, or go from REM to Stage 2 and then back to REM. Also, the time between REM and non-REM is highly variable, differing from person to person and also within any given individual.

The purpose of REM sleep is still a matter of debate, but clearly it does have a purpose. If you wake people every time they lapse into REM sleep, nothing dramatic will happen. When finally allowed to sleep normally, however, they will spend a much longer time than usual in the REM phase. Electrical brain activity associated with REM may burst through into quiet sleep and even into wakefulness. The subjects seem to be making up for something they were deprived of. Many people think that in adults, at least, this "something" has to do with dreaming.

The Dreaming Brain

When adults are in REM sleep, their eyes seem to track dream images, actions, and events (J. H. Herman, 1992; Schatzman, Worsley, & Fenwick, 1988). But why do these dream images arise? Why doesn't the brain just *rest*, switching off all thoughts and images and launching us into a coma? Why, instead, do we spend our nights flying through the air, battling monsters, or flirting with an old flame in the fantasy world of our dreams?

Most theories of dreaming have been psychological. They propose, for example, that we dream to gratify unconscious wishes and longings, often sexual (Freud, 1900/1953), or to deal with the ongoing emotional preoccupations of waking life, such as concerns over relationships, work, sex, or health (Webb & Cartwright, 1978). But some theories put the emphasis instead on brain physiology. One, the **activation–synthesis theory,** was first proposed by Allan Hobson and Robert McCarley (1977) and later elaborated by Hobson (1988, 1990). According to this theory, dreams are not, in Shakespeare's words, "children of an idle brain." Rather, they are the result of neurons firing spontaneously in the lower part of the brain, in the pons. These neurons control eye movement, gaze, balance, and posture, and they send messages to areas of the cerebral cortex responsible during wakefulness for visual processing and voluntary action. Such sleeptime signals have no psychological meaning in themselves, but the cortex tries to make sense of them by *synthesizing* (combining) them with existing knowledge and memories to produce some sort of coherent interpretation—just as it would if the signals had come from sense organs during wakefulness.

Thus, according to the activation–synthesis theory, when neurons fire in the part of the brain that handles balance, the cortex may generate a dream about falling. When signals occur that would ordinarily produce running, the cortex may manufacture a dream about being chased. Because the signals themselves lack coherence, the interpretation—the dream—is also likely to be incoherent and confusing. And because cortical neurons that control storage of new memories are turned off during sleep (because certain neurotransmitter levels are low), we typically forget our dreams upon waking unless we write them down or immediately recount them to someone else.

Hobson (1988) explains why REM sleep and dreaming do not occur continuously through the night. Giant cells in the reticular activating system of the pons, cells that are sensitive to the neurotransmitter acetylcholine, appear to initiate REM sleep. They then proceed to fire in unrestrained bursts, like a machine gun. Eventually, however, the gun's magazine is emptied, and other neurons, which inhibit REM sleep, take over. "If synapses are like cartridges," writes Hobson, "it may be that is why REM sleep ends; no more synaptic ammunition." Only when the neurons "reload" can firing, and REM

---

activation–synthesis theory The theory that dreaming results from the cortical synthesis and interpretation of neural signals triggered by activity in the lower part of the brain.

sleep, resume. In support of this hypothesis, Hobson notes that when sleeping volunteers are injected with drugs that enhance the action of acetylcholine, REM sleep and dreaming increase. Conversely, when volunteers are injected with a drug that blocks the effects of acetylcholine, REM sleep and dreaming decrease (Gillin et al., 1985).

Wishes, according to Hobson, do not cause dreams; brain-stem mechanisms do. But that doesn't mean that dreams are meaningless. According to Hobson (1988), the brain "is so inexorably bent upon the quest for meaning that it attributes and even creates meaning when there is little or none to be found in the data it is asked to process." By studying these attributed meanings, you can learn about your unique perceptions, conflicts, and concerns—not by trying to dig below the surface of the dream, as Freud would, but by examining the surface itself. Or you can relax and enjoy the nightly entertainment that dreams provide.

The activation–synthesis model has its critics. In a review of findings on dreams and sleep, John Antrobus (1991) concluded that contrary to most theories, including Hobson's, dreaming is really just a modification of what goes on when we are awake. The difference is that during sleep, we are cut off from sensory input and feedback from our own movements; the only input to the processing areas of the brain is their own output. It is this restricted input, argues Antrobus, that accounts for the bizarre imagery in dreams. Antrobus cites research in his laboratory suggesting that mental activity during wakefulness would be much like that during dreaming—with the same hallucinatory quality—if the person could be totally cut off from all external stimulation. Older studies have found the same thing (Heron, 1957), and outside the laboratory, some people have reported mild hallucinations while relaxing in saltwater "flotation tanks."

Advocates of purely psychological explanations of dreams have not conceded defeat. We all know from experience that not all dreams are alike: Some clearly address daily problems, some are "anxiety dreams" that occur when we are tense and worried, some are nebulous and incoherent. Perhaps it will turn out that different kinds of dreams have different purposes and origins. Much remains to be learned about the purpose of dreaming and even of sleep itself.

WHAT DO YOU KNOW?

A. Match each term with the appropriate phrase:

1. REM periods   a. delta waves and talking in one's sleep
2. alpha   b. irregular brain waves and light sleep
3. Stage 4 sleep   c. relaxed but awake
4. Stage 1 sleep   d. active brain, inactive muscles

B. According to the activation–synthesis theory, dreams arise because of signals initiated in the _____ of the brain, and these signals are then synthesized with existing knowledge by the _____ to produce an interpretation.

ANSWERS:

A.1.d 2.c 3.a 4.b B. pons, cerebral cortex

THE OLDEST QUESTION

When we think about the remarkable blob of tissue in our heads that allows us to remember, to dream, and to think—the blob that can make our existence a hideous nightmare when it is diseased—we are led, inevitably, to the oldest question of all: Where, exactly, is the mind?

When you say, "I am feeling unhappy," your amygdala, your serotonin receptors, your endorphins, and all sorts of other brain parts and processes are active, but who, exactly, is the "I" doing the feeling? When you say, "I've decided to have a hot dog instead of a hamburger," who is the "I" doing the choosing? When you say, "My mind is playing tricks on me," who is the "me" watching your mind play those tricks, and who is it that's being tricked? How can the self observe itself? Isn't that a little like a finger pointing at its own tip?

Most modern brain scientists, with some notable exceptions, consider mind to be a matter of matter. Although they may have personal religious convictions about a soul, most assume that "mind" or "self-awareness" can be explained in physical terms as a product of the activities of the cerebral cortex. They regard the brain as a fabulous, exceedingly complex machine that will one day be understood in terms of its parts, without reference to some invisible manager pulling the levers; in the words of the British philosopher Gilbert Ryle (1949), there is no "ghost in the machine." If that is so, then it makes no sense, really, to say "I have a brain" or "We think with our brains" or "Boy, she's really using her brain"—although we all use such everyday constructions— because we *are* our brains! There's no one else in there.

Some scientists believe that the sense of self is merely a reflection, a kind of by-product, of some sort of overall control mechanism in the brain. Many others, however, think there is no such mechanism. Neurologist Richard Restak (1983, 1994) has noted that many of our actions and choices seem to occur without direction by a conscious self. He concludes that "There is not a center in the brain involved in the exercise of will any more than there is a center in the brain of the swan responsible for the beauty and complexity of its flight. Rather, the brains of all creatures are probably organized along the lines of multiple centers and various levels." Likewise, brain researcher Michael Gazzaniga (1985) has proposed that the brain is organized as a loose confederation of independent "modules," or mental systems, all working in parallel. The sense of a unified self or consciousness is an illusion; it occurs because the one verbal module, an "interpreter" (usually in the left hemisphere), is constantly coming up with theories to explain the actions, moods, and thoughts of the others.

Such views come close to those of Eastern spiritual traditions. Buddhism, for example, teaches that the "self" is not a unified "thing" but rather a collection of thoughts, perceptions, concepts, and feelings that shift and change from moment to moment. In this view, the unity and the permanence of the self are a mirage. Such notions are contrary, of course, to what most people in the West, including psychologists, have always assumed about their "selves."

We are not about to settle here a question that has plagued philosophers for thousands of years. Inevitably, though, as we think about the brain, we must think about how the brain can think about itself. What do you think about the existence and location of your "self" . . . and who, by the way, is doing the thinking?

♦ ♦ ♦

Summary

1. The brain is the origin of consciousness, perception, memory, emotion, and reasoning. People debate what language to use in describing the brain, and where the "you" is that is "using" your brain.

2. The function of the nervous system is to gather and process information, produce responses to stimuli, and coordinate the workings of different cells. Scientists divide it into the *central nervous system (CNS)* and the *peripheral nervous system (PNS)*. The CNS, which includes the brain and spinal cord, receives, processes, interprets, and stores incoming sensory information and sends messages destined for muscles, glands, and organs. The PNS transmits information to and from the CNS by way of sensory and motor nerves.

3. The peripheral nervous system is made up of the *somatic nervous system,* which permits sensation and voluntary action; and the *autonomic nervous system,* which regulates the functioning of blood vessels, glands, and internal (visceral) organs. Some people can learn to heighten or suppress autonomic responses intentionally, using *biofeedback* techniques, but it is unclear whether this control is direct or indirect.

4. The autonomic nervous system is divided into the *sympathetic nervous system,* which mobilizes the body for action, and the *parasympathetic nervous system,* which conserves energy.

5. *Neurons,* supported by *glial cells,* are the basic units of the nervous system. Each neuron consists of *dendrites,* a *cell body,* and an *axon.* In the peripheral nervous system, axons (and sometimes dendrites) are collected together in bundles called *nerves.* Many axons are insulated by a *myelin sheath* that speeds up the conduction of neural impulses and prevents signals in adjacent cells from interfering with one another. Recent research has challenged the old assumption that neurons in the human central nervous system cannot be induced to regenerate or multiply.

6. Communication between two neurons occurs at the *synapse.* Many synapses have not yet formed at birth. During development, axons and dendrites continue to grow as a result of both physical maturation and experience with the world, and throughout life, new learning results in new synaptic connections in the brain. Long-term memory involves permanent structural changes in neurons and synapses and an increase in the strength of synaptic response called *long-term potentiation.* Thus, the brain's circuits are not fixed and immutable; they are continually changing in response to information, challenges, and changes in the environment.

7. When a wave of electrical voltage (action potential) reaches the end of a transmitting axon, *neurotransmitter* molecules are released into the *synaptic cleft.* When these molecules bind to *receptor sites* on the receiving neuron, that neuron becomes either more or less likely to fire. The message that reaches a final destina-

tion depends on how frequently particular neurons are firing, how many are firing, what types are firing, and where they are located.

8. Through their effects on nerve circuits, neurotransmitters play a critical role in mood, memory, and psychological well-being. Deficits in neurotransmitters have been implicated in several disorders, including Alzheimer's disease and Parkinson's disease.

9. *Endorphins,* which act primarily as *neuromodulators* that affect the actions of neurotransmitters, reduce pain and promote pleasure. Endorphin levels seem to shoot up when an animal or person is either afraid or under stress. Endorphins may also be linked to the pleasures of social contact.

10. *Hormone* levels affect, and are affected by, the nervous system. Psychologists are especially interested in the *adrenal hormones,* which are involved in emotion and stress, and which appear to enhance memory at moderate levels; *melatonin,* which appears to regulate certain biological rhythms, including the sleep–wake cycle; and the *sex hormones,* which are involved in the physical changes of puberty, the menstrual cycle (estrogen), and sexual arousal (testosterone).

11. Researchers study the brain by observing patients with brain damage; by using the *lesion method* with animals; and by using such techniques as electroencephalograms (*EEGs*), positron-emission tomography (*PET scans*), and magnetic resonance imaging (*MRI*).

12. The more reflexive or automatic a behavior is, the more likely it is to be controlled by the lower areas of the brain. The *brain stem* controls automatic functions such as heartbeat and breathing; the *reticular activating system (RAS)* screens incoming information and is responsible for alertness. The *cerebellum* contributes to balance and muscle coordination, and to the learning and storage of some skills and simple responses. The *thalamus* directs sensory messages to appropriate higher centers in the brain. The *hypothalamus* is involved in emotion and in drives associated with survival, controls the complex operations of the autonomic nervous system, and sends to the *pituitary gland* chemicals that tell it when to "talk" to other endocrine glands.

13. The *limbic system* is involved in emotions that we share with other animals, and it contains pathways involved in pleasure. Within this system, the *amygdala* appears to be responsible for evaluating sensory information and quickly determining its emotional importance, and also for the initial decision to approach or withdraw from a person or situation. The *hippocampus* has been called the "gateway to memory" because it plays a critical role in the formation of long-term *declarative memories.*

14. Much of the brain's circuitry is packed into the *cerebrum,* which is divided into two hemispheres and is covered by thin layers of densely packed cells known collectively as the *cerebral cortex.* The *occipital, parietal, temporal,* and *frontal lobes* of the cortex have specialized (but partially overlapping) functions. The *association cortex* appears to be responsible for higher mental processes. The frontal lobes, particularly areas in the *prefrontal cortex,* are involved in social judgment, the making and carrying out of plans, and decision making.

15. Studies of split-brain patients, who have had the *corpus callosum* cut, show that the two cerebral hemispheres have somewhat different talents. In most people, language is processed mainly in the left hemisphere, which generally is specialized for logical, symbolic, and sequential tasks. The right hemisphere is associated with spatial-visual tasks, facial recognition, and the creation and appreciation of art and music. Regions of the left hemisphere seem to be specialized for the processing of positive emotions and regions of the right hemisphere for negative emotions. However, in most mental activities, the two hemispheres cooperate, with each making a valuable contribution.

16. Most scientists believe that the neural changes associated with specific memories are *localized,* but another view holds that the information is *distributed* across large areas of the cerebral cortex. These two views can be reconciled by recognizing that the typical memory consists of many pieces of information, which may be stored at separate sites, with all the sites participating in the representation of an object or event.

17. Biological research offers insights into sleeping and dreaming. Sleep seems necessary not only for bodily restoration but also for normal brain function. During sleep, periods of *rapid eye movement,* or *REM,* alternate with non-REM periods. Non-REM sleep is divided into four stages associated with characteristic brain-wave patterns. During REM sleep, the brain is active, and there are other signs of arousal, yet most of the skeletal muscles are limp. Dreams are reported most often during REM sleep.

18. The *activation–synthesis theory* of dreaming holds that dreams occur when the cerebral cortex tries to make sense of spontaneous neural firing initiated in the pons. The resulting interpretation is a dream. In this view, dreams do not disguise unconscious wishes, but they can reveal a person's conflicts and concerns. Alternative theories that emphasize brain physiology have also been proposed.

19. Most modern brain scientists assume that "mind" or self-awareness can be explained in physical terms as a product of the activities of the cerebral cortex. Many believe that the brain is a loose confederation of independent modules working in parallel, and that the sense of a unified self is an illusion. The biological perspective raises the oldest question: Where, exactly, is the self?

Key Terms

neuropsychology *126*

central nervous system *127*

peripheral nervous system *127*

sensory nerves *127*

motor nerves *127*

somatic nervous system *128*

autonomic nervous system *129*

biofeedback *129*

sympathetic nervous system *129*

parasympathetic nervous system *129*

neurons *130*

glial cells *130*

dendrites *131*

cell body *131*

axon *131*

axon terminals *132*

nerves *132*

myelin sheath *133*

synaptic cleft *134*

synapse *134*

spines *135*

long-term potentiation *135*

plasticity *135*

action potential *136*

synaptic end bulb *136*

synaptic vesicles *136*

neurotransmitter *136*

receptor sites *136*

excitatory and inhibitory effects *136*

serotonin *138*

dopamine *138*

acetylcholine *138*

norepinephrine *138*

GABA *138*

glutamate *138*

endorphins *139*

neuromodulators *139*

hormones *140*

endocrine glands *140*

neuroendocrine system *140*

adrenal hormones (cortisol, epinephrine, norepinephrine) *141*

adrenal cortex and medulla *141*

melatonin *142*

pineal body *142*

biological rhythm *142*

circadian rhythm *143*

sex hormones (androgens, estrogens, progesterone) *143*

lesion method *145*

electrodes *145*

electroencephalogram (EEG) *145*

evoked potentials *145*

PET scan (positron-emission tomography) *146*

MRI (magnetic resonance imaging) *146*

brain stem *147*

medulla *147*

pons *147*

reticular activating system (RAS) *147*

cerebellum *148*

thalamus *149*

olfactory bulb *149*

hypothalamus *149*

pituitary gland *149*

limbic system *149*

amygdala *150*

hippocampus *151*

declarative memories *151*

cerebrum *152*

cerebral hemispheres *152*

corpus callosum *152*

lateralization *152*

cerebral cortex *152*

occipital lobes *153*

visual cortex *153*

parietal lobes *153*

somatosensory cortex *153*

temporal lobes *153*

auditory cortex *153*

frontal lobes *153*

motor cortex *153*

association cortex *154*

prefrontal cortex *154*

split-brain studies *156*

Broca's area *156*

Wernicke's area *156*

localized versus distributed processing *160*

rapid eye movement (REM) sleep *163*

non-REM sleep *163*

alpha waves *163*

delta waves *164*

activation–synthesis theory *166*

CHAPTER 5
Evaluating the Biological Perspective

*T*hirty years ago, biological psychology was still in its infancy. Endorphins were unknown, and neurotransmitters were just being discovered. There were no PET scans or MRIs to help scientists peer into the brain. Dementia in the elderly was an enigma. People suffering from brain disorders were often misdiagnosed as having psychological problems. The idea of identifying every single human gene would have been ridiculed as science fiction.

No longer. In only a few decades, understanding of the nervous system and brain chemistry has expanded astronomically; more has probably been learned about the brain in the past 20 years than in the past 200 years. The biological perspective is giving psychologists a new appreciation for the impact of physiology on temperaments, abilities, mental disorders, emotions, and many other aspects of human psychology. Sometimes, as in the study of body weight or autism, biological theories are making purely psychological theories passé. And every month sees new discoveries in genetic research. An international collaboration of researchers is now rushing to map the entire human genome—all 3 billion units of DNA—and some optimistic scientists expect success within only a few years.

CONTRIBUTIONS OF THIS PERSPECTIVE

As biological findings have accumulated, psychology has been moving closer to the life sciences in general, and to biology and neuroscience in particular. Here are a few of the biological perspective's major contributions to psychological science:

1 **REJECTION OF EXTREME ENVIRONMENTALISM.** For three decades following World War II, the prevailing doctrine in psychology was that culture and environment are the primary if not the sole determinants of personality, intelligence, and behavior. This extreme environmentalism was probably influenced by three interlocking factors: the popularity of behaviorism (see Chapter 6), the Western belief in equality and the perfectibility of human nature, and the historical association of biological explanations with racism.

Earlier in the century, eugenicists in Europe and North America had argued that government should help improve humanity by discouraging births among the lower socioeconomic classes and others presumed to have genetically inferior traits. Some within the eugenics movement called for the forced sterilization of people with low IQs and for strict limits on immigration. They were inspired by *Social Darwinism,* the theory that the prevailing social order reflects the "survival of the fittest" (the phrase was coined by the English political philosopher Herbert Spencer in the 1840s). These ideas were taken to their extreme during the 1930s and 1940s by the Nazis, who used them as a rationale for exterminating 12 million people in the Holocaust. When the extent of the Nazi atrocities became known, most scholars turned away in disgust from all biological explanations of human abilities and behavior.

But now the pendulum is swinging back. The findings of behavioral geneticists and neuroscientists are showing that we cannot hope to understand human personality and performance without taking the brain, the body, and genes into account. The biological perspective further reminds us that in spite of our intricate neural wiring and our spectacular mental achievements, human beings have much in common with other species. Like other animals, we are constrained by our evolutionary past: It's easier for us to learn a fear of spiders, snakes, or heights than a fear of butterflies, flowers, or toasters, no doubt because during human evolution the former objects presented a danger.

2 AN APPRECIATION FOR THE ROLE OF PHYSICAL HEALTH IN PSYCHOLOGICAL FUNCTIONING. The biological perspective teaches us that our bodies and brains need proper care and maintenance to work properly; we interfere with the fine calibration of our biological systems at our peril. Lack of exercise, irregular sleep habits, or work shifts that interfere with normal biological rhythms can all affect how we function mentally and emotionally. Conversely, good health habits tone the mind as well as the body. Aerobic exercise, for example, is associated with a decrease in physiological arousal to stress (Brown, 1991). In a study of preschoolers, children who did aerobic exercises daily for eight weeks not only had better cardiovascular fitness and agility than children who spent the same time in free play, but also had higher self-esteem (Alpert et al., 1990). Many studies have shown that exercise alleviates anxiety and depression (Taylor, 1995), and may even boost mental functioning.

Ordinary foods can also affect mood and alertness because certain nutrients are the precursors for neurotransmitters (Wurtman, 1982). For example, tyrosine, an amino acid found in protein-rich foods such as dairy products and meat, is a precursor of norepinephrine, epinephrine, and dopamine; and choline, a component of the lecithin found in egg yolks, soy products, and liver, is a precursor of acetylcholine. Because mental functioning and mood involve many different neurotransmitters, restrictive fad diets—the ones that eliminate all protein, or all carbohydrates, or all whatever—are probably a bad idea both in physiological and psychological terms. So is reliance on whatever health food or wonder drug is being promoted at the moment (the latest example being melatonin, the long-term risks of which are unknown). The best "brain food" and probably the best "mood food," too, is a well-balanced diet—the sort of diet that many children do not get because of poor eating habits or poverty and neglect.

Similarly, environmental toxins can affect mental abilities. One longitudinal study showed that exposure to high levels of lead in early childhood is associated later on, in adolescence, with low vocabulary and grammatical-reasoning scores, slow reaction times, poor hand–eye coordination, and low reading scores, even after other possible factors are taken into account (Needleman et al., 1990). And a recent study of boys ages 7 to 11 found that high lead concentrations in the bones of some of the boys was associated with attention problems and with aggression and delinquency; these links remained even after the researchers took into account the mothers' IQs, occupations, schooling, and child-rearing practices (Needleman et al., 1996). Such findings are disheartening because, although house paint no longer contains lead, poor children often live in run-down buildings with old, peeling, lead-based paint. Here is a case where biological findings can illuminate a major social issue—the effects of poverty on a nation's level of intelligence and the incidence of behavior problems.

3 NEW INSIGHTS INTO BIOLOGICAL CONTRIBUTIONS TO MENTAL AND EMOTIONAL DISORDERS. Because of advances in biology and biological psychology, it is now clear that many disorders once considered to be purely psychological or the normal result of aging in fact involve genetic, neurological, or biochemical abnormalities. For example, senility used to be regarded as an inevitable part of growing old. Now scientists realize that it results from various diseases, such as Alzheimer's. The brains of Alzheimer's patients contain abnormal deposits of beta-amyloid, a protein that, in certain forms, appears to be toxic to nerve cells or to activate other toxic compounds. Some scientists think that these deposits cause the brain degeneration in Alzheimer's patients (although a number of other proteins may also be accomplices or major causes; see Pennisi, 1994).

Several genes have been implicated in Alzheimer's. Recently, researchers used the linkage method to identify one of these genes, on chromosome 14. When mutated, this gene may cause up to 80 percent of early-onset familial (inherited) Alzheimer's cases (Sherrington et al., 1995). (This form of the disease, which can strike as early as age 40, accounts for about 10 percent of all Alzheimer's cases.) Interestingly, the normal version of the gene produces a protein that could play a role in the production of beta-amyloid. Another recently discovered gene, on chromosome 1, may account for most of the remaining early-onset familial Alzheimer's cases; it is closely related to the gene on chromosome 14 (Levy-Lahad et al., 1995a, 1995b). Still another gene, on chromosome 19, seems to increase the risk of late-onset Alzheimer's (Corder et al., 1993). Further research on the functions of these genes will greatly help researchers in their efforts to understand and cure this terrible illness.

Advances in biological psychology have been so dazzling that it is easy to get carried away by them. Soon, we think, we'll know the genes for everything from TV watching to math genius! Soon we'll have a drug to fix any part of our personalities we want to change! Soon we'll know just which part of the brain makes some people violent! But hold on; before we go galloping off on the biological highway, we need to consider some potholes that people often stumble into when interpreting and applying the message of this perspective.

MISUSES AND LIMITATIONS OF THIS PERSPECTIVE

In the two preceding chapters, we saw that most scientists emphasize the interaction of biology and the environment. Yet when considering the accomplishments of this perspective, people often fall victim to *biological reductionism,* the tendency to explain complex personal and social problems solely in terms of a few physiological mechanisms.

Reductionism of any kind distorts and limits our understanding of human behavior, and we will be discussing other forms of reductionism when we evaluate other perspectives. But in today's world, biological reductionism has a special appeal. One reason is that it promises quick fixes—a pill, a hormone injection, a brain tissue transplant—for what have seemed to be intractable problems. Another is that biological reductionism allows some individuals to feel free of responsibility for their actions. In England, a woman murdered her boyfriend—she rammed him into a utility pole with her car—and pleaded not guilty because she suffered from "premenstrual syndrome." (She was acquitted.) In San Antonio, Texas, a rapist tried to claim that he was not responsible for his crime because he had a high testosterone level. (He was convicted.) The idea that hormones can *cause* murder or rape in a simple, direct way—"It wasn't me; my hormones made me do it"—is an extreme example of biological reductionism. And these cases also show the profound legal issues it raises.

Biological reductionism leads to three common errors in the interpretation of biological findings:

1 **PREMATURE CONCLUSIONS.** Science is a slow, painstaking process, but sudden dramatic breakthroughs make better headlines. As a result, the media often overstate biological findings or leap to conclusions on the basis of only one or two studies. And the public, eager for quick answers, follows suit.

For example, studies of twins and adopted children suggest that there may be a genetic component in **bipolar disorder** ("manic depression"), a mood disorder involving alternating episodes of extreme depression and abnormal states of exhilaration. A decade ago, some researchers reported that a specific gene had been implicated, variously identified as a gene on the X chromosome or on chromosome 6 or 11 (Baron

---

bipolar disorder A mood disorder in which depression alternates with mania.

et al., 1987; Egeland et al., 1987). The findings quickly made headlines. However, subsequent research failed to find chromosome abnormalities in people with bipolar disorder (Faraone, Kremen, & Tsuang, 1990; Kelsoe et al., 1989). Apparently, the differences initially reported had been coincidental or unique to the people being studied. Efforts to pin down the genetic contribution to bipolar disorder are continuing at several research centers, but so far they have not been successful. As Nick Martin, an Australian behavioral geneticist, noted, "All those guys are starting to get depressed themselves" (quoted in Aldhouse, 1992).

The story has been the same with findings on biological factors in **schizophrenia,** a severe but mysterious disorder that causes hallucinations, delusions, extreme emotional abnormalities, speech that is full of incoherent word associations, grossly disorganized and inappropriate behavior, and, sometimes, withdrawal into an inner world. Almost everyone studying this disorder believes that schizophrenia is a brain disease of some sort. Some patients have abnormalities in neurotransmitters, especially dopamine; eye-movement abnormalities; decreased brain weight; reduced numbers of neurons in specific layers of the prefrontal cortex; a decrease in the volume of the temporal lobe or limbic regions; enlargement of the *ventricles,* the spaces in the brain that are filled with cerebrospinal fluid; or abnormalities in the thalamus, the brain's traffic-control center for incoming sensations (Andreasen et al., 1994; Heinrichs, 1993; Meltzer, 1987; Raz & Raz, 1990).

Some researchers have even found evidence that an infectious virus during prenatal development is the culprit (Bracha et al., 1991; Torrey et al., 1994). A longitudinal study that began decades ago found a significant association between exposure to influenza virus during the second trimester of gestation and adult schizophrenia 20 to 30 years later (Mednick, Huttunen, & Machón, 1994). Genes may also be involved; children have a greater risk of schizophrenia if an identical twin develops the disorder, if one parent has the disorder, and especially if both parents are schizophrenic—even if the child is reared apart from the affected relative (Gottesman, 1994). As we write this, geneticists are working to find the genes that may play a role.

Yet so far, no explanation of schizophrenia can account for all cases. One reason seems to be that the disease comes in many varieties (Heinrichs, 1993). Another is that several factors are probably involved, and that biological factors interact with environmental ones. We should not conclude that the biological influences on mental disorders will never be found. However, we do need to be cautious about interpreting the significance of any single study that makes the news and wait patiently for the many replications that will be needed to confirm or negate early findings.

The same moral applies to findings that seem to confirm common assumptions about "hot" issues, such as sex differences. In 1982, two anthropologists autopsied 14 human brains and reported an average sex difference in the size and shape of the

---

schizophrenia A mental disorder or group of disorders marked by some or all of these symptoms: delusions, hallucinations, disorganized and incoherent speech, severe emotional abnormalities, inappropriate behavior, and withdrawal into an inner world.

splenium, a small section at the end of the corpus callosum (the bundle of fibers dividing the two hemispheres) (de Lacoste-Utamsing & Holloway, 1982). The researchers concluded that "The female brain is less well lateralized—that is, manifests less hemispheric specialization—than the male brain" for certain functions, such as visual-spatial ability. In some quarters this news was received with as much excitement as if another Dead Sea Scroll had just been discovered. It quickly made its way into newspapers, magazines, and even textbooks as a verified sex difference.

Now that more than a decade of research has passed, however, the picture is different. Neuroscientist William Byne (1993), in a review of the available studies, found that only the 1982 study reported the splenium to be larger in women. Two very early studies (in 1906 and 1909) found that it was larger in men, and 21 later studies found no sex differences at all. Findings on the shape of the splenium are also mixed: Four studies find the splenium to be more bulb-shaped in women; one study finds it to be more bulbous in men; and six studies find no sex difference.

Recently, Sandra Witelson and her colleagues, who studied nine brains from autopsied bodies, reported that the women had an average of 11 percent more cells in areas of the cortex associated with the processing of auditory information; all of the women had more of these cells than any of the men (Witelson, Glazer, & Kigar, 1994). Other researchers are using high-tech methods to search for average sex differences in the brain areas that are active when people work on a particular task. In one study, 19 men and 19 women were asked to say whether pairs of nonsense words rhymed; MRI scans showed that in both sexes, an area at the front of the left hemisphere was activated. But in 11 of the women and none of the men, the corresponding area in the right hemisphere was also active (Shaywitz et al., 1995). At present, however, no one knows what such differences might mean, or how they might be related to general abilities. (In the MRI study, there was no difference in how women and men actually performed on the rhyme-judgment task.) Speculations are as plentiful as ants at a picnic, but at present they remain just that—speculations (Hoptman & Davidson, 1994).

While it is important, therefore, to keep an open mind about new biological findings, it is also important to keep a cautious attitude about how such findings might be exaggerated or misused.

2 UNWARRANTED INFERENCES ABOUT CAUSE AND EFFECT. Although the brain affects how we experience the world, we must never forget that experience also shapes and alters the brain. Whenever people evaluate findings from biological psychology, especially correlational findings, they need to ask: In this case, is biology influencing behavior, or is it the other way around? Or both?

Often, experience alters biology. For example, early social deprivation or trauma in monkeys, and probably in humans, too, can create neurotransmitter abnormalities (Kraemer et al., 1984; Kramer, 1993). And dozens of animal studies show that a stimulating environment can actually change the structure of the brain in a beneficial way. Rats that learn complicated tasks or that grow up playing with lots of challenging rat toys develop thicker and heavier cortexes and richer networks of synaptic connections in certain brain areas than do rats in unchallenging environments (Diamond, 1993;

Greenough & Anderson, 1991; Greenough & Black, 1992; Rosenzweig, 1984). These changes continue throughout life, as long as the animal is in an enriched environment.

Mental stimulation enhances the human brain as well, in children and adults. In a study called the Abecedarian Project, researchers found that inner-city children who got lots of mental enrichment, starting in infancy and lasting throughout childhood, had higher IQs by age 12 than did children in a control group (Campbell & Ramey, 1994, 1995). The increases were not trivial: They averaged 15 to 30 points.

There is also evidence that practice on specific tasks can make the brain more efficient. PET-scan studies show that during certain intellectual tasks, the brains of high performers are less active, metabolizing glucose at a lower rate than those of low performers (Haier et al., 1988; Parks et al., 1988). But is such a neurologically efficient brain the cause or the result of superior performance? The second interpretation is supported by a study in which people played a computer game over a period of several weeks. As the study progressed, their glucose metabolism rates during the sessions gradually fell (Haier et al., 1992).

This is amazing stuff, and it points to an exciting and wholly unexpected contribution of the biological perspective. Whereas many people assume that biology determines intelligence, this work suggests that the kinds of experiences and environments we have actually affect our brains, to our detriment or our advantage.

3 EXAGGERATING THE POWER OF GENES. When reading about genetic contributions to a behavior or a disorder, it is all too easy to assume that genes are *the* cause and the only cause. People make this mistake in part because of the language that researchers themselves sometimes use. As biologist Ruth Hubbard and writer Elijah Wald (1993) have observed, when scientists or journalists say that genes "control," "program," or "determine" behavior, or refer to genes "for" this or that trait, their words imply an inevitability that does not actually exist and obscure the interaction of biological and social processes. (We have made a concerted effort to avoid such deterministic language in this book.) Any complex behavior is bound to depend on many factors, as most genetics researchers are the first to recognize.

Consider the issue of sexual orientation. Many researchers are persuaded that sexual orientation has a genetic basis, and that certain brain areas, hormones, and neuroendocrine processes differ in homosexual and heterosexual men and women (Gladue, 1994). For example, women with a history of prenatal exposure to synthetic sex hormones are more likely than others to become bisexual or lesbian (Meyer-Bahlburg et al., 1995). Simon LeVay (1991) made headlines when he announced that he had found a difference in specific brain structures of homosexual and heterosexual men. Others have reported that sexual orientation is moderately heritable, both in men and in women (Bailey & Pillard, 1991; Bailey & Benishay, 1993; Bailey et al., 1993; Hershberger, Lykken, & McGue, 1995; Whitam, Diamond, & Martin, 1993). And in 1993 Dean Hamer and his associates caused a stir when they reported a genetic linkage study that found a shared stretch of DNA on the X chromosome in 33 of 40 pairs of gay brothers—a rate above what one would expect in siblings by chance. Two years later, another study by the same group got similar results (Hu et al., 1995).

These scientists are excited about such findings because efforts by psychologists from other perspectives to find the "origins" of homosexuality (or, for that matter, of heterosexuality) have failed.* Contrary to what psychoanalysts have claimed, having a homosexual orientation is unrelated to bad mothering, absent fathering, or individual psychopathology (Bell, Weinberg, & Hammersmith, 1981; Garnets & Kimmel, 1993). Contrary to what learning theorists have argued, it is unrelated to socialization practices or parental role models (Bailey et al., 1995; Patterson, 1992). And, although the *expression* of sexual orientation is affected by cultural norms and practices, having a homosexual or heterosexual orientation in the first place does not seem to be affected by culture, as sociocultural psychologists have learned. So it is understandable that many people now look to biology for answers.

However, as by now you might expect, in order to evaluate this sensitive and complex issue, it is necessary to keep a few things in mind. First, the studies claiming to find differences in the brain and evidence of heritability have important limitations. Dean Hamer's genetics studies, for example, were based on samples of gay brothers; but the majority of gays and lesbians do *not* have a close gay relative. This research is controversial and has yet to be replicated. A key problem in Simon LeVay's study was that all of the gay men in his sample had died of AIDS. AIDS itself, and also some of the medical treatments given for the disease, creates endocrine abnormalities that can affect brain structures. The differences LeVay observed, therefore, might have been a result of AIDS rather than a cause of sexual orientation (Byne, 1993).

Second, homosexuality and heterosexuality are not two opposite, mutually exclusive conditions; human sexual orientation is complicated and variable. Some people are exclusively gay, lesbian, or straight their whole lives, but others are not. Such evidence suggests that sexual orientation involves a complex interaction of biology, culture, experiences, and opportunities; and it also suggests that the route to sexual identity for one person may not be the same for another (Gladue, 1994; Patterson, 1995). As Dean Hamer told the *New York Times:* "Sexual orientation is too complex to be determined by a single gene. The main value of this work is that it opens a window into understanding how genes, the brain and the environment interact to mold human behavior" (July 16, 1993).

One reason it is so important to understand these errors of biological reductionism is that biological findings are often used for political purposes. No research is conducted in a social and moral vacuum, nor could it be. But biological findings, which have so much promise, also have great potential for being misinterpreted and abused

---

*It is worth noting that although same-sex sexual attraction seems to have existed throughout history in various forms, it was not considered a distinct medical or psychological entity to be studied and "explained" until the nineteenth century. The words *heterosexuality* and *homosexuality* were not even invented until then (Katz, 1995). Today, the question of whether gay or straight sexual identities are essentially, fundamentally different or whether sexual identity is socially and psychologically created by experience and culture is still being hotly debated (Baumrind, 1995).

(Fausto-Sterling, 1985; Gould, 1981; Hubbard & Wald, 1993). That is why they often generate such controversy.

For example, many gay men and lesbians themselves welcome the new biological research on sexual orientation, on the grounds that it supports what they have been saying all along: that sexual orientation is not a matter of choice, but a fact of nature. But people who are prejudiced against homosexuals regard the same research as evidence that gay people have a biological "defect" that should be eradicated or "cured." Other gay men and lesbians strongly oppose biological arguments and their implication of essential differences between gays and straights (Kitzinger & Wilkinson, 1995); but so do many antigay people, who argue that homosexuality is a "preference" or "choice" that can and should be "unchosen."

Similar controversy surrounds findings on a possible link between genes and criminal violence. A few years ago, Dutch researchers reported evidence, from one large family, for a possible "aggression gene," in particular a mutation in a recessive gene on the X chromosome associated with the enzyme monoamine oxidase-A, or MAOA. They argued that this enzyme, which assists in the breakdown of various neurotransmitters, is implicated in the violent behavior of at least some males (Brunner et al., 1993). In addition, behavioral-genetics research suggests a possible genetic contribution to impulsivity and other traits that could increase the risk of delinquency (Nigg & Goldsmith, 1994). Critics fear that such research will be used to foster racism, stigmatize poor people, and draw attention (and resources) away from the economic and environmental causes of despair, aggression, and crime. When the University of Maryland hosted a 1995 interdisciplinary conference on "The Meaning and Significance of Research on Genetics and Criminal Behavior," protesters disrupted the proceedings, even though the conference participants included critics as well as supporters of such research.

Biological researchers respond that knowledge is worth having for its own sake and that the potential for misusing knowledge is no justification for ignorance or censorship. In their view, a society bent on eliminating its enemies or suppressing some minority will use any information it can to justify its ends. Hitler chose "the ugly language of eugenics" to rationalize the Holocaust, says Michael Bailey (1993), but Joseph Stalin didn't choose "biological inferiority" as a reason to massacre millions; instead, he summoned the virtuous language of revolution.

A society's intentions, Bailey believes, affect what it makes of biological research. Evidence that homosexuality has a hereditary component, which his own research suggests, can be used to reduce homophobia and make discrimination against gay men and lesbians illegal; or it can be used as evidence of a biological "defect" to be corrected. Evidence that some extremely violent delinquents are brain damaged (perhaps as a result of parental blows to the head, drugs, or even a genetic mutation) can be used to prevent or treat this problem; or it can be used to screen and stigmatize children who are merely "potentially" aggressive. And genetic engineering, which is revolutionizing the biomedical world, can be used to eradicate horrendous diseases; or it can be used to eradicate perfectly normal human variations that some people regard as a social disadvantage, such as being shorter than average.

As you can see, the biological perspective raises many ethical, social, and practical concerns. We turn now to three controversial issues that illustrate the appeal of the biological perspective, the dangers of biological reductionism, and the problems of biological politics: "PMS," sociobiology, and drug treatments for mental disorders.

WHAT DO YOU KNOW?

1. Name three major contributions of the biological perspective.
2. Biological reductionism is (a) the tendency to minimize the importance of biology in human functioning, (b) the reduction of complicated biological findings to a few psychological principles, c) the reduction of complex social and personal issues to a few biological mechanisms, (d) the successful explanation of psychological findings in terms of biological processes.
3. What three errors does biological reductionism often lead to?

ANSWERS:

1. rejection of extreme environmentalism; evidence for the role of physical health in psychological functioning; new insights into the biological contributions to mental and emotional disorders.   2. c   3. premature conclusions; unwarranted inferences about cause and effect; exaggeration of the power of genes

---

ISSUE 1: THE MENSTRUAL CYCLE, MOOD, AND BEHAVIOR

Long-term biological rhythms have been observed in everything from the threshold for tooth pain to conception rates, but no long-term cycle has raised as much controversy as the menstrual cycle, which is characterized by the ebb and flow of estrogen and progesterone over a period of roughly 28 days. For psychologists, the interesting question is whether these physical changes are correlated with emotional or intellectual changes—as folklore and tradition would have us believe.

Since the 1970s, a cluster of symptoms associated with the days preceding menstruation—including fatigue, backache, headache, irritability, and depression—has come to be thought of as an illness and has been given a label, "premenstrual syndrome (PMS)." Some books refer to "millions" of sufferers or assert that most women have "PMS," although there are no statistics to back up such claims. Proposed explanations of the syndrome include progesterone deficiency, estrogen/progesterone imbalance, water retention, high sodium, and a fall in the level of endorphins, the brain's natural opiates. Yet biomedical research provides no consistent support for *any* of these theories, and it offers evidence against some of them. For example, in one study, researchers gave "PMS" patients a drug that blocks the hormonal changes that normally occur premenstrually; yet the women still reported symptoms, indicating that hormone changes could not be responsible (Schmidt et al., 1991). Further, despite many anecdotes and testimonials, no treatment—including progesterone, the most commonly prescribed remedy—works better than a placebo (Freeman et al., 1990).

Discussions of "PMS" often fail to distinguish between physical and emotional symptoms, and this distinction is crucial. No one disputes that physical symptoms are associated with menstruation, including cramps, breast tenderness, and water retention, although women vary tremendously; some have no symptoms and others have many. But there is reason to question claims that *emotional* symptoms are reliably and universally tied to the menstrual cycle. Many women do report such symptoms, but self-reports can be a poor guide to reality, no matter how valid they feel to the person doing the reporting. A woman might easily attribute a blue mood to her impending period, although at other times of the month she would blame a stressful day or a poor grade on an English paper. She might notice that she feels depressed or irritable when these moods happen to occur premenstrually but overlook times when such moods are *absent* premenstrually.

A woman's perceptions of her own emotional ups and downs can also be influenced by her expectations and attitudes toward menstruation and by menstrual myths prevalent in popular culture. Even the name of the questionnaire used in a study can bias a woman's perceptions—the typical title, "Menstrual Distress Questionnaire," gets different results from "Menstrual Joy Questionnaire" (Chrisler et al., 1994)! To get around these problems, some psychologists have polled women about their psychological and physical well-being *without revealing the true purpose of the study* (Alagna & Hamilton, 1986; Burke, Burnett, & Levenstein, 1978; Englander-Golden, Whitmore, & Dienstbier, 1978; Parlee, 1982; Slade, 1984; Vila & Beech, 1980). Using a double-blind procedure, these researchers have had women report symptoms for a single day and have then gone back to see what phase of the cycle the women were in; or they have had women keep daily records over an extended period of time. And some studies have included a control group that is usually excluded from research on hormones and moods: men! Here are some of the major findings:

✦Overall, women and men *do not differ* significantly in the emotional symptoms they report or the number of mood swings they experience in the course of a month, as you can see in Figure 5.1 on the next page (McFarlane, Martin, & Williams, 1988).

✦A few women do become more irritable or depressed before menstruation; others become happier or more energetic. But for most women, the relationship between cycle stage and symptoms is weak or nonexistent. They may recall their moods as having been more unpleasant before or during menstruation, but, as you can also see in Figure 5.1, their own daily reports fail to bear them out.

✦Even when women know that menstruation is being studied, most do not consistently report negative (or positive) psychological changes from one cycle to the next. Their moods and emotional symptoms vary far more in degree and

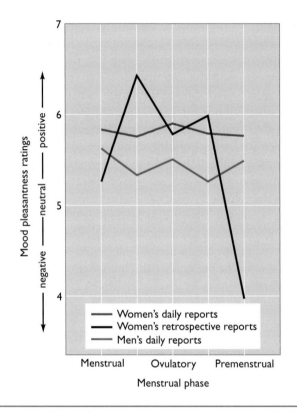

Figure 5.1 *In a study that challenged stereotypes about "PMS," college women and men recorded their moods daily for 70 days without knowing the purpose of the study. This graph shows the surprising results: First, when women were asked to recall their moods, they said their moods had been more negative premenstrually, when in fact they were not. Second, both sexes reported only moderate mood changes—and there were no significant differences between women and men at any time of the month (McFarlane, Martin, & Williams, 1988).*

direction than we would expect if predictable hormonal fluctuations were the main reason for these changes (Walker, 1994).

✦There is *no* reliable relationship between cycle stage and work efficiency, problem solving, motor performance, college exam scores, creativity, or any other behavior that matters in real life (Golub, 1992).

Do these findings surprise you? Results such as these, reported many times since the 1980s, are unknown to most people and are often ignored by doctors, therapists, and the media (Tavris, 1992). And many women still insist that they do have PMS. So what is going on here? One answer is that premenstrual symptoms are created by an *interaction* between mind and body. To be sure, certain hormonal conditions may produce psychological symptoms, just as a brain tumor or thyroid problem might, and chronic pain or discomfort can make anyone miserable, depressed, and grumpy. But the body only provides the clay for our symptoms; learning and culture mold that clay, by teaching us which symptoms are important or worrisome and which are not. The impact of any bodily change depends on how we interpret it and how we respond to it. Thus an increased state of arousal or sensitivity may contribute to nervousness and restlessness, or to creative energy and vitality.

The story of "PMS" also shows the importance of the social and political context of research. When the PMS label was first proposed, many women welcomed it as a validation of the normal physical changes of the menstrual cycle and a sign that women's health concerns were finally being taken seriously. But during the 1980s, the medical and psychiatric establishments welcomed "PMS" as another disorder suitable for treatment and insurance compensation. Critics point out that instead of validating women's normal experience, the PMS label fits right into the old superstition that hormones make women emotionally unstable, and thus is often used to stigmatize women or dismiss their legitimate grievances (Gise, 1988; Koeske, 1987; Caplan, 1995).

The critical thinker may wonder why only women's moods constitute a "syndrome," and why only women, not men, are viewed as being at the mercy of their fluctuating hormones. Sharon Golub (1992) notes that although many studies have tried to find a link between menstruation and women's mental performance, no one has ever asked how men's testosterone levels, which peak in the morning and fall in the evening, might affect *their* thinking skills or test scores. In a study of 4,462 men, James Dabbs and Robin Morris (1990) found that high testosterone levels were associated with delinquency, drug use, having many sex partners, abusiveness, and violence—and were not associated with any positive behaviors. Why, then, is so much attention and funding devoted to "PMS" and not to, say, "HTS"—HyperTestosterone Syndrome?

We do not wish to imply that men are victims of their hormones any more than women are. The reasons for antisocial behavior are far more complicated than simple testosterone levels, and besides, the Dabbs and Morris findings were only correlational. But it is interesting to ask why the hormonal excuse for the goose is not the same for the gander. Why do you think that is?

WHAT DO YOU KNOW?

There are no hormonal excuses for avoiding this quiz!

1. For most women, the days before menstruation are reliably associated with (a) depression, (b) irritability, (c) elation, (d) creativity, (e) none of these, (f) few of these.

2. Rosalyn, who is expecting her period in a few days, is in an irritable frame of mind. "It must be my hormones," she says. Rosalyn's explanation illustrates biological _____.

3. A researcher studying testosterone in men tells her subjects that the hormone peaks in the morning and that it probably causes hostility. She then asks them to fill out a "HyperTestosterone Syndrome (HTS) Survey" in the morning and again at night. Based on menstrual-cycle findings, what results might she get? How could she improve her study?

ANSWERS:

women should be added, to see whether their hostility levels vary in the same way as men's do.
and late in the day (since individuals vary in the timing of their peaks). Also, a control group of
tionnaire (say, "Health and Mood Checklist"), and measure their actual hormone levels early
would be better to keep them in the dark about the hypothesis, use a neutral title on the ques-
now have about testosterone, they may be biased to report more hostility in the morning. It
1. e 2. reductionism (can you explain why?) 3. Because of the expectations that the men

ISSUE 2: SOCIOBIOLOGY AND THE GENETIC LEASH

Many of the earliest psychologists believed that human behavior is motivated largely by *instincts,* complex chains of reflexes that are relatively uninfluenced by learning and that occur in every member of the species. Nowadays, most psychologists acknowledge that certain simple behaviors, such as smiling or a preference for sweet tastes, do resemble instincts (or, as they are now called, *fixed action patterns*). Most would agree that human beings inherit some of their cognitive, perceptual, emotional, and linguistic capacities. There is great disagreement, however, about the biological and evolutionary origins of complex social customs, such as those surrounding sexuality and marriage.

The evolutionary viewpoint on mating practices has been strongly influenced by the writings of **sociobiologists,** a group that includes scientists from psychology, sociology, anthropology, biology, zoology, and other disciplines. Sociobiologists contend that evolution has bred into each of us a tendency to act in ways that maximize our chances of passing on our genes, and to help our close biological relatives, with whom we share many genes, do the same. This impulse to act in ways that ensure the survival of our personal genetic code, sociobiologists argue, is the primary motivation behind much of our social behavior, from altruism (concern for others) to xenophobia (fear of strangers) (Wilson, 1975, 1978). In the sociobiological view, just as nature has selected physical characteristics that have proved adaptive, so it has selected psychological traits and social customs that aid individuals in propagating their genes. Customs that enhance the odds of such transmission survive in the form of kinship bonds, courtship rituals, dominance arrangements, taboos against female adultery, and many other aspects of social life.

Sociobiologists believe that because the males and females of most species have faced different kinds of survival and mating problems, the sexes have evolved to differ

---

sociobiology An interdisciplinary field of study that emphasizes evolutionary explanations of social behavior in animals, including human beings.

profoundly in aggressiveness, social dominance, and sexual strategies (Symons, 1979; Trivers, 1972). In this view, it pays for males to compete with other males for access to young and fertile females, and to try to win and then inseminate as many females as possible. The more females a male mates with, the more genes he can pass along. But females need to shop for the best genetic deal, as it were, because they can conceive and bear only a limited number of offspring. Having such a large investment in each pregnancy, they can't afford to make mistakes. Besides, mating with a lot of different males would produce no more offspring than staying with just one.

So, according to sociobiologists, females try to attach themselves to dominant males, who have resources and status and are likely to have "superior" genes. The result of these two opposite sexual strategies is that, in general, males want sex more than females do; males are often fickle and promiscuous, whereas females are usually devoted and faithful; males are drawn to sexual novelty and even rape, whereas females want stability and security; males are relatively undiscriminating in their choice of partners, whereas females are cautious and choosy; and males are competitive and concerned about dominance, whereas females are less so.

Evolutionary psychologists agree with much of this argument. However, unlike the sociobiologists, most evolutionary psychologists do not consider human beings to be "reproductive-fitness maximizers" whose main motive is to perpetuate their genes. As evolutionary psychologist David Buss (1995) points out, if men had a conscious or unconscious motive to maximize their reproductive fitness, they would be lining up to make donations to sperm banks! Instead, say evolutionary psychologists, evolved behavioral tendencies are simply the end products of two evolutionary processes. One is *natural selection,* which occurs when characteristics increase in frequency because they help individuals survive (see Chapter 3). The other is *sexual selection,* which occurs when characteristics increase in frequency because they help individuals compete for or attract sexual partners.

According to evolutionary psychologists, some of the "end products" of these processes are mating preferences and strategies similar to those described by sociobiologists. They cite evidence from hundreds of studies, such as one massive project in which 50 scientists studied 10,000 people in 37 cultures located on six continents and five islands (Buss, 1994). Such studies have found that around the world, men are more violent than women, more socially dominant, more interested in the youth and beauty of their sexual partners (presumably because youth is associated with fertility), more sexually jealous and possessive of their partners (presumably because males can never be 100 percent sure that their children are really theirs genetically), less discriminating in their choice of partners, quicker to have sex with partners they don't know well, and more inclined toward polygamy and promiscuity (Bailey et al., 1994; Buss, 1994, 1996; Buunk et al., 1996; Daly & Wilson, 1983; Kenrick & Trost, 1993; Sprecher, Sullivan, & Hatfield, 1994).

It is no accident, say evolutionary psychologists, that the sex differences found so often in human societies are the very ones found among other mammals. Douglas Kenrick and Melanie Trost (1993) observe that hamadryas baboons and Ugandan kob antelopes are unlikely to have been influenced by human social customs, so some other explanation of the similarities between such animals and our own species is necessary. That explanation, they believe, starts with our genes.

Critics of the evolutionary approach acknowledge that sex differences exist, but they differ in how they explain those differences. It is a mistake, they say, to argue by analogy. Two species may behave in a similar fashion, but this does not necessarily mean that the _origins_ of the behavior are the same in both species. For example, a male scorpionfly that coerces a female into copulation can hardly have the same motives as a human rapist, but some sociobiologists use the word _rape_ to apply to the behavior of both the fly and the man (Thornhill, 1980). In this way, says geneticist Richard Lewontin (1993), "human categories are laid on animals by analogy, partly as a matter of convenience of language, and then these traits are 'discovered' in animals and laid back on humans as if they had a common origin."

Moreover, not all animal behavior conforms to the stereotypes of the sexually promiscuous male and the coy and choosy female (Hrdy, 1994; Hubbard, 1990). In many species—including birds, fish, mammals, and primates—females are sexually ardent and often have many male partners. In these species, the female's sexual behavior does not seem to depend simply on the goal of being fertilized by the male, because females actively solicit males when the females are not ovulating and even when they are already pregnant! And in many primate species, males do not just mate and run; they stick around, feeding the infants, carrying them on their backs, and protecting them against predators (Hrdy, 1988; Taub, 1984). These findings have sent evolutionary theorists scurrying to figure out the evolutionary benefits of female promiscuity and male nurturance.

But critics of evolutionary theories take exception to this entire line of reasoning. The evidence of female promiscuity in other species, they say, has no more relevance to human behavior than does evidence of female fidelity. Among human beings, sexual behavior is extremely varied and changeable. Human cultures range from those in which women have many children to those in which they have very few; from those in which men are intimately involved in child rearing to those in which they do nothing at all; from those in which women may have many lovers to those in which women may be killed if they have sex outside of marriage. Even within a culture, there are large variations in people's sexual attitudes and practices (Laumann et al., 1994). These variations, say the critics, argue against a single, genetically determined sexual strategy. In rebuttal, evolutionary theorists reply that cultural variation does not negate the importance of biology. "Evolutionary theorists do not deny that there is a great variation in the range of human social behavior," observe Kenrick and Trost (1993), but "they believe that, underneath all the variation, it is possible to discern some regularities in human behavior."

This may seem like a reasonable enough conclusion, but debate over these matters can get quite heated. Critics worry that evolutionary arguments will be used to justify existing social and political arrangements and behavior patterns. Why do some men rape women? The evolutionary perspective could be used to argue that rape is a biological imperative—modifiable, perhaps, but impossible to eliminate. Why do men control business and politics everywhere? Well, given the history of our species, one could argue that that's just the way it's turned out; after all, who are we to question thousands of years of evolution? Indeed, Edward Wilson (1975), one of the leading proponents of sociobiology, once wrote that because of genetics, "Even with identical education and equal access to all professions [for both sexes], men are likely to continue to play a disproportionate role in political life, business, and science." This is not a message that people who hope for gender equality welcome! In 1978, demonstrators at a meeting of the American Association for the Advancement of Science dumped water on Wilson's head, chanting, "Wilson, you're all wet!" The American Anthropological Association even considered censuring him until Margaret Mead, an ardent environmentalist if ever there was one, defended him by reminding the association that censure would be equivalent to book burning (Wilson, 1994).

Ultimately, the central issue in this debate has to do with the relative power of biology and culture. In *On Human Nature* (1978), Wilson argued that genes hold culture on a leash. The big question, replied paleontologist Stephen Jay Gould (1987), is this: How long and tight is that leash? Is it only one foot long, in which case a society doesn't have much room to maneuver and change, or is it ten feet long, in which case biology merely establishes a broad range of possibilities? To some sociobiologists, the near universality of certain human customs is evidence that the leash is short and tight. To most psychologists who take a nonevolutionary approach, the enormous variation among individuals and societies is evidence that the leash is long and flexible. Most evolutionary psychologists seem to fall somewhere in the middle. They emphasize the adaptive nature of mating and courtship tendencies in the environments in which our species originally evolved, but they also acknowledge that some of these customs may no longer be adaptive or intelligent in our current environments. And they believe that human beings have evolved to be flexible enough to change when environmental demands change (Buss, 1995; Mealey, 1996).

WHAT DO YOU KNOW?

How is your understanding of the biological perspective evolving?

1. According to sociobiologists, human customs reflect a motive of individuals to act in ways that ensure the survival of (a) the species, (b) their particular ethnic or national group, (c) their personal genetic code.
2. Which of the following would an evolutionary psychologist expect to be more typical of males than of females? (a) promiscuity, (b) choosiness about sexual partners, (c) concern with dominance, (d) interest in young partners, (e) emphasis on physical attractiveness of partners

ANSWERS:

1. c 2. all but b

ISSUE 3: MEDICATING THE MIND

Raphael Osheroff had a thriving medical practice until he became severely depressed and could no longer work. He was not having a garden-variety blue mood; this was **major depression,** a serious disorder that involves chronic misery, decreased self-esteem, apathy, and a pervasive sense of hopelessness. Osheroff decided to admit himself to a private psychiatric hospital, where he received daily intensive psychotherapy. After seven months of ineffective treatment, he switched to another hospital, where he was given antidepressant medication. Within a few months, he was fully recovered (Shuchman & Wilkes, 1990).

As the Osheroff case illustrates, the biological perspective has made important contributions to the treatment of emotional disorders in some people. Drug treatments for depression, anxiety, schizophrenia, and other mental disorders have become popular partly because of new research on the brain, drugs, and genetics, and partly because of the failure of traditional psychotherapies to help chronic sufferers of many disorders. Like findings about the discovery of new genes, stories about dramatic cures such as Raphael Osheroff's abound in the media. An educated consumer of psychological research should know what these drugs are, what they do, and why they aren't always so miraculous.

Antipsychotic drugs, or *major tranquilizers,* include chlorpromazine (Thorazine), haloperidol (Haldol), clozapine (Clozaril), and risperidone. These drugs have transformed the treatment of schizophrenia and other **psychoses** (extreme mental disorders that involve distorted perceptions and irrational behavior). Before the introduction of such drugs, hospital staffs controlled psychotic patients with physical restraints, including straitjackets, or put them in padded cells to keep them from hurting others or themselves during states of extreme agitation and delusion. When given to people who are acutely ill with schizophrenia and likely to improve spontaneously within a few weeks or months, antipsychotic drugs can reduce agitation and delusions, and they shorten the schizophrenic episode (Kane, 1987). Some people on clozapine have "awakened" after a decade of illness and resumed their former lives.

However, antipsychotic drugs are not a cure. For some patients, they remove or lessen the most dramatic symptoms, such as incoherence, delusions, and hallucinations, but they usually cannot restore normal thought patterns or relationships. They allow many people to be released from hospitals, but often these individuals cannot care for themselves, or they fail to take their medication because of its unpleasant

---

major depression A mood disorder involving disturbances in emotion (excessive sadness); behavior (loss of interest in one's usual activities); cognition (distorted thoughts of hopelessness and low self-esteem); and body function (fatigue and loss of appetite).

antipsychotic drugs Major tranquilizers used primarily in the treatment of schizophrenia and other psychotic disorders.

psychosis (pl. psychoses) An extreme mental disturbance involving distorted perceptions and irrational behavior; it may have psychological or physiological causes.

unintended effects. The overall success of these drugs is modest, and some individuals diagnosed as schizophrenic deteriorate when they take them (Breggin, 1991; Karon, 1994).

Antidepressant drugs are used primarily in treating mood disorders such as depression, anxiety, and phobias (irrational fears), and symptoms of **obsessive–compulsive disorder,** such as endless hand washing and hair pulling (Swedo & Rapoport, 1991). There are three types of antidepressants. *Monoamine oxidase (MAO) inhibitors* elevate the level of norepinephrine and serotonin in the brain by blocking or inhibiting the enzyme that deactivates these neurotransmitters. *Tricyclic antidepressants,* which are more commonly used, prevent the normal reabsorption, or "reuptake," of norepinephrine and serotonin by the cells that release them. *Selective seratonin reuptake inhibitors (SSRIs),* such as *fluoxetine* (Prozac), work on the same principle as the tricyclics but specifically target serotonin. Antidepressants are nonaddictive, but they can produce unpleasant physical reactions such as dry mouth, headaches, constipation, nausea, weight gain, and reduced sexual desire. Prozac has fewer disagreeable effects, but it does make some people headachy, nauseated, or restless.

"Minor" tranquilizers, such as diazepam (Valium) and alprazolam (Xanax), are the drugs most frequently prescribed by family physicians for patients who complain of unhappiness, anxiety, or **panic attacks** (brief episodes of intense fear and feelings of impending doom or death, accompanied by intense physiological arousal). Unfortunately, they are the least effective drugs for these emotional disorders, which are often more effectively treated by cognitive-behavioral therapy (see Chapter 11). In addition, a small but significant percentage of people who take tranquilizers overuse the drugs and develop problems with *tolerance* (they need larger and larger doses) and withdrawal (Lader, 1989; Lader & Morton, 1991).

Finally, a special category of drug, a salt called *lithium carbonate,* is often successful in calming people who suffer from bipolar disorder. It must be given in exactly the right dose because too little won't help and too much is toxic. The patient's blood levels of lithium must be carefully monitored.

Drugs have helped many people who might otherwise have gone from therapy to therapy without relief. Without question, they have rescued some people from institutionalization, suicide, or a life of suffering and incapacity. Although medication cannot magically eliminate depressed people's real-life problems, it can be a useful first step in treatment: By improving sleep patterns, appetite, and energy, it may help people concentrate on solving their problems.

---

antidepressant drugs A category of drugs that are used primarily in the treatment of mood disorders, especially depression and anxiety.

obsessive–compulsive disorder An anxiety disorder in which a person feels trapped in repetitive, persistent thoughts (obsessions) and repetitive, ritualized behaviors (compulsions) designed to reduce anxiety.

"minor" tranquilizers Depressants commonly but often inappropriately prescribed for patients who complain of unhappiness or worry; they are the least effective drugs for treating emotional disorders.

panic attack A brief feeling of intense fear and impending doom or death, accompanied by intense physiological symptoms such as rapid breathing and pulse, and dizziness.

Yet, despite these benefits, some words of caution are in order. Many psychologists are worried about the *routine* prescription of medications, which are often dispensed without accompanying therapy for the person's problems. Some physicians are tempted to prescribe drugs indiscriminately, without finding out what the patient might be angry, depressed, or anxious about. And many psychiatrists and drug companies trumpet the benefits of medication without informing the public of its limitations (Fisher & Greenberg, 1989). Here are some of them:

1. **THE PLACEBO EFFECT.** New drugs promise quick and effective cures, as was the case with the arrival of Clozaril, Xanax, and Prozac. Yet the placebo effect ensures that some people will respond positively to new drugs just because of the enthusiasm surrounding them. After a while, when placebo effects decline, many drugs turn out to be neither as effective as promised nor as widely applicable. Research cannot always rule out the placebo effect, because in supposedly double-blind studies, patients can usually tell if they are being given an active drug or a placebo. The reason is that virtually all of the drugs we have described produce physical effects, whereas inert placebos do not. Patients and researchers therefore often figure out who is getting the genuine drug, and this knowledge can affect the patients' responses—and judgments of the treatment's success (Carroll et al., 1994). When true double-blind studies are done, using *active placebos* that mimic the physical effects of real drugs, there is often little difference between the real drug and the placebo (Fisher & Greenberg, 1993).

2. **RELAPSE AND DROPOUT RATES.** A person may have short-term success with antipsychotic and antidepressant drugs. However, in part perhaps because these medications have some unpleasant effects, the percentage of people who stop taking them is very high—between 50 and 67 percent (McGrath et al., 1990; Torrey, 1988). People who take antidepressants without learning how to cope with their problems are also more likely to relapse and again become depressed.

3. **DOSAGE PROBLEMS.** The challenge with drugs is to find the "therapeutic window," the amount that is enough but not too much. Many questions remain about which drug best suits which problem, what the proper dose should be, how long the drug should and can be taken, and so forth (Gutheil, 1993). The same dose is not necessarily suitable for men and women, for all ages, or for all racial groups.

4. **LONG-TERM RISKS, KNOWN AND UNKNOWN.** Antipsychotic drugs are among the safest in medicine, but if they are taken over many years they can have some dangerous effects. One is the development of a neurological disorder called *tardive* (late-appearing) *dyskinesia,* which is characterized by involuntary muscle movements. About one-fourth of all adults who take antipsychotics develop this disorder, and fully one-third of elderly adults do (Saltz et al., 1991). And in a small percentage of cases, antipsychotic drugs cause *neuroleptic malignant syndrome,* which produces fever, delirium, coma, and sometimes death. Clozapine has produced, in about two percent of cases, a potentially fatal condition in which there is a sharp decrease in certain white blood cells.

   Antidepressants are likewise said to be safe, but at present, few longitudinal studies have been done. No one knows the long-term effects of Prozac, for example, although it is prescribed widely, especially to women of childbearing age (Kramer, 1993). Caution is wise, especially considering that several kinds of psychotherapy work as well as drugs, or even better, for many people who have panic attacks, phobias, anxiety, or depression (Chambless, 1995). We will be considering these treatments in Chapter 11.

In *Listening to Prozac* (1993), psychiatrist Peter Kramer raised provocative questions about the use of drugs to treat psychological problems. Kramer himself is an enthusiastic advocate of psychopharmacology, particularly Prozac. Watching his patients thrive on the drug changed the way he viewed the causes of behavior. "I had come to see inborn, biologically determined temperament," he wrote, "where before I had seen slowly acquired, history-laden character." Kramer chronicled the effects of Prozac not only on the symptoms of serious emotional disorders but also on troubling but more ordinary problems, such as perfectionism, low self-esteem, shyness, irritability, anxiety, hypersensitivity to rejection, a need for attention, lack of assertiveness, inability to take risks, inhibition of pleasure, sluggishness of thought, and *dysthymia,* a condition of chronic melancholy. He believes that drugs will one day "modify inborn predisposition" and "repair traumatic damage to personality."

However, Kramer admits that Prozac and other drugs create a dilemma. Should mental-health professionals provide medication for reasons of "cosmetic psychopharmacology"—not for treating debilitating mental illness but simply to help patients think more sharply, feel perkier, or gain an emotional edge at work? He wonders whether we will end up with "psychic steroids for mental gymnastics, medicinal attacks on the humors, antiwallflower compound—these might be hard to resist." He recognizes that the possibility of reaching into the personality to alter a single trait—to prop up self-esteem, perhaps, or mental agility—has troubling implications "not only as regards the arrogance of doctors but as regards the subtly coercive power of convention."

Moreover, as Kramer pointed out in his book, thousands of individual decisions to take a mood-altering drug could have unforeseen consequences for society. Do we

Drawing by Lorenz; © 1993 The New Yorker Magazine, Inc.

"Before Prozac, she <u>loathed</u> company."

really want a brave new world in which no one ever feels miserable or has chronic complaints? At first glance, the answer might seem "yes." But the French have a proverb: *Les heureux ne font pas d'histoire* (Happy people don't make history). "Much of the insight and creative achievement of the human race," points out Kramer, "is due to the discontent, guilt, and critical eye of dysthymics."

Underlying these concerns is what we call the Jurassic Park Question: Just because we *can* do something (clone DNA, medicate the mind), does that mean we *should* do it? Kramer believes that people's suspicions about drugs will save them from overmedicating their personalities. Is his optimism warranted? Already, too many people are willing to take amphetamines to reduce their weight, although these drugs are ineffective in the long run; too many athletes are taking steroids to improve performance, although these drugs are dangerous in the long run. What, then, is to prevent too many people from taking "cosmetic drugs" to shake the blues and improve their motivation, even if these drugs have long-term risks?

Economic forces are already shaping people's individual decisions. In the United States, many health plans are more willing to reimburse mental-health professionals for "medication management" than for doing psychotherapy, which takes longer. Drug companies, of course, have a vested interest in persuading professionals and the public that drugs are the way to go in the treatment of all emotional and personality problems. When we "listen to Prozac" or to any other psychoactive medication, we must be sure that we are hearing the whole message.

WHAT DO YOU KNOW?

A. Match the treatment with the problem(s) for which it is most typically used.

1.	antipsychotic drugs	a.	bipolar disorder
2.	antidepressant drugs	b.	schizophrenia
3.	lithium carbonate	c.	depression and anxiety
		d.	obsessive–compulsive symptoms

B. Give four reasons that the public should be cautious about concluding that drugs for psychological disorders are miracle cures.

C. Suppose you read that PET scans show changes in cerebral brain activity in patients with obsessive–compulsive symptoms after treatment with Prozac. Why shouldn't you conclude that the only appropriate treatment is medical?

ANSWERS:

A. 1. b   2. c, d   3. a   B. Placebo effects are common; dropout and relapse rates are high; appropriate dosages are difficult to determine; and some drugs have long-term risks. C. The brain changes may or may not be related to improvement. Moreover, similar changes in the brain may occur after nonmedical forms of therapy. Indeed, studies have found that behavior therapy produces the same effects on the brain as drug treatments do (Schwartz et al., 1996)—another reminder that although the brain affects behavior, behavior also affects the brain.

The biological perspective has vastly broadened our understanding of mental disorders and normal functioning. There is no disputing that the more we know about our physical selves, the better we will understand our psychological selves. The challenge is to learn from biology without oversimplifying it. In evaluating the biological perspective, therefore, we must be wary of media hype, avoid unwarranted conclusions, examine political implications, and resist the temptation to "overbiologize."

Analyzing a human being in terms of physiology alone is like analyzing the Taj Mahal solely in terms of the materials that were used to build it. Physiological findings are always most illuminating when they are integrated with what we know about personal development and cultural context. Even if we could monitor every cell and circuit of the brain, we still would want to understand the circumstances, thoughts, and social rules that affect whether we are gripped by hatred, consumed by grief, lifted by love, or transported by joy.

◆　◆　◆

Summary

1. The biological perspective is giving people a new appreciation for the role of physiology in temperaments, abilities, mental disorders, emotions, and many other aspects of psychology. It shows that human beings, like other animals, are constrained by their evolutionary past and are a product, in part, of their genes and neurons.

2. Among this perspective's major contributions to psychology are the rejection of extreme environmentalism, an appreciation for the role of physical health in psychological functioning, and new insights into biochemical and genetic factors in mental and emotional disorders.

3. To understand the contributions and the limitations of the biological perspective, we need to be on guard for *biological reductionism,* the tendency to explain complex personal and social problems solely in terms of a few physiological mechanisms.

4. Biological reductionism leads to three common errors in interpreting biological findings: (a) premature conclusions (e.g., about biological factors in bipolar disorder and schizophrenia and the implications of reported sex differences in the brain); (b) unwarranted conclusions about cause and effect (e.g., assuming that the brain affects performance on mental tasks without also considering that experience and training affect brain efficiency); and (c) exaggerating the power of genes (e.g., in the development of sexual orientation).

5. Biological findings have great potential for being misinterpreted and misused politically. A society's intentions affect what it makes of biological research on, for example, aggression or sexual orientation.

6. One issue that illustrates the pitfalls of biological reductionism and the nature of biological politics is that of "premenstrual syndrome (PMS)." The physical symptoms associated with the menstrual cycle are not in dispute, but emotional symptoms are. Well-controlled double-blind studies show that for most women, the relationship between cycle stage and emotional symptoms is weak or nonexistent.

Overall, women and men do not differ in the emotional symptoms reported or in the number of mood swings they experience over the course of a month. Expectations and learning affect how people experience bodily and emotional changes; few people of either sex are likely to undergo dramatic mood swings or personality changes because of hormones. The "PMS" label can be used to help women by validating the normal physical changes of the menstrual cycle, but it can also be used to stigmatize women and to trivialize their genuine complaints.

7. Controversy exists about the biological and evolutionary origins of sexual and mating practices. *Sociobiologists* maintain that people's tendency to act in ways that ensure the survival of their personal genetic code is the primary motivation behind most social customs, including those related to sexual behavior. In this view, males and females have developed different reproductive strategies, so that, for example, males are on the average more promiscuous than females. Most evolutionary psychologists reject the notion of a motive for reproductive fitness, but they agree that different kinds of mating and survival problems faced by the sexes in the past have resulted in sex differences. Critics of the evolutionary approach question the relevance of animal data and argue that human sexual behavior is too varied and changeable to fit a single evolutionary explanation. They also worry that evolutionary arguments will be used politically to justify inequality between the sexes.

8. Drug treatments for depression, anxiety, schizophrenia, and other problems have helped some people with these disorders. These medications include *antipsychotic drugs* (major tranquilizers), used in treating schizophrenia and other psychotic disorders; *antidepressants,* used in treating depression and anxiety disorders; *"minor" tranquilizers,* often inappropriately prescribed for emotional problems; and *lithium carbonate,* used to treat bipolar disorder. But drug treatments also have limitations, including placebo effects, high relapse and dropout rates, uncertainties about appropriate dosages, and long-term risks. Critics believe that medication is prescribed too routinely and indiscriminately. The widespread use of Prozac raises many questions about the potential for overmedication and the possible negative consequences for individuals and for society.

Key Terms

Social Darwinism *174*

biological reductionism *176*

bipolar disorder *176*

schizophrenia *177*

"premenstrual syndrome (PMS)" *182*

instincts (fixed action patterns) *186*

sociobiology *186*

sexual selection *187*

major depression *190*

antipsychotic drugs (major tranquilizers) *190*

psychosis *190*

antidepressant drugs *191*

obsessive–compulsive disorder *191*

monoamine oxidase (MAO) inhibitors *191*

tricyclic antidepressants *191*

PART III
THE LEARNING PERSPECTIVE

On a hot summer day, James Peters shot and killed his next-door neighbor, Ralph Galluccio. Peters had reached the end of his patience in an acrimonious ten-year dispute with Galluccio over their common property line. Shocked friends insisted that this feud was not predictable from the men's personalities. Galluccio, his employer reported, was "a likable person with a good, even disposition." Peters, said his employer, was a "very mild-mannered, cooperative" man, an "all-around good guy."

How on earth could such two "nice" men as James Peters and Ralph Galluccio get into such an irrational and ultimately tragic argument? Whereas a psychologist in the biological perspective might look for clues in the men's brain chemistries or their inherited temperaments, a psychologist in the learning perspective would emphasize each man's past learning and present environment. In this view, it is because of our learning histories that each of us winds up with the hundreds of qualities and talents that commonly go by the name "personality." From a learning perspective, we become liberals, conservatives, rock fans, Bach buffs, gourmet cooks, fast-food fanatics, optimists, or pessimists in large part because of our experiences and what we have learned from them. A learning theorist, therefore, would want to know about the particular circumstances of the Peters–Galluccio feud, as well as each man's past, to explain why, when hurled insults and then hurled eggs failed to bring about a resolution, all they knew how to do was to behave more violently.

Research in the learning perspective has been heavily influenced by *behaviorism,* the school of psychology that accounts for behavior in terms of observable events, without reference to such hypothetical mental entities as "mind" or "will." Indeed, for almost half a century, until the 1960s, behaviorism was *the* approach to learning. (Detractors of behaviorism like to say that during this period, psychology "lost its mind.") Today, other approaches, collectively known as *social-learning theories,* continue to recognize the importance of the environment but hold that omitting mental processes from explanations of human learning is like omitting passion from descriptions of sex: You may explain the form, but you miss the substance.

In Chapter 6, we are going to take a look at some of the many important principles of learning uncovered by behavioral studies, including the work of two remarkable scientists, Ivan Pavlov and B. F. Skinner. Then, in Chapter 7, we will see how social-learning theorists and other researchers have expanded on behavioral principles and added social and cognitive variables to the learning equation.

CHAPTER 6

Behavioral Learning

$\mathcal{A}$ dentist decided to soothe the fears of his youngest patients by showing them animated cartoons while he drilled their teeth. He no doubt thought that if the children were distracted, they would relax and lose their fear. But decades later, a former patient, now an adult, described an unforeseen result in a letter to *Science News:* "After all these years," he wrote, "I still can't stand watching cartoons."

A dog owner, fed up with his pet's annoying habit of defecating on the carpet while he was away, wanted to teach the pooch a lesson. "Bad dog," he shouted sternly, as he forced the dog's nose close to one of the piles on the floor. Then he fed the animal and went to clean up. This routine continued for several days. One evening, the owner came home to find the usual smelly mess, but with one surprising difference: In each pile, there was the clear imprint of a dog's nose.

A young mother was beside herself because her two daughters were constantly whining and quarreling. Mornings had become intolerable. "When I awakened the girls," the mother later recalled, "Karen's reaction was to snarl, 'You woke me too late.' Then she'd demand, 'What's for breakfast? Where are my shoes?' Finally she'd order her six-year-old sister: 'Debbie, get out of my room!'" Sometimes, the mother responded by flying into a screaming rage herself. At other times, she tried to smother her anger and help them resolve their conflicts. Their misbehavior only increased (Seif, 1979).

In each of these cases, a lesson missed its mark. The reason, a **behaviorist** would say, was that the dentist, the dog owner, and the mother all misapplied or ignored certain basic laws of learning—laws that you are going to read about in this chapter.

In ordinary speech, the word *learning* often refers to classroom activities, such as memorizing the facts of geography, or to the acquisition of practical skills, such as carpentry or sewing. But to psychologists, learning is *any* relatively permanent change in behavior that occurs because of experience (excluding changes due to maturation, fatigue, injury, or disease). For psychologists in the learning tradition, experience is the

---

behaviorism An approach to psychology that emphasizes the study of observable behavior and the role of the environment as a determinant of behavior.

greatest teacher, providing the essential link between the past and the future and enabling an organism to adapt to changing circumstances in order to survive and thrive. Our species is more dependent on learning than is any other, but learning is a fundamental process in all animals, from the lowliest backyard bug to the most eminent human scholar.

In this chapter, we are going to explore a basic kind of learning called **conditioning,** which involves associations between environmental stimuli and responses. Behaviorists have shown that two types of conditioning can explain much of human behavior: classical conditioning and operant conditioning.

CLASSICAL CONDITIONING

At the turn of the century, the great Russian physiologist Ivan Pavlov (1849–1936) was studying salivation in dogs as part of a research program on digestion. His work would shortly win him the Nobel Prize in physiology and medicine. One of Pavlov's procedures was to make a surgical opening in a dog's cheek and insert a tube that conducted saliva away from the animal's salivary gland so that the saliva could be measured. To stimulate the reflexive flow of the saliva, Pavlov placed meat powder or other food in the dog's mouth. This procedure was later refined by others, who used an apparatus like the one in Figure 6.1, in which salivation was measured by the movement of a needle on a revolving drum.

Pavlov was a truly dedicated scientific observer. Many years later, as he lay dying, he even dictated his sensations for posterity! During his salivation studies, Pavlov noticed something that most people would have overlooked or dismissed as trivial. After a dog had been brought to the laboratory a number of times, it would start to salivate *before* the food was placed in its mouth. The sight or smell of the food, the dish in which the food was kept, even the sight of the person who delivered the food or the sound of the person's footsteps were enough to start the dog's mouth watering. This new salivary response clearly was not inborn but was acquired through experience.

At first, Pavlov treated the dog's drooling as an annoying "psychic secretion." But after reviewing the literature on reflexes, he realized that he had stumbled onto an important phenomenon, one that he came to believe was the basis of all learning in human beings and other animals. He called that phenomenon a "conditional" reflex—conditional because it depended on environmental conditions. Later, an error in the translation of his writings transformed *conditional* into *conditioned,* the word that is most commonly used today.

Pavlov soon dropped what he had been doing and turned to the study of conditioned reflexes, to which he would devote the last three decades of his life. Why were

---

conditioning A basic kind of learning that involves associations between environmental stimuli and the organism's responses.

Figure 6.1   *A modification of Pavlov's method.*

his dogs salivating to aspects of the environment other than food? Pavlov decided that it was pointless to speculate about his dogs' thoughts, wishes, or memories. Instead, he analyzed the environment in which the conditioned reflex arose. The original salivary reflex, according to Pavlov, consisted of an **unconditioned stimulus (US)**, food, and an **unconditioned response (UR),** salivation. By an unconditioned stimulus, Pavlov meant an event or thing that elicits a response automatically or reflexively. By an unconditioned response, he meant the response that is automatically produced:

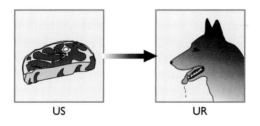

Learning occurs, Pavlov said, when some neutral stimulus is regularly paired with an unconditioned stimulus. The neutral stimulus then becomes a **conditioned stimulus (CS),** which elicits a learned or **conditioned response (CR)** that is usually similar

---

unconditioned stimulus (US) The classical-conditioning term for a stimulus that elicits a reflexive response in the absence of learning.

unconditioned response (UR) The classical-conditioning term for a reflexive response elicited by a stimulus in the absence of learning.

conditioned stimulus (CS) The classical-conditioning term for an initially neutral stimulus that comes to elicit a conditioned response after being associated with an unconditioned stimulus.

conditioned response (CR) The classical-conditioning term for a response that is elicited by a conditioned stimulus; occurs after the conditioned stimulus is associated with an unconditioned stimulus.

to the original, unlearned one. In Pavlov's laboratory, the sight of the food dish, which had not previously elicited salivation, became a CS for salivation:

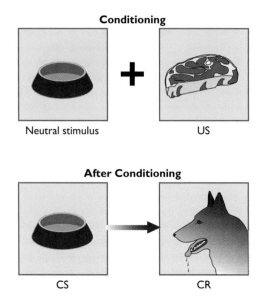

In a series of experiments, Pavlov showed that a wide variety of stimuli can become a conditioned stimulus for salivation—the ticking of a metronome, the musical tone of a tuning fork, the vibrating sound of a buzzer, a flashing light, a triangle drawn on a large card, even a pinprick or an electric shock. None of these stimuli naturally elicits salivation, but if paired with food, all of them will (although some associations are easier to establish than others). The optimal interval between the presentation of the neutral stimulus and the presentation of the US depends on the kind of response being conditioned; in the laboratory, it is often less than a second.

The process by which a neutral stimulus becomes a conditioned stimulus has become known as **classical conditioning** and is also sometimes called *Pavlovian* or *respondent conditioning*. Because the terminology of classical condition can be hard to learn, let's pause for a quiz before going on.

What Do You Know?

See whether you can name the four components of classical conditioning in these two situations.

1. Five-year-old Samantha is watching a storm from her window. A huge bolt of lightning is followed by a tremendous thunderclap, and Samantha jumps at the noise. This happens several more times. There is a brief lull and then another lightning bolt. Samantha jumps in response to the bolt.

---

classical conditioning The process by which a previously neutral stimulus acquires the capacity to elicit a response through association with a stimulus that already elicits a similar or related response; also called *Pavlovian* or *respondent conditioning*.

2. Gregory's mouth waters whenever he eats anything with lemon in it. One day, while reading an ad that shows a big glass of lemonade, Gregory notices his mouth watering.

ANSWERS:

1. US = the thunderclap; UR = jumping elicited by the noise; CS = the sight of the lightning; CR = jumping elicited by the lightning.   2. US = the taste of lemon; UR = salivation elicited by the taste of lemon; CS = the picture of a glass of lemonade; CR = salivation elicited by the picture.

Since Pavlov's day, researchers have established that nearly any involuntary response can become a conditioned response—for example, heartbeat, stomach secretions, blood pressure, reflexive movements, blinking, or muscle contractions. For optimal conditioning, the neutral stimulus should precede the unconditioned stimulus, rather than follow it or occur simultaneously. This makes sense, because in classical conditioning, the conditioned stimulus becomes a kind of signal for the unconditioned stimulus. It enables the organism to *prepare* for an event that is about to happen. In Pavlov's studies, for instance, a bell or buzzer was a signal that meat was coming, and the dog's salivation was preparation for digesting food.

Indeed, today many psychologists contend that what an animal or person actually learns in classical conditioning is not merely an association that is formed between two paired stimuli because they occur close together in time, but rather *information* conveyed by one stimulus about another. In studies supporting this view, Robert Rescorla showed that the mere pairing of an unconditioned stimulus and a neutral stimulus is not sufficient to produce learning; for conditioning to take place, the neutral stimulus must reliably *signal*, or *predict*, the unconditioned one (Rescorla, 1968, 1988; Rescorla & Wagner, 1972).

Suppose you are a budding behaviorist and you want to teach a rat to fear a tone. Following the usual procedure, you repeatedly sound the tone before an unconditioned stimulus for fear, such as a mild electric shock: tone, shock, tone, shock, tone, shock. . . . After 20 such pairings, the rat shows signs of fear on hearing the tone. Now suppose you do this experiment again—on 20 trials, the tone precedes the shock—but this time you randomly intersperse an additional 20 trials in which the shock occurs *without* the tone. With this method, the tone is paired with the shock just as often as in the standard procedure, but it signals shock only half of the time. In other words, the shock is equally likely to occur when the tone is absent as when it is present. Under these conditions, the tone does not provide any information about the shock, and hardly any conditioning occurs.

From this and similar findings, Rescorla (1988) concluded that "Pavlovian conditioning is not a stupid process by which the organism willy-nilly forms associations between any two stimuli that happen to co-occur. Rather, the organism is better seen as an information seeker using logical and perceptual relations among events, along with its own preconceptions, to form a sophisticated representation of its world." Not all learning theorists agree with this conclusion or with the findings on which it is based; an orthodox behaviorist would say that it's silly to talk about the preconceptions of a rat. The important point, however, is that for some researchers, concepts such as "information seeking," "preconceptions," and "representations of the world" have opened the door to a more cognitive view of classical conditioning.

Principles of Classical Conditioning

The processes involved in the learning of classically conditioned responses are common to all species, from worms to *Homo sapiens*. Among the most important are extinction, higher-order conditioning, and stimulus generalization and discrimination.

Extinction. Conditioned responses do not necessarily last forever. If, after conditioning, the conditioned stimulus is repeatedly presented without the unconditioned stimulus, the conditioned response eventually disappears, and **extinction** is said to have occurred. Suppose that you train a dog to salivate to the sound of a bell, but then you ring the bell every five minutes and do not follow it with food. The dog will salivate less and less to the bell and will soon stop salivating altogether; salivation has been extinguished. However, if you come back the next day and ring the bell, the dog may salivate again for a few trials. The reappearance of the response, which is called **spontaneous recovery,** explains why eliminating a conditioned response usually requires more than one extinction session.

Higher-Order Conditioning. Sometimes a neutral stimulus can become a conditioned stimulus by being paired with an already established CS, a procedure known as **higher-order conditioning.** Say that a dog has learned to salivate to the ringing of a bell. Now you present a flash of light before ringing the bell. With repeated pairings of the light and the bell, the dog may learn to salivate to the light, although the light will probably elicit less salivation than the bell does. The procedure is shown in Figure 6.2.

It may be that words acquire their emotional meanings through a process of higher-order conditioning. When they are paired with objects or other words that already elicit some emotional response, they, too, may come to elicit that response (Chance, 1994; Staats & Staats, 1957). For example, a child may learn a positive response to the word *birthday* because of its association with gifts and attention. Conversely, the child may learn a negative response to ethnic or national labels—such as *Swede, Turk,* or *Jew*—if those words are paired with already disagreeable words, such as

---

extinction The weakening and eventual disappearance of a learned response; in classical conditioning, it occurs when the conditioned stimulus is no longer paired with the unconditioned stimulus.

spontaneous recovery The reappearance of a learned response after its apparent extinction.

higher-order conditioning In classical conditioning, a procedure in which a neutral stimulus becomes a conditioned stimulus through association with an already established conditioned stimulus.

Higher-Order Conditioning

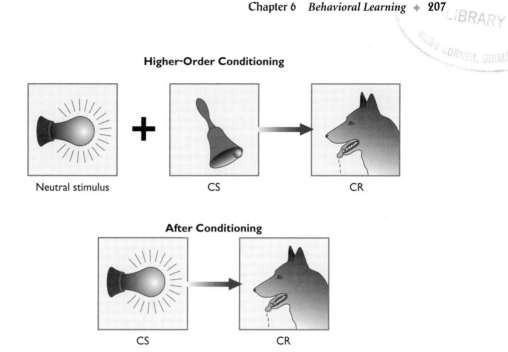

Figure 6.2 *An example of higher-order conditioning.*

dumb or *dirty*. Higher-order conditioning, in other words, may contribute to the formation of prejudices.

Stimulus Generalization and Discrimination. After a stimulus becomes a conditioned stimulus for some response, other, similar stimuli may produce a similar reaction—a phenomenon known as **stimulus generalization.** For example, a dog conditioned to salivate to middle C on the piano may also salivate to D, which is one tone above C, even though D was not paired with food. Stimulus generalization is described nicely by an old English proverb: "He who hath been bitten by a snake fears a rope."

The mirror image of stimulus generalization is **stimulus discrimination,** in which *different* responses are made to stimuli that resemble the conditioned stimulus in some way. Suppose that you condition your poodle to salivate to middle C on the piano. Now you play middle C on a guitar, *without* following it by food (but you continue to follow C on the piano by food). Eventually, the dog will learn to salivate to a C on the piano and not to salivate to the same note on the guitar; that is, the animal will discriminate between the two sounds.

---

stimulus generalization After conditioning, the tendency to respond to a stimulus that resembles one involved in the original conditioning; in classical conditioning, it occurs when a stimulus that resembles the conditioned stimulus elicits the conditioned response.

stimulus discrimination The tendency to respond differently to two or more similar stimuli; in classical conditioning, it occurs when a stimulus similar to the CS fails to evoke the CR.

Classical Conditioning in Real Life

If a dog can learn to salivate to the ringing of a bell, so can you. In fact, you probably have learned to salivate to the sound of a lunch bell, not to mention the sight of the refrigerator, the phrase *hot fudge sundae,* "mouth-watering" pictures of food in magazines, the sight of a waiter in a restaurant, and a voice calling out, "Dinner's ready!" But the role of classical conditioning goes far beyond the learning of simple observable reflexes; conditioning affects us every day in many ways.

Accounting for Taste. We probably learn to like and dislike many things, including particular foods, through a process of classical conditioning. In the laboratory, researchers have taught animals to dislike various foods or odors by pairing them with drugs that cause nausea or other unpleasant symptoms. One researcher trained slugs to associate the smell of carrots, which slugs normally like, with a bitter-tasting chemical that they detest. Soon the slugs were avoiding the smell of carrots. The researcher then demonstrated higher-order conditioning by pairing the smell of carrots with the smell of potato. Sure enough, the slugs began to avoid the smell of potato as well (Sahley, Rudy, & Gelperin, 1981).

Martin Seligman, who has studied learned behavior in the laboratory for many years, tells how he himself was conditioned to hate béarnaise sauce. One night, shortly after he and his wife ate a delicious meal of filet mignon with béarnaise sauce, he came down with the flu. Naturally, he felt wretched. His misery had nothing to do with the béarnaise sauce, of course, yet the next time he tried it, he found he disliked the taste (Seligman & Hager, 1972). Similar conditioned food aversions may occur in cancer patients when a meal is followed by nausea-inducing chemotherapy (Bernstein, 1985).

Sometimes we like a food, but our bodies refuse to tolerate it. This happens with allergies: You adore chocolate, say, but your skin breaks out in hives whenever you eat it. Some allergic reactions may be classically conditioned. In a study with guinea pigs, researchers paired the smell of either fish or sulphur with injection of a substance to which the animals were already allergic. After only ten pairings, the animals became allergic to the odor alone. Their blood histamine levels rose, just as they would have done after exposure to a true allergen (Russell et al., 1984). People, too, may learn to be allergic to certain substances that have been associated with substances to which they are already sensitive. A century ago, a physician reported that he used an artificial rose to provoke asthmatic symptoms in an allergic patient, and since then, several studies have confirmed that nonallergenic objects previously associated with allergens can induce asthmatic symptoms in some people (Ader & Cohen, 1993).

Learning to Love—and to Like. Classical conditioning involves involuntary bodily responses, and many such responses are part and parcel of human emotions. It follows that this type of learning may explain how we acquire emotional responses to particular objects and events.

One of the first psychologists to recognize this implication of Pavlovian theory was John B. Watson, who founded American behaviorism and was an enthusiastic promoter of Pavlov's ideas. Watson believed that emotions were no more than collections of gut-level muscular and glandular responses, a view later detractors derided as "muscle-twitch psychology" (Hunt, 1993). A few such responses, said Watson, are inborn. For the sake of convenience he called them fear, rage, and love, but he was really referring to patterns of movement and changes in breathing, circulation, and digestion, and not to subjective feelings. In Watson's analysis, "love" included the smiling and burbling that babies do when they are stroked and cuddled. The stroking and cuddling are unconditioned stimuli; the smiling and burbling are unconditioned responses. According to Watson, an infant learns to "love" other things when those things are paired with stroking and cuddling. The thing most likely to be paired with stroking and cuddling is, of course, a parent. Learning to love a parent (or anyone else, for that matter), is really no different from learning to salivate to the sound of a bell—at least in Watson's view.

A similar process may help explain unusual desires and preferences, such as masochism, the enjoyment of pain. We mentioned earlier that Pavlov could condition dogs to salivate to a pinprick or an electric shock. The animals showed none of the bodily upset usually associated with these painful stimuli. In fact, they seemed to enjoy being pricked or shocked. Similarly, masochism in human beings may result when painful stimuli are associated with an unconditioned stimulus for pleasure or satisfaction, such as sexual arousal and orgasm.

Classical conditioning can also help account for other positive responses to images and inanimate objects. For example, consumer psychologists have shown that many of Madison Avenue's techniques for getting us to like their products are based on the principles first demonstrated by Pavlov, whether advertising executives realize it or not. In one study, college students looked at slides of either a beige pen or a blue pen. During the presentation, half the students heard a song from a recent musical film, and half heard a selection of traditional music from India. (The experimenter made the reasonable assumption that the show tune would be more appealing to most young Americans.) Later, the students were allowed to choose one of the pens. Almost three-fourths of those who heard the popular music chose a pen that was the same color as the one they had seen in the slides. An equal number of those who heard the Indian music chose a pen that *differed* in color from the one they had seen (Gorn, 1982). In classical-conditioning terms, the music was an unconditioned stimulus for internal responses associated with pleasure or displeasure, and the pens became conditioned stimuli for similar responses. You can see why television commercials often pair their products with music, attractive people, or other appealing sounds and images.

Conditioned Fears. Dislikes and negative emotions such as fear, as we saw in our discussion of higher-order conditioning, can also be classically conditioned. According to behaviorists, most fears are conditioned responses to stimuli that were originally neutral. The original conditioning incident does not have to be remembered in order for the fear to persist.

When a fear of a specific object or situation is irrational and interferes with normal activities, it qualifies as a *phobia*. Common phobias include fear of heights (acrophobia); fear of closed spaces (claustrophobia); fear of dirt and germs (mysophobia); fear of such animals as snakes, dogs, insects, and mice (zoophobia); fear of speaking or performing in public, using public restrooms, or eating in public (social phobias); and fear of being away from a safe place or person (agoraphobia). There are also more idiosyncratic fears, such as fear of the color purple (porphyrophobia), fear of thunder (brontophobia), and fear of the number 13 (triskaidekaphobia). (Memorize these terms if you want to impress your friends.)

To demonstrate how a phobia might be acquired, John B. Watson and Rosalie Rayner (1920) deliberately established a rat phobia in an 11-month-old boy named Albert. The ethics, procedures, and findings of their study have since been questioned, and no behaviorist today would perform such a demonstration. Nevertheless, the study remains a classic, and its main conclusion, that fears can be conditioned, is still well accepted.

"Little Albert" was a rather placid tyke who rarely cried. When Watson and Rayner gave him a furry white rat to play with (a live one, not a toy), Albert showed no fear; in fact, he was delighted. However, like most children, Albert was afraid of loud noises. Whenever a steel bar behind his head was struck with a hammer, he would jump and fall sideways onto the mattress he was sitting on. The noise was an unconditioned stimulus for the unconditioned response of fear.

Having established that Albert liked rats, Watson and Rayner set about teaching him to fear them. Again they offered him a rat, but this time, as Albert reached for it, one of the researchers struck the steel bar. Startled, Albert fell onto the mattress. The researchers repeated this procedure several times. Albert began to whimper and tremble. Finally, the rat was offered alone, without the noise. Albert fell over, cried, and crawled away as fast as he could; the rat had become a conditioned stimulus for fear. Further tests showed that Albert's fear had generalized to other hairy or furry objects, including white rabbits, cotton wool, a Santa Claus mask, and even John Watson's hair.

Unfortunately, Watson and Rayner did not have an opportunity to reverse the conditioning, for reasons that are unclear. Later, however, Watson and Mary Cover Jones did accomplish a reversal in a three-year-old named Peter (Jones, 1924). Peter was deathly afraid of rabbits. His fear was, as Watson put it, "home-grown" rather than psychologist induced. Watson and Jones eliminated it with a method called **counterconditioning,** which involved pairing the rabbit with another stimulus—a snack of milk and crackers—that produced pleasant feelings incompatible with the conditioned response of fear. At first, the researchers kept the rabbit some distance from Peter, so that his fear would remain at a low level. Otherwise, Peter might have learned to fear milk and crackers (just as the child in our opening story about the dentist learned to fear cartoons). But gradually, over several days, they brought the rabbit closer and closer. Eventually Peter was able to sit with the rabbit in his lap, playing with it with one hand while he ate with the other. A variation of this procedure, called *systematic desensitization,* was later devised for treating phobias in adults, as we will see in Chapter 8, when we evaluate the learning perspective.

Learning theorists, then, see classical conditioning as the invisible mechanism behind many of our likes and dislikes, tastes, and emotional reactions. But to under-

---

counterconditioning In classical conditioning, the process of pairing a conditioned stimulus with a stimulus that elicits a response that is incompatible with an unwanted conditioned response.

stand behavior, we also need to understand a second type of conditioning, to which we now turn.

WHAT DO YOU KNOW?

Supply the correct term to describe the outcome in each situation:

1. After a child learns to fear spiders, he also responds with fear to ants, beetles, and other crawling bugs.
2. A toddler is afraid of the bath, so her father puts just a little water in the tub and gives the child a lollipop to suck on while she is being washed. Soon, the little girl loses her fear of the bath.
3. A factory worker notices that his mouth waters whenever a noontime bell signals the beginning of his lunch break. One day the bell goes haywire and rings every half hour. By the end of the day, the worker has stopped salivating to the bell.

ANSWERS:

1. stimulus generalization   2. counterconditioning   3. extinction

---

OPERANT CONDITIONING

If you follow tennis, you know that John McEnroe was famous for his on-court antics and spectacular temper tantrums; he was the bad boy of the tennis circuit. Once, when McEnroe noticed a small microphone that could pick up what the players were saying, he walked over and hit it with his racquet, breaking a string. Then he strolled to the sidelines and got a new racquet. There was no penalty for this little episode. In fact, it seemed to work to his advantage: He got all charged up for the game, while his opponent's performance suffered from the interruption. McEnroe also received plenty of attention from fans and the media, who loved him or loved to hate him.

In contrast, Bjorn Borg, another tennis champion, was controlled and civilized on the court. "Once I was like John [McEnroe]," he told a reporter. "Worse. Swearing and throwing rackets. Real bad temper. Ask anyone who knew me in Sweden then, 10 or 11 years ago. Then, when I was 13, my club suspended me for six months. My parents locked my racket in a cupboard for six months. Half a year I could not play. It was terrible. But it was a very good lesson. I never opened my mouth on the court again. I still get really mad, but I keep my emotions inside" (quoted in Collins, 1981).

Some people might attribute the opposite emotional styles of these two athletes to their inborn temperaments. But a learning theorist would say that McEnroe's temper and Borg's calm deportment illustrate one of the most basic laws of learning, that *behavior becomes more or less likely depending on its consequences.* McEnroe's outbursts got him what he wanted, so they continued. Borg's outbursts kept him from playing his beloved sport, so they stopped.

An emphasis on consequences is at the heart of **operant conditioning** (also called *instrumental conditioning*), the second kind of conditioning studied by behaviorists. In classical conditioning, the animal's or person's behavior does not have any environmental consequences; in Pavlov's procedure, the dog got food whether it salivated or not. But in operant conditioning, the organism's response (a tantrum by John McEnroe, for example) *operates* or produces effects on the environment. These effects, in turn, influence whether the response will occur again. Classical and operant conditioning also tend to differ in the types of responses they involve. In classical conditioning, the response is reflexive, an automatic reaction to something happening in the environment, such as the sight of food or the sound of a bell. Generally, responses in operant conditioning are complex and not reflexive, involving the entire organism— for instance, riding a bicycle, writing a letter, climbing a mountain, . . . or breaking your tennis racket in a fit of temper.

Operant conditioning has been studied since the turn of the century, although it wasn't called "operant" until later. Edward Thorndike (1898), then a young doctoral candidate, set the stage by observing cats as they tried to escape from a "puzzle box" in order to reach a scrap of fish that was just outside the box. At first, the cat would engage in trial and error, scratching, biting, or swatting at parts of the cage in an unorganized way. Then, after a few minutes, the animal would chance on the successful response (loosening a bolt, pulling on a loop of string, hitting a button) and rush out to get the reward. Placed in the box again, the cat now took a little less time to escape, and after several trials, it immediately made the correct response. According to Thorndike's *law of effect*, the correct response had been "stamped in" by its satisfying effects (getting the food). In contrast, annoying or unsatisfying effects "stamped out" behavior. Behavior, said Thorndike, is controlled by its consequences.

the neighborhood by Jerry Van Amerongen. Reprinted with special permission of King Features Syndicate, Inc.

An instantaneous learning experience.

---

operant conditioning The process by which a response becomes more or less likely to occur, depending on its consequences.

This general principle was elaborated and extended to more complex forms of behavior by B. F. (Burrhus Frederic) Skinner (1904–1990). Calling his approach "radical behaviorism," to distinguish it from the behaviorism of John Watson, Skinner argued that what we need to know to understand behavior are the external causes of an action and the action's consequences. Skinner was careful to avoid such terms as "satisfying" and "annoying," which reflect assumptions about what an organism feels and wants. Focusing on intentions, values, or states of mind, said Skinner, is "prescientific" and a waste of time. Likewise, said Skinner, what we usually call "personality" is really just a collection of behavioral patterns. Labels for supposed personality traits, such as aggressiveness or extroversion, merely reflect the fact that different people learn to respond in different ways when they are in particular kinds of situations. For Skinner, the explanation of behavior was to be found by looking outside the individual rather than within—a position he continued to defend until his death in 1990.

Skinner has often been called the greatest of all American psychologists, and certainly he is one of the best known. Yet despite his fame, or perhaps because of it, his position is often distorted by the general public, psychology students, and even some psychologists. For example, many people think that Skinner denied the existence of human consciousness and the value of studying it. It is true that Skinner's predecessor John Watson thought that psychologists should study only public (external) events, not private (internal) ones. But Skinner maintained that we *can* study private events, by observing our own sensory responses and the verbal reports of others, and the conditions under which they occur. For Skinner, the private events we "see" when we examine our own "consciousness" are simply the early stages of behavior, before the behavior begins to act on the environment. These private events are as real or physical as public ones, Skinner said, although they are less accessible and harder to describe (Skinner, 1972, 1990).

Another misconception is that Skinner denied the influence of genetics and biology. Skinner knew as well as anyone that physical characteristics place limits on what an organism can learn; a fish cannot be trained to climb a ladder. Although Skinner himself did not say much about biological influences, behaviorists in recent years have been paying more attention to the importance of innate tendencies and have integrated these factors into their theories.

One of Skinner's most controversial positions was on the matter of free will. Whereas some other psychologists, notably the humanists, have argued for the existence of free will, Skinner regarded free will as an illusion and steadfastly argued in favor of *determinism*. Environmental consequences may not automatically "stamp in" operant behavior, he said, but they do determine the probability that an action will occur. Skinner refused to credit traits, such as curiosity, or mental events, such as goals and motives, for his own or anyone else's accomplishments. Indeed, he regarded himself not as a "self" but as a "repertoire of behaviors" resulting from an environment that encouraged looking, searching, and investigating (Bjork, 1993). "So far as I know," he wrote in his autobiography (1983), "my behavior at any given moment has been nothing more than the product of my genetic endowment, my personal history, and the current setting."

Reinforcement and Punishment

In Skinner's analysis, which has inspired an immense body of research, a response ("operant") can lead to one of three types of consequences. The first type is neutral as far as future behavior is concerned: It neither increases nor decreases the probability that the behavior will recur. If a door handle squeaks each time you turn it, and the sound does not affect whether you turn the door handle again in the future, the squeak is a neutral consequence.

A second type of consequence involves **reinforcement.** In reinforcement, a reinforcing stimulus—or *reinforcer*—strengthens or increases the probability of the response that it follows. When you are training your dog to heel, and you offer it a doggie biscuit or a pat on the head when it keeps pace with you, you are trying to reinforce the good behavior.

Reinforcers are roughly equivalent to rewards, and many psychologists have no objection to the use of the words *reward* and *reinforcer* as approximate synonyms. However, strict behaviorists avoid *reward* because it is the organism, not the response, that is rewarded; the response is *strengthened.* Also, in common usage, a reward is something earned that results in happiness or satisfaction. But technically, any stimulus is a reinforcer if it strengthens the preceding behavior, whether or not the organism experiences pleasure or any other positive state. And conversely, no matter how pleasurable a stimulus is, it is not a reinforcer if it does not increase the likelihood of a response. It's pleasurable to get a paycheck, but if you get paid regardless of the effort you put into your work, the money will not reinforce "hard-work behavior."

The third type of consequence involves **punishment.** Punishment occurs when the stimulus or event that follows a response weakens it or makes it less likely to recur. Any aversive (unpleasant) stimulus or event may be a *punisher.* A dog that runs into the street and is nearly hit by a passing car will be less likely to run into the street in the future when cars are around. Later, we will see that deliberate punishment as a way of controlling behavior has many drawbacks.

In a way, operant conditioning is a kind of natural selection applied to the constantly changing behavior of individuals. As we saw in Chapter 3, because natural selection operates during evolution, some genetically influenced characteristics are selected by the environment and become more common in a population over time. Similarly, in operant conditioning, some actions of an individual are "selected" by their environmental consequences, and these responses become more frequent in the behavior of the individual.

Positive and Negative Reinforcers and Punishers

The great seventeenth-century English philosopher John Locke wrote that "Reward and punishment . . . are the spur and reins whereby all mankind are set on work, and

---

reinforcement The process by which a stimulus or event strengthens the response that it follows, increasing the probability of the response.
punishment The process by which a stimulus or event weakens the response that it follows, reducing the probability of the response.

guided." Today we talk about the carrot and the stick as being the two great motivators. But reward and punishment are not quite so simple as they seem. In our example of reinforcement, something pleasant (a doggie biscuit or a pat on the dog's head) followed the dog's response (heeling). This type of procedure is known as **positive reinforcement.** But there is another brand of reinforcement, **negative reinforcement,** which involves the *removal* of something *unpleasant.* If you politely ask your roommate to turn off some music you can't stand, and your roommate immediately complies, the likelihood of your being polite when making similar requests will probably increase. Your politeness has been strengthened (negatively reinforced) by the removal of the unpleasant music.

As Table 6.1 shows, the positive–negative distinction can also be applied to punishment: Something unpleasant may occur (positive punishment), or something pleasant may be removed (negative punishment). However, the terms "positive" and "negative" are more often applied to reinforcement.

The distinction between positive and negative reinforcement has been a source of confusion and frustration for generations of students, and has been known to turn strong and confident people into quivering heaps. We can assure you that if we had been around when these terms were first coined, we would have complained loudly. One eminent behaviorist, Gregory Kimble (1993), has argued that it's still not too late to change their meanings so that they conform better to ordinary usage. But we doubt that changing the definitions at this point would help much because students who went on in psychology would still have to read articles and books using the old defini-

TABLE 6.1   ◆   Types of Reinforcement and Punishment

| | | **WHAT EVENT FOLLOWS THE RESPONSE?** | |
		Stimulus Presented	*Stimulus Removed*
WHAT HAPPENS TO THE RESPONSE?	*Response Increases*	**Positive reinforcement** Example: Completion of homework increases when followed by praise.	**Negative reinforcement** Example: Use of aspirin increases when followed by reduction of headache pain.
	Response Decreases	**Positive punishment** Example: Nail biting decreaseswhen followed by the taste of a bitter substance painted on the nails.	**Negative punishment** Example: Parking in "no parking" zone decreases when followed by loss of money (a fine).

---

positive reinforcement A reinforcement procedure in which a response is followed by the presentation of, or increase in intensity of, a pleasant stimulus; as a result, the response becomes stronger or more likely to occur.
negative reinforcement A reinforcement procedure in which a response is followed by the removal, delay, or decrease in intensity of an unpleasant stimulus; as a result, the response becomes stronger or more likely to occur.

tions, and, in introductory courses, some books would be teaching one set of definitions and others a different set. That is why as textbook authors, we've resigned ourselves to the traditional terms, irksome though they are.

You will master these terms more quickly if you understand that "positive" and "negative" have nothing to do with "good" or "bad." These words refer to *procedures*—giving something or taking something away. *With either positive or negative reinforcement, a response becomes more likely.* If you praise Ludwig for doing his homework, and he starts studying more, that is positive reinforcement (of studying). If you nag Ludwig to study more and you stop nagging when he starts doing his homework, that is negative reinforcement (of studying). Think of a positive reinforcer as something pleasant that is added or obtained, and a negative reinforcer as avoidance of or escape from something unpleasant.

Recall again what happened with Little Albert. Albert learned to fear rats through a process of classical conditioning. Then, after he acquired this fear, crawling away (an operant behavior) was negatively reinforced by escape from the now-fearsome rodent. The negative reinforcement that results from escaping or avoiding something unpleasant explains why so many fears and anxieties are long-lasting. When you evade a feared object or situation, you also cut off all opportunities for extinguishing your fear.

Here's an example. Suppose that a young man is worried that his girlfriend will leave him. He is afraid to talk to her about his feelings because he believes that doing so would reveal unmanly weakness. Instead, every time his feelings of insecurity arise, he goes out drinking with his buddies. Soon he has learned a habit: "When I feel anxious, I'll drink." In behavioral terms, the young man has learned to avoid his feelings by distracting himself; drinking has been negatively reinforced. You can see how negative reinforcement might help explain behaviors that appear to be self-defeating or injurious.

Understandably, people often confuse negative reinforcement with positive punishment, because both involve an unpleasant stimulus. To keep the two straight, remember that punishment *decreases* the likelihood of the response it follows. Reinforcement—either positive or negative—*increases* it. In real life, positive punishment and negative reinforcement often go hand in hand. If you use a choke collar on your dog to teach it to heel, a yank on the collar punishes the act of walking. But release of the collar negatively reinforces the act of standing still by your side.

Primary and Secondary Reinforcers and Punishers

Food, water, light stroking of the skin, and a comfortable air temperature are naturally reinforcing because they satisfy biological needs. They are therefore known as **primary reinforcers.** Similarly, pain and extreme heat or cold are inherently punishing and are therefore known as **primary punishers.** Primary reinforcers and punishers are very

---

primary reinforcer A stimulus that is inherently reinforcing, typically satisfying a physiological need; an example is food.
primary punisher A stimulus that is inherently punishing; an example is electric shock.

effective for controlling behavior, but they also have their drawbacks. The organism may have to be in a deprived state for a stimulus to act as a primary reinforcer; a glass of water isn't much of a reward to someone who just drank three glasses. Also, there are ethical problems with using primary punishers or taking away primary reinforcers.

Fortunately, behavior can be controlled just as effectively by **secondary reinforcers** and **secondary punishers,** which are learned. Money, praise, applause, good grades, awards, and gold stars are common secondary reinforcers. Criticism, demerits, catcalls, scoldings, fines, and bad grades are common secondary punishers. Most behaviorists believe that secondary reinforcers and punishers acquire their ability to influence behavior by being paired with primary reinforcers and punishers. If that reminds you of classical conditioning, reinforce your excellent thinking with a pat on the head! Indeed, secondary reinforcers and punishers are often called *conditioned* reinforcers and punishers.

Just because a reinforcer or punisher is a secondary one doesn't mean that it is any less potent than a primary one. Money has considerable power over most people's behavior; not only can it be exchanged for primary reinforcers such as food and shelter, but it also brings with it other secondary reinforcers, such as praise and respect. Still, like any conditioned stimulus, a secondary reinforcer such as money will eventually lose its ability to affect behavior if it cannot be paired at least occasionally with one of the stimuli originally associated with it. In 1930, a child who found a penny would have been thrilled at the goodies it could buy. Today, U.S. pennies are considered so worthless that billions of them go out of circulation each year because people throw them away or leave them on the ground when they drop.

WHAT DO YOU KNOW?

A. Which kind of consequence is illustrated by each of the following? (You may want to refer back to Table 6.1 if you have difficulty with the first three items.)

1. A child nags her father for a cookie; he keeps refusing, but she keeps pleading. Finally, unable to stand the whining any longer, he hands over the cookie. For him, the ending of the child's pleas is a _____. For the child, the cookie is a _____.

2. A woman wants her husband to take more responsibility for household chores. One night, he clears the dishes. She touches him affectionately on the arm. The next night, he again clears the dishes. Her touch was probably a _____.

3. A hungry toddler gleefully eats his oatmeal with his hands after being told not to. His mother promptly removes the cereal and takes the messy offender out of the high chair. The removal of the cereal is a _____.

---

secondary reinforcer A stimulus that has acquired reinforcing properties through association with other reinforcers.
secondary punisher A stimulus that has acquired punishing properties through association with other punishers.

B. Which of the following are secondary (conditioned) reinforcers: quarters spilling from a slot machine, a winner's blue ribbon, a piece of candy, an A on an exam, "frequent flyer" points.

C. During "happy hours" in bars and restaurants, typically held in the late afternoon, drinks are sold at a reduced price, and appetizers are often free. What undesirable behavior may be rewarded by this practice?

ANSWERS:

A. 1. negative reinforcer; positive reinforcer   **2.** positive reinforcer   **3.** punisher (or more precisely, a negative punisher)   **B.** All but the candy are secondary reinforcers.   **C.** One possible answer: The reduced prices, free appetizers, and convivial atmosphere all reinforce heavy alcohol consumption just before the commuter rush hour, thus possibly contributing to drunk driving (see Geller & Lehman, 1988).

Principles of Operant Conditioning

Thousands of studies have been done on operant conditioning, many using animals. A favorite experimental tool is the *Skinner box,* a cage equipped with a device (called a "magazine") that delivers food or water into a dish when an animal makes a desired response (see Figure 6.3). A *cumulative recorder* connected to the cage automatically records each response and produces a graph showing the cumulative number of responses across time. Skinner is said to have originally created this apparatus by modifying a Sears, Roebuck ice chest.

Early in his career, Skinner (1938) used the Skinner box for a classic demonstration of operant conditioning. A rat that had previously learned to eat from the magazine was placed in the box. Because no food was present, the animal proceeded to do typically ratlike things, scurrying around the box, sniffing here and there, and randomly touching parts of the floor and walls. Quite by accident, it happened to press a lever mounted on one wall, and immediately a pellet of tasty rat food fell into the food dish. The rat continued its movements and again happened to press the bar, causing

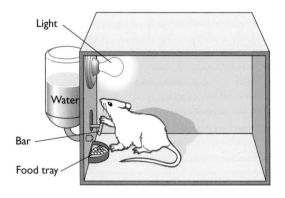

Figure 6.3 *A Skinner box.*

another pellet to fall into the tray. With additional repetitions of bar pressing followed by food, the animal began to behave less randomly, and to press the bar more consistently. Eventually, Skinner had the rat pressing the bar as fast as it could turn away from the magazine.

A cartoon well known to behaviorists, originally published in a student newspaper, shows two rats in a Skinner box, with one saying to the other, "Boy, do we have this guy conditioned. Every time I press the bar down he drops a pellet in." But, in characteristic fashion, Skinner didn't think it was a joke. To Skinner, the environment was a place where organisms reinforced and punished each other, *reciprocally:* Yes, he conditioned the rat—but the rat also conditioned him (Bjork, 1993).

Skinner's favorite experimental animals were pigeons, which usually are trained to peck at a disk or key, but most behaviorists have worked with rats. By using the Skinner box and similar devices, behavioral researchers have discovered many principles and techniques of operant conditioning.

Extinction. In operant conditioning, as in classical, **extinction** is a procedure that causes a previously learned response to stop occurring. In operant conditioning, extinction takes place when the reinforcer that maintained the response is removed or is no longer available. At first, there may be a spurt of responding, but then the responses gradually taper off and eventually cease. Suppose you put a coin in a vending machine and get nothing back. You may throw in another coin, or perhaps even two, but then you will probably stop trying. The next day you may put in yet another coin, an example of *spontaneous recovery.* Eventually, however, you will probably give up on that machine. Your response has been extinguished.

The harried mother in our opening story learned, with the help of a behavior therapist, to extinguish the yelling, whining, and arguments of her two daughters. The therapist pointed out that both parents were overinvolved in their children's lives; they were actually rewarding the girls' misbehavior with their attention, which is why the misbehavior continued. His recommendation to the mother was to stay out of her daughters' quarrels. At first, as a behaviorist would predict, the girls' fighting, shouting, and griping actually escalated, as they tried to regain the mother's attention. But the parents had been warned that this would happen, and they remained steadfast in their new policy of noninvolvement. After a couple of difficult weeks, the girls began to take responsibility for their problems and ceased their fighting and hollering (Seif, 1979).

Immediate Versus Delayed Consequences. In general, the sooner a reinforcer or punisher follows a response, the greater its effect. This principle applies especially to animals and children, but human adults also respond more reliably when they don't have to wait too long for a paycheck, a smile, or a grade. When there is a delay, other responses occur in the interval, and the connection between the desired or undesired response and the consequence may not be made.

---

extinction The weakening and eventual disappearance of a learned response; in operant conditioning, it occurs when a response is no longer followed by a reinforcer.

Recall the pooch that defecated on the rug. Because the owner didn't discover the messes the dog made until much later, punishment was not effective; the dog could not associate the punishment with its behavior. Then, after the owner held the animal's nose to the feces on the floor, he made matters worse by immediately feeding the dog, thus rewarding it for having its nose in that position—which is why those mysterious nose imprints appeared. In operant conditioning, timing is everything.

Normally, immediate rewards tend to outweigh the effects of delayed punishment, so it is hard for people to do what they know they ought to. For example, do you have a problem with credit-card bills you can never pay off? A behaviorist would say that handing over your card to a salesperson is immediately rewarded by the delivery of a desired item into your hands, whereas the payment isn't due until much later. Thus, through a process of operant conditioning, credit-card use becomes more likely, despite your resolve to pay off your debts. To curb impulse buying, you might leave your credit cards at home and take with you only what you can afford to spend.

Here's another example. We bet that you already know the main rules for protecting your health: get enough sleep; get regular exercise; eat a nutritious diet; if you drink alcohol, do so only in moderation; do not overeat; do not go on starvation diets; and do not smoke cigarettes. Well, then, why aren't you following all these rules? One obstacle is the fact that smoking, eating rich food, and sitting around watching TV bring immediate rewards, whereas their negative effects may not be apparent for years. As a result, many people feel that they are invulnerable and therefore persist in their unhealthy habits. Perhaps you can think of some way to reward yourself—immediately!—for adopting good health practices.

Stimulus Generalization and Discrimination. In operant conditioning, as in classical, **stimulus generalization** may occur. That is, responses may generalize to stimuli not present during the original learning situation that resemble the original stimuli. For example, a pigeon that has been trained to peck at a picture of a circle may also peck at a slightly oval figure. But if you wanted to train the bird to discriminate between the two shapes, you would present both the circle and the oval, giving reinforcers whenever the bird pecked at the circle and withholding reinforcers whenever it pecked at the oval. Eventually, **stimulus discrimination** would occur.

A somewhat different kind of discrimination occurs when an animal or human being learns to respond to a stimulus only when some other stimulus, called a **discriminative stimulus,** is present. The discriminative stimulus signals whether a response, if made, will "pay off." In a Skinner box containing a pigeon, a light may serve as a discriminative stimulus for pecking at a circle. When the light is on, pecking

---

stimulus generalization In operant conditioning, the tendency for a response that has been reinforced (or punished) in the presence of one stimulus to occur (or be suppressed) in the presence of other, similar stimuli.

stimulus discrimination In operant conditioning, the tendency for a response to occur in the presence of one stimulus but not in the presence of other, similar stimuli that differ from it on some dimension.

discriminative stimulus A stimulus that signals when a particular response is likely to be followed by a certain type of consequence.

brings a reward; when it is off, pecking is futile. The light is said to exert **stimulus control** over the pecking by setting the occasion for reinforcement to occur if the response is made. However, the response is not *compelled,* as salivation was compelled by the ringing of the bell in Pavlov's classical-conditioning studies. It merely becomes more probable (or occurs at a greater rate) in the presence of the discriminative stimulus.

Human behavior is controlled by many discriminative stimuli, both verbal ("Store hours are 9 to 5") and nonverbal (traffic lights, doorbells, the ring of a telephone, the facial expressions of others). Learning to respond correctly when these stimuli are present is an essential part of a person's socialization. In a public place, if you have to go to the bathroom, the words *Women* and *Men* are discriminative stimuli for entering one door or the other. One word tells you that the response will be rewarded by an opportunity to empty a full bladder, the other that it will be punished by the jeers or protests of others.

The failure to make appropriate discriminations can lead to accidents and errors. A behaviorist would say that when we go into the next room to do something and then can't remember why we're there, it is because the discriminative stimuli for the response are no longer present (Salzinger, 1990). But insufficient generalization also causes problems. For example, "personal growth" workshops provide participants with lots of reinforcement for emotional expressiveness and self-disclosure. Participants often feel that their way of interacting with others has been dramatically transformed. But when they return home and to work, where the environment is full of the same old reinforcers, punishers, and discriminative stimuli, they may be disappointed to find that their new responses have failed to generalize. A grumpy boss or cranky spouse may still be able to "push their buttons"—a relapse that is predictable from behavioral principles.

Learning on Schedule. Reinforcers can be delivered according to different schedules, or patterns over time. When a response is first acquired, learning is usually most rapid if the response is reinforced each time it occurs; this procedure is called **continuous reinforcement.** However, once a response has become reliable, it will be more resistant to extinction if it is rewarded on a **partial** or **intermittent schedule of reinforcement,** which involves reinforcing only some responses, not all of them. Skinner (1956) reported that he first happened on this property of partial reinforcement when he ran short of food pellets for his rats and was forced to deliver reinforcers less often. (Not all scientific discoveries are planned!) Years later, when he was asked how he could tolerate being misunderstood so often, he replied that he only needed to be understood three or four times a year—his own intermittent schedule of reinforcement.

---

stimulus control Control over the occurrence of a response by a discriminative stimulus.
continuous reinforcement A reinforcement schedule in which a particular response is always reinforced.
intermittent (partial) schedule of reinforcement A reinforcement schedule in which a particular response is sometimes but not always reinforced.

Many kinds of intermittent schedules have been studied. *Ratio schedules* deliver a reinforcer after a certain number of responses have occurred. *Interval schedules* deliver a reinforcer if a response is made after the passage of a certain amount of time since the last reinforcer. The number of responses that must occur or the amount of time that must pass before the payoff may be *fixed* (constant) or *variable*. Combining the ratio/interval patterns and fixed/variable patterns yields four types of intermittent schedules. These variations in how the reinforcers are delivered have characteristic effects on the rate, form, and timing of behavior:

1. **FIXED-RATIO (FR) SCHEDULE.** *On this schedule, reinforcement occurs after a fixed number of responses.* An FR-2 schedule delivers a reinforcer after every other response, an FR-3 schedule delivers a reinforcer after every third response, and so forth. Fixed-ratio schedules produce very high rates of responding. In the laboratory, a rat may rapidly press a bar several hundred times to get a single reward. Outside the laboratory, fixed-ratio schedules are often used by employers to increase productivity. A salesperson who must sell a certain number of items before getting a commission or a factory worker who must produce a certain number of products before earning a given amount of pay (a system known as "piecework") are on fixed-ratio schedules. An interesting feature of high fixed-ratio schedules is that performance drops off just after reinforcement. If a writer must complete four chapters before getting a check, interest and motivation will sag right after the check is received.

2. **VARIABLE-RATIO (VR) SCHEDULE.** *On this schedule, reinforcement occurs after some average number of responses, but the number varies from reinforcement to reinforcement.* A VR-5 schedule would deliver a reinforcer *on the average* after every fifth response but sometimes after one, two, six, or seven responses, or any other number, as long as the average was five. Variable-ratio schedules produce extremely high, steady rates of responding. The responses are more resistant to extinction than when a fixed-ratio schedule is used. The prime example of a variable-ratio schedule outside the laboratory is delivery of payoffs by a slot machine. The player knows that the average number of responses necessary to win is set at a level that makes money for the house. Hope springs eternal, though. The gambler takes a chance on being in front of the machine during one of those lucky moments when fewer responses bring a payoff.

3. **FIXED-INTERVAL (FI) SCHEDULE.** *On this schedule, reinforcement of a response occurs only if a fixed amount of time has passed since the previous reinforcer.* A rat on a FI-10-second schedule gets a food pellet the first time it presses the bar after the passage of a 10-second interval. Pressing the bar earlier does not hasten the reward. Animals on fixed-interval schedules seem to develop a sharp sense of time. After a reinforcer is delivered, they often stop responding altogether. Then as the end of the interval approaches, responding again picks up, reaching a maximum rate right before reinforcement. Outside the laboratory, fixed-interval schedules are not common, but some behavior patterns do resemble those seen on such schedules. Suppose your sweetheart, who is away for a month, promises to

send you a love note by e-mail every day at dinnertime. You'll probably start checking for messages around 5 p.m., and keep checking until the message arrives. Once you get it, you won't look again until the next day.

4. VARIABLE-INTERVAL (VI) SCHEDULE. *On this schedule, reinforcement of a response occurs only if a variable amount of time has passed since the previous reinforcer.* A VI-10-second schedule means that the interval will average 10 seconds but will vary from reinforcement to reinforcement. Because the animal or person cannot predict when a reward will come, responding is relatively low but steady. When your sweetheart sends you ten e-mail messages every morning, playfully spacing them at unpredictable intervals, you may check your e-mail every half hour.

The different patterns resulting from these schedules—known as *learning curves*—can be plotted with a cumulative recorder. Each time a response occurs, a pen moves up a notch on a moving strip of paper. The faster the rate of responding, the steeper the curve. Figure 6.4 shows typical learning curves for the four basic schedules of reinforcement; each crosshatch indicates the delivery of a reinforcer.

A basic principle of operant conditioning is that if you want a response to persist after it has been learned, you should reinforce it intermittently, not continuously. If an animal has been receiving continuous reinforcement for some response and then the reinforcement suddenly stops, the animal will soon stop responding. Because the change in reinforcement is large, from continuous to none at all, the animal will easily discern the change. But if reinforcement has been intermittent, the change will not be so dramatic, and the animal will keep responding for some period of time. Pigeons,

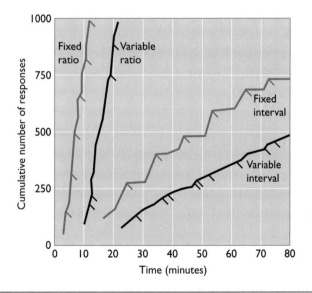

Figure 6.4 *Different schedules of reinforcement produce different learning curves, or patterns of responding over time. For example, when a fixed-interval schedule is used, responses drop off immediately after reinforcement, resulting in a scalloped curve. (Adapted from Skinner, 1961.)*

rats, and people on intermittent schedules of reinforcement have responded in the laboratory thousands of times without reinforcement before throwing in the towel, especially on variable schedules. Animals will sometimes work so hard for an unpredictable, infrequent bit of food that the energy they expend is greater than that from the reward; theoretically, the animal could actually work itself to death.

It follows that if you want to get rid of a response, you should be careful not to reinforce it intermittently. If you are going to extinguish undesirable behavior by ignoring it—a child's tantrums, a friend's midnight phone calls, a parent's unasked-for advice—you must be *absolutely consistent* in withholding reinforcement (your attention). Otherwise, you will probably only make matters worse. The other person will learn that if he or she keeps up the screaming, calling, or advice giving long enough, it will eventually be rewarded. One of the most common errors people make, from a behavioral point of view, is to reward intermittently the responses they would like to eliminate.

Shaping. For a response to be reinforced, it must first occur. But suppose you want to train a rat to pick up a marble, or a dog to stand on its hind legs and turn around, or a child to use a knife and fork properly, or a friend to play terrific tennis. Such behaviors, and most others in everyday life, have almost no probability of appearing spontaneously. You could grow old and gray waiting for them to occur so that you could then reinforce them. The operant solution to this dilemma is a procedure called **shaping.**

In shaping, you start by reinforcing a tendency in the right direction, then gradually require responses that are more and more similar to the final, desired response. The responses that you reinforce on the way to the final one are called **successive approximations.** In the case of the rat and the marble, you might deliver a food pellet if the rat merely turns toward the marble. Once this response is well established, you might then reward the rat for taking a step toward the marble. After that, you could reward it for approaching the marble, then for touching the marble, then for putting both paws on the marble, and finally for holding it. With the achievement of each approximation, the next one would become more likely, making it available for reinforcement.

Using shaping and other techniques, Skinner was able to train pigeons to play Ping-Pong with their beaks and to "bowl" in a miniature alley, complete with a wooden ball and tiny bowling pins. Rats have learned equally impressive behaviors. Animal trainers routinely use shaping to teach dogs to act as the "eyes" of the blind and to do such amazing things for their owners as turning on light switches, opening refrigerator

---

shaping An operant conditioning procedure in which successive approximations of a desired response are reinforced; it is used when the desired response has a low probability of occurring spontaneously.

successive approximations In the operant-conditioning procedure of shaping, behaviors that are ordered in terms of increasing similarity or closeness to the desired response.

Behavioral principles have many practical applications. This capuchin monkey has been trained to assist her paralyzed owner by picking up objects, opening doors, helping with feeding, and performing other everyday tasks.

doors, and reaching for boxes on supermarket shelves. According to one story (probably apocryphal), some university students once used the reinforcer of eye contact to shape the behavior of a famous professor who was an expert on operant conditioning. They decided to get him to deliver his lecture from a corner of the room. Each time he moved in that direction, they looked at him; otherwise, they averted their gaze. Eventually, the professor was backed into the corner, never suspecting that his behavior had been shaped.

What Do You Know?

Are you ready to apply the principles of operant conditioning? In each of the following situations, choose the best alternative and give your reason for choosing it:

1. You want your two-year-old to ask for water with a word instead of a grunt. Should you give him water when he says "wa-wa" or wait until his pronunciation improves?

2. Your roommate keeps interrupting you while you are studying even though you have asked her to stop. Should you ignore her completely or occasionally respond for the sake of good manners?

3. Your father, who rarely writes to you, has finally sent a letter. Should you reply quickly or wait a while so he will know how it feels to be ignored?

ANSWERS:

1. You should reinforce "wa-wa," an approximation of *water,* because complex behaviors need to be shaped. 2. You should ignore her completely because intermittent reinforcement (attention) could cause her interruptions to persist. 3. You should reply quickly if you want to encourage letter writing, because immediate reinforcement is more effective than delayed reinforcement.

OPERANT CONDITIONING IN REAL LIFE

Over the years, behaviorists have carried operant principles out of the narrow world of the Skinner box and into the wider world of the classroom, athletic field, prison, mental hospital, nursing home, rehabilitation ward, child-care center, factory, and office. The use of operant techniques (and also classical ones) in such real-world settings is called **behavior modification.**

Many behavior-modification programs rely on a technique called the **token economy.** *Tokens* are secondary reinforcers, such as points or scrip money, that have no real value in themselves but that are exchangeable for primary reinforcers or for other secondary reinforcers. They provide an easy way to reinforce behavior on a continuous schedule. Once a particular behavior is established, tokens can be phased out and replaced by more natural intermittent reinforcers, such as praise.

Behavior modification has had some enormous successes. Behaviorists have taught parents how to toilet train their children in only a few sessions (Azrin & Foxx, 1974) and have taught teachers how to be "behavioral change agents" (Besalel-Azrin, Azrin, & Armstrong, 1977). They have taught autistic children who have never before spoken to use a vocabulary of several hundred words (Lovaas, 1977). They have trained disturbed and mentally retarded adults to communicate, mingle socially with others, and earn a living in the community (Lent, 1968; McLeod, 1985). They have taught brain-damaged patients to control inappropriate behavior, focus attention, and improve their language abilities (McGlynn, 1990). And they have helped ordinary folk eliminate unwanted habits, such as smoking and nail biting, or acquire wanted ones, such as practicing the piano or studying.

---

behavior modification The application of conditioning techniques to teach new responses or to reduce or eliminate maladaptive or problematic behavior.

token economy A behavior-modification technique in which secondary reinforcers called *tokens,* which can be collected and exchanged for primary or other secondary reinforcers, are used to shape behavior.

Yet when people try to apply the principles of conditioning to commonplace problems, their efforts sometimes fail or backfire. Both punishment and reinforcement have their pitfalls, as we are about to see.

The Problem with Punishment

In a perfect world, according to behaviorists, reinforcers would be used so wisely that undesirable behavior would be rare. Unfortunately, we do not live in a perfect world. Bloopers, bad habits, and antisocial acts abound. Then we are faced with how to get rid of all those bad habits and behaviors.

An obvious approach might seem to be punishment. In the United States, the physical punishment of children has roots in the religious belief that you must beat children, or their innate wickedness will land them in hell (Greven, 1991). Most Western countries have banned corporal (physical) punishment of schoolchildren by principals and teachers, but in the United States, 24 states still permit it (Hyman, 1994), and other states are considering restoring this penalty for disruptive behavior, graffiti vandalism, and other problems that plague many schools. Boys, minority children, and poor white children are the most likely to be hit.

The American penal system, too, has become more severe in the punishments it metes out for crime; the United States has a higher proportion of its citizens in jail for nonviolent crimes (e.g., drug use) than any other developed country. The latest rallying cry is "three strikes and you're out"—committing a third felony requires that you be sent to prison for life, even, as in a recent case in California, when the "third strike" is a theft of $24 worth of food. (As of this writing, the constitutionality of three-strike legislation is in doubt.)

And of course in daily life, people punish one another constantly, by yelling, scolding, fining, and sulking. Many people feel rewarded by a temporary feeling of control and power when they punish others in these ways. But does all this punishment work?

Sometimes punishment is unquestionably effective. Some highly disturbed children have been known to chew their own fingers to the bone, stick objects in their eyes, or tear out their hair. You can't ignore such behavior because the children are seriously injuring themselves. You can't respond with concern and affection because you may unwittingly reward the behavior. In this case, immediately punishing the self-destructive behavior eliminates it (Lovaas, 1977; Lovaas, Schreibman, & Koegel, 1974). Mild punishers, such as a spray of water in the face, are often just as effective as strong ones, such as electric shock; sometimes they are even more effective. A firm "No!" can also be established as a conditioned punisher.

The effects of punishment, however, are far less predictable than many people realize, as we can see in reactions to domestic violence. In a widely publicized real-life experimental intervention, men who were arrested for assaulting their wives or girlfriends were less likely to repeat the offense within six months than men who were merely talked to by the police or ordered to stay away from the victim for a few hours (Sherman & Berk, 1984). On the basis of these results, police departments across the United States adopted mandatory-arrest policies in cases of domestic assault. Then more research came along showing that the conclusions were premature: Although arrests do temporarily prevent a repeat attack, they do not usually deter domestic violence *in the long run* (Dunford, Huizinga, & Elliott, 1990; Hirschel et al., 1990; Sherman, 1992).

Further, sociologist Lawrence Sherman and his colleagues (Sherman, 1992; Sherman et al., 1991) have noted that if arrest is the aspirin of criminal justice, the pill has different effects on different people at different doses. They found that brief arrests of two or three hours were generally most effective in initially reducing the chances of renewed domestic violence (when compared with a warning), although this effect disappeared within a few weeks. However, for unemployed men in the inner city, being arrested actually *increased* the long-term chances of a repeat attack. The researchers speculated that for these men, the initial fear of being arrested again wore off quickly and was replaced by anger at the woman who "caused" the arrest or at all women. The policy of arresting violent men, therefore, poses a dilemma—between the need to rescue the victim right after the violent episode and punish her attacker and the long-term need to reduce the risk of further harm to her.*

Because of such complexities, simplistic efforts to "crack down" on wrongdoers often fail to work. Laboratory and field studies show that punishment also has other disadvantages as a method of behavior control:

1. **PEOPLE OFTEN ADMINISTER PUNISHMENT INAPPROPRIATELY OR WHEN THEY ARE SO ENRAGED THAT THEY ARE UNABLE TO THINK THROUGH WHAT THEY ARE DOING AND HOW THEY ARE DOING IT.** They swing blindly or yell wildly, applying punishment so broadly that it covers all sorts of irrelevant behaviors. Even when people are not carried away by anger, they often misunderstand the proper application of punishment. One student told us that his parents used to punish their children before leaving them alone for the evening because of all the naughty things they were *going* to do. Naturally, the children didn't bother to behave like angels.

2. **THE RECIPIENT OF PUNISHMENT OFTEN RESPONDS WITH ANXIETY, FEAR, OR RAGE.** Through a process of classical conditioning, these emotional side effects may then generalize to the entire situation in which the punishment occurs—the place, the person delivering the punishment, and the circumstances. Negative emotional reactions tend to create more problems than the punishment solves. For example, instead of becoming obedient or respectful, a teenager who has been severely punished may strike back or run away. As we saw in the case of domestic violence, emotional reactions to punishment may even produce an increase in the undesirable behavior that the punishment was intended to eliminate. That may be why the physical punishment of children is correlated with high rates of violence in children; violence breeds violence (Hyman, 1994; McCord, 1991; Straus, 1991; Weiss et al., 1992).

3. **THE EFFECTS OF PUNISHMENT ARE SOMETIMES TEMPORARY, DEPENDING HEAVILY ON THE PRESENCE OF THE PUNISHING PERSON OR CIRCUMSTANCES.** All of us can

---

*Of course, punishment in the criminal-justice system is not aimed only at changing behavior; it also serves as a penalty for wrongdoing and as a means of retribution.

probably remember some transgressions of childhood that we never dared commit when our parents were around but that we promptly resumed as soon as they were gone. All we learned was not to get caught.

4. **MOST MISBEHAVIOR IS HARD TO PUNISH IMMEDIATELY.** Recall that punishment, like reinforcement, works best if it quickly follows a response, especially with animals and children. Outside the laboratory, immediate punishment is often hard to achieve.

5. **PUNISHMENT CONVEYS LITTLE INFORMATION.** If it immediately follows the misbehavior, it may tell the recipient what *not* to do. But it doesn't communicate what the person (or animal) *should* do. For example, spanking a toddler for messing in his pants will not teach him to use the potty chair. As Skinner (1968) wrote, "We do not teach [a student] to learn quickly by punishing him when he learns slowly, or to recall what he has learned by punishing him when he forgets, or to think logically by punishing him when he is illogical."

6. **AN ACTION INTENDED TO PUNISH MAY INSTEAD BE REINFORCING BECAUSE IT BRINGS ATTENTION.** Indeed, angry attention may be just what the offender is after. If a mother yells at a child who is throwing a tantrum, the very act of yelling may give him what he wants—a reaction from her. In the schoolroom, teachers who scold children in front of other students, thus putting them in the limelight, often unwittingly reward the misbehavior they are trying to eliminate.

Because of these drawbacks, most psychologists believe that punishment, especially severe punishment, is a poor way to eliminate unwanted behavior and in general should be regarded only as a last resort. When punishment is used, it should not involve physical abuse, it should be accompanied by information about what kind of behavior would be appropriate, and it should be followed, whenever possible, by the reinforcement of desirable behavior.

Fortunately, in most situations there is a good alternative to punishment: extinction of the responses you want to discourage. Of course, extinction is sometimes difficult to achieve. It is hard to ignore a child nagging for a cookie before dinner, a roommate interrupting your concentration, or a dog barking its head off. Moreover, the simplest form of extinction—ignoring the behavior—is not always appropriate. A teacher cannot ignore a child who is hitting a playmate. The dog owner who ignores Fido's backyard barking may soon hear some "barking" of another sort—from the neighbors. A parent whose child is a TV addict can't ignore the behavior because television is rewarding to the child. One solution: Combine extinction of undesirable acts with reinforcement of alternative ones. If a child is addicted to TV, the parent might ignore the child's pleas for "just one more program" and at the same time encourage behavior that is incompatible with television watching, such as playing outdoors or building a model airplane.

It is also important to understand the reasons for a person's misbehavior before deciding how to respond to it. Edward Carr and Mark Durand (1985) found, for example, that when autistic and other disturbed children throw tantrums, attack their teachers, or do self-destructive things such as punching or poking themselves, it is often because difficult demands are being placed on them or because they are bored and frustrated. Their bizarre behavior is a way of saying, "Hey, let me out of here!" And because the behavior often works, or is reinforced by attention from adults, it tends to persist. When these children are taught to use words to ask for praise or help ("Am I doing good work?" "I don't understand"), their problem behavior decreases and often even disappears. Similarly, a child screaming in a supermarket may be saying, "I'm going out of my head with boredom. Help!" A lover who sulks may be saying, "I'm not sure you really care about me; I'm frightened." Once we understand the purpose or meaning of behavior we dislike, we may be more effective in dealing with it.

The Problem with Reward

Researchers have conditioned rats thousands of times, and as far as we know, none of the rats ever refused to cooperate or felt that they were being manipulated. Human beings are different. A little girl we know came home from school one day in a huff after her teacher announced that good performance would be rewarded with play money that could later be exchanged for privileges. "Doesn't she think I can learn without being bribed?" the child asked her mother indignantly.

This child's reaction illustrates a complication in the use of reinforcers. So far, most of our examples of operant conditioning have involved **extrinsic reinforcers,** reinforcers that come from an outside source and are unrelated to the activity being reinforced. Money, praise, gold stars, applause, hugs, and thumbs-up signs are all extrinsic reinforcers. But people (and probably some other animals, too) also work for **intrinsic reinforcers,** such as enjoyment of the task and the satisfaction of accomplishment. As psychologists have applied operant conditioning in real-world settings, they have sometimes found that extrinsic reinforcement, if you focus on it exclusively, can become too much of a good thing, because in some circumstances, it can kill the pleasure of doing something for its own sake.

Consider what happened when psychologists gave nursery-school children the chance to draw with felt-tip pens (Lepper, Greene, & Nisbett, 1973). The children already liked this activity and readily took it up during free play. First, the researchers recorded how long each child spontaneously played with the pens. Then they told some of the children that if they would draw with felt-tip pens for a man who had come "to see what kinds of pictures boys and girls like to draw with Magic Markers," there would be a prize, a "Good Player Award," complete with gold seal and red ribbon. After drawing for six minutes, each child got the award, as promised. Other children did not expect a reward and were not given one. A week later, the researchers again observed the children's free play. Those children who had expected and received a reward were spending much less time with the pens than they had before the start of the experiment. Children who were not given an award continued to show as much

---

extrinsic reinforcers Reinforcers that are not inherently related to the activity being reinforced, such as money, prizes, and praise.
intrinsic reinforcers Reinforcers that are inherently related to the activity being reinforced, such as enjoyment of the task and the satisfaction of accomplishment.

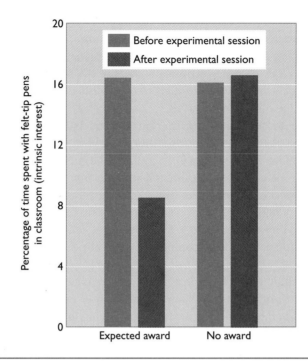

Figure 6.5 *When preschoolers were promised a prize for drawing with felt-tipped pens, the behavior temporarily increased, but after receiving the prize, the children spent less time with the pens than they had before the study began (Lepper, Greene, & Nisbett, 1973). Such results suggest that extrinsic rewards can sometimes reduce intrinsic motivation.*

interest in the activity as they had shown initially (see Figure 6.5). Similar results occurred when older children were or were not rewarded for working on academic tasks.

More recently, in an ongoing longitudinal study, researchers divided nine-year-old children into two groups, one in which mothers encouraged the children to learn for the intrinsic pleasure of it and another in which mothers rewarded high grades and punished low ones. By the time they were ten years old, the children in the first group had higher motivation and better school performance. Extrinsic rewards and punishments actually seemed to impede the children's academic achievement (Gottfried, Fleming, & Gottfried, 1994).

Why should extrinsic rewards undermine intrinsic motivation? Some researchers suggest that when we are paid for an activity, we interpret it as work. It is as if we say to ourselves, "I'm doing this because I'm being paid for it. Because I'm being paid, it must be something I wouldn't do if I didn't have to." When the reward is withdrawn, we refuse to "work" any longer. Others argue that extrinsic rewards are seen as controlling, and therefore they reduce a person's sense of autonomy and choice ("I guess I should do only what I'm told to do") (Deci & Ryan, 1987). A third, more behavioral explanation is that extrinsic reinforcement sometimes raises the rate of responding above some optimal, enjoyable level. Then the activity really does become work.

There is a trade-off, then, between the short-term effectiveness of extrinsic rewards and the long-term effectiveness of intrinsic ones. Extrinsic rewards work:

How many people would trudge off to work every morning if they never got paid? In the classroom, a teacher who offers incentives to an unmotivated student may be taking the only course of action open. Further, you have to have the skill to do something before the activity can become intrinsically pleasurable (Chance, 1992). Reading a good novel may be intrinsically rewarding, but the painstaking process of learning, as a first-grader, to sound out words is less so.

If a behavior is to last when the teacher isn't around, however, extrinsic reinforcers eventually must be phased out. As one mother once wrote in a *Newsweek* essay, "The winners [of prizes for school work] will . . . suffer if they don't discover for themselves that they can gain the pleasure of health and strength from exercise, the joy of music from songs, the power of mathematics from counting and all of human wisdom from reading" (Skreslet, 1987). The fact that our school system relies heavily on grades may help explain why the average college graduate reads few books. Like all extrinsic rewards, grades induce temporary compliance but not necessarily a lifelong disposition to learn.

We do not want to leave the impression, however, that extrinsic reinforcers always decrease the pleasure of an activity. Many businesses now recognize that workers' productivity depends both on pay incentives *and* on having interesting, challenging, and varied kinds of work to do. Money and praise do not necessarily interfere with intrinsic motivation when these extrinsic rewards are clearly tied to competence rather that mere performance and when the activity is already well learned (Dickinson, 1989). Also, people who are extremely interested in an activity or task to begin with are likely to keep doing it even when external rewards are withdrawn (Mawhinney, 1990). Extrinsic rewards can even increase creativity, as long as they are given only for high-quality performance and are not so salient that they distract a person from the task at hand (Eisenberger & Selbst, 1994).

WHAT DO YOU KNOW?

A. According to behavioral principles, what is happening here?

1. An adolescent whose parents have hit him for minor transgressions since he was small runs away from home.
2. A young woman whose parents paid her to clean her room while she was growing up is a slob when she moves to her own apartment.
3. Two parents scold their young daughter every time they catch her sucking her thumb. The thumb sucking continues anyway.

B. In a fee-for-service system of health care, doctors are paid for each visit by a patient or for each service performed, and the longer the visit, the higher the fee. In contrast, some health-maintenance organizations (HMOs) pay their doctors a fixed amount per patient for the entire year. If the amount actually expended is less, the physician gets a bonus, and in some systems, if the amount expended is more, the physician is financially penalized. Given what you know about operant conditioning, what are the advantages and disadvantages of each system?

THE WORLD AS THE BEHAVIORIST VIEWS IT

In 1913, John Watson's paper "Psychology as the Behaviorist Views It"—sometimes called "the behaviorist manifesto"—transformed American psychology. It immediately appealed to Americans' love of the practical and pragmatic. Today, behavioral concepts continue to offer down-to-earth explanations of events that to others might seem complicated. Let us look at the world as the behaviorist views it, by examining two phenomena not usually attributed to conditioning: the persistence of superstitions and the lightning bolt of insight. In explaining these phenomena, or any others, behaviorists argue for the application of Occam's razor: the rule, mentioned in Chapter 1, which says that the best explanation is the one requiring the fewest assumptions.

Superstition

Do you use a "lucky pen" when you take exams? Have you ever avoided walking under a ladder because doing so "brings bad luck"? Do you have a little "lucky charm" in your car to protect you against accidents? Even if you have never done these things, you probably know someone who has. Why do people hold such superstitions?

The answer, say behaviorists, has to do partly with the nature of reinforcement. Although many reinforcers are a direct result of the responses they follow (a rat's bar pressing brings food), reinforcement can be effective even when it is entirely coincidental. Skinner (1948) first demonstrated this fact by putting eight pigeons in boxes and rigging the boxes so that food was delivered every 15 seconds, even if the bird didn't lift a feather. Pigeons, like rats, are often in motion, so when the food came, the animals were likely to be doing *something*. That something was then reinforced by the food. The behavior, of course, was reinforced entirely by chance, but it still became more likely to occur, and thus to be reinforced again. Within a short time, six of the pigeons were practicing some sort of consistent ritual—turning in counterclockwise circles, bobbing the head up and down, swinging the head to and fro, or making brushing movements toward the floor. None of these actions had the least effect on the delivery of the reinforcer; the birds were behaving "superstitiously." It was as if they thought their movements were responsible for bringing the food.

You can see how coincidental reinforcement might account for certain human superstitions. A baseball pitcher happens to scratch his left ear, then strikes out a star batter on the other team; ever after, he scratches his left ear before pitching. A student uses a purple pen on the first exam of the semester, gets an A, and from then on uses only purple pens for taking tests. Why, though, don't such superstitions extinguish? After all, the pitcher isn't going to strike out every batter, nor is the student always going to be brilliant. One answer: Intermittent reinforcement may make the response resistant to extinction. If coincidental reinforcement occurs occasionally, the superstitious behavior may continue indefinitely (Schwartz & Reilly, 1985). Ironically, to everyone but behaviorists, the fact that our little rituals "work" only some of the time ensures that we will keep using them.

Of course, there are other reasons that superstitions persist. Many superstitions are part of one's culture and are reinforced by the agreement, approval, or attention of others. You don't have to have an accident after walking beneath a ladder, spilling the salt, or breaking a mirror to believe that these actions bring bad luck. Some superstitions are reinforced by the feeling of control over events that they provide. And people often look for evidence to justify their superstitions but ignore contrary evidence. As Paul Chance (1988) has pointed out, if a child finds a four-leaf clover and a few days later trips over a dollar, adults may point to the four-leaf clover's power; but if nothing particularly lucky happens to the child until puberty, no one points to the clover's failure. As for good-luck charms and the like, as long as nothing awful happens when a person is carrying the charm, the person is likely to credit it with protective powers, but if something bad does occur, the person can always say that the charm has lost its powers. Yet even when we know the reasons for our superstitions, they can be hard to shake. Chance says that he himself no longer has any superstitions. "A black cat means nothing to me now, nor does a broken mirror. There are no little plastic icons on the dashboard of my car, and I carry no rabbit's foot. I am free of all such nonsense, and I am happy to report no ill effects—knock wood."

Insight

Insight is learning that seems to occur in a flash: You suddenly "see" how to solve an equation, assemble a cabinet that came with unintelligible instructions, or finish a puzzle. The human species is not the only one capable of insight. In the 1920s, Wolfgang Köhler (1925) put chimpanzees in situations in which some tempting bananas were just out of reach, then he watched to see what the apes would do. Most did nothing, but a few turned out to be very clever. If the bananas were outside the cage, the animal might pull them in with a stick. If the bananas were hung overhead, and there were boxes in the cage, the chimpanzee might pile up the boxes and climb on top of

---

insight A form of learning that occurs in problem solving and appears to involve the (often sudden) understanding of how elements of a situation are related or can be reorganized to achieve a solution.

them to reach the fruit. Often the solution came after the animal had been sitting quietly for a while without actively trying to reach the bananas. It appeared as though the animal had been thinking about the problem and suddenly saw the answer.

To most people, insight seems to be an entirely cognitive phenomenon—a new way of perceiving logical and cause-and-effect relationships—in which a person or animal does not simply respond to a stimulus but instead solves a problem. But behaviorists argue that insight can be explained in terms of an organism's reinforcement history, without resorting to cognitive explanations (Windholz & Lamal, 1985). To a behaviorist, insight is just a label for a sudden change in behavior; it does not *explain* the behavior. In this view, nothing is to be gained by resorting to mentalistic notions. What seems to be "insight" is the combination of previously learned patterns.

Behaviorists point out that even animals not usually credited with higher mental processes seem capable of what looks suspiciously like "insight" if they have had certain experiences. In one ingenious study, Robert Epstein and his colleagues (1984) taught four pigeons to perform three separate behaviors, during different training sessions: to push boxes in a particular direction, to climb onto a box, and to peck at a toy banana in order to obtain grain. The birds were also taught not to fly or jump at the banana; those behaviors were extinguished. Then the pigeons were left alone with the banana suspended just out of reach overhead and the box at the edge of the cage.

"At first," the researchers observed, "each pigeon appeared to be 'confused'; it stretched and turned beneath the banana, looked back and forth from banana to box, and so on. Then each subject began rather suddenly to push the box in what was clearly the direction of the banana" (Epstein et al., 1984). Just as Köhler's chimps had done, the birds quickly solved their feeding problem by pushing the box beneath the banana and climbing onto it (see Figure 6.6), yet few people would want to credit pigeons with complex thought processes. Epstein (1990) has since devised a computer model that is amazingly accurate in predicting the pigeons' behavior in the banana-and-box situation, using only behavioral concepts.

(a)   (b)   (c)

Figure 6.6 *A pigeon looks at a cluster of toy bananas strung overhead (a), pushes a small box beneath the bananas (b), and then climbs on the box to peck at them (c). The bird had previously learned separate components of this sequence through a process of operant conditioning. Behaviorists view this accomplishment as evidence against the cognitive view of insight. What do you think?*

Most psychologists maintain that although insight may require the use of previously learned responses to solve problems, in human beings (and possibly chimpanzees), it requires mentally combining these responses in new ways. To behaviorists, however, insight is the *result* of learning, not a way of learning.

The learning perspective suggests that many behaviors that we regard as perplexing, self-defeating, or just plain natural may, in fact, be the result of patterns of reinforcement—and that these patterns, once understood, can be manipulated to alter behaviors and improve our lives. (We will discuss some practical efforts to do just this in Chapter 8.) But behaviorists and their goals have often been misunderstood. Skinner was a special target of public hostility. In the 1970s, after Skinner's book *Beyond Freedom and Dignity* put him on the cover of *Time* magazine, scholars, theologians, and even politicians rushed to attack him. Poet Stephen Spender called the book "fascism without tears." The Chicago *Tribune* ran a picture of a rat with Skinner-like features.

In reality, Skinner was a quiet and mild-mannered person, who cared passionately about the wise application of behavioral principles. He adamantly opposed the use of coercion and punishment and was greatly concerned with issues of social justice (Dinsmoor, 1992). Long before the modern feminist movement, he advocated a world of sexual equality in which work is not assigned by gender. Skinner was, in fact, a humanist in the broadest sense of the term, which is why the American Humanist Association once gave him its Humanist of the Year Award. Toward the end of his life, in a book called *Enjoy Old Age,* he offered all sorts of useful tips on how the elderly could make their lives easier (Skinner & Vaughan, 1984). And in 1990, just a week before his death, ailing and frail, he addressed an overflow crowd at the annual meeting of the American Psychological Association, making the case one last time for the approach he was convinced could create a better society.

When you see the world as the behaviorist views it, Skinner was saying, you see the folly of human behavior, but you also see the possibility of improving it.

◆ ◆ ◆

Summary

1. For almost half a century, until the 1960s, *behaviorism* was the dominant approach to the study of learning. Behaviorists have shown that two types of conditioning can explain much of human behavior: classical conditioning and operant conditioning.

2. *Classical conditioning* was first studied by Russian physiologist Ivan Pavlov. In this type of learning, when a neutral stimulus is regularly paired with an *unconditioned stimulus (US)* that elicits some reflexive *unconditioned response (UR),* the neutral stimulus comes to elicit a similar or related response. The neutral stimulus is then called a *conditioned stimulus (CS),* and the response it elicits, a *conditioned response (CR).* In classical conditioning, the CS becomes a kind of signal for the US; it enables the organism to prepare for an event that is about to happen. Nearly any kind of involuntary response can become a CR.

3. Today, many theorists believe that what an animal or person learns in classical conditioning is not just an association between the unconditioned and conditioned

stimulus, but information conveyed by one stimulus about another. They cite evidence that the neutral stimulus does not become a CS unless it reliably signals or predicts the US.

4. In *extinction,* the conditioned stimulus is repeatedly presented without the unconditioned stimulus, and the conditioned response eventually disappears. In *higher-order conditioning,* a neutral stimulus becomes a conditioned stimulus by being paired with an already established conditioned stimulus. In *stimulus generalization,* after a stimulus becomes a conditioned stimulus for some response, similar stimuli produce a similar reaction. In *stimulus discrimination,* different responses are made to stimuli that resemble the conditioned stimulus in some way.

5. Classical conditioning may help account for the acquisition of likes and dislikes, emotional responses to particular objects and events, unusual desires, consumer preferences, and fears and phobias. John Watson showed how fears may be learned and then unlearned through a process of *counterconditioning.*

6. The basic principle of *operant conditioning* is that behavior becomes more or less likely to occur, depending on its consequences. Responses in operant conditioning are generally not reflexive and are more complex than in classical conditioning. Research on operant conditioning is closely associated with B. F. Skinner.

7. In the Skinnerian analysis, a response ("operant") can lead to one of three consequences: neutral, reinforcing, or punishing. *Reinforcement* strengthens or increases the probability of a response. *Punishment* weakens or decreases the probability of a response. Reinforcement (and punishment) may be positive or negative. *Positive reinforcement* occurs when something pleasant follows a response. *Negative reinforcement* occurs when something *un*pleasant is removed. Reinforcement is called *primary* when the reinforcer is naturally reinforcing (for instance, satisfying a biological need) and *secondary* when the reinforcer has acquired its ability to strengthen a response through association with other reinforcers. A similar distinction is made for punishers.

8. By using the Skinner box and similar devices, behaviorists have shown that extinction, stimulus generalization, and stimulus discrimination occur in operant, as well as in classical, conditioning. They have also found that immediate consequences usually have a greater effect on a response than do delayed consequences.

9. The pattern of responding in operant conditioning depends in part on the *schedule of reinforcement. Continuous* reinforcement leads to the most rapid learning, but *intermittent,* or *partial,* reinforcement makes a response resistant to extinction. Intermittent schedules deliver a reinforcer after a certain amount of time has passed since the last reinforcer (*interval schedules*) or after a certain number of responses have been made (*ratio schedules*). Such schedules may be *fixed* or *variable.* One of the most common errors people make is to reward intermittently the responses they would like to eliminate.

10. *Shaping* is used to train behaviors that have a low probability of occurring spontaneously. Reinforcers are given for *successive approximations* to the desired response, until the desired response is achieved.

11. *Behavior modification,* the application of operant principles, has been used successfully in many settings, often by applying a *token economy.* But reinforcement and punishment both have their pitfalls.

12. Punishment has many drawbacks and may have unintended consequences. It is often administered inappropriately because of the emotion of the moment; it may produce rage and fear; it is hard to administer immediately; its effects are often only temporary; it conveys little information about what kind of behavior is desired; and an action intended to punish may instead be reinforcing because of the attention it brings. Extinction of undesirable behavior, combined with reinforcement of desired behavior, is generally preferable to the use of punishment. It is also important to understand the reasons for a person's misbehavior instead of simply trying to get rid of it without knowing why it occurs.

13. In real-world settings, an exclusive reliance on *extrinsic reinforcement* can sometimes undermine the power of *intrinsic reinforcement*. But money and praise do not usually interfere with intrinsic pleasure when a person is rewarded for succeeding or making progress rather than for merely participating in an activity, or when a person is already extremely interested in the activity.

14. Behaviorists explain superstitions by noting that accidental or coincidental reinforcement can effectively strengthen a behavior even though it is not a direct result of the response it follows. In this view, when superstitions do not extinguish, the reason is that they are reinforced intermittently. Superstitious behaviors are also reinforced by the agreement or approval of others, and by the illusion of control that they bring.

15. Behaviorists explain *insight* in terms of a person's or an animal's history of reinforcement. In their view, insight simply involves the combination of previously learned patterns; it is the result of learning, not a way of learning.

16. Because behaviorists believe that the environment can and should be manipulated to alter behavior, some critics have portrayed them as cold-blooded and even dangerous. Behaviorists reply that people are constantly manipulating the environment, whether in a planned or an unplanned way; society should therefore use learning principles wisely to achieve humane goals.

Key Terms

behaviorism *201*

conditioning *202*

Ivan Pavlov *202*

unconditioned stimulus (US) *203*

unconditioned response (UR) *203*

conditioned stimulus (CS) *203*

conditioned response (CR) *203*

classical conditioning *204*

extinction (in classical conditioning) *206*

spontaneous recovery (in classical conditioning) *206*

higher-order conditioning *206*

stimulus generalization (in classical conditioning) *206*

stimulus discrimination (in classical conditioning) *206*

John B. Watson *208*

phobia *209*

counterconditioning *210*

CHAPTER 7

Social and Cognitive Learning

*I*n 1903, an Irish journalist named Frank Skeffington married a young woman named Hanna Sheehy. To demonstrate his commitment to women's rights, he added her name to his, becoming Frank Sheehy-Skeffington; wore a large "Votes for Women" badge; and resigned as registrar of University College, Dublin, when the university refused to grant women equal status with men. Throughout their lives, Frank and Hanna Sheehy-Skeffington never wavered in their commitment to unpopular causes—women's rights, Irish independence, and nonviolence—despite public ridicule, harassment, and even time in jail. In 1915, with World War I raging, Frank wrote to a friend,

> European militarism has drenched Europe in blood; Irish militarism may only crimson the fields of Ireland. . . . I advocate no mere servile lazy acquiescence in injustice. I am, and always will be, a fighter. But I want to see the age-long fight against injustice clothe itself in new forms suited to a new age. I want to see the manhood of Ireland no longer hypnotised by the glamour of "the glory of arms," no longer blind to the horrors of organised murder. (Quoted in Levenson, 1983)

Why do individuals such as the Sheehy-Skeffingtons care little for the conventional boundaries of masculinity and femininity? What keeps people working for long-term dreams that might never pay off in their lifetimes? How does behavior become so self-rewarding that it does not depend on the immediate reinforcers of society? After all, few of this couple's actions were rewarded; on the contrary, most of their actions were followed by negative consequences. Why did they never lose their commitment to unpopular causes?

To most psychologists, principles of classical and operant conditioning do not offer adequate answers. Even during the early glory years of behaviorism, a few behaviorists were rebelling against explanations that relied solely on conditioning principles. In the 1940s, two social scientists proposed a modification they called *social-learning theory* (Dollard & Miller, 1950). In human beings, they argued, most learning is social—that is, acquired by observing other people in social context.

By the 1960s and 1970s, social-learning theory was in full bloom, and a new element had been added: the human capacity for higher-level cognitive processes. Its proponents agreed with behaviorists that human beings, along with the rat and the rabbit, are subject to the laws of operant and classical conditioning. But they added that human beings, unlike the rat and the rabbit, are full of attitudes, beliefs, and expectations that affect the way they acquire information, make decisions, reason, and solve problems. All of these mental processes affect what individuals will do at any given moment and also, more generally, the kinds of people they become.

Social-learning theories remain linked to their origins in behaviorism in stressing the influence of the immediate environment on a person's actions. And because rewards and punishers differ in different circumstances, all learning approaches to behavior correctly predict that people often will behave inconsistently across situations (Mischel, 1984, 1990). Situational reinforcers are the reason that employees may be honest at work and cheat on their taxes, or that teenagers may behave dutifully and lovingly to their parents but commit thefts and vandalism with their buddies. ("But he's such a good boy," the mother always says at her son's trial—and to her, he might very well have been just that.)

However, social-learning theorists differ from radical behaviorists by arguing that people often choose what situations to get into in the first place. A party imposes a general requirement to be sociable, but sociable people are more likely to go to parties than hermits are. Moreover, simply counting behaviors (say, acts of honesty) can lead to mistaken conclusions. You might not cheat on an exam in class but ask a friend to help you on a take-home essay; your actions may seem inconsistent to an observer, yet you may believe you are doing the honest thing in both cases. When researchers assess the *psychological meaning* of an act to the individual, they find greater consistency across situations than a strictly behavioral approach would predict (Funder & Colvin, 1991). In social-learning approaches, therefore, behavior cannot be separated from its psychological meaning. People bring their unique perceptions and expectations to all situations, which is why you can find sulkers at the happiest occasions and optimists in the midst of disasters.

Thus social-learning approaches differ from behaviorism in the way they see the *interaction* between individuals and their environments. Radical behaviorists regard the relationship of environment to behavior primarily as a straight line, like this:

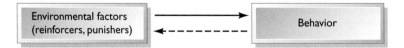

But social-learning theorists see the environment, a person's qualities, and his or her behavior as forming a circle in which all elements mutually affect each other. This interaction of the person and the environment, called *reciprocal determinism* (Bandura, 1986), looks like this:

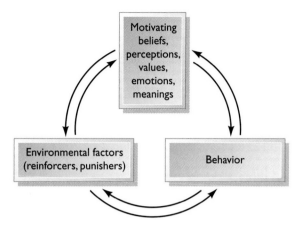

We speak of **social-learning theories** in the plural because they do not represent a single unified approach to behavior in the way that traditional behaviorism does. Researchers in this field differ, for example, in the emphasis they place on cognitive processes. Some continue to call themselves "social-learning theorists," but the two leading proponents of this approach, Walter Mischel and Albert Bandura, call their theories *cognitive social-learning theory* (Mischel, 1973) and *social cognitive theory* (Bandura, 1986, 1994), respectively. Social-learning psychologists also differ in how much they distance themselves from behaviorism. One reviewer of this chapter, who studies how boys and girls learn the rules of masculine and feminine behavior, said that the "most important theme in social-learning theory is its insistence on understanding how the environment is organized, which then provides a person with feedback that in turn elicits and maintains certain behaviors." But another, who studies people's capacities to monitor and change their own behavior, said, "I explicitly reject the view that people's beliefs and behavior are determined by the cumulative effect of their history of reinforcement." To make matters more complicated, many psychologists do research that supports a social-learning model without calling themselves "social-learning theorists" or "social cognitive theorists" or anything similar! We include their work nonetheless because it illustrates the major components of this general approach to how people learn.

In the first half of this chapter, we will consider the distinguishing features of social-learning approaches to behavior. Then we will see how they might help us understand two complex aspects of child development: how children learn the rules of gender and how they become moral and helpful members of society.

---

social-learning theories Theories of learning that typically emphasize a person's reciprocal interaction with the environment and that focus on observational learning, cognitive processes, and motivational beliefs.

Beyond Behaviorism

Modern social-learning theories emphasize three phenomena that distinguish them from traditional behaviorism: (1) observational learning and the role of models; (2) cognitive processes such as perceptions and interpretations of events; and (3) motivating beliefs, such as enduring expectations of success or failure, and confidence or doubt in one's ability to master new skills and achieve goals. We want to emphasize again, however, that individual social-learning theorists differ in the relative attention they pay to these three factors.

Observational Learning

Late one night, a friend who lives in a rural area was awakened by a loud clattering and banging. Her whole family raced outside to find the source of the commotion. A raccoon had knocked over a "raccoon-proof" garbage can and seemed to be demonstrating to an assembly of other raccoons how to open it: If you jump up and down on the can's side, the lid will pop off.

According to our friend, the observing raccoons learned from this episode how to open stubborn garbage cans, and the observing humans learned how smart raccoons can be. In short, they all benefited from **observational learning** (which behaviorists call *vicarious conditioning*): learning by watching what others do and what happens to them for doing it. Social-learning theorists argue that operant conditioning can and often does occur vicariously, when an animal or person observes a *model* (another animal or person) behaving in certain ways and then experiencing the consequences. Sometimes the learner imitates the responses shortly after observing them. At other times the learning remains latent until circumstances allow or require it to be expressed in performance. A little boy may observe a parent setting the table, threading a needle, or tightening a screw, but he may not act on this learning for years. Then the child finds that he knows how to do these things, even though he has never before done them. He did not learn by doing, but by watching.

None of us would last long without observational learning. We would have to learn to avoid oncoming cars by walking into traffic and suffering the consequences or to swim by jumping into a deep pool and flailing around. Learning would be not only dangerous but also inefficient. Parents and teachers would be busy 24 hours a day shaping children's behavior. Bosses would have to stand over their employees' desks, rewarding every little link in the complex behavioral chains we call typing, report writing, and accounting. Observational learning also explains why parents who hit their children for hitting other kids tend to rear children who are hitters, and why yellers ("Be quiet!") tend to rear yellers. The children do as their parents do, not as they say (Grusec, Saas-Kortsaak, & Simutis, 1978).

---

observational learning A learning process in which an individual learns new responses by observing the behavior of another (a model) rather than through direct experience; in behaviorism, it is called *vicarious conditioning*.

Many years ago, Albert Bandura and his colleagues showed just how important observational learning is, especially for children who are learning the rules of social behavior (Bandura, Ross, & Ross, 1963). In their study, nursery-school children watched a short film of two men, Rocky and Johnny, playing with toys. (Apparently, the children did not think this behavior was odd.) In the film, Johnny refuses to share his toys, and Rocky responds by clobbering him. Rocky's actions are rewarded because he winds up with all the toys. Poor Johnny sits dejectedly in the corner, while Rocky marches off with a sack full of his loot and a hobbyhorse under his arm. After viewing the film, each child was left alone for 20 minutes in a playroom full of toys, including some of the items shown in the film. Watching through a one-way mirror, the researchers found that these children were much more aggressive in their play than were a control group of children who had not seen the film. Sometimes the children's behavior was a direct imitation of Rocky's. At the end of the session, one little girl even asked the experimenter for a sack!

Of course, children imitate positive activities, too. Matt Groening, the creator of the cartoon *The Simpsons,* decided it would be funny if the Simpsons' 8-year-old daughter Lisa played the baritone sax. Sure enough, across the country little girls began imitating her. Cynthia Sikes, a saxophone teacher in New York, told *The New York Times* (January 14, 1996) that "When the show started, I got an influx of girls coming up to me saying, 'I want to play the saxophone because Lisa Simpson plays the saxophone.'" And Groening says his mail regularly includes photos of girls holding up their saxophones.

Observational learning begins very early. Recent studies have found that even children who are too young to speak are natural mimics who learn by observing and imitating the behavior of others. In three experiments, Elizabeth Hanna and Andrew Meltzoff (1993) demonstrated that one-year-olds will imitate their peers, and this learning is robust enough to persist over time and in different situations. The researchers designed five simple toys that a one-year-old could not have seen elsewhere. With one toy, the baby had to learn to poke a finger through a hole in a box to activate a buzzer. Another was a plastic cup made of rings; the trick was to collapse the cup by pressing it down with the palm of the hand.

In the first experiment with sixty 14-month-old babies, several babies learned to be "experts" by sitting on their mothers' laps and watching an experimenter demonstrate the toys. The babies then got to play with the toys themselves and were praised (rewarded!) for using them correctly. Next, the now-"expert" babies showed three fellow toddlers how the toys worked. When the babies who watched were given a chance to play with the toys, they did so correctly two-thirds of the time, within 20 seconds. This was significantly more often than a baseline control group of toddlers who hadn't observed the expert, and significantly more often than another control group that had watched a toddler who played with the toys but did not solve the toys' tricks.

In two other experiments with toddlers ranging from 14 to 18 months of age, the researchers found that children not only learn from their peers but also are able to transfer that learning from one setting to another, even after two days have elapsed. "Expert" babies demonstrated each toy, just once, to other children who observed them either in a calm laboratory or in the busy and distracting environment of a child-care center. Two days later, the observing children got the chance to play with the toys themselves, but this time in their own homes. Even though they had observed the solution to each toy only once, they played correctly with the toys 72 percent of the time—again, far more often than did those in the two control groups. These studies clearly illustrated observational learning: The toddlers saw the demonstration and then remembered what they had seen.

Behaviorists have always acknowledged the importance of observational learning; they just think that it can be explained in stimulus–response terms. But social-learning theorists believe that in human beings, observational learning cannot be fully understood without taking into account the thought processes of the learner (Meltzoff & Gopnik, 1993).

Cognitive Processes

Behaviorists, of course, are interested in the external stimuli that cause an animal or human being to respond a certain way. Whatever might be going on mentally, between the stimulus and the response, is of little interest to them. As behaviorist William Baum (1994) explains, "I no more have a mind than I have a fairy godmother. I can talk to you about my mind or about my fairy godmother; that cannot make either of them less fictional. No one has ever seen either one . . . such talk is no help in a science."

Early behaviorists liked to compare the mind to an engineer's hypothetical "black box," a device whose workings must be inferred because they can't be observed directly. To the behaviorists, the box of the mind contained irrelevant wiring; it was enough for them to know that pushing a button on the box would produce a predictable response. But even as early as the 1930s, a few behaviorists could not resist peeking into that black box. Edward Tolman (1938) committed virtual heresy at the time by noting that his rats, when pausing at turning points in a maze, seemed to be *deciding* which way to go. In his studies, Tolman found that sometimes the animals didn't behave as conditioning principles would predict. Sometimes the animals were clearly learning without any obvious behavioral change. What, he wondered, was going on in their little rat brains that might account for this puzzle?

In a classic experiment, Tolman and Chase Honzik (1930) placed three groups of rats in mazes and observed their behavior each day for more than two weeks. The rats in Group 1 always found food at the end of the maze. Group 2 never found food. Group 3 found no food for ten days but then received food on the eleventh. The Group 1 rats, which had been reinforced with food, quickly learned to head straight for the end of the maze without going down blind alleys, whereas Group 2 rats did not learn to go to the end. But the Group 3 rats were different. For ten days they appeared to follow no particular route. Then, on the eleventh day, when food was introduced, they quickly learned to run to the end of the maze. By the next day they were doing as well as those in Group 1.

Group 3 had demonstrated **latent learning,** learning that is not immediately expressed. A great deal of human learning also remains latent until circumstances allow or require it to be expressed, as we saw in our discussion of observational learning. But latent learning poses problems for behavioral theories. Not only does it occur in the

---

latent learning A form of learning that is not immediately expressed in an overt response; it occurs without obvious reinforcement.

absence of any obvious reinforcer, but it also raises questions about what, exactly, is learned during learning. The rats that were not given food until the eleventh day had no reason to run toward the end during their first ten days in the maze. Yet clearly they had learned *something*.

Tolman (1948) argued that this "something" was a **cognitive map,** a mental representation of the spatial layout of the environment. You have a cognitive map of your neighborhood, which is what allows you to find your way to Fourth and Kumquat streets even if you have never done so; and you have a cognitive map of the city you live in, which enables you to take three different unfamiliar routes across town to the movies and still get there. More generally, according to social-learning theories, what the learner learns in observational and latent learning is not a response but *knowledge* about responses and their consequences. We learn how the world is organized, which paths lead to which places, and which actions can produce which payoffs. This knowledge permits us to be creative and flexible in reaching our goals.

Social-learning theories also emphasize the importance of people's *perceptions* in what they learn: perceptions of the models they observe and also perceptions of themselves. As we will see in the cognitive perspective, two people may observe the same event and come away with entirely different interpretations of it; they have learned, we might say, two different lessons from it. Individuals also bring different knowledge and assumptions to an event, and they notice and pay attention to different aspects of a situation. Imagine two people trying to learn how to do a perfect "tush push" in country-western line dancing: One is paying careful attention to the instructor who is modeling the complex steps, but another is distracted by an appealing tush-pusher down the line. And of course the two novices may differ in how much they want to learn the new dance. People make thousands of observations every day and theoretically could learn something from all of them; but if they don't *want* to learn what is being modeled, they could watch a hundred teachers and not get anywhere at all (Bandura, 1986).

Individual differences in perceptions and interpretations help explain why violence in the media does not have the same effects on all viewers. No one disputes that movies and television programs are powerful shapers of values, attitudes, and reactions to events, including violent events. Much research since the classic Rocky and Johnny study has found that some children do become more aggressive by imitating the aggression they observe on television and in movies (Comstock et al., 1978; Eron, 1980, 1995; Singer & Singer, 1988). A task force assembled by the American Psychological Association to study this issue concluded that "There is absolutely no doubt that higher levels of viewing violence on television are correlated with increased acceptance of aggressive attitudes and increased aggressive behavior" (APA Commission on Violence and Youth, 1993).

Leonard Eron (1995), who has been conducting longitudinal research on this issue for many years, has found support for this conclusion in studies of girls and boys in countries as diverse as Australia, Finland, Israel, and Poland. Eron thinks the reason for the link between heavy childhood viewing of TV violence and later aggressive

---

cognitive map A mental representation of the environment.

habits is that TV violence teaches children certain attitudes, norms of behavior, and ways of solving problems (that is, aggressive ways—yelling, calling people names, hitting, and destroying the enemy in graphic ways). TV violence, he argues, is different from violence in Shakespeare, the movies, or fairy tales; in contrast to these forms of entertainment, which are clearly absorbed as "fantasy," TV images are pervasive, repetitive, and incessant because in most homes, the TV is nearly always on.

But other psychologists point out that in most studies, the relationship between media violence and real violence is not strong (Freedman, 1988; Milavsky, 1988). Cognitive social-learning theory helps explain why. Children watch many kinds of programs and movies, and they have many models to observe besides those they see in the media; their parents and peers are also influential. Moreover, not everyone draws the same lessons from the violence they perceive. One person who watches Arnold Schwarzenegger destroy the bad guys might regard Arnold as the greatest hero of all time, while another sees him as an overpaid weight lifter who should take acting lessons. One person may learn from seeing people being "blown away" in a film that violence is cool and masculine; another may conclude that violence is ugly, stupid, and self-defeating.

As a series of three experiments recently demonstrated, individuals who are habitually aggressive seek out violent media—and are more affected by violent media—than are nonaggressive people. Given a choice of films to see, they prefer the violent ones; when they actually watch violent films, they feel angrier afterward than nonaggressive people do; and if given the chance to behave aggressively toward others after watching a violent film, they are more likely to do so than nonaggressive people are (Bushman, 1995). Perhaps people should be prevented from seeing a violent movie on the basis not of their age, but their scores on an aggression test!

Eron responds to these findings by noting that "The size of the relation [between television violence and aggression] is about the same as that between smoking and lung cancer. Not everyone who smokes gets lung cancer and not everybody who has lung cancer ever smoked. But no one outside the tobacco industry would deny that smoking causes cancer. Similarly, not everyone who watches violent TV becomes aggressive and not everyone who is aggressive watches television. But that doesn't mean television violence is not a cause of aggression." Nevertheless, as Eron himself acknowledges, the relationship between TV violence and aggression is a two-way street: TV violence makes some children more aggressive, but highly aggressive children are also more likely to watch violent television. Also, a person prone to aggression may find "justification" to behave violently from *anything* he or she sees. Some years ago, a German named Heinrich Pommerencke went to the movies, where, watching women dancing on screen, he became convinced that all women were immoral and deserved to die. He went on to commit four brutal rape–murders before he was caught. The film that set him off was Cecil B. DeMille's *The Ten Commandments.*

In social-learning theories, therefore, cognitive processes of perception and interpretation, along with other dispositions such as aggressiveness (or, in the case of people like Pommerencke, mental illness), are crucial factors that intervene between what we see and how we respond.

Motivating Beliefs

Behaviorists would say that the thing we call "personality" is a set of habits and beliefs that have been rewarded over a person's lifetime. Social-learning theorists, however, maintain that these learned habits and beliefs eventually acquire a life of their own, coming to exert their own effects on behavior. In fact, they may even supersede the power of external rewards and punishers.

Let's take the question of why people work. One obvious answer is survival; people work for food and shelter. Yet survival needs do not explain what motivates LeRoy to work to put caviar on his table and Duane to work to put peanut butter on his. It doesn't explain why some people want to do their work well, and others want just to get it done. It doesn't explain the difference between Aristotle's view ("All paid employments absorb and degrade the mind") and Noël Coward's ("Work is more fun than fun"). According to social-learning theories, to understand why some people work hard, persisting even when they repeatedly fail, we need to understand their motivating beliefs and the goals they set for themselves.

In psychology, **motivation** refers to an inferred process within a person or animal that causes that organism to move toward a goal. With physiological motives, the goal

---

motivation An inferred process within a person or animal that causes that individual to move toward a goal.

is to satisfy a biological need, as in eating a sandwich to reduce hunger. But psychological motives involve incentives such as becoming the best in a field, earning nine zillion dollars, or reaching the pinnacle of fame. According to the learning perspective, no one is born with the ambition to be the best in a field. Behaviorists would say that this ambition, like any other, is a result of a history of reinforcers. When we say, "Pat is motivated to become famous," we are really saying that fame is positively reinforcing to Pat, which is why Pat continues to strive for it. But in the social-learning view, Pat's motivation eventually becomes internalized and self-directing. As Bandura (1994) puts it, people motivate themselves and evaluate their actions by setting goals, anticipating results, and planning courses of action. Some of the most important beliefs that motivate behavior, in the cognitive social-learning view, are the sense of control that people feel they have over their lives, their degree of optimism or pessimism, and how much confidence they have in their own abilities.

Locus of Control. Julian Rotter (1966, 1982, 1990) is a psychologist who, in his long career, has demonstrated the benefits of integrating more than one psychological perspective. When Rotter was first developing his social-learning approach to personality in the 1950s, he was working as both a psychotherapist and a researcher. He was a behaviorist in the laboratory, but he was also treating clients who weren't behaving according to behavioral principles. They kept having troubling emotions and irrational beliefs (Hunt, 1993). Rotter saw that his clients had formed certain entrenched attitudes as a result of their lifetimes of experience, and these attitudes were affecting their decisions and actions.

Over time, Rotter observed, people learn that certain of their acts will be rewarded and others punished, and thus they develop *generalized expectancies* about which situations and acts will be rewarding. A child who studies hard and gets good grades, attention from teachers, admiration from friends, and loving praise from parents will come to expect that hard work in other situations will also pay off. A child who studies hard and gets poor grades, is ignored by teachers, is rejected by friends for being a grind, or earns no support or praise from parents will come to expect that hard work isn't worth it. One child may learn that if she speaks her mind, she can expect praise and attention. Another may learn that if she speaks her mind, she can expect to irritate her parents, who want her to be quiet and obedient.

Once acquired, these expectations often create a **self-fulfilling prophecy,** in which a person predicts how he or she will do and then behaves in such a way as to make the prediction come true (Jones, 1977). You expect to do well, so you study hard, and then you do well. You expect to fail, so you don't do much work, and then you do poorly. In either case, you have fulfilled your expectation of yourself. One early experiment showed how quickly a self-fulfilling prophecy can be created. Young women were asked to solve 15 anagram puzzles. Before working on each one, they had to estimate

---

self-fulfilling prophecy An expectation that comes true because of the tendency of the person holding it to act in ways that confirm it.

their chances of solving it. Half of the women started off with five very simple anagrams, but half began with five insoluble ones. Sure enough, those who started with
the easy ones increased their estimates of success on later ones. Those who began with
the impossible ones decided that they would *all* be impossible. These expectations, in
turn, affected the young women's ability to solve the last ten anagrams, which were the
same for everyone. The higher the expectation of success, the more anagrams the
women solved (Feather, 1966).

Rotter and his colleagues demonstrated the power of expectancies in many experiments. At the same time, both in his private practice and in his experiments, Rotter
was observing people whose expectations of success never went up *even when they
were actually successful.* "Oh, that was just a fluke," they would say, or "I was lucky; it
will never happen again."

"At that point I put together the two sides of my work—as practitioner and as scientist," recalled Rotter, "and hypothesized that some people feel that what happens to
them is governed by external forces of one kind or another, while others feel that what
happens to them is governed largely by their own efforts and skills" (quoted in Hunt,
1993). Rotter used the term **locus of control** to refer to people's beliefs about whether
the results of their actions are under their own control. Such beliefs, he concluded, are
as important as the actual reinforcers and punishers in the environment. People who
have an *internal* locus of control ("internals") tend to believe that they are responsible
for what happens to them, that they control their own destiny. People who have an
external locus of control ("externals") tend to believe that they are victims (or sometimes beneficiaries) of luck, fate, or other people.

To measure these attitudes, Rotter (1966) developed an *Internal/External (I/E)
scale,* consisting of pairs of statements. People had to choose the statement in each pair
with which they most strongly agreed, as in these two items:

1. a. Many of the unhappy things in people's lives are partly due to bad luck.
    b. People's misfortunes result from the mistakes they make.

2. a. Becoming a success is a matter of hard work; luck has little or nothing to do
       with it.
    b. Getting a good job depends mainly on being in the right place at the right
       time.

Research on locus of control took off like a hot rod, and over the years more than
2,000 studies based on the I/E scale have been published (Hunt, 1993). Having an
internal locus of control has important advantages, both psychological and even physical. For example, it helps to reduce chronic pain, speed adjustment to surgery and illness, and hasten recovery from some diseases (Marshall, 1991; Taylor, 1995). In a study
of patients recovering from heart attacks, those who thought their illness was due to

---

locus of control A general expectation about whether the results of one's actions are under one's own control
(*internal* locus) or beyond one's control (*external* locus).

bad luck or fate—factors outside their control—were less likely to generate active plans for recovery and more likely to resume their old unhealthy habits. But those who thought that the heart attack occurred because they smoked, didn't exercise, or had a stressful job—factors within their control—were more likely to change their bad habits and recover more quickly (Affleck et al., 1987).

Cultures differ in their degree of fatalism and in their beliefs about whether it is possible to take control of one's health, and these cultural attitudes actually seem to be related to mortality rates. Researchers examined the deaths of 28,169 adult Chinese-Americans and 412,632 randomly selected, matched control subjects whose death certificates identified them as "white." In traditional Chinese astrology, certain birth years are considered bad luck, and people born in those years often acquire a fatalistic attitude toward bad fortune. This expectation can become a self-fulfilling prophecy. Chinese-Americans died significantly earlier than whites who had the same disease—by a margin of one to five years!—if they were born in a year traditionally considered to be ill-fated. The more strongly traditional the Chinese were, the more years of life they lost. These results held for nearly all causes of death studied, even when the researchers controlled for how well the patients took care of themselves and the kinds of medical treatments they received (Phillips, Ruth, & Wagner, 1993).

To date, dozens of studies conducted in different cultures and ethnic groups, with people of different ages, have confirmed that internal locus of control is also strongly related to achievement, especially academic achievement. More than 700 studies using a children's version of the I/E scale have been done, and this research shows that internal control and its effects emerge at an early age (Strickland, 1989).

However, although having an internal locus of control has advantages, it is not necessarily beneficial to everyone, in all situations. The reason may be clear if we ask: Control over what? Some goals in life are not attainable even with the most determined effort, so a person who is unrealistically confident may be devastated by failure. Some psychologists maintain that the very notion of being in control of your destiny reflects a middle-class and Western view of life: Work hard enough, and anything is possible (Markus & Kitayama, 1991). For some poor people and minorities, in contrast, having an external locus of control is one way to preserve self-esteem and cope with objective difficulties. They say, in effect, "I am a good and worthy person; my lot in life is a result of prejudice, fate, or the system" (Crocker & Major, 1989).

Such findings suggest that locus of control is affected by one's position and experiences in society—and, in turn, that it has the potential to motivate people to make changes in society. As Rotter was developing his ideas about locus of control in the 1960s, the civil rights movement was gathering steam. At that time, civil-rights activists and black student leaders were more likely to score at the internal end of the scale than control groups who were uninvolved in civil-rights efforts (Gore & Rotter, 1963; Strickland, 1965). By the 1970s, however—after the assassinations of Martin Luther King, Jr., Malcolm X, and John and Robert Kennedy, after riots had devastated many black communities, and with the nation embroiled in the Vietnam War—American self-confidence in social progress had been deeply shaken. Accordingly, scores on the locus-of-control scale changed. Civil-rights leaders and college students became less internal—that is, less confident that they, as individuals, could improve social conditions (Phares, 1976; Sank & Strickland, 1973; Strickland, 1989). Where would you place your own locus of control today? How do you think it reflects your experiences? How does it affect your beliefs about the possibility of personal and social change?

Explanatory Style. The findings on locus of control suggest that most people find an ego-enhancing balance between internal and external explanations, saying, in essence, "I'm responsible for the good things that happen to me, but rotten luck is responsible for the bad things." Depressed people, however, typically do the reverse: They say that the good things that happen to them are accidents and that the bad things are their own fault. Where do they get these self-defeating ideas?

Martin Seligman (1975), who was a graduate student when Rotter published his I/E scale, proposed that the answer was "learned helplessness": People become depressed when their efforts to control the environment fail, when they cannot escape pain and unhappiness. This behavioral explanation seemed to explain the burnout and apathy of depressed people. But it proved to have a fatal flaw: Not all depressed people have actually failed in their lives, and many people live though painful experiences that they can't do anything about, yet they don't become depressed.

Eventually, Seligman (1991) combined learned helplessness with locus of control, producing a theory of *explanatory style*—the typical ways that people account for unexpected bad events that befall them. People who have a *pessimistic* explanatory style tend to explain such events as internal ("It's all my fault"), stable ("This misery is going to last forever"), and global ("It's going to affect everything I do"). People who have an *optimistic* explanatory style regard the same events as external ("I couldn't have done anything"), unstable ("Things will improve"), and limited in impact ("At least the rest of my life is OK").

Optimism is a remarkable predictor of achievement and resilience. For example, studies have found that optimistic life-insurance agents sell more insurance than pessimistic agents; and optimistic Olympic-level swimmers recover from defeat and later swim even faster, whereas pessimistic swimmers, following defeat, get slower (Seligman, 1991). When faced with a serious problem—such as deciding about a risky operation, coping with traumatic events, or overcoming drug abuse or alcoholism—optimists tend to focus on what they can *do* rather than on how they *feel.* They keep their senses of humor, plan for the future, and reinterpret the situation in a positive light (Carver, Scheier, & Weintraub, 1989). When researchers followed a sample of people in Florida who had suffered devastating losses as a result of Hurricane Andrew, they found that pessimism was a significant predictor of continued distress six months after the disaster, whereas loss of resources was not (Carver et al., 1993). It's not how much you lose, apparently, but how you think about that loss that makes the most difference to your state of mind.

Optimists, by definition, expect to recover from adversity eventually, and they expect to be successful at whatever they do, so they work much harder to reach their goals than pessimists do. Thus is another self-fulfilling prophecy created.

Self-efficacy. The third and perhaps most important motivating belief in social-learning theory is a person's sense of competence (Sternberg & Kolligian, 1990; White, 1959). Albert Bandura (1990, 1994) maintains that competence is based on **self-efficacy,** the conviction that you can successfully accomplish what you set out to do. Dozens of studies have found that self-efficacy affects how well people do on a task, how persistently they pursue goals, the kind of career choices they make, their ability to solve complex problems at work, their health habits, their athletic performance, and how they respond to stress (Hackett et al., 1992; Kamin et al., 1995; Sadri & Robertson, 1993).

According to Bandura (1994), people acquire self-efficacy from four sources:

1. EXPERIENCES IN MASTERING NEW SKILLS AND OVERCOMING OBSTACLES ON THE PATH TO ACHIEVEMENT. Occasional failures are necessary for a robust sense of self-efficacy because people who experience only success learn to expect quick results and tend to be easily discouraged by normal difficulties.

2. VICARIOUS EXPERIENCES PROVIDED BY SUCCESSFUL AND COMPETENT PEOPLE (MODELS) WHO ARE SIMILAR TO OURSELVES. For example, if an African-American boy learns that a black man, Garrett Morgan, invented the traffic light, his belief that he too could be an engineer might be strengthened. By observing the competence of a person similar to oneself, an individual learns that the task is possible and how to do it. In contrast, negative modeling can undermine self-efficacy. If other people in their own group seem to keep failing, people may come to doubt that they can succeed.

3. ENCOURAGEMENT AND PERSUASION FROM OTHERS. People acquire a sense of self-efficacy when they are in an environment in which other people persuade them that they have what it takes to "make it," reward their capabilities, allow them to succeed, and do not subject them to repeated failure.

4. JUDGMENTS OF ONE'S OWN PHYSIOLOGICAL STATE. People feel more competent when they are calm and relaxed than when they are tense or under extreme stress. People who have high self-efficacy are also able to use states of arousal and tension productively. For example, instead of interpreting normal feelings of stage fright as evidence that they are going to make fools of themselves when they give a talk, they regard these jitters as a source of energy that will help them perform better.

Notice that the first entry on Bandura's list of the origins of self-efficacy includes not only experiences with success but also experiences with failure. This is a very important point. Behaviorists, after all, would predict that repeated experiences with failure will eventually extinguish "achievement behavior." But to cognitive social-learning theorists, *everything depends on how people interpret their failures.* Imagine that two people are faced with a difficult problem, and both do poorly. The one who is

---

self-efficacy The belief that one is capable of producing, through one's own efforts, desired results, such as mastering new skills and reaching goals.

low in self-efficacy is likely to give up, whereas the one who is high in self-efficacy keeps striving to master it. The difference between them has nothing to do with their abilities; many talented people lack the self-efficacy to persist in the face of failure, and their talents are lost to history. The difference is that a person with high self-efficacy interprets failure as an opportunity to learn from mistakes, and a person with low self-efficacy interprets failure as an embarrassing disaster.

Another way of describing this difference is in terms of the way people think of their goals. According to Carol Dweck (1990, 1992), people who are motivated by **performance goals** are concerned with doing well, being judged highly, and avoiding criticism. When such people are focused on how well they are performing and then do poorly, they often decide that the fault is theirs, and they stop trying to improve. Because their goal is to demonstrate their abilities, they set themselves up for grief when they temporarily fail—as all of us must if we are to learn anything new.

In contrast, those who are motivated by **learning (mastery) goals** are concerned with increasing their competence and skills. Therefore, they regard failure as a source of useful information that will help them improve. Failure and criticism do not discourage them because they know that learning takes time; focusing on specific ways of mastering a goal raises intrinsic motivation and satisfaction. These attitudes emerge in early childhood. In one study of first-, third-, and fifth-graders, sizable percentages were already motivated by performance goals, giving up when they failed to solve a difficult puzzle; such children had already come to regard "intelligence" as fixed and did not see their grades as having much to do with their efforts or abilities (Cain & Dweck, 1995).

Bandura (1994) observes that because ordinary life is "full of impediments, adversities, setbacks, frustrations, and inequities," having an "optimistic sense of personal efficacy" is needed to sustain the effort to persist and succeed. Such a sense lies somewhere between having unrealistic delusions that all things are possible, and having cynical beliefs that nothing ever can be done.

The three factors of locus of control, explanatory style, and self-efficacy are, as you might have noticed, closely interrelated. When a team of researchers conducted a factor analysis of many personality inventories and measures of psychological and physical health, they found that the first key factor was "optimistic control": a sense of optimism, hope, faith in one's abilities (self-efficacy), self-esteem, and an internal locus of control (Marshall et al., 1994). Together, these concepts take us a long way from strict behaviorism. In the social-learning view, behavioral principles are important, but they omit the motivating beliefs that keep some people chasing their dreams while others dream their lives away.

---

performance goals Motivational goals that emphasize external rewards, such as doing well, being judged highly, and avoiding criticism.
learning (mastery) goals Motivational goals that emphasize the intrinsic satisfaction of increasing one's competence and skills.

WHAT DO YOU KNOW?

You can increase your sense of control over the material in this section by answering these questions.

1. In general, high achievement is associated with having an (internal/external) locus of control.
2. "I'll never find anyone else to love because I'm not good-looking; that one romance was a fluke" illustrates a(n) _____ explanatory style.
3. Expecting to fail in a class and then making no effort to do well can result in a _____.
4. You are a schoolteacher, and you would like your students to have self-efficacy. You should (a) be sure that they never fail in their efforts; (b) provide competent role models whom the students can relate to; (c) withhold praise so that they don't get conceited; (d) avoid all criticism.
5. Ramón and Ramona are learning to ski. Every time she falls down, Ramona says, "This is the most humiliating experience I've ever had! Everyone is watching me behave like a clumsy dolt!" Ramón says, "&*!!@*$@! I'll show these dratted skis who's boss!" Why is Ramona more likely than Ramón to give up? She is (a) a clumsy dolt; (b) less competent at skiing; (c) focused on performance; (d) focused on learning.

ANSWERS:

1. internal   2. pessimistic   3. self-fulfilling prophecy   4. b   5. c

---

LEARNING THE RULES OF GENDER

The following conversation was overheard in the infant department of a large store, between a female clerk and a customer buying a receiving blanket for her friend's new-born baby:

Buyer: I'd like this receiving blanket, please.

Clerk: Is the baby a boy or girl?

Buyer: A boy.

Clerk: In that case, I'd suggest a different pattern. How about this one, with the little cowboys and guns?

Buyer: But I like the clowns—they're so colorful and cute.

Clerk: Trust me, honey. I get lots of dads in here, and you can't imagine how much time they spend choosing colors and patterns. They all say the cowboys are more masculine.

Most babies, unless they have rare abnormalities, are born unambiguously male or female—a biological distinction. But, according to psychologists in the learning perspective, children must learn to be masculine or feminine—a psychological distinction. This learning, as the clerk realized, starts at the moment of birth, when the newborn is enveloped in the clothes, colors, and toys the parents think are appropriate for its sex. No parent ever excitedly calls a relative to exclaim, "It's a baby! It's a seven-and-a-half-pound, black-haired baby!"

To distinguish what is anatomically given from what is learned, many psychologists distinguish *sex* from *gender* (Deaux, 1985; Lott & Maluso, 1993; Unger, 1990). *Sex* refers to the anatomical and physiological attributes of, well, the sexes; thus these psychologists would speak of a "sex difference" in frequencies of baldness and color blindness. But they use *gender* to refer to the cultural and psychological attributes that children learn are appropriate for the sexes. Thus they would speak of a "gender difference" in sexual attitudes, dishwashing, and willingness to read romance novels. (In Chapter 13 this distinction will turn up again, when we consider, from the sociocultural perspective, why cultures differ in the gender rules they establish for their members.)

Social-learning theories have been applied to the question of how children develop a **gender identity,** a fundamental sense of maleness or femaleness that exists regardless of what one wears or does. (*Transsexuals* are people whose gender identity is out of sync with their biological sex: A transsexual man, for example, feels that he is a woman trapped in a man's body.) The social-learning approach also tries to account for **gender socialization** (sometimes called *sex typing*), the psychological process by which boys and girls learn what it means to be masculine or feminine, including the abilities, interests, personality traits, actions, and self-concepts that their culture says are appropriate for males or females. A person can have a strong gender identity and not be sex typed: A man may be confident in his maleness and not feel threatened by doing "unmasculine" things, such as needlepointing a pillow; a woman may be confident in her femaleness and not feel threatened by doing "unfeminine" things, such as serving in combat. For others, gender identity seems to depend on adhering to rules of sex typing; they get very nervous when asked to do something that they think a "real man" or a "real woman" would never do.

Modern social-learning theorists account for the emergence of gender identity and for gender socialization by emphasizing principles of learning, cognitive processes, and situational influences (Lott & Maluso, 1993).

Behavioral Learning

Early social-learning theories assumed that the child was a relatively passive participant in his or her own upbringing. They emphasized the rewards and punishments that children get for behaving appropriately or inappropriately for their sex, the adult models they observe, and the lessons they learn from seeing what happens to men and

---

gender identity   The fundamental sense of being male or female, regardless of whether one conforms to the rules of sex typing.

gender socialization (sex typing)   The process by which children learn the behaviors, attitudes, and expectations associated with being masculine or feminine in their culture.

women who break gender rules (Mischel, 1966). In these early formulations, the child absorbed whatever rules and lessons the parents and other adults transmitted. Researchers showed that most adults start sex typing as soon as a baby is born, offering dolls to infants they believe are girls and toy footballs or hammers to infants they believe are boys, even when they don't know the infant's sex (Stern & Karraker, 1989). It followed that if parents wanted to raise children who were free of gender stereotypes, they had only to treat sons and daughters equally and reward the same behaviors in both sexes.

Before long, it became apparent that something was wrong with this argument. Parents (some of whom were psychologists) insisted that they *were* treating their sons and daughters equally, yet their toddler sons still preferred mechanical toys while their toddler daughters wanted tea sets. In a meta-analysis of 172 studies, Hugh Lytton and David Romney (1991) found that in 18 domains of parental socialization—including warmth and responsiveness, encouragement of achievement, encouragement of dependency, restrictiveness, use of reasoning, and general amount of interaction—there was no evidence that parents treat sons and daughters any differently. And yet children often stubbornly act out masculine and feminine stereotypes anyway. One couple we know wouldn't let a toy gun in their house, yet their four-year-old son bit his sandwich into the shape of a gun and proceeded to "shoot" his brother. And a female friend who is a physician herself wondered why her own three-year-old daughter absolutely, positively knew that only boys can be doctors.

There were other problems with early social-learning approaches (Jacklin & Reynolds, 1993). One was that children are not passive imitators. They *select* whom they wish to imitate, and they are terribly conformist about this. Children are unlikely to copy an adult of the same sex who is doing something different from other adults, even if the nonconformist is their own parent. (Hence the physician and her daughter.) Another problem was that reinforcement works only when certain people administer it. In nursery and elementary school, for example, girls respond to reinforcers given by teachers but not to those given by boys. Boys, though, respond better to reinforcers given by other boys than to those given by teachers or by girls (Fagot, 1985). A third problem was that parents respond to their children's interests and behavior, as

Cathy *Copyright © 1986 Cathy Guisewite. Reprinted with permission of Universal Press Syndicate. All rights reserved.*

well as shape them. Children express preferences for what they want to do and play with at a very early age, and parents react to those preferences (Snow, Jacklin, & Maccoby, 1983).

Today, most social-learning theorists still emphasize the importance of the obvious reinforcers and consequences of behavior in the process of gender socialization, but they also focus on identifying some of the *subtle* reinforcers that might explain the foregoing findings. They find that although many parents and teachers insist that they treat boys and girls equally, and although in many ways they do, adults are often unaware of the hidden gender messages in their behavior. For example, many parents believe that males are naturally more aggressive than females and that this difference appears too early to be a result of systematic patterns of reinforcement. But even at one year of age, boys and girls *whose behavior is the same* are treated differently by adults. In one study, Beverly Fagot and her colleagues (1985) observed the reactions of teachers to "assertive acts" and "communicative acts" of 12- to 16-month-old children. Although there were no differences between the boys and girls in the frequency of these acts, the teachers responded far more often to assertive boys than to shy ones and more often to talkative girls than to less verbal ones. When the researchers observed the same children a year later, a gender difference was now apparent, with boys behaving more assertively and girls talking more to teachers.

Similarly, the aggressiveness of boys gets more attention and other rewards from teachers and peers than does aggressiveness in girls, again even when the children start out being equally aggressive. In one observational study of preschool children, peers or teachers paid attention to the aggression of boys 81 percent of the time, compared with only 24 percent of the time for the girls' aggression. When girls and boys behaved dependently, however, such as by calling for help from the teacher, the girls got attention far more often than the boys did (Fagot, 1984). In another study, highly aggressive fourth- to seventh-grade boys and girls were more likely than unaggressive children to report that they expected tangible rewards to result from their aggressive acts. They already knew that their behavior was paying off for them (Perry, Perry, & Rasmussen, 1986). "Behaviors given attention are maintained," Fagot (1984) summarized, "while those that result in being ignored tend to drop out"—just as any good behaviorist would predict.

The hidden messages conveyed by parents, teachers, and other adults affect older children as well. In the early 1980s, Janis Jacobs and Jacquelynne Eccles (1985) were conducting a longitudinal study of seventh- and ninth-grade children's math achievement. At the start of the study, the children were equal in math ability, as determined by test scores and teachers' evaluations. Jacobs and Eccles found that parents who believed that boys had a natural superiority in math were unintentionally communicating this message to their children. For instance, parents would say of their sons' good math grades, "You're a natural math whiz, Johnny!" But if their daughters got identically good grades, they would say, "Boy, you really worked hard in math, Janey, and it shows!" The implication, not lost on the children, was clear: When girls do well, it is because of concerted effort; when boys do well, it is because they have a natural gift. Over time, this attitude was related to the reduced likelihood that the girls would take further math courses, remain interested in math, and value math in general. Why should they, if the subject is going to be so hard, take so much effort, and isn't natural to females anyway? The eventual divergence between boys and girls in their grades and enrollment in math courses, the researchers found, was unrelated to aptitude, because all of the children started out being equally competent in math. In subsequent longitudinal studies, Eccles has found that parents' stereotypical expectations about their children's talents in math, English, and sports strongly influence their children's performance and feelings of competence in these areas (Eccles, 1993; Eccles, Jacobs, & Harold, 1990).

Gender Schemas

The second element in modern social-learning approaches to gender is the role of children's unfolding cognitive abilities. In this view, once a boy has a concept of himself as male, he automatically values "boy things" and dislikes "girl things," without being taught. In accordance with reciprocal determinism, children acquire their beliefs about correct sex-typed behavior from what they observe in their environments; then they internalize those beliefs, which in turn regulate their future behavior.

As children mature, they develop a **gender schema;** that is, they begin to divide people into the fundamental categories of male or female (Archer & Lloyd, 1982; Bem, 1985; Fagot, 1985; Kohlberg, 1966). "It is inarguable," said Janet Spence (1985), "that gender is one of the earliest and most central components of the self-concept and serves as an organizing principle through which many experiences and perceptions of self and other are filtered." Gender as a cognitive "organizing principle" begins early in life—indeed, well before children can speak. By the age of only nine months, most babies can discriminate male and female faces, even if they vary according to hairstyle and facial expression (Fagot & Leinbach, 1993), and they can match female faces with female voices (Poulin-Dubois et al., 1994).

Fagot (1993), who did so much to show how children's sex-typed behavior is affected by external reinforcers, has in recent years turned to studying the cognitive processes that are also involved in sex typing. Once children acquire the ability to distinguish male and female, she finds, it is not long before they can label themselves as "boy" or "girl." And once they can do that, they begin to prefer same-sex playmates and sex-typed toys.

In Fagot's studies, 18-month-old children *did not differ* on several behavioral measures in which sex differences are often taken for granted: large motor activity (running, jumping, climbing), play with sex-typed toys (such as trucks for boys, dolls for girls), aggression, and verbal skills. Nine months later, at age 27 months, half of the children could correctly distinguish boys from girls on a test in which they had to assign gender labels to pictures of boys and girls, and men and women. That is, they

---

gender schema A cognitive schema (mental network) of knowledge, beliefs, metaphors, and expectations about what it means to be male or female.

had acquired a gender schema. These "early-labeling" children were now more sex-typed in their toy play and the other categories than were children who still were not consistently labeling males and females. Most notably, early-labeling girls showed less aggression than late-labeling girls. It was as if the girls were going along, behaving as aggressively and as actively as boys, until they knew they were girls. At that moment, but not until that moment, they seemed to decide, "Girls don't do this; I'm a girl; I'd better not either." The late-labeling children eventually also showed the consistent use of labels to distinguish between males and females, and then their behavior, too, became more sex-typed.

The period between ages 2 and 4 is especially important for the development of gender schemas. Children begin to divide the world up into objects and attributes that are "male" and those that are "female," even though they have never been specifically reinforced for making these connections. Later, their gender schemas expand beyond preferences for dolls or jungle gyms to include many more meanings and associations (Fagot & Leinbach, 1993). Children between the ages of 4 and 7, for instance, will usually say that the following things are "masculine": bears, fire, anger, the color black, spiky and angular shapes, dogs, fir trees, and rough textures. "Feminine" things are butterflies, hearts, the color pink, flowers, cats, birds, rabbits, and soft textures. (Crayons, maple trees, cameras, and telephones are neutral.)

According to Fagot (1993), children at this age are learning the *metaphors* of gender, associating qualities such as strength or dangerousness with males, and gentler qualities with females. By age 5, all children can differentiate male from female solely on the basis of these qualities. In fact, Fagot is finding, the metaphors of gender are enough to override the actual nature of objects. When she takes a "girl's toy," such as a tea set, and gives it "masculine" attributes—making it black, angular, and spiky—boys say they would play with it! Perhaps this research explains the popularity of Barney among little girls; he is a dinosaur, but he's soft and cuddly. Toy manufacturers may yet come up with Terminator tea sets for boys.

By the age of 4 or 5, children have developed a secure gender identity; they are cognitively capable of understanding that a girl remains a girl even if she can climb a tree, and a boy remains a boy even if he has a ponytail. With increasing experience, knowledge, and mental sophistication, children construct their own standards of what boys and girls may or may not do. They begin to give themselves approval for sex-typed behavior and criticize themselves for behaving like the other sex. According to Bandura, these self-evaluations, or internalized standards, best predict how sex-typed their actual behavior will be. One of his experiments, illustrated in Figure 7.1 on the next page, found that younger children (about 3 years old) did not differ significantly in how they expected to feel—approving or critical—if they played with "masculine" or "feminine" toys. But 4-year-olds, especially boys, were already anticipating that they would feel good about themselves for playing with same-sex toys and bad for playing with cross-sex toys (Bussey & Bandura, 1992). These self-evaluations, the researchers found, accurately predicted which toys the children played with.

However, there is a problem in the idea that children voluntarily sex-type themselves. Repeated studies find that boys express stronger preferences for "masculine"

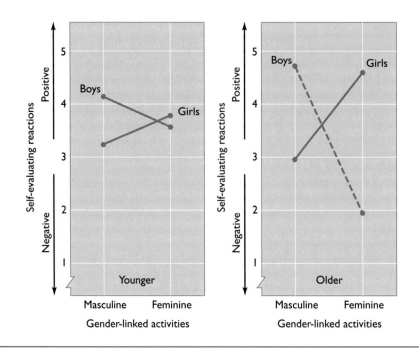

Figure 7.1 *This experiment shows the internalization of sex typing in children between the ages of 3 and 4. The graph on the left shows that 3-year-olds did not significantly differ in how they felt about playing with "boys' toys" or "girls' toys." The graph on the right shows that 4-year-olds, especially boys, already felt far better about playing with toys associated with their sex than with those associated with the other sex (Bussey & Bandura, 1992).*

toys and activities than girls do for "feminine" ones, and boys are harsher on themselves if they fail to behave in sex-typed ways. Some researchers think that this gender difference reflects the fact that "masculine" activities, occupations, and traits hold more value in society than "feminine" ones do. Thus when boys behave like or play with girls, they lose status, whereas when girls behave like boys, they gain status (Serbin, Powlishta, & Gulko, 1993). Preschoolers are already aware of gender differences in status: When asked to observe two furry rabbit puppets acting out a story and then to identify the genders of the rabbits, 4- and 5-year-olds identified as a female the rabbit that was deferent, had its opinions overruled, and was less likely to have its advice followed (Ward, 1994).

As their abilities further mature, children understand the exceptions to their gender schemas—for instance, that women can be engineers and men can be cooks. From middle childhood through adolescence, they become more flexible about what they will be able to do as women or men, and about people who are nontraditional, especially if they have friends of the other sex and if their environments encourage such flexibility (Katz & Ksansnak, 1994). But internalized beliefs about gender continue to have an effect throughout adulthood. When the behavior or the occupation of a man or a woman violates an observer's gender schema, the observer is often uncomfortable and reacts negatively. For example, people evaluate female leaders in traditionally male domains, such as business and athletics, more harshly than male leaders who are otherwise described in identical terms (Eagly, Makhijani, & Klonsky, 1990). Gender schemas can and do change, but they continue to wield a strong influence.

The Specific Situation

Finally, social-learning theories of gender emphasize the influence of situation and circumstance in shaping and maintaining behavior (Deaux & Major, 1987, 1990). Although most people come to think of "feminine" and "masculine" qualities and talents as being stable aspects of personality, the fact is that in their everyday lives, men and women, and boys and girls, often behave in "feminine" ways *and* in "masculine" ways. Some situations, such as a date, evoke sex-typed behavior: Which partner pays? Who asks whom out? Who makes the sexual overtures? In other situations, such as working on an assembly line, gender is irrelevant and sex-typed behavior disappears. Many studies now confirm that if you want to predict how people will behave in a particular situation, you would do better to know the details of the situation than what sex they are (Deaux & Major, 1990; Eagly, 1987; Eagly & Wood, 1991; Lott & Maluso, 1993).

For example, Eleanor Maccoby (1990), reviewing many studies, found that boys and girls do not consistently differ in the traits of passivity or activity; *their behavior depends on the gender of the child they are playing with.* Among preschoolers, girls are seldom passive with one another; however, when paired with boys, girls typically stand on the sidelines and let the boys monopolize the toys. This behavior, Maccoby found, is unrelated to the individual traits or temperaments of the children. Instead, it is related to the fact that when a boy and a girl compete for a shared toy, the boy dominates—unless there is an adult in the room. Girls in mixed classrooms stay nearer to the teacher, Maccoby found, not because they are more dependent but because they want a chance at the toys! Girls play just as independently as boys when they are in all-girl groups, and they will actually sit farther from the teacher than boys in all-boy groups do.

Because of the importance of situations in evoking or minimizing sex-typed behavior, social-learning theorists hold that the gender rules acquired in childhood do not always last (Lott & Maluso, 1993). Consider the fascinating results of a meta-analysis of 65 studies, involving more than 9,000 people (Cohn, 1991). Gender differences in personality, moral reasoning, "maturity of thought," conformity, and other characteristics were greatest among junior- and senior-high-school students, largely because girls mature earlier than boys. But most of these differences declined significantly among college-age adults and disappeared entirely among older men and women.

Such research supports the social-learning view that early experiences are not necessarily a blueprint for life because people continue to have new experiences. This is why children can grow up in an extremely sex-typed family and yet, as adults, find themselves in careers or relationships they might never have imagined for themselves. Of course, some people feel torn between the gender rules of their family's culture and the gender rules of the larger society. A Filipina student said she desperately wanted an education and a career in biology, but she also didn't want to be disobedient to her parents, who wanted her to return home and get married.

Social-learning theorists find that the importance of gender itself depends on the situation. If you have ever been the only man in a group of women, or the only woman in a group of men, you know what we mean. Your sex—because of its uniqueness—will be what everyone notices and cites to account for your behavior (Geis, 1993; Kanter, 1977/1993). (Similarly, if you have ever been the only black in a group of whites, or the only disabled person, or the only young person, you will be familiar with the experience of being treated as a representative of an entire group instead of as an individual.) When women achieve a certain critical density in a group and are no longer tokens or a very small percentage, however, they are perceived as having all the diverse qualities and abilities that any group contains.

Modern social-learning approaches to gender remind us of the importance of the models that children and adults are constantly observing. They recognize the role of cognitive factors such as gender schemas in how children and adults become sex-typed, and in how they become un-sex-typed. They show how sex-typed behavior becomes internalized, regulated not by external rules but by internally motivated standards. But by also emphasizing the power of our experiences and the situations in which we find ourselves, the learning perspective suggests that masculinity and femininity are not permanent qualities but flexible standards that can change from childhood to adulthood and again throughout our lives.

What Do You Know?

Are you socialized yet into the habit of taking quizzes?

1. Most parents say that they treat their sons and daughters in exactly the same way, but their children prefer stereotypically sex-typed toys anyway. How might a cognitive social-learning theorist explain this phenomenon?
2. A seven-year-old girl who is quiet and passive in class, but active and independent in her all-girl Brownie troop, illustrates which social-learning influence on gender development? (a) gender schemas, (b) imitation, (c) the specific situation, (d) adult reinforcers
3. Which statement about gender schemas is *false?* (a) They are present in early form by age one; (b) they are permanent conceptualizations of what it means to be masculine or feminine; (c) they eventually expand to include metaphors associated with male and female.
4. Herb really wants to be a doctor, but he doesn't get into medical school. A friend suggests he become a nurse. "Yipes!" says Herb. "Real men aren't nurses!" Herb (a) has a strong gender identity and is sex-typed, (b) has a strong gender identity but isn't sex-typed, (c) is strongly sex-typed but has a weak gender identity, (d) isn't sex-typed and has a weak gender identity.

Answers:

1. Adults who think they treat boys and girls the same are often unaware of the hidden gender messages they convey and the influence of subtle reinforcers on children's sex-typed behavior (e.g., rewarding aggressiveness in boys while ignoring it in girls). However, a cognitive social-learning theorist might also agree with the parents' claim, pointing out that when very young children are developing a gender schema, they can be quite inflexible about the rules and metaphors of sex-typed behavior. (These schemas can change as children develop.) 2. c 3. b 4. a

LEARNING TO BE MORAL

What does it mean to be a moral human being? This question has been the subject of philosophical and religious debate over the ages, but we like the answer offered by psychologists Michael Schulman and Eva Mekler (1994): A moral person is someone who strives to be kind, fair, and responsible. Helping your friend cheat on a test may be kind to him but it is not fair, and therefore it is not a moral act. Treating all of your siblings in an equally mean and hurtful way may be fair, but it is not kind, and therefore it is not a moral act. A moral person takes responsibility for his or her occasional lapses of kindness and fair play; he or she doesn't rely on excuses and lies. Finally, moral behavior rests on good intentions. If you visit your 95-year-old aunt only because you hope to inherit her estate, your kindness is not a moral act.

As this definition shows, morality is a complex phenomenon involving empathy for others, intentions, the inner voice of conscience, and behaving in considerate and responsible ways (Kurtines & Gewirtz, 1991). Every perspective in psychology has had something to say about one or another of the facts of morality: the emotions of empathy, guilt, and shame that act as internal regulators of behavior; the cognitive ability to evaluate moral dilemmas; or people's behavior in situations in which the easiest course of action is to cheat, lie, or behave selfishly. Biologically minded researchers believe that empathy, altruism, and cooperation are rooted in our evolutionary heritage (Batson, 1990; Plutchik, 1987). Psychodynamic psychologists explore the unconscious sources of guilt, egotism, and aggression, as well as the mechanisms by which conscience becomes internalized. Cognitive psychologists study the development and nature of moral reasoning. Cultural psychologists investigate how a society's values and traditions affect its definitions of moral behavior. And social psychologists, as we will see in the sociocultural perspective, find that forces in society often compel people to behave in unethical ways, in complete contradiction to what an individual might personally wish to do. In this section, our goal is to show how social-learning theories, with their multifaceted approach to behavior, extend our understanding of moral development beyond explanations based on biology, behaviorism, or cognition alone.

Behavioral and Cognitive Theories

Moral behavior has always posed a problem for behaviorism. Behaviorists would argue that children's moral behavior depends on the rewards and punishments they get as they grow up. Indeed, when children are rewarded for aggressive and competitive acts, such behavior does prevail over cooperation and altruism (Kohn, 1992). But directly rewarding children for being helpful does not necessarily produce helpful children because, for one thing, the point of altruism is to do good with no thought of getting a reward. Moreover, behaviorism overlooks the importance of developing cognitive categories of right and wrong, good and bad, that can be applied in new situations where rewards may be absent. Finally, as we saw in the previous chapter, punishment is often ineffective and can actually be counterproductive in teaching children or adults how to behave. You can't always make people good by causing them to fear being bad.

For many years, the dominant alternative to the behavioral analysis of morality was a cognitive one, based on the child's development of reasoning abilities. The most famous and influential of the cognitive theories of morality was developed by Lawrence Kohlberg in the 1960s. Kohlberg was a charismatic psychologist whose ideas became highly influential both for the research they generated and for their applications (Darley, 1993). In order to show you what is wrong with purely cognitive approaches to moral behavior, we need to begin with what was so appealing about Kohlberg's ideas.

Kohlberg outlined a stage theory based on how people reason about moral dilemmas. He did not observe how children or adults *actually* treat one another; his implicit assumption seemed to be that if people think right, they will do right. Your moral stage, said Kohlberg, can be determined by the answers you give to hypothetical moral dilemmas. For example, a man's wife is dying and needs a special drug. The man can't afford the drug and the druggist won't lower his price. Should the man steal the drug? What if he no longer loves his wife? If the man is caught, should the judge be lenient? To Kohlberg, the reasoning behind the answers was more important than the decisions themselves.

Kohlberg (1964, 1976, 1984) proposed three universal levels of moral development, each divided into two stages. At Kohlberg's first level, *preconventional morality,* young children obey rules because they fear being punished if they disobey (Stage 1), and later because they think it is in their best interest to obey (Stage 2). Stage 2 reasoning is also hedonistic, self-centered, and lacking in empathy; what is right is what feels good. At about ages 10 or 11, according to Kohlberg, children shift to the second level, the *conventional morality* of adult society. At Stage 3, conventional morality is based on trust, conformity, and loyalty to others; morality means "don't hurt others; don't rock the boat." Most people then advance to Stage 4, a "law-and-order orientation," based on understanding the social order, law, justice, and duty.

In late adolescence and early adulthood, said Kohlberg, some people realize that there is a level of moral judgment that transcends human laws. They see that some laws—such as those that legitimize the systematic mistreatment or segregation of minorities—are themselves immoral. Such awareness moves them to the highest moral level, *postconventional (principled) morality.* At Stage 5, they realize that values and laws are relative, that people hold different standards, and that laws are important but can be changed. A few great individuals reach Stage 6, developing a moral standard based on universal human rights. When faced with a conflict between law and conscience, such people follow conscience, even at personal risk.

Hundreds of studies have been done, on samples all over the world, to test Kohlberg's theory (Eckensberger, 1994; Shweder, Mahapatra, & Miller, 1990). The results show that Stages 5 and 6 are rare, but the others do indeed develop sequentially in many cultures. Some developmental psychologists are persuaded therefore that children's moral reasoning does evolve according to Kohlberg's stages, or at least most of them (Bee, 1997).

In the early 1980s, Carol Gilligan (1982) countered Kohlberg's cognitive approach to moral development with one of her own. She argued that men tend to base their moral choices on abstract principles of law and justice, asking questions such as "Whose rights should take precedence here?" whereas women tend to base their moral decisions on principles of compassion and care, asking questions such as "Who will be hurt least?" Some studies have supported Gilligan's view, finding that men care more about justice and women care more about caring (Bussey & Maughan, 1982; Gilligan & Wiggins, 1987; Walker, 1989). Most research, however, finds no gender differences in moral reasoning, especially when people are allowed to rank *all* the reasons behind their moral judgments (Clopton & Sorell, 1993; Cohn, 1991; Friedman, Robinson, & Friedman, 1987; Thoma, 1986). Both men and women say that they base their moral decisions on compassion *and* on abstract principles of justice; they worry about feelings *and* fairness. As social-learning theory would predict, how they reason also depends significantly on the *situation they are reasoning about*. Women and men tend to use "justice" reasoning when they are thinking about highly abstract ethical dilemmas, and "care" reasoning when they are thinking about intimate dilemmas in their own lives (Clopton & Sorell, 1993; Walker, de Vries, & Trevethan, 1987).

Kohlberg's and Gilligan's theories of moral reasoning generated dozens of studies and much animated discussion. Many people enjoy speculating about which stage of reasoning they might be at and arguing about whether the sexes really differ in how they think about moral problems. Social-learning theorists and other critics, however, regard all stage theories of moral reasoning as inherently limited, for three major reasons:

1. STAGE THEORIES TEND TO OVERLOOK CULTURAL AND EDUCATIONAL INFLUENCES ON MORAL REASONING. Many critics argue that Kohlberg's hierarchy of stages reflects verbal ability and education, not moral judgment, and in a Western cultural context at that (Shweder, Mahapatra, & Miller, 1990). In Iceland and Germany, for example, among children who are supposedly at only a Stage 2 level, concern for others is far more important than the theory would predict; and because Stage 4 is heavily based on formal legal conceptions, unschooled members of many cultures do not achieve it (Eckensberger, 1994). College-educated people give "higher-level" explanations of moral decisions than people who have not attended college, but all that shows, say Kohlberg's critics, is that they are more verbally sophisticated. Likewise, adults have a greater understanding of law than children do, but this knowledge does not necessarily make their moral reasoning better. A child who says "The judge should be lenient because [the husband] acted unselfishly" will score lower than the adult who says "The judge should be lenient because he or she can find a precedent or rule that reflects what is right." As Schulman and Mekler (1994) note, in Kohlberg's system the cruelest lawyer will get a higher score than the kindest 8-year-old.

2. PEOPLE'S MORAL REASONING IS OFTEN INCONSISTENT ACROSS SITUATIONS; ONCE PEOPLE REACH A HIGHER LEVEL, THEY DON'T NECESSARILY STAY THERE. On the contrary, in most people's lives moral reasoning depends on the situation (Colby et al., 1983; Kagan, 1993). You might do something charitable out of sympathetic feelings one day, and not another; behave cooperatively and selflessly in one situation, and not another (Knight et al., 1994). You might show conventional morality by overlooking a racial slur at a dinner party because you don't want to upset everyone else, but you reveal postconventional reasoning by protesting a governmental policy you regard as immoral. College students usually draw on higher levels—principles of justice and fair play—to justify moral decisions, yet about one-

third of American and Canadian college men say they would force a woman into sexual acts if they could "get away with it" (Malamuth & Dean, 1990), an admission that reveals the lowest form of moral reasoning.

As developmental psychologist Jerome Kagan (1993) has pointed out, a 7-year-old, when asked why he should not steal, will typically reply that he wants to avoid punishment, whereas a 15-year-old will typically say that the stability of society would be destroyed if everyone stole. Yet, says Kagan, fear of punishment is not the main reason that 7-year-olds don't steal; as we will see, dozens of research studies show that very young children are capable of moral feelings, of behaving kindly and considerately, of understanding that their actions have consequences. Conversely, adolescents are by no means indifferent to being punished by their parents or the police!

Even those admirable people who reach Kohlberg's sixth stage are not consistent across all situations. Mohandas Gandhi, for example, reached the highest moral stage because of his commitment to universal principles of peace, justice, and nonviolence. But as Gandhi's biographers have pointed out, he was *also* a man who was aloof from his family and followers, whom he often treated in the harshest and most callous manner. Vietnam war hero John Vann performed astonishing feats of bravery during the war, time and again rescuing soldiers from certain death. But he was also an obsessive seducer who abandoned his wife and five children without supporting them, and he lied to avoid being court-martialed for seducing a 15-year-old girl (Sheehan, 1988). The social-learning approach accurately predicts that only a few saints can be expected to be fair, just, and responsible across all situations.

3. **PEOPLE'S MORAL REASONING AND THEIR BEHAVIOR ARE OFTEN UNRELATED.** The third and most important criticism of cognitive theories of moral reasoning, in the social-learning view, is that these theories do not necessarily predict whether people will actually *behave* in kind, just, and responsible ways. People can know what is right and come up with all sorts of highfalutin' rationalizations for not doing it. "We can reach high levels of moral reasoning," said Thomas Lickona (1983), "and still behave like scoundrels." Indeed, as Kagan (1993) observes, "Although the quality of moral reasoning increases dramatically from school entrance to high school graduation, so, too, do cheating and cruelty." This observation suggests to us that Kohlberg could just as well have proposed a stage theory of "immoral development," based on the child's increasing cognitive abilities to rationalize immoral acts.

Social-Learning Theories

Cognitive theories of morality imply that children evolve in their ability to reason about moral choices; something inherent in their age or gender causes them to reason in certain ways. In the social-learning view, children must *learn* to avoid the temptations to steal, lie, cheat, and otherwise behave as they might like. They do this through social-learning processes that are missing in strictly behavioral and cognitive explanations, such as by observing the behavior of public figures—what they do, and what they get away with. Does a person commit an illegal act and then earn a fortune from movie deals and a tell-all autobiography? Does a sports hero get away with cheating because it helped the team win? Does a scientist falsify results in order to earn fame and awards?

Social-learning explanations of moral development also emphasize the processes by which children internalize parental standards of right or wrong. The capacity for moral feeling, like that for language and attachment, seems to be inborn. As Jerome Kagan (1984) says, "Without this fundamental human capacity, which nineteenth-century observers called a *moral sense,* the child could not be socialized." The "moral sense" develops out of children's attachment to their parents. According to social-learning theory, because children need to give love to and receive love from their parents, they are motivated to adopt the parents' standards of good and bad behavior. Children who break the parents' rules are afraid not just of being punished, but also of losing their parents' love. Children shift from obeying rules for external reasons, such as fear of punishment, to obeying rules for internal reasons, because they will feel guilty or ashamed of behaving badly or disappointing the loved parent (Bandura, 1991).

The internalization of moral standards begins with *empathy,* the ability to feel bad about another person's unhappiness and to feel good about another's joy. Social-learning theorists have examined how parents and societies can encourage or inhibit children's natural empathy. Whether a 4-year-old boy will feel empathy toward a new-born sister's wails depends on the experience he has in taking care of her. And whether he will feel empathy or animosity toward homeless people depends on how he has learned to interpret their suffering.

According to research by Martin Hoffman (1987, 1989), empathy takes different forms, depending on a child's age and cognitive abilities. In the first year, before infants even have a sense of themselves as distinct from others, they feel *global empathy,* general distress at another person's misery. At times, they act as though what happened to the other happened to themselves. One 11-month-old girl in Hoffman's research, seeing an older child fall and cry, behaved as if *she* had been hurt. She looked as if she were about to cry, put her thumb in her mouth, and buried her head in her mother's lap.

As toddlers develop a sense of self (ages 1 to 2), they also develop *egocentric empathy.* Children now understand that someone else is in distress, but they assume that the other person must feel as they do. Two-year-olds can be impulsive and egocentric, but they are able to feel sad when another child or adult is unhappy and to try to make the person feel better. In one touching instance, a 13-month-old child offered her own beloved doll to a sad adult (Hoffman, 1977).

By the age of 2 or 3, children are capable of *empathy for another's feelings* that are different from their own. For example, they can empathize with another child's feelings of shame, and they know when the child wants to be left alone. They are able to feel angry or sad on someone else's behalf. A toddler in one study said, "You sad, Mommy. What Daddy do?" (Bretherton & Beeghly, 1982).

The final stage of empathy, *empathy for another's life condition,* emerges by late childhood. Children are able to understand that people have different experiences and histories and to feel empathy toward whole groups of individuals who are less fortunate than they.

Although people might like a life without shame or guilt, these emotions, too, are essential to the social learning of morality. They help maintain rules and standards, and they encourage moral action. *Shame* is a wound to the self-concept. It comes from perceiving that others have seen you doing something wrong and that they will like you less for having done it. As soon as the toddler has a sense of self, shame is quick to follow (Lewis, 1992). *Guilt,* in contrast, is the emotion you feel when you have not lived up to your own internal standards; it is remorse for real or imagined wrongdoings, a kind of self-inflicted punishment.

Because of attachment, empathy, and the development of a sense of self, by the time children are 2 years old, they are aware of standards of behavior, and at this tender age, they react with anxious concern or distress when a standard has been violated. By the age of 3 or 4, children associate a bad act with being a "bad boy" or "bad girl" and begin to regulate their moral behavior. In every culture around the world, children at this age judge their thoughts, feelings, and behavior against the standards they know are right (Edwards, 1987; Hoffman, 1994; Kagan & Lamb, 1987). In turn, adults begin to treat children differently, expecting them to follow the moral standards the adults hold appropriate.

According to social-learning theorists, children internalize moral standards as much from *how* their parents interact with them as from the content of their parents' lessons. When you did something wrong as a child, what did the adults in your family do about it? Did they shout at you, punish you, or explain the error of your ways? One of the most common methods that many parents use is **power assertion,** which consists of punitive measures such as threats, physical punishment, depriving the child of privileges, and generally taking advantage of being bigger, stronger, and more powerful ("Do it because I say so"). Yet power assertion, which is based on the child's fear of punishment, is associated with a *lack* of moral feeling and behavior in children.

But perhaps aggressive, self-absorbed children are hard to discipline consistently, so the parent must respond with efforts to assert power. For many years, Gerald Patterson and his colleagues have been conducting longitudinal and observational studies of parents and children, often in the family's home, to try to separate the causes and effects of parental practices (Patterson, 1994; Patterson, DeBaryshe, & Ramsey, 1989; Patterson, Reid, & Dishion, 1992). They find that parents of aggressive children use a great deal of punishment (shouting, scolding, spanking), yet fail to make the punishment contingent on the child's behavior. They do not state clear rules, require compliance, consistently punish violations, or praise good behavior. Instead, they nag and shout at the child, occasionally and unpredictably tossing in a slap or loss of privileges. This combination of power assertion with a pattern of intermittent discipline causes the children's aggressiveness to increase and eventually get out of hand. The child becomes withdrawn, manipulative, and difficult to control, which causes the parents to assert their power even more forcefully, which makes the child angrier . . . and a vicious cycle is generated.

---

power assertion A method of correcting a child's behavior in which the parent uses punishment and authority.

In contrast to power assertion, a far more successful method for teaching moral behavior is **induction,** in which the parent appeals to the child's own resources, affection for others, and sense of responsibility. For example, a mother may tell her child that the child's actions will harm, inconvenience, or disappoint another person. Induction tends to produce children who behave morally on five different measures: They feel guilty if they hurt others; they internalize standards of right and wrong, instead of just following orders; they confess rather than lie if they misbehave; they accept responsibility for their misbehavior; and they are considerate of others (Hoffman & Saltzstein, 1967; Schulman & Mekler, 1994).

In a study of children only 15 to 20 months old, some were already more helpful than others. If their behavior caused a friend to feel unhappy, afraid, or hurt, they would try to bring comfort by offering a toy, hugging the friend, or going to get help. It turned out that the mothers of these little Samaritans were using particular techniques of induction when their children misbehaved. They would *moralize* ("You made Doug cry; it's not nice to bite") or prohibit bad behavior with *explanations* or *statements of principle* ("You must never poke anyone's eyes because that could hurt them seriously"). Neutral reprimands were ineffective ("Tina is crying because you pushed her"), and the techniques that produced the *lowest* amount of helping were unexplained prohibitions ("Stop that!") and punishment, such as spanking and hitting (Zahn-Waxler, Radke-Yarrow, & King, 1979). Other studies, too, find that punishment, such as a forceful reprimand or a time-out, is effective *primarily if accompanied by an explanation* ("You can't play with that toy for a while because you hit people with it") (Schulman & Mekler, 1994).

In numerous longitudinal studies, child-rearing practices have been linked to children's moral behavior and their internalization of parental standards (Hoffman, 1994). In a large study designed to investigate the origins of male delinquency, for example, the researchers found many factors that predicted which boys would avoid a life of crime. These included, among others, consistent discipline, parental affection, a low level of aggressiveness in the father, restrictions on the son's behavior, and high parental standards and expectations (McCord, 1990). In the families that scored below the median on these factors, 58 percent of the sons eventually went on to commit serious crimes, compared to only 15 percent of those who came from families above the median. (In the next chapter, we will look at how to apply social-learning findings on moral development to child-rearing practices.)

Ultimately, the greatest influence on children's moral behavior is, as all learning theories would predict, what adults expect of them. In a large-scale study of children in Kenya, India, the Philippines, Okinawa, Mexico, and the United States, Beatrice and John Whiting (1975) measured how often children behaved altruistically (offering help and support to others) or egoistically (seeking help and attention or wanting to dominate others). This study was later reanalyzed and five new cultures were added to it (Whiting & Edwards, 1988). American children were the least altruistic and the most

---

induction A method of correcting a child's behavior in which the parent appeals to the child's own abilities, sense of responsibility, and feelings for others.

egoistic on all of the measures. The most altruistic children came from societies in which

- ◆children are assigned many tasks, such as caring for younger children and helping to gather and prepare food;
- ◆children know that their work makes a genuine contribution to the well-being or economic survival of the family;
- ◆parents depend on their children's contributions;
- ◆mothers have many responsibilities inside and outside the home;
- ◆children respect parental authority.

In summary, in accounting for how children learn to become (or fail to become) kind, helpful, and responsible members of society, social-learning approaches move beyond simple rewards and punishments or having the sophisticated verbal ability to justify moral decisions. They direct us to the importance of the moral emotions of empathy, shame, and guilt; the role of attachment; the societal models and values that children observe; the styles of child rearing that foster or inhibit moral standards and behavior; and the importance of the behavior that is expected and required of children in everyday situations.

WHAT DO YOU KNOW?

A. To raise children who are kind and helpful, parents and parents-to-be should be able to answer the following questions.

1. LaVerne, age 14 months, feels sad when she sees her mother crying during a tearjerker, and she starts to cry, too. LaVerne has developed (a) global empathy, (b) egocentric empathy, (c) empathy for another's feelings.
2. Shame and guilt are (a) unconscious emotions in infancy, (b) necessary for internalizing moral standards, (c) destructive emotions that should be stamped out as soon as possible.
3. Which method of parental discipline tends to create children who have internalized values of helpfulness and empathy? (a) induction, (b) punishment, (c) power assertion, (d) ignoring bad behavior and praising good behavior
4. Which form of family life tends to create helpful children? (a) Every family member "does his or her own thing"; (b) children contribute to the family welfare; (c) parents remind children often about the importance of being helpful; (d) children don't have to interrupt their schoolwork with family tasks.

B. In Chapter 3, you read that many personality traits have a genetic component, are resistant to change, and emerge almost regardless of what parents do. Yet social-learning theorists offer evidence that what parents do *does* make a difference. How might these two lines of research be reconciled?

Principles of social and cognitive learning have much to offer in understanding Frank and Hanna Sheehy-Skeffington, whose story opened this chapter. Their parents were models of people who practiced what they preached. They held high standards for all of their children and did not require them to conform to gender stereotypes. Frank's father wanted to instill in him habits of "order, virtue, morality, and feelings of kindliness for others" (quoted in Levenson, 1983). Hanna grew up in a politically active household in which all the daughters were educated and encouraged to develop their own interests. By the time they were young adults, Frank and Hanna had developed a commitment toward others less fortunate than they, as well as a set of motivating beliefs that allowed them to act on that commitment. Like human-rights activists before and after them, they had a strong internal locus of control, a sense of self-efficacy, and optimism; they were confident of their ability to affect the course of history. But they were also influenced by the times and situations in which they found themselves, particularly the Irish movement for independence from Britain and the struggle for women's suffrage.

Frank Sheehy-Skeffington died as he had lived, committed to pacifism in violent times. During the Easter Uprising against the British in 1916, Frank, who was thoroughly sympathetic to Ireland's cause, ran to the aid of a British officer who lay bleeding in a cross fire of shells. When Hanna admonished him for risking his life, he said, "I could not let anyone bleed to death while I could help." Later, while posting notices advising the populace not to riot or loot, he was arrested, taken to prison, and there murdered on the whim of a fanatical British captain. Hanna continually assailed the English military and government until the true circumstances of Frank's death were revealed and his murderer was punished. She lived another 30 years as her husband had lived, a tireless campaigner for equality for women and justice for everyone.

◆ ◆ ◆

Summary

1. Even during the heyday of behaviorism, a few behaviorists were rebelling against explanations that relied solely on conditioning principles. One result was *social-learning theory,* whose proponents study not only environmental influences on behavior but also the impact of higher-level cognitive processes, the psychological meaning of an act to the individual, and the interaction between individuals and their environments (*reciprocal determinism*). Two leading proponents of this

approach, Walter Mischel and Albert Bandura, call their theories *cognitive social-learning theory* and *social cognitive theory*, respectively.

2. In general, social-learning theories emphasize observational learning and the role of models; cognitive processes such as perceptions and interpretations of events; and motivating beliefs, such as enduring expectations of success or failure. Social-learning theorists differ in the factors they emphasize most strongly and the extent to which they distance themselves from behaviorism.

3. In *observational learning*, one learns by watching what others do and what happens to them for doing it. Sometimes the learner imitates the responses shortly after observing them; at other times the learning remains latent until circumstances allow or require it to be expressed. Observational learning begins in infancy.

4. Behaviorist Edward Tolman demonstrated *latent learning* in maze studies with rats and concluded that what was learned was not a response but a *cognitive map*. Social-learning theories hold that observational and latent learning reflect knowledge about responses and their consequences. Individual differences in perceptions and interpretations—for example, of violence in the media—help explain why observational learning does not produce the same results in all observers.

5. In contrast to behaviorists, social-learning theorists maintain that learned habits and beliefs can eventually begin to exert their own effects on behavior and may even supersede the power of external rewards and punishers. In this view, motivation depends not simply on one's history of reinforcement but also on motivating beliefs that are internalized and self-directing.

6. People develop *generalized expectancies* about which situations and acts will be rewarding, and these expectations often create a *self-fulfilling prophecy.* People who have an *internal locus of control* tend to believe that they are responsible for what happens to them; those with an *external locus of control* tend to believe that they are pawns of luck, fate, or other people. Having an internal locus of control has important psychological and even physical advantages. Locus of control is affected by one's position and experiences in society and in turn affects people's motivation to change society.

7. People with an *optimistic explanatory style* differ from those with a *pessimistic explanatory style* in how they explain unexpected bad events that befall them. Optimism is a predictor of achievement and resilience.

8. *Self-efficacy,* the belief that one is competent and can accomplish one's goals, affects many kinds of behavior. According to Albert Bandura, self-efficacy comes from experience in mastering new skills, having successful role models, receiving encouragement from others, and making judgments of one's own physical state. A person with high self-efficacy interprets failure as an opportunity to learn from mistakes, and a person with low self-efficacy interprets failure as a disaster. Another way of describing this difference is in terms of the way people think of their goals. People who set *performance goals* may become discouraged when they temporarily fail (as everyone occasionally does); those who set *learning goals* regard failure as a source of useful information and are less easily discouraged.

9. Social-learning theories have been applied to the question of how children develop a *gender identity* and to the process of *gender socialization* (sex typing). Early social-

learning theories assumed that the child was a passive participant in his or her upbringing and that equal treatment of boys and girls would result in children who were not sex-typed. Today, researchers recognize the active role played by the child and the subtle reinforcers that can affect children's gender-related behavior. Gender socialization is affected by children's *gender schemas*, self-labeling, acquisition of the metaphors of gender, and construction of internalized standards for male and female behavior. Situations also play a role in shaping and maintaining gender-related behavior and account for the adaptability people often show. Masculinity and femininity are not necessarily ingrained personality traits but involve flexible standards that can change over time.

10. For many years, the dominant approach to the study of morality was either behavioral or cognitive. Lawrence Kohlberg's theory of the development of moral reasoning (preconventional, conventional, and postconventional levels, each divided into two stages) was especially influential. Another cognitive theory has been proposed by Carol Gilligan, who argues that women tend to base moral decisions on principles of compassion, whereas men tend to base theirs on abstract principles of justice. Most research, however, finds no gender differences in moral reasoning.

11. Evidence supports the universality of Kohlberg's middle three stages, but social-learning theorists and other critics regard cognitive theories as inadequate for three reasons: (1) They tend to overlook the influence of culture and education, which means that people who are verbally sophisticated may score higher on moral reasoning than those less well educated or verbally skilled; (2) moral reasoning is inconsistent across situations and ages, and people often "regress" to a lower stage of reasoning, depending on the situation; and, most important, (3) moral reasoning and actual moral behavior are often unrelated.

12. In the social-learning view, children learn to behave morally by observing the behavior of others and its consequences and by internalizing moral standards based on their attachment to caregivers and the development of a *moral sense*. Parents and societies can encourage or inhibit children's natural *empathy*, which takes different forms as children grow older and their cognitive abilities mature. "Moral emotions," such as *shame* and *guilt*, are essential to the social learning of morality.

13. Children's moral development is strongly affected by how their parents interact with them, as well as what parents teach. *Induction* has many advantages over *power assertion* as a method of teaching children to be kind and ethical. Parents who require children to behave in helpful ways tend to raise altruistic children. In accounting for how people learn to become kind, just, and responsible, social-learning approaches move beyond simple rewards and punishments or the sophisticated ability to justify moral decisions.

Key Terms

reciprocal determinism *242*

social-learning theories *243*

observational learning *244*

model *244*

latent learning *246*

cognitive map *247*

.

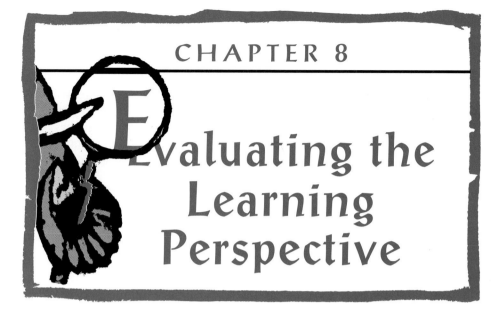

CHAPTER 8

Evaluating the Learning Perspective

B. F. Skinner aroused controversy the way a comedian provokes laughter. One famous controversy involved an enclosed "living space" that he designed for his younger daughter, Deborah, when she was an infant. Skinner noticed that when babies cry, it is often because they are wet, hot, cold, or confined by blankets and clothing. The Skinners could not be on hand every moment to relieve these discomforts, so Skinner invented the "baby tender" or "Air-Crib" (the public came to call it the "baby box") to do it for them. The baby tender had a safety-glass front, a stretched canvas floor, and temperature and humidity controls that maintained a cozy climate so that Deborah could wear just a diaper and move around freely. A long strip of sheeting passed over the canvas, and the Skinners could crank a clean section into place within seconds. The baby box was an example of learning principles in action: If you want to change behavior, you must change the environment.

After writing about his invention in a *Ladies' Home Journal* article, Skinner decided to try marketing it to other parents. Did the world rush to his door in gratitude? Hardly. Although some people did order the Air-Crib, and others built their own with Skinner's plans, in the end the baby box bombed. Many people regarded it as a cage, an oversized "Skinner box" in which Skinner experimented with his own child the way he might with a rat or a pigeon (Skinner, 1978). People imagined, incorrectly, that the Skinners were leaving their child in the Air-Crib day and night, without giving her the cuddling and "contact comfort" that are essential to healthy development. For years, rumors circulated that Deborah had gone insane or killed herself. Actually, both of Skinner's daughters turned out to be perfectly normal. Deborah became a successful artist and writer. Julie became a behaviorist and raised her own two daughters in an Air-Crib.

CONTRIBUTIONS OF THIS PERSPECTIVE

The brouhaha over the baby box illustrates the suspicion with which many people regard the learning perspective, especially the behavioral part of it. These critics, although they acknowledge the power of the environment, regard deliberate efforts to alter behavior as manipulative and cold-blooded, and they are offended by behaviorism's mechanistic language. Such complaints make learning theorists want to throw up their hands in despair. Behavioral studies are among the most reliable in all of psychology, they point out, and learning principles, when properly understood, have many useful applications. The many contributions of the learning perspective include the following:

1 THE RECOGNITION THAT WE ALL INFLUENCE OTHERS, AND IN TURN ARE INFLUENCED BY OTHERS, EVERY DAY OF OUR LIVES, WHETHER WE KNOW IT OR NOT. The last time you flirted, had a political argument, or asked someone to do something, you were trying to affect someone's behavior. Even the most easygoing people inevitably influence others by their actions, responses, facial expressions, and silences. We all respond to reinforcers and punishers, and produce them in response to the behavior of others; we all observe and imitate models, and act as models for the behavior of others. Because we cannot avoid the laws of learning, say psychologists in the learning perspective, we ought to apply them intelligently in order to improve our lives and the lives of others. People are constantly manipulating the environment, whether in a planned or an unplanned way; the important question, to a learning theorist, is whether society is willing to use learning principles wisely to achieve humane goals.

As early as 1948, in his novel *Walden Two*, B. F. Skinner created his own vision of an ideal society organized and run according to behavioral principles (Skinner, 1948/1976). (He called his society Walden Two because he regarded it as an advance on Thoreau's visionary Walden.) Many people, including the eminent critic Joseph Wood Krutch, disliked this book for what they regarded as its promotion of a "calculated" utopia. In response to Krutch's vituperative review, Skinner wrote,

> If Krutch came across a culture like Walden Two, say on a mesa in Arizona—where people chose their own line of work, where children were educated for the life they were to lead, where music and art flourished, where economic problems were solved by designing a modest life à la Thoreau, he would be shouting to the house-tops, "This is it!" But what bothers him about Walden Two is simply that somebody planned it that way! Let the accidents of history work out a pattern and it's fine. Let someone try it as an experimental plan and that's evil. (Quoted in Bjork, 1993)

2 THE UNDERSTANDING THAT MERELY NAMING A BEHAVIOR DOES NOT EXPLAIN IT. By studying the specific mechanisms that cause behavior to be perpetuated or to become extinguished, the behavioral tradition put pressure on all psychologists to be scientific and focused in their explanations of behavior. Behaviorists continually remind us that labeling someone's behavior does not explain it. What do we learn from saying that a man cannot control his drinking because he is an "alcoholic"? We might as well say that the man drinks too much because he drinks too much! Likewise, learning theorists observe, to say that a boy puts off cleaning his room because of an internal disposition called "laziness" is circular (he's lazy because of laziness) and tells us nothing, certainly not what to do about the behavior. A behaviorist would want to know what is reinforcing the boy's "laziness": an opportunity to do something that's more fun, perhaps lying on the bed and watching TV? A social-learning theorist would want to know about the boy's models (perhaps his parents are slobs too), his attitudes (perhaps he can't see a single good reason for keeping his room clean), and his gender socialization (perhaps he has learned that real boys don't vacuum).

3 A WIDE RANGE OF PRACTICAL APPLICATIONS. The learning perspective is probably best known for its down-to-earth applicability to people's lives. Other kinds of psychologists might give you pep talks and sermons, analyze your motives, or encourage you to live with the traits you were born with; the learning perspective tells you what to *do.* Learning theorists have sometimes been accused of regarding people as passive pawns of the environment, but that accusation is unfair; psychologists in this perspective, behaviorists and social-learning theorists alike, have said again and again that people can and should play an active role in creating new and better environments for themselves and others. If we want emotionally healthy children, we should learn how to rear them in ways that promote emotional health. If we want a peaceful world, we had better not wait around for people's personalities to change; instead, we had better change circumstances so that cooperation is modeled and rewarded, cheaters don't win, and aggressors don't stay in power.

In Chapter 6, we saw that behavior-modification techniques have been applied successfully in homes, schools, offices, and many other settings. Social-learning theories, too, have had great applicability to the solution of personal and social problems because of their emphasis on the interaction of the person and the environment—on the attitudes and expectations that a person can develop, for example, to acquire the motivation to change that environment. Following are just a few benefits of the research discussed in Chapter 7:

✦RAISING SELF-EFFICACY. Self-efficacy can be acquired and improved in children and adults, through programs and experiences that teach skills and provide models and appropriate rewards (Ozer & Bandura, 1990). In one study of 24 graduate students in business, for example, some students were taught to perceive the ability to make managerial decisions as a skill that can be learned and improved through practice; others were encouraged to believe that managerial ability reflects "basic cognitive processes" that people either have in abundance or don't have (Wood & Bandura, 1989). Learning to see managerial ability as a learned skill, the researchers found, "fostered a highly resilient sense of personal efficacy," which in turn caused these students to continue to strive for challenging organizational goals, which in turn improved their performance, which confirmed their self-efficacy.

✦SETTING GOALS. People can achieve more by learning to set goals that are demanding but that they can realistically achieve. Given two people of equal ability, the one who sets specific and moderately difficult goals will work longer and achieve more than the one who sets vague, easy goals or none at all (Locke & Latham, 1990). If a goal is too vague, as in "I'm going to work harder," you don't know what action to take to reach it or how to know when you've attained it (what does "harder" mean?). If your goal is concrete, as in "I am going to study two hours every evening instead of one, and read 25 pages instead of 15," you have specified both a course of action and a goal you can recognize. Moreover, as we saw in the previous chapter, people whose goals are focused more on *learning* than on *performance* are more likely to persist in the face of failure and develop intrinsic satisfaction from mastering a new skill.

✦IMPROVING HEALTH HABITS. How can you get people to change their health habits and take better care of themselves, especially if they already have health problems such as diabetes or heart disease, or are at high risk of contracting certain diseases? Popular solutions are to scare them or inundate them with information, but social-learning approaches have been far more successful: Raise their self-efficacy and sense of internal control; provide them with models of people who demonstrate how to cope with setbacks and lapses; and teach them new ways of perceiving their physical symptoms and coping with them (Meyerowitz & Chaiken, 1987; Taylor, 1995).

Perhaps the clearest evidence of the learning perspective's usefulness is how often advertisers and businesses rely on learning principles to get their customers to change their behavior. Their efforts are apparent everywhere: in the free trips we get from frequent-flyer programs, in rebates offered by car companies, in reduced insurance premiums for nonsmokers and good drivers.

LIMITATIONS AND MISUSES
OF THIS PERSPECTIVE

Of all the perspectives in psychology, the learning perspective probably seems the most obviously "true." Reward, punishment, imitation, values, expectations, self-efficacy— these influences on behavior all seem indisputable and self-evident.

Yet the very success of the learning perspective also highlights one of its inherent limitations. Behavioral and social-learning researchers tend to study one influence on learning at a time: a parental model, a teacher's reactions, the pattern of reinforcers in a particular situation, media images, self-efficacy, locus of control, and so forth. In real life, as the examples of gender socialization and the effects of media violence show, a person is surrounded by hundreds of potential influences, all of them interacting in complicated ways. This fact presents a difficult problem for researchers in the learning perspective: When nearly anything *can* have an influence on a specific behavior, it can be frustratingly difficult to show that any one thing actually *is* having an influence. It's like trying to grab a fistful of fog; you know it's there, but somehow it's out of your grasp. This is why some learning explanations of complex phenomena, such as personality traits, gender preferences, or aggression, can seem elusive. Learning researchers have to say, "Well, your parents play a role, and your attitudes, and unusual experiences you had, and what you observe in your culture, and what your religion teaches, and. . . ."

Of course, the fact that "the environment" consists of many interacting factors isn't a fault of behaviorism or social-learning theories. (The other perspectives are complex in their own ways, too.) But it does mean that we have to be careful to avoid misusing the learning perspective, as is commonly done in the following ways:

1 ENVIRONMENTAL REDUCTIONISM. Some people misinterpret the learning perspective, especially its behavioral branch, and conclude that individuals are as pliable as jellyfish, or that with the right environment, anyone can become anything. Just as it's a mistake to try to reduce all human behavior to biology, so it's a mistake to try to reduce everything to environmental influences. Genetic dispositions and biological attributes place definite limits on what individuals and species can learn.

Modern learning theorists, including behaviorists, recognize this fact and have incorporated it into their theories. For example, they recognize that all organisms seem to be biologically prepared to learn some responses more easily than others, and that conditioning procedures work best when they capitalize on these inborn tendencies. Years ago, Keller and Marian Breland (1961), psychologists who became animal trainers, described what happens when biological constraints are ignored. The Brelands found that animals often had trouble learning tasks that should have been easy. For example, a pig was supposed to drop large wooden coins into a box. Instead, the pig would drop the coin, push at it with its snout, throw it into the air, and push at it some more. This odd behavior actually delayed the delivery of the reinforcer, so it was hard to explain in terms of operant principles. Apparently, the pig's rooting instinct— its tendency to use its snout to uncover edible roots—was keeping it from learning the task. The Brelands called such a reversion to instinctive behavior **instinctive drift.**

In human beings, too, inborn tendencies affect how quickly learning occurs, or even whether it occurs at all. You may remember the psychologist in Chapter 6 who learned, through a process of classical conditioning, to hate béarnaise sauce. In the laboratory, conditioning usually takes several trials, and it is most likely to occur if the unconditioned stimulus immediately follows the conditioned one. But in the béarnaise-sauce incident, learning took place after only one pairing of the sauce with illness and with a considerable delay between the conditioned and unconditioned stimuli. Moreover, neither the psychologist's wife nor the plate from which he ate became a conditioned stimulus for nausea, even though they, too, were paired with illness. Controlled research suggests that human beings, and certain other animals as well, are biologically prepared to associate sickness with taste rather than, say, with light and sound (Garcia & Koelling, 1966; Seligman & Hager, 1972). This tendency enhances the species' survival: Eating bad food is more likely to be followed by illness than are sights or sounds. Thus, conditioning in the béarnaise-sauce incident was rapid and occurred despite the delay. Conversely, when efforts to alter human behavior have ignored biology, they have sometimes been disappointing, as we will see later in this evaluation.

2 THE ERROR OF ASSUMING THAT IF SOMETHING IS LEARNED, IT CAN EASILY BE CHANGED. Just as people often wrongly assume that biologically influenced characteristics must be permanent and immutable, so people often wrongly believe that learned behavior must always be flexible and reversible. Actually, as research in the biological perspective shows, even behavior and attributes that are strongly influenced

---

instinctive drift The tendency of an organism to revert to an instinctive behavior over time; it can interfere with learning.

by genetics can change, within limits, over a person's lifetime, because of a person's efforts, attitudes, culture, and experience. And, conversely, behavior and attributes that are entirely learned can become deeply ingrained and almost impossible to change—such as people's religious commitments and cultural practices.

Beliefs about the possibility or impossibility of change have important political implications. Throughout history, as we noted in evaluating the biological perspective (Chapter 5), people have resorted to "biological politics," using biological arguments to justify the subordination of women, legitimize racial inequities, and defend the social and political status quo (Fausto-Sterling, 1985; Gould, 1981; Hubbard, 1990). People who advocate egalitarianism and social change, on the other hand, are drawn to the learning perspective. Liberals who wish for a less prejudiced and sex-typed world, for example, can take solace in the idea that human nature is malleable and that what is learned can be unlearned. But just as political motivations underlying a biological view of the world can lead to an incomplete view of human behavior, so can those underlying a learning view.

For example, some psychologists argue that "learning politics" have blinded egalitarian-minded people to the persistence of sex differences in certain skills and learning abilities (McGuinness, 1993). Consider again the complex matter of how children become sex-typed and whether they can become *un*-sex-typed. Naturally, many feminist psychologists and biological psychologists often find themselves on opposite sides of this issue. The former think that virtually all gender differences—in levels of aggression, physical risk-taking, preferences for certain toys, occupational interests such as math or nursing, and skills such as flying planes or knitting sweaters—are learned from the lessons and roles of society at large, media images, and adult treatment of boys versus girls. There is no gene, they observe, for becoming a doctor, which women are more likely than men to do in Russia, or for wearing a skirt, which Scottish men do on formal occasions. They also point to the studies discussed in Chapter 7, showing that many of the reinforcers that matter most in gender socialization are subtle; parents and teachers may think they are treating boys and girls equally, but often they are not. The assumption of people who share the learning view is that most gender differences will eventually fade and disappear if we change sexist images in books, on television, and in popular music; teach parents and teachers to recognize and eliminate the practices that promote sex typing; and instill in children egalitarian values.

Biological psychologists, in contrast, argue that many differences between the sexes are largely a matter of hormones, genes, and brain lateralization; parents and society *reflect* gender differences rather than *causing* them. Supporters of this view cite studies in which girls who were exposed to prenatal androgens (masculinizing hormones) in the womb* were later more likely than nonexposed girls to prefer "boys' toys," such as cars, fire engines, and Lincoln Logs (Berenbaum & Hines, 1992). Such

---

*Such unusual exposure can occur if the mother has an adrenal or ovarian tumor that secretes androgens or if the fetus has a genetic condition that causes the adrenal glands to secrete too much androgen. In addition, in the 1950s, some mothers were given hormones during pregnancy for medical reasons, before it was known that the fetus would be affected too.

findings, along with evidence that on many dimensions parents *don't* treat sons and daughters differently, indicate to biological advocates that there is a "biological sub-strate for toy and play preferences" (Lytton & Romney, 1991). And so the debate over the origins of gender differences goes on, with egalitarians tending to line up on the learning side and traditionalists on the biological side.

But perhaps it is possible to break out of the dichotomous thinking that has char-acterized this debate for so long. Let's suppose there is a "biological substrate" for children's toy preferences. What does that tell us about *adult* occupational interests and gender schemas? The answer: not much—because children grow up and change, and because most adult occupational interests have little or nothing to do with biolo-gy and far more to do with what jobs people perceive are available and possible for them (Kanter, 1977/1993). Or suppose that biology contributes to some of the *aver-age* differences in certain skills between the sexes; why should that fact have anything to do with an *individual* woman's or man's educational or occupational opportuni-ties? Girls, on the average, have a disadvantage in certain kinds of spatial–visual rea-soning, compared with boys. Why should this finding mean that women who are as good as or better than men in this skill should be discouraged from careers in math and science, as so many now are? Are there other ways to teach girls that might help more of them do better? Likewise, boys, on the average, are more likely than girls to have reading disabilities. Shouldn't this finding be used to develop better programs to help boys read?

Some egalitarians fear that acknowledging these differences implies a biological cause, which in turn implies no hope for change. In fact, learning theorists and biolog-ical theorists alike can agree that it is only by acknowledging gender differences, and being open-minded about their many possible causes, that we can hope to find the best ways of reducing or eliminating them.

3 OVERSIMPLIFICATION IN APPLYING LEARNING TECHNIQUES. By emphasizing the complexity of elements affecting a person's life, social-learning theories alert us to another misuse of the learning perspective: a tendency to oversimplify. When people try to apply learning principles to problems in the classroom, the workplace, or the home, they often reduce the entire perspective to a simplistic kind of pop behaviorism. Alfie Kohn (1993) observes that bribes and threats become the only rule: "Do this and you'll get that." American workplaces, Kohn complains, have become "enormous Skin-ner boxes with parking lots," places where simple-minded, competitive incentive plans have replaced responsible management. There is an unspoken assumption that the only way to motivate people is to use the carrot and the stick.

The results of this attitude, says Kohn, often backfire. Children learn to fear their teachers or grow dependent on them, and employees feel the same way about their bosses. Everyone is so worried about failing that no one is willing to take risks. When only a few students can earn A's or only a few workers can be employee of the month, people become mistrustful of one another, demoralized when they "lose," and unwill-ing to work cooperatively. No one stops to ask what the source of poor performance is in the first place. No one stops to ask whether the behavior that is being rewarded is worth doing.

We think that Skinner would have disapproved of pop behaviorism as much as Kohn does. Skinner certainly never advocated the mindless use of extrinsic reinforcers that are bribes in disguise. On the contrary, Skinner (1987) bemoaned the fact that so many people are bored and depressed. One reason, he said, is that a life based on the pleasures of acquisition—shopping, going to the movies, driving a nice car—can thwart a life of intrinsic satisfaction. "People look at beautiful things, listen to beautiful music, and watch exciting entertainments," said Skinner, "but the only behavior reinforced is looking, listening, and watching." Too rarely, he added, are people reinforced for creativity, risk, participation, taking gambles. Too rarely are they given an opportunity to take pride in the products of their work, or to exercise initiative in their choice of pleasures. Skinner, as you can see, was fully aware of the importance of intrinsic rewards.

Still, many of Kohn's criticisms of how learning principles are applied and misapplied in the everyday world are worth thinking about. As we saw in our discussion of performance versus learning goals, when people are worried about *how* they are doing, they may never get fully absorbed in *what* they're doing. Substituting bribes for punishments, says Kohn, is not necessarily a better way to motivate people, because "The question is not whether more flies can be caught with honey than with vinegar, but *why* the flies are being caught in either case—and how this feels to the fly."

Despite these problems, behaviorists and social-learning theorists believe that society could take much better advantage of learning principles than it presently does, and be a far better place for it. We can understand the promise of this perspective, as well as some barriers that prevent it from fulfilling that promise, by examining the implications of learning principles in three important areas: psychotherapy, education, and child rearing.

WHAT DO YOU KNOW?

1. Name three contributions of the learning perspective and three of its potential misuses.
2. An old advertisement for a weight-training program used to promise to transform even a timid, mild-tempered "90-pound weakling" into an aggressive, brave, muscle-bound hunk. What misuse of the learning perspective did this ad illustrate?

ANSWERS:

1. Contributions include making people aware of the ways they influence, and are influenced by, others; the lesson that naming or labeling behavior doesn't explain it; and the practicality of the perspective's findings in solving personal and social problems. Misuses include environmental reductionism; the error of assuming that anything learned can be easily changed (which often occurs because of "learning politics"); and oversimplification in applying learning techniques.   2. environmental reductionism, because the ad overlooked the possibility of genetic and anatomical constraints on temperament and on body weight and shape.

ISSUE 1: PSYCHOTHERAPY

When people want to change their behavior, often they turn to a psychotherapist, so it's not surprising that psychotherapy has been a major beneficiary of behavioral findings. Psychologists who practice *behavior therapy* don't spend their time delving into the depths of a person's psyche. Instead, they focus on helping the client change troublesome behaviors and attitudes, using a variety of methods derived from behavioral principles.

1. BEHAVIORAL RECORDS AND CONTRACTS are used for helping clients identify the rewards that keep an unwanted habit going and make commitments to better forms of behavior. For example, a man who wants to curb his overeating may not be aware of how much he eats throughout the day; a behavioral record might show that he eats more junk food in the late afternoon than he realized. A student who procrastinates might not be aware of how she actually spends her time when she is avoiding her studies. Afraid that she hasn't time to do everything, she does nothing. Keeping a behavioral diary would tell her exactly how she spends her time, and how much time she can realistically allot to a project. (Procrastinators often are poor judges of how much time it takes to do things.)

   Once the unwanted behavior is identified, along with the reinforcers that keep it going, a treatment program can be designed to change it. The therapist can help the person set *behavioral goals,* small step by small step. A husband and wife who fight over housework, for instance, might be asked to draw up a contract indicating who will do what, with specified rewards for carrying out their duties. With such a contract, they can't fall back on mutual accusations, such as "You never do anything around here!"

2. SYSTEMATIC DESENSITIZATION is a step-by-step process of "desensitizing" a person to a feared object or experience. It combines relaxation training with a systematic hierarchy of stimuli, sometimes in imagined situations and sometimes in real ones, leading gradually to the one that is most feared. The sequence for a person who is terrified of flying might be to read about airplane safety, visit an airport, sit in a plane while it is on the ground, take a short flight, and then take a long flight. At each step the person must become comfortable before going on. This procedure is based on the same principles that guided John Watson and Mary Cover Jones's *counterconditioning* of Peter's fear of rabbits (see Chapter 6).

3. AVERSIVE CONDITIONING substitutes punishment for the reinforcement that has perpetuated a bad habit. Suppose that a woman who bites her nails is reinforced each time she does so by the relief of her anxiety and a brief good feeling. A behavior therapist might have her wear a rubber band around her wrist and ask her to snap it (hard!) each time she bites her nails or feels the desire to do so. The goal is to make sure that there is no opportunity for the undesirable behavior to be rewarded.

4. FLOODING OR EXPOSURE TREATMENTS take the client right into a feared situation, but the therapist goes along to show that the situation isn't going to kill either of

Two behavioral therapists assist a phobic woman who is afraid of stairs. In exposure treatments, a therapist takes the client directly into the feared situation in order to extinguish his or her fear. What situations would you have to put yourself in to extinguish your own fears? Public speaking? Visiting the spider display at a zoo? Looking down from the top of the Empire State Building?

them. For example, a person suffering from **agoraphobia** (a fear of leaving a safe place and being in an unfamiliar, unprotected situation) would be taken right into a new situation—a procedure called "in vivo" exposure—and would remain there, with the therapist, until the panic and anxiety decline.

5. **Skills training** provides practice in specific acts that are necessary for achieving the person's goals. It's not enough to tell someone "Don't be shy" if the person doesn't know how to make companionable small talk when meeting other people. There are countless skills-training programs available—for parents who don't know how to discipline children, for people with social anxieties, for children and adults who don't know how to control angry feelings, and so on.

Hundreds of controlled studies have established the effectiveness of behavior therapy in contrast to doing nothing at all or to being in "depth" therapies that analyze the deep-seated causes of one's problems (Chambless, 1995; Lazarus, 1990; Weisz et al., 1995). (We will discuss cognitive therapy, which is often combined with behavioral techniques, in Chapter 11, and we will evaluate the general effectiveness of all kinds of therapy in Chapter 16.) Behavior therapy has been especially successful in helping people manage

---

agoraphobia A set of phobias (irrational fears) involving the basic fear of being away from a safe place or person.

chronic pain, helping people eliminate unwanted habits, and treating behavior problems in children and teenagers. Exposure treatments have proved particularly effective in treating fears, agoraphobia, posttraumatic stress disorder, and other anxiety problems; a meta-analysis of 88 studies found that exposure techniques for reducing fear were more effective than any other treatment (Kaplan, Randolph, & Lemli, 1991). And researchers who conducted a meta-analysis of 108 outcome studies of children and adolescents reported that "behavioral treatments proved more effective than nonbehavioral treatments regardless of client age, therapist experience, or treated problem" (Weisz et al., 1987).

Some of the individual cases of successful behavior therapy make for fascinating reading. In one, a 10-year-old boy named Jim had a scratching problem. He had started scratching himself during a case of poison oak and then continued even after the rash cleared up. Eventually, he was covered with scars and sores. Behavioral records showed that almost all of Jim's scratching occurred at home and that his parents were rewarding it with attention. Because the parents were unable to ignore the scratching for long, treatment consisted of sending Jim to a "time-out" room for 20 minutes whenever he scratched, and rewarding him each week with a favored activity, such as roller skating, if his sores decreased. Nine months after treatment ended, Jim had only two sores, both almost completely healed (Carr & McDowell, 1980).

In addition to such successes, however, therapies and interventions based on learning principles have also had their failures (Foa & Emmelkamp, 1983). They are generally not the best way to recover from trauma or severe depression. They are not highly effective with people who do not really want to change and who are not motivated to carry out a behavioral program. And they do not necessarily have long-lasting effects when peer pressures and other environmental demands overwhelm the best efforts of a person to change. One cognitive-behavioral intervention program, for example, had had stunning success in lowering rates of using alcohol and other drugs, raising self-esteem, and improving the social skills of a group of highly aggressive boys. But by the three-year follow-up, there were no effects of the intervention on delinquency or classroom disruptiveness, except for one group of boys who continued to attend booster sessions (Lochman, 1992).

Moreover, some kinds of behavior are so biologically or psychologically ingrained that they resist change by any means, including the behavior therapist's impressive arsenal of behavior-change techniques. One such category is sex offenses, including exhibitionism, child molestation, rape, and incest. Behavior therapists have tried using aversive conditioning to treat pedophiles, pairing an unpleasant stimulus, such as electric shock or injections of a nausea-inducing drug, with images of naked children. They have also tried using desensitization techniques to reduce the anxiety that sex offenders often feel in ordinary sexual encounters. And they have tried to "recondition" deviant sexual fantasies by pairing images and thoughts of appropriate behavior with a pleasant stimulus or experience (such as masturbation). None of these techniques, when used alone, has had much success. The most promising treatment for sex offenders combines cognitive therapy, aversive conditioning, sex education, group therapy, reconditioning of sexual fantasies, and social-skills training—and even so, it works only when the offenders are highly motivated to change and are not just trying to reduce their prison sentences (Abel et al., 1988; Kaplan, Morales, & Becker, 1993).

Another problem that resists any kind of treatment, including behavior therapy, is **antisocial personality disorder,** a condition that many researchers believe involves biological abnormalities (Hare, 1993; Holmes, 1994; Luengo et al., 1994). People with this disorder (sometimes called "psychopaths" or "sociopaths") have no conscience. They can lie, charm, seduce, and manipulate others, and then drop them without a qualm. Some antisocial persons are sadistic, with a history of criminal or cruel behavior that began in childhood. They can kill anyone—an intended victim, a child, a bystander—without a twinge of regret. Others direct their energy into con games or career advancement, abusing other people emotionally rather than physically.

For unknown reasons, this disorder is far more common in males than in females; according to survey evidence, it is estimated to occur among 3 to 5 percent of all males and less than 1 percent of all females (Robins, Tipp, & Przybeck, 1991). Although these percentages are small, antisocial individuals create a lot of havoc: They are believed to account for more than half of all serious crimes committed in the United States* (Hare, 1993).

Some people with antisocial personality disorder can be very "sociable," charming everyone around them, but they have no emotional connection to other people, and no guilt about their wrongdoing. Their inability to feel emotional arousal—empathy, guilt, fear of punishment, anxiety under stress—implies some abnormality in the central nervous system. Antisocial individuals do not respond to punishments that would affect other people, such as threat of physical harm or loss of approval. This fact may explain why antisocial persons fail to learn that their actions will have unpleasant consequences (Hare, 1993). Normally, when a person is anticipating danger, pain, or shock, the electrical conductance of the skin changes—a classically conditioned response that indicates anxiety or fear. But in several experiments, people with antisocial personality disorder were slow to develop such responses. As you can see in Figure 8.1, it is as if they aren't "wired" to feel the anxiety necessary for avoidance learning.

Some researchers believe that there is a common inherited condition among people who are labeled antisocial, hyperactive, or overly extroverted (Luengo et al., 1994). All three conditions involve problems in *behavioral inhibition*—the ability to control responses to frustration or to inhibit a pleasurable action that may have unpleasant consequences. Another biological possibility, supported by studies of violent criminals compared with nonviolent criminals, and by longitudinal studies that follow people from birth to adulthood, is that some extremely violent individuals have central-nervous-system impairments as a result of genetic factors, complications during birth, or physical abuse (Holmes, 1994; Moffitt, 1993; Raine, Brennan, & Mednick, 1994). Of course, many environmental factors contribute to antisocial personality disorder, including parental

---

antisocial personality disorder A disorder characterized by antisocial behavior such as lying, stealing, manipulating others, and sometimes violence; a lack of social emotions (guilt, shame, and empathy); and impulsivity. (Sometimes called "psychopathy" or "sociopathy.")

*A person who commits antisocial *behavior* does not necessarily have an antisocial personality *disorder*. Most kinds of criminal behavior—homicide, rape, robbery, assault, burglary, and auto theft—are carried out by young men whose criminal activities drop off sharply by their late twenties. The personality disorder characterizes a much smaller number of males, who begin displaying antisocial behavior in early childhood, are drawn to criminal environments, and never develop emotional connections to other people (Moffitt, 1993).

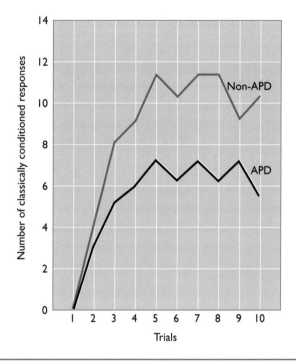

Figure 8.1   *In several experiments such as this one, people with antisocial personality disorder (APD) were slow to develop classically conditioned responses to anticipated danger, pain, or shock—the normal responses that indicate anxiety (Hare, 1965). This deficit may be related to the ability of these people to behave in destructive ways without remorse or regard for the consequences (Hare, 1993).*

neglect, observing and being rewarded by role models, and experiences with violence. But biological abnormalities may help explain why people with antisocial personalities do not learn to control their impulsive actions, do not acquire the usual social values, and seem impervious to normal social learning, as well as to behavioral therapies.

WHAT DO YOU KNOW?

Match each behavior problem on the left with the behavior-therapy technique best suited to it:

1. Shyness at parties
2. Fear of flying
3. Marital quarrels about housework
4. Agoraphobia
5. Nail-biting

a. behavioral contract
b. aversive conditioning
c. exposure (flooding)
d. systematic desensitization
e. skills training

ANSWERS:

1. e   2. d   3. a   4. c   5. b

ISSUE 2: EDUCATION

If learning principles would apply anywhere, surely it is the classroom, where learning is, after all, the primary goal. Indeed, classroom learning was one of B. F. Skinner's chief interests. In 1943, during a visit to his daughter's fourth-grade class, Skinner noticed that the teacher was unable to give her students immediate feedback on their work and that all the students were being pushed to learn at the same pace, regardless of their academic preparation or ability. It occurred to Skinner that operant techniques could be used to design better instruction. So he went home and invented the first teaching machine, a mechanical contraption that helped inspire the educational technique called *programmed instruction.*

In programmed instruction, the material to be learned is broken down into small chunks or "frames," and the student is tested on each chunk. Each level of learning builds on what is already known; in behavioral terms, the student's behavior is shaped. A correct response brings an immediate reinforcer in the form of feedback ("You're right!"), and the student is then led on to more difficult items. An incorrect response brings a review of the material or an easier problem to try. Programmed instruction was the direct forerunner of the computerized drill-and-practice programs that are now used in many schools.

Since Skinner's day, behaviorists concerned with classroom learning have designed many programs using an operant approach. In one program, instructors at the Morningside Academy in Seattle (kindergarten through eighth grade) and at Malcolm X College in Chicago were trained to teach basic skills and to drill students on these skills until the students could perform them quickly, easily, and automatically. More complex kinds of skills often then emerged *without further instruction.* For example, four college students in a summer remedial program initially could not solve mathematical word problems involving fractions. After intensive training on whole-number word problems and fraction-computation skills, the students were able to solve fraction word problems on their own. At the Morningside Academy, children in the program who have been diagnosed as learning disabled have typically gained from two to three grade levels a year in such subjects as math, reading, and writing (Johnson & Layng, 1992).

Unfortunately, say behaviorists, many educational systems have failed to use behavioral principles properly and effectively. Skinner himself regarded behaviorism's lack of success in improving education and increasing children's enjoyment of learning as the greatest disappointment of his life (Bjork, 1993).

One barrier has been the extra work required of teachers when they are asked to use frequent reinforcers in the conventional classroom. Teachers often use study periods to sit at their desks and mark papers, but if they are to watch for behaviors to reinforce, they must leave their desks and move about the room. This means, of course, that they will have to wait until after school to grade papers. This may be why, in some studies, teachers learned to use reinforcers successfully, yet they reverted to their former style of teaching as soon as the study ended (Hopkins, 1987). Their use of reinforcement was not reinforced!

Psychologist and educator Paul Chance (personal communication) notes that there are few rewards for teachers who take the extra steps necessary to implement operant procedures. Teaching awards, he says, often go to teachers who are popular or innovative, rather than to those whose students are actually improving in their performance. Teachers themselves have resisted merit pay, fearing an intrusion of administrators into their classrooms and the development of hostile competition among teachers. Chance believes that the way around these problems is to base merit pay on the average performance of all the children in a school. If performance improved, bonuses would go to all the teachers and administrators, thus promoting cooperation rather than competition. A few school districts are now moving in this direction.

Another barrier to the implementation of learning principles is the heavy emphasis in most schools on grades. Like all extrinsic rewards, grades induce temporary compliance but not necessarily a lifelong disposition to learn. There is evidence that as children get older, they become more and more dependent on grades and the teacher's approval and less and less concerned with satisfying their own curiosity (Harter & Jackson, 1992). Sadly, in the process they lose the natural inquisitiveness and need to explore that all children seem to be born with. Although teachers commonly believe that gold stars, extra privileges, and grades will boost performance, children who are concerned mainly about rewards and approval actually use less sophisticated learning strategies and score lower on standardized achievement tests than children who are interested in learning for its own sake (Boggiano et al., 1992). A cognitive social-learning theorist would observe that this outcome is predictable from the finding that learning goals are more effective than performance goals for fostering persistence and mastery.

Some teachers have tried to boost self-esteem in their students by being lavish both with high grades and with praise, in the hope that as children learn to feel good about themselves their academic performance will improve. In one middle school, when teachers tried to use a cutoff of a 3.5 grade-point average for membership in a new academic honor society, they found that *two-thirds* of the school's 600 students were eligible, even though they were not all doing A work (Celis, 1993). The teachers apparently felt obligated to give high grades, whether the students deserved them or not. Grade inflation has infiltrated higher education as well; in some colleges and universities, C's, which once meant average or satisfactory, are nearly extinct. The problem, from a learning-theory point of view, is that to be effective, rewards must be tied to the behavior you're trying to increase. When rewards are dispensed indiscriminately, they become meaningless; they are no longer reinforcing. And when teachers praise mediocre work, that is what they are likely to get.

There is another problem with praise when the praise is not tied to good performance. If a teacher gushes over work on a task that was actually easy, the hidden message may be that the child isn't very smart ("Gee, Minnie, you certainly did a *fantastic* job . . . of adding two and two"). Even when the task is challenging, praise, if delivered too dramatically, may carry an unintended message—that the student's good work was a surprise ("Gee, Robert, you *really* did *well* on that paper [and who would have

"That is the correct answer, Billy, but I'm afraid
you don't win anything for it."

ever thought you could do it?]"). The result is likely to be lower, not higher, self-esteem, and reduced expectations of doing well.

Although many people believe that self-esteem is the main ingredient of success and achievement, and its absence a major reason that children fail, there is actually no evidence to support this idea, in spite of concerted efforts to find some (Dawes, 1994; Smelser, Vasconcellos, & Mecca, 1989). Lilian Katz (1993), a professor of early childhood education who has headed the National Association for the Education of Young People, argues that "feel good about yourself" programs in schools tend to confuse self-esteem with self-involvement. Children are taught to turn their attention on themselves and to focus on their own gratification and self-celebration. Program after program asks children to write about such superficial things as physical attributes and consumer preferences ("What I like to watch on TV" or "What I like to eat"). In one typical curriculum she examined, Katz says, "Not once was the child asked to assume the role of producer, investigator, initiator, explorer, experimenter, wonderer, or problem-solver." Children never had to write essays on such topics as "What I want to know more about," or "What I am curious about," or on what they wanted to explore, find out, solve, figure out, or make. Real self-esteem, Katz argues, does not come from "cheap success in a succession of trivial tasks," from phony flattery by a teacher, or from gold stars and happy faces. It emerges from effort, persistence, and the gradual acquisition of skills, and it is nurtured by a teacher's genuine appreciation of the *content* of the child's work.

What Katz is really arguing for is the promotion of self-efficacy. A social-learning theorist would say that when schools either use praise indiscriminately or punish all failures, they are actually decreasing students' self-efficacy. As Albert Bandura and others have emphasized, occasional failures are necessary opportunities for learning the value of persistence, and they also teach students where they need to improve.

Self-efficacy is important not only for students, but also for teachers. In one classroom field study of 48 teachers in four high schools, researchers measured the teachers' sense of self-efficacy as teachers, made classroom observations of "climate and atmosphere," and assessed student achievement. They found that "teachers with a greater sense of self-efficacy tend to maintain a positive emotional climate in their classrooms, avoiding the harsh modes of behavior control that tend to characterize low-efficacy teachers." Even better, the students of teachers who were high in self-efficacy scored higher on standardized math tests than students in other classrooms (Ashton & Webb, 1986).

In recent years, study after study has revealed an appalling level of illiteracy in the United States. Some high-school graduates cannot read well enough to decipher a bus schedule or a warning on a nonprescription medication. Millions of people have such poor arithmetic skills that they cannot balance a checkbook or verify the change they get at the supermarket. Many students are unaware that their writing and math skills are deficient; how could they know, since they have always received high grades? The time certainly seems right to rethink the way children are taught and schools are organized.

WHAT DO YOU KNOW?

Now that you are familiar with behavioral and social-learning principles, what would *you* do as a teacher to design a classroom that fosters achievement, competence, self-efficacy, and an intrinsic love of learning?

ANSWERS:

There are many possible answers. You might start by eliminating grades on some assignments, and having students assess their own interests, strengths, and weaknesses. You might reward students who show improvement in their weakest skills. You might give students free time in each class hour to pursue their own individual projects. You would try to be a role model who demonstrates enthusiasm and love of learning, and who doesn't dispense different subtle messages or rewards to boys and girls for classroom participation. You would help students to set individual goals for themselves that were difficult but realistic. You would teach students that criticism of their work is not the same as criticism of *them*, and that honest feedback is necessary for improvement. You would encourage students to regard their failures as learning experiences instead of catastrophes. And you would try to get your school system to reward you for behaving this way!

ISSUE 3: CHILD REARING

We turn now to an area where the potential contribution of the learning perspective may be the greatest: in the rearing of competent, responsible, emotionally healthy children. The learning perspective addresses the questions that all parents have: How should they treat their children? Should they be strict or lenient, powerful or permissive? Should they require their children to stop having tantrums, clean up their rooms, and be polite, or just wait for these behaviors to emerge naturally?

Parents, of course, are not the only influence on children: Friends, television images, teachers, and a child's own temperament, beliefs, and expectations all affect how the child turns out. But parents do provide role models for their children and convey important lessons about morality, responsibility, and the consequences of behavior. For example, in Chapter 7, we saw that aggressive behavior in boys is due, in part, to parents who shout, scold, and spank, but who don't make punishment contingent on the child's behavior. Other research, too, shows that violence is first learned in the family. In a 22-year study of boys and girls who were first observed at age 8, parents who used the harshest discipline had the most aggressive and disruptive children. By the time they were 30, many of the aggressive children had grown into violent adults, many with criminal records, and they were, as parents, more likely than others to use harsh physical punishment with their own children (Huesmann et al., 1984).

There must be a better way, and the learning perspective can help us find it. In a program of research spanning three decades, Diana Baumrind (1966, 1971, 1973, 1989, 1991) has identified three general styles of child rearing and their effects on children.

1. AUTHORITARIAN PARENTS exercise too much power and give too little nurturance. Communication is all one way: The parent uses power assertion to get the child to behave, issuing orders ("Stop that!" "Do it because I say so!"), and the child is expected to listen and obey. The children of these parents tend to be less socially skilled than other children, have lower self-esteem, and do more poorly in school. Some are overly timid and others are overly aggressive.

2. PERMISSIVE PARENTS are nurturant, but they exercise too little control and don't make strong demands for mature and responsible behavior on the part of their children. They fail to state rules clearly and consistently, and they have poor communication with their kids. Their children, compared with the offspring of other kinds of parents, are likely to be impulsive, immature, irresponsible, and academically unmotivated.

3. AUTHORITATIVE PARENTS travel a middle road. They know when and how to discipline their children. They set high but reasonable expectations and teach their children how to meet them. They also give their children emotional support and encourage two-way communication; when they correct their children's behavior, they use *induction* (see page 271). Children of authoritative parents tend to have self-control, high self-esteem, and high self-efficacy, and they are the most likely to be socially mature, successful in school, cheerful, and helpful to others.

Other learning theorists have suggested some modifications of Baumrind's categories. Eleanor Maccoby and John Martin (1983) have proposed that the permissive style actually comes in two varieties, *indulgent* and *neglecting*. Indulgent parents make few demands on their children but at least are responsive to them, reinforcing them for desirable behavior. Neglecting parents neither make demands nor give appropriate reinforcement. The children of neglecting parents have the most severe problems of all: They tend to be much more impulsive and belligerent and much less achievement oriented than other children (Block, 1971; Pulkkinen, 1982).

Of course, as social-learning theorists would be the first to admit, these parental practices occur in a social context. Their effectiveness depends not only on what the parents do but also on the child's temperament, cognitive abilities (such as an understanding of rules and another person's feelings), and *perceptions* of the parent's intentions (Fabes et al., 1994; Grusec & Goodnow, 1994). A parent who sets harsh and authoritarian rules may be perceived as acting in an arbitrary, mean way, or as acting out of love and concern. As Diana Baumrind (1991) observed, "Parental practices that would be overly restrictive in a benign middle-class environment may provide optimum supervision in an urban ghetto." The meaning and implications of any parenting style depend on the circumstances of people's lives and what succeeds for them in their own neighborhoods and culture.

In a review of the research on parenting, Nancy Darling and Laurence Steinberg (1993) distinguish between parenting *styles,* defined as clusters of attitudes that create a certain emotional climate in the family, and parenting *practices,* defined as specific actions—helping a child with homework, spanking the child, talking to the child about problems with friends, taking the child to museums, and so forth. A parent's practices directly affect many of the child's behaviors, from cooking to studying, as well as the child's values and level of self-esteem. The parent's style affects the child indirectly, by making the parent's practices more or less effective, and by making the child more or less open to those practices. The child's openness, in turn, affects the influence of the parent's practices on the child's development. The following figure shows these interacting relationships:

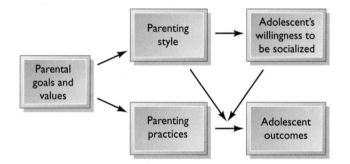

Complicated, isn't it? That's the nature of learning approaches to behavior, because so much is going on in what we blithely call "the environment." Yet even though we still don't know exactly how parental styles, goals, and practices and the child's own qualities all interact to produce certain results, behavioral and cognitive social-learning findings allow us to draw a picture of the kind of parenting that is apt to produce happy children who like themselves and are considerate of others:

◆**CONSISTENCY IN ENFORCING RULES AND DEMANDS.** Effective parents, as we have seen, do not give in to a child's whining or tantrums. Inconsistency—letting the child draw on the walls on Tuesday but not on Thursday—encourages the child's misbehavior by reinforcing it intermittently.

◆**MODELING OF DESIRABLE BEHAVIOR.** Children often do as their parents do instead of as their parents say. Thus telling a child to be generous and share with others will not work if the parents themselves behave in selfish and self-centered ways (Grusec, Saas-Kortsaak, & Simutis, 1978).

◆**HIGH EXPECTATIONS.** Good parents set high expectations and teach a child how to meet them. However, their demands must be appropriate to the child's age. Before you can expect children to get up on time by themselves, they have to be old enough to know how to work an alarm clock.

◆**RESPECT FOR THE CHILD.** Although effective parents require compliance with certain rules, they do not regard themselves as infallible or hem their children in with a bunch of arbitrary restrictions and requirements. They respect the child's individual temperament, interests, and abilities.

◆**EXPLANATIONS FOR RULES.** Explanations help children to internalize rules and standards. Verbal give-and-take between a parent and child also teaches the child to reason and rewards curiosity and open-mindedness (Schulman, 1991). This does not mean that parents have to argue with a 4-year-old about the merits of table manners. Parents can set standards while also allowing children to express disagreements and feelings.

◆**APPROVAL AND REINFORCEMENT OF DESIRABLE BEHAVIOR.** Because punishment has so many drawbacks, a better approach to socializing children is to accentuate the positive by noticing and praising desirable behavior. Instead of constantly scolding a child for wetting the bed, parents can give praise for dry sheets in the morning. Rewards, however, as we have seen, are not the same as insincere gushing about every tiny step in the right direction, which can cause praise to lose its value and "up the ante" so that soon nothing less than a standing ovation will do.

◆**THE USE OF INDUCTION RATHER THAN POWER ASSERTION.** As we saw in Chapter 7, parents who want a child to have empathy and consideration for others will call the child's attention to the effects of hurtful actions on others and will teach the child to take another person's point of view. In other words, they will use induction. For boys, especially, there is a strong negative relationship between aggression and empathy—the higher the one, the lower the other (Feshbach et al., 1983).

We realize that not everyone is ready to accept these guidelines. Many people get huffy at the notion of using induction with their children, saying, "My parents spanked me, and I turned out okay, so why shouldn't I do the same with my kids?" Some people think that power assertion is the only way to keep kids from turning into little monsters, and they scoff at the idea of explaining rules to a 6-year-old. All of us have learned and internalized our own culture's standards of what makes a good parent, and these standards don't always correspond to an authoritative style. People often care deeply for even the most authoritarian of parents, and therefore they may equate criticisms of the authoritarian approach with criticisms of their parents, who, after all, may only have been doing their best. But if we are willing to examine the evidence and question some cultural assumptions, we will be open to the important lessons that the learning perspective has to offer.

WHAT DO YOU KNOW?

1. Which statement illustrates a parent's use of induction? (a) "Stop pinching your sister right now, or else." (b) "Pinching hurts your sister; big boys like you don't need to pinch." (c) "Go to your room at once."
2. A parent who uses power assertion and punishment to make children obey is relying on an _____ style; a parent who uses induction and explanation is relying on an _____ style.
3. Parents who have a _____ style tend to have children with the most severe behavioral and academic problems.

ANSWERS:

1. b 2. authoritarian; authoritative 3. neglecting

The learning perspective has specific lessons for us, and it also assures us that we are never too old to learn them. In this respect, the learning perspective is, by its nature, an optimistic one. We can change for the better if only we will turn our attention to ways of fashioning better environments for ourselves, our children, and our fellow human beings. In Skinner's *Walden Two,* the main character, Frazier, exclaims, "The one fact that I would cry from every housetop is this: The Good Life is waiting for us—here and now! We have the necessary techniques, both material and psychological, to create a full and satisfying life for everyone."

Frazier was overstating his case, which was his prerogative; he was, after all, a character in a utopian novel. The rest of us need to be wary of his environmental reductionism. But we can take with us his ultimate message: With patience, care, and forethought, we can learn to apply the learning perspective in our own lives.

✦ ✦ ✦

Summary

1. Behavioral studies are among the most reliable in all of psychology, and learning principles have many useful applications. Major contributions of this perspective include making people aware of the ways they influence, and are influenced by, others; showing that the naming or labeling of behavior doesn't explain it; and solving real-life problems because of the practical applications of the perspective's findings. Social-learning theories have had particular applicability to personal and social problems, because of their emphasis on the interaction of the person and the environment—for example, in helping people to achieve self-efficacy, set goals, and improve health habits.

2. Rewards, punishment, imitation, values, expectations, and self-efficacy all are indisputable influences on behavior. Yet the learning perspective has an inherent limitation because in real life, there are often so many interacting influences on any given behavior or social problem that it can be difficult to demonstrate the role of any one factor. Misuses of the learning perspective include *environmental*

reductionism, the tendency to reduce all behavior to environmental influences and ignore biological and cultural contributions; the belief that if something is learned, it is easily changeable (a belief fostered by "learning politics"), which can lead to an incomplete view of a problem and an exaggeration of the possibilities for rapid changes in behavior; and oversimplification in applying learning techniques and principles, as in the mindless use of extrinsic reinforcers that are thinly disguised bribes.

3. Psychotherapy has been a major beneficiary of behavioral findings. Behavioral therapists use *behavioral records and contracts, systematic desensitization, aversive conditioning, flooding or exposure treatments,* and *skills training* with their clients. Behavior therapies have been especially successful in treating fears and phobias (including *agoraphobia*), helping people to manage chronic pain, helping people to eliminate unwanted habits, and treating behavior problems in children and teenagers. But therapies and interventions based on learning principles are not effective for all problems or all individuals. Behavior therapies alone have not been successful with sex offenders or people with *antisocial personality disorder.* Some kinds of behaviors may be so biologically or psychologically ingrained that they resist the behavior therapist's arsenal of behavior-change techniques.

4. Behaviorists concerned with classroom learning have designed many programs using an operant approach, but critics believe that many educational systems have failed to use behavioral principles properly and effectively. An important barrier to the implementation of learning principles is the heavy emphasis on grades. Programs aimed at boosting the self-esteem of students tend to ignore behavioral principles (because praise is not always tied to good performance) and social-learning principles (because teachers and administrators overlook the importance of instilling self-efficacy).

5. The contribution of the learning perspective may be greatest in the rearing of children. Parents provide important role models for their children and convey important lessons about morality, responsibility, and the consequences of behavior. In general, an *authoritative* style of child rearing is superior to an *authoritarian* or *permissive* (indulgent or neglecting) style, but it is necessary to consider the family and cultural context in which parents and children live. Beneficial parental techniques include consistency in enforcing rules and demands; modeling desirable behavior; setting high expectations; respecting the child; explaining rules; approving and reinforcing desirable behavior; and using induction rather than power assertion.

Key Terms

environmental reductionism *281*

instinctive drift *281*

behavioral records and contracts *285*

systematic desensitization *285*

aversive conditioning *285*

flooding/exposure treatments *285*

agoraphobia *286*

skills training *286*

PART IV

THE COGNITIVE PERSPECTIVE

The scene: Japan, long ago. A man is leading a horse down a narrow wooded path. On the horse sits his elegant wife, heavily veiled. Suddenly the two are attacked by a bandit, who ties up the man and rapes the woman. And then . . . well, and then it depends on who is telling the story.

The thief, when captured, says that the woman tried valiantly to defend herself with a dagger hidden in her clothes. After the assault, he says, she told him that either he or her husband must die, to keep her from being "doubly disgraced." The thief then freed the husband and engaged him in a sword fight, killing him. But when he looked around, the woman was gone.

No, no, that's not what happened at all, says the woman. After the attack, the thief freed the husband and fled. Feeling disgraced and desperate, she ran to her husband, hoping to be comforted. But when she looked into his eyes she saw not sorrow but hatred. She picked up the dagger and begged her husband to kill her, but he sat there unmoved. In despair, she fainted and when she came to, the dagger was in her husband's chest.

Wait, that's not what happened either, says the husband (speaking through a medium, since he is now dead). After the attack, the bandit asked the woman to go away with him. She said she would if the bandit would kill her husband. The bandit was shocked at this request. "What should I do with her?" he asked the husband, at which point the woman ran off, with the bandit in pursuit. Hours later, the bandit returned, cut the husband's bonds, and left. The husband, consumed by grief, used the dagger to kill himself.

Wrong, says a passerby who witnessed the crime. After the assault, the thief begged the woman for forgiveness and offered to marry her. She replied that the men must decide her fate in a duel. Reluctantly, they began to fight. At last, the thief managed to kill the husband, but when he went to claim his prize, the woman had run away.

One incident, four different accounts, and you will find them all in Akira Kurosawa's classic film *Rashomon*. (Rashomon was the south entrance gate to Kyoto, a place where travelers used to meet and tell stories.) Kurosawa's parable teaches that the truth is elusive, that, as one character says, human beings must "create stories" that deceive not only others but also themselves. Our needs, motives, and desire to protect ourselves—all these determine the kinds of narratives we construct about our lives. That is the message of the cognitive perspective as well. As George Gerbner (1988) once observed, we human beings differ from all other species because we tell stories— and live by the stories we tell. In Chapter 9, we will see how the human mind thinks and reasons, sometimes rationally, sometimes not so rationally. In Chapter 10, we will confront the mystery of memory and find out why it is often difficult to know which of our stories are right.

CHAPTER 9

Thinking and Reasoning

*H*ere's a little test for you to try: For 30 seconds or so, look away from this page and *don't think about anything.* Don't think about what you have to do this week. Don't think about what you ate for breakfast. Don't think about your personal problems. Don't think about the weather. Don't think about reading this chapter. Don't think about politics. Don't think about this test. Don't think about psychology and don't think about elephants. *Don't even think about not thinking.* Okay, ready? Begin.

Couldn't do it, could you? Well, this is a test that everyone flunks—with the possible exception of some experienced meditators who have spent years taming the jumpy and restless nature of what Buddhists call the "monkey mind." To be human is to think thoughts from morning until night, and then to keep right on thinking, even during sleep. Descartes' famous declaration "I think, therefore I am" could just as well have been reversed: "I am, therefore I think." Not a day goes by when we don't make plans, solve problems, draw inferences, analyze relationships, concoct explanations, and organize and reorganize the flotsam and jetsam of our mental world. We can't help it.

Think about what thinking does for us. It frees us from the confines of the immediate present: We can think about a trip taken three years ago, a party planned for next Saturday, or the War of 1812. It carries us beyond the boundaries of reality: We can imagine unicorns and utopias, Martians and magic. Because we think, we do not need to grope our way blindly through our problems but, with some effort and knowledge, can solve them intelligently and creatively.

To explain such abilities, many cognitive psychologists liken the human mind to an information processor, somewhat analogous to a computer but far more complex. Information-processing approaches have been useful because they capture the fact that the brain does not passively record information but actively alters and organizes it. When we take action, we physically manipulate the environment; when we think, we *mentally* manipulate internal representations of objects, activities, and situations. However, we do not manipulate all the information potentially available to us; if we did, making the simplest decision or solving the most trivial problem would be time-consuming and perhaps impossible. Imagine trying to decide whether to go out for a hamburger if that meant thinking about every hamburger you ever ate, saw a commercial for, or watched someone eat. Thinking is possible because our internal representations simplify and summarize information that reaches us from the environment.

One type of representation, or unit of thought, is the **concept.** Essentially, a concept is a mental category that groups objects, relations, activities, abstractions, or qualities having common properties. The instances of a concept are seen as roughly similar. For example, *golden retriever, cocker spaniel,* and *Weimaraner* are instances of the concept *dog;* and *anger, joy,* and *sadness* are instances of the concept *emotion.* Because concepts simplify the world, we do not need to learn a new name for each thing, relation, activity, abstract state, or quality we encounter, nor do we need to treat each instance as though it were unique. You may never have seen a *basenji* or eaten *escargots,* but if you know that the first is an instance of *dog* and the second an instance of *food,* you will know, roughly, how to respond.

We form concepts through direct contact with objects and situations and also by contact with *symbols,* things that represent or stand for something else. Symbolic representations include words, mathematical formulas, maps, graphs, pictures, and even gestures. Symbols stand not only for objects but also for operations (e.g., the symbols + and ÷), relationships (e.g., = and <), and qualities (e.g., the dot in musical notation that symbolizes an abrupt or staccato quality).

Concepts are the building blocks of thought, but they would be of limited use if we simply stacked them up mentally. We must also represent their relationships to one

---

concept A mental category that groups objects, relations, activities, abstractions, or qualities having common properties.

another. One way we accomplish this may be by storing and using **propositions,** units of meaning that are made up of concepts and that express a unitary idea. A proposition can express nearly any sort of knowledge (e.g., "Hortense raises basenjis") or belief (e.g., "Basenjis are beautiful"). Propositions, in turn, may be linked together in complicated networks of knowledge, beliefs, associations, and expectations. These networks, which psychologists call **cognitive schemas,** serve as mental models of aspects of the world. For example, as we saw in Chapter 7, gender schemas represent a person's beliefs and expectations about what it means to be male or female. People also have schemas about cultures, occupations, animals, geographical locations, and many other features of the social and natural environment.

Most cognitive psychologists believe that visual images, pictures in the mind's eye, are also important in thinking. Although no one can directly "see" another person's images, psychologists are able to study them indirectly. One method is to measure how long it takes people to rotate an image, scan from one point to another in an image, or "read off" some detail from an image. The results suggest that visual images are much like images on a television screen: We can manipulate them; they occur in a mental "space" of a fixed size; and small ones contain less detail than larger ones (Kosslyn, 1980; Shepard & Metzler, 1971). People's visual imagery skills may be affected by experience. In one study, deaf and hearing users of American Sign Language (ASL) were more skilled at generating complex visual images and recognizing mirror-image reversals than were nonsigners, presumably because signing enhances these skills (Emmorey, Kosslyn, & Bellugi, 1993). In another study, young children were not as adept at generating, scanning, and rotating objects mentally as older children and adults were (Kosslyn et al., 1990a).

In addition to visual images, most people also report auditory images (for instance, when thinking about a song or a conversation), and many report images in other sensory modalities—touch, taste, smell, or pain. Some even report kinesthetic images, feelings in the muscles and joints. Although mental images often have no obvious purpose, people do sometimes use them to visualize the possible outcomes of a decision, understand or formulate verbal descriptions, boost motivation, or improve mood (Kosslyn et al., 1990b). Imagining yourself performing an athletic skill, such as diving or sprinting, may even improve your actual performance (Druckman & Swets, 1988). A recent brain-scan study suggests that this mental practice activates most of the brain circuits involved in the activity itself (Stephan et al., 1995).

Albert Einstein relied heavily on visual and kinesthetic imagery for formulating ideas. The happiest thought of his life, he once recalled, occurred in 1907, when he suddenly imagined a man falling freely from the roof of a house and realized that the man would not experience a gravitational field in his immediate vicinity. This insight led eventually to Einstein's formulation of the principle of general relativity, and physics was never again the same.

---

proposition A unit of meaning that is made up of concepts and expresses a unitary idea.
cognitive schema An integrated mental network of knowledge, beliefs, and expectations concerning a particular topic or aspect of the world.

HOW CONSCIOUS IS THOUGHT?

When we think about thinking, most of us have in mind those mental activities, such as solving problems or making decisions, that are carried out in a deliberate way with a conscious goal in mind. However, not all mental processing is conscious.

Subconscious processes lie outside of awareness but can be brought into consciousness when necessary. These processes allow us to handle more information and perform more complex tasks than if we depended entirely on conscious thought, and they enable us to perform more than one task simultaneously (Kahneman & Treisman, 1984). Consider all the automatic routines performed "without thinking," though they might once have required careful, conscious attention: knitting, typing, driving a car, decoding the letters in a word in order to read it. Because of the capacity for automatic processing, with proper training, people can even learn to perform simultaneously such complex tasks as reading and taking dictation (Hirst, Neisser, & Spelke, 1978).

Nonconscious processes remain outside of awareness but nonetheless affect behavior. For example, most of us have had the odd experience of having a solution to a problem "pop into mind" after we have given up trying to find one. Similarly, people will often say that they rely on intuition rather than on conscious reasoning to solve a problem. Research suggests that the experience of intuition is actually an orderly process involving two stages (Bowers et al., 1990). In the first stage, clues in the problem automatically activate certain memories or knowledge, and you begin to see a pattern or structure in the problem, although you can't yet say what it is. This nonconscious process guides you toward a hunch or hypothesis. Then, in the second stage, your thinking becomes conscious and you become aware of a possible solution. This stage may feel like a sudden revelation ("Aha, I've got it!"), but considerable mental work has already occurred, even though you are not aware of it.

Some decisions to act also seem to be made without awareness. In a fascinating study, physiologist Benjamin Libet (1985) told volunteers to flex a wrist or finger whenever they felt like it. As soon as the urge to flex occurred, the person noted the position of a dot revolving on a clocklike screen. Electrodes monitored changes in brain activity occurring immediately before the volunteers' muscular movements, changes known as "readiness potentials." Libet found that readiness potentials occurred about half a second before muscle movement, but conscious awareness of an intention to move the muscle (as inferred from reports of dot position) occurred about three-tenths of a second *after* that. In other words, one part of the brain seemed to be initiating action before another part—the aware part—knew it.

Libet drew an analogy between these results and what happens when a sprinter hears a starter's pistol go off. The sprinter will take off in less than a tenth of a second after the gun fires, yet that is too short a time to perceive the sound consciously.

---

subconscious processes Mental processes occurring outside of conscious awareness but accessible to consciousness when necessary.

nonconscious processes Mental processes occurring outside of and not available to conscious awareness.

According to Libet, the runner must be responding unconsciously. Then, after the sound enters awareness, the mind corrects the sequence, so the person thinks that he or she heard the sound before actually moving.

Usually, of course, much of our thinking is conscious—but we may not be thinking very *hard*. We may act, speak, and make decisions out of habit, without stopping to analyze what we are doing or why we are doing it. Ellen Langer (1989) has called this mental inertia *mindlessness*. She notes that mindless processing keeps people from recognizing when a change in context requires a change in behavior. In one study by Langer and her associates, a researcher approached people as they were about to use a photocopier and made one of three requests: "Excuse me, may I use the Xerox machine?" "Excuse me, may I use the Xerox machine, because I have to make copies?" or "Excuse me, may I use the Xerox machine, because I'm in a rush?" Normally, people will let someone go before them only if the person has a legitimate reason, as in the third request. In this study, however, people also complied when the reason sounded like an authentic explanation but was actually meaningless ("because I have to make copies"). They heard the form of the request, but not its content, and mindlessly stepped aside (Langer, Blank, & Chanowitz, 1978). This sort of mindlessness may occur more often that we would like to think, as the cartoon on this page suggests.

The mindless processing of information has benefits: If we stopped to think twice about everything we did, we would get nothing done ("Okay, now I'm reaching for my toothbrush; now I'm putting a quarter-inch of toothpaste on it; now I'm brushing my upper-right molars"). But mindlessness can also lead to errors and mishaps, ranging from the trivial (putting the butter in the dishwasher or locking yourself out of the car) to the serious (driving carelessly while on "automatic pilot"). Jerome Kagan (1989) argues that fully conscious awareness is really needed only when we must make

Drawing by Weber; © 1989 The New Yorker Magazine Inc.

"This CD player costs less than players selling for twice as much."

Mindlessness is a common source of irrationality.

a deliberate choice, when events happen that can't be handled automatically, and when unexpected moods and feelings arise. "Consciousness," he says, "can be likened to the staff of a fire department. Most of the time, it is quietly playing pinochle in the back room; it performs [only] when the alarm sounds." That may be so, but most of us would probably benefit if our mental firefighters paid a bit more attention to their jobs. Cognitive psychologists have, therefore, devoted a great deal of study to mindful, conscious thought and the capacity to reason.

What Do You Know?

1. Stuffing your mouth with cotton candy, licking a lollipop, and chewing on a piece of beef jerky are all instances of the _____ *eating*.
2. In addition to concepts and images, _____ have been proposed as a basic form of mental representation.
3. Peter's mental representation of "Thanksgiving" includes many associations (e.g., to turkeys), attitudes ("People should be with relatives at Thanksgiving"), and expectations ("I'm going to gain weight from all that eating"). They are all part of his _____ for the holiday.
4. Zelda discovers that she has dialed her boyfriend's number instead of her mother's, as she had intended. Her error can be attributed to _____.

Answers:

1. concept 2. propositions 3. cognitive schema 4. mindlessness

---

Reasoning and Creativity

Reasoning is purposeful mental activity that involves operating on information in order to reach conclusions. Unlike impulsive or nonconscious responding, reasoning requires us to draw specific inferences from observations, facts, or assumptions. Two of the most basic types of reasoning are deductive reasoning and inductive reasoning, which both involve drawing conclusions from a series of observations or propositions (*premises*).

In **deductive reasoning,** if the premises are true then the conclusion must be true. Deductive reasoning often takes the form of a *syllogism,* a simple argument consisting of two premises and a conclusion:

premise   *All human beings are mortal.*

premise   *I am a human being.*

conclusion *Therefore I am mortal.*

---

deductive reasoning A form of reasoning in which a conclusion follows necessarily from certain premises; if the premises are true, the conclusion must be true.

We all think in syllogisms, although many of our premises are implicit rather than explicitly spelled out: "I never have to work on Saturday. Today is Saturday. Therefore, I don't have to work today." However, applying deductive reasoning to abstract problems that are divorced from everyday life does not seem to come so naturally; it depends on experience and schooling.

In **inductive reasoning,** the premises provide support for a conclusion, but the conclusion *could* still be false; the conclusion does not follow necessarily from the premises, as it does in deductive reasoning. Often, people think of inductive reasoning as the drawing of general conclusions from specific observations, as when you generalize from experience: "I had three good meals at that restaurant; they sure have great food." But an inductive argument can also have general premises. Two logicians (Copi & Burgess-Jackson, 1992) give this example:

> *All cows are mammals and have lungs.*
> *All whales are mammals and have lungs.*
> *All humans are mammals and have lungs.*
> *Therefore probably all mammals have lungs.*

Conversely, inductive arguments can have specific conclusions:

> *Most people with season tickets to the concert love music.*
> *Jeannine has season tickets to the concert.*
> *Therefore Jeannine probably loves music.*

Science depends heavily on inductive reasoning. In their studies, scientists make many careful observations and then draw some conclusions that they think are probably true. But in inductive reasoning, no matter how much supporting evidence you gather, it is always possible that new information will turn up to show that you are wrong. For example, you might discover that the three good meals you ate at that restaurant were not at all typical—that, in fact, all the other dishes on the menu are awful. Or you might learn that Jeannine bought season tickets to the concert only to impress a friend. Similarly, new scientific information may show that previous conclusions were faulty and must therefore be revised.

Almost everyone has trouble thinking logically under some circumstances. For example, some people will say that the following syllogism is valid, though it is not:

> *All rich people live in big, fancy houses.*
> *That person lives in a big, fancy house.*
> *Therefore that person is rich.*

"That person" may well be rich, but the conclusion does not follow from the premises, because some people may live in big, fancy houses for other reasons—perhaps they inherited one or bought it when it was inexpensive. Errors of this type occur

---

inductive reasoning A form of reasoning in which the premises provide support for a certain conclusion, but it is still possible for the conclusion to be false.

because people mentally reverse a premise. In this case, they convert "All rich people live in big, fancy houses" to "All people who live in big, fancy houses are rich." The reversed premise is plausible, but it is not the one that was given.

Logic is a crucial weapon to have in your cognitive arsenal, but logic alone is often inadequate for solving psychological difficulties and social problems. One reason is that different people may reach different conclusions even when their logic is impeccable, if they start out with different premises. Logic only tells us that *if* the premises are true, then a certain conclusion must follow (in deductive reasoning) or is probably true (in inductive reasoning). Logic does not tell us whether the premises are, in fact, true. Controversial issues tend to be those in which premises cannot be proven true or false to everyone's satisfaction. For example, your position on abortion rights will depend on your premises about when meaningful human life begins, what rights an embryo has, and what rights a woman has. People on opposing sides even disagree on how the premises should be phrased, because they have different emotional reactions to terms such as "rights," "meaningful life," and "control over one's body."

Even when we feel fairly confident about our premises, there may be no clearly correct solution to a problem. In formal reasoning problems—the kind you might find, say, on an intelligence test or a college entrance exam—the information you need for drawing a conclusion is specified clearly, and there is a single right answer. Deductive and inductive reasoning are useful for these kinds of problems. But in *informal* reasoning problems, information may be incomplete; many approaches and viewpoints may compete, and you have to decide which one is most reasonable, based on what you know, even though there is no clear-cut solution. Philosophers call such problems "ill-structured." For example, should the government raise taxes or lower them? What is the best way to improve public education? Is this a good time to buy a car?

To think rationally about such issues, you need more than inductive and deductive logic. You also need to think dialectically. **Dialectical reasoning** is the ability to evaluate opposing points of view. Philosopher Richard Paul (1984) described it as the process of moving "up and back between contradictory lines of reasoning, using each to critically cross-examine the other." This is just what juries are supposed to do to arrive at a verdict. Ideally, a jury decision is not reached by applying some formula or set of procedures, but rather by open-minded consideration of arguments for and against, point and counterpoint. Many people have trouble with dialectical reasoning because their self-esteem depends on being right and on having their beliefs accepted by others.

Real-world problem solving can also benefit from another ability, the ability to think creatively. When certain strategies and rules have been successful in the past, they often become habitual: A person develops a **mental set,** a tendency to try to solve new problems by using the same procedures that worked before. Mental sets make

---

dialectical reasoning A process in which opposing facts or ideas are weighed and compared, with a view to determining the best solution or to resolving differences.
mental set A tendency to solve problems using procedures that worked before on similar problems.

human learning and problem solving efficient; because of them, we do not have to keep reinventing the wheel. But mental sets are not helpful when a problem calls for fresh insights and methods. They cause us to cling to the same old assumptions, hypotheses, and strategies, blinding us to breakthroughs that would lead to better, more accurate, or more rapid solutions. Such mental rigidity is a major impediment to effective thinking.

Here's an exercise that illustrates this point. Copy the following figure, and see whether you can connect the dots by using no more than four straight lines, without lifting the pencil from the paper. A line must pass through each point. Can you do it?

```
•   •   •

•   •   •

•   •   •
```

Most people have difficulty solving this problem because they are mentally prepared to perceive patterns, and they interpret the arrangement of dots as a square. Once having done so, they assume that they can't extend a line beyond the "boundaries" of the square. A tendency to perceive patterns enables us to make sense of the world, but in this case, a correct solution requires that you resist the tendency. Now that you know this, you might try again if you haven't yet solved the puzzle. (Some possible solutions are given on page 342.)

People who are creative are able to break free of rigid patterns of perceiving and thinking in order to produce new solutions. They exercise **divergent thinking;** instead of stubbornly sticking to one tried-and-true path, they explore some side alleys and generate several possible solutions. They come up with new hypotheses, imagine alternative interpretations, and look for connections that may not be immediately obvious. As a result, they are able to use familiar concepts in unexpected ways. In contrast, less creative individuals rely solely on **convergent thinking,** following a particular set of steps that they think will converge on one correct solution.

Edward de Bono (1971) once illustrated the nature of creative problem solving by asking children ages 4 to 14 to design a dog-exercising machine. One child came up with the simple idea of having the dog chase a bone held always out of reach by a harness on the dog's back—frustrating for the dog, but effective (see Figure 9.1a on the next page). Another child devised a more sophisticated solution (see Figure 9.1b). When the dog barks into a "speaking tube," the energy of its barking activates a system of rods and springs, causing the wheels of the cart to turn. An "eye tube" allows the poor pooch to see where it is going, but this is only a courtesy, because a periscope automatically "sees" obstacles and a "transformer box" adjusts the steering accordingly. The more the dog barks, the faster the cart moves.

---

divergent thinking Mental exploration of unconventional alternatives in solving problems; it tends to enhance creativity.
convergent thinking Thinking aimed at finding a single correct answer to a problem.

(a)　　　　　　　　　　　　　(b)

Figure 9.1 *When Edward de Bono asked children to design a dog-exercising machine, their solutions showed that they could use familiar concepts in new and imaginative ways. What kind of dog-exercising machine can you create?*

In the laboratory, psychologists have traditionally studied creativity by using tests that measure fluency, flexibility, and originality in generating solutions to problems (Guilford, 1950). One, the Alternate Uses Test, asks you to think of as many uses as possible for common items, such as a brick or a paper clip. Another, the Remote Associates Test (Mednick, 1962), presents sets of three words and asks you to find an associated word for each set. For example, an appropriate answer for the set *news–clip–wall* is *paper*. Associating elements in new ways by finding a common connection among them is thought to be an important component of creativity. Can you find associates for the following word sets? (The answers are given on page 341.)

1. piggy–green–lash
2. surprise–line–birthday
3. mark–shelf–telephone
4. stick–maker–tennis
5. blue–cottage–cloth

More recent approaches to measuring creativity rely on personality tests and assessments of a person's actual history of creativity in work and leisure activities. For example, using a questionnaire called the Lifetime Creativity Scales (Richards et al., 1988), a skilled interviewer can obtain detailed information about the person's creative accomplishments, including those that may not have been generally recognized. The Lifetime Creativity Scales measure both *peak creativity* (as reflected by major enterprises or activities) and *extent of involvement* (the pervasiveness of creative activity in a person's life). The invention of an unusual machine or the writing of a distinctive novel would earn you a high peak-creativity score. The ongoing diagnosis and repair of automobiles or the writing of colorful letters to the editor would show some creativity. The routine assembly of mechanical parts according to a prescribed pattern or the proofreading of a manuscript would demonstrate "insignificant" creativity. This approach assumes that creative thinking enhances survival by helping us adapt to constantly changing conditions, and that it is not confined to traditional creative arts, such as painting or music. It can be found in the auto mechanic who invents a new tool, the mother who designs and makes her children's clothes, the office manager who devises a clever way to streamline work flow, or the amateur chef who concocts unusual gourmet meals (Richards, 1991).

Why, though, are some people able to think creatively, whereas others can't climb out of their mental ruts? Most people answer this question by assuming that creativity must be entirely in the person. But certain situations can also foster creativity and inspire people to escape the trap of mental rigidity. Research shows that creativity tends to flourish when people (1) have control over how to perform a task or solve a problem; (2) are evaluated unobtrusively, instead of being constantly observed and judged; and (3) work independently (Amabile, 1983). In addition, organizations encourage creativity when they let people take risks, give them plenty of time to think about problems, and welcome innovation. These are the very same working conditions that promote high achievement (see Chapter 7).

Various personality traits are also associated with the ability to think creatively. They include, among others, the following (Helson, Roberts, & Agronick, 1995; MacKinnon, 1968; McCrae, 1987; Schank, 1988):

1. NONCONFORMITY. Creative individuals are not overly concerned about what others think of them. They are willing to risk ridicule by proposing ideas that may initially appear foolish or off the mark.
2. INDEPENDENCE. Highly creative people tend to prefer working alone instead of in a group. During childhood, they are often encouraged to solve problems themselves instead of depending on others.
3. CONFIDENCE. In general, creative people neither fear failure nor overvalue success. They are therefore able to enjoy the challenge of a complex, ambiguous, or difficult problem. They do not let the emotional turmoil that can sometimes accompany intellectual or artistic uncertainty deter them.
4. CURIOSITY. Creative people usually have a wide range of interests and therefore accumulate a broad base of knowledge. They are open to new experiences and look into everyday puzzles that others would ignore. As Roger Schank (1988) writes, "They notice things and ask questions about them"—which, you may remember, is the first step in thinking critically. "They wonder why butterflies have to be caterpillars first. They wonder why the drugstore on the corner always does well and why the one across the street from it seems to be up for sale every two years. . . . They notice things and ask questions about them."
5. PERSISTENCE. This is perhaps the most important attribute of the creative person. After that imaginary lightbulb goes on over your head, you still have to work to make the illumination last. Or as Thomas Edison, inventor of the real lightbulb, put it, "Genius is one percent inspiration and ninety-nine percent perspiration."

These characteristics of creativity are apparent in the biographies of successful artists, writers, scientists, and inventors. Consider the story of Georges de Mestral, a Swiss inventor, who was hunting one day in the late 1940s when he and his dog accidentally brushed up against a bush that left them both covered with burrs. When de Mestral tried to remove the burrs, they clung stubbornly to his clothes. This would be merely a minor annoyance to most of us, but de Mestral was curious about why the burrs were so hard to remove. After he got home, he studied them under a microscope and discovered that hundreds of tiny hooks on each burr had snagged on the threads of his pants. Burrs, he thought, would make great fasteners.

That was the inspiration. There then followed several years of perspiration as de Mestral tried to figure out how to attach tiny hooks to pieces of tape in such a way that they would stay lined up (Madigan & Elwood, 1984). He also struggled to find a way of producing equally tiny loops for the hooks to attach to. After testing many methods, he finally succeeded. The result: Velcro fasteners, now used on millions of items, from blood-pressure cuffs to tennis shoes.

What Do You Know?

1. Most of the items Mervin bought as holiday gifts this year cost more than they did last year, so he concludes that inflation is increasing. Is he using inductive, deductive, or dialectical reasoning?
2. Yvonne is arguing with Henrietta about whether real estate is a better investment than stocks. "You can't convince me," says Yvonne. "I just know I'm right." Yvonne needs training in _____ reasoning.
3. For many years, if you wanted to avoid carrying a heavy suitcase while traveling, you had to use a collapsible device with wheels on it. Then someone got the brilliant idea of attaching wheels to the case itself. This insight was an example of (convergent/divergent) thinking.
4. Which of the personality traits associated with creativity did Georges de Mestral exemplify?

Answers:

1. inductive **2.** dialectical **3.** divergent **4.** Nonconformity, independence, confidence, curiosity, and persistence—in other words, all of them.

The Development of Thought and Reasoning

The ability to think and reason begins in early infancy. But as anyone who has ever observed a young child knows, children do not think the way adults do. At age two, they may call all large animals by one name (say, *horsie*) and all small animals by another (say, *bug*). At four, they may protest that a sibling has "more" fruit juice when it is only the shapes of the glasses that differ, not the amount of juice.

In the 1920s, the Swiss psychologist Jean Piaget (Zhan Pee-ah-ZHAY; 1896–1980), who started out observing his own children and later interviewed many others, proposed a new theory of cognitive development to explain these childish mistakes. Piaget's great insight was that children's errors are as interesting as their correct responses. The strategies children use to understand concepts and solve problems are not random or incomprehensible, said Piaget; rather, they reflect an interaction between the child's developmental stage and the child's experience in the world. Although many of Piaget's ideas have since been challenged and modified, they caused a revolution in thinking about how thinking develops, and they continue to exert a profound influence on researchers.

Piaget's Stages: How Children Think

Piaget (1929/1960, 1952, 1984) proposed that mental functioning depends on two biological processes. One is *organization:* All human beings are designed to organize their observations and experiences into a coherent set of meanings. The other is *adaptation* to new observations and experiences. Adaptation, said Piaget, takes two forms, which he called "assimilation" and "accommodation."

Assimilation is what you do when you fit new information into your existing mental schemas. Suppose that little Harry learns the concept *dog* by playing with the family schnauzer. If he then sees the neighbor's chihuahua and says "doggie!" he has assimilated the new information about the neighbor's pet into his mental schema for *dogs.* **Accommodation** is what you do when, as a result of undeniable new information, you must change or modify your existing schemas. If Harry sees the neighbor's Siamese cat and still says "doggie!" his parents are likely to laugh and correct him. Harry will have to modify his schema for *dogs* to exclude cats, and he will have to create a new schema for *cats.* In this way, he accommodates the new information that a Siamese cat is not a dog.

Using these concepts, Piaget proposed that all children go through four stages of cognitive development:

1. THE SENSORIMOTOR STAGE (BIRTH TO AGE TWO). In this stage, the infant learns through concrete actions: looking, touching, hearing, putting things in the mouth, sucking, grasping. "Thinking" consists of coordinating sensory information with bodily movements. Soon these movements become more purposeful, as the child actively explores the environment and learns that specific movements will produce specific results. Swatting a cloth away will reveal a hidden toy; releasing one's grasp of a fuzzy duck will cause the duck to drop out of reach; banging on the table with a spoon will produce dinner (or mom, taking the spoon away).

---

assimilation In Piaget's theory, the process of absorbing new information into existing cognitive structures.
accommodation In Piaget's theory, the process of modifying existing cognitive structures in response to experience and new information.

One of the baby's major accomplishments at this stage, said Piaget, is **object permanence,** the understanding that something continues to exist even if you can't see or touch it. In the first few months of life, he observed, infants seem to follow the motto "out of sight, out of mind." They will look intently at a little toy, but if you hide it behind a piece of paper, they will not look behind the paper or make an effort to get the toy. By about 6 months of age, infants begin to grasp the idea that a toy exists and the family cat exists, whether they can see the toy, or the cat, or not. If a baby of this age drops a toy from her playpen, she will look for it; she also will look under a cloth for a toy that is partially hidden. By 1 year of age, most babies have developed an awareness of the permanence of (some) objects. This is when they love to play peek-a-boo.

Object permanence, said Piaget, represents the beginning of *representational thought,* the capacity for using mental imagery and other symbolic systems. The child is now able to hold a concept in mind—for instance, to understand that the word *fly* represents an annoying, buzzing creature, and that *daddy* represents a friendly, playful one. These developments during the sensorimotor stage occur at a similar rate and sequence across a wide range of cultures.

2. THE PREOPERATIONAL STAGE (AGES TWO TO SEVEN). During this stage, the use of symbols and language accelerates, in play and in imitation of adult behavior. A 2-year-old is able to pretend, for instance, that a large box is a house, table, or train. Piaget described this stage largely in terms of what (he thought) the child cannot do. Children can think, said Piaget, but they cannot reason. They do not yet have the kinds of mental abilities that allow them to understand abstract principles or cause and effect. Piaget called these missing abilities **operations,** by which he meant reversible actions performed in the mind. An operation is a sort of "train of thought" that can be run backward or forward. Multiplying 2 times 6 to get 12 is an operation; so is the reverse, dividing 12 by 6 to get 2.

Children at the preoperational stage, Piaget believed, rely on primitive or "magical" reasoning based on the evidence of their own senses, which can be misleading. If a tree moves in the wind, it must be alive. If the wind blows while the child is walking, then walking must make the wind blow. Piaget also believed (mistakenly, as we will see) that children of this age cannot take another person's point of view because their thinking is **egocentric.** They see the world only from their own frame of reference. They cannot imagine that you see things differently, that events happen to others that do not happen to them, that the world does not exist solely for them. "Why are there mountains [with lakes]?" Piaget asked a preoperational Swiss child. "So that we can skate," answered the child.

---

object permanence The understanding, which develops in the first year of life, that an object continues to exist even when you can't see it or touch it.
operations In Piaget's theory, mental actions that are cognitively reversible.
egocentric thinking Seeing the world from only one's own point of view; the inability to take another person's perspective.
conservation The understanding that the physical properties of objects—such as the number of items in a cluster or the amount of liquid in a glass—can remain the same even when their form or appearance changes.

Figure 9.2   *In this test for conservation of number, the child is asked if one of the sets of blocks has "more." His answer shows whether he understands that the two sets contain the same number even though the larger blocks in one of the sets take up more space.*

Further, said Piaget, preoperational children cannot grasp the concept of **conservation**—the notion that physical properties do not change when their form or appearance changes. They are unable to understand that an amount of liquid, a number of pennies, or a length of rope remains the same even if you pour the liquid from one glass to another, stack the pennies, or coil the rope. If there is an equal number of blocks in each of two sets of blocks, but the blocks in one set are larger and take up more space—as in Figure 9.2—a preoperational child will say that the set with the larger blocks has "more" blocks. Similarly, if you transfer liquid from a short, fat glass into a tall, narrow glass—as in Figure 9.3—a preoperational child will say that there is more liquid in the second glass. At this stage, the child attends to the appearance of the liquid (its height in the glass) instead of its fixed quantity.

Figure 9.3   *In a test for conservation of quantity, the child is asked if one glass has more liquid. Her answer shows whether she understands that pouring liquid from a short, fat glass into a tall, narrow one does not change the amount of liquid.*

3. THE CONCRETE-OPERATIONS STAGE (ABOUT AGE SIX OR SEVEN TO ELEVEN). At this stage, the nature and quality of children's thought change significantly. According to Piaget, during these years children come to understand the principles of conservation, reversibility, and cause and effect. They also understand the nature of *identity*; they know that a girl doesn't turn into a boy by wearing a boy's hat, and that a brother will always be a brother, even if he grows up. They learn mental operations, such as addition, subtraction, multiplication, division, and categorization—not just of numbers, but also of people, events, and actions. They learn a few abstract concepts, such as *serial ordering*—the idea that things can be ranked from smallest to largest, lightest to darkest, shortest to tallest. But, according to Piaget, children's thinking at this stage is "concrete" because it is still grounded primarily in concrete experiences and concepts, rather than in abstractions or logical deductions. They can use their imaginations to try to solve problems, but not in a systematic and logical way.

4. THE FORMAL-OPERATIONS STAGE (AGE TWELVE THROUGH ADULTHOOD). This stage, said Piaget, marks the development of abstract reasoning. Teenagers understand that ideas can be compared and classified, just as objects can. They are able to reason about situations they have not experienced firsthand, and they can think about future possibilities. They are able to search systematically for answers to problems. They are able to shift from concrete operations to deductive reasoning, using premises common to their culture and experience.

Here, then, is a summary of Piaget's four stages:

STAGE	MAJOR ACCOMPLISHMENTS
Sensorimotor (0–2)	Object permanence Beginning of representational thought
Preoperational (2–7)	Accelerated use of symbols and language
Concrete operations (6–11)	Understanding of conservation Understanding of identity Understanding of serial ordering
Formal operations (12–)	Abstract reasoning Ability to compare and classify ideas

Piaget's work has had a powerful impact. Most researchers today accept his major point, that new reasoning abilities depend on the emergence of previous ones. You can't study algebra before you can count, and you can't study philosophy before you understand logic. And even Piaget's critics agree with him that children are not passive vessels into which education and experience are poured. Children actively interpret their worlds. They bring to their experiences their own perceptions and modes of thought and try to figure things out using their existing schemas.

However, research has called into question several aspects of Piaget's theory. As we will see in Chapter 14, culture and environment play a large role in the pace of children's cognitive development and in the particular skills that are fostered. Within our own culture, the changes from one stage to another are neither as clear-cut nor as sweeping as Piaget implied. At any given age, a child may use several different strategies for trying to solve a problem, some more complex or accurate than others—a finding that has prompted one researcher to suggest that cognitive ability develops in overlapping waves rather than discrete steps (Siegler, 1996). Children's reasoning ability often depends on the circumstances—who is asking them questions, the specific words used, the materials used, and so forth. Further, young children often demonstrate more cognitive skills than Piaget gave them credit for; for example, as we saw in Chapter 3, there is some evidence that young infants have a primitive grasp of certain fundamental laws of physics and a rudimentary ability to add and subtract. Here are some other findings that show that children understand more than Piaget realized:

✦ Piaget believed that the ability of a baby to play peek-a-boo illustrates object permanence. But infants as young as 9 months of age also understand the *rules* of peek-a-boo. In one study, when adults failed to take their turns in the exchange, the infants were clearly startled and distressed. The babies reacted by pointing to or touching the adults, repeating their own turns, or offering toys to the adults (Ross & Lollis, 1987).

✦ Infants as young as 2½ to 3½ months understand some of the physical properties of objects hidden from view. Renée Baillargeon (1991) discovered this by observing how long a baby will pay attention to an obscured ball or toy, rather than, as Piaget had, observing whether the baby would reach for the hidden toy. She reasoned that infants might understand that objects continue to exist when hidden but not be able to reach for them or know how to search for them. Infants, she summarizes, "are aware that objects continue to exist when masked by other objects, that objects cannot remain stable without support, that objects move along spatially continuous paths, and that objects cannot move through the space occupied by other objects" (Baillargeon, 1994).

✦ Children advance rapidly in their symbolic abilities much earlier than Piaget thought—between the ages of 2½ and 3. As one experiment showed, within that six-month period, toddlers become able to think of a miniature model of a room in two ways at once: as a room in its own right and as a symbol of the larger room it represents (DeLoache, 1987). This ability is a big step toward adult symbolic thought, in which anything can stand for anything else—a flag for a country, a dove for world peace.

✦ Most 3- and 4-year-olds *can* take another person's perspective and draw inferences about other people's behavior. When 4-year-olds play with 2-year-olds, for example, they modify and simplify their speech so that the younger child will understand (Shatz & Gelman, 1973). As we saw in Chapter 7, even very young children are capable of astonishing acts of empathy. They are not always egocentric; their answers depend on the questions you ask them. One 5-year-old showed her teacher a picture she had drawn of a cat and an unidentifiable blob. "The cat is lovely," said the teacher, "but what is this thing here?" "That has nothing to do with you," said the child. "That's what the *cat* is looking at."

This shift in perspective-taking, according to John Flavell (1993), is part of a broader change in how the child understands appearance and reality. Two- and three-year-olds judge by appearance; if you put a dog mask on a cat, they will say it's a dog. By age 5, however, they know it's "really" a cat. Even more important, at age 4 or 5, they understand that someone else might be fooled into thinking it's a dog and even act on that false belief. They understand that you can't predict what a person will do just by observing the actual situation or the "facts"; you have to know what the person is feeling and thinking. In short, by then children have developed a **theory of mind,** a theory about how one's own and other people's minds work and how people are affected by their beliefs and feelings (Astington & Gopnik, 1991; Flavell, Green, & Flavell, 1990).

If Piaget underestimated the cognitive skills of young children, he also *over*estimated those of many adults. Research shows that not all adolescents develop the ability for formal operational thought or reasoning about moral issues. Even as adults, some people never develop these capacities, and others continue to think "concretely" unless a specific problem requires abstract thought. And the ability to handle formal operations is not the culmination of cognitive development, as we are about to see.

Beyond Piaget: How Adults Think

Where do you stand on the issue of nuclear power? How safe do you consider food additives to be? Do you think stories in the news are reported objectively? Over a period of many years, Karen Kitchener and Patricia King have been asking people of all ages and occupations about these and other issues. Kitchener and King are not interested in how much people know about such issues, or even how they feel about them, but rather in how they think. More specifically, these researchers want to know whether people use *reflective judgment* in thinking about everyday problems (King & Kitchener, 1994; Kitchener & King, 1990). As mentioned in Chapter 1, reflective judgment is basically what we have called "critical thinking": the ability to evaluate and integrate evidence, relate that evidence to a theory or opinion, and reach a conclusion that can be defended as reasonable or plausible. To think reflectively, you must question assumptions, consider alternative interpretations, and stand ready to reassess your conclusions in the face of new information.

To date, King and Kitchener and their colleagues have interviewed more than 1,700 adolescents and adults, ranging in age from 14 to 65. (Some of this research has followed the same individuals for up to a decade.) First the researchers provide the

---

theory of mind A theory about how one's own mind and other people's minds work and how people are affected by their beliefs and feelings.

interviewee with statements that describe opposing viewpoints on topics such as those we mentioned. Then the interviewer asks some questions: What do you think about these statements? How did you come to hold that point of view? On what do you base your point of view? Can you ever know for sure that your position is correct? Do you think there are definite right and wrong answers? Why do you suppose disagreement exists about this issue?

This research finds that a person may reach Piaget's last stage of cognitive development, the stage of formal operations, without being able to think reflectively. King and Kitchener have also identified seven additional cognitive stages, some occurring in childhood and others unfolding throughout adolescence and adulthood. At each stage, people make certain kinds of assumptions about how things are known and use certain ways of justifying or defending their beliefs. Each stage builds on the skills of the prior one and lays a foundation for successive ones.

We will not be concerned here with the details of these stages, but only in their broad outlines. In general, according to Kitchener and King, people in the early, *prereflective* stages assume that a correct answer always exists and that it can be obtained directly through the senses ("I know what I've seen") or from authorities ("They said so on the news"; "That's what I was brought up to believe"). If authorities don't yet have the truth, prereflective thinkers tend to reach conclusions on the basis of what "feels right" at the moment. They do not distinguish between knowledge and belief, or between belief and evidence, and they don't see any reason for justifying a belief (King & Kitchener, 1994):

Interviewer: Can you ever know for sure that your position [on evolution] is correct?

Respondent: Well, some people believe that we evolved from apes and that's the way they want to believe. But I would never believe that way and nobody could talk me out of the way I believe because I believe the way that it's told in the Bible.

Interviewer: In this case, then, is one view right and one point of view wrong?

Respondent: Well, I think the evolved one is wrong.

During the middle, *quasi-reflective* stages, people recognize that some things cannot be known with absolute certainty, but they are not sure how to deal with these situations. They realize that judgments should be supported by reasons, but they pay attention only to evidence that fits what they already believe. They know that there are alternative viewpoints, but they seem to think that because knowledge is uncertain, any judgment about the evidence is purely subjective. Quasi-reflective thinkers will defend a position by saying that "Everyone has a right to his or her opinion," as if all opinions were created equal. Here is the response of a college student who uses quasi-reflective reasoning:

Interviewer: Can you say you will ever know for sure that chemicals [in foods] are safe?

Student: No, I don't think so.

Interviewer: Can you tell me why you'll never know for sure?

Student: Because they test them in little animals, and they haven't really tested them in humans, as far as I know. And I don't think anything is for sure.

Interviewer: When people differ about matters such as this, is it the case that one opinion is right and one is wrong?

Student: No. I think it just depends on how you feel personally because people make their decisions based upon how they feel and what research they've seen. So what one person thinks is right, another person might think is wrong. But that doesn't make it wrong. It has to be a personal decision. If I feel that chemicals cause cancer and you feel that food is unsafe without it, your opinion might be right to you and my opinion is right to me.

In the last stages, a person becomes capable of *reflective* judgment. He or she understands that knowing is an active, continual process of inquiry, and that although some things can never be known with certainty, certain judgments are more valid than others, depending on their coherence, their fit with the evidence, their usefulness, and so on. People at these stages are willing to consider evidence from a variety of sources and to reason dialectically. At the very highest stage, they are able to defend their conclusions as representing the most complete, plausible, or compelling understanding of an issue, based on currently available evidence. This interview with a graduate student illustrates reflective thinking:

Interviewer: Can you ever say you know for sure that your point of view on chemical additives is correct?

Student: No, I don't think so. I think ... [that] even if the internal argument in your system is completely consistent, it might be that the assumptions are wrong. So, just from this standpoint, we can't always be sure. I think we can usually be reasonably certain, given the information we have now, and considering our methodologies.

Interviewer: Is there anything else that contributes to not being able to be sure?

Student: Yes. Aside from assumptions, it might be that the research wasn't conducted rigorously enough. In other words, we might have flaws in our data or sample, things like that.

Interviewer: How then would you identify the "better" opinion?

Student: One that takes as many factors as possible into consideration. I mean one that uses the higher percentage of the data that we have, and perhaps that uses the methodology that has been most reliable.

Interviewer: And how do you come to a conclusion about what the evidence suggests?

Student: I think you have to take a look at the different opinions and studies that are offered by different groups. Maybe some studies offered by the chemical industry, some studies by the government, some private studies. . . . You wouldn't trust, for instance, a study funded by the tobacco industry that proved that cigarette smoking is not harmful. You wouldn't base your point of view entirely upon that study. . . . You have to try to interpret people's motives and that makes it a more complex soup to try to strain out.

Most people do not show evidence of reflective judgment until their middle or late twenties—if at all. That doesn't mean they're incapable of it; most studies have measured people's typical performance, not their *optimal* performance. When students get support for thinking reflectively and opportunities for practice, their thinking tends to become more complex, sophisticated, and well grounded (Kitchener et al., 1993). This may be one reason that higher education seems to move people gradually closer to reflective judgment. Most undergraduates, whatever their age, tend to score at Stage 3 during their first year of college, and at Stage 4 as seniors; most graduate students score at Stage 4 or 5, and many advanced doctoral students perform consistently at Stage 6 (King & Kitchener, 1994). Longitudinal studies suggest that these differences do not occur simply because lower-level thinkers are more likely to drop out along the way.

The gradual development of thinking skills among undergraduates, says Barry Kroll (1992), represents an abandonment of "ignorant certainty" in favor of "intelligent confusion." It may not seem so, but this is a big step forward! You can see why, in this book, we emphasize thinking about and evaluating the different perspectives in psychology, and not just memorizing their findings.

What Do You Know?

What stage have you reached in your study of cognitive development?

1. Understanding that two groups of six pennies are equal in number, even though one group is laid out flat and the other is stacked up, is an example of _____.

2. Understanding that a toy exists even after Mom puts it in her purse is an example of _____, which, according to Piaget, develops during the _____ stage.

3. Research shows that Piaget _____ the cognitive abilities of children and _____ those of adults.

4. Seymour thinks the media have a liberal bias, and Sophie thinks they're too conservative. "Well," says Seymour, "I have my truth and you have yours. It's purely subjective." Which of King and Kitchener's levels of thinking describes Seymour?

5. What kind of evidence might resolve the issue that Seymour and Sophie are arguing about?

ANSWERS:

expect to perceive.
impressions, might not be informative, because people perceive often only what they want or
newspapers were slanted in one direction or the other, based solely on their own subjective
think of other strategies as well. However, having people judge whether *entire* TV programs or
country and evaluate the editorials as liberal or conservative in outlook. You can probably
viewpoints. Or raters could read a random sample of newspaper editorials from all over the
shows and measure the amount of time devoted to conservative and liberal politicians or
4. quasi-reflective **5.** Researchers might have raters watch a random sample of TV news
1. conservation **2.** object permanence, sensorimotor **3.** underestimated, overestimated

BARRIERS TO LOGICAL
AND CREATIVE THOUGHT

The human mind, which has managed to come up with poetry, penicillin, and panty-hose, is a miraculous thing. But the human mind has also managed to come up with traffic jams, junk mail, and war. To better understand why the same species that figured out how to get to the moon is also capable of breathtaking bumbling here on earth, cognitive psychologists have studied the cognitive barriers that hinder reasoning.

As we have seen, people must often make judgments and decisions under conditions of uncertainty. To solve a problem in long division, you need only apply a certain **algorithm**—a method guaranteed to produce a solution even if you don't really know how it works. To make a cake, you need only apply an algorithm called a *recipe*. But to solve most common problems, in addition to having a capacity for reflective judgment, dialectical reasoning, and creativity, you need a knowledge of **heuristics**—rules of thumb that suggest a course of action without guaranteeing an optimal solution. Heuristics are often used as shortcuts in solving complex problems. An investor trying to predict the stock market, a renter trying to decide whether to lease an apartment, a doctor trying to determine the best treatment for a patient, a marriage counselor advising a troubled couple, a factory owner trying to boost production: All are faced with incomplete information on which to base a judgment or decision and must therefore rely on heuristics.

Usually, our heuristics are helpful and appropriate, but some are subject to predictable cognitive biases. Psychologists have shown that these biases frequently affect personal, economic, and political decision making (Simon, 1973; Tversky & Kahne-

---

algorithm A problem-solving strategy guaranteed to produce a solution even if the user does not know how it works.
heuristic A rule of thumb that suggests a course of action or guides problem solving but does not guarantee an optimal solution.

man, 1986). There are dozens of such biases in the way people think and make decisions; here we report a few of them.

Exaggerating the Improbable

One bias is the inclination to exaggerate the probability of very rare events—a bias that explains why so many people enter lotteries and why they buy airline disaster insurance.

People are especially likely to exaggerate the likelihood of a rare event if its consequences are catastrophic. One reason is the **availability heuristic,** the tendency to judge the probability of an event by how easy it is to think of examples or instances. Catastrophes stand out in our minds and are therefore more "available" than other kinds of events. For example, in one study, people overestimated the frequency of deaths from tornadoes and underestimated the frequency of deaths from asthma, which occur 20 times as often but do not make headlines. And these same people estimated deaths from accidents and disease to be equally frequent, even though 16 times as many people die each year from disease as from accidents (Lichtenstein et al., 1978).

People will sometimes work themselves up into a froth about unlikely events, such as dying in an airplane crash, yet they will irrationally ignore real dangers that are harder to visualize, such as a growth in cancer rates due to depletion of the ozone layer in the earth's atmosphere. Similarly, parents are often more frightened about real but unlikely threats to their children, such as their being kidnapped by a stranger or having a fatal reaction to an immunization (both horrible but extremely unlikely), than they are about problems that are far more common in children, such as depression, delinquency, or poor grades (Stickler et al., 1991).

Loss Aversion

In general, people making decisions try to avoid or minimize risks and losses. For example, suppose you had to choose between two health programs to combat a disease expected to kill 600 people. Which would you prefer, a program that would definitely save 200 people, or one with a one-third probability of saving all 600 people and a two-thirds probability of saving none? (See Figure 9.4a.) When subjects (including physicians) were asked this question, most said they preferred the first program. In other words, they rejected the riskier but potentially more rewarding solution in favor of a sure gain. The same study, however, found that people *will* take a risk if they see it as a way to *avoid loss.* Subjects were asked to choose between a program in which 400 people would definitely die and a program in which there was a one-third probability of nobody dying and a two-thirds probability that all 600 would die. If you think

---

availability heuristic The tendency to judge the probability of a type of event by how easy it is to think of examples or instances.

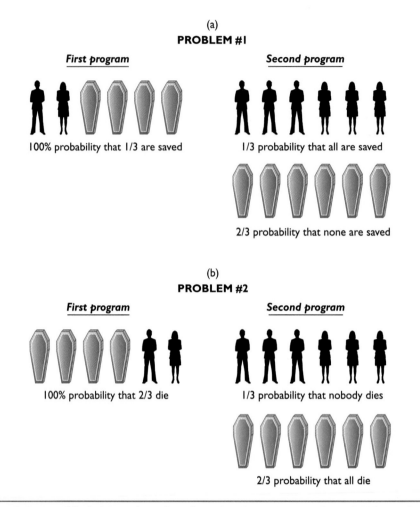

Figure 9.4 *People's decisions depend on how the alternatives are framed. When asked to choose between the programs in (a), which are described in terms of lives saved, most people choose the first program. When asked to choose between the programs in (b), which are described in terms of lives lost, most people choose the second program. Yet the alternatives in (a) are actually identical to those in (b).*

about it for a while, you will see that these alternatives are exactly the same as in the first problem; they are merely worded differently (see Figure 9.4b). Yet this time, most people chose the second solution. They rejected risk when they thought of the outcome in terms of lives saved, but they accepted risk when they thought of the outcome in terms of lives lost (Tversky & Kahneman, 1981).

Few of us will have to face a decision involving hundreds of lives, but we may have to choose between different medical treatments for ourselves or a relative. Our decision may be affected by whether the doctor frames the choice in terms of mortality or survival.

The Confirmation Bias

When our primary objective is to make an accurate judgment, we will usually try to encode relevant information thoroughly and think about it carefully. But when our main motive is to reach a particular conclusion about ourselves, other people, or circumstances, we may give in to the **confirmation bias:** We pay attention to evidence that confirms what we want to believe while ignoring or finding fault with evidence that points in a different direction (Kunda, 1990). We may think we are being rational and impartial, but we are only fooling ourselves.

You can see the confirmation bias at work in yourself, friends, politicians, and editorial writers—whenever people are defending their beliefs and seeking to justify them. Politicians, for example, are likely to accept economic news that confirms their philosophies and to dismiss counterevidence as biased or unimportant. Police officers who are convinced of a suspect's guilt are likely to take anything the suspect says or does as evidence that confirms it. Unfortunately, the confirmation bias also affects many jury members. Deanna Kuhn and her colleagues had people listen to an audiotaped reenactment of an actual murder trial, then say how they would have voted and why. Instead of considering and weighing possible verdicts against the evidence, many people quickly constructed a story about what had happened and then considered only the evidence that supported their version of events. These same people were the most confident in their decisions and were most likely to vote for an extreme verdict (Kuhn, Weinstock, & Flaton, 1994).

The confirmation bias can also affect how students react to what they learn. When students read about scientific findings that dispute one of their own cherished beliefs, or that challenge the wisdom of their own actions, they tend to acknowledge but minimize the strengths of the research. In contrast, when a study supports their view, they will acknowledge any flaws (such as a small sample or a reliance on self-reports) but will give these flaws less weight than they would otherwise (Sherman & Kunda, 1989). It seems that in thinking critically, people apply a double standard: They think most critically about results they don't like.

The confirmation bias even affects how we perceive the physical world. Suppose you spot a round object hovering high in the sky. If you believe that extraterrestrials occasionally visit the earth, you may "see" the object as a spaceship and decide that your belief is correct. But if you think such notions are hogwash, you are more likely to see a weather balloon. An image of a crucified Jesus on a garage door in Santa Fe Springs, California, caused great excitement among people who were ready to believe that divine messages can be found in the mundane world. The image was found to be caused by two streetlights that merged the shadows of a bush and a "For Sale" sign in the yard. But that fact did not dissuade those who wanted to see confirmation of their belief.

---

confirmation bias The tendency to look for or to pay attention only to information that confirms one's beliefs.

Biases Due to Expectations

Expectations also affect how we perceive the world. The tendency to perceive what you expect is called a *perceptual set.* Perceptaul sets can come in handy; they help us fill in words in sentences, for example, when we haven't really heard every one. But they can also cause misperceptions. In Center Harbor, Maine, local legend has it that veteran newscaster Walter Cronkite was sailing into port one day when he heard a small crowd on shore shouting, "Hello, Walter . . . Hello, Walter." Pleased, he waved and took a bow. Only when he ran aground did he realize that they had really been shouting, "Low water . . . low water." (By the way, there is a misspelled word in this paragraph. Did you notice it? If not, probably it was because you expected all the words in this book to be spelled correctly.)

Expectations also affect what we do with information once we've perceived it. On July 3, 1988, a U.S. warship shot down an Iranian passenger jet taking off over the Persian Gulf, killing several hundred people aboard. The warship's computer system had at first misread the plane's altitude and identified it as an F-14 fighter jet, but then it corrected itself. Unfortunately, by that time, the initial information had created an expectation of an attack. The skipper therefore paid more attention to his crew's reports of an emergency than to new information being generated by the computer. The earlier information was never reevaluated, and the crew assumed that the airliner was descending rather than ascending—with tragic results (Nisbett, 1988).

Hindsight

Would you have been able to predict, beforehand, that in 1996 Prince Charles and Princess Diana of England would agree to divorce, or that Magic Johnson would return to pro basketball—and then retire again? People who learn about the outcome of an event (or the answer to a question) tend to be sure that they "knew it all along." Armed with the wisdom of hindsight, they see the outcome that actually occurred as having been inevitable, and they overestimate the probability that they could have predicted what happened. Compared with judgments made *before* an event takes place, their judgments about their own ability to have predicted the event are inflated (Fischhoff, 1975; Hawkins & Hastie, 1990).

This **hindsight bias** shows up in all kinds of judgments, including political judgments ("I always knew my candidate would win"), medical judgments ("I could have told you that mole was cancerous"), and evaluations of other people's job performance ("The officers in charge of Pearl Harbor in 1941 should have known it would be attacked"). In 1991, when a blinding dust storm along a stretch of highway in California caused the worst multicar crash in U.S. history, many people angrily concluded that the highway patrol should have recognized the danger and closed the road. But

---

hindsight bias The tendency to overestimate one's ability to have predicted an event, once the outcome is known; the "I knew it all along" phenomenon.

from the highway patrol's standpoint, the situation was ambiguous: There were plenty of dust storms that people had gotten through perfectly well by slowing down or pulling off the road. Hindsight no doubt made the situation seem more straightforward in retrospect than it was at the time.

Hindsight biases may be a side effect of adaptive learning. When we try to predict the future, we consider many possible scenarios. But when we try to make sense of the past, we focus on explaining just one outcome—the one that actually occurred. This is efficient: Explaining outcomes that didn't occur can be a waste of time. According to Scott Hawkins and Reid Hastie (1990), hindsight biases represent "the dark side of successful learning and judgment." They are the dark side because when we are sure we knew something "all along," we are less willing to find out what we need to know in order to make accurate predictions in the future. In medical conferences, for example, when doctors are told what the postmortem findings were for a patient who died, they tend to think that the case was easier than it actually was ("I would have known it was a brain tumor"), and so they learn less from the case than they should (Dawson et al., 1988).

Cognitive-Dissonance Reduction

In 1994, Americans were stunned when football legend O. J. Simpson was charged with murdering his former wife Nicole Brown Simpson and her friend Ron Goldman. Glued to their television sets, viewers watched in shock as Simpson, who had always seemed the quintessential nice guy, was pursued by a caravan of police on a Los Angeles freeway, then arrested at his home and led away in handcuffs. Some reacted by quickly revising their opinion of their fallen hero. Others, however, groped to make sense of the unimaginable. Perhaps Simpson had run from the police not because he was guilty but because he was suicidal with grief over his ex-wife's death. Perhaps one of the police investigators had planted incriminating evidence (an argument later used successfully by the defense). Perhaps the media were exploiting the case by exaggerating the evidence against Simpson. Perhaps he did kill Nicole, but only after she provoked the attack by taunting him and trying to extort money from him.

To psychologists, such strategies for coming to terms with information that conflicts with one's existing ideas are predictable. They can be explained, said Leon Festinger (1957), by the theory of **cognitive dissonance.** "Dissonance," the opposite of consistency ("consonance"), is a state of tension that occurs when a person simultaneously holds two cognitions (beliefs, thoughts, attitudes) that are psychologically inconsistent, or holds a belief that is incongruent with the person's behavior. This tension is uncomfortable, and someone in a state of dissonance will be motivated to reduce it—by rejecting or changing a belief, by changing a behavior, by adding new beliefs, or by rationalizing (Harmon-Jones et al., 1996).

---

cognitive dissonance A state of tension that occurs when a person simultaneously holds two cognitions that are psychologically inconsistent, or when a person's belief is incongruent with his or her behavior.

For example, cigarette smoking is dissonant with the awareness that smoking causes illness. To reduce the dissonance, the smoker might change the behavior and try to quit; reject the cognition "smoking is bad"; persuade herself that she will quit later on ("after these exams"); emphasize the benefits of smoking ("A cigarette helps me relax"); or decide that she doesn't want a long life, anyhow ("It will be shorter, but sweeter"). In an actual study of people who had gone to a clinic to quit smoking, those who later relapsed had to reduce the dissonance between "I tried to quit smoking because it's bad for me" and "I couldn't do it." Can you predict what they did? In contrast to the successful quitters, most of them lowered their perceptions of the health risks of smoking ("It's not really so dangerous") (Gibbons, McGovern, & Lando, 1991).

You can see cognitive dissonance reduction at work among the growing number of true believers who are predicting that doomsday is at hand. Such predictions are especially popular at the end of every century, so we predict that you will be hearing some lulus as the year 2000 approaches. Have you ever wondered what happens to true believers when a doomsday prophecy fails? Do they ever say, "Boy, what a jerk I was"? What would dissonance theory predict?

Many years ago, Festinger and two associates were able to explore people's reactions to failed prophecies by taking advantage of an opportunity to observe a group of people who thought the world would end on December 21 (Festinger, Riecken, & Schachter, 1956). The group's leader, whom the researchers called Marian Keech, promised that the faithful would be picked up by a flying saucer and whisked to safety at midnight on December 20. Many of her followers quit their jobs and spent all their savings, waiting for the end. What would they do or say, Festinger and his colleagues wondered, to reduce the dissonance between "The world is still muddling along on the 21st" and "I expected the end of the world and sold all my worldly possessions"?

The researchers predicted that believers who had made no public commitment to the prophecy, who awaited "the end of the world" by themselves at home, would simply lose their faith. But those who acted on their conviction, waiting with Keech for the spaceship, would be in a state of dissonance. They would, said the researchers, have to *increase* their religious belief to avoid the intolerable realization that they had behaved foolishly. That is just what happened. At 4:45 A.M., long past the appointed hour of the saucer's arrival, the leader had a new vision. The world had been spared, she said, because of the impressive faith of her little band.

Cognitive-dissonance theory thus predicts how people will receive and process information that conflicts with their existing ideas. They don't always do so "rationally," by accepting new facts that are well documented; instead, they resist or rationalize the information. Subsequent research has specified the conditions under which people are particularly likely to be motivated to reduce dissonance (Aronson, Wilson, & Akert, 1994; Taylor, Peplau, & Sears, 1997):

1. **WHEN PEOPLE FEEL THAT THEY HAVE FREELY MADE A DECISION.** If you do not think you freely chose to join a group, sell your possessions, or smoke a cigarette, you will not feel dissonance if these actions prove to be seriously misguided. There is no dissonance between "The army drafted me; I had no choice about being here" and "I hate basic training."

2. **WHEN PEOPLE FEEL THAT THE DECISION IS IMPORTANT AND IRREVOCABLE.** If you know that you can always change your mind about a decision you have made, or if you have a lackluster commitment to it, you will not feel dissonance if the decision proves foolhardy. There is no dissonance between "I just spent a fortune on ski equipment" and "I hate skiing" if you know you can return your ski gear and get your money back.

3. **WHEN PEOPLE FEEL PERSONALLY RESPONSIBLE FOR THE NEGATIVE CONSEQUENCES OF THEIR BEHAVIOR.** If you choose a course of action that leads to disastrous but unforeseen results, you will not feel dissonance unless you feel responsible for the consequences. There is no necessary dissonance between "I took my vacation in Hawaii" and "It rained the whole week I was there" if you don't feel personally responsible for causing the rain.

4. **WHEN WHAT PEOPLE DO THREATENS THEIR SELF-CONCEPT.** If you are in a political discussion at a party and you pretend to agree with the position of the majority for the sake of social harmony, you will experience dissonance only if you have a concept of yourself as honest and true to your convictions. If you are a pathological liar and you know it (and don't care), there will be no dissonance, even if your words contradict your beliefs (Thibodeau & Aronson, 1992).

5. **WHEN PEOPLE HAVE PUT A LOT OF EFFORT INTO A DECISION OR ACTIVITY, ONLY TO FIND THE RESULTS LESS THAN THEY HOPED FOR.** The harder you work to achieve a goal, or the more you suffer for it, the more you will reduce dissonance by convincing yourself that you value the goal, even if the goal itself isn't so great after all (Aronson & Mills, 1959). This explains why hazing, whether in social clubs or in the military, turns new recruits into loyal members. The cognition "I went through a lot of awful stuff to join this group" is dissonant with the cognition ". . . only to find that I hate the group." Therefore people must decide either that the hazing wasn't so bad or that they really like the group. This mental reevaluation is called the *justification of effort,* and it is one of the most popular methods of reducing dissonance.

There are limitations to dissonance theory. It can be hard to know when two cognitions are inconsistent: What is dissonant to you may be neutral or pleasingly paradoxical to another. Moreover, some people reduce dissonance by admitting their mistakes instead of rationalizing them. Still, there is vast evidence of a motive for cognitive consistency under certain conditions, and this motive can lead to irrational decisions and actions as well as rational ones.

Biases in Attributions

According to **attribution theory,** all of us are constantly searching for causes to which we might attribute our own behavior or the behavior of others. We generally consider

---

attribution theory The theory that people are motivated to explain their own and other people's behaviors by attributing causes of those behaviors either to a situation or to a disposition.

two kinds of causes: We make a *situational attribution*, identifying the cause of an action as something in the environment ("John stole the money because his family is starving"), or we make a *dispositional attribution*, identifying the cause of an action as something in the person, such as a trait or motive ("Joe stole the money because he is a born thief").

Most human actions are determined by a combination of situational and dispositional factors. But when people try to find reasons for someone else's behavior, they often overestimate personality factors and underestimate the influence of the situation (Nisbett & Ross, 1980). This tendency has been called the **fundamental attribution error.** People are especially likely to make this error when they are distracted or preoccupied and don't have time to stop and ask themselves, "Why, exactly, is Aurelia behaving like a dork today?" Instead, they leap to the easiest attribution, which is dispositional: Aurelia simply has a dorklike personality (Gilbert, Pelham, & Krull, 1988). People will often make a dispositional attribution even when they know that a person had no choice in a particular setting (Taylor, Peplau, & Sears, 1997).

The fundamental attribution error is prevalent in Western nations, where middle-class people tend to believe that individuals are responsible for their own actions. But this error is by no means universal. In countries such as India, for example, where everyone is deeply embedded in caste and family networks, and China, where people are more group oriented than they are in the West, people are likely to recognize situational constraints on behavior (J. G. Miller, 1984; Morris & Peng, 1994). If someone is behaving oddly, therefore, an Indian or Chinese is likely to make a situational attribution of the problem rather than a dispositional one.

The fundamental attribution error occurs mostly when people judge the actions of others. When it comes to explaining their own behavior, however, people often choose attributions that are favorable to them. Because of this **self-serving bias,** people are likely to take credit for their good actions (a dispositional attribution) and let the situation account for their bad ones. For instance, most of us will say, "I am furious for good reason—this situation is intolerable!" We are less likely to say, "I am furious because I am an ill-tempered grinch." If we do something admirable, though, such as donating money to charity, we attribute our motives to personality ("I'm the generous type") instead of to the situation ("The fund raiser pressured me into it"). Self-serving attributions, however, are highly influenced by cultural expectations: When people are expected or required to take responsibility for their mistakes, as in Japan, they often will do so (Markus & Kitayama, 1991).

As you can see, the decisions that people make, and the feelings of regret or pleasure that follow, are not always logical. This fact has enormous implications for deci-

---

fundamental attribution error The tendency, in explaining other people's behavior, to overestimate personality factors and to underestimate the influence of the situation.
self-serving bias The tendency, in explaining one's own behavior, to take credit for one's good actions and to rationalize one's mistakes.

sion makers in the legal system, business, medicine, government, and the market-place—in fact, in all areas. But before you despair about the human ability to think clearly and rationally, we should tell you that the situation is not hopeless. People are not equally irrational in all situations. When they are doing things they have some expertise in, or making decisions that have serious consequences, cognitive biases often diminish. Accountants who audit companies' books, for example, are less subject to the confirmation bias than are undergraduates in psychology experiments, perhaps because auditors can be sued if they overestimate a firm's profitability or economic health (Smith & Kida, 1991).

Further, once we understand a bias, we may be able to reduce or eliminate it. For example, we have seen that doctors are vulnerable to the hindsight bias if they already know what caused a patient's death. But Hal Arkes and his colleagues (1988) were able to reduce a similar bias in neuropsychologists. The psychologists were given a case study and asked to state one reason why each of three possible diagnoses—alcohol withdrawal, Alzheimer's disease, and brain damage—might have been applicable. This procedure forced the psychologists to consider all the evidence, not just evidence that supported the "correct" diagnosis. The hindsight bias evaporated, apparently because the psychologists saw that the correct diagnosis had not been so obvious at the time the patient was being treated.

WHAT DO YOU KNOW?

Think rationally to answer these questions.

A. Stu takes a study break and meets a young woman at the student cafeteria. They hit it off, start seeing each other, and eventually get married. Says Stu, "I knew that day, when I headed for the cafeteria, that something special was about to happen." What cognitive bias is affecting Stu's thinking?

B. In a classic study of cognitive dissonance (Festinger & Carlsmith, 1959), students did some boring, repetitive tasks and then had to tell another student, who was waiting to participate in the study, that the work was interesting and fun. Half the students were offered $20 for telling this lie and the others only $1. Which students who lied later decided that the tasks had been fun after all?

C. What kind of attribution is being made in each case, situational (S) or disposition-al (D)?

   1. A jury decides that a congressman accepted a bribe because FBI agents set up a sting operation to trap him.
   2. A man says, "My wife has sure become a grouchy person."
   3. The same man says, "I'm grouchy because I've had a bad day at the office."
   4. A woman reads that unemployment is very high in inner-city communities. "Well, if those people weren't so lazy, they would find work," she says.

D. What kinds of biases are suggested by items 2 and 3 in the preceding question?

ANIMAL MINDS

We have seen that human beings can be remarkably creative. Sometimes other animals seem to share this creativity. A green heron swipes some bread from a picnicker's table and scatters the crumbs on a nearby stream. When a minnow rises to the bait, the heron strikes, swallowing its prey before you can say "hook, line, and sinker." A sea otter, floating calmly on its back, bangs a mussel shell against a stone that is resting on its stomach. When the shell cracks apart, the otter devours the tasty morsel inside, tucks the stone under its flipper, and dives for another shell, which it will open in the same way. In Africa, a lioness appears behind a herd of wildebeests and chases them toward a ditch. Another lioness, lying in wait at the ditch, leaps up and kills one of the passing wildebeests. The first lioness then joins her companion for the feast.

Incidents such as these, summarized nicely in Donald Griffin's *Animal Minds* (1992), have convinced some biologists, psychologists, and ethologists that we are not the only animals with cognitive abilities—that "dumb beasts" are far smarter than we may think. For many years, any scientist who claimed that animals could think was likely to get laughed at, or worse; today, however, the interdisciplinary field of **cognitive ethology,** the study of cognitive processes in nonhuman animals, is gaining increased attention (Gould & Gould, 1995; Griffin, 1992; Ristau, 1991). Cognitive ethologists argue that some animals can remember past events, anticipate future ones, make plans and choices, and coordinate their activities with those of their comrades. The versatility of these animals in meeting new challenges in the environment, say these researchers, suggests that they are, indeed, capable of thought.

Other scientists are not so certain, noting that even complex behavior can be genetically prewired and performed without cognitive processes or conscious intention. The assassin bug of South America catches termites by gluing nest material on its back as camouflage, but it is hard to imagine how the bug's tiny dab of brain tissue could enable it to plan this strategy consciously. Even trees and plants, which few people credit with consciousness, do things that *appear* intelligent. When willow trees are attacked by insects, they release into the air a chemical that causes leaves on nearby

---

cognitive ethology The study of cognitive processes in nonhuman animals.

healthy willow trees to change chemically and become less palatable to the insects (Rhoades, 1985). Their "communication" does not imply thought; it is a genetically controlled adaptation to the environment.

Even many cognitive ethologists are cautious about how *much* cognition they are willing to read into an animal's behavior. An animal could be "conscious," they argue, in the sense of being aware of its environment and "knowing" some things, without knowing that it knows and without being able to think about its own thoughts in the way that human beings do (Cheney & Seyfarth, 1990; Crook, 1987).

But explanations of animal behavior that leave out any sort of consciousness at all and that attribute animal actions entirely to instinct leave many questions unanswered. Like the otter who uses a stone to crack mussel shells, many animals are capable of using objects in the natural environment as rudimentary tools. For example, mother chimpanzees occasionally show their young how to use stone tools to open hard nuts (Boesch, 1991). In the laboratory, too, nonhuman primates have accomplished some truly surprising things. In one study, chimpanzees compared two pairs of food wells containing chocolate chips. One pair might contain, say, five chips and three chips, the other four chips and three chips. Allowed to choose which pair they wanted, the chimps almost always chose the one with the higher total, showing some sort of summing ability (Rumbaugh, Savage-Rumbaugh, & Pate, 1988). Other chimps have learned to use numerals to label quantities of items and simple sums (Boysen & Berntson, 1989; Washburn & Rumbaugh, 1991).

A primary ingredient in human cognition is language, the ability to combine elements that are themselves meaningless into an infinite number of utterances that convey meaning. Language is often thought of as the last bastion of human uniqueness, a result of the evolutionary forces that produced our species (see Chapter 3). Of course, other animals do communicate, using gestures, body postures, facial expressions, vocalizations, and odors. And some of these signals have more specific meanings than was previously thought. For example, vervet monkeys seem to have separate calls to warn about leopards versus eagles versus snakes (Cheney & Seyfarth, 1985). But the sounds made by other animals are not combined to produce entirely novel utterances.

Perhaps, however, some animals could acquire language if they got a little help from their human friends, beginning early in life. Dozens of researchers have tried to provide chimpanzees with just such help. Because the vocal tract of a chimpanzee does not permit speech, early efforts to teach chimpanzees spoken language were failures, though some comprehension on the part of the animals did occur. During the 1960s and 1970s, researchers tried different approaches that relied on vision rather than speech (an example of divergent, creative thinking!). In one project, chimpanzees learned to use as words geometric plastic shapes arranged on a magnetic board (Premack & Premack, 1983). In another, they learned to punch symbols on a computer keyboard (Rumbaugh, 1977). In yet another, they learned hundreds of signs from ASL (Fouts & Rigby, 1977; Gardner & Gardner, 1969). The animals in these and other studies learned to follow instructions, answer questions, and make requests. More important, they combined individual signs or symbols into longer utterances that they had never seen before. In general, their linguistic abilities appeared to resemble those of a two-year-old child.

As you can imagine, accounts of the apes' abilities caused quite a stir. The animals were apparently using their newfound skills to apologize for being disobedient, scold their trainers, and even talk to themselves. Koko, a lowland gorilla, reportedly used signs to say that she felt happy or sad, to refer to past and future events, to mourn for a dead pet kitten named All-Ball, and to convey her yearning for a baby. She even lied on occasion, when she did something naughty (Patterson & Linden, 1981).

The animals in these studies were lovable, the findings appealing. But soon skeptics and some of the researchers themselves began to point out serious problems (Seidenberg & Petitto, 1979; Terrace, 1985). In their desire to talk to the animals and their affection for their primate friends, researchers had failed to be objective. They had overinterpreted the animals' utterances, reading all sorts of meanings and intentions into a single sign. In videotapes, they could be seen unwittingly giving nonverbal cues that might enable the apes to respond correctly. Further, the animals appeared to be stringing signs and symbols together in no particular order to earn a reward, instead of using grammatical rules to produce novel utterances. "Me eat banana" seemed to be no different for them than "Banana eat me." Longer utterances did not bring greater complexity in syntax, but mere repetition: "Give orange me give eat orange me eat orange give me eat orange give me you" (R. Brown, 1986).

Recent studies have benefited from such criticisms and are a marked improvement on past research. Carefully controlled experiments have established that after training, chimps can acquire the ability to use symbols to refer to objects (Savage-Rumbaugh, 1986). In some projects, chimpanzees have spontaneously used signs to converse with one another, suggesting that they are not merely imitating or trying to get a reward (Van Cantfort & Rimpau, 1982). A young chimp named Loulis has learned dozens of signs from Washoe, the original signing chimp (Fouts, Fouts, & Van Cantfort, 1989).

Bonobo (pygmy) chimps are even more adept at language than are common chimpanzees. One bonobo named Kanzi has learned to understand English words and short sentences, and to understand keyboard symbols, *without specific training* (Savage-Rumbaugh & Lewin, 1994; Savage-Rumbaugh, Shanker, & Taylor, 1996). He responds correctly to commands such as "Put the key in the refrigerator" and "Go get the ball that is outdoors." Kanzi picked up language as children do—by observing others using it, and through normal social interaction. He has also learned, with training, to manipulate keyboard symbols to request foods or activities (games, TV, visits to friends) or to announce his intentions, and he seems to use some simple grammatical ordering rules to convey meaning.

Other research suggests that even certain nonprimates can acquire some aspects of language. In Hawaii, Louis Herman and his colleagues have taught dolphins to respond to sentencelike requests made in two artificial languages, one consisting of computer-generated whistles and another of hand and arm gestures (Herman, 1987; Herman, Kucazj, & Holder, 1993). To interpret a request correctly, the dolphins must take into account both the meaning of the individual symbols in a string of whistles or

Researchers have used innovative methods in their efforts to teach apes language. Kanzi, a bonobo chimp with the most advanced linguistic skills yet acquired by a nonhuman primate, can answer questions and make requests by punching symbols on a specially designed computer keyboard.

gestures and the order of the symbols (syntax). For example, they must understand the difference between "To left Frisbee, right surfboard take" and "To right surfboard, left Frisbee take."

In another fascinating project, Irene Pepperberg (1990, 1994) has taught an African gray parrot named Alex to count, classify, and compare objects by vocalizing English words. When the bird is shown up to six items and is asked how many there are, he responds with spoken (squawked?) English phrases, such as "two cork(s)" or "four key(s)." He can even respond correctly to questions about items specified on two dimensions, as in "How many blue key(s)?" Alex can also make requests ("Want pasta") and can answer simple questions about objects ("What color? Which is bigger?"). When presented with a blue cork and a blue key and asked "What's the same?" he will correctly respond "Color." He actually scores slightly better with new objects than with familiar ones, suggesting that he is not merely memorizing a set of stock phrases.

These recent results on animal language and cognition are certainly impressive, but scientists are still divided over just what the animals in these studies are doing. Do they have language, or are they merely performing tricks to earn rewards? Are they "thinking," in human terms? On one side are those who worry about *anthropomorphism,* the tendency to falsely attribute human qualities to nonhuman beings. They tell the story of Clever Hans, a "wonder horse" at the turn of the century, who was said to possess mathematical abilities and other intellectual talents (Fernald, 1984). Clever Hans would answer math problems by stamping his hoof the appropriate number of times, and respond to other questions by tapping in an established code. But a little careful experimentation by a psychologist, Oskar Pfungst (1911/1965), revealed that when Hans was prevented from seeing his questioners, or the questioners did not know the answers themselves, his "powers" left him. It seems that questioners were staring at the animal's feet and leaning forward expectantly after stating the problem, then lifting their eyes and relaxing as soon as he completed the right number of taps. Clever Hans was indeed clever, but not at math or other human skills. He was simply responding to nonverbal signals that people were inadvertently providing.

On the other side are those who warn against *anthropocentrism,* the tendency to think, falsely, that human beings have nothing in common with other animals. The need to see our own species as unique, they say, may keep us from recognizing that other species, too, have cognitive abilities, even if not as intricate as our own. Those who take this position point out that most modern researchers have gone to great lengths to avoid the Clever Hans problem.

The outcome of this debate is bound to have an effect on how we view ourselves and our place among other species on the planet. As Donald Griffin (1992) writes, "Cognitive ethology presents us with one of the supreme scientific challenges of our times, and it calls for our best efforts of critical and imaginative investigation."

What Do You Know?

After learning about research methods in Chapter 2 and reading in this chapter about the problems that marred early research on the capacity of animals for language, what would you want to keep in mind if you had to design a study of this issue?

Answers:

In general, you would want to use procedures that ensure your own objectivity and help you avoid the confirmation bias. For example, to avoid experimenter effects when testing an animal's understanding of English words, you could have the animal listen to the words through headphones and be sure the researcher does not know which ones are being tested. Or you could have the researcher wear a mask to prevent the animal from reading cues in the person's facial expressions. (Both of these procedures have been used with Kanzi.) To test for grammatical comprehension, you could present words in different orders, some correct and some not. To evaluate whether the animal is using syntactical rules in producing utterances, you could use raters who know the language (e.g., ASL) but are not involved in the animal's training and care. Can you think of any other measures you might take?

Our powers of thought led our forebears to give our species the immodest name *Homo sapiens,* Latin for wise or rational man. Yet as we have seen in this chapter, sometimes we humans are not nearly as "sapiens" as we would like to think. We may be the smartest species around, in terms of our ability to adapt to changing environments and come up with novel solutions to problems, but we are neither unique nor as savvy as we might suppose. Still, there is one crowning accomplishment we can boast of: *We are the only species that tries to understand its own misunderstandings.* This capacity for self-examination is perhaps our greatest accomplishment and the best reason to remain optimistic about our cognitive capacities.

In the next chapter, we invite you to exercise your own powers of understanding as we turn to an aspect of human cognition that is widely misunderstood—the mystery of memory.

✦ ✦ ✦

Summary

1. Thinking is the mental manipulation of information. Our mental representations of objects, activities, and situations simplify and summarize information from the environment.

2. One type of representation, or unit of thought, is the *concept,* which groups objects, relations, activities, abstractions, or qualities that share certain properties. *Propositions* are units of meaning that are made up of concepts and that express a unitary idea. Propositions may be linked together in networks of knowledge, beliefs, and expectations called *cognitive schemas,* which serve as mental models of aspects of the world. Visual images and other sensory images also play a role in thinking.

3. Not all mental processing is conscious. *Subconscious processes* lie outside of awareness but can be brought into consciousness when necessary. *Nonconscious processes* remain outside of awareness but nonetheless affect behavior and may be involved in what we call "intuition." Conscious processing may be carried out in a mindless fashion if we overlook changes in context that call for a change in behavior.

4. *Reasoning* is purposeful mental activity that involves drawing inferences from observations, facts, or assumptions (premises). In *deductive reasoning,* which often takes the form of a syllogism, if the premises are true then the conclusion must be true. In *inductive reasoning,* the premises provide support for a conclusion, but the conclusion could still be false. Science depends heavily on inductive reasoning.

5. Logic alone is often inadequate for solving human problems. People make logical errors, or disagree with others about basic premises. In informal reasoning problems, information may be incomplete, and there may be no clear-cut solution; in such cases, one needs to be able to reason *dialectically* about opposing points of view.

6. Creative problem solving requires us to overcome *mental sets* and to exercise *divergent* as well as *convergent thinking.* Traditional creativity tests measure fluency, flexibility, and originality in generating solutions to problems; more recent approaches rely on personality tests or assess a person's actual history of creativity in a broad range of work and leisure activities. Certain situations, such as being evaluated unobtrusively, can foster creativity and inspire people to break out of the rigidity of mental sets. Personality traits, including nonconformity, independence, confidence, curiosity, and persistence, also play a role in creativity.

7. Children do not think the way adults do. Jean Piaget argued that children's cognitive development depends on their current developmental stage and their experience in the world. Children's thinking, he said, adapts and changes through the processes of *assimilation* and *accommodation*. Piaget proposed four stages of cognitive development: *sensorimotor* (birth to age 2), during which the child learns *object permanence*, which represents the beginning of *representational thought*; *preoperational* (ages 2 to 7), during which language and symbolic thought develop; *concrete operations* (ages 6 or 7 to 11), during which children come to understand the principles of *conservation, identity, serial ordering,* and cause and effect; and *formal operations* (age 12 through adulthood), which marks the development of abstract reasoning and logic.

8. Most researchers today accept Piaget's major point, that new reasoning abilities depend on the emergence of previous ones. However, changes from one stage to another are neither as clear-cut nor as sweeping as Piaget implied; they depend on culture and experience, as well as on cognitive maturation; and many young children demonstrate more cognitive skills than Piaget gave them credit for. Piaget also overestimated the cognitive abilities of many adults.

9. Studies of *reflective judgment* find that a person may reach the Piagetian stage of formal operations without being able to think dialectically. People in the *prereflective* stages assume that a correct answer always exists; they do not distinguish between knowledge and belief, or between belief and evidence. Those in the *quasireflective* stages think that because knowledge is uncertain, any judgment about the evidence is purely subjective. Those who think *reflectively* understand that although some things can never be known with certainty, certain judgments are more valid than others, depending on their coherence, usefulness, fit with the evidence, and so on. Higher education seems to move people gradually closer to reflective judgment.

10. The *heuristics* that people use to make decisions are often influenced by cognitive biases and the way choices are framed. People tend to exaggerate the likelihood of improbable events (in part because of the *availability heuristic*); to be swayed in their choices by the desire to minimize loss; to attend to evidence that confirms what they want to believe (the *confirmation bias*); to perceive what they expect; and to overestimate their ability to have made accurate predictions (the *hindsight bias*). The theory of *cognitive dissonance* holds that people are also motivated to reduce the tension that exists when two cognitions are in conflict—by rejecting or changing a belief, changing their behavior, or rationalizing. Further, when people try to explain someone else's behavior, they often overestimate personality factors and underestimate the influence of the situation, a tendency called the *fundamental attribution error*. In explaining their own behavior, however, they prefer attributions that are favorable to themselves (the *self-serving bias*).

11. Some researchers, including many *cognitive ethologists,* argue that nonhuman animals have greater cognitive abilities than is usually thought. Many animals can use objects as rudimentary tools. Chimpanzees have learned to use numerals to label quantities of items and symbols to refer to objects. Several researchers have used

visual symbol systems, ASL, and other linguistic systems to teach primates language skills, and some animals (even nonprimates) seem able to use simple grammatical ordering rules to convey meaning. However, scientists are still divided on how to interpret these findings.

Key Terms

concept *304*

symbols *304*

propositions *305*

cognitive schemas *305*

mental image *305*

subconscious processes *306*

nonconscious processes *306*

mindlessness *307*

reasoning *308*

premises *308*

deductive reasoning *308*

syllogism *308*

inductive reasoning *309*

informal reasoning problems *310*

dialectical reasoning *310*

creativity *310*

mental sets *310*

divergent/convergent thinking *310*

Jean Piaget *315*

assimilation *315*

accommodation *315*

sensorimotor stage *315*

object permanence *316*

representational thought *316*

preoperational stage *316*

operations *316*

egocentric thinking *316*

conservation *317*

concrete-operations stage *318*

identity *318*

serial ordering *318*

formal-operations stage *318*

theory of mind *320*

reflective judgment *320*

prereflective stages *321*

quasi-reflective stages *321*

algorithm *324*

heuristic *324*

availability heuristic *325*

loss aversion *325*

confirmation bias *327*

perceptual set *328*

hindsight bias *328*

cognitive dissonance *329*

justification of effort *331*

attribution theory *331*

   situational attribution *332*

   dispositional attribution *332*

   fundamental attribution error *332*

self-serving bias *332*

cognitive ethology *334*

anthropomorphism *337*

anthropocentrism *338*

Answers to the Remote Associates Test on page 312: (1) back, (2) party, (3) book, (4) match, (5) cheese.

Some solutions to the nine-dot problem on page 311 (from Adams, 1986):

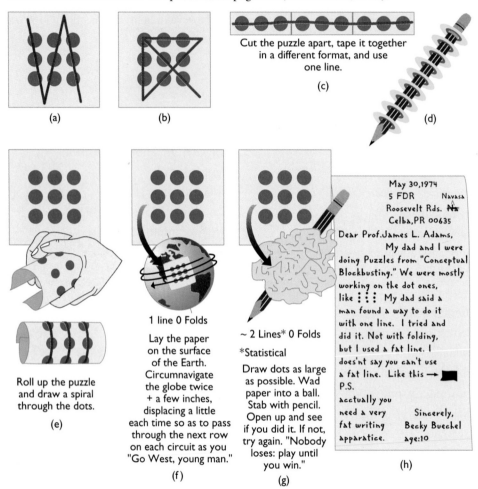

(a)

(b)

Cut the puzzle apart, tape it together in a different format, and use one line.

(c)

(d)

1 line 0 Folds

Lay the paper on the surface of the Earth. Circumnavigate the globe twice + a few inches, displacing a little each time so as to pass through the next row on each circuit as you "Go West, young man."

(f)

Roll up the puzzle and draw a spiral through the dots.

(e)

~ 2 Lines* 0 Folds

*Statistical

Draw dots as large as possible. Wad paper into a ball. Stab with pencil. Open up and see if you did it. If not, try again. "Nobody loses: play until you win."

(g)

May 30,1974
5 FDR   Navasa
Roosevelt Rds. N̶s̶
Celba, PR 00635
Dear Prof.James L. Adams,
    My dad and I were
doing Puzzles from "Conceptual
Blockbusting." We were mostly
working on the dot ones,
like ⦂⦂⦂ My dad said a
man found a way to do it
with one line. I tried and
did it. Not with folding,
but I used a fat line. I
does'nt say you can't use
a fat line. Like this ➝ ▰
P.S.
acctually you
need a very   Sincerely,
fat writing   Becky Buechel
apparatice.   age:10

(h)

CHAPTER 10

Memory

*I*n 1983, a writer we know took a trip to Italy with her husband and spent a few days exploring the beautiful city of Florence. Not long afterward, she read and saw the film of E. M. Forster's novel *A Room with a View,* which is set in Florence. Years went by, and a decade after her Italian vacation, she sat down on a winter's eve to rewatch the film of *A Room with a View.* During the movie, a long camera shot of the Piazza Signoria suddenly brought back a flood of memories, one of them violent. Our friend remembered that during her trip, while she and her husband were in that piazza, a wild fight had broken out and a young man had been seriously injured. In her mind's eye, she once again saw the crowd, the commotion, the blood on the man's shirt. "At that moment," she says, "I would have sworn in a court of law that we had seen a fight in the Piazza Signoria."

Then, suddenly, she found herself watching, right up there on her television screen, the very same fight that she recalled witnessing a decade earlier. The fight she was so sure she had actually observed was a scene from the novel! Perhaps, she thought, some other violent event had occurred during her visit. Checking her journal of the trip, she found that on the day she and her husband were in the Piazza Signoria, they had spent some time admiring the sculptures, had sipped lemonade at a sidewalk café, and had watched a prostitute idly solicit business. But there had been no fight, no disturbance—only a typical, peaceful Florentine morning in the Piazza Signoria.

Our friend's story illustrates an all-too-common glitch in the process of remembering an event: She imported information acquired after the fact and assumed that the result was her own personal memory. How could our friend, who is known for her keen intelligence and devotion to accuracy, have been so wrong? Are such memory malfunctions the exception to the rule, or might they be the norm? If memory can be so unreliable, how can any of us be sure we know the story of our own life? How can we hope to understand the past?

In this chapter, we will see how psychologists in the cognitive perspective investigate these uncomfortable questions. Cognitive researchers want to know how a person can "remember" things that never happened. They also want to know why, despite our best efforts, we all forget many (perhaps most) events that did take place. They want to know why even very recent memories can evaporate like the morning dew: why we watch the evening news, and half an hour later, can't recall the main story; why we enjoy a meal and quickly forget what we ate; why, as students, we may study our heads off for an exam, only to find that some of the information we studied isn't there when we need it most.

But psychologists in the cognitive tradition also study the many astonishing feats of memory that all human beings are capable of—for, despite its lapses, on most occasions memory serves us remarkably well. A mathematician once calculated that over the course of a lifetime, we store 500 times as much information as there is in the entire *Encyclopaedia Britannica* (Griffith, in Horn & Hinde, 1970). It is knowledge stored in memory that enables us to recognize a friend on the street even when she is wearing a new outfit and just had her hair permed; or to realize that in "Mary had a little lamb," Mary owned the lamb rather than eating it or giving birth to it. These kinds of seemingly mundane accomplishments, which are actually quite impressive when you stop to think about them, depend on remembering an enormous amount of information about the world. Memory, the capacity to retain and retrieve information, confers competence; without it, we would be as helpless as newborns, unable to negotiate even the most trivial of our daily tasks. It also confers a sense of identity; we are each the sum total of our personal recollections, which is why we feel so threatened when others challenge the accuracy of our memories. Individuals and cultures alike rely on a remembered history for a sense of coherence and meaning; memory preserves the past and guides the future.

RECONSTRUCTING THE PAST

In ancient times, philosophers compared memory to a tablet of hot wax that would preserve anything that chanced to make an imprint on it. Then, with the advent of the printing press, they began to think of memory as a sheet of paper, with all our memories filed away in a sort of giant mental filing cabinet, awaiting retrieval. Today, in the audiovisual age, many people think of memory as a tape recorder or video camera, automatically recording each and every moment of their lives. One psychotherapist, who apparently never studied introductory psychology, expressed the modern pop-psych view of memory this way (Fiore, 1989): "The subconscious mind has a memory bank of everything we ever experienced, exactly as we perceived it. Every thought, emotion, sound of music, word, taste and sight. Everything is faithfully recorded somehow in your mind. Your subconscious mind's memory is perfect, infallible."

Popular and appealing though this belief about memory is, however, it is utterly, absolutely wrong. As Robyn Dawes (1994) points out, this therapist has managed to ignore "every study that has ever been conducted on the nature of human memory." What those studies show is that *not* everything that happens to us or impinges on our senses is tucked away for later use. If it were, our minds would be cluttered with all sorts of mental junk—the temperature at noon Thursday, the price of turnips two years ago, a phone number needed only once. Memory must be selective. And recovering a memory, as we are about to see, is not at all like replaying a film of an event; it is more like watching a few unconnected frames and then figuring out what the rest of the scene must have been like.

The Manufacture of Memory

In 1932, the British psychologist Sir Frederic Bartlett asked people to read lengthy, unfamiliar stories from other cultures and then tell the stories back to him. Bartlett found that as the volunteers tried to retrieve the stories from memory, they made interesting errors. They often eliminated details that didn't make sense to them and added other details to make the story coherent. Memory, Bartlett concluded, must therefore be largely a *reconstructive* process. (Psychologists today sometimes call the this process *confabulation.*) We may reproduce some kinds of simple information by rote, said Bartlett, but when we remember complex information, we typically add, delete, and change elements in ways that help us make sense of the material, based on what we already know, or think we know. Since Bartlett's time, hundreds of memory studies have found his conclusion to be true for everything from stories to conversations.

You can see the process of reconstruction at work in the tragic case of H. M., which we described in Chapter 4 (page 151). Ever since 1953, when much of H. M.'s hippocampus and the adjacent cortex were surgically removed, he has suffered from **anterograde amnesia,** the inability to form lasting memories for new events and facts (Hilts, 1995; Ogden & Corkin, 1991). He cannot remember much of anything that has happened since 1953, or recognize anyone he has met, including the people who have studied him for more than four decades. To cope with his devastating condition, H. M. will sometimes try to reconstruct events. On one occasion, after eating a large chocolate Valentine's Day heart, H. M. stuck the shiny red wrapping in his shirt pocket. Two hours later, while searching for his handkerchief, he pulled out the paper and looked at it in puzzlement. When researcher Jenni Ogden asked why he had the paper in his pocket, he replied, "Well, it could have been wrapped around a big chocolate heart. It must be Valentine's Day!" Ogden could hardly contain her excitement about H. M.'s apparent recall of a recent episode. But a short time later, when she asked him to take out the paper again and say why he had it in his pocket, he replied, "Well, it might have been wrapped around a big chocolate rabbit. It must be Easter!"

Of course, H. M. *had* to reconstruct the past; his damaged brain could not recall it in any other way. But those of us with normal memory abilities also reconstruct far, far more than we realize. Suppose someone asks you to describe one of your early birthday parties. You may have some direct recollection of the event, especially if it was emotionally significant. But you have also stored information gleaned from family stories, photographs, or home videos. You may take all these bits and pieces and build one integrated account from them, and, like the writer who "remembered" a fight in a

---

anterograde amnesia The inability to form lasting memories for new events and facts.

peaceful piazza, later you may not be able to separate what you originally experienced from what you have added after the fact—a phenomenon that psychologists call *source amnesia*.

In studies done over the past two decades, Marcia Johnson and her colleagues have found that certain conditions are associated with confusions between imagined events and actual ones (Johnson, 1995). An imagined event or experience is most likely to be misremembered as real under the following conditions:

✦ THE PERSON HAS THOUGHT ABOUT THE IMAGINED EVENT MANY TIMES. Suppose, at family gatherings over the years, you keep hearing about the time that Uncle Sam scared everyone at a New Year's party by pounding a hammer into the wall so hard that the wall collapsed. It's such a colorful story—Uncle Sam in a rage—that you can practically see it in your mind's eye. The more you think about this event, the more likely you are to believe that you were there, even if you were actually sound asleep in another house altogether.

✦ THE IMAGE OF THE EVENT CONTAINS A LOT OF DETAILS. Ordinarily, we can distinguish an imagined event from a real one by the amount of detail in our memory of the event; real events tend to produce more detailed memories. However, the more you think about an imagined event, the more details you are likely to add to it—what Sam was wearing, the fact that he'd had too much to drink, the crumbling plaster, people standing around in party hats—and these details may in turn persuade you that the event really happened.

✦ IT IS EASY TO IMAGINE THE EVENT. If forming an image of an event takes little effort (e.g., a man pounding a wall with a hammer is easy to imagine), then we tend to think that the event was real. In contrast, when we have to make an effort to form an image—for example, of being in a place we have never seen or doing something that is utterly foreign to us—the cognitive operations we perform apparently serve later as a cue that the event did not really take place.

✦ THE PERSON FOCUSES ON HIS OR HER EMOTIONAL REACTIONS TO THE EVENT RATHER THAN ON WHAT ACTUALLY HAPPENED. Emotional reactions to an imagined event can resemble those that would have occurred in response to a real event; therefore the fact that a person has a strong emotional feeling about an event is not a reliable cue to the event's reality. Let's take our Sam story again—which happens to be true. A woman we know believed for years that she had been present in the room (as an eight-year-old child) when her uncle destroyed the wall. Because the story was so vivid and upsetting to her, she felt angry at him for what she thought was his mean and violent behavior, and felt that she must have been angry with him at the time. Then, as an adult, she learned two things: (1) She wasn't at the party at all, but had simply heard about it repeatedly from the family over the years; and (2) Sam hadn't pounded the wall in anger, but as a joke—to tell the assembled friends and family that he and his wife were about to remodel their house. Nevertheless, our friend's family has had a terrible time convincing her that her "memory" of this event is entirely wrong, and they aren't sure she believes them yet.

As this last story illustrates, and as laboratory research shows, false memories can be as stable over time as true ones, or even more so (Brainerd, Reyna, & Brandse, 1995; Poole, 1995; Roediger & McDermott, 1995). Yet, despite the wealth of evidence for the reconstructive nature of memory, some people still believe that memories are permanently stored somewhere in the brain with perfect accuracy. As evidence, they will cite studies of recall under hypnosis, studies of electrical brain stimulation, and studies of the recall of emotionally powerful memories (e.g., of the *Challenger* explosion). Researchers have found that all three of these lines of evidence are seriously flawed.

Hypnosis and Memory. Consider, first, the frequent claim that under hypnosis, people can relive a long-ago childhood event or recall a forgotten experience. Stage hypnotists, "past-lives channelers," and some psychotherapists have reported dramatic performances by people who have been "age-regressed" to earlier years or even earlier centuries. A few therapists claim that hypnosis has helped their patients recall alleged abductions by extraterrestrials (Fiore, 1989). The assumption is that any memory recovered by hypnosis must be accurate, and that therefore total recall is possible. But is that true?

Michael Nash (1987), who reviewed six decades of scientific studies on hypnotic age regression, found that when people are regressed to an earlier age, their mental and moral performance remains "essentially adult in nature." Their brain-wave patterns and reflexes do not become childish; they do not show any signs of outgrown emotional disorders; they do not reason as children do or show child-sized IQs. Nor does hypnosis reliably improve memory for specific early experiences, even though hypnotized people often swear that it does. In one of Nash's own studies, hypnotized subjects tried to recall what their favorite comforting object had been (a teddy bear, a blanket, or the like) at age three. Only 23 percent were accurate, compared with 70 percent of a nonhypnotized control group! (Mothers independently verified the accuracy of these memories.)

It is true, Nash says, that people undergo dramatic changes in behavior and subjective experience when they are hypnotically regressed; they may use baby talk or report that they feel four years old again. But the reason is not that they *are* four; they are simply willing to play the role. They will do the same when they are hypnotically *progressed* ahead—say, to age 70 or 80—or regressed to "past lives." Their belief that they are 7 or 70 or 7,000 years old may be sincere and convincing, but it is based on confabulation.

Under hypnosis, the natural tendency to confuse fact and speculation is increased by a desire to please the hypnotist and by the fact that hypnosis encourages fantasy and detailed images. Therefore, although hypnosis does sometimes boost the amount of information recalled about an actual event, it also increases errors, perhaps because hypnotized people are more willing than nonhypnotized people to guess, or because they mistake vividly imagined possibilities for actual memories (Dinges et al., 1992; Kihlstrom, 1994; Nash & Nadon, 1996).

In a fascinating series of studies that dramatically demonstrated how false memories can be constructed under hypnosis, Nicholas Spanos and his colleagues (1991) directed hypnotized Canadian university students to regress past their own birth to a previous life. About a third of the students reported that they could do so. But when they were asked, while supposedly "reliving" a past life, to name the leader of their country, say whether the country was at peace or at war, or describe the money used in their community, the students could not do it. One young man, who thought he was Julius Caesar, said the year was A.D. 50 and he was emperor of Rome—but Caesar died in 44 B.C. and was never crowned emperor (and besides, identifying years as A.D. or B.C. did not begin until several centuries later).

In these studies, all of the students who believed they were reliving a past life were actually weaving events, places, and persons from their present lives into their accounts. Their descriptions and their acceptance of their regression experiences as real were also influenced by the instructions of the hypnotist. The researchers concluded that the act of "remembering" another "self" involves the construction of a fantasy that accords not only with one's own beliefs but also with the beliefs of others.

A similar process occurs when people under hypnosis report spirit possession or "memories" of UFO abductions (Baker, 1992; Dawes, 1994; Spanos, Burgess, & Burgess, 1994). Often, the hypnotist shapes the person's story by giving subtle and not-so-subtle hints about what the person should say. Here is an exchange between one therapist who believes in UFO abductions and a supposed abductee who has been hypnotized (from Fiore, 1989, quoted in Newman & Baumeister, 1994):

Dr. Fiore: Now I'm going to ask you a few questions at this point. You will remember everything because you want to remember. When you were being poked everywhere, did they do any kind of vaginal examination?

Sandi: I don't think they did.

Dr. Fiore: Now you're going to let yourself know if they put a needle in any part of your body, other than the rectum.

Sandi: No. They were carrying needles around, big ones, and I was scared for a while they were going to put one in me, but they didn't. [*Body tenses.*]

Dr. Fiore: Now just let yourself relax. At the count of three you're going to remember whether they did put one of those big needles in you. If they did, know that you're safe, and it's all over, isn't it. And if they didn't, you're going to remember that too, at the count of three. One . . . two . . . three.

Sandi: They did.

Brain Stimulation and Memory. Another line of evidence often cited by those who believe that all memories are accurately and permanently stored in the brain comes from studies of electrical brain stimulation carried out during the 1960s by neurosurgeon Wilder Penfield. Penfield reported that stimulating parts of the brain before surgery, while the patient was conscious, would sometimes evoke reports of what seemed to be sharp memories from the distant past, thought by the patient to be long forgotten (Penfield & Perot, 1963). In one case, a woman told of rehearing a concert she had attended years before; she even hummed along with the music. Another woman said, "I hear voices. It is late at night, around the carnival somewhere—some sort of traveling circus."

For years, many psychologists unquestioningly accepted Penfield's brain-stimulation research as persuasive support for the permanent storage of memories. Then Elizabeth Loftus (1980) decided to look at his work more critically. First, she observed that although Penfield had electrically stimulated the brains of about 1,100 patients, only 40 of them—3.5 percent—reported having a "memory." Of those 40, most claimed to hear nothing more than some music or a person singing—hardly a memory of anything. As for the few patients who seemed to have more elaborate memories, closer examination suggested that they were not actually "reliving" a long-forgotten experience at all. Instead, they were re-creating one, drawing in part on actual memories and in part on their current interpretations of such memories, much as they might do while dreaming. One woman's "memories" turned out to consist of whatever thoughts or bits of conversation had taken place just before and during the time of stimulation.

Loftus also pointed out what in retrospect should have been obvious: The recovery of *some* information stored long ago does not mean that *all* memories remain available and reflect what truly happened. According to Loftus, there is no solid evidence that all memories last forever. On the contrary, she argues, information in memory can be completely wiped out by new, misleading information, or it can become permanently inaccessible. Although it is true that we can all produce many familiar facts without much reconstruction, literal recall of events is probably the exception, not the rule.

Flashbulb Memories. But, you may say, what about those surprising, shocking, or emotional events that hold a special place in memory? Such experiences seem like moments frozen in time, with all the details intact (Conway et al., 1994). Years ago, Roger Brown and James Kulik (1977) labeled these memories **flashbulb memories** because that term captures the surprise, illumination, and seemingly photographic detail that characterize them. Brown and Kulik speculated that the capacity for flashbulb memories may have evolved because such memories had survival value. Remembering the details of a surprising or dangerous experience could have helped our ancestors avoid similar situations in the future. This interpretation fits well with the finding, reported in Chapter 4, that certain hormones released during emotional arousal enhance memory.

Yet despite their intensity, even flashbulb memories are not always complete or accurate records of the past (Wright, 1993). Many people who were alive when John F. Kennedy was killed swear that they saw the assassination on television, as he was riding

---

flashbulb memory A vivid, detailed recollection of a significant or startling event, or the circumstances in which a person learned of such an event.

More facts of nature: All forest animals, to this very day, remember where they were and what they were doing when they heard that Bambi's mother had been shot.

in his motorcade. In reality, no television cameras were present during the assassination, and the only film of the event, made by a bystander, was not shown until much later. Similarly, many people now over age 25 say that they know exactly where they were and what they were doing when they learned of the 1986 explosion of the space shuttle *Challenger,* as well as who told them the news and what their own reactions were. Yet several studies done since the tragedy show that even these "unforgettable" memories often grow dim with time (Bohannon, 1988; McCloskey, Wible, & Cohen, 1988). In one such study, college students, on the morning after the event, reported how they had heard the news. Three years later, when they again recalled how they learned about the explosion, not one student was entirely correct and a third of them were *completely wrong,* although they felt that they were remembering accurately (Neisser & Harsch, 1992).

Some shocking or surprising events do remain extremely memorable, especially when the person doing the remembering was personally involved in the event. Research finds, for example, that people who were living in the San Francisco Bay Area in 1989 are likely to remember accurately where they were and what they were doing when the Loma Prieta earthquake hit on October 17 and what they did right afterward (Neisser, Winograd, & Weldon, 1991; Palmer, Schreiber, & Fox, 1991). Even with flash-bulb memories, however, facts tend to get mixed with a little fiction. These findings remind us, once again, that remembering is an *active* process; it involves not only dredging up stored information but also putting two and two together to reconstruct the past.

When Seeing Isn't Believing

The reconstructive nature of memory helps the mind work efficiently. We can store just the essentials of an experience, then use our knowledge of the world to figure out the specifics when we need them. But sometimes the same process gets us into hot water, and this raises problems in legal cases that involve eyewitness testimony.

Imagine that as you leave an office building, you see a man running in the direction of a blue Dodge. You glance away for a moment, and when you look back, you see that someone in the Dodge is pulling away from the curb. You are not paying much attention to this chain of events; why should you? But just then, a woman emerges from the building, points wildly at the departing car, and shouts, "Stop that man, he stole my purse!" Soon the police arrive and ask you to tell what you saw.

If we again compare memory to a film, you have actually seen only some of the frames: a man running toward a car, the car pulling away. Asked now for a description of what happened, you are likely to fill in the frames that are missing, the ones that would presumably show the man climbing into the car. In other words, you *infer* (deduce) what must have happened: "I saw a brown-haired man, about 5 feet 10 inches tall, with a mustache, and wearing a blue shirt, run over to the blue Dodge, get in, and drive away." To make matters worse, some aspects of this episode were undoubtedly hazy or incomplete, so you have probably gone back and "retouched" them, adding a little color here, a little detail there.

Will any harm result from your reconstruction? That depends. Perhaps the man you saw really did drive off in the car. Then again, perhaps someone else was the purse snatcher, and the man you saw was someone else. Because memory is reconstructive, eyewitness testimony is not always reliable, even when the witness feels completely confident in the accuracy of his or her report (Bothwell et al., 1987; Sporer et al., 1995). There is no easy solution to this problem. It does little good to give a polygraph ("lie detector") test to a witness who is unwittingly reconstructing an event. For one thing, polygraph results are highly unreliable (see Chapter 2); for another, someone who is trying to reconstruct the past is not deliberately lying and should therefore pass the test. Nor, as we've seen, will hypnosis necessarily help. In fact, because pseudomemories and errors are so common in hypnotically induced recall, the American Psychological Association and the American Medical Association oppose the use of "hypnotically refreshed" testimony in courts of law.

Of course, the accounts of eyewitnesses play a vital role in our justice system; without them, many guilty people would go free. But convictions based solely or mostly on such testimony occasionally turn out to be tragic mistakes. Errors are especially likely to occur when the suspect's race differs from that of the witness, perhaps because prejudices or lack of familiarity prevent people from attending to the distinctive features of members of other races (Brigham & Malpass, 1985; Chance & Goldstein, 1995).

To complicate matters further, our reconstructions of past events are heavily influenced by the way in which questions about those events are put to us, as we saw in our discussion of hypnosis. In a classic study of leading questions, Elizabeth Loftus and John Palmer (1974) showed people short films depicting car collisions. Afterward, the researchers asked some of the viewers, "About how fast were the cars going when they *hit* each other?" Other viewers were asked the same question, but with the verb changed to *smashed, collided, bumped,* or *contacted.* These words imply different speeds, with *smashed* implying the greatest speed and *contacted* the least. Sure enough, the estimates of how fast the cars were going varied, depending on which word was used. *Smashed* produced the highest average speed estimates (40.8 mph), followed by *collided* (39.3 mph), *bumped* (38.1 mph), *hit* (34.0 mph), and *contacted* (31.8 mph).

In a similar study, the researchers asked some participants "Did you see a broken headlight?" but asked of others "Did you see the broken headlight?" (Loftus & Zanni, 1975). Two other pairs of questions also differed only in the use of *a* or *the.* Note that the question with *the* presupposes a broken headlight and merely asks whether the witness saw it, whereas the question with *a* makes no such presupposition. The researchers found that people who received questions with *the* were far more likely to report having seen something that had not really appeared in the film than were those who received questions with *a.* If a tiny word like *the* can lead people to "remember" what they didn't see, you can imagine how the leading questions of police detectives and courtroom lawyers might influence a witness's recall.

Misleading information from any source can alter what we remember. In a third study (Loftus & Greene, 1980), participants saw the face of a young man who had straight hair, then heard a description of the face supposedly written by another witness—a description that wrongly described the man as having light curly hair. When these subjects reconstructed the face using a kit containing different features, 33 percent of their reconstructions contained the misleading detail, whereas only 5 percent contained it when curly hair was not mentioned. The face on the left shows one person's reconstruction in the absence of the misleading information; on the right is another person's reconstruction of the same face after exposure to the misleading information:

No misleading information   *Exposure to misleading information*

Even when people are told the purpose of such research, they often continue to report seeing things they never saw. For example, Loftus and her colleagues used leading questions to get people to think they had seen a yield sign or a stop sign while viewing slides of a traffic accident. A control group was not misled in this way. Later, all of the subjects were told the purpose of the study and were asked to guess whether they had been misled. Almost all of those who were misled continued to insist they had *really, truly* seen the sign whose existence had been planted in their minds (Loftus, Miller, & Burns, 1978). These people were entirely confident about the accuracy of their memories—and they were dead wrong.

What Do You Know?

See whether you can reconstruct what you have read to answer these questions.

1. Memory can be compared most accurately to (a) a wax tablet, (b) a giant file cabinet, (c) a videorecorder, (d) none of these.
2. In the children's game "telephone," one person tells another a story, the second person relates the story to a third, and so on. By the end of the game, the story will have changed considerably, which illustrates the principle that memory is
   _____.
3. According to psychological research, which statement about hypnosis is correct? (a) It reduces errors in memory. (b) It enables people to relive memories from infancy. (c) It permits people to relive a former life. (d) Along with the existence of flashbulb memories, it demonstrates that memories are permanently and accurately stored in the brain.
4. In psychotherapy, hundreds of people have claimed to recall long-buried memories of having taken part in bizarre satanic rituals involving animal and human torture and sacrifice, even though (as we noted in Chapter 2) none of these reports has ever been confirmed. Based on what you have learned so far, how might you explain such "memories"?

Answers:

which can produce "source amnesia" and the conviction that the memory is real. therapist might then probe for more details and emotions associated with the alleged memory. The descriptions from fictionalized accounts or from other traumatic experiences in their lives. The interpretations, may then "remember" experiences that did not happen, "borrowing" ideas and comments to their patients (Ganaway, 1991). Patients, who are susceptible to their therapists' assume that satanic abuse cults are widespread may ask leading questions and make leading **1.** d **2.** reconstructive **3.** None of the statements is true. **4.** Therapists who uncritically

MEASURING MEMORY

Now that we have seen how memory *doesn't* work, we turn to studies of how it *does* work. To understand how memory operates, however, you must know a little about how psychologists measure it. The ability to remember is not an absolute talent; it depends on the type of performance being called for. Students who express a preference for multiple-choice, essay, or true-false exams already know this.

Conscious recollection of an event or an item of information is called **explicit memory.** It is usually measured using one of two methods. The first tests for **recall,** the ability to retrieve and reproduce information encountered earlier. Essay and fill-in-the-blank exams and memory games such as Trivial Pursuit or Jeopardy require recall. The second tests for **recognition,** the ability to identify information you have previously observed, read, or heard about. The information is given to you, and all you have to do is say whether it is old or new, or perhaps correct or incorrect, or pick it out of a set of alternatives. The task, in other words, is to compare the information you are given with the information stored in your memory. True-false and multiple-choice tests call for recognition.

For example, pause for a moment and try to name the seven dwarfs who befriended Snow White. How many can you come up with? That's a test of recall. Now look at this list of 14 names, and pick out the 7 correct ones:

Dopey	Doc
Dumbo	Wheezy
Sneezy	Grumpy
Sleepy	Dumpy
Surly	Happy
Horny	Cheerful
Bashful	Mork

That's a test of recognition. (You can find the answers at the end of this chapter.)

As all students know, recognition tests can be difficult (some might say "tricky"), especially when false items closely resemble correct ones. Under most circumstances, however, recall is the greater challenge. This difference was once demonstrated in a study of people's memories of their high-school classmates (Bahrick, Bahrick, & Wittlinger, 1975). The subjects, ages 17 to 74, first wrote down the names of as many classmates as they could remember. Recall was poor; most recent graduates could write only a few dozen names, and those out of school for 40 years or more recalled an average of only 19. Even when prompted with yearbook pictures, the youngest participants failed to name almost 30 percent of their classmates, and the oldest ones failed to name more than 80 percent. Recognition, however, was far better. The task was to look at ten cards, each containing five photographs, and to say which picture on each card was that of a former classmate. Recent graduates were right 90 percent of the time, but so were people who had graduated 35 years earlier! Even those out of high school for

---

explicit memory Conscious, intentional recollection of an event or of an item of information.
recall The ability to retrieve and reproduce from memory previously encountered material.
recognition The ability to identify previously encountered material.

more than 40 years could identify three-fourths of their classmates, and the ability to recognize names was nearly as impressive.

Sometimes, information is retained and affects our thoughts and actions even when there is no conscious or intentional remembering—a phenomenon known as **implicit memory** (Graf & Schacter, 1985; Schacter, Chiu, & Ochsner, 1993). To get at this subtle sort of knowledge, researchers must rely on indirect methods. One common method, **priming,** asks you to read or listen to some information and then tests you later to see whether the information affects your performance on another type of task. For example, you might read a list of words, then later try to complete word stems (such as *def-*) with the first word that comes to mind (such as *define* or *defend*). Even when recognition or recall for the original list is poor, people who see the original list are more likely than control subjects to complete the word fragments with words from the list. The fact that the original words "prime" (make more available) certain responses on the word-completion task shows that people can retain more implicit knowledge about the past than they realize. They know more than they know that they know (Richardson-Klavehn & Bjork, 1988; Roediger, 1990).

This finding is true even for patients who have anterograde amnesia and cannot remember learning material. H. M., for example, performs on tests of priming just as people with normal memories do (Keane, Gabrieli, & Corkin, 1987). Some psychologists conclude that there must be separate systems in the brain for implicit and explicit tasks, a view that has been supported by PET scans showing differences in the location of brain activity when people perform such tasks (Squire et al., 1992).

Researchers often show great ingenuity in uncovering elusive evidence of implicit memory. One group of researchers played an audiotaped list of word pairs (such as *ocean–water*) while surgical patients were apparently unconscious. After their operations, the patients could not recall the word pairs, but when they were given the first word from each pair and asked to say any word that popped into mind, they were somewhat more likely than they would otherwise have been to respond with the associated words they "heard" during surgery (Kihlstrom et al., 1990). Equally fascinating research has been done with patients who, because of damage to the brain, cannot identify familiar faces. In one study, two patients shown photographs of familiar and unfamiliar people could not consciously identify the faces of people they knew. Yet electrical conductance of the skin (a measure of autonomic-nervous-system arousal) changed while they were looking at the familiar faces, indicating that implicit, nonconscious recognition must have been taking place (Tranel & Damasio, 1985).

Yet another method of measuring memory, the **relearning method** (also called the *savings method*) seems to straddle the boundary between implicit and explicit tests.

---

implicit memory Unconscious retention in memory, as evidenced by the effect of a previous experience or previously encountered information on current thoughts or actions.

priming A method for measuring implicit memory in which a person reads or listens to information and is later tested to see whether the information is "activated" on another type of task.

relearning method A method for measuring retention that compares the time required to relearn material with the time required for the initial learning of the material.

Devised by Hermann Ebbinghaus (1885/1913) more than a century ago, the relearning method requires you to relearn information or a task that you learned earlier. If you fail to recall or recognize some or all of the material, yet you master it more quickly the second time around, you must be remembering something from the first experience. One eminent memory researcher whom we consulted said that he considers the relearning method to be a test of explicit memory. Another, however, maintained that it can sometimes function as a test of implicit memory, if the learner is unaware that the material being relearned was ever learned earlier.

MODELS OF MEMORY

Although people usually refer to memory as if it were a single faculty, as in "I must be losing my memory" or "He has a memory like an elephant's," the term *memory* actually covers a complex collection of abilities, processes, and mental systems. If tape recorders and video cameras aren't accurate metaphors for capturing these diverse components of memory, then what metaphor would be better?

As we saw in Chapter 9, many cognitive psychologists liken the mind to an information processor, along the lines of a computer, though more complex. They have constructed *information-processing* models of memory, often borrowing liberally from the language of computer programming by referring, for example, to inputs, output, accessing, and information retrieval. According to information-processing theories, remembering begins with **encoding,** the conversion of information to a form that the brain can process and store. Our memories are not exact replicas of experience. Sensory information is changed in form almost as soon as it is detected, and the form retained for the long run differs from the original stimulus. One reason is that whenever we encounter new information, we integrate it with what we already know or believe, incorporating it into an existing web of knowledge called a **cognitive schema** (see Chapter 9).

Often such schemas are useful because they help us make sense of separate pieces of information and thus remember them better. For example, having an overall schema of the story of American history, and of the major issues and conflicts involved, makes it easier to remember specific dates, facts, and events. However, cognitive schemas can also lead to misremembering, because people often distort new information in order to make it fit their existing schemas. And if the new information doesn't fit, they may ignore it or forget it—a popular way of reducing cognitive dissonance.

Even when we don't distort, we simplify. For example, when you hear a lecture, you may hang on every word, but you do not store those words verbatim. Instead, you convert sentences to units of meaning, possibly in the form of propositions (Anderson

---

encoding The conversion of information into a form that can be stored in and retrieved from memory.
cognitive schema An integrated network of knowledge, beliefs, and expectations about a particular topic or aspect of the world.

& Bower, 1973). Propositions, as we saw in Chapter 9, are similar to sentences, but they express unitary ideas and are made up of abstract concepts rather than words. Thus the sentence "The clever psychologist made an amazing discovery" contains three propositions that can be expressed by the words *the psychologist was clever, the psychologist made a discovery,* and *the discovery was amazing.* A man who emigrated from Germany at a young age and forgot all his German would still remember facts that he learned in Germany because such information is stored as propositions, not as strings of German (or English) words.

Most psychologists believe that information is also stored in the form of auditory or visual images—melodies, sounds, "pictures in the mind's eye." Visual images are often particularly memorable. In one study, Roger Shepard (1967) had students look at 612 color slides. Then he paired those pictures with new ones, and the students had to select the ones they had previously seen. Immediately after seeing the original slides, the students identified 96.7 percent of them, and four months later, they still recognized more than 50 percent. Subsequent research showed that even if the original set of slides contained 2,560 different photographs, recognition remained high (Haber, 1970).

Other forms of encoding may also be possible. For example, memories for specific motor skills, such as those involved in swimming or riding a bicycle, may be encoded and stored as sets of kinesthetic (muscular) instructions. Memories for motor skills are extremely long-lasting. If you learned to swim as a child, you will still know how to swim at age 30, even if you haven't been in a pool or lake for 22 years.

With some kinds of information, encoding takes place automatically; you don't have to make a deliberate effort. Think about where you usually sit in your psychology class. When were you last there? You can probably provide this information easily, even though you never made a deliberate effort to encode it. In general, people automatically encode their location in space and time and the frequency with which they experience various situations (Hasher & Zacks, 1984). But other kinds of information require *effortful* encoding. To retain such information, you might have to label it, associate it with other material, or rehearse it until it is familiar. A friend of ours tells us that in her ballet class, she knows exactly what to do when asked to perform a *pas de bourrée,* yet she often has trouble recalling the term itself. Because she rarely uses it, she probably has not bothered to encode it well.

Unfortunately, people sometimes count on automatic encoding when effortful encoding is needed. For example, when students study, they may assume that they can encode the material in a textbook as effortlessly as they encode where they usually sit in the classroom. Or they may assume that the ability to remember and perform well on tests is innate and that effort won't make any difference (Devolder & Pressley, 1989). As a result, they wind up in trouble at test time. Experienced students know that most of the information in a college course requires effortful encoding.

After encoding takes place, the next steps are *storage,* the maintenance of the material over time, and *retrieval,* the recovery of stored material (or what a computer programmer might call the "accessing" of information). In most information-processing theories, these processes occur in three separate, interacting systems: *sensory memory,* which retains incoming sensory information for a second or two, until it can be processed further; *short-term memory* (STM), which holds a limited amount of information for a brief period of time, perhaps up to 30 seconds or so, unless a conscious effort is made to keep it there longer; and *long-term memory* (LTM), which accounts for longer storage—from a few minutes to decades. This model, which is sometimes informally called the "three-box model," has dominated research on memory for three decades. According to two of its leading proponents, Richard Atkinson and Richard Shiffrin (1968, 1971), information can pass from sensory memory to short-term memory and in either direction between short-term and long-term memory, as illustrated in Figure 10.1.

The three-box model, however, does not explain all the findings on memory, and competing information-processing models also exist. Advocates of these models disagree about how information passes from one kind of memory system to another and how information gets encoded and stored in each system. Some question the very notion of distinct memory systems. They argue that there is just one system, with different mental processes called on for different tasks.

Further, although many psychologists agree with Philip Johnson-Laird (1988) that "the computer is the last metaphor for the mind," others are doubting the usefulness of this metaphor. They argue that the human brain does not operate like your average computer. Most computers process instructions sequentially and work on a single stream of data, so information-processing models of memory have also represented mental processing as sequential. The human brain, however, performs many operations simultaneously—that is, in parallel. It recognizes patterns all at once rather than as a sequence of information bits. It monitors bodily functions, perceives the environment, produces

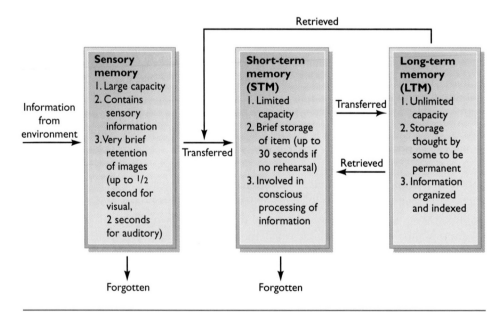

Figure 10.1 *In the "three-box" model of memory, information that does not transfer out of sensory memory or short-term memory is assumed to be forgotten forever. Once in long-term memory, information can be retrieved for use in analyzing incoming sensory information or for temporary mental operations performed in short-term memory.*

speech, and searches memory all at the same time. It can do this because millions of neurons are active at once, and each neuron communicates with hundreds or thousands of others, which in turn communicate with millions more. Although no single neuron is terribly smart or terribly fast, millions of them working simultaneously produce the complexities of cognition.

Some cognitive scientists, therefore, have rejected the traditional information-processing approach in favor of a **parallel distributed processing (PDP)** or *connectionist* model (Bechtel & Abrahamsen, 1990; McClelland, 1994; Rumelhart, McClelland, & The PDP Research Group, 1986). In PDP models, knowledge is represented not as propositions or images but as connections among thousands and thousands of interacting processing units, distributed in a vast network and all operating in parallel—just like the neurons of the brain. As new information comes into the system, the ability of these units to excite or inhibit one another is constantly adjusted to reflect new knowledge.

Although the details of PDP theory are beyond the scope of this book, we want to point out that it reverses the notion that the human brain can be modeled after a computer. PDP theorists say that for computers to be truly intelligent, they must be modeled after the human brain. Indeed, computer scientists are now designing machines called *neural networks* that attempt to imitate the brain's vast grid of densely connected neurons (Anderson & Rosenfeld, 1988; Levine, 1990). In these machines, thousands of simple processing units are linked up to one another in a weblike system, interacting with one another and operating in parallel. On the software side, researchers in the multidisciplinary field of *artificial intelligence* have been writing programs that simulate the way in which PDP theorists believe the human mind works. Like human beings, these programs do not always find the best solution to a problem, but they do tend to find a good solution quickly. They also have the potential to learn from experience by adjusting the strengths of their "neural" connections in response to new information.

It is not clear whether the connectionist approach will be an improvement on the more traditional information-processing models. Both approaches can explain many findings about memory, but neither one can explain all the findings. PDP models have the virtue of resembling the brain's actual wiring, and they are applicable not just to memory but also to perception, language, and decision making. But traditional information-processing models do a better job, at least for now, of explaining memory for a single event (Schacter, 1990). They are also better at explaining why well-learned information is sometimes forgotten when new information is learned (McCloskey & Cohen, 1989; Ratcliff, 1990).

In this chapter, we have decided to retain the information-processing model of three separate memory systems—sensory, short-term, and long-term—because it offers a convenient way to organize the major findings on memory, does a good job of accounting for those findings, and is consistent with biological facts about memory. But keep in mind that it is only a metaphor, one that might someday be as outdated as the metaphor of memory as a camera.

---

parallel distributed processing (PDP)   An alternative to the information-processing model of memory, in which knowledge is represented not as propositions or images but as connections among thousands of interacting processing units, distributed in a vast network and all operating in parallel.

How well have you encoded what you just learned?

1. Alberta solved a crossword puzzle a few days ago. She no longer has any conscious recollection of the words that were in the puzzle, but while playing a game of Scrabble with her brother, she unconsciously tends to form words that were in the puzzle, showing that she has _____ memories for some of the words.
2. The three basic memory processes are _____, storage, and _____.
3. Do the preceding two questions ask for recall, recognition, or relearning? (And what about *this* question?)
4. One objection to traditional information-processing theories of memory is that unlike most computers, which process information _____, the brain performs many independent operations _____.

ANSWERS:

1. implicit 2. encoding, retrieval 3. The first two questions both measure recall; the third measures recognition. 4. sequentially; simultaneously, or in parallel

THE THREE-BOX MODEL

The fact that most information-processing theories refer to three interacting systems of memory does not necessarily mean that there are three entirely separate places in the brain corresponding to the three memory storehouses. Talking about memory systems as places is merely a convenience. The three systems are actually clusters of mental processes that occur at different stages.

Sensory Memory

In the three-box model, all incoming sensory information must make a brief stop in **sensory memory,** the entryway of memory. Sensory memory includes a number of separate memory subsystems, or *sensory registers*—as many as there are senses. Information in sensory memory is short-lived. Visual images, or *icons,* remain for a maximum of half a second in a visual register. Auditory images, or *echoes,* remain for a slightly longer time, by most estimates up to two seconds or so, in an auditory register.

Sensory memory acts as a holding bin, retaining information just until we can select items for attention from the stream of stimuli bombarding our senses. *Pattern recognition,* the preliminary identification of a stimulus on the basis of information already contained in long-term memory, occurs during the transfer of information

---

sensory memory A memory system that momentarily preserves extremely accurate images of sensory information.

from sensory memory to short-term memory. Information that does not go on to short-term memory vanishes forever, like a message written in disappearing ink.

Images in sensory memory are fairly complete. How do we know that? In a clever experiment, George Sperling (1960) briefly showed people visual arrays of letters that looked like this:

$$
\begin{array}{cccc}
X & K & C & Q \\
N & D & X & G \\
T & F & R & J
\end{array}
$$

In previous studies, subjects had been able to recall only four or five letters, no matter how many they initially saw. Yet many people insisted that they had actually seen more items. Some of the letters, they said, seemed to slip away before they could be reported. To overcome this problem, Sperling devised a method of "partial report." He had people report the first row of letters when they heard a high tone, the middle row when they heard a medium tone, and the third row when they heard a low tone:

$$
\begin{array}{cccc}
X & K & C & Q \quad \longleftarrow \text{ High tone} \\
N & D & X & G \quad \longleftarrow \text{ Medium tone} \\
T & F & R & J \quad \longleftarrow \text{ Low tone}
\end{array}
$$

If the tone occurred right after they saw the array, people could recall about three letters from a row. Because they did not know beforehand which row they would have to report, they therefore must have had most of the letters in sensory memory right after viewing them. However, if the tone occurred after a delay of even one second, people remembered very little of what they had seen. The letters had slipped away.

In normal processing, too, sensory memory needs to clear quickly to prevent sensory "double exposures." It also acts as a filter, keeping out extraneous and unimportant information. Our brains store trillions of bits of information during our lifetimes. Processing everything detected by our senses, including irrelevancies, would lead to inefficiency and confusion.

Short-term Memory

Like sensory memory, **short-term memory (STM)** retains information only temporarily—for up to about 30 seconds by most estimates, although some think that the

---

short-term memory (STM) In the three-box model of memory, a limited-capacity memory system involved in the retention of information for brief periods; it is also used to hold information retrieved from long-term memory for temporary use.

maximum interval may extend to a few minutes. This impermanence has its basis in biology: Whereas long-term retention involves permanent structural changes in the brain (see Chapter 4), short-term memory appears to involve only temporary changes within neurons that increase or decrease the ability of these cells to release neurotransmitters (Kandel & Schwartz, 1982). In short-term memory, the material is no longer an exact sensory image but an encoding of one, such as a word or a number. This material either transfers into long-term memory or decays and is lost forever. There are, however, ways to keep material in short-term memory beyond the usual limits, as we will see.

Certain cases of brain injury demonstrate the importance of transferring new information from short-term memory into long-term memory. H. M.'s case is again instructive. H. M., you will recall, can store information on a short-term basis; he can hold a conversation and appears normal when you first meet him. He also retains implicit memories. However, for the most part H. M. cannot retain information about new facts and events for longer than a few minutes. H. M.'s problem is not in retaining information in long-term memory after it gets there; he, and other patients like him, can learn some new visual information if they have extra time to study it, and then forgetting follows a normal course (McKee & Squire, 1992). Therefore, H. M.'s terrible memory deficits probably involve a problem in transferring explicit memories from short-term storage into long-term storage in the first place.

Besides retaining new information for brief periods, short-term memory also holds information that has been retrieved from long-term memory for temporary use. For this reason, short-term memory is often called *working memory*. When you do an arithmetic problem, working memory contains the numbers and the rules for doing the necessary operations ("Add the right-hand column, carry the 2"), plus the intermediate results from each step. The ability to bring information from long-term memory into working memory is not disrupted in patients such as H. M. They can do arithmetic, converse, relate events that occurred before their injury, and do anything else that requires retrieval of information from long-term into short-term memory.

People such as H. M. fall at the extreme end on a continuum of forgetfulness, but even those of us with normal memories know from personal experience how frustratingly brief short-term retention can be. We look up a telephone number, dial it, get a busy signal, and then find after only a moment that the number has vanished from our minds. We meet someone at a party and two minutes later find ourselves groping unsuccessfully for her name. Is it any wonder that short-term memory has been called a "leaky bucket"?

According to most memory models, if the bucket did not leak it would quickly overflow, because at any given moment, short-term memory can hold only so many items. Years ago, George Miller (1956) estimated its capacity to be "the magical number 7 plus or minus 2." Five-number ZIP codes and 7-digit telephone numbers fall conveniently in this range; 15-digit credit-card numbers do not. But some researchers have questioned whether Miller's magical number is so magical after all. Estimates of STM's capacity have ranged from 2 items to 20, with most of the estimates at the lower end. Some cognitive psychologists believe that it is not STM per se that is limited, but rather the processing capacity available to the entire memory system at any one time. Everyone agrees, however, that the number of items that short-term memory can handle at a given time is quite small.

If this is so, then how do we remember the beginning of a spoken sentence until the speaker reaches the end? After all, most sentences are longer than just a few words. According to most models of memory, we overcome this problem by grouping small bits of information into larger units, or **chunks.** The real capacity of STM, it turns out, is not a few bits of information but a few chunks. A chunk may be a word, a phrase, a sentence, or even a visual image, and it depends on previous experience. For most of us, the abbreviation *FBI* is one chunk, not three, and the date *1492* is one chunk, not four. In contrast, the number *9214* is four chunks and *IBF* is three—unless your address is 9214 or your initials are IBF. Take another, more visual example: If you are not familiar with football and you look at a field full of players, you probably won't be able to remember their positions when you look away. But if you are a fan of the game, you may see a single chunk of information—say, a wishbone formation—and be able to retain it.

Even chunking, however, cannot keep short-term memory from eventually filling up. Fortunately, much of the information we encounter during the day is needed for only a few moments. If you are multiplying two numbers, you need to remember them only until you have the answer. If you are talking to someone, you need to keep the person's words in mind only until you have understood them. But some information is needed for longer periods and must be transferred to long-term memory. Items that are particularly meaningful, have an emotional impact, or link up to something already in long-term memory may enter long-term storage easily, with only a brief stay in STM. The destiny of other items depends on how soon new information displaces them in short-term memory. Material in short-term memory is easily displaced unless we do something to keep it there, as we will see.

Long-term Memory

The third box in the information-processing model of memory is the largest: **long-term memory (LTM).** The capacity of long-term memory seems to have no practical limits. The vast amount of information stored there enables us to learn, get around in the environment, and build a sense of identity and personal history.

Organization in Long-term Memory. Because long-term memory contains so much information, we cannot search through it exhaustively, as we can through short-term memory. According to most models of memory, the information must be organized and indexed, just as items in a library are, so that we can find it. One way to

---

chunk A meaningful unit of information; it may be composed of smaller units.
long-term memory (LTM) In the three-box model of memory, the memory system involved in the long-term storage of information.

index words (or the concepts they represent) is by the semantic categories to which they belong. *Chair,* for example, belongs to the category *furniture.* In a classic study, people had to memorize 60 words that came from four semantic categories: animals, vegetables, names, and professions. The words were presented in random order, but when people were allowed to recall them in any order they wished, they tended to recall them in clusters corresponding to the four categories (Bousfield, 1953). This finding has since been replicated many times.

Evidence on the storage of information by semantic category also comes from case studies of people with brain damage. In one study (Hart, Berndt, & Caramazza, 1985), a patient called M. D. appeared to have made a complete recovery two years after suffering several strokes, with one odd exception: He had trouble remembering the names of fruits and vegetables. M. D. could easily name a picture of an abacus or a sphinx but not a picture of an orange or a carrot. He could sort pictures of animals, vehicles, and other objects into their appropriate categories but did poorly with pictures of fruits and vegetables. On the other hand, when M. D. was *given* the names of fruits and vegetables, he immediately pointed to the corresponding pictures. Apparently, he still had a store of information about fruits and vegetables, but his brain lesion prevented him from using their names to get to the information when he needed it, unless the names were provided by someone else. Such evidence supports the idea that information about a particular concept (e.g., *orange*) is linked in some way to information about the concept's semantic category (e.g., *fruit*).

Many models of long-term memory represent its contents as a vast network or grid of interrelated concepts (Collins & Loftus, 1975) and propositions (Anderson, 1990). A small part of a conceptual grid for *animal* might look something like Figure 10.2. Network models assume that semantic networks are a universal way of organizing information. The way people use these networks, however, depends on experience and education. For example, cross-cultural studies of rural children in Liberia and Guatemala have shown that the more schooling children have, the more likely they are to use semantic categories in recalling lists of objects (Cole & Cole, 1993). This makes sense, because in school, children must memorize a lot of information in a short time, and semantic grouping can help. Unschooled children, having less need to memorize lists, do not cluster items and do not remember them as well. But this does not mean that unschooled children have poor memories. When the task is meaningful to them—say, recalling objects that were in a story or a village scene—they remember extremely well (Mistry & Rogoff, 1994).

We organize information in long-term memory not only by semantic groupings but also in terms of the way words sound or look. Have you ever tried to recall some word that was on the "tip of your tongue"? Nearly everyone experiences such a *tip-of-the-tongue state,* especially when trying to recall the names of acquaintances or famous persons, the names of objects or places, or the titles of movies or books (Burke et al., 1991). It is reported even by users of sign language, who call it the tip-of-the-finger experience! One way to study this frustrating state is to have people record tip-of-the-tongue episodes in daily diaries. Another method is to give people the definitions of uncommon words and ask them to supply the words themselves. When a word is on

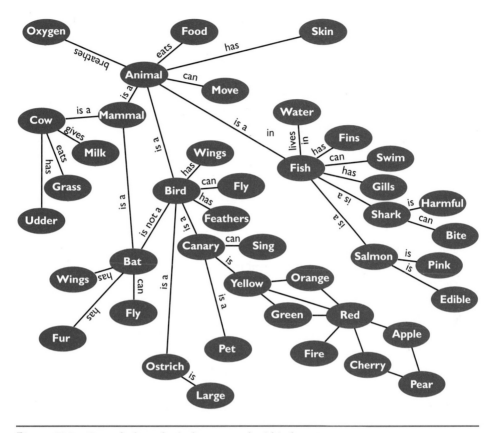

Figure 10.2 *Part of a hypothetical conceptual grid in long-term memory.*

the tip of the tongue, people tend to come up with words that are similar in meaning to the right word before they finally recall it. For example, for "patronage bestowed on a relative, in business or politics" a person might say "favoritism" rather than the correct response, "nepotism." But verbal information in long-term memory also seems to be indexed by sound and form, and it is retrievable on that basis. Thus, incorrect guesses often have the correct number of syllables, the correct stress pattern, the correct first letter, or the correct prefix or suffix (A. Brown, 1991; Brown & McNeill, 1966). For example, for the target word *sampan* (an Asian boat), a person might say "Siam" or "sarong."

Researchers are studying other ways in which we organize information in long-term memory, such as by its familiarity, personal relevance, or association with other information. The method a person uses in any given instance probably depends on the nature of the memory; you would no doubt store information about the major cities of Europe differently from information about your first date. To understand the organization of long-term memory, then, we must know what kinds of information can be stored there.

The Contents of Long-term Memory. Most theories of memory distinguish skills or habits ("knowing how") from abstract or representational knowledge ("knowing that"). **Procedural memories** are memories of knowing how—for example, knowing how to comb your hair, use a pencil, solve a jigsaw puzzle, knit a sweater, or swim. Some researchers believe that procedural memories are implicit rather than explicit, because once skills and habits are well-learned, they do not require much conscious processing. **Declarative memories** are memories of "knowing that," and they are usually assumed to be explicit. Declarative memories, in turn, come in two varieties, semantic memories and episodic memories (Tulving, 1985). **Semantic memories** are internal representations of the world, independent of any particular context. They include facts, rules, and concepts—items of general knowledge. On the basis of your semantic memory of the concept *cat*, you can describe a cat as a small, furry mammal that typically spends its time eating, sleeping, prowling, and staring into space, even though a cat may not be present when you give this description, and you probably won't know how or when you first learned it. **Episodic memories,** on the other hand, are internal representations of personally experienced events. When you remember how your cat once surprised you in the middle of the night by pouncing on your face as you slept, you are retrieving an episodic memory. Figure 10.3 summarizes these distinctions.

As we saw in Chapter 4, patients such as H. M., who cannot form new declarative memories because of damage to the hippocampus, can, with sufficient practice, acquire new procedural memories, including those necessary for manual, perceptual, and problem-solving skills. They can learn to solve a puzzle, read mirror-reversed words, or play tennis—even though they do not remember the training sessions in which they learned these skills. Apparently, the parts of the brain involved in acquiring procedural memories have remained intact.

From Short-term to Long-term Memory: A Riddle. The three-box model of memory has been invoked to explain an interesting phenomenon called the **serial-position effect.** If you are shown a list of items and are then immediately asked to recall them, your retention of any particular item will depend on its position in the list (Glanzer & Cunitz, 1966). Recall is best for items at the beginning of the list (the *primacy effect*) and at the end of the list (the *recency effect*). When retention of all the items is plotted, the result is a U-shaped curve, as shown in Figure 10.4. A serial-position effect occurs when you are introduced to a roomful of people and find that you can recall the names of the first few people and the last, but almost no one in the middle.

---

procedural memories Memories for the performance of actions or skills ("knowing how").
declarative memories Memories of facts, rules, concepts, and events ("knowing that"); they include semantic and episodic memories.
semantic memories Memories of general knowledge, including facts, rules, concepts, and propositions.
episodic memories Memories for personally experienced events and the contexts in which they occurred.
serial-position effect The tendency for recall of the first and last items on a list to surpass recall of items in the middle of the list.

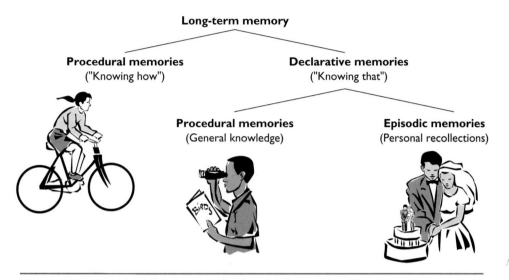

Figure 10.3 *You might draw on procedural memories to ride a bike, semantic memories to identify a bird, and episodic memories to recall your wedding. Can you come up with some other examples for each type of memory?*

According to the three-box model, the first few items on a list are remembered well because they have the best chance of getting into long-term memory. Because short-term memory was relatively "empty" when they entered, there was little competition among these items to make it into long-term memory. They were verbally processed, so they remain memorable. The last few items are remembered for a different reason: At the time of recall, they are still sitting in short-term memory and can just be "dumped." The items in the middle of a list, however, are not so well retained

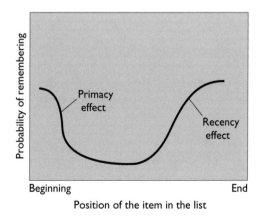

Figure 10.4 *The serial position effect.*

because by the time they get into short-term memory it is already crowded. As a result, many of these items drop out of short-term memory before they can be stored in long-term memory.

This explanation makes sense except for two things. First, under certain conditions, the last items on a list are well remembered even when the test is delayed past the time when short-term memory has presumably been "emptied" and filled with other information (Greene, 1986). In other words, the recency effect occurs even when, according to the three-box model, it should not.

Second, in some studies, serial-position curves occur in animals that have to remember a series of places in a maze or cage; these animals include even rats and birds (Crystal & Shettleworth, 1994; Kesner, Chiba, & Jackson-Smith, 1994). Therefore, the primary and recency effects can't be due to human verbal memory strategies alone. Whatever is producing these effects, researchers are not yet sure what it is—another puzzle of memory.

What Do You Know?

Find out whether the findings discussed in the previous section have transferred from your short-term memory to your long-term memory.

1. _____ memory holds images for a fraction of a second.
2. For most people, the abbreviation *U.S.A.* consists of _____ informational "chunk(s)."
3. Suppose you must memorize a long list of words that includes the following: *desk, pig, gold, dog, chair, silver, table, rooster, bed, copper,* and *horse.* If you can recall the words in any order you wish, how are you likely to group them in recall? Why?
4. When you roller-skate, are you relying on procedural, semantic, or episodic memory? How about when you recall the months of the year? How about when you remember falling off your roller skates on an icy January day?
5. If a child is trying to memorize the alphabet, which sequence should present the greatest difficulty: *abcdefg, klmnopq,* or *tuvwxyz?* Why?

Answers:

1. Sensory 2. one 3. *Desk, chair, table,* and *bed* would probably form one cluster; *pig, dog, rooster,* and *horse* a second; and *gold, silver,* and *copper* a third. Concepts tend to be organized in long-term memory by semantic categories, such as *furniture, animals,* and *metals.* 4. procedural; semantic; episodic 5. *klmnopq,* because of the serial-position effect

How to Remember

Once we understand how memory works, we can use that understanding to remember better. One important technique for keeping information in short-term memory and increasing the chances of long-term retention is *rehearsal,* the review or practice of

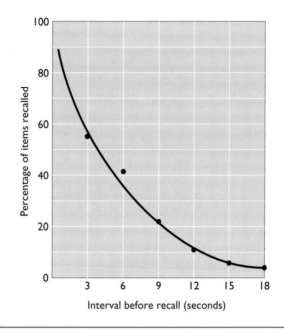

Figure 10.5 *Without rehearsal, the ability to recall information in short-term memory quickly falls off.*

material. When people are prevented from rehearsing, the contents of their short-term memories quickly fade. In an early study of this phenomenon, people had to memorize meaningless groups of letters. Immediately afterward, they had to start counting backward by threes from an arbitrary number; the counting prevented them from rehearsing the letter groups. Within only 18 seconds, the subjects forgot most of the items, as you can see in Figure 10.5. But when they did not have to count backward, their performance was much better, probably because they were rehearsing the items to themselves (Peterson & Peterson, 1959). Similarly, if you repeat a telephone number over and over, you will be able to retain it in short-term memory for as long as you like; but if you look up a number and then get into a conversation with someone, you are apt to forget the number almost immediately.

A dramatic and poignant demonstration of the power of rehearsal once occurred during a research session with H. M. (Ogden & Corkin, 1991). The experimenter gave H. M. five digits to repeat and remember, but then she was unexpectedly called away. When she returned after more than an hour, H. M. was able to repeat the five digits correctly. He had been rehearsing them the entire time!

Short-term memory holds many kinds of information, including visual information and abstract meanings. In fact, some theorists believe that there are several STMs, each specializing in a particular type of information. But most people—or at least most hearing people—seem to favor speech for rehearsing the contents of short-term memory. The speech may be spoken aloud or to oneself. When people make errors on short-term-memory tests that use letters or words, they often confuse items that sound the same or similar, such as *b* and *t,* or *bear* and *bare.* These errors suggest that they have been rehearsing verbally.

Some strategies for rehearsing are more effective than others. **Maintenance rehearsal** involves merely the rote repetition of the material. This kind of rehearsal is fine for maintaining information in STM, but it will not always lead to long-term retention. A better strategy if you want to remember for the long haul is **elaborative rehearsal,** also called *elaboration of encoding* (Cermak & Craik, 1979; Craik & Tulving, 1975). Elaboration involves associating new items of information either with items that have already been stored or with other new items. It can also involve analyzing the various physical, sensory, or semantic features of an item.

Suppose, for example, that you are studying the concept *hypothalamus* in Chapter 4 of this book. Impoverished encoding of the concept might look something like this:

In contrast, elaborative encoding, which would promote better retention, might look like this:

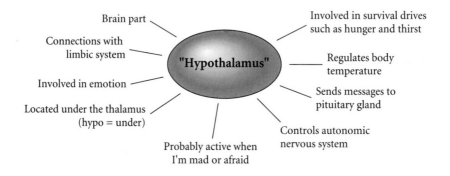

Similarly, if you are studying the concept of reinforcement in Chapter 6, simply rehearsing the definition in a rote manner is unlikely to transfer the information you

---

maintenance rehearsal Rote repetition of material in order to maintain its availability in memory.
elaborative rehearsal Association of new information with other knowledge and analysis of the new information to make it memorable.

need from short-term to long-term memory. Instead, when going over (rehearsing) the concept, you could encode the information that a reinforcer follows a response, strengthens the response, and is similar to a reward. You might also note that the word *reinforcer* starts with the same two letters as *reward*. And you might think up some examples of reinforcement and of how you have used it in your own life and could use it in the future. The more you elaborate the concept of reinforcement, the better you will remember it.

A related strategy for prolonging retention is **deep processing,** or the processing of meaning. If you process only the physical or sensory features of a stimulus, such as how the word *reinforcement* is spelled and how it sounds, your processing will be shallow even if it is elaborated. If you recognize patterns and assign labels to objects or events ("Reinforcement is an operant procedure"), your processing will be somewhat deeper. If you fully analyze the meaning of what you are trying to remember, your processing will be deeper yet. Unfortunately, students (and other people) often try to remember information that has little or no meaning for them, which explains why the information doesn't stick.

In addition to using elaborative rehearsal and deep processing, people who want to give their powers of memory a boost sometimes rely on **mnemonics** [neh-MON-iks], formal strategies and tricks for encoding, storing, and retaining information. (Mnemosyne—neh-MOZ-eh-nee—was the ancient Greek goddess of memory.) Some mnemonics take the form of easily memorized rhymes ("Thirty days hath September / April, June, and November . . ."). Others use formulas (e.g., "Every **g**ood **b**oy **d**oes **f**ine" for remembering which notes are on the lines of the treble clef in musical notation). Still others use visual images or word associations, which increase retention.

The best mnemonics force you to encode material actively and thoroughly. They may also reduce the amount of information by "chunking" it (as in the phone number 466-3293, which corresponds to the letters in GOOD-BYE—appropriate, perhaps, for a travel agency). Or they may make the material meaningful and thus easier to store and retrieve; facts and words to be memorized are often more memorable, for example, if they are woven into a coherent story (Bower & Clark, 1969). If you needed to remember the parts of the digestive system for a physiology course, you could construct a narrative about what happens to a piece of food after it enters a person's mouth, then repeat the narrative out loud to yourself, a roommate, or a study partner.

Some stage performers with amazing recall rely on more complicated mnemonics. We are not going to spend time on them here, because for ordinary memory tasks, such tricks are often no more effective than rote rehearsal, and sometimes they are actually worse (Wang, Thomas, & Ouellette, 1992). In one survey of memory researchers, most said they did not use complicated mnemonics themselves (Park,

---

deep processing In the encoding of information, the processing of meaning rather than of simply the physical or sensory features of a stimulus.
mnemonics Strategies and tricks for improving memory, such as the use of a verse or a formula.

Smith, & Cavanaugh, 1990). After all, why bother to memorize a grocery list using a fancy mnemonic when you can write down what you need to buy?

The fastest route to a good memory is to follow the principles suggested by the findings in this section and by other research on memory. Encode elaboratively, and try to make the material as meaningful as possible. Take your time: Leisurely learning, spread out over several sessions, usually produces better results than harried cramming (although *reviewing* material just before a test can be helpful). In terms of hours spent, "distributed" (spaced) learning sessions are more efficient than "massed" ones. Thus you may find that you retain information better after three separate one-hour sessions than after one session of three hours. You don't want to wait until the night before the test to start learning material for the first time. Just as concrete takes time to set, the neural and synaptic changes in the brain that underlie long-term memory take time to develop. This is why memories require a period of *consolidation,* or stabilization, before they "solidify" and become resistant to disruption.

It is also helpful to keep monitoring your learning. People who remember well tend to score well on tests of *metamemory,* the ability to monitor and be aware of one's own retention. By testing yourself frequently, rehearsing thoroughly, and reviewing periodically, you will have a better idea of how you are doing. Don't just evaluate your learning immediately after reading the material, though; because the information is still in short-term memory, you are likely to feel a false sense of confidence about your ability to recall it later. If you delay making a judgment for at least a few minutes, your evaluation will probably be more accurate (Nelson & Dunlosky, 1991). Finally, try to overlearn the material. You can't remember something you never learned well in the first place. Overlearning—studying even after you think you know the material—is one of the best ways to ensure that you'll remember it.

Whatever strategies you use, you will find that active learning produces more comprehension and therefore more retention than passive reading or listening. As the great philosopher Confucius said, "I hear and I forget. I see and I remember. I do and I understand." In contrast, popular books and tapes that promise you a "perfect," "photographic" memory or "instant recall" of everything you've read fly in the face of what psychology knows about how the mind operates. Our advice: Forget them.

WHAT DO YOU KNOW?

Camille is furious with her history professor. "I read the chapter three times, but I still failed the quiz," she fumes. "The quiz must have been unfair." What's wrong with Camille's reasoning, and what are some other possible explanations for her poor performance, based on what you have learned so far in this chapter?

ANSWERS:

Camille is reasoning emotionally and is not examining the assumptions underlying her explanations. Perhaps she relied on automatic rather than effortful encoding, used maintenance instead of elaborative rehearsal, and used shallow instead of deep processing when she studied. She may also have tried to encode everything, instead of being selective.

WHY WE FORGET

Have you ever, in the heat of some deliriously happy moment, said to yourself, "I'll never forget this, never, *never*, NEVER"? Do you find that you can more clearly remember saying those words than the deliriously happy moment itself? Sometimes you encode an event, you rehearse it, you analyze its meaning, you tuck it away in long-term memory—and still, despite all these efforts, you forget it. Is it any wonder that most of us have wished, at one time or another, that memory really was as accurate as a video camera?

Actually, having a perfect long-term memory is not the blessing that you might suppose. The Russian psychologist Alexander Luria (1968) once told of a journalist, S., who could remember giant grids of numbers and could reproduce them both forward and backward, even after the passage of 15 years. S. also remembered the exact circumstances under which he had originally learned the material. He used mnemonics to accomplish his astonishing feats, many involving the formation of visual images. But you shouldn't envy him, for he had a serious problem: He could not forget even when he wanted to. Along with the diamonds of experience, he kept dredging up the pebbles. Images he had formed in order to remember kept creeping into consciousness, distracting him and interfering with his ability to concentrate. At times, he even had trouble holding a conversation because the other person's words would set off a jumble of associations. In fact, Luria called him "rather dull-witted." Eventually, unable to work at his profession, S. took to supporting himself by traveling from place to place, demonstrating his mnemonic abilities for audiences.

Like remembering, then, a certain degree of forgetting enhances our mental functioning. It also contributes to our survival and our sanity, for some things are probably better forgotten. (Think back; would you really want to recall every angry argument, every embarrassing episode, every painful moment in your life?) Nonetheless, most of us forget more than we would like to.

Over a century ago, in an effort to measure pure memory loss independent of personal experience, Hermann Ebbinghaus (1885/1913) memorized long lists of nonsense syllables, such as *bok, waf,* or *ged,* and then tested his retention over a period of several weeks. He reported that most forgetting occurred soon after the initial learning and then leveled off (see Figure 10.6a on the next page). Ebbinghaus's method of studying memory was adopted by generations of psychologists, even though it didn't tell them much about the kinds of memories that people care about most—memories for personal experiences, important ideas, and practical information.

A century later, Marigold Linton decided to find out how people forget real events rather than nonsense syllables. Like Ebbinghaus, she used herself as a subject, but she charted the curve of forgetting over years rather than days. Every day for 12 years she recorded on a 4- × 6-inch card two or more things that had happened to her that day. Eventually, she accumulated a catalogue of thousands of discrete events, both trivial ("I have dinner at the Canton Kitchen: delicious lobster dish") and significant ("I land at Orly Airport in Paris"). Once a month, she took a random sampling of all the cards accumulated to that point, noted whether she could remember the events on them,

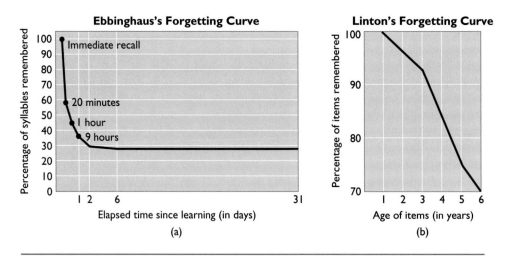

Figure 10.6 *Ebbinghaus's forgetting curve (a) shows that forgetting of nonsense syllables is rapid at first and then tapers off. In contrast, the forgetting curve obtained by Marigold Linton (b), who tested her own memory for personal events over a period of several years, is quite different from that of Ebbinghaus. Her retention was excellent at first, but then it fell off at a gradual but steady rate.*

and tried to date the events. Reporting on the results from the first six years of the study, Linton (1978) told how she had expected the kind of rapid forgetting reported by Ebbinghaus. Instead, as you can see in Figure 10.6b, she found that long-term forgetting was slower and proceeded at a much more constant pace, as details dropped out of her memories.

Of course, some personal memories never lose their distinctiveness. Events that mark important transitions (marriage, getting a first job, having an operation, buying a house) are more memorable than others. But why did Marigold Linton, like the rest of us, forget so many details? Psychologists have proposed several theories to account for forgetting.

The Decay Theory. One commonsense view, the **decay theory,** holds that memory traces fade with time if they are not "accessed" now and then. We have already seen that decay occurs in sensory memory, and that it seems to occur in short-term memory as well, if we don't rehearse the material. However, the mere passage of time does not account so well for forgetting in long-term memory. People commonly forget something that happened only yesterday while still remembering events from many years ago. Indeed, some knowledge remains accessible decades after learning. One

---

decay theory The theory that information in memory eventually disappears if it is not accessed; it applies more to short-term than to long-term memory.

study found that people still did well on a Spanish test as long as 50 years after taking Spanish in high school, although most had hardly used Spanish at all in the intervening years (Bahrick, 1984). Decay alone, then, cannot explain lapses in long-term memory.

New Memories for Old. Another explanation holds that new information can completely wipe out old information, just as rerecording on an audiotape or videotape will obliterate the original material. Recall the study by Elizabeth Loftus and her colleagues, described earlier on page 353, in which people who had been misled into thinking that they had seen a stop sign or a yield sign continued to insist that their memories were accurate even after being told the purpose of the study. These findings suggest that the subjects' original perception may have been "erased" by the misleading information.

Interference. A third theory holds that forgetting occurs because similar items of information interfere with one another in either storage or retrieval; the information is in memory, but it becomes confused with other information. This type of forgetting, which occurs in both short- and long-term memory, is especially common when you have to recall isolated facts.

Suppose you are at a party and you meet someone named Julie. A half hour later you meet someone named Judy. You go on to talk to other people, and after an hour, you again bump into Julie, but by mistake you call her Judy. The second name has interfered with your memory for the first. This type of interference, in which new information interferes with the ability to remember similiar information stored previously, is called **retroactive** (see Figure 10.7a). Retroactive interference is sometimes illustrated by a story about an absent-minded professor of ichthyology (the study of fish) who complained that whenever he learned the name of a new student he forgot the name of a fish.

Because new information is constantly entering memory, we are all vulnerable to the effects of retroactive interference—or at least most of us are. Studies of H. M. find that his memories of childhood and adolescence are unusually detailed and clear, and they rarely change. H. M. can remember actors and singers famous in his childhood, the films they were in, and who their costars were. He knows the names of friends from the second grade. Presumably, these declarative memories from early in life have not been subject to interference from new memories since the operation—because there have been no new memories!

Interference also works in the opposite direction. Old information (such as the Spanish you learned in high school) may interfere with the ability to remember new information (such as the French you're trying to learn now). This type of interference is called **proactive** (see Figure 10.7b). Over a period of weeks, months, and years,

---

retroactive interference Forgetting that occurs when recently learned material interferes with the ability to remember similar material stored previously.

proactive interference Forgetting that occurs when previously stored material interferes with the ability to remember similar, more recently learned material.

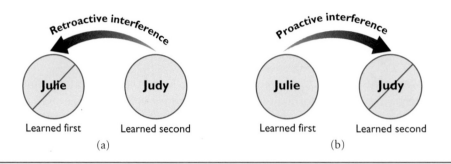

Figure 10.7 *Retroactive interference (a) occurs when new information interferes with memory for previously stored material. Proactive interference (b) occurs when previously stored material interferes with memory for new information.*

proactive interference may cause more forgetting than retroactive interference does, because we have stored up so much information that can potentially interfere with anything new. Fortunately, we can also use our old information to elaboratively encode new information and thus improve our ability to remember.

Motivated Forgetting. Sigmund Freud maintained that people forget because they block from consciousness those memories that are too threatening or painful to live with, and he called this self-protective process *repression.* Today, many psychologists prefer a more general term, **motivated forgetting,** and they argue that a person might be motivated to forget certain events for many reasons, including embarrassment, guilt, shock, and a desire to protect one's pride. Motivated forgetting could explain some cases of **retrograde amnesia,** in which people can remember historical incidents and form new memories but forget friends, relatives, or painful experiences from the past.

The concepts of repression and motivated forgetting are based mostly on clinical reports of people in psychotherapy who appear to recall long-buried memories, typically of traumatic events in childhood. Only rarely, however, have such memories been corroborated by objective evidence, so it is difficult and often impossible to know whether the recollections have been accurately retrieved or reconstructed. This is why the concept of repression remains extremely controversial among psychological scientists (Holmes, 1990). We will discuss repression further in Chapter 16, in evaluating the psychodynamic perspective.

Cue-dependent Forgetting. Often, when we need to remember, we rely on *retrieval cues,* items of information that can help us find the specific information we're looking for. When we lack such cues, we may feel as if we have lost the call number for an entry

---

motivated forgetting Forgetting that occurs because of a desire to eliminate awareness of painful, embarrassing, or otherwise unpleasant experiences.

retrograde amnesia Loss of the ability to remember events or experiences that occurred before some particular point in time.

in the mind's library. This type of memory failure, which psychologists call **cue-dependent forgetting,** may be the most common type of all. Willem Wagenaar (1986), who, like Marigold Linton, recorded critical details about events in his life, found that within a year, he had forgotten 20 percent of those details, and after five years, he had forgotten 60 percent. However, when he gathered cues from witnesses about ten events that he thought he had nearly forgotten, he was able to recall more about all ten, which suggests that some of his forgetting was cue-dependent.

Cognitive psychologists think that retrieval cues work by getting us into the general area of memory where an item is stored, or by making a match with information that is linked in memory with the item in question. Thus, if you are trying to remember the last name of an actor, knowing the person's first name or the name of a recent movie the actor starred in might help. Cues that were present at the time you learned a new fact or had an experience are apt to be especially useful as retrieval aids. That may explain why remembering is often easier when you are in the same physical environment as you were when an event occurred: Cues in the present context match those from the past. Many people have suggested that the overlap between present and past cues may also lead to a *false* sense of having been in exactly the same situation before; this is the eerie phenomenon of *déjà vu* (which means "already seen" in French). Ordinarily, however, contextual cues help us remember the past more accurately.

Because of this finding, many police departments have altered the way they interview witnesses to a crime. The old way was to direct a set of linear questions at the witness: "Then what did he do? And then what happened after that?" The new way is to encourage witnesses to reconstruct the circumstances of the crime and to recall *without interruption* everything they can about what they saw, even details that seem unimportant. Such "cognitive interview" strategies often increase the number of available retrieval cues and produce better recall than standard "and-then-what-did-he-do" techniques (Fisher & Geiselman, 1992).

Your mental or physical state may also act as a retrieval cue, evoking a **state-dependent memory.** For example, if you are intoxicated when something happens, you may remember it better when you once again have had a few drinks than when you are sober. (This is not an endorsement of drunkenness! Your memory will be best if you are sober during both encoding and recall.) Likewise, if your emotional arousal is especially high or low at the time of an event, you may remember that event best when you are once again in the same emotional state. When victims of violent crimes have trouble recalling details of the experience, it may be in part because they are far less emotionally aroused than they were at the time of the crime (Clark, Milberg, & Erber, 1987).

Some researchers have proposed that retrieval of a memory is also more likely when a person's *mood* is the same as it was when the memory was first encoded and stored, presumably because mood serves as a retrieval cue. Findings on this notion,

---

cue-dependent forgetting The inability to retrieve information stored in memory because of insufficient cues for recall.

state-dependent memory The tendency to remember something when one is in the same physical or mental state as during the original learning or experience.

however, have been frustratingly inconsistent, possibly because the effect depends on many factors, such as the strength and sincerity of the mood, the nature of the event, and the way the memory is retrieved (Eich, 1995). Clearer support exists for a somewhat different idea, that what really counts is the match between your current mood and the *kind of material* being remembered. In most studies, this effect has been modest but reliable. It is strongest when people are feeling happy; in other words, you are more likely to remember happy events or ideas when you are feeling happy than when you are feeling sad (Mayer, McCormick, & Strong, 1995).

What Do You Know?

If you haven't repressed what you just read, try these questions.

1. Ever since she read *Even Cowgirls Get the Blues* many years ago, Wilma has loved the novels of Tom Robbins. Nowadays, one of her favorite actors is Tim Robbins, but every time she tries to recall his name she calls him "Tom." Why?
2. When a man at his twentieth high school reunion sees his old friends, he recalls incidents he had thought were long forgotten. Why?

Answers:

1. proactive interference   2. The sight of his friends has provided retrieval cues for the incidents.

Autobiographical Memories

Memory provides each of us with a sense of identity that evolves and changes as we build up a store of episodic memories about events we have experienced firsthand. For most of us, the memories we have of our own lives are by far the most fascinating. We use them as entertainment ("Did I ever tell you about the time . . . ?"); we manipulate them—some people even publish them—in order to create a certain image; we analyze them to learn more about who we are (Ross, 1989).

Childhood Amnesia

One curious aspect of autobiographical memory is that most adults cannot recall any events from earlier than the third or fourth year of life. A few people apparently can recall momentous experiences that occurred when they were as young as two years old, such as the birth of a sibling, but not earlier (Usher & Neisser, 1993). Of course, we all retain many procedural memories from the toddler stage, when we first learned to use a fork, drink from a cup, and pull a wagon. We also retain semantic memories acquired early in life: the rules of counting, the names of people and things, knowledge about all manner of objects in the world. But as adults, we cannot remember being fed in infancy by our parents, taking our first steps, or uttering our first halting sentences. We are victims of **childhood amnesia** (sometimes called *infantile amnesia*).

People often find childhood amnesia difficult to accept. There is something disturbing about the fact that our early years are beyond recall—so disturbing that some people adamantly deny it, claiming to remember events from the second or even the first year of life. But most psychologists believe these memories are merely reconstructions based on photographs, family stories, and imagination. The "remembered" event may not even have taken place.

Swiss psychologist Jean Piaget (1951) once reported a memory of nearly being kidnapped at the age of 2. Piaget remembered sitting in his pram, watching his nurse as she bravely defended him from the kidnapper. He remembered the scratches she received on her face. He remembered a police officer with a short cloak and white baton who finally chased the kidnapper away. There was only one small problem: None of it happened. When Piaget was 15, his nurse wrote to his parents confessing that she had made up the entire story. Piaget noted, "I therefore must have heard, as a child, the account of this story . . . and projected it into the past in the form of a visual memory, which was a memory of a memory, but false."

Some biological researchers believe that childhood amnesia occurs because either hippocampal or cortical areas involved in the formation or storage of events are not well developed until a few years after birth (McKee & Squire, 1993; Nadel & Zola-Morgan, 1984; Schacter & Moscovitch, 1984). In contrast, cognitive scientists emphasize possible cognitive reasons for the amnesia of the first years. For example, Mark Howe and Mary Courage (1993) argue that "It is the emergence of the cognitive self that is pivotal to the establishment of autobiographical memory." As this hypothesis would predict, age differences in the emergence of a self-concept, not chronological age per se, are related to the age at which autobiographical memories begin (Howe, Courage, & Peterson, 1994).

Cognitive theories of childhood amnesia can help solve an interesting riddle: Some babies who are only one to two years old do remember past experiences, and some four-year-olds can remember experiences that occurred before age two and a half (Bauer & Dow, 1994; Bauer & Fivush, 1992; Bauer & Hertsgaard, 1993; McDonough & Mandler, 1995). But these memories are not preserved into later childhood or adulthood. Why? One answer is that as adults, we use very different cognitive schemas from those we used in early childhood; these adult schemas are not useful for reconstructing early events from the memory fragments we stored at the time (Howe & Courage, 1993). Only after we enter school do we learn to think as adults do, using language to organize our memories and storing not only events but also what we think about them. In addition, as preschoolers, we may encode our experiences far less elaborately than we do as

---

childhood (infantile) amnesia   The inability to remember events and experiences that occurred during the first two or three years of life.

adults because our information-processing abilities are still limited. As a result, we may have few cues for retrieving our early memories later on in life (White & Pillemer, 1979).

Longitudinal research with children suggests still other cognitive explanations for the puzzling loss of early memories. Preschoolers are trying to figure out how the world works, and they tend to focus on the routine, familiar aspects of an experience (eating lunch, going to sleep, playing with toys) rather than the distinctive aspects that make the event memorable in the long run. Also, young children have not yet mastered the social conventions for reporting events; they do not know what is important and interesting to others. Instead, they tend to rely on adults' questions to provide retrieval cues ("Where did we go for breakfast?" "Who did you go trick-or-treating with?"), and this dependency on adults may prevent them from building up a stable core of remembered material that will continue to be available when they are older (Fivush & Hamond, 1991).

Whatever the explanation for childhood amnesia, our first memories may provide some useful insights into our personalities. Some psychologists believe that these memories are not random but instead reflect our concerns, ambitions, and attitudes toward life (Kihlstrom & Harackiewicz, 1982). What are your own first memories? Do you think the kinds of events and experiences you recall reveal anything important about you? The early psychologist Lloyd Morgan once wrote that an autobiography "is a story of oneself in the past, read in the light of one's present self." That is just what our private memories are.

Memory and Narrative: The Stories of Our Lives

In the introduction to this perspective, we noted George Gerbner's observation that our species is unique because we tell stories and live by the stories we tell. This view of human beings as the "storytelling animal" is sweeping cognitive psychology and related fields (Sarbin, 1986). Researchers find that the narratives we compose to make sense of our lives have a profound influence on us: Our plans, memories, love affairs, hatreds, ambitions, and dreams are all guided by plot outlines. "Understanding one's past, interpreting one's actions, evaluating future possibilities—each is filtered through these stories," writes Mary Gergen (1992).

Thus we say, "I am this way because, as a small child, this happened to me, and then my parents . . ." We say, "Let me tell you the story of how we fell in love." We say, "When you hear what happened, you'll understand why I felt entitled to take such cold-hearted revenge." These stories are not necessarily fictions, as in the child's meaning of "tell me a story." Rather, they are narratives that provide a unifying theme to organize the events of our lives and give them meaning.

But because the narratives of our lives rely on memory, and because memories are constructed and dynamic, constantly shifting in response to present needs and experiences, our stories are also, to some degree, works of interpretation and imagination. Adult memories thus reveal as much about the present as they do about the past. From his own research and that of others, Michael Ross (1989) has concluded that even when we appear to remember what we said, did, or believed months or years ago, many of our memories are actually based on our present traits and beliefs, and also on our *implicit theories* about how much certain traits or beliefs can change. The theories are "implicit" because we may never have expressed them to anyone, even ourselves.

For example, Ross finds that most people have an implicit theory that feelings and attitudes are consistent over time. As a result, whether recalling their past opinions of a dating partner, their past drug use, or their past incomes, they tend to think that they have not changed much—even when the evidence shows that they have. In one study, 91 percent of people who had changed their political affiliations in a four-year period reported that they had *not* changed (Niemi, Katz, & Newman, 1980). Remarkably, if they were currently Republicans, they forgot that they had only recently voted Democratic, and vice versa!

Conversely, when people's implicit theories do predict change, they are likely to forget evidence that they haven't really changed much at all. An implicit theory predicting change, Ross observes, seems to explain why (as we saw in Chapter 5) many women "remember" mood changes associated with their menstrual cycles, even when their own daily diaries fail to confirm such changes. Implicit theories of change also raise a problem in evaluating self-help programs, because most people have an implicit theory that these programs will improve their lives. As a result, they remember themselves as having been worse off before the program than they really were (Conway & Ross, 1984).

An understanding of the importance of narrative helps us appreciate some features of how memory works and why it fails. As we age, certain periods of our lives stand out; old people remember more from adolescence and early adulthood than from midlife, a phenomenon known as the "reminiscence bump" (Fitzgerald, 1988; MacKavey, Malley, & Stewart, 1991). Perhaps the younger years are especially memorable because they are full of memorable transitions. Or perhaps, as narrative research suggests, people are especially likely to weave events from their youth into a coherent story and thus remember them better ("After I graduated from college I met the love of my life, who dumped me in the most cruel and heartless fashion, and before I knew it . . .").

Yet, as we have seen throughout this chapter, many of the details of our memories, even those we are sure we remember so clearly, probably are added after the event. By now, you should not be surprised that memory can be as fickle as it can be accurate. As cognitive psychologists have shown repeatedly, we are not merely actors in our personal life dramas. We also write the scripts.

✦ ✦ ✦

Summary

1. Memory, the capacity to retain and retrieve information, confers competence and personal identity. Unlike a tape recorder or video camera, it is highly selective and is *reconstructive*: People add, delete, and change elements in ways that help them

make sense of information and events. Because memory is reconstructive, people sometimes confuse imagined events with actual ones, especially when the person has thought about the imagined event many times; the image of the event contains many details; it is easy to imagine the event; and the person focuses on his or her emotional reactions rather than what actually happened.

2. People who mistakenly believe that all memories are permanently stored with perfect accuracy often cite studies of recall under hypnosis, studies of electrical brain stimulation, and studies of emotionally powerful memories that seem permanent (*flashbulb memories*). All three lines of evidence, however, fail to support such a belief. Under hypnosis, people confabulate, and the same is true in studies of electrical brain stimulation. Even flashbulb memories may be embellished or distorted, and they tend to change over time.

3. The reconstructive nature of memory raises problems in legal cases involving eyewitness testimony. Errors are especially likely when the suspect's race differs from that of the witness and when leading questions are put to witnesses.

4. The ability to remember depends in part on the type of performance being called for. In tests of *explicit memory* (conscious recollection), *recognition* is usually better than *recall.* In tests of *implicit memory,* which is measured by indirect methods such as *priming,* past experiences may affect current thoughts or actions even when these experiences are not consciously and intentionally remembered. The *relearning method* seems to straddle the boundary between explicit and implicit tests.

5. *Information-processing models* depict memory as the encoding, storage, and retrieval of information. In these models, sensory information is changed in form almost as soon as it is detected, as a person integrates the information into existing *cognitive schemas* and simplifies the information by storing it in the form of propositions, images, or sets of instructions. Some kinds of information require effortful, as opposed to automatic, encoding.

6. The "three-box model" has dominated research on memory for three decades, but it does not explain all the findings on memory, and competing models also exist. Some cognitive scientists have rejected the traditional information-processing approach and computer metaphors for the mind in favor of a *parallel distributed processing (PDP)* or *connectionist* model. In PDP models, knowledge is represented as connections among numerous interacting processing units, distributed in a vast network and all operating in parallel. Computer scientists are now designing machines called *neural networks* that attempt to imitate the brain's grid of densely connected neurons, and researchers in the field of *artificial intelligence* have been writing programs that simulate the way PDP theorists believe the human mind works. Nonetheless, the three-box model continues to offer a convenient way to organize the major findings on memory, and it fits the known biological facts about memory.

7. In most information-processing models of memory, incoming sensory information makes a brief stop in *sensory memory,* which temporarily retains it in the form of literal sensory images, such as *icons* and *echoes,* so that it can be further

processed. Pattern recognition occurs during the transfer of information from sensory memory to short-term memory. Sensory memory acts as a filter, keeping out extraneous and unimportant information.

8. *Short-term memory (STM)* retains new information for up to 30 seconds by most estimates (unless *rehearsal* takes place) and also acts as a *working memory* for the processing of information retrieved from long-term memory for temporary use. The capacity of STM is extremely limited but can be extended if information is organized into larger units by *chunking*. Items that are meaningful, have an emotional impact, or link up to something already in long-term memory may enter long-term storage easily with only a brief stay in STM.

9. *Long-term memory (LTM)* contains a vast amount of information that must be organized and indexed. For example, words (or the concepts they represent) seem to be organized by semantic categories. Many models of long-term memory represent its contents as a network of interrelated concepts and propositions. The way people use these networks depends on experience and education. Words are also indexed in LTM in terms of sound and form.

10. *Procedural memories* are memories for how to perform specific actions; *declarative memories* are memories for abstract or representational knowledge. Declarative memories include *semantic memories* and *episodic memories.*

11. The three-box model has often been invoked to explain the *serial-position effect* in memory, but it cannot explain why a *recency effect* sometimes occurs when it shouldn't and why even rats and birds show the serial-position effect.

12. Rehearsal is a technique for keeping information in short-term memory and increasing the chances of long-term retention. *Elaborative rehearsal* is more likely to result in transfer to long-term memory than is *maintenance rehearsal,* and *deep processing* is usually a more effective retention strategy than *shallow processing.* *Mnemonics* can also enhance retention by promoting elaborative encoding and making material meaningful, but for ordinary memory tasks, complex memory tricks are often ineffective or even counterproductive. People who do well on tests of *metamemory* tend to remember well.

13. Forgetting can occur for several reasons. Information in sensory and short-term memory appears to *decay* if it does not receive further processing. New information may "erase" old information in long-term memory. *Proactive* and *retroactive* interference may occur. Some lapses in long-term memory may be due to *motivated forgetting,* although it is hard to confirm the validity of "repressed" memories that are subsequently recalled. Finally, *cue-dependent forgetting* may occur when retrieval cues are inadequate. The most effective retrieval cues are those that were present at the time of the initial experience. A person's mood or physical state may also act as a retrieval cue, evoking a *state-dependent memory.*

14. Because of *childhood (infantile) amnesia,* most people cannot recall any events from earlier than the third or fourth year of life. The reason may be biological, but many cognitive explanations have also been proposed: the lack of a "cognitive self" in the first few years of life; the child's reliance on cognitive schemas that differ from those used later; the fact that young children encode experiences less

elaboratively; and children's focus on routine rather than distinctive aspects of an experience.

15. A person's narrative or "life story" organizes the events of his or her life and gives it meaning. Narratives change as people build up a store of episodic memories. Many memories seem to be based on people's current traits and beliefs, and also on their *implicit theories* of how much particular traits or beliefs can change. Life stories are, to some degree, works of interpretation and imagination.

Key Terms

reconstruction (in memory) *345*

anterograde amnesia *345*

source amnesia *346*

flashbulb memories *349*

leading questions *352*

explicit memory *354*

recall *354*

recognition *354*

implicit memory *355*

priming *355*

relearning method *355*

information-processing models *356*

encoding *356*

cognitive schema *356*

proposition *357*

effortful/automatic encoding *357*

storage *357*

retrieval *357*

"three-box model" *358*

parallel distributed processing (PDP) models *359*

neural networks *359*

artificial intelligence *359*

sensory memory *360*

sensory registers *360*

   icons *360*

   echoes *360*

pattern recognition *360*

short-term memory (STM) *361*

working memory *362*

chunks *363*

long-term memory (LTM) *363*

semantic categories *364*

tip-of-the-tongue state *364*

procedural memories *366*

declarative memories *366*

   semantic memories *366*

   episodic memories *366*

serial-position effect *366*

primacy and recency effects *366*

rehearsal *368*

   maintenance rehearsal *370*

   elaborative rehearsal *370*

deep versus shallow processing *371*

mnemonics *371*

metamemory *372*

decay theory *374*

retroactive interference *375*

proactive interference *375*

motivated forgetting/repression *376*

retrograde amnesia *376*

cue-dependent forgetting *377*

retrieval cues *377*

Answers to the "Seven Dwarfs" test on page 354: Dopey, Sneezy, Sleepy, Bashful, Doc, Grumpy, and Happy.

CHAPTER 11

Evaluating the Cognitive Perspective

$\mathcal{H}$ave you ever found yourself in one of these situations?

You have a big job interview tomorrow, and you want to be sure to get a good night's sleep, but you are having difficulty dozing off. You tell yourself to relax, forget your worries, and just *sleep*. But the more you worry about falling asleep, the wider awake you feel. Or . . .

You want to lose a few pounds, so you vow to distract yourself and not even *think* about food. But the more distracted you try to get, the more your thoughts keep returning to the refrigerator and mouth-watering visions of your favorite fattening foods. Or . . .

You have read the same paragraph three times and still don't know what it said. Your eyes are tracking the words, but your brain seems to be out to lunch. You tell yourself to really, really concentrate this time. But the more you try to concentrate, the more you "gray out" mentally. Or . . .

You get the idea. We have all had annoying experiences like these, when we not only fail to do what we want but also actually find ourselves doing the opposite. As Daniel Wegner (1994) writes, "Our attempts at mental control fall short so often that we may stop to wonder . . . whether there is some part of our minds, an imp of the perverse, that ironically strives to compel our errors." As Wegner wryly adds, "It does not take a great deal of psychological sophistication to notice that people have serious deficiencies in the ability to control their mental activities."

The cognitive perspective, however, goes beyond this obvious fact. By building models of how the mind operates, it helps us to understand our mental shortcomings, and even overcome them.

CONTRIBUTIONS OF THIS PERSPECTIVE

Since the turn toward cognitive explanations of behavior in the 1960s, the cognitive perspective has dramatically transformed the study of psychology. Here are just a few of this perspective's major contributions to the field:

1 INNOVATIVE METHODS FOR EXPLORING THE "BLACK BOX" OF THE MIND. As we saw in Chapter 7, behaviorists have sometimes compared the mind to an engineer's hypothetical "black box"; the processes within the box, they argue, are irrelevant for understanding human behavior, and in any case, they cannot be known. Cognitive psychologists, however, have challenged that claim by devising ingenious methods for peering into the black box. Jean Piaget asked children to compare different quantities, and from their performance, he was able to draw inferences about the mental processes necessary for understanding conservation. Karen Kitchener and Patricia King had adolescents and adults explain their positions on a variety of issues, and from the responses, they were able to discern differences in the reasoning processes of prereflective, quasi-reflective, and reflective thinkers. Leon Festinger and his associates infiltrated a doomsday group and found out how people respond to new information when it conflicts with their existing beliefs. Nicholas Spanos and his colleagues hypnotized college students and discovered that the students' accounts of "past lives" were affected by their knowledge (or ignorance) of history. Elizabeth Loftus and her associates asked people leading questions and showed that the mind incorporates misinformation into its reconstructions of events. Other memory researchers have used the subtle method of priming to uncover implicit memories that cannot be consciously retrieved but that nonetheless continue to affect behavior. And these are only a few of the many creative strategies devised by researchers in the cognitive perspective.

2 AN UNDERSTANDING OF HOW COGNITION AFFECTS BEHAVIOR. Behaviorists, you may recall, have never denied that people think and remember, but they have denied that these internal events *explain* behavior. In the behaviorist view, cognitions are themselves simply behaviors, to be accounted for in terms of reinforcement and punishment. Psychologists who take a cognitive perspective, however, have produced convincing evidence that cognitions often do, in fact, explain the way people act and feel.

Consider, for example, the influence of attributions, which we discussed in Chapter 9 (page 332). One place where attributions affect behavior is in marriage: Unhappy spouses are more likely than happy ones to attribute marital problems to their partners' stable *dispositions,* blaming the person's selfishness, meanness, or thoughtlessness. Happy spouses, in contrast, are more likely to attribute marital problems to the *situation,* blaming the stress the partner is under, a lack of time together because of work and family obligations, and so forth. Although it's probably true that being happy or dissatisfied can affect each partner's attributions, longitudinal research shows that attributions also affect the happiness of marriage partners and the long-term success of their marriages (Fincham & Bradbury, 1993; Karney et al., 1994).

Here's another example of how attributions can influence actions. In a clever study done two decades ago, researchers set out to convince fifth-grade children not to litter. Children in one class were subjected to standard persuasion techniques: lectures on how littering increases pollution, a visit by the principal to discuss the need for tidy classrooms, posters saying "Don't be a litterbug," a reminder from the janitor to pick up papers on the floor, and so forth. (Parents and teachers, of course, often rely on scolding and lecturing; kids call it "nagging.") In a second class, the attribution group, the teacher sought to instill a dispositional attribution in the students—"We are the sort of people who don't litter." The teacher pointed out some paper on the floor, saying, "Our class is clean and would not do that"; the principal commented on how orderly the classroom looked; a poster saying "We are Andersen's Litter-Conscious Class" was pinned to the bulletin board; the janitor left a note saying the room was easy to clean. On the tenth day, an experimenter posing as a marketing representative for a candy company told the children she was testing the tastiness of a new brand of candy and gave each student a piece. During recess, the experimenters simply counted the number of candy wrappers in the wastebaskets, on the floor, and in desk seats. The result: Littering in the attribution group fell much more than in the persuasion group or in a control group that got neither treatment, presumably because the children felt a need to avoid cognitive dissonance and live up to their new self-concept as "nonlitterers" (Miller, Brickman, & Bolen, 1975).

Many other studies have confirmed that if you want people to make long-lasting changes in their behavior, you often need to give them an opportunity to construct their own internal justifications for the desired actions. Lectures and extrinsic reinforces aren't enough: You need to change their attitudes and attributions.

3 STRATEGIES FOR IMPROVING MENTAL ABILITIES. One of the most important lessons from the cognitive perspective is the value of intellectual humility and the danger of intellectual arrogance. As cognitive research has shown so clearly, we are far from being rational creatures; our reasoning can go awry, we may get mired in mental ruts, and our memories are frighteningly fallible. Overcoming the many barriers to clear and effective thought is a lifelong process. Yet even as this perspective makes us aware of our mental limitations, it offers techniques for overcoming them. We can immunize ourselves against biases; we can create the conditions that allow creativity to blossom; we can learn to reason dialectically and to make judgments reflectively; we can adopt strategies that make our memories more reliable.

Research on memory, for example, has not only helped individuals remember more accurately but has also contributed to better identification techniques in criminal cases. The traditional method, asking witnesses to look at individuals in a lineup and pick out the perpetrator, has a serious drawback: Sometimes witnesses pick the one most like the person they saw, even when *all* the participants in the lineup are innocent (Wells, 1993). Cognitive research has found the solution: The witness views the lineup members one at a time, without being told how many will be viewed, and must respond to each one individually, without ever going back to an earlier member. That way, the witness compares each person with his or her memory of the offender and not with the other participants in the lineup. This procedure reduces false identifications without reducing correct ones (Wells, Luus, & Windschitl, 1994).

Findings from the cognitive perspective can also help people make wiser decisions, solve problems, and understand the development of cognitive abilities—their own and those of their children. For example, cognitive research shows that, as Piaget said, children are not always ready to learn what adults want to teach them. On the other hand, research also shows that parents can do a great deal to nurture and enhance their children's cognitive development. Children's mental abilities improve when parents spend time with them; encourage them to think things through; read to them; provide toys and field trips; and expect them to do well (Bradley & Caldwell,

1984; Bradley et al., 1989; Lewis, 1993). Children's cognitive skills also develop more rapidly when their parents *talk* to them about many topics and describe things accurately and fully (Clarke-Stewart, VanderStoep & Killian, 1979; Sigman et al., 1988). By answering their children's questions and responding to their actions, parents can show their children that their efforts matter.

Fortunately, these parenting skills can be taught. In one study, 30 middle-class parents learned, during two brief training sessions, to ask open-ended questions when reading to their toddlers ("What is the cat doing?") instead of merely asking the children to point out objects or answer yes–no type questions ("Is the cat asleep?"). The parents also learned to expand on the children's answers, provide alternative responses, correct inaccurate responses, and give plenty of praise. Parents in a control group read just as often to their children but did not get the special instruction. After only a month, the children in the experimental group were eight and a half months ahead of those in the control group in their expressive language skills and six months ahead of them in vocabulary skills (Whitehurst et al., 1988). A similar study, in which parents and child-care teachers read interactively with low-income children, also produced highly significant vocabulary gains (Whitehurst et al., 1994). The implications are enormous when you consider that by one estimate, the average low-income child enters first grade with only 25 hours of one-on-one picture-book reading, compared to 1,000 to 1,700 hours for middle-class children (Adams, 1990).

The cognitive perspective also alerts us to other influences on mental abilities, such as technology. For example, a review of studies found that because television supplies the viewer with ready-made visual images, it often suppresses the development of imagination and novel ideas (Valkenburg & van der Voort, 1994). Children remember more details of a story when they see it on TV than when they hear it on radio, because visual images help memory; but their thinking becomes more *imaginative* when they hear the story on radio, because they have to imagine what the characters look like and what they are doing (Greenfield & Beagles-Roos, 1988). The replacement of reading by television watching may also be contributing to a growing inability of young people to use dialectical reasoning and reflective judgment, and an unwillingness to spend time searching for answers to intellectual problems (Suedfield et al., 1986). Television, say its critics, gives us "sound bites" instead of well-developed arguments, and thus it discourages people from analyzing issues and weighing opposing points of view in order to reach thoughtful conclusions. In contrast, reading requires us to sit still and follow extended arguments; it gives us the opportunity to examine connections among statements and to spot contradictions. As writer Mitchell Stephens (1991) notes, "All television demands is our gaze."

Yet the cognitive perspective also suggests antidotes to the mindlessness of television. One is *mindful* television viewing, in which you analyze and discuss with others what you are seeing. Studies find that mindful watching can be intellectually enriching (Langer & Piper, 1988). Another is careful selection of programs. A study of preschoolers in a low-income area found that children who watched educational programs such as *Sesame Street* did better at age 5 than would have been expected on tests of math and verbal skills, school readiness, and vocabulary, whereas preschoolers who watched mainly adult shows and cartoons did worse (Huston & Wright, 1995).

Research from this perspective, then, can equip us to act more intelligently, avoid tripping over mental roadblocks, and help children fulfill their intellectual potential.

MISUSES AND MISINTERPRETATIONS
OF THIS PERSPECTIVE

Despite its many contributions, this perspective, like every other, has its limitations. Perhaps the most common criticism of the cognitive approach is that its models of the mind are all based on metaphors—a problem that behaviorists have been pointing out for years. Are there really three "boxes" for sensory, short-term, and long-term memory? Does the mind work like a computer? Do implicit and explicit memories involve different brain systems, or simply different encoding strategies? At present, many competing models seem equally convincing. Cognitive psychologist Howard Gardner (1985) has noted that without a decisive way to distinguish one information-processing model from another, cognitive psychology might end up with as many convincing diagrams of the mind as there are ingenious researchers to think them up!

Further, the cognitive perspective, like all others, can be misused when its findings are poorly understood or incorrectly applied. Misuse of this perspective results in three common errors:

1 COGNITIVE REDUCTIONISM. Enthusiasm about the cognitive revolution has caused some people to reduce all human behavior to what goes on in people's minds. Those who are inclined to think in a reductionist fashion may infer that to solve personal problems or the world's problems, all we need to do is think a little differently about things. Many self-help and transformational programs preach just this kind of simplistic message, which can lead people to feel responsible for bad experiences that are entirely beyond their control.

Some pop-psych writers even claim that "No one gets sick unless they want to be sick" and conversely that "The power of positive thinking can always get you well." It is true that cognitive factors—such as having a sense of humor, being optimistic, and feeling in control of events—have a powerful effect on behavior, mental and physical health, and the speed of recovery from illness, as we saw in Chapter 7. Yet the fact that cognition plays an important role in health does not mean that cognitive factors are the *only* factors of importance. Serious diseases, poverty, unemployment, and injustice cannot be treated with jokes and positive thinking alone. Mind does matter, but it is not all that matters.

2 ERRORS OF CAUSE AND EFFECT. In their understandable excitement about the power of attitudes, reasoning, and beliefs to influence behavior, some people overlook the fact that the relationship between mind and body, or between thoughts and circumstances, is a two-way street. Believing that you have control over your life may affect your health, but the state of your health also affects how much control you think you have (Rodin, 1988). High motivation and the "right attitude" can help people get out of miserable circumstances, but miserable circumstances—such as living with chronic poverty, violence, drug abuse, or unemployment—can also suppress motivation and optimism. Cognitive psychologists have shown how "life stories" or narratives influence a person's decisions and goals, but actual events also shape those narratives (Howard, 1991). Negative, pessimistic thoughts can cause depression, but being depressed also makes people more likely to hold negative, pessimistic thoughts.

3 COGNITIVE RELATIVISM. Another misreading of the cognitive perspective leads to cognitive relativism: the assumption that all ideas, thoughts, or memories have an equal claim to be taken seriously. This belief is the very *opposite* of what cognitive research shows. As we have seen, some thinking is rational and reflective, and some is not; some beliefs are based on evidence, and some are not; some memories are accurate, and some are not; some ways of managing problems are creative and fruitful, and some are not. However, as findings from the cognitive perspective make their way into the popular media, people sometimes draw the erroneous conclusion that if cognitions are important, they must also be valid—that if your interpretation of events is true for you, that's all that matters; never mind what the evidence shows. This is an example of the quasi-reflective thinking that Patricia King and Karen Kitchener (1994) have studied (see Chapter 9).

Cognitive relativism leads to the belief that there are at least two sides to every issues, and that all sides must have equal merit. For example, as we saw in Chapter 1, some people claim that the Holocaust never happened; but there are not two equally valid sides to this question, any more than there are two sides to whether the United States had a civil war. Similarly, some religious fundamentalists (but not most other religious people) believe that the earth and all its species were created in six days, just a few thousand years ago. They argue that "creation science" should get equal time with evolution in biology and geology classes; indeed, "equal treatment" laws have been passed in several states. But from a scientific point of view, there are not two sides to this issue, because creationist doctrine is refuted by all known facts about the development of the earth and its species (Shermer, 1997). Scientists may and do debate the nature and pace of evolution; but they do so based on evidence and scholarship.

If we take the cognitive perspective seriously, we must be prepared to analyze not only the beliefs, biases, memories, and reasoning processes of others but also our own. The cognitive perspective teaches us to reject mindlessness and to become more aware of why we think and behave as we do. Let's look now at three issues that show the promise of this perspective: improving intelligence; cognitive psychotherapy and emotional well-being; and children's eyewitness testimony.

WHAT DO YOU KNOW?

1. Name three contributions of the cognitive perspective and three common errors resulting from its misuse.

2. A motivational speaker exhorts his audience to think more positively about becoming wealthy; getting rich, he says, is all a matter of having the right attitudes. What error, discussed in the previous section, is the speaker making?

ANSWERS:

money the person has to begin with.
opportunities, the general state of the economy, the needs of the marketplace, and how much
but attitudes alone cannot guarantee wealth. Amassing wealth also depends on an individual's
2. The speaker is guilty of cognitive reductionism. Attitudes are important to financial success,
Errors include cognitive reductionism, confusion of cause and effect, and cognitive relativism.
understanding of how cognition affects behavior, and strategies for improving mental abilities.
1. Contributions include innovative methods for exploring the "black box" of the mind, an

---

ISSUE 1: BECOMING MORE INTELLIGENT

Most of us would not mind being a little smarter. But until recently, psychologists have been better at measuring intelligence than at improving it. Most test constructors have taken a *psychometric* approach to mental abilities, focusing on how well people perform—that is, on whether they get the right answers—and not on changing that performance. Newer approaches, however, inspired by cognitive findings and information-processing models of the mind, recognize that intelligence involves many skills, such as encoding problems, noticing similarities and differences, spotting fallacies, and "reading" the environment and other people. These approaches therefore emphasize the *strategies* people use to solve problems. The goal is not merely to measure mental ability but also to understand it and help people use it.

One promising theory, Robert Sternberg's *triarchic theory of intelligence* (1988), distinguishes three aspects of intelligence:

1. COMPONENTIAL INTELLIGENCE includes information-processing strategies that go on inside a person's head when the person is thinking intelligently about a problem. These mental "components" include recognizing the problem, selecting a method for solving it, mastering and carrying out the strategy, and evaluating the result. People who are strong in componential intelligence tend to do well on conventional tests of intelligence.

2. EXPERIENTIAL INTELLIGENCE refers to how well you transfer skills to new situations. People with experiential intelligence cope well with novelty and learn quickly to make new tasks automatic; those who are lacking in this area perform well only under a narrow set of circumstances. For example, a student may do well in school, where assignments have due dates and feedback is immediate, but may be less successful after graduation if her job requires her to set her own deadlines, and her employer doesn't tell her how she is doing.

3. CONTEXTUAL INTELLIGENCE refers to the practical application of intelligence, which requires you to take into account different contexts in which you find yourself. If you are strong in contextual intelligence, you know when to adapt to the environment (you are in a dangerous neighborhood, so you become more vigilant); when to change environments (you had planned to be a teacher, but you

find you don't enjoy working with kids, so you switch to accounting); and when to try to fix the environment (your marriage is rocky, so you and your spouse go for counseling).

Most intelligence tests do not measure the experiential and contextual aspects of intelligence, yet these aspects, which together constitute what many call *practical intelligence,* have a powerful effect on an individual's personal and occupational success. As Sternberg (1986) observes, people "can come into the world with some of the best intellectual gifts heredity has to offer, or they can be brought up in a highly advanced environment . . . and they can still routinely make a mess of their lives." Without practical intelligence, you won't have the kind of savvy that allows you to pick up **tacit knowledge**—action-oriented strategies for success that usually are not formally taught but instead must be inferred (Sternberg et al., 1995). Tacit knowledge can be measured by asking people to solve real-life problems associated with work situations. In studies of college professors, business managers, and salespeople, scores on tests of tacit knowledge do not correlate strongly with conventional ability-test scores, but they do predict effectiveness on the job (Sternberg, Wagner, & Okagaki, 1993). Tacit knowledge about how to be a student—how to take notes during lectures, prepare for tests, write papers—predicts college success as well as academic tests do (Sternberg & Wagner, 1989).

Some of the operations that make up Sternberg's componential intelligence require **metacognition,** the knowledge or awareness of one's own cognitive processes. (Metamemory, the ability to monitor your own retention, which we discussed in Chapter 10, is one aspect of metacognition.) Increasingly, psychologists are recognizing the important role that metacognitive skills play in intelligent behavior. For example, before you can solve a problem, you have to recognize that one exists—a metacognitive skill. Some students, however, fail to notice when a textbook contains incomplete or inconsistent information, or when a passage is especially difficult. As a result, they don't study the difficult material enough, and they spend more time than necessary on material they already know (Nelson & Leonesio, 1988). Poor learners also tend to go through the motions of reading without realizing when they have failed to understand the material; good students are better at assessing what they do and don't know. They check their comprehension by restating what they have read, backtracking when necessary, and questioning what they are reading (Bereiter & Bird, 1985). (If they are reading this textbook, they also take the periodic quizzes!)

In other ways, too, cognitive approaches are expanding our ideas about what it means to be intelligent. Howard Gardner (1983), in his *theory of multiple intelligences,* suggests that there are actually seven "intelligences" or domains of talent: *linguistic, logical-mathematical, spatial, musical, bodily-kinesthetic* (which actors, athletes, and dancers have), *intrapersonal* (insight into yourself), and *interpersonal* (understanding of others). These talents are relatively independent, and each may have its own neural structures. Often, people with brain damage lose one of the seven without losing their competence in the others. And some autistic and retarded individuals, known by the

---

tacit knowledge Strategies for success that are not explicitly taught but instead must be inferred.
metacognition The knowledge or awareness of one's own cognitive processes.

unfortunate label "idiot savants" (*savant* means "learned" in French), have exceptional talents in one area—such as music, art, or rapid mathematical computation—despite poor functioning in all others.

Gardner's last two "intelligences" correspond to what many theorists call *emotional intelligence:* the ability to know how to identify your own and other people's emotions, express your emotions clearly, and regulate emotions in yourself and others (Goleman, 1995; Mayer & Salovey, 1993). People who are low in emotional intelligence are often confused about their own emotions; they may insist that they're not angry, for example, while shouting and slamming doors. They express emotions inappropriately, such as by acting violently when they are suffering from grief or anxiety. And they misread nonverbal signals from others—for example, they may give a long-winded account of all their problems even when the listener is obviously bored.

People with high emotional intelligence use their emotions in adaptive ways, to motivate themselves and others or to spur creative thinking. Emotional intelligence even contributes to school achievement. One study of more than 1,000 children found that although difficulty in interpreting nonverbal emotional signals from others was not related to IQ, it was related to low academic achievement, especially in boys. Another study compared children whose parents had taught them to analyze and manage feelings of anger with children who had comparable IQs and socioeconomic backgrounds but whose parents were not good "emotional coaches." Those who had learned to understand their own emotions as preschoolers tended at age eight to score higher on math and reading tests and to have longer attention spans (Hooven, Gottman, & Katz, 1995). It may be that children who can't read emotional cues from their teachers and classmates, or who can't control their own emotions, have trouble learning because they feel anxious, confused, or angry (Goleman, 1995).

People with emotional intelligence are skilled at reading nonverbal emotional cues. Which of these children do you think feels the most relaxed and self-assured, and which is the most anxious? What cues are you using to answer?

Cognitive research on "intelligences" is starting to have practical benefits. Robert Sternberg and Howard Gardner have worked together with others to develop a practical-intelligence curriculum now being used in hundreds of classrooms (Sternberg, Okagaki, & Jackson, 1990; Williams et al., 1996). The curriculum teaches children three kinds of tacit knowledge necessary for success in school: how to manage themselves (e.g., by avoiding procrastination); how to manage tasks (e.g., by using different strategies when studying for multiple-choice versus essay tests); and how to get along with others (e.g., by convincing a teacher that an idea is worthwhile). Children receiving the curriculum have shown greater increases in reading, writing, homework performance, and test-taking ability than those not receiving it (Sternberg et al., 1995).

Other schools are trying to incorporate Gardner's ideas about "intelligences" to allow children to capitalize on their particular strengths (Gardner, 1993; Scarnati, Kent, & MacKenzie, 1993). One little boy in Modesto, California, had trouble reading but was good in music; his teacher used folk songs such as "Fifteen Miles on the Erie Canal" to help him recall facts about the Erie Canal and the westward movement (Woo, 1995). Future research will assess the effectiveness of these new approaches.

Other researchers are finding ways of boosting the mental abilities of older people. In longitudinal studies spanning more than four decades, K. Warner Schaie and his associates have examined how people's intellectual abilities change as they grow older (Schaie, 1993). They have found that some abilities, such as verbal skill, do not decline much between one's 20s and one's 80s. Other abilities decline modestly in most people after age 60 and fall off more noticeably after age 80 or so, but some people maintain high levels of intellectual functioning all their lives. One reason, Schaie and his colleagues believe, is that high-performing older people remain involved in stimulating activities, such as reading, traveling, attending cultural events, taking continuing-education classes, and participating in clubs and professional organizations (Gribbin, Schaie, & Parham, 1980; Schaie, 1984). Based on what they have learned about cognition, these researchers have designed programs to improve inductive reasoning and spatial abilities in elderly people. In one study, most participants improved after only five 1-hour sessions, and about 40 percent of those who had declined significantly returned to the level at which they had been functioning 14 years previously (Schaie & Willis, 1986). A follow-up found that people who received the special training retained a significant advantage over control subjects even after the passage of seven years (Schaie, 1993).

"Too soon old," goes an old Jewish lament, "and too late smart." The cognitive perspective, however, is more optimistic. It shows us that if we apply the lessons of the perspective, it is never too late to get smart—or at least a little smarter.

What Do You Know?

1. What goal do cognitive theories of intelligence have that psychometric approaches do not?
2. Logan understands the material in his statistics class, but on tests, he plans his time poorly: He spends the entire period on the most difficult problems, never even getting to those he can solve easily. According to the triarchic theory of intelligence, which aspects of intelligence does he need to improve?

3. Tracy does not have an unusually high IQ and was not an A student when she was in school, but at work, she was quickly promoted because she knew how to make others feel valued, set priorities, and communicate with top management. Tracy has _____ intelligence, characterized by _____ knowledge.

ANSWERS:

3. practical, tacit

2. componential intelligence (which involves metacognition)

1. to understand people's strategies for solving problems and to use this information to improve mental performance

ISSUE 2: COGNITIVE PSYCHOTHERAPY AND EMOTIONAL WELL-BEING

Suppose you have had a crush for weeks on a fellow student in your English class. Heart pounding, palms sweating, you cheerfully say, "Hi, there!" Before you can add another word, the student has walked right past you without even a nod. What emotion do you feel? Your answer will depend on how you explain the student's behavior:

Angry: "What a rude thing to do, to ignore me like that!"

Sad: "I knew it; I'm no good. No one will ever like me."

Embarrassed: "Oh, no! Everyone saw how I was humiliated!"

Relieved: "Thank goodness; I wasn't sure I wanted to get involved, anyway."

As you can see, your emotion in this situation depends as much on your *interpretation* of the event as on the event itself—and this discovery lies at the heart of the cognitive perspective's contribution to the study of emotion and the practice of psychotherapy.

Many studies over the years have demonstrated the role of thoughts, attributions, values, and expectations in generating emotions, from joy and euphoria to grief and anger. Researchers in the cognitive perspective have discovered that emotions are not only a physiological matter but also a mental one. In the 1960s, Stanley Schachter and Jerome Singer (1962) argued that emotion depends on two factors: hormonal arousal and the *cognitive interpretation* of that arousal. Your body may be churning away in high gear, but unless you can interpret, explain, and label those changes, they said, you won't feel an "emotion."

Schachter and Singer's own experiments were not successfully replicated, and today it is known that the physiology of emotion involves more than the simple activation of hormonal arousal; indeed, each of the basic emotions is associated with a somewhat different pattern of activity in the brain and autonomic nervous system (Davidson et al., 1990; Levenson, 1992). Further, certain primitive emotions occur independently of conscious cognitive processes, which is why people can be afraid for no "rational" reason or can have pleasant feelings about a familiar object without knowing why (Izard, 1994a; Murphy & Zajonc, 1993). Nevertheless, the physical changes caused by the autonomic nervous system cannot explain the experience of most emotions—or why, of two students about to take an exam, one feels psyched up, and the other feels overwhelmed by anxiety. Schachter and Singer's ideas launched scores of studies designed to identify the kinds of cognitions that are involved in the experience of emotions.

For example, most people assume that success on a project brings happiness, and failure brings unhappiness. But cognitive research shows that people's emotions depend on how they *explain* their success or failure. In one series of experiments, students reported times when they had done well on or failed an exam for a particular reason, such as help from others or lack of effort, and they described the emotions they felt on each of these occasions. Their emotions were more closely associated with their explanations than with the outcome of the test (Weiner, 1986). Students who believed they did well because of their own efforts and abilities tended to feel proud, competent, and satisfied. Those who believed that they did well because of chance or a lucky fluke tended to feel gratitude, surprise, or guilt ("I don't deserve this"). Those who believed that their failures were their own fault tended to feel regret, guilt, or resignation. And those who blamed others for their failures tended to feel angry or hostile.

The cognitions that are involved in emotion range from your immediate perceptions of a specific event to your general philosophy of life. If you believe that winning is everything and that trying your best counts for nothing, you may feel depressed rather than happy if you "only" come in second. If you think a friend's criticism is intentionally mean rather than well-meaning, you may respond with anger rather than gratitude. If you believe that intense emotions are what life is all about, you may ride a roller coaster of ups and downs; if you follow the Zen philosophy that an ideal life requires the mastery of feeling, you may follow a path of emotional calm. This is why almost all theories of emotion agree that cognitive appraisals, the *meanings* people give to events, are essential in the creation of emotion (Frijda, 1988; Lazarus, 1991; Oatley, 1993; Ortony, Clore, & Collins, 1988). Our emotions cannot be separated from our mental lives.

Perhaps you can already imagine the implications of such theories for the practice of psychotherapy. In *cognitive therapies,* the aim is to help clients identify the thoughts, beliefs, and expectations that might be unnecessarily prolonging their unhappiness, loneliness, conflicts, and other problems. When people feel depressed, angry, or anxious, they can learn how their thinking affects their emotions and can try to change their thinking (and emotions) accordingly. They can ask themselves what the evidence is for their belief that the world will collapse if they get a C in biology, that no one loves them, that a colleague is intentionally sabotaging their work, or that they will always be lonely. They can notice whether they have a tendency to "catastrophize" by turning molehills into mountains. And they can reject the self-fulfilling prophecy that their problems are permanent and beyond their control ("I'm ugly and unlikable, and that's just the way it is"; "My office is an unfriendly place and always will be").

One of the oldest and best-known of the cognitive therapies is Albert Ellis's rational emotive therapy, which he now calls *rational emotive behavior therapy* (Ellis, 1993). This approach is based on the assumption that unrealistic beliefs and demands on

The ultimate example of how interpretations of an event can differ.

oneself lead to irrational, self-defeating behavior. The therapist works to change the client's beliefs by challenging them with rational arguments. Another approach was devised by Aaron Beck to treat depression and, later, anxiety and phobias (Beck, 1976, 1991). The therapist does not challenge the client's illogical beliefs directly but instead encourages the person to test those beliefs against the evidence. And a third approach, devised by Donald Meichenbaum (1975), relies on *self-instruction;* the client learns to substitute positive thoughts for self-defeating ones that the client habitually has when under stress. In all of these therapies, the goal is to replace false or exaggerated beliefs and thoughts with more positive ones, and to help the client learn to seek out situations that confirm these new ways of thinking. To cognitive therapists, expressing emotions is not enough to get rid of them, if the thoughts behind the emotions remain. Such therapists are teaching metacognitive skills.

In cognitive therapy, clients may be asked to write down their thoughts, read the thoughts as if someone else had said them, and then write a rational response to each one. This technique is useful because many people have unrealistic notions of what they "must" or "should" do in their lives, and often they do not pause to examine the validity of these notions. Consider a student who cannot get himself to turn in a term paper because each time he writes a sentence, he imagines every possible criticism of it. Believing that his essay will not stand up to these criticisms, he ends up handing in nothing at all. A cognitive therapist would help this student examine his thoughts and feelings:

Negative thought:	"This paper isn't good enough; I'd better rewrite it for the twentieth time."
Rational response:	"Good enough for what? True, it won't win a Pulitzer Prize, but if I look at it objectively, I see it is a pretty good paper."

Negative thought: "If I don't get an A+ on this paper, my life will be ruined."

Rational response: "My life will be a lot worse if I keep getting incompletes. It's better to get a B or even a C than to do nothing at all."

Negative thought: "My professor is going to think I'm an idiot when he reads this. I'll feel humiliated by his criticism."

Rational response: "He's never accused me of being an idiot before. If he makes some criticisms, I can learn from them and do better next time."

The techniques of cognitive therapy have become extremely popular in recent years, but they are not without their critics. Robert Fancher (1995), a psychodynamic therapist, argues that despite its name, cognitive therapy does not actually incorporate many findings from cognitive science, instead relying on a commonsense view of cognition and a false assumption that the therapist can identify "wrong thinking." Moreover, what may seem illogical or irrational to the therapist, writes Fancher, may not be so irrational in terms of the client's own experience. Many depressed people, he notes, *have* been unsuccessful in love and work; they are troubled not by unrealistic appraisals but by truly troubling events in their lives. To ask a person to change his or her interpretations without considering the person's actual history—*that,* argues Fancher, is what is irrational. To assume that the source of a person's unhappiness is exclusively cognitive, he is saying, is to fall into the trap of cognitive reductionism.

The best cognitive therapy, however, avoids these pitfalls. Indeed, research finds that cognitive therapy is often highly effective, especially when combined with behavioral techniques (Chambless, 1995; Lambert & Bergin, 1994). Its greatest success has been in the treatment of mood disorders, particularly panic attacks, anxiety, and moderate depression (Black et al., 1993). Reviews and meta-analyses find that cognitive therapy is often more effective than antidepressant drugs in preventing relapses of depression and panic (Barlow, 1994; Chambless, 1995; McNally, 1994; Whisman, 1993). Cognitive-behavioral therapies have also been highly effective in helping people live with physical pain (J. Skinner et al., 1990) and chronic fatigue syndrome (Butler et al., 1991), and in treating eating disorders (Wilson & Fairburn, 1993).

Cognitive techniques have even been used successfully to prevent serious depression in children before it develops. Fifth- and sixth-graders who, tests showed, were at risk of depression met in small groups, where they learned to identify their pessimistic beliefs, evaluate the evidence for and against those beliefs, and generate more optimistic alternatives. The children also learned to think about their goals before acting, generate lots of solutions for problems, and make decisions by weighing pros and cons. During a two-year followup period, these children were much less depressed than were children in a control group, and the effect actually increased over time. The researchers believe that such cognitive interventions can give children a "psychological immunization" against depression as they begin to encounter the difficulties of puberty and adolescence (Gillham et al., 1995).

For many centuries, Western philosophers regarded emotion as the opposite of thinking, and an inferior opposite at that; the heart was said to go its own way, in spite of what the head wanted. The cognitive perspective shows us, however, that the head–heart dichotomy is a false one: Thoughts influence our emotions, and emotional arousal influences our thoughts. The more we understand about how emotions really work, say cognitive psychologists, the better equipped we will be to live with them.

WHAT DO YOU KNOW?

1. Emotion depends not only on physiological changes in the body but also on _____.

2. Suppose you go to a cognitive therapist because your irrational jealousy is sabotaging all of your close relationships. As an example, you describe how you were flooded with jealousy recently when your date merely chatted briefly with your best friend. What would the therapist especially want to know about the incident, and why? How would the therapist then proceed?

ANSWERS:

1. cognitions (interpretations, values, expectations, explanations, etc.)   2. The therapist would want to know your thoughts about your date's behavior: Thoughts such as "My date finds other people more attractive" or "My date's behavior is humiliating me" could be increasing your jealousy. If so, the therapist might encourage you to consider other ways of thinking, such as "It's a compliment to me that other people find my date interesting."

ISSUE 3: CHILDREN'S EYEWITNESS TESTIMONY

A four-year-old boy was having his temperature taken rectally at the doctor's office when he told a nurse, "That's what my teacher does to me at school." The child's mother notified the state's child protective agency, and an assistant prosecutor interviewed the boy. During the interview, the child put his finger into the rectum of an anatomically realistic doll and said that two other boys had also "had their temperature taken." Although the other boys denied this claim, one said that their nursery-school teacher, Kelly Michaels, had touched his penis. The first mother then told another parent, who questioned his own son, who said that Michaels had touched his penis with a spoon.

More allegations soon followed, some of them bizarre: that Michaels had licked peanut butter off children's genitals, had made children drink her urine and eat her feces, and had raped and assaulted the children with knives, forks, and Lego blocks. These shocking acts were said to have occurred during school hours over a period of seven months, although no adult had ever noticed them, no child had complained, and none of the parents had noticed any symptoms or problems in their children. Was Kelly Michaels guilty of horrible acts, or had the children been somehow persuaded to make up fanciful stories about her?

In recent years, few questions have aroused more heartfelt debate than the question of whether children are capable of making up stories about sexual abuse. Some people argue that no child would ever lie about or misremember such a traumatic experience. Others say that you can't trust a child's testimony because children can't distinguish reality from fantasy and because they tend to say whatever adults expect. The two sides in this controversy hold different assumptions about what children know, what they remember, and what they can be induced to say. This is a debate in which findings from the cognitive perspective can have a tremendous impact. Since 1979, there have been more than 100 studies on children's ability to give accurate testimony. After carefully reviewing this research, Stephen Ceci and Maggie Bruck (1993, 1995) have concluded that extremists on both sides of the debate are wrong.

Of course, you can't randomly assign some children to a sexual-abuse group and others to a control group. So some researchers have tested children's accuracy by questioning them about other kinds of potentially embarrassing experiences. In one study by Gail Goodman and her associates (Saywitz et al., 1991), the children, ages five and seven, had all undergone routine physical checkups. Half had been examined genitally and anally for rashes, infections, wounds, and other signs of trauma. The others had been examined for scoliosis (curvature of the spine). The researchers began by asking the children to act out what happened during the exam, using dolls and doctor toys. Then they interrogated the children with some intentionally misleading questions, such as "How many times did the doctor kiss you?" They found that children whose genitals had been touched did not usually reveal that fact spontaneously during the doll play. On the other hand, children whose genitals had not been touched almost never said they had, even when prompted to do so by leading questions.

Other studies, too, show that children, like adults, are able to remember the essential facts about an important event with great accuracy, especially if they were personally involved in the event (Fivush, 1993; Goodman et al., 1990). Even preschoolers are able to provide accurate testimony when they are questioned properly. According to Ceci and Bruck (1993), "In most of the studies [on children's memories] that have been reported during the past decade, young children were able to accurately recollect the majority of the information they observed."

On the other hand, some children *will* say something happened when it did not. Like adults, they can be influenced to report an event in a certain way, depending on the frequency of the suggestions and the insistence of the person making them. Sometimes very young children give misleading responses because they don't understand the terms used by an adult; one little girl in Goodman's study thought "private parts" meant her elbows! Occasionally a child will spontaneously give a false report about being touched or undressed without any prompting by an adult. And occasionally, to avoid punishment, protect a loved one, or keep a promise, a child may lie or deliberately withhold information (Clarke-Stewart, Thompson, & Lepore, 1989; Peters, 1991; Pipe & Goodman, 1991).

Researchers still disagree about how often false reports of abuse occur. Some believe that lying about abuse is rare and that most accusations by children can be trusted. Others note that in some studies, between a quarter and a third of all three-year-olds have given false answers to misleading questions about physical contact (questions such as "She touched your bottom, didn't she?" and "How many times did he spank you?"). They therefore urge caution in the acceptance of children's accounts. The debate is stormy because the possible consequences of believing or not believing a child are so serious. Children's advocates worry that their hard-won reforms will be lost and abusers will go free if people once again come to distrust the accounts of children. Others worry that the automatic, uncritical acceptance of *everything* children report will lead—in fact, has already led—to the destruction of innocent defendants' lives.

Ceci and Bruck suggest that instead of asking, "Are children suggestible?" or "Do children lie?" and then staking out extreme positions, we need to recognize that *all people* can be suggestible under certain circumstances, as findings on the reconstructive nature of memory would predict. A more useful question is, "Under what conditions are children apt to be suggestible?" Here are a few of those conditions:

✦ **WHEN THE CHILD IS VERY YOUNG.** Ceci and Bruck found that in 83 percent of all studies that looked at age differences, preschoolers were more vulnerable to suggestion than were school-aged children and adults.

✦ **WHEN THE CHILD IS INFLUENCED BY PRECONCEPTIONS.** The recollections of children, like those of adults, are often influenced by their stereotypes or beliefs about people. In one compelling study, researchers repeatedly described a man named Sam Stone to young children (Ceci, 1994). Sam, they said, was clumsy and always broke things that weren't his. Later, a person pretending to be "Sam" visited the children's nursery school, where he spent a couple of minutes talking with the children. During this visit, he did not behave in a clumsy manner, and he did not break anything. Then, once every other week for ten weeks, the researchers interviewed the children about a ripped book and a soiled teddy bear, each time asking them two leading questions: "I wonder if Sam Stone got the teddy bear dirty on purpose or by accident?" and "I wonder whether Sam Stone was wearing long pants or short pants when he ripped the book?"

At the end of ten weeks, a new interviewer asked the children what had happened during Sam's visit. Almost *three-fourths* of the three- and four-year-olds said Sam had ruined the bear or the book, and 45 percent said they had actually seen Sam do it. Almost 20 percent of the children stood by their stories even when the interviewer tried to talk them out of it. Some children provided details about Sam's misbehavior: For example, they said he had painted melted chocolate on the teddy bear, or that he was mad and had ripped the book apart with his hands. Older children, ages five and six, were less likely to make such false reports, as were children in a control group who had not heard about Sam before he visited.

✦ **WHEN THE SITUATION IS EMOTIONALLY INTENSE.** Children usually know the difference between reality and fantasy, but in emotionally intense situations, the boundary may blur. In one study, four- and six-year-olds were told to imagine a pretend character (such as a rabbit or a monster) sitting on an empty box. Before long, some of them began to act as if the character were real. When the experimenter said she had to leave the room, some of the younger children, apparently afraid, didn't want her to go. And when she returned, questioning revealed that a quarter of the children believed that pretend creatures could become real (Harris et al., 1991). This finding is important because in some abuse cases, including the Kelly Michaels case, children's allegations have become more and more peculiar and unlikely over time. As Ceci & Bruck (1995) note, the interviewers in such cases have often encouraged the blurring of fantasy and reality: ". . . when young children with fragile fantasy–reality boundaries are asked to 'pretend' about some events, even ones that seem bizarre, they may eventually become confused about what is real and what is pretend, especially when the interviewer fails to bring the child back to reality."

✦ **WHEN THE CHILD HAS A DESIRE TO PLEASE AN INTERVIEWER.** When children are questioned by adults, they will sometimes give answers that they think the adult wants rather than answers based on their own knowledge of an event. Children tend to regard an adult interviewer as truthful and trustworthy, and they want to cooperate. Moreover, when an adult repeatedly asks the same question during an interview, children (especially preschoolers) will often change their answers, apparently because they interpret the repetition to mean that their initial answer was wrong or unacceptable (Cassel & Bjorklund, 1992; Poole & White, 1991). In some cases, the result may be a drop in accuracy from the first answer to the second, especially among younger children (Moston, 1987). This finding, too, has troubling implications for sexual-abuse prosecutions, because interviewers have sometimes used extremely questionable interview techniques. In one highly publicized case in Jordan, Minnesota, in which scores of parents were accused of horrific acts of abuse and murder, one child eventually admitted that he had made up detailed stories of abuse because "I could tell what they wanted me to say by the way they asked the questions" (Benedek & Schetky, 1987).

✦ **WHEN THE CHILD IS PRESSURED BY ADULTS.** If the interviewer's manner is urgent or perceived as coercive, children may feel pressured to say what the adult wants them to say. In one study, three- and six-year-old children played with an unfamiliar man for five minutes while seated across the table from him (Goodman et al., 1989). Four *years* later, the researchers interviewed the children, telling them they were being questioned about "an important event" and that they would "feel better once they had told about it." Of course, few children actually remembered the episode. Yet five of the 15 children, in response to a leading question, said that the man had hugged or kissed them; two agreed that he had taken pictures of them in the bathroom; and one little girl agreed that he had given her a bath.

Goodman noted that no children in this study claimed that the man removed their clothes or touched them in "a bad way," despite misleading questions about such actions. She feels that the chances of an erroneous conviction based on a child's testimony are small. However, in court cases, interrogators and social workers are sometimes far more insistent than researchers are; some have made threats, offered bribes, or repeatedly accused children of lying if they don't give the "right" answers. In the Kelly Michaels case, for instance, the children underwent relentless, intimidating interviews. Here is an excerpt from one such interview, conducted by a social worker and a detective (from Ceci & Bruck, 1993):

Social worker:	Don't be so unfriendly. I thought we were buddies last time.
Child:	Nope, not any more.
Social worker:	We have gotten a lot of other kids to help us since I last saw you. . . . Did we tell you that Kelly is in jail?
Child:	Yes, my mother already told me.
Social worker:	Did I tell you that this [the detective] is the guy that arrested her? . . . Well, we can get out of here quick if you just tell me what you told me the last time, when we met.
Child:	I forgot.
Social worker:	No, you didn't. I know you didn't.
Child:	I did! I did! . . .
Social worker:	Oh, come on. We talked to a few more of your buddies. And everyone told me about the nap room, and the bathroom stuff, and the music room stuff, and the choir stuff, and the peanut butter stuff, and everything. . . . All your buddies [talked]. . . . Come on, do you want to help us out? Do you want to keep her in jail? I'll let you hear your voice and play with the tape recorder. . . . Real quick, will you just tell me what happened with the wooden spoon? Let's go.
Child:	I forgot.
Detective:	Now listen, you have to behave.
Social worker:	Do you want me to tell him to behave? Are you going to be a good boy, huh? While you were here, did [the detective] show you his badge and his handcuffs? . . . Back to what happened to you with the spoon. If you don't remember words, maybe you can show me [with some anatomically realistic dolls].
Child:	I forgot what happened, too.
Social worker:	You remember. You told your mommy about everything about the music room and the nap room, and all that stuff. You want to help [Michaels] stay in jail, don't you? So she doesn't bother you anymore and so she doesn't tell you any more scary stories.

Kelly Michaels was eventually convicted of 115 counts of sexual abuse against 20 preschoolers, and sentenced to 47 years in prison. After serving 5 years, she was released when an appeals court ruled that she had not received a fair trial because of the way the children were interrogated; the district attorney declined to retry her.

Investigators who must interview children in cases of suspected sexual abuse, therefore, face a dilemma: They must somehow persuade a child who might be shy, embarrassed, or verbally unsophisticated to tell the truth about what happened, while avoiding questions that are coercive or that lead the child into making a false report or confusing an imagined event with a real one. Investigators must also overcome their own confirmation bias, the tendency to seek only confirming evidence for their belief that abuse did (or did not) occur.

Some therapists in the child-protection field have tried to overcome these problems by observing how children play with anatomically detailed dolls, on the assumption that abused children will pay excessive attention to the dolls' genitals, perhaps reenacting the abuse they experienced. However, when researchers have studied how abused children play with the dolls, *comparing them to a control group of nonabused children,* they have learned that this method is not reliable. Even nonabused children will play with the dolls in a sexual manner, and independent raters often cannot distinguish abused and nonabused children on the basis of how they play with the dolls (Ceci & Bruck, 1993; Koocher et al., 1995). With preschoolers, who have difficulty understanding that a doll can represent a real person, the use of dolls may even increase memory errors (DeLoache, 1995). Indeed, recent research finds a high rate of false reporting of sexual touching when dolls are used to question young children (Bruck et al., 1995). Researchers are now testing approaches for interviewing children that take into account the findings we have discussed. They hope to find better ways to help children be as accurate and truthful as possible.

Research on children's play with anatomically detailed dolls shows why control groups are such an essential part of the scientific method. Although abused children sometimes become preoccupied with the dolls' genitals, so do children who have never been abused. Doll play, then, is not a reliable technique for diagnosing sexual abuse—a finding of great significance in legal cases.

For the moment, it seems that the wisest course to take about children's testimony is to be open-minded but cautious, and to avoid extreme positions. Children, like adults, can be accurate in what they report; and also like adults, they can distort, forget, fantasize, and be misled. As research in the cognitive perspective shows, their memory processes are only human.

WHAT DO YOU KNOW?

1. Research suggests that the best way to encourage truthful testimony by children about possible sexual abuse is to (a) have them play with anatomically detailed dolls; (b) repeatedly ask them the same questions; (c) gently question them without pressuring; (d) refuse to accept answers you believe are wrong.

2. "Children never lie about abuse," says one person. "Children's reports of abuse can never be trusted," says another. What critical-thinking guideline are these individuals violating? What other ways of thinking about child abuse could they adopt?

ANSWERS:

1. c   2. Both individuals are oversimplifying (specifically, by thinking in either–or terms). Instead, they could be asking questions such as, "In this particular case, how was the child interviewed? By whom? How often? Did the leading questions become repetitive and coercive? Was there any corroborating evidence?"

The findings of the cognitive perspective, as we have seen, have consequences for intellectual development, emotional well-being, social problems, and legal policies. Much remains to be learned, however, about how people think, deliberate, entertain ideas, ponder decisions, recall the past, and convey the results of all this mental effort to others. We can draw the "boxes" of memory, and we can reach for ever more sophisticated metaphors of the mind, but there is much we still do not understand about consciousness, which makes human thought so different from the "cognition" of a computer. Cognitive scientist Daniel Dennett (1991) notes that "No mere machine, no matter how accurately it mimicked the brain processes of the human wine taster, would be capable of appreciating a wine, or a Beethoven sonata, or a basketball game. For appreciation, you need consciousness—something no mere machine has."

Ultimately, Dennett believes, the mystery of the mind will fall to science. Some people would rather it did not; like love, they say, consciousness will become a duller, less magnificent thing if we ever truly comprehend it. But the demystification of the mind need not diminish our wonder at its workings. "Fiery gods driving golden chariots across the skies are simpleminded comic-book fare compared to the ravishing strangeness of contemporary cosmology," writes Dennett. "When we understand consciousness—when there is no more mystery—consciousness will be different, but there will still be beauty, and more room than ever for awe."

◆ ◆ ◆

Summary

1. Since the 1960s, the cognitive perspective has transformed the study of psychology. Its contributions include innovative methods for exploring the mind; an understanding of how cognition affects behavior; and strategies for improving mental abilities, including techniques for improving memory, making better decisions, solving problems, and enhancing the mental development of children.

2. A common criticism of the cognitive perspective is that its models of the mind rely on metaphors, and it is often difficult to choose which models are the most convincing. In addition, misuse of the perspective can lead to three common errors: *cognitive reductionism,* the tendency to reduce all human behavior to what goes on in people's minds; errors of cause and effect, when people fail to realize that the relationship between the mind and the body, or the mind and circumstances, runs in both directions; and *cognitive relativism,* the mistaken assumption that all ideas, thoughts, or memories have an equal claim to be taken seriously.

3. In contrast to traditional *psychometric approaches* to intelligence testing, new cognitive approaches focus on the strategies people use to solve problems and not just on whether they get the right answers. Sternberg's *triarchic theory of intelligence* proposes three aspects of intelligence: componential, experiential, and contextual. Most intelligence tests do not measure the experiential and contextual aspects of intelligence, yet these contribute to *practical intelligence,* which enables a person to pick up the tacit knowledge necessary for personal and occupational success. *Metacognition,* the knowledge or awareness of one's own cognitive processes, also plays an important part in intelligent behavior.

4. Gardner, in his *theory of multiple intelligences,* argues that there are seven independent domains of talent: *linguistic, logical-mathematical, spatial, musical, bodily-kinesthetic, intrapersonal,* and *interpersonal.* The last two correspond to what others have called *emotional intelligence,* which is related to personal and academic success.

5. Cognitive work on the many aspects of intelligence is beginning to have practical benefits, as researchers apply their theories to the classroom. Psychologists are also finding ways to improve the mental abilities of older people.

6. Emotions are not only a physiological matter but also a cognitive one: Cognitive appraisals, attributions, values, and expectations affect the emotions that people feel. *Cognitive therapies* aim to help clients identify the thoughts, unrealistic expectations, and self-defeating beliefs that might be prolonging their unhappiness and loneliness. The goal is to replace false or exaggerated beliefs and thoughts with more positive ones, and to help the client learn to seek situations that confirm these new ways of thinking. Critics argue that cognitive therapists falsely assume that they can identify "wrong thinking" and often ignore a person's actual history. But cognitive therapy is often highly effective, especially when combined with behavioral techniques. It is particularly successful in treating mood disorders.

7. Findings from the cognitive perspective help clarify the issues in the debate about whether children are capable of making up accounts of sexual abuse. Children, like adults, are often able to remember the essential facts about an important

event with great accuracy, especially if they were personally involved. However, like adults' memories, children's recollections can be influenced by leading questions and by stereotypes and preconceptions. In emotionally intense situations, the boundary between fantasy and reality may blur. Children will sometimes give answers that they think the adult wants rather than answers based on their own knowledge of an event, especially when they are pressured to respond. Efforts to overcome these problems by observing children as they play with anatomically detailed dolls have not been successful, but researchers are now exploring other methods for interviewing children that take cognitive findings into account.

Key Terms

cognitive reductionism *391*

cognitive relativism *392*

psychometric approach *393*

triarchic theory of intelligence *393*

   componential intelligence *393*

   experiential intelligence *393*

   contextual intelligence *393*

practical intelligence *394*

tacit knowledge *394*

metacognition *394*

theory of multiple intelligences *394*

emotional intelligence *395*

cognitive therapies *398*

rational emotive behavior therapy *398*

self-instruction *399*

PART V

THE SOCIOCULTURAL PERSPECTIVE

In an English class for foreign students, an Arab student was describing a tradition of his home country. Something he said embarrassed a Japanese student, who did what was customary in his culture to disguise his shame: He smiled. The Arab student demanded to know what was so funny about Arab customs. The Japanese student, now feeling publicly humiliated, giggled. The Arab student, enraged, hit the Japanese student, who he felt had insulted him. What went wrong here?

During the Nazi occupation of France, people living in the impoverished Protestant village of Le Chambon, led by their pastor André Trocmé and his wife, Magda, rescued some 5,000 Jewish children from being sent to their deaths. In Los Angeles in 1992, Terri Barnett and Gregory Alan Williams, along with other African-Americans, rescued whites during the violence and looting that followed the first trial of the police officers who had beaten Rodney King. In both Le Chambon and Los Angeles, the rescuers rose above the temptation to do nothing, choosing instead to save fellow human beings in trouble. Why did they do it?

In Waco, Texas, in 1993, a charismatic cult leader named David Koresh, claiming that Armageddon was at hand, led dozens of his followers to their deaths rather than surrender to the police. The members of the cult had come from all walks of life, and some were highly educated professionals. Why did so many adults hand over their minds and lives, and those of their children, to such a leader?

Psychologists working in the sociocultural perspective explore these and many other questions by examining the individual in a social context. They focus on all the possible things outside the person that affect how we think, perceive, feel, and act—for example, the rules and roles of society, the impact of groups and situations, and the subtle yet dramatic power of culture. The basic assumption of researchers in the sociocultural perspective is that as human beings, we are constantly being influenced by other people and by the requirements of society, even when we believe we are acting independently. Without a social context, a person is like a Rockette without her chorus line or a quarterback having a huddle by himself. We all depend on others of our kind, and we constantly adjust our behavior to what others are doing. It's hard to find true loners. Even Batman has Robin.

CHAPTER 12

The Social Context

$\mathcal{A}$ man was on trial for murder, although he personally had never killed anyone. Six psychiatrists examined him and found him sane. His family life was normal, and he had deep feelings of love for his wife, children, and parents. Two observers, after reviewing transcripts of his 275-hour interrogation, described him as "an average man of middle-class origins and normal middle-class upbringing, a man without identifiable criminal tendencies" (Von Lang & Sibyll, 1984).

The man was Adolf Eichmann, a Nazi SS officer who had supervised the deportation and death of millions of Jews during World War II. Eichmann was proud of his efficiency and his ability to resist the temptation to feel pity for his victims. But he insisted that he was not anti-Semitic: He had had a Jewish mistress for a while, and he had personally arranged for the protection of his Jewish half-cousin, both dangerous crimes for an SS officer. Shortly before his execution by hanging, Eichmann said, "I am not the monster I am made out to be. I am the victim of a fallacy."

The fallacy to which Eichmann referred was the widespread belief that a person who does monstrous deeds must be a monster—someone sick, insane, evil, sadistic. The Nazis, who used technology to carry mass slaughter to horrendous new extremes, have understandably come to symbolize the most monstrous of human beings. Perhaps for this reason, some people today regard them as an aberration, a story safely buried in the past. Yet "monstrous" behavior, far from being abnormal and rare, is common in human history. Virtually no nation can claim to have bloodless hands, to be innocent of ever having committed torture, genocide, and mass killings: Americans slaughtered native cultures, Turks slaughtered Armenians, the Khmer Rouge slaughtered millions of fellow Cambodians, the Spanish slaughtered native Mexicans, Idi Amin waged a reign of terror against his own people in Uganda, the Japanese slaughtered Koreans and Chinese, Iraqis slaughtered Kurds, Iranians slaughtered members of the Baha'i religion, and despotic regimes in Argentina and Chile launched mass killings ("disappearances") of dissidents and rebels. In a 1994 bloodbath in Rwanda, hundreds of thousands of Tutsis were shot or hacked to death with machetes by members of the rival Hutu tribe; and in the former Yugoslavia, Bosnian Serbs exterminated entire villages of Bosnian Muslims in the name of "ethnic cleansing." The systematic destruction of people defined as the enemy has been and continues to be a widespread practice (Staub, 1989, 1990).

Of course, human history is also marked by acts of bravery and self-sacrifice. In Nazi Germany, people risked their lives to aid and shelter victims or to disobey orders in other ways. A German physician, known to history only as Dr. Marie L., refused Nazi requests that she participate in sadistic experiments on prisoners in concentration camps. One Nazi doctor, Eduard Wirths, tried to persuade her by pointing out that the Jews to be operated on were subhuman beings. "Can you not see," he asked, "that these people are different from you?" She replied that many people were different from her, starting with Dr. Wirths (Lifton, 1986). And Oskar Schindler was a member of the Nazi Party who made enormous fortunes profiteering from the underpaid labor of Jews in his factory. But by the end of the war, having seen firsthand the atrocities committed against the Jews in the ghettos and concentration camps, he jeopardized his own safety and spent his entire fortune to rescue his 1,200 employees (Keneally, 1982/1993).

What gave Dr. L. and Oskar Schindler their courage? Why, in contrast, do most people do what they are told without thinking twice about it? Why do most people go along with the crowd, even when the crowd is committing morally reprehensible acts? Why do some people behave in helpful and cooperative ways, and others in hurtful or destructive ones?

Psychologists who take one of the other perspectives discussed in this book would answer in terms of the qualities of each individual. Aggressive behavior might result from a genetic predisposition to be violent; it might be a learned response to provocation; it might be an unconscious defense against anxiety. Researchers working in the social side of the sociocultural perspective, however—those in the specialties of *social psychology* and *industrial/organizational psychology*—are interested in the social and situational forces that influence behavior, thoughts, and feelings. In this chapter, we will see what they have found about the importance of the roles we play and the groups we belong to, the social origins of attitudes, and the environmental origins of our dreams and motivations.

ROLES AND RULES

"We are all fragile creatures entwined in a cobweb of social constraints," said social psychologist Stanley Milgram. This cobweb snares people in two ways. First, people are expected to follow social **norms,** or rules. Norms are the conventions of everyday life that make our interactions with other people predictable and orderly. Some are matters of law, such as "A person may not beat up another person, except in self-defense." Some come from a group's cultural values and standards, such as "A man may beat up another man who insults his masculinity." Some are tiny, unspoken regulations that people learn to follow unconsciously, such as "You may not sing at the top of your lungs on a public bus."

---

norms Social conventions that regulate human life, including explicit laws and implicit cultural standards.

Second, people fill a variety of social **roles.** A role is a position in society that is regulated by norms about how a person in that position should behave. In modern life, most people play many roles. Gender roles define the proper behavior for a man and a woman. Organizational roles determine the correct behavior for a manager and an employee, a professor and a student. Family roles set tasks for parent and child, husband and wife. Certain aspects of every role must be carried out. As a student, for instance, you know just what you have to do to pass a course.

How might you identify a role requirement? One way is simply by violating it. For instance, in your family whose job is it to buy gifts for parents, send greeting cards to friends, organize parties and prepare the food, remember an elderly aunt's birthday, and call friends to see how they're doing? Chances are you are thinking of a woman. These activities are considered part of the woman's role in most cultures. Therefore it will be the woman in the family, not the man, who is blamed if these responsibilities are not carried out (di Leonardo, 1987; Lott & Maluso, 1993).

Similarly, what is likely to happen to a man who reveals his fears and worries when his culture's male gender role considers such revelations a sign of weakness or vulnerability? Men who deviate from the masculine role by disclosing their emotions and fears are frequently regarded by both sexes as being "too feminine" and "poorly adjusted" (Peplau & Gordon, 1985; Taffel, 1990). In one study, 47 therapists were randomly assigned to evaluate a videotaped simulation of a depressed man. The tapes were identical except for the man's occupational and family roles, which were portrayed as either traditional (he was the breadwinner) or nontraditional (he was a househusband whose wife earned the family income). Most of the therapists evaluated the nontraditional man as being more disturbed than the traditional man and recommended more severe treatment for him (Robertson & Fitzgerald, 1990).

Naturally, people bring their own personalities and interests to the roles they play. Although two actresses who play the role of Cleopatra must follow the same script, you can bet that Demi Moore and Whitney Houston will have different interpretations. Yet, as we will see next, the requirements of a role can cause a person to behave in ways that violate his or her deeply held feelings, personal wishes, and fundamental sense of self.

The Power of Roles

In the early 1960s, Stanley Milgram (1963, 1974) designed a study that was to become one of the most famous in all of psychology. Participants in Milgram's study thought they were part of an experiment on the effects of punishment on learning. Each was assigned, apparently at random, to the role of "teacher." Another person, introduced as a fellow volunteer, was the "learner." When the learner, seated in an adjoining room, made an error in reciting a list of word pairs he was supposed to have memorized, the teacher had to give him an electric shock by depressing a lever on an ominous-looking

---

role A given social position that is governed by a set of norms for proper behavior.

Figure 12.1 *On the left is Milgram's shock machine. On the right, you see the "learner" being strapped into his chair by the experimenter and the "teacher" (the subject).*

machine (see Figure 12.1). With each error, the voltage (marked from 0 to 450) was to be increased by another 15 volts. The shock levels on the machine were labeled from SLIGHT SHOCK to DANGER—SEVERE SHOCK and, finally, ominously, XXX. In reality, the learners were confederates of Milgram and did *not* receive any shocks, but none of the teachers ever realized this during the experiment. The actor–victims played their parts convincingly: As the study continued, they shouted in pain and pleaded to be released, all according to a prearranged script.

When Milgram first designed this experiment, he asked a number of psychiatrists, students, and middle-class adults how many people they thought would "go all the way" to XXX on orders from the experimenter. The psychiatrists predicted that most people would refuse to go beyond 150 volts, the point at which the learner first demanded to be freed, and that only one person in a thousand, someone who was emotionally disturbed and sadistic, would administer the highest voltage. The nonprofessionals agreed with this prediction, and all of them said that they personally would disobey early in the experiment.

In fact, however, every subject in the study administered some shock to the learner, and about two-thirds, of all ages and from all walks of life, obeyed the experimenter to the fullest extent. They obeyed no matter how much the victim shouted for them to stop and no matter how painful the shocks seemed to be. They obeyed even when they themselves were anguished about the pain they believed they were causing. They obeyed even as they wept, implored the experimenter to release them from further participation, and argued with themselves. Milgram noted that many would "sweat, tremble, stutter, bite their lips, groan, and dig their fingernails into their flesh"; yet they continued.

More than a thousand participants at several universities eventually went through the Milgram experiment. Most of them, men and women equally, inflicted what they thought were dangerous amounts of shock to another person. (Seven of eight subsequent replications of the study also found the obedience rates of men and women to be identical [Blass, 1993].) Many protested to the experimenter, but they backed down when he merely asserted, "The experiment requires that you continue."

Milgram and his team next set up several variations of the basic experiment to determine the conditions under which people might disobey the experimenter. They found that virtually *nothing the victim did or said changed the likelihood of the person's compliance*—even when the victim said he had a heart condition, screamed in agony, or stopped responding entirely as if he had collapsed. However, people were more likely to disobey under the following conditions:

◆ **WHEN THE EXPERIMENTER LEFT THE ROOM.** Many people then subverted authority by giving low levels of shock but reporting that they had followed orders.

◆ **WHEN TWO EXPERIMENTERS ISSUED CONFLICTING DEMANDS TO CONTINUE THE EXPERIMENT OR TO STOP AT ONCE.** In this case, no one kept inflicting shock.

◆ **WHEN THE PERSON ORDERING THEM TO CONTINUE WAS AN ORDINARY MAN, APPARENTLY ANOTHER VOLUNTEER, INSTEAD OF THE AUTHORITATIVE EXPERIMENTER.**

◆ **WHEN THE SUBJECT WORKED WITH PEERS WHO REFUSED TO GO FURTHER.** Seeing someone else rebel gave subjects the courage to disobey.

◆ **WHEN THE VICTIM WAS RIGHT THERE IN THE ROOM, AND THE TEACHER HAD TO ADMINISTER THE SHOCK DIRECTLY TO THE VICTIM'S BODY.**

Obedience, then, was more a function of the situation than of the particular personalities of the participants. "The key to the behavior of subjects," Milgram (1974) summarized, "lies not in pent-up anger or aggression but in the nature of their relationship to authority. They have given themselves to the authority; they see themselves as instruments for the execution of his wishes; once so defined, they are unable to break free."

The Milgram experiment has had its critics. Some believe it was unethical, both because of Milgram's deception in not telling subjects what was really happening (of course, such honesty in advance would have invalidated the study) and because the study caused so many of the subjects such emotional pain (Milgram countered that the subjects wouldn't have felt pain if they had disobeyed instructions). Others argue that there are plenty of examples of obedience to immoral authority in history without having to set up such an unreal laboratory scenario. Still others question Milgram's assertion that the situation often overrules personality. Subsequent studies find that certain personality traits, such as hostility and authoritarianism, do increase obedience to authority in real life (Blass, 1993). Yet this experiment had a tremendous influence on public awareness of the dangers of uncritical obedience. And it vividly illustrated the power of roles and obligations to influence, even overturn, the preferences of individuals.

A decade later, in the early 1970s, Philip Zimbardo and his colleagues designed an entirely different, but equally compelling, demonstration of the power of roles (Haney, Banks, & Zimbardo, 1973). They wanted to know what would happen when ordinary college students took on the roles of prisoners and guards for a two-week stint. The young men who volunteered for this experiment were paid a nice daily fee. They were randomly assigned to be prisoners or guards, but other than that, they were given no instructions.

The study was designed to be as true to life as possible. If you had been assigned to be a prisoner, for example, you would have been "arrested" unexpectedly, perhaps as you were walking home from school. A police car would pull up, and two uniformed officers would take you to an authentic-looking prison cell in the basement of a university building. There you would be stripped of your clothes, sprayed with a delousing fluid, given a uniform, photographed with your prison number, and put behind bars.

Within a very short time, the prisoners in this study became distressed, helpless, and panicky. They developed emotional symptoms and psychosomatic ailments. Some became depressed, tearful, and apathetic. Others became rebellious and angry. After a few days, half of the prisoners begged to be let out. Most were more than willing to forfeit their pay for early release.

Within an equally short time, the guards adjusted to their new power. Some tried to be nice, helping the prisoners and doing little favors for them. Some were "tough but fair," holding strictly to "the rules." But about a third of the guards became tyrannical. Although they had complete freedom to use any method to maintain order, they almost always chose to be abusive, even when prisoners were not resisting in any way. One guard, unaware that he was being observed by the experimenters, paced the corridor while the prisoners were sleeping, pounding his nightstick into his hand. Another guard put a prisoner in solitary confinement (a small closet) and tried to keep him there all night, concealing this information from the researchers, who, he thought, were "too soft" on the prisoners. Many guards were willing to work overtime without additional pay.

The researchers, who had not expected such a speedy and terrifying transformation of normal students, ended this study after only six days. The prisoners were relieved by this decision, but most of the guards were disappointed. They had enjoyed their short-lived authority.

Critics of this study, as of Milgram's, maintain that you can't learn much from such an artificial setup. In their view, the volunteers knew very well—from movies, TV, and games—how they were supposed to behave. They acted their parts to the hilt, in order to have fun and not disappoint the experimenters. Their behavior was no more surprising than if young men had been dressed in football gear and then had been found to be willing to bruise one another. The critics agree that the prison study makes a great story, but it isn't *research* (Festinger, 1980). That is, it did not carefully investigate relationships between variables; for all its drama, the study provided no new information.

Zimbardo responded that these criticisms support his point: People's behavior depends to a large extent on the roles they are asked to play. *Real* prisoners and guards know their parts, too. Moreover, if the students were having so much fun, why did the prisoners beg for early release? Why did the guards lose sight of the "game" and behave as if they were doing a real job? Even if the prison study was a dramatization, Zimbardo believes, it illustrates the power of roles in a way that a short-lived experiment cannot. The behavior of the prisoners and guards varied (some prisoners were more rebellious than others, some guards were more abusive than others), but ultimately, what people did depended on the roles they were assigned.

When people in the Milgram study believed they had to follow the orders of authority, most of them put aside their personal values and administered the highest levels of shock. When students in the Zimbardo study believed they had been given the authority to issue orders, many of them put aside their personal values and treated their prisoners harshly. The roles that people were assigned in these studies determined their power to compel obedience from others or their obligation to obey.

All societies depend on the obedience of their members. And all societies impose consequences on those who fail to obey, from a slap on the wrist to complete ostracism. A nation could not function if everyone ignored traffic signals, cheated on their taxes, dumped garbage wherever they chose, or assaulted one another. But obedience also has a darker aspect. Throughout history, the plea "I was only following orders" has been offered to excuse actions carried out on behalf of orders that were foolish, destructive, or illegal. The writer C. P. Snow observed that "More hideous crimes have been committed in the name of obedience than in the name of rebellion."

Most people follow orders because of the obvious consequences of disobedience: They can be suspended from school, fired from their jobs, or arrested. In addition, they obey because they respect the authority who is giving orders; because they want to be liked; or because they hope to gain personal advantages. They obey without thinking critically about the authority's right to issue orders or because they are confident that the authority knows more than they do. But what about those obedient people in Milgram's experiment who felt they were doing wrong, who wished they were free, but who could not untangle themselves from the cobweb of social constraints? Why do people obey when it is not in their interest, or when obedience requires them to ignore their own values or even commit a crime?

Social psychologists Herbert Kelman and Lee Hamilton (1989) have studied "crimes of obedience," ranging from military massacres of civilians to bureaucratic crimes such as Watergate and Iran-Contra. They and other researchers draw our attention to several factors that cause people to obey when they would rather not:

1. **LEGITIMIZATION OF THE AUTHORITY.** Legitimization of authority allows people to feel absolved of the responsibility for their actions. In Milgram's experiment, many people who administered the highest levels of shock gave up their own accountability to the demands of the experiment. A 37-year-old welder explained that the experimenter was responsible for any pain the victim might suffer "for the simple reason that I was paid for doing this. I had to follow orders. That's how I figured it." In contrast, the people who refused to give high levels of shock took credit for their actions and refused to grant the authority legitimacy. "One of the things I think is very cowardly," said a 32-year-old engineer, "is to try to shove the

responsibility onto someone else. See, if I now turned around and said, 'It's your fault . . . it's not mine,' I would call that cowardly" (Milgram, 1974).

2. **ROUTINIZATION.** Routinization is the process of defining the activity in terms of routine duties and roles so that one's behavior becomes normalized, a job to be done, and there is little opportunity to raise doubts or ethical questions. In the Milgram study, some people became so fixated on the "learning task" that they shut out any moral concerns about the learner's demands to be let out.

3. **THE RULES OF GOOD MANNERS.** Good manners, of course, are the honey of relationships and the grease of civilization; they smooth over the rough spots of interaction and protect good feelings. Once people are caught in what they perceive to be legitimate roles and are obeying a legitimate authority, good manners further ensnare them into obedience. Most people don't like to rock the boat, appear to doubt the experts, or be rude, because they know they will be disliked (Sabini & Silver, 1985). Indeed, when students watch a videotape of the Milgram procedure, they are much more favorably inclined toward dissenters who politely disobey than those who get furiously riled up and morally indignant. The psychologist who reported these findings, Barry Collins (1993), observes that they dispel the typical fantasy that people have about "What *I* would have liked to have done as a Milgram subject."

   Because of good manners, many people literally *lack a language of protest.* To have gotten up from your chair in the Milgram study and walked out would have been embarrassing, and you would have had to justify your "rudeness." Many literally lack the words to do so. One woman kept apologizing to the experimenter, trying not to offend him with her worries for the victim: "Do I go right to the end, sir? I hope there's nothing wrong with him there." (She did go right to the end.) A man repeatedly protested, but he, too, obeyed, even when the victim had apparently collapsed in pain. "He thinks he is killing someone," Milgram (1974) commented, "yet he uses the language of the tea table."

4. **ENTRAPMENT.** Although obedience often seems to be an either–or matter—you obey or you do not—the fact is that obedience usually escalates through a process called **entrapment.** In entrapment, individuals increase their commitment to a course of action in order to justify their investment in it (Brockner & Rubin, 1985). You are trapped at the point at which you are heavily invested in an activity, and it costs too much to get out. The first steps of entrapment pose no difficult choices. But one step leads to another, and before the person realizes it, he or she has become committed to a course of action that does pose problems. In Milgram's study, once subjects had given a 15-volt shock, they had committed themselves to the experiment. The next level was "only" 30 volts. Before they knew it, they were administering what they believed were dangerously high shocks. At that point, it was difficult to explain a sudden decision to quit.

---

entrapment A gradual process in which individuals escalate their commitment to a course of action to justify their investment of time, money, or effort.

Everyone is vulnerable to the process of entrapment. A job requires, at first, only a "little" cheating, and, besides, "everyone else is doing it," and before long you are enmeshed in the company's dishonest policies. You start dating someone you like moderately. Before you know it, you have been together so long that you can't break up, although you don't want to become committed, either. Or you visit Las Vegas and quickly lose the $50 you allotted yourself for gambling. So you decide to keep going "just a little longer" in hopes of recovering the lost money. Before long, you're out $500 and have to go home a day early.

Entrapment can lead to aggressive and violent actions by individuals and nations, and examples of it appear frequently in the news. A young man decides to ride along with some gang members but does not intend to do anything illegal. Soon he is scrawling graffiti, then stealing tires, then dealing drugs, although he would rather not do any of these things. Government leaders start a war they think will end quickly. Years later, the nation has lost so many soldiers and so much money that the leaders believe they cannot retreat without losing face.

A chilling study of entrapment was conducted with 25 men who had served in the Greek military police during the authoritarian regime that ended in 1974 (Haritos-Fatouros, 1988). A psychologist who interviewed the men identified the steps used in training them to use torture in questioning prisoners. First the men were ordered to stand guard outside the interrogation and torture cells. Then they stood guard in the detention rooms, where they observed the torture of prisoners. Then they "helped" beat up prisoners. Once they had obediently followed these orders and become actively involved, the torturers found their actions easier to carry out.

Many people expect the answers to moral problems to fall into two clear categories, with right on one side and wrong on the other. But in everyday life, as in the Milgram study, people often set out on a path that is morally ambiguous, only to find that they have traveled a long way toward violating their own principles (Sabini & Silver, 1985). From Greece's bad torturers to Milgram's good subjects, people share the difficult task of drawing a line beyond which they will not go. People who mindlessly succumb to the power of roles are less likely to hear the voice of conscience.

The Role of Power

The role relationships we have discussed so far—of experimenter and subject, prisoner and guard—have a common denominator: One person has more power than the other, by virtue of the authority vested in the role itself. This power imbalance is typical of many role relations: teacher and student, physician and patient, police officer and motorist. Of course, students, patients, and motorists are not entirely powerless. There are many ways they can make their influence felt, as individuals or collectively. But the *role* does not confer the authority on them to do so.

Power imbalances affect people's behavior and feelings, even in close relationships, which most people want to believe are free from power issues and role playing.

For example, sociocultural research shows that many of the differences between the sexes that appear to be in the nature of women and men actually reflect gender-role obligations and differences in power, both of which change over time in response to changes in society and the economy.

Consider a gender stereotype that is common among many North Americans: To get their way, women are manipulative and indirect, whereas men are straightforward and say what's on their minds. The stereotype has some truth; studies find that, on the average, women and men do differ in the strategies they use to try to influence others. Women are more likely than men to use methods that are indirect and one-sided, such as pouting, crying, manipulation, or withdrawing (Lakoff, 1990). Men are more likely to be direct, asking outright for what they want, using techniques of persuasion and reason, and using force if necessary. Men are also more likely to use what researchers call "hard" strategies (demanding, shouting, being assertive), whereas women are more likely to use "soft" strategies (acting nice, flattering the other person) (Hatfield & Rapson, 1993; Kipnis & Schmidt, 1985).

Where do these differences come from? Many laypeople assume that the answer has something to do with the essential nature or personality of the sexes. But in the Malagasy tribe of Madagascar, a remote society in which nothing much happens, news of any kind is a valued commodity—and the ability to hoard information is a sign of power. Therefore Malagasy men, to display their power, speak in ways that seem deliberately misleading and vague to Westerners. Women, in contrast, speak directly and to the point—evidence, according to Malagasy men, that women just don't know how to communicate (Lakoff, 1990).

Cross-cultural studies on many different societies, as well as experiments in the United States and Canada, show that gender differences in communication styles are related less to the fact of being male or female than to *power* and the *social norms for expressing power* (Carli, 1990; Lakoff, 1990; Lips, 1991). In most Western countries, direct strategies ("Bring me the book") are typically used by people who have the greater power and status in a relationship, whatever their gender, ethnicity, or sexual orientation. Powerless people tend to use indirect strategies ("Sweetie, if you're not too busy would you mind possibly remembering to bring me the book?") in order to avoid angering their partners by direct confrontation. Think for a moment about relationships in which you feel free to say what you think and what you want, and those in which you feel you have to be indirect and manipulative. What makes the difference?

If influence strategies depend on who has the power, it follows that women will use different strategies when speaking with men than when speaking with women—because men tend to be perceived as having more power (and often do have more power, by virtue of their roles). To test this idea, Linda Carli (1990) asked randomly assigned pairs of individuals—male–male, male–female, and female–female—to discuss a topic on which they disagreed. Women spoke more tentatively than men did, she found, only when they were speaking to men. With men, they offered more disclaimers ("I'm no expert," "I may be wrong," "I suppose," "I'm not sure"). They used more hedges and moderating terms, such as the use of "like" ("Drinking and driving is, like, dangerous"). And they used more tag questions—rhetorical questions at the ends of statements—to solicit agreement ("It's unfair to prevent 18-year-olds from drinking when they can be drafted and killed in war, isn't it?").

Carli even discovered why many women use such hesitations and tags when speaking with men: They work! "Women who spoke tentatively were more influential with men and less influential with women," she reported. Tag questions and hesitations annoyed other women but seemed to reassure the men. Even though the men regarded an assertive woman as being more knowledgeable and competent than a woman who said the same thing hesitantly, they were more influenced by a woman who spoke tentatively. They liked her more and found her more trustworthy. When a woman speaks hesitantly to a man, Carli concluded, she may be communicating that she has no wish to enhance her own status or challenge his. Even former British Prime Minister Margaret Thatcher revealed, on the television show *20/20,* that she tailored her way of speaking depending on the man she was talking to. With Ronald Reagan, she said, she could communicate directly. But George Bush, she said, was more responsive to her arguments when she was indirect and used qualifying language.

Power differences, rather than gender, also help account for the common belief that women are better than men at reading other people's feelings and are therefore more intuitive than men. In two experiments, Sara Snodgrass (1985, 1992) concluded that "women's intuition" should really be called "subordinate's intuition." In male–female pairs, the person assigned to the subordinate (follower) position was more sensitive to the leader's nonverbal signals than the leader was to the follower's cues. This difference occurred whether a man or a woman was the leader or the follower. Differences due to social role, Snodgrass found, almost totally overrode gender differences.

If you think critically for a moment about the purpose and meaning of intuition, you may see why. For self-advancement and self-protection, less powerful people must learn to read the more powerful person's signals; powerful people don't need to pay attention to the moods of subordinates (Fiske, 1993; Lakoff, 1990). Prisoners learn, for their survival, to read the moods of their captors. Children quickly learn to read the moods of alcoholic or abusive parents. Adult employees of both sexes learn to read the moods of an unpredictable or despotic employer. As the research on the power of roles and the role of power illustrates, there is nothing special to women about "women's intuition."

What Do You Know?

A. 1. About how many people in Milgram's study administered the highest levels of shock? (a) two-thirds, (b) one-half, (c) one-third, (d) one-tenth
    2. Which of the following actions by the "learner" reduced the likelihood of being shocked by the "teacher"? (a) protesting noisily, (b) screaming in pain, (c) complaining of an heart ailment, (d) nothing he did made a difference
    3. In the Zimbardo and Milgram studies, people's behavior was predicted most strongly by (a) their personality traits, (b) the dictates of conscience, (c) their assigned roles, (d) norms codified in law.

B. What social-psychological concept does each story illustrate?

1. A friend of yours, who is moving, asks you to bring over a few boxes. Because you are there anyway, he asks you to fill them with books. Before you know it, you have packed up his entire kitchen, living room, and den.
2. Sam is having dinner with a group of fellow students when one of his friends tells a joke about how dumb women are. Sam is angry and disgusted but doesn't say anything. Later, in the shower, he thinks of what he should have said.

C. Which member of each pair is more likely to have what's often called "women's intuition"? (1) female teacher, female student (2) female teacher, male student (3) father, son

Answers:

C. 1. female student   2. male student   3. son
A. 1. a   2. d   3. c   B. 1. entrapment   2. rules of manners and lacking a language of protest

Groups

Something happens to individuals when they collect in groups. They act differently from the way they would act on their own, and this is true for every social species.

In 1937, S. C. Chen set up an experiment in which he could observe ants working alone and working in groups of two or three. Chen found that the amount of work an ant did increased sharply in the presence of another ant. Two ants would hang around idly for about 28 minutes and then get to work building a nest. But a solo ant would dawdle (or whatever the ant equivalent of dawdling is) for 192 minutes before starting its nest. Chen's ant study—since repeated many times with rats, cockroaches, puppies, parakeets, human beings, and many other creatures—demonstrated *social facilitation,* in which the mere presence of another member of the same species perks up performance. The animal or person will eat more, run faster, work harder, sing longer.

However, sometimes the mere presence of another member of one's species makes performance worse, a phenomenon called *social inhibition.* One factor that predicts whether the presence of others facilitates or inhibits behavior is, simply, whether you know what you're doing (Zajonc, 1965). The presence of others improves well-learned activities, which is why actors, trained athletes, and practiced trial lawyers all do better in front of an audience than they do on their own. But when you have to do something that requires complex skills or skills you haven't mastered, the presence of others is likely to get you flustered and make your performance worse. In an observational study of college students shooting pool at the student union, researchers first secretly identified the above-average and below-average players. Then they gathered, in groups of four, around the pool tables to watch the action. The good players' scores improved, but the poor players' scores worsened (Michaels et al., 1982).

If people's performance can be affected by the mere presence of another human being, imagine the effects of being in an organized work group that must cooperate to reach decisions, or in a massive crowd of spectators gathered to celebrate the new year. Research in the sociocultural perspective suggests that a group's actions depend less on the personalities of its members than on the nature of the group itself.

Conformity and Groupthink

One thing that happens in groups is that people conform; that is, they take action or adopt attitudes as a result of real or imagined group pressure.

Test line   A   B   C

Suppose that you are required to appear at your professor's laboratory for an experiment on perception. You join seven other students who are already seated, and the study begins. You are shown a ten-inch line and asked which of three other lines is identical to it. The correct answer, line A, is obvious, so you are amused when the first person in the group chooses line B. "Bad eyesight," you say to yourself. "He's off by two whole inches!" The second person also chooses line B. "What a dope," you think. But by the time the fifth person has chosen line B, you are beginning to doubt yourself. The sixth and seventh students also choose line B, and now you are worried about your own eyesight. The experimenter looks at you. "Your turn," he says. Do you follow the evidence of your own eyes or the collective judgment of the group?

This was the basic design for a series of classic studies of conformity conducted by Solomon Asch (1952, 1965). The seven "nearsighted" students were actually Asch's confederates. Asch wanted to know what people would do when a group unanimously contradicted an obvious fact. He found that when people made the line comparisons on their own, they were almost always accurate. But in the group, only 20 percent of the students remained completely independent on every trial, and they were often apologetic for not agreeing with the group. One-third conformed to the group's incorrect decision more than half the time, and the rest conformed at least some of the time. Conformers and independents often felt uncertain regardless of their decision. As one participant later said, "I felt disturbed, puzzled, separated, like an outcast from the rest."

Asch's experiment has been replicated many times over the years, in the United States and many other countries. A recent meta-analysis of 133 studies in 17 countries reported three general conclusions (Bond & Smith, 1996). First, in America, conformity has declined since the 1950s, when Asch first did his work, suggesting that conformity reflects prevailing social norms. Second, people in "individualistic" cultures, such as the United States, are less likely to conform than are people in group-oriented cultures, where social harmony is considered more important than individual assertiveness (as we will see in the next chapter). Third, regardless of culture, conformity increases under certain conditions: the more ambiguous the stimulus is; the larger the size of the majority who disagree with the subject; and the more homogenous the majority is.

Like obedience, conformity has both its positive and its negative sides. It allows people to feel connected to one another. Society runs more smoothly when people know how to behave in a given situation, when they go along with the rules of dress and manners. But conformity can also suppress critical thinking and creativity. People often do destructive and even self-destructive things because "everyone else does it." As decades of research now confirm, many people will, in a group, deny their private beliefs, agree with silly notions, and act in ways that violate their own values (Aronson, 1995; Cialdini, 1993). Some do so because they identify with group members and want to be like them in dress, attitudes, or behavior. Some conform because they believe the group has knowledge or abilities that are superior to their own. Some conform in order to keep their jobs, win promotions, or win votes. Some conform for the same reason they obey; they wish to be liked and know that disagreeing with a group can make them unpopular. For their part, groups are often uncomfortable with nonconformists, and their members will try to persuade a deviant to conform. If pleasant persuasion fails, the group may punish, isolate, or reject the deviant altogether (Moscovici, 1985).

Group members who like one another and conform to one another's attitudes often work well together. But close, friendly groups are also subject to a problem that Irving Janis (1982, 1989) called **groupthink,** the tendency for all members of the group to think alike and suppress dissent. According to Janis, groupthink occurs when a group's need for total agreement overwhelms its need to make the wisest decision, and when the members' needs to be liked and accepted overwhelm their ability to disagree with a bad decision. Two instances of groupthink in American history resulted in disastrous military decisions. In 1961, President John F. Kennedy, after meeting with his advisers, approved a CIA plan to invade Cuba at the Bay of Pigs and overthrow the government of Fidel Castro. The invasion was a disaster, and the United States was humiliated. In the mid-1960s, President Lyndon Johnson and his cabinet kept escalating the war in Vietnam in spite of obvious signs that further bombing and increased troops were not bringing the war to an end.

To study groupthink, Janis (1982) examined the historical records pertaining to these two decisions. He argued that groupthink has several identifiable features. First, to preserve harmony and to stay in the leader's good graces, group members avoid thinking of alternatives to the leader's initial preference. Instead of generating as many solutions to a problem as possible, they stick with the first one. Second, members don't want to disagree with one another or make their friends look bad, so they don't examine this initial preference closely for errors or flaws. They suppress their own misgivings, and their silence creates an illusion of unanimity. Third, the group avoids getting any outside information from experts that might challenge its views, and it suppresses dissent within the group. (President Johnson, who favored increased bombing of North Vietnam, ridiculed his adviser Bill Moyers by greeting him with "Well, here comes Mr. Stop-the-Bombing.") Groupthink can be counteracted, however, under several conditions: when group members are explicitly encouraged to express doubt and dissent (Janis, 1989); when group members are not worried about how they are being evaluated by others (Paulus & Dzindolet, 1993); and when the group's decision is based on majority rule

---

groupthink In close-knit groups, the tendency for all members to think alike for the sake of harmony and conformity and to suppress dissent.

instead of a demand for unanimity (Kameda & Sugimori, 1993).

Some researchers dislike the term *groupthink* because, catchy and compelling though it is, they believe that it oversimplifies the complexities of group decision making and implies that conformity is always a bad thing. Ramon Aldag and Sally Fuller (1993) argue that it is easy to see *retrospectively* how conformity contributes to making a bad decision, as Janis did in studying disastrous political decisions. It is harder to specify the complex conditions under which a group will make good or bad decisions in the future. Conformity and cohesion are not the only contributions to such decisions. In reviewing the decade of research since Janis's study, Aldag and Fuller consider the many factors that affect a group's decision. These include the group's history; how cohesive and homogeneous it is; the nature of the decision to be made; the characteristics of the leader; the context in which the group is making the decision; whether the group is permanent or temporary; whether the group is subject to outside pressures; the members' political agendas; organizational politics and policies; and so forth. Nevertheless, Janis certainly put his finger on a phenomenon that many people have experienced in groups: individual members' suppression of their real opinions and doubts so as to be a good team player.

Of course, some people are more afraid than others to resist group pressure. People who have a strong need for social approval, who are highly rigid, or who have low self-esteem are all more likely to conform than people who are more individualistic, self-assured, and creative (Whitney, Sagrestano, & Maslach, 1994). Most instances of conformity, however, depend on the situation. Everyone conforms in some degree to work rules, to their friends' social habits, and to the standards of groups that mean something to them. Some teenagers may do everything in their power not to conform to their parents' values, dress, and musical tastes, yet they may conform slavishly to the values, dress, and musical tastes of their friends. Conformity, therefore, is not just a matter of joining the herd. People follow different herds at different times.

Anonymity and Responsibility

Many years ago, in a case that received much public attention, a woman named Kitty Genovese was stabbed repeatedly in front of her apartment building. She screamed for help for more than half an hour, but not one of the 38 neighbors who heard her, who came to their windows to watch, even called the police.

Kitty Genovese was a victim of a process called the **diffusion of responsibility,** in which responsibility for an outcome is diffused, or spread, among many people. Individuals fail to take action because they believe that someone else will do so. The many reports of *bystander apathy* in the news—people watching as a woman is attacked, as a man burns himself to death, as a car hits a child and drives away—reflect the diffusion of responsibility on a large scale.

In work groups, the diffusion of responsibility sometimes takes the form of *social loafing:* Each member of a team loafs along, letting others work harder (Karau &

---

diffusion of responsibility In organized or anonymous groups, the tendency of members to avoid taking responsibility for actions or decisions, assuming that others will do so.

Williams, 1993; Latané, Williams, & Harkins, 1979). This slowdown of effort and abdication of personal responsibility does not happen in all groups. It occurs primarily when individual group members are not responsible or accountable for the work they do, when people feel that working harder would only duplicate their colleagues' efforts, or when the work itself is uninteresting. When the challenge of the job is increased or when each member of the group has a different, important job to do, the sense of individual responsibility rises, and loafing declines. Loafing also declines when people know they will have to evaluate their own performance later, or when they know their group's performance will be evaluated against that of another group (Harkins & Szymanski, 1989). And if people are working on a group project that really matters to them, they may even work harder than they would on their own to compensate for some of their loafing buddies (Williams & Karau, 1991).

The most extreme instances of the diffusion of responsibility occur in groups in which people lose all awareness of their individuality and sense of self, a state called **deindividuation** (Festinger, Pepitone, & Newcomb, 1952). Deindividuated people do not take responsibility for their own actions; they "forget themselves" in responding to the immediate situation. They are more likely to act mindlessly, and their behavior becomes disconnected from their values. They may break store windows, loot, get into fights, riot at a sports event, or commit rape and torture. But sometimes deindividuated people become more friendly; think of all the chatty people on buses and planes who reveal things to their seatmates they would never tell anyone they knew.

Deindividuation increases under conditions of anonymity. It is more likely to occur, for instance, when a person is in a large city rather than a small town; in a faceless mob rather than an intimate group; when signs of individuality are covered by uniforms or masks; or in a large and impersonal class of hundreds of students rather than a small class of only 15. (Having taught in both situations, we have noticed that a student who would never think of taking a nap in a small class—where his or her behavior would be immediately apparent—thinks nothing of snoozing away in a large lecture hall. The snoozing is still apparent to the lecturer, but the student feels invisible, deindividuated.)

The power of the situation to influence what deindividuated people do has been demonstrated repeatedly in experiments. In one, women who wore Ku Klux Klan–like disguises delivered twice as much apparent electric shock to another woman as did women who not only were undisguised but also wore large name tags (Zimbardo, 1970). In a second study, women who were wearing nurses' uniforms gave *less* shock than did women in regular dress (Johnson & Downing, 1979). Evidently, the KKK disguise was a signal to behave aggressively; the nurses' uniforms were a signal to behave nurturantly.

As these studies suggest, deindividuated women are perfectly capable of behaving aggressively, in spite of the stereotype that women are less aggressive than men. Indeed, two experiments found that the commonly observed sex difference in aggressiveness has more to do with *gender roles* than with supposedly natural male and female inclinations—and that being in a state of deindividuation can overrule the influence of those roles (Lightdale & Prentice, 1994). In these studies, men behaved more aggressively

---

deindividuation In groups or crowds, the loss of awareness of one's own individuality and the abdication of mindful action.

Women who were "deindividuated" by being covered in Ku Klux Klan–like disguises gave more shocks to another woman than did women who were not disguised or who were identified with name tags (Zimbardo, 1970).

than did women in a competitive video war game when they were individuated—that is, when their names and background information about them were spoken aloud, heard by all subjects, and recorded publicly by the experimenter. But when the subjects believed they were anonymous to their fellow students and to the experimenter—when they were deindividuated—there were no gender differences in aggression.

The point to keep in mind, from the sociocultural perspective, is that mob violence, bystander apathy, groupthink, and deindividuation cannot be reduced by appeals to reason and individual responsibility. Because these persistent problems in social life stem from the structure of groups, according to this perspective, solutions must involve restructuring groups and situations rather than fixing individuals.

The Conditions of Independent Action

In 1942, Wladyslaw Misiuna, a young man from Radom, Poland, was ordered by the Germans to supervise inmates at a concentration camp. Misiuna stuffed his pockets with bread, milk, and potatoes and smuggled the food to the 30 women in his charge. One day, one of his workers, Devora Salzberg, came to see him about an infection that had covered her arms with open lesions. Misiuna knew that if the Germans discovered her illness, they would kill her; but there was no way he could get a doctor to the camp to treat her. So Misiuna did the only thing he could think of: He infected himself with her blood, contracted the lesions himself, and went to a doctor. Then he shared with Devora the medication he was given. Both were cured, and both survived the war (Fogelman, 1994).

Throughout history, men and women have not always obeyed orders or conformed to ideas that they believed to be misguided or immoral; sometimes they have

Sometimes a lone dissenter can inspire a conforming majority. In 1956 in Montgomery, Alabama, Rosa Parks, weary after a hard day's work, refused to give up her seat and move to the back of a bus, as the segregation laws of the time required. She was arrested, fingerprinted, and convicted of violating the law. Her calm defiance touched off a boycott in which the black citizens of Montgomery refused to ride city buses. It took them more than a year, but they won—and the civil rights movement to abolish segregation began.

resisted them, and their actions have changed the course of history. *Altruism,* the willingness to take selfless or dangerous action on behalf of others, is in part a matter of personal belief and conscience. The Quakers and other white abolitionists who risked their lives to help blacks escape their captors before the Civil War did so because they believed in the inherent evil of slavery. Studies of rescuers throughout history find that two motives sustain them: deeply held moral values or personal feelings for the victims (Fogelman, 1994; Oliner & Oliner, 1988).

However, just as there are many social and situational reasons for obedience and conformity, there are many social and situational influences on a person's decision to dissent, speak up for an unpopular opinion, or help a stranger in trouble. Instead of condemning bystanders and conformists for their laziness or cowardice, social psychologists study the situational factors that predict independent action. They have used a variety of methods to do so.

For example, some have set up experimental situations in which they can vary the conditions under which a bystander observes another person in trouble—alone or with other people, when the victim is anonymous or when the bystander empathizes with the victim, and so forth (Dovidio, Allen, & Schroeder, 1990; Latané & Darley, 1976). Others have gone into the field and interviewed people in actual work settings. In a study of 8,587 federal government employees, employees were asked whether they had observed any wrongdoing at work, whether they told anyone about it, and what happened if they told (Graham, 1986). Nearly half of the sample had personally observed some serious cases of wrongdoing, such as someone stealing federal funds, accepting bribes, or creating a situation that was dangerous to public safety. Of that half, 72 percent had done nothing at all. What made the rest different?

According to evidence from many field and laboratory studies, several factors predict independent action such as whistle-blowing and altruism:

1. **THE INDIVIDUAL PERCEIVES THE NEED FOR INTERVENTION OR HELP.** Many bystanders see no need to help someone in trouble. Sometimes this willful blindness is used to justify inaction; the German citizens of Dachau didn't "see" the local Nazi concentration camp, although it was in plain view. Similarly, many employees choose not to see flagrant examples of bribery and other illegal actions.

    Sometimes, however, the blindness is an inevitable result of screening out too many demands on attention. People who live in a big city cannot stop to help everyone who seems to need it; people who have many demands on their time at work cannot stop to correct every problem they notice. Indeed, a study of 36 small, medium, and large American cities found that the strongest predictor of whether people would help strangers with small favors (such as making change for a quarter or helping a person with a leg brace pick up a heavy stack of spilled magazines) was not population *size,* but population *density* (Levine et al., 1994). Density both increases the sensory overload on people and makes them more deindividuated.

2. **THE INDIVIDUAL DECIDES TO TAKE RESPONSIBILITY.** In a large crowd of observers or in a large organization, it is easy for people to avoid action. Crowds of anonymous people encourage the diffusion of responsibility because everyone assumes that someone else will take charge. When people are alone and hear someone call for help, they usually do intervene (Latané & Darley, 1976). Bystanders are also more likely to take responsibility when they are in a good mood—and when they are thinking of themselves as kind people (Brown & Smart, 1991). Similarly, whistle-blowers take personal responsibility for doing something about ethical violations they observe (Glazer & Glazer, 1990).

3. **THE INDIVIDUAL HAS AN ALLY.** In Asch's experiment, the presence of one other person who gave the correct answer was enough to overcome conformity to the incorrect majority. In Milgram's experiment too, the presence of a peer who disobeyed sharply increased the number of subjects who also disobeyed. One dissenting member of a group may be viewed as a troublemaker, but two dissenting members are a coalition, and enough dissenting members can become a majority. Having an ally reassures a person of the rightness of the protest, and their combined efforts may eventually persuade the rest of the group (Moscovici, 1985).

4. **THE INDIVIDUAL DECIDES THAT THE COSTS OF DOING NOTHING OUTWEIGH THE COSTS OF GETTING INVOLVED.** The cost of helping or protesting might be embarrassment and wasted time or, more seriously, lost income, loss of friends, and even personal danger. The cost of not helping or remaining silent might be guilt, blame from others, loss of honor, or even responsibility for the injury or death of others. Although three courageous whistle-blowers from Rockwell International tried to inform NASA that the space shuttle *Challenger* was not safe, the NASA authorities

remained silent; no one was prepared to take responsibility for the costly decision to postpone the launch. The cost of their silence was a disastrous explosion and the deaths of the entire crew.

5. **THE INDIVIDUAL BECOMES ENTRAPPED.** Once having taken the initial step of getting involved, most people will increase their commitment. In the study of federal employees who had witnessed wrongdoing, 28 percent reported the problem to their immediate supervisors. Once they had taken that step, nearly 60 percent of the whistle-blowers eventually took the matter to higher authorities (Graham, 1986). Many non-Jewish rescuers of Jews said that once they had taken action to aid one person, even in a small way, they could not avoid helping others. Because they could be arrested or shot for helping one Jew, they reasoned, they might as well rescue as many as possible (Fogelman, 1994).

As you can see, independent and moral action is not just a spontaneous or selfless expression of a desire to do the right thing. There are social conditions that make altruism and individual protest more likely to occur, just as there are conditions that suppress them. Some psychologists believe that all acts of helpfulness and protest are ultimately selfish, even if one person helps another in order to feel like a moral and decent soul. Others argue that life is full of countless illustrations of true altruism, in which people help others out of empathy and concern without weighing costs or benefits at all (Batson, 1990). But today many people are suspicious of rescuers, whistle-blowers, and others who follow conscience over safety. When Eva Fogelman (1994) began lecturing on the non-Jewish rescuers of Jews during the Holocaust, she noticed that her stories "had a disquieting effect on many listeners. Rescuers' altruistic behavior throws people off balance by calling into question their own vision of themselves as good people. As they listen, they cannot help but wonder, 'What would I have done? Would I have had the courage to defy authority? Would I have risked my life? My family's lives?'" How would you answer?

WHAT DO YOU KNOW?

Identify which phenomenon—deindividuation, social facilitation, diffusion of responsibility, or groupthink—is represented in each of the following four situations.

1. The president's closest advisers are afraid to disagree with his views on arms negotiations.
2. You are at a Halloween party wearing a silly gorilla suit. When you see a chance to play a practical joke on the host, you do it.
3. You are repainting your apartment, but it's taking you two hours to do a single wall. When some friends come over to help you, you find you can do one wall in half the time.
4. Walking down a busy street, you see that fire has broken out in a store window. "Someone else must have called the fire department already," you say.

ANSWERS:

1. groupthink   2. deindividuation   3. social facilitation   4. diffusion of responsibility

THE SOCIAL ORIGINS OF ATTITUDES

People have attitudes about all sorts of things—politics, people, food, children, movies, sports heroes, you name it. An *attitude* is a relatively stable opinion containing a cognitive element (your perceptions and beliefs about the topic, including any stereotypes you may have) and an emotional element (your feelings about the topic, which may range from negative and hostile to positive and loving). Attitudes range from shallow, changeable opinions to major convictions.

Most people think that their attitudes are based on thinking, a reasoned conclusion about how things work. Sometimes, of course, that's true. But social psychologists have found that some attitudes are a result of not thinking at all. They are a result of conformity, habit, rationalization, economic self-interest, and many subtle social and environmental influences.

For example, attitudes can be created simply by virtue of "the cohort effect." Each generation, or *age cohort*, has its own experiences and economic concerns, and therefore its own characteristic attitudes. The ages of 16 to 24 appear to be critical for the formation of a *generational identity* that lasts throughout adulthood (Inglehart, 1990). In one survey of a cross-section of the American population, researchers found that the major political events and social changes that occur during these years make deeper impressions and exert more lasting influence than those that happen later (Schuman & Scott, 1989). Some of the key events that have affected generational cohorts in this century include the Great Depression (1930s), World War II (1940s), the dropping of the atomic bomb on Hiroshima (1945), the rise of the civil rights movement (1950s–1960s), the assassination of John F. Kennedy (1963), the Vietnam War (1965–1973), the rebirth of the women's rights movement (1970s), and the legalization of abortion (1973). People who were between 16 and 24 when these events occurred regard them as "peak memories" that have shaped their political philosophy, values, and attitudes about life. What do you think might be the critical generational events affecting the attitudes of your cohort?

Friendly Persuasion

All around you, every day, advertisers, politicians, and friends are trying to get you to change your attitudes. Changing one's attitudes is not, in and of itself, good or bad; but people need to know why they are doing so. When persuasive tactics go beyond the use of reasoned argument, people are vulnerable to being manipulated. The best defense against manipulation is not rigid thinking and the refusal to accept new ideas; it is critical thinking, as well as the ability to identify some of the social forces that influence the formation of attitudes.

One force is the drip, drip, drip of a repeated idea. In fact, repeated exposure even to a nonsense syllable such as *zug* is enough to make a person have a more positive attitude toward it (Zajonc, 1968). The effectiveness of familiarity has long been known to politicians and advertisers: Repeat something often enough, even the basest lie, and eventually the public will believe it. The effect of familiarity on attitudes is the reason that advertisements are repeated so often—many people even spend four times as much for a familiar brand of aspirin as for an unfamiliar one, even though the cheaper product is just as good.

The formal name for this phenomenon is the **validity effect.** In a series of experiments, Hal Arkes and his associates demonstrated how the validity effect operates (Arkes, 1991; Arkes, Boehm, & Xu, 1991). In one typical study, people read a list of statements, such as "Mercury has a higher boiling point than copper" or "Over 400 Hollywood films were produced in 1948." They had to rate each statement for its validity, where "1" meant that the rater thought the statement was definitely false and "7" that it was definitely true. A week or two later, subjects again rated the validity of some of these statements and rated others that they hadn't seen previously. The result: Mere repetition increased the perception that the familiar statements were true. The validity effect also occurred for other kinds of statements: for unverifiable opinions, such as "At least 75 percent of all politicians are basically dishonest," for opinions that subjects initially felt were true, and even for those they initially felt were false. "Note that no attempt has been made to persuade," wrote Arkes (1991). "No supporting arguments are offered. We just have subjects rate the statements. Mere repetition seems to increase rated validity. This is scary." Further experiments have ruled out competing explanations, confirming that the simple familiarity of an argument is sufficient to make many people believe that it is valid (Boehm, 1994).

When Arkes discussed this research with a student from the People's Republic of China, she was not surprised. She told him how her government made use of the validity effect by distributing posters claiming, for example, that the 1989 protest for democracy in Tienanmen Square had been organized by a small band of traitors. At first, no one believed these lies. But over time, with repetition, the government's assertions became more plausible.

People are also more easily persuaded to change their minds when they hear arguments from someone they admire or think is attractive, which is why advertisements are full of beautiful models, sports heroes, and experts (Cialdini, 1993). Advertisers and politicians spend more to convince the public that they can be trusted than to educate the public about their products or their ideas. Persuaders will also try to link their message with a good feeling. In one study, students who were given peanuts and Pepsi while listening to an argument were more likely to be convinced than were students who listened to the same words without the pleasant munchies and soft drinks (Janis, Kaye, & Kirschner, 1965). Perhaps this is why so much business is conducted over lunch, and so many seductions over dinner!

The emotion of fear, in contrast, can cause people to resist arguments that are in their own best interest (Pratkanis & Aronson, 1992). Fear tactics are often used to try to persuade people to quit smoking cigarettes or abusing other drugs, drive only when sober, use condoms to avoid AIDS and other sexually transmitted diseases, check for signs of cancer, and prepare for earthquakes. However, fear works only if people are

---

validity effect The tendency of people to believe that a statement is true or valid simply because it has been repeated many times.

moderately anxious, not scared to death, *and* if the message is combined with information about what a person can do to avoid the danger (Leventhal, 1970). When messages about an impending disaster are too terrifying and when people believe that there is nothing they can do to avoid it, they tend to deny the danger.

Sometimes, however, efforts to change attitudes go beyond exposing people to a new idea and persuading them to accept it. The manipulator uses more severe tactics, not just hoping that people may change their minds but also attempting to force them to do so.

Coercive Persuasion

The term *brainwashing* was first used during the Korean War to describe techniques used on American prisoners of war to get them to collaborate with their Chinese communist captors and endorse anti-American propaganda. It has since been used to account for the sympathy that some hostages develop toward their captors and the fanatical attachment of some members of religious, political, or psychological sects to their leaders.

Many psychologists dislike the word *brainwashing* and prefer *coercive persuasion.* "Brainwashing," they argue, implies that a person has a sudden change of mind and is unaware of what is happening. It sounds mysterious and powerful. In fact, the methods involved are neither mysterious nor unusual. The difference between "persuasion" and "brainwashing" is often only a matter of degree and the observer's bias, just as a group that is a crazy cult to one person is a group of devoutly religious people to another.

How, then, might we distinguish coercive persuasion from the usual techniques of persuasion that occur in daily life? Persuasion techniques become coercive when they suppress an individual's ability to reason and make choices in his or her own best interests. Studies of religious, political, and other cults have identified some of the processes by which individuals, singly or in groups, can be coerced (Galanter, 1989; Mithers, 1994; Ofshe & Watters, 1994; Singer, Temerlin, & Langone, 1990; Zimbardo & Leippe, 1991):

1. THE PERSON IS PUT UNDER PHYSICAL OR EMOTIONAL DURESS. The individual may not be allowed to eat, sleep, or exercise. He or she may be isolated in a dark room with no stimulation or food prior to joining the group. In the group, the person may be induced into a trancelike state through repetitive chanting, hypnosis, deep relaxation, or fatigue. A participant who is already under stress, perhaps feeling lonely or troubled, is especially likely to be primed to accept the ideas of the leader or group.

2. THE PERSON'S PROBLEMS ARE DEFINED IN SIMPLISTIC TERMS, AND SIMPLE ANSWERS ARE OFFERED REPEATEDLY. There are as many of these answers as there are persuasive groups, but here are some real examples: Do you have problems with your marriage? A long-term marriage is an addiction; better break the habit. Are you afraid or unhappy? It all stems from the pain of being born. Are you worried about homeless earthquake victims? It's not your problem; victims are

responsible for everything that happens to them. Are your parents giving you a hard time? Reject them completely. Are you struggling financially? It's your fault for not wanting to be rich fervently enough.

3. **THE LEADER OFFERS UNCONDITIONAL LOVE, ACCEPTANCE, AND ATTENTION.** The new recruit may be given a "love bath" from the group—constant praise, support, applause, and affection. Positive emotions of euphoria and well-being are generated. In exchange, the leader demands everyone's attachment, adoration, and idealization.

4. **A NEW IDENTITY BASED ON THE GROUP IS CREATED.** The recruit is told that he or she is part of the chosen, the elite, the redeemed. To foster this new identity, many cults require a severe initiation rite; require their members to wear identifying clothes or eat special diets; and assign new names. All members of the Philadelphia group MOVE were given the last name "Africa"; all members of the Church of Armageddon took the last name "Israel." Conversely, members are taught to hate certain "evil" enemies: parents, capitalists, blacks, whites, nonbelievers.

5. **THE PERSON IS SUBJECTED TO ENTRAPMENT.** "There is no contract up front that says 'I agree to become a beggar and give up my family,'" says Philip Zimbardo. Instead, the person agrees to small things: to spend a weekend with the group, then another weekend, then take weekly seminars, then advanced courses. During the Korean War, the Chinese first got the American POWs to agree with mild remarks such as "The United States is not perfect." Then the POWs had to supply their own examples of the imperfections. At the end they were signing their names to anti-American broadcasts (Schein, Schneier, & Barker, 1961).

6. **ONCE A PERSON ACCEPTS THE NEW PHILOSOPHY, HIS OR HER ACCESS TO DISCREPANT INFORMATION IS SEVERELY CONTROLLED.** As soon as a person is a committed believer or follower, the group limits his or her choices, denigrates critical thinking and makes fun of doubts, defines the outside world as evil, and insists that any private distress is due to lack of belief in the group. The person may be isolated from the outside world and thus from antidotes to the leader's ideas. Total conformity is demanded.

All of these techniques were apparent in the Branch Davidian cult led by David Koresh. By moving his group to a virtually self-sufficient compound in Waco, Texas, Koresh physically isolated his followers from their families and from other people who could have offered them a different interpretation of Koresh's paranoid beliefs. He subjected them to exhausting all-night vigils and lectures. He offered them simple answers for their complex lives: "Believe in me; you will be saved; you will no longer be unhappy; I will take care of you." He entrapped them in an escalating series of obligations and commitments. Koresh never said to new recruits, "Follow me, and you will have to give up your marriages, your homes, your children, and your lives"; but by the end, that is just what they did.

Some people may be more vulnerable than others to coercive tactics. But these techniques are powerful enough to overwhelm even strong individuals. Unless people understand how these methods work, few can resist their effects.

What Do You Know?

1. Candidate A spends $3 million to make sure his name is seen and heard frequently, and to repeat unverified charges that his opponent is a thief. What psychological process is he relying on to win?

2. Your best friend urges you to join a "life-renewal" group called "The Feeling Life." Your friend has been spending increasing amounts of time with her fellow Feelies, and you have some doubts about them. What questions would you want to have answered before joining up?

Answers:

1. The validity effect   2. A few things to consider: Is there a single autocratic leader who tolerates no dissent or criticism, while rationalizing this practice as a benefit for members? ("Doubt and disbelief are signs that your feeling side is being repressed.") Have long-standing members given up their friends and families, their interests and ambitions, for this group? Does the leader offer simple but unrealistic promises to repair your life and all that troubles you? Are members required to make extreme personal sacrifices by donating large amounts of money and breaking off their outside relationships?

The Social Origins of Motivation

Suppose that you live in a town that has one famous company, Boopsie's Biscuits and Buns. Everyone in the town is grateful for the 3B company and goes to work there with high hopes. Soon, however, an odd thing starts happening to many employees. They complain of fatigue and irritability. They are taking lots of sick leave. Productivity declines. What's going on at Boopsie's? Is everybody suffering from sheer laziness?

When people contemplate why it is that some individuals are motivated to achieve and others seem not to care, they usually think of qualities within the person. But sociocultural research finds that as conditions and opportunities change within a society, people's motivations change as well. For example, in the early 1970s, some psychologists hypothesized that women had an internal motive called "fear of success" (Horner, 1972). This idea caught on like wildfire; many popular articles and seminars offered ways to help women identify their "FOS" motive and cure it. As opportunities for women improved throughout the 1970s and 1980s, however, studies began to find that this apparent motive was fast fading. Because of the historical evidence that *motivation* to succeed depends in part on having the *opportunity* to achieve, some psychologists have criticized the idea that achievement depends mainly on internal motives—on enduring, unchanging qualities of the individual. This notion, they say, leads to the incorrect inference that people who don't make it have only themselves to blame (Morrison & Von Glinow, 1990). Some people undoubtedly do lack motivation, but research in the sociocultural perspective finds that accomplishment does not depend on motives alone. It can be nurtured or reduced by the work you do and the conditions under which you do it.

The Conditions of Work

If you had to list the ideal conditions of a job that would make you happy and productive, what would they be? Think carefully, because working conditions affect a person's satisfaction, mood, health, and motivation to work hard.

In an important longitudinal study, researchers interviewed a random sample of American workers over a period of ten years (Kohn & Schooler, 1983). Comparing results of the first interviews with later ones, they found that many aspects of the work (such as fringe benefits, complexity of daily tasks, pace, pressure, and how routine or varied the work was) significantly changed the workers' self-esteem, job commitment, and motivation. The degree of job flexibility was especially important. People who have a chance to set their own hours, make decisions, vary their tasks, and solve problems are likely to rise to the challenge. They tend to become more flexible in their thinking and feel better about themselves and their work than if they are stuck in a routine, boring job that gives them no control over what they do. As a result, their work motivation rises, and stress drops (Karasek & Theorell, 1990; Locke & Latham, 1990). Conversely, when people with high power or achievement motivation are put in situations that frustrate their desire and ability to express these ambitions, they become dissatisfied and stressed, and their power and achievement motives decline (Jenkins, 1994).

American culture emphasizes money as the great motivator, but actually work motivation is not related to the amount of money you get, but how and when you get it. The strongest motivator is *incentive pay,* that is, bonuses that are given on completion of a goal and not as an automatic part of salary (Smither, 1994). If you think about it, you can see why this might be so. Incentive pay increases people's feelings of self-efficacy and sense of accomplishment ("I got this raise because I deserved it"). This doesn't mean that people should accept low pay so they will like their jobs better, or that they should never demand cost-of-living raises!

Ultimately, achievement ambitions are related to people's *chances* of achieving. Reviewing studies of opportunity and ambition, Rosabeth Kanter (1977/1993) found

Work motivation can be squelched by authoritarian employers!

that men and women who work in dead-end jobs with no prospect of promotion behave the same way. They play down the importance of achievement, fantasize about quitting, or emphasize the social benefits of their jobs instead of the intellectual and financial benefits. Yet if opportunities are created for such people, if the structure of work changes, their motivation often changes too.

For instance, in Kanter's research, a woman who had been a secretary for 20 years reported that she had never had a desire to be anything else. Then, because of an affirmative-action program, she was offered a management job. Although she felt insecure about her ability, she accepted it. She did superbly, and her motives changed. "Now I'm ambitious," she told the interviewer, "probably overly so. I will probably work 20 more years, and I expect to move at least six grade levels, maybe to vice-president. . . . You know, as you do, you learn you can, so you want to do more."

In contrast, consider the following comments from a man who realized in his mid-30s that he was never going to be promoted to top management and who scaled down his ambitions accordingly (Scofield, 1993). As organizational psychologists would predict, he began to emphasize the benefits of not achieving: "I'm freer to speak my mind," "I can choose not to play office politics," and "I don't volunteer for lousy assignments." He had time, he learned, for coaching Little League and could stay home when the kids were sick. "Of course," he wrote, "if I ever had any chance for upward corporate mobility it's gone now. I couldn't take the grind. Whether real or imagined, that glass ceiling has become an invisible shield."

Many groups who fall outside the dominant culture of corporate life encounter that "glass ceiling"—a barrier to promotion that is so subtle as to be transparent, yet strong enough to prevent advancement to the top levels of management (Morrison & Von Glinow, 1990). A study of Asian-Americans in professional and managerial positions, for instance, found that their education and work experience did not predict advancement as they do for white American men (Cabezas et al., 1989). And in a study of African-Americans in the banking industry, the three most significant problems reported were racism; not being "in the network," and therefore not being told what was going on; and an inability to find a mentor (Irons & Moore, 1985).

Work motivation and satisfaction depend on the right fit between qualities of the individual and conditions of the work. Psychologists in this perspective are trying to determine how best to structure work so that the increasing diversity of workers will result in worker satisfaction, achievement, and effectiveness rather than conflict, bitterness, and prejudice on both sides.

Competition and Cooperation

If you want to make some money, play the dollar auction with a few friends. Everyone must bid for your dollar in 5-cent increases, and the auction is over when there is no new bid for 30 seconds. The catch is this: The second-highest bidder must also pay you, although he or she will get nothing in return. Usually, the bidding starts quickly and soon narrows to two competitors. After one of them has bid $1.00, the other decides to bid $1.05, because she would rather pay $1.05 for your dollar than give you

$.95 for nothing. Following the same logic, the person who bid $1.00 decides to go to $1.10. By the time they quit, you may have won $5 or $6. Your bidders will have been trapped by the nature of competition. Both will want to "win"; both will fear losing; both will try to save face. Had they thought of cooperation, however, they would both have won. The bidders could have agreed to set a limit on the bidding (say, 45 cents) and split the profits.

During a competitive game, participants and spectators are involved and energized, and they have a good time. Competition in business and science can lead to better services and products and new inventions. Yet there are some psychological hazards to competition. When winning is everything, competitors may find no joy in being second or even in being in the activity at all. After reviewing the huge number of studies on the effects of competition, Alfie Kohn (1992) concluded that "The phrase *healthy competition* is a contradiction in terms." Competition, research shows, often decreases work motivation. It makes people feel insecure and anxious, even if they win; it fosters jealousy and hostility; and it can stifle achievement. Because competition is "the common denominator of American life," Kohn maintains, we rarely pause to notice its negative effects. And we rarely notice that in practice, most businesses depend on cooperation among employees, and cooperation often earns the biggest prizes. In 1993, three rival companies that had been competing for the right to develop high-definition television (HDTV) agreed to join forces to design a single approach. With that decision, they avoided bitter litigation that would have delayed HDTV for years.

Years ago, Muzafer Sherif and his colleagues used a natural setting, a Boy Scout camp called Robbers Cave, to conduct an experiment on the contrasting results of cooperation and competition (Sherif, 1958; Sherif et al., 1961). Sherif randomly assigned 11- and 12-year-old boys to two groups, the Eagles and the Rattlers. To build team spirit, each group worked on communal projects, such as making a rope bridge and building a diving board. Sherif then put the teams in competition for prizes. During fierce games of football, baseball, and tug-of-war, the boys whipped up a competitive fever that spilled off the playing fields. They began to raid each other's cabins, call each other names, and start fistfights. No one dared to have a friend from the opposite gang. Before long, the Rattlers and the Eagles were as hostile toward each other as any two rival gangs fighting for turf, any two siblings fighting for a parent's attention, and any two nations fighting for dominance. Their hostility continued even when they were just sitting around together watching movies.

Then Sherif determined to undo the hostility he had created and to make peace between the Eagles and the Rattlers. Instead of focusing on the boys' personalities, lecturing them on the evils of fighting, or doing psychotherapy, the experimenters decided to restructure the situation. They set up a series of predicaments in which both groups needed to work together to reach a desired goal. The boys had to cooperate to get the water-supply system working. They had to pool their resources to get a movie they all wanted to see. When the staff truck broke down on a camping trip, they all had to join forces to pull the truck up a steep hill and get it started again. This policy of *interdependence in reaching mutual goals* was highly successful in reducing the boys' hostility and competitiveness. The boys eventually made friends with their former enemies.

Interdependence has a similar effect in adult groups. When adults work together in a cooperative group in which teamwork is rewarded, they often like one another better and are less hostile than when they are competing for individual success (Deutsch, 1949, 1980). Cooperation causes people to think of themselves as members of one big group instead of two opposed groups, *us* and *them* (Gaertner et al., 1990). Organizational psychologists have found that in many companies, employees do better and their motivation is higher when they work in cohesive work teams than when they work competitively or alone. For example, an alternative to the standard assembly line is to have factory employees work in groups and handle different aspects of assembling the product instead of one repeated routine. This approach has been tried successfully by Volvo, General Foods, Sherwin-Williams, and Saab (Sundstrom, De Meuse, & Futrell, 1990).

Teamwork produces many benefits, including better problem solving, greater satisfaction, and increased participation. Of course, as we saw, teams must be careful to avoid groupthink and to reward individual innovation. Certain conditions of the group raise members' motivation and reduce the risk of groupthink: clarity of purpose, autonomy for each member, prompt feedback on individual performance, a physical environment that permits informal face-to-face meetings, and a system of rewards and recognition in which the benefits to individual members depend on the whole team's performance (Smither, 1994; Sundstrom, De Meuse, & Futrell, 1990).

And so we have come to the end of a long list of the social conditions that affect motivation. In the sociocultural perspective, these conditions help explain (a) why competent employees might slow down and get bored at work, and also why they might become enthusiastic, innovative workers; and (b) how easily two groups can become enemies, and also how they might find common ground. The sociocultural perspective shows that what appears to be a simple question—"Why is Horace knocking himself out at his new job when he used to be such a slug at his old one?"—has many answers, and not all of them are in Horace.

What Do You Know?

Imagine that you are the chief executive officer (CEO) of a new electric car company. You want your employees to feel free to offer their suggestions and criticisms to improve productivity and satisfaction, and to inform managers if they find any evidence that your cars are unsafe, even if that means delaying production. What concepts from this chapter could you use in setting company policy?

Answers:

Some possibilities: Set up cooperative production teams based on teamwork and interdependence in reaching mutual goals rather than competition; reduce social loafing by rewarding individual innovation, paying attention to each worker's suggestions, and implementing the best suggestions; encourage deviant ideas; stimulate commitment to the task (e.g., building a car that will solve the world's pollution problem!); establish a written policy to protect whistle-blowers. What else can you think of?

The Question of Human Nature

Psychologists, like everyone else, like to debate whether human beings are, at heart, good, helpful, cooperative, and hardworking, or selfish, cruel, aggressive, and lazy. Those who believe that people are basically decent and kind often rely on moral persuasion as a tactic for making the world less hostile. Those who believe that people are governed by aggressive, even death-seeking instincts hope that we can find constructive ways of displacing or channeling our violent energies.

Psychologists working in the sociocultural perspective would phrase the question differently. It is in our nature, they would say, to behave both generously and savagely, to be selfish and altruistic, to be lazy and to work hard, to be mindless and to be mindful, to conform and to behave independently. The task is to identify the conditions that make these reactions likely to occur. To do so, we must understand such normal psychological processes and circumstances as roles, obedience to authority, conformity, entrapment, deindividuation, working conditions, and competition and cooperation.

At the beginning of this chapter, we reported Adolf Eichmann's claim that he was "not the monster I am made out to be." Philosopher Hannah Arendt (1963), who observed his trial and later wrote about it, agreed with him, describing his actions as evidence of "the banality of evil." (*Banal* means "commonplace" or "unoriginal.") Eichmann and his fellow Nazis were ordinary men, Arendt wrote, just doing their jobs. The banality of evil is one of the most important lessons of the sociocultural perspective in psychology. Most people want to believe that harm to others is done only by evil people who are bad down to their bones. It is reassuring to divide the world into those who are good or bad, kind or mean, moral or immoral. Yet this perspective reminds us that perfectly nice people can behave in cruel, aggressive, and mindless ways if the situation demands it. Conversely, situations can be created that encourage considerate and helpful behavior, independent action, and dissent. Studies of rescuers and helpful bystanders find plenty of evidence for the "banality of virtue"—for everyday, often anonymous acts of kindness, selflessness, and generosity.

This is good news and bad news. The bad news is that bad behavior cannot be eliminated by getting rid of a few "bad" people (or nations) because cruelty and cowardice are often a result of normal, everyday social processes. The good news, from the sociocultural perspective, is that all that human nature gives us is potential. It's up to us to create the social situations that allow us to use it well.

✦ ✦ ✦

Summary

1. Psychologists working in the sociocultural perspective explore psychological questions by examining the individual in a social context. The social side of this perspective, which includes the specialties of *social psychology* and *industrial/organizational psychology,* focuses on the social and situational influences on behavior, thoughts, and feelings.

2. *Norms* and *roles* place powerful constraints on human behavior, and role requirements can cause a person to behave in ways that violate his or her feelings, person-

al wishes, and sense of self. In Milgram's obedience study, most people in the role of "teacher" inflicted what they thought was extreme shock to another person in the role of "learner." In Zimbardo's prison study, college students randomly assigned to the role of "prisoner" or "guard" quickly began to behave as they thought the roles required.

3. All societies depend on the obedience of their members, but obedience also has a darker aspect. People follow orders because of the obvious consequences of disobedience, out of respect for authority, and to gain advantages. Even when they would rather not, they may obey because they believe the authority is legitimate; because the role is routinized into duties that are performed mindlessly; because they are embarrassed to break the rules of good manners and lack a language of protest to do so; or because they have become *entrapped*. Entrapment can lead to aggressive actions by individuals and nations.

4. A power imbalance is typical of many role relations. In the sociocultural view, many differences between the sexes, including differences in influence strategies and ways of communicating, actually reflect gender-role obligations and differences in power rather than anything intrinsic to the natures of women and men. Power differences, rather than gender per se, also help account for the common belief that women are better than men at reading other people's moods and feelings and are thus naturally more intuitive than men.

5. Individuals act differently in groups from the way they would on their own. Sometimes groups produce *social facilitation*, especially of well-learned activities; sometimes groups produce *social inhibition*, especially when a task requires skills not yet mastered. A group's actions depend less on the personalities of its members than on the nature of the group itself.

6. Conformity results from real or imagined group pressure and has both positive and negative aspects. People conform because they want to identify with a group, want to be accurate, desire personal gain, and wish to be liked. Close, friendly groups are subject to *groupthink*, the tendency for all members to think alike and suppress dissent, but many other factors also affect a group's decision and whether the outcome is favorable.

7. *Diffusion of responsibility* in a group can lead to inaction on the part of individuals—to *bystander apathy*, and, in work groups, *social loafing*. The most extreme instances of the diffusion of responsibility occur in *deindividuation*, when people lose all awareness of their individuality. Deindividuation increases under conditions of anonymity.

8. From the sociocultural perspective, mob violence, bystander apathy, groupthink, and deindividuation stem from the structure of groups, so solutions must involve restructuring groups and situations rather than fixing individuals. Although the willingness to take independent, selfless, or dangerous action is in part a matter of personal belief and conscience, several social and situational factors also predict independent action. These include seeing a need for help; deciding to take responsibility; having an ally; weighing the costs of getting involved; and becoming entrapped in a commitment.

9. People have many *attitudes*, which include cognitive elements and emotional elements. Attitudes are formed and change in social interaction, and they are influenced by one's age *cohort* and *generational identity*. When persuasive tactics go beyond the use of reasoned argument, people are vulnerable to being manipulated; for example, because of the *validity effect*, people may come to believe that a statement is true simply because it has been repeated many times. People are most easily persuaded to change their minds when they hear arguments from someone they admire or think is attractive. The emotion of fear, in contrast, can cause people to resist good arguments. Certain conditions make people especially vulnerable to *coercive persuasion*, including being put under physical or emotional distress and being subjected to entrapment.

10. As conditions and opportunities change within a society, people's work motivations change as well. Commitment to a job and motivation to achieve can be nurtured or reduced by working conditions and the degree of job flexibility. Many groups that fall outside the dominant culture of corporate life encounter a "glass ceiling" that can prevent advancement.

11. Competition in business and science can lead to better services and products and new inventions, but it can also decrease work motivation, make people feel insecure, and foster hostility. Conflict and hostility between groups can be reduced by promoting *interdependence in reaching mutual goals*. In business, cooperative teamwork can produce better problem solving, worker satisfaction, and increased performance, as long as groupthink is avoided and individual innovation also rewarded.

12. Psychologists working in the sociocultural perspective argue that it is "human nature" to behave both generously and savagely, to be both selfish and altruistic, to be lazy and to work hard, to be mindless and to be mindful, and to conform and to behave independently. The task is to identify the conditions that make these reactions likely to occur.

Key Terms

social psychology *414*

industrial–organizational psychology *414*

norms (rules) *414*

roles *415*

Milgram's study of obedience *415*

Zimbardo's prison study *417*

entrapment *420*

social facilitation *424*

social inhibition *424*

conformity *425*

groupthink *426*

diffusion of responsibility *427*

bystander apathy *427*

social loafing *427*

deindividuation *428*

altruism *430*

attitude *433*

age cohort *433*

generational identity *433*

validity effect *434*

coercive persuasion *435*

"glass ceiling" *439*

competition *440*

cooperation *440*

CHAPTER 13

The Cultural Context

*I*n a suburb of Baton Rouge, Louisiana, Yoshihiro Hattori, a 16-year-old Japanese exchange student, went along with his friend Webb Haymaker to a Halloween party. They mistakenly stopped in front of a house covered in Halloween decorations and rang the bell. Hearing no answer, Yoshihiro went around the side of the house to see if the party might be in the backyard. The home owner, Bonnie Peairs, opened the front door, saw Webb in a Halloween costume, and then saw Yoshihiro running back toward her waving an object, which turned out to be a camera. She panicked and called for her husband to get his gun. Rodney Peairs grabbed a loaded .44 Magnum and shouted at Yoshihiro to "freeze." Yoshi, not understanding the word, did not stop. Peairs shot him in the heart, killing him instantly. Little more than a minute had passed between the time that Yoshihiro Hattori rang the doorbell and the time that Rodney Peairs shot him to death.

When the case came to trial, the jury acquitted Rodney Peairs of manslaughter after only three hours of deliberation.

If ever a tragic misunderstanding illustrated the power of cultural differences, this one is it. To the Japanese news media, the story illustrated everything that is wrong with America. It is a nation rife with guns and violence—a "developing nation," as one commentator put it, that is still growing out of its Wild-West past. Japanese television reporters, in amazement, showed their viewers American gun stores, restaurants that display guns on the walls, and racks of gun magazines. The Japanese cannot imagine a nation in which private individuals are allowed to keep guns. In Japan in 1991, 74 people were killed with guns, almost all of them members of organized crime; in the United States, a person is fatally shot every 16 minutes.

"I think for Japanese the most remarkable thing is that you could get a jury of Americans together, and they could conclude that shooting someone before you even talked to him was reasonable behavior," Masako Notoji, a professor of American cultural studies in Tokyo, told *The New York Times* (May 25, 1993). "We are more civilized. We rely on words."

In contrast, the citizens of Baton Rouge were surprised that the case came to trial at all. What is more right and natural, they said, than protecting oneself and one's family from intruders? "A man's home is his castle," said one potential juror, expressing puzzlement that Peairs had even been arrested. "That's my question—why [was he arrested]?" A local man, joining the many sympathizers of Rodney Peairs, said, "It would be to me what a normal person would do under those circumstances."

Bonnie Peairs wept on the witness stand. "There was no thinking involved," she said. "I wish I could have thought. If I could have just thought."

The clash of American and Japanese cultures, which is so clear in this sad case, shows why it is important to understand what culture means and how it influences us. Defining culture is more easily said than done, however. As cross-cultural psychologist Walter Lonner (1995) observes, "It ranks right up there with truth, beauty, justice, and intelligence as abstract and fuzzy constructs whose precise definitions challenge even the most insightful thinkers." Nevertheless, Lonner himself and most other researchers would agree that **culture** can be defined both as a program of shared rules that govern the behavior of members of a community or society and as a set of values, beliefs, and attitudes shared by most members of that community. Culture includes a system of rules, passed from one generation to another, for just about everything in the human-made environment: for getting along with other people, for raising children, for making decisions, and for using artifacts (e.g., an ax or computer) and symbols (e.g., written words or painted images) (Cole, 1990; Lonner, 1995; Lonner & Malpass, 1994; Shweder, 1990).

Cultural psychologists study the many ways in which people are affected by the culture in which they live. *Cross-cultural psychologists* compare members of different societies, searching both for their human commonalities and their specific cultural differences. Cultural psychology is similar to *cultural anthropology,* the cross-cultural study of human groups, and indeed we will be reporting some research from anthropologists. But whereas anthropologists tend to study the economy and customs of a cultural unit as a whole, cultural psychologists are more interested in how culture affects individual psychological and physiological processes, such as the motivation to achieve or infant and child development.

Until recently, most Western psychologists were uninterested in the influence of culture on psychological processes. In contrast to physiology, which they treated as real and tangible, they regarded culture as if it were merely a light veneer on human behavior, or perhaps as a charming source of stories or information for tourist travel ("Did you know that in Spain people eat dinner at 10 P.M.?"). As a result, students and teachers knew little about the psychological characteristics of people living in other societies and assumed that they could safely generalize from studies of people in their own culture to people everywhere (Betancourt & López, 1993; Cole, 1984).

Today researchers in the sociocultural perspective are demonstrating that culture is just as powerful an influence on human behavior as any biological process. In fact, culture affects biological processes. Everyone needs to eat, for instance; but culture affects how often people eat, what they eat, and with whom they eat. Depending on your culture, you might eat lots of little meals throughout the day or only one large

---

culture A program of shared rules that govern the behavior of members of a community or society, and a set of values, beliefs, and attitudes shared by most members of that community.

meal. You will eat food that your culture calls delicious—whale meat in Inuit communities, lizards in South America, locusts in Africa, horses in France, dogs in Asia—and you are likely to find everyone else's food preferences disgusting. You won't eat foods that your culture calls taboo: pigs among Muslims and Orthodox Jews, cows in India, horses in America, deer among the Tapirapé (Harris, 1985). And your culture affects your choice of dining companions. People generally don't eat with those they consider their social inferiors, such as servants; in some cultures, men do not eat with children or women.

These cultural influences on a process as essential as eating can cause people to eat when they aren't hungry (to be sociable) or not to eat when they *are* hungry (because the company or the food is culturally unappetizing). Sometimes, cultural pressures are in direct conflict with biological dispositions. Evolution has programmed women to maintain a reserve of fat necessary for healthy childbearing, nursing, and, after menopause, the production and storage of the hormone estrogen. And, as we saw in Chapter 3, genes influence body shape and weight. Yet the contemporary cultural ideal for many North American women is a boyishly slim body, an ideal that is by no means universal across cultures or historical epochs. The result of the battle between biological design and cultural standards is that many women are obsessed with weight, continually dieting, excessively exercising, or suffering from eating disorders such as *anorexia nervosa* (self-starvation) or *bulimia* (bingeing and vomiting) (Rodin, Silberstein, & Striegel-Moore, 1990; Silverstein & Perlick, 1995).

If culture can so powerfully affect a person's belief in what is proper behavior, you can imagine why misunderstandings between cultures are so frequent. "Many people have the well-meaning delusion that if they could only get to know people in another culture, they would realize how alike they are," said anthropologist Edward T. Hall. "The truth is that the more you get to know people from another culture, the more you realize how *different* they are" (quoted in Tavris, 1987). In this chapter, we will try to show you what Hall meant.

We begin with a discussion of some unique difficulties that the study of culture poses for psychologists. We will then consider some studies that illustrate the influence of culture on a wide range of psychological processes and behaviors, from the gestures you make to support your favorite football team to your personal goals and your very identity. However, although describing individual cultural customs is a fascinating project on its own, cultural psychologists want to do more than just tote up examples of different practices as if they were a stack of potato chips. As we will see, sociocultural researchers also try to explain these practices—where they come from, why they change, and what purpose they serve for the society as a whole.

THE STUDY OF CULTURE

The study of culture is challenging for both methodological and psychological reasons. Four issues in particular make this kind of research different from other methods and approaches in psychology:

1. **THE PROBLEM OF METHODS AND SAMPLES.** Devising good methods and getting good samples is difficult enough when you are studying just one culture; these tasks are even more daunting when you are dealing with many societies and hope to make cultural comparisons. Cross-cultural psychologists must consider many different criteria in selecting their samples: societal (e.g., How many societies or cultures should I have?), community (How many groups within each society do I need?), individual (How many individuals within each community shall I select?), and behavioral (Which specific actions or attitudes should I measure?) (Lonner & Malpass, 1994).

Some cultural differences can be measured indirectly, by drawing inferences from data about collective behavior, such as the frequency of domestic violence, traffic accidents, or suicides (Hofstede & Bond, 1988). In New York, for example, almost everyone jaywalks, but in German cities almost no one jaywalks, a finding that implies a cultural difference in attitudes toward breaking a law governing public behavior. However, indirect measurements permit different interpretations: Perhaps the jaywalking difference doesn't reflect attitudes toward the law but rather the density of pedestrians and the number of cars per clogged street.

For this reason, many cross-cultural psychologists prefer to use direct measures, such as questionnaires or observations of *matched samples* of respondents from different countries. Matching means that an effort is made to study samples of individuals who are similar in all aspects of their lives except their nationalities, including age, economic status, and education. For example, two researchers, Michael Bond (a psychologist and cross-cultural management trainer for multinational corporations in Hong Kong) and Geert Hofstede (an anthropologist and director of the Institute for Research on International Cooperation in the Netherlands), were able to make use of a remarkable databank of directly obtained cross-cultural information. The IBM corporation had been surveying its employees worldwide, in 53 different cultures and in 20 languages, using standardized questionnaires. Analyzing this rich mine of data on matched samples of IBM employees, Hofstede and Bond (1988) found that members of these 53 cultures differ across four key dimensions: the extent to which they accept and expect an unequal distribution of power in organizations and families; the extent to which they are integrated into groups or are expected to be "individualistic"; the extent to which they endorse "masculine" values of assertiveness or "feminine" values of nurturance; and, interestingly, the extent to which they can tolerate uncertainty. Cultures that try to minimize or avoid uncertainty, say Hofstede and Bond, tend to adhere to strict laws, rules, and safety and security measures; and, philosophically and religiously, they tend to believe that "There can be only one truth, and we have it." People in cultures that are more tolerant of uncertainty are more accepting of differing behavior, opinions, and religious views.

These differences in values, attitudes toward life and institutions, and beliefs about one's place in society, Hofstede and Bond learned, have implications for business practices (e.g., whether group loyalty or individual ambition is rewarded, and what style of leadership is most effective) and for people's motivations (e.g., competition is more effective in "masculine" cultures). By identifying and measuring the precise components of cultural beliefs and practices, they were able to show how "culture" translates into behavior.

2. **THE PROBLEM OF INTERPRETING RESULTS.** A second concern in cross-cultural research is linguistic and functional equivalence: You must make sure that your questionnaires and interviews convey the same meanings in every language. This is hard to do. The meaning of "Mary had a little lamb" is obvious to an English speaker, who knows that she owned the lamb and did not give birth to it, eat it, or have an affair with it! But translations can be difficult. Sometimes, a concept that is tremendously important in one culture cannot easily be translated into an equivalent term in another culture. The Chinese Value Survey, for instance, contains items that seem strange to many Westerners, such as "filial piety," defined as "honoring of ancestors and obedience to, respect for, and financial support of parents" (Hofstede & Bond, 1988).

Moreover, a custom in one culture might not have the same meaning or purpose as the same practice elsewhere. For example, the circumcision of male babies has a religious purpose among Jews and serves to strengthen identification with the group, but the same practice became widespread in Europe and America during the Victorian era for a very different reason: It was (mistakenly) believed that circumcised boys wouldn't masturbate and thus succumb to "masturbatory insanity" (Paige & Paige, 1981). In addition, a custom may persist long after its original function or intention has been abandoned. Circumcision continued in North America, but not in Europe, decades after masturbatory insanity was forgotten as its rationale, because the medical establishment endorsed the procedure in the name of hygiene.

3. **THE PROBLEM OF STEREOTYPING.** A third problem in studying culture is how to identify and describe average differences across societies without stereotyping. As

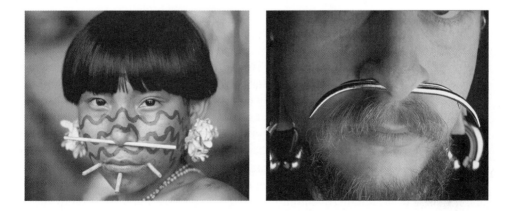

The same behavior may have different functions in different cultures. For the Yanomamo Indians, nose piercing is a part of normal facial decoration and display, but a Westerner might do it to be unusual, rebellious, or shocking.

one student of ours put it, "How come when we students speak of 'the' Japanese or 'the' blacks or 'the' whites or 'the' Latinos, it's called stereotyping, and when you do it, it's called 'cross-cultural psychology'?" This question shows excellent critical thinking! The study of culture does not rest on the assumption, implicit in stereotypes, that *all* members of a culture behave the same way. (Later in this chapter we will discuss the functions and consequences of stereotypes.) As the other psychological perspectives have shown, individuals vary within every culture according to their heredity, beliefs, and learning histories. Just as people play their social roles differently, they read their cultural scripts differently. But the fact that people carry out their roles in individual ways does not negate the reality of role requirements in general. Likewise, the fact that individuals vary within a culture does not negate the existence of cultural rules that, overall, make Swedes different from Bedouins or Cambodians different from Italians.

4. **The reification of culture.** To *reify* means to regard an intangible process, such as an emotion, as if it were a literal object. For example, when people say, "I have a lot of anger buried in me," they are reifying anger—treating it as a thing that sits inside them like a kidney, instead of as a complex cluster of mental and physical reactions that come and go. In the study of cultural psychology, there is a tendency to reify the concept of culture—that is, to regard it as an explanation without identifying the specific mechanisms or aspects of culture that influence behavior (Betancourt & López, 1993). To say "The Japanese work hard because of their culture" or "The Americans are violent because of their culture" shows circular reasoning. "Using a label as an explanation doesn't help our understanding very much," observe Lonner and Malpass (1994). It is, they say, like telling a man with a leg injury that he can't walk because he is lame. We may observe that Culture A behaves more aggressively than Culture B, but we don't get to say that Culture A frequently attacks its neighbors because it is a warlike culture. Instead, we need to ask what is going on in Culture A that makes it different from Culture B. "To say that the difference is cultural," say Lonner and Malpass, "just means that we have to look for the explanation in the details of how people live."

As if these methodological problems in the study of culture were not enough, we then have to deal with the political and emotional sensitivity of many cross-cultural findings. It is often difficult for people to talk about cultural differences when they feel uncomfortable and suspicious about other groups and defensive about their own. Emotions run high. For example, some time ago we were talking with students about average differences in the kinds of questions that southern African-American adults and southern white adults ask children. (This interesting study will be discussed later in this chapter.) Later, a white student came up to us and asked why we had "trashed" the white parents, and a black student argued that the study was invalid because no one *she* knew in *her* southern community talked to children that way. Both of these students were letting their feelings and tensions about race get in the way of their ability to hear the point of the research. Of course we weren't trashing the white parents, or the black parents either; neither was the study's author. But the students were unable to distinguish an objective difference from a value judgment. No one said that one parental style was better than the other, but these students heard it that way.

Social and cultural psychologists have studied why discussions of culture so often deteriorate into judgmental and emotional language. As we will see, they also explore the reasons for the universal habit of assuming that one's own culture is the best. Must cultural differences always be sources of conflict and misunderstanding, or can people learn to accept their differences? And must differences always be evaluated in terms of better and worse, or can they just be . . . differences?

What Do You Know?

1. Dr. Livingston does research on Americans' habit of making frequent geographical moves and how it affects their attitudes toward friendship and sociability. Dr. Livingston can best be described as a (cultural/cross-cultural) psychologist.
2. Like eating, sleeping is a biological process that is influenced in many ways by culture. Can you think of some of these ways?
3. Several decades ago, a study compared arranged marriages in Japan with marriages for love in the United States; after ten years of married life, there were no differences between the two groups in their self-rankings of marital satisfaction and love. What might be a problem in interpreting these findings?

Answers:

1. cultural   2. Culture affects what time people go to sleep and get up in the morning; the kind of bed, cot, or mat they sleep on; what they wear, if anything, while sleeping; whether they rely on an artificial signal (e.g., an alarm clock) to wake them up; whether they permit their infants or older children to sleep with them; and whether they take afternoon naps. (This list is not exhaustive.)   3. One problem is that "satisfaction" and "love" might have had different meanings in the two cultures, or they might have been measured in different ways.

THE RULES OF CULTURE

People learn their culture's rules as effortlessly as they learn its language. Just as they can speak without being able to state the rules of grammar, most people follow their culture's prescriptions without being aware of them. In this section, we will consider some of those invisible rules.

Context and Communication

Fiorello La Guardia, who was mayor of New York City from 1933 to 1945, was fluent in three languages: English, Italian, and Yiddish. La Guardia knew more than the words of those languages; he also knew the gestures that went along with each one. Researchers who studied films of his speeches could tell which language he was speaking with the sound turned off! They could do so by reading his *body language,* the nonverbal signals of body movement, posture, gesture, and gaze that people constantly express (Birdwhistell, 1970). Italians and Jews embellish their speech with circular movements of their arms and hands, and by measuring the radius of those movements, you can actually predict whether a speaker is of Italian or Jewish descent: The larger the radius, the more likely the speaker is Italian (Keating, 1994).

Some signals of body language, like some facial expressions, seem to be "spoken" universally. Across cultures, people generally recognize body movements that reveal pleasure or displeasure, liking or dislike, tension or relaxation, and high status or low status (Buck, 1984; Keating, 1994). When people are depressed, it shows in their walk, stance, and head position. However, most aspects of body language are specific to particular verbal languages and cultures.

For example, the smile is universally recognized as a sign of friendliness, yet it also has many culture-specific meanings. Americans smile more often than Germans do; this does not mean that Americans are friendlier than Germans but that they differ in their notions of when a smile is appropriate. After a German-American business session, Americans often complain that their German counterparts are cold and aloof. In turn, Germans often complain that the Americans are excessively cheerful, hiding their real feelings under the mask of a smile (Hall & Hall, 1990). The Japanese smile even more than the Americans, to disguise anger, embarrassment, or other negative emotions whose public display is considered rude and incorrect; this behavior is what got the Japanese student of our story on page 411 in hot water with his Arab classmate. In America, "looking someone in the eye" is a sign of honesty and forthrightness; but in many countries, such as Korea, Japan, and Thailand, it is a sign of disrespect, surliness, and aggressiveness.

Be careful where you make this gesture

Even the simplest gesture is subject to misunderstanding and offense. The sign of the University of Texas football team, the Longhorns, is to extend the index finger and the pinkie. In Italy and other parts of Europe this gesture means a man's wife has been unfaithful to him—a serious insult! Anita Rowe, a consultant who advises businesses on cross-cultural customs, tells of a newly hired Asian engineer in a California company. As the man left his office to lead the first meeting of his project team, his secretary crossed her fingers to wish him luck. Instead of reassuring him, her gesture thoroughly confused him: In his home country, crossing one's fingers is a sexual proposition (Gregor, 1993).

When a nonverbal rule is broken, a person is likely to feel extremely uncomfortable without knowing why. One such rule governs *conversational distance:* how close people normally stand to one another when they are speaking (Hall, 1959, 1976). Arabs like to stand close enough to feel your breath, touch your arm, and see your eyes—a distance that makes white North Americans and northern Europeans uneasy, unless they are talking intimately with a lover. Cross-cultural researchers have found that white North Americans, the English, and the Swedes stand farthest apart when they converse; southern Europeans stand closer; and South Americans and Arabs stand the closest (Keating, 1994; Sommer, 1969).

Knowing about cultural differences, though, doesn't make it easy to change one's own rules. Caroline Keating (1994), an American cross-cultural psychologist, tells of walking with a Pakistani colleague: "I found myself clumsily stepping off the sidewalk. Without realizing it, the closer my Muslim colleague moved toward me (seeking the interpersonal closeness he was comfortable with) the more I moved over streetside (seeking the interpersonal distance I was comfortable with). . . . I would suddenly disappear from his view, having fallen into the street; perhaps not 'the ugly American,' but a clumsy one!"

People from different cultures differ in how attentive they are to body language and nonverbal signals, and they differ in how much attention they pay to the context of the conversation (Goldman, 1994; Gudykunst & Ting-Toomey, 1988; Hall, 1983). In **high-context cultures,** which are generally homogeneous and close-knit, such as Japan and Middle Eastern nations, people pay close attention to nonverbal signs such as posture and distance between speakers. They assume a shared knowledge and history, so things don't have to be spelled out directly. In Japan, for instance, people will rarely say, "No, I can't do that" right to your face; it would be considered too direct and too insulting. They are more likely to say, "That is difficult" or "We will see."

In **low-context cultures,** such as Germany and most regions of the United States, people pay far more attention to words than to nonverbal signals. They assume no shared knowledge and history, so everything has to be explained and stated directly. When low-context Americans talk to high-context Japanese, both sides may come away dissatisfied. Americans will have difficulty knowing what their Japanese colleagues meant, and why they meandered around the subject instead of getting to the point. The Japanese, who think that intelligent human beings should be able to discover the point of a conversation from its context, will think the direct-speaking Americans are talking down to them.

The importance of knowing the difference between high- and low-context cultures cannot be overestimated: Misunderstandings between them can lead to war (Triandis, 1994). On January 9, 1991, the Foreign Minister of Iraq, Tariq Aziz, met with the American Secretary of State, James Baker, to discuss Iraq's invasion of Kuwait. Seated next to Aziz was the half brother of Iraq's president, Saddam Hussein. Baker said, "If you do not move out of Kuwait we will attack you." An unmistakable statement, right? But his *nonverbal* language was that of a low-context American diplomat, moderate and polite. He didn't roar, stamp his feet, or wave his hands. Saddam Hussein's brother, for his part, behaved like a normal, high-context Iraqi: He paid attention to Baker's nonverbal language, which he considered the important form of communication. He reported to Saddam Hussein that Baker was "not at all angry. The Americans are just talking, and they will not attack." Saddam therefore instructed Aziz to be

---

high-context cultures Cultures in which people pay close attention to nonverbal forms of communication and assume a shared context for their interactions—a common history and set of attitudes.
low-context cultures Cultures in which people do not take a shared context for granted and instead emphasize direct verbal communication.

inflexible and yield nothing. This misunderstanding contributed to the outbreak of a bloody war in which untold thousands of people died.

The Organization of Time

Imagine that you have arranged to meet a friend for lunch at noon. The friend has not arrived at 12:15, 12:30, or even 12:45. Please answer these questions: What time would *you* have arrived? Would you have been "on time"? How long would you wait for your friend before you started to feel worried or annoyed? When would you leave?

In most parts of the United States and Canada, the answers are obvious. You would have been there pretty close to noon and would not have waited much past 12:30. That is because these countries, along with northern European nations, are **monochronic cultures:** Time is organized into linear segments in which people do one thing "at a time" (Hall, 1983; Hall & Hall, 1990). The day is divided into appointments, schedules, and routines, and because time is a precious commodity, people don't like to "waste" time or "spend" too much time on any one activity. In such cultures, therefore, it is considered the height of rudeness (or high status) to keep someone waiting. But the farther south you go in Europe, South America, and Africa, the more likely you are to find **polychronic cultures.** Here, time is organized along parallel lines. People do many things at once, and the demands of friends and family supersede those of the appointment book. People in Latin America and the Middle East think nothing of waiting all day, or even a week, to see someone. The idea of having to be somewhere "on time," as if time were more important than a person, is unthinkable. Here is a summary of the differences between the two cultural styles (Hall & Hall, 1990):

MONOCHRONIC PEOPLE	POLYCHRONIC PEOPLE
Are low-context	Are high-context
Do one thing at a time	Do many things at once
Concentrate on the job	Are highly distractible and subject to interruptions
Take time commitments seriously	Consider time commitments an objective to be achieved if possible
Give the job first priority	Give people first priority
Adhere religiously to plans	Change plans often and easily
Are concerned about not disturbing others; value privacy	Are more concerned with relationships than with privacy; may not even have a word for privacy
Like "own space" or private office to work in	Freely share working space, which increases flow of information

monochronic cultures Cultures in which time is organized sequentially; schedules and deadlines are valued over people.
polychronic cultures Cultures in which time is organized horizontally; people tend to do several things at once and value relationships over schedules.

Monochronic People	Polychronic People
Show great respect for private property; seldom borrow or lend	Borrow and lend things often
Emphasize promptness	Care less about own promptness than other people's needs; are almost never "on time"
Develop many short-term relationships	Build lifetime relationships

The Japanese have one of the few cultures to combine elements of both systems. With the American occupation that followed World War II, they started being monochronic as a way of creating harmony with the *gaijin* (foreigners). Today they are extremely monochronic about schedules, but in every other way they are high-context and polychronic. For instance, they are loyal to long-term business relationships, and employees and managers share office space and information freely (Hall & Hall, 1990).

In diverse North America, the two time systems keep bumping into each other. Business, government, and other institutions are organized monochronically, but Native Americans, Latinos, and others tend to operate on polychronic principles. The result is repeated misunderstandings. A white judge in Miami got into hot water when he observed that "Cubans always show up two hours late for weddings"—late in his culture's terms, that is. The judge was accurate in his observation; the problem was his implication that there was something wrong with Cubans for being "late." And late compared with what, by the way? The Cubans were perfectly on time for Cubans.

A culture's way of organizing time does not develop arbitrarily. It stems from the culture's economic system, social organization, political history, and ecology. The monochronic structure of time emerged as a result of the Industrial Revolution in England (Hall, 1983). That makes sense: When thousands of people began working in factories and assembly lines, their efforts had to become coordinated. Moreover, factories have no intrinsic rhythms; people can and do work day or night in them.

But in rural economies, where work is based on the rhythms of nature, people think of time differently. When Edward Hall (1983) worked on a Hopi reservation many decades ago, he found that the Hopi were behaving in ways that were mysterious and silly to the Anglos. The Hopi were always leaving work undone; they would start to build a dam, a house, or a road, and stop in the middle. To the Anglos, the Hopi were shiftless and lazy. To the Hopi, the Anglos were rigid, arbitrary, and compulsive. What was so important about building dams, houses, and roads? Unlike the maturing of sheep or the ripening of corn, said the Hopi, building a house had no inherent timetable. What did matter was working in their fields and completing seasonal religious ceremonies, activities that indeed had to be done on time—nature's time, not human time.

The Self and Self-identity

Who are you? Take as much time as you like to complete this sentence: "I am _____."

One of the most important ways in which cultures differ has to do with whether the individual or the group is given the greater emphasis (Hofstede & Bond, 1988; Markus & Kitayama, 1991; Triandis, 1995). This difference, in turn, affects people's concepts of the self and personality (see Figure 13.1.) The idea of defining the "self" as a collection of personality traits (e.g., "I am extroverted, agreeable, and ambitious") is inherent in *individual-centered* cultures. In *collectivist* or *group-centered* cultures, the self is seen as something embedded in a community and is defined that way (e.g., "I am descended from three generations of storytellers on my mother's side and five generations of farmers on my father's side, and their ancestors first came to this village two hundred years ago . . .").

In a revealing study comparing Japanese and Americans, the Americans reported that their sense of self changes only 5 to 10 percent in different situations, whereas the Japanese said that 90 to 99 percent of their sense of self changes (de Rivera, 1989). For the Japanese, it is important to enact *tachiba*—to perform one's social roles correctly so that there will be harmony with others. (As we just noted, this was one reason they adopted the American monochronic system of time after World War II.) Americans, in contrast, tend to value "being true to yourself" and having a "core identity." Similarly, in cross-cultural studies of how people respond to the "I am . . ." cue, people from collectivist cultures typically answer in terms of family (e.g., "I am an uncle, a cousin, a son") or nation, whereas people from individualist cultures tend to answer in terms of personality traits or occupation (Triandis, 1994, 1995). The way that people define the self affects many aspects of individual psychology, including people's personalities, emotions, motivations, and relationships (Campbell et al., 1996; Trafimow, Triandis, & Goto, 1991).

The perception of the self also affects how people perceive their need for relationships (Kashima et al., 1995). All human beings are dependent on others, but just as individuals vary—some like lots of "space" whereas others like to be surrounded by friends—cultures vary in the value they place on dependency versus autonomy. Amer-

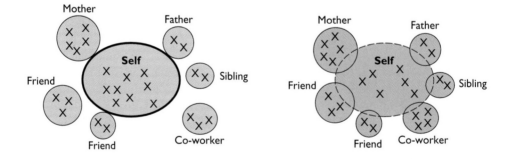

Figure 13.1 *The Western view of the independent self is illustrated on the left, and the Eastern view of the interdependent self is on the right. The Xs represent aspects of the self or others, such as "I am creative" or "My friend is kind." In collectivist cultures, the boundaries between the self and others are more permeable and shifting; people feel that they change across situations more than Westerners do (from Markus & Kitayama, 1991).*

ican culture emphasizes independence and self-reliance, but other cultures, such as the Latino and Japanese, emphasize family cohesiveness, group interdependence, and teamwork. In many parts of American society, *dependence* is practically a dirty word, especially for men, but in Japan the need for dependence and nurturant concern for another is assumed to be a powerful and lifelong motive for both sexes (Doi, 1973). Latinos tend to rely on their extended families for emotional support much more than Anglo-Americans do, and they feel more anxiety when separated from them. Perhaps for this reason, rates of homelessness are very low among Latinos living in the United States and Canada. Anglos have more casual networks, even listing co-workers among those they depend on (Griffith & Villavicencio, 1985).

In the low-context United States, where mobility is prized and people move many times in their lives, the ability to make friends quickly and develop a surface sociability is adaptive and valuable. In collectivist cultures, where people rarely change homes and neighborhoods, friendship develops slowly; it takes a long time to flower, but then it blooms for life. The difference between these two styles shows clearly in reactions to the proverb "A rolling stone gathers no moss." In America, it means keep moving; don't let anything cling to you. In Japan, it means stay where you are; if you keep moving you will never acquire the beauty of stability.

In collectivist cultures, the strongest human bond is usually not between husband and wife but between parent and child or among siblings (Triandis, 1995). In China, the most valued and celebrated relationship is the father–son bond; in India, Mexico, Ireland, and Greece, it is mother–son; in parts of Africa, it is older brother–younger brother; among the Tiwi of North Australia, it is mother-in-law and son-in-law (no mother-in-law jokes among the Tiwi!). In addition, child rearing in collectivist cultures is a communal matter. Everyone has a say in correcting the child's behavior; as an African proverb says, "It takes a whole village to raise a child." The idea of privacy for children is unknown, and the goal is to raise children who are obedient, hardworking, and dutiful toward their parents. Can you predict what will happen if a collectivist man marries an individualist woman? The chances are high that the husband will regard his relationship with one or both of his parents as most important, whereas his wife will expect his relationship to her to be the most important. And they are likely to disagree intensely, without knowing why, about such matters as letting their children have their own rooms, speak their minds, make their own choices, talk back, and become independent.

Everyone develops a *personal* identity—a sense of who one is—that is based on his or her individual traits and unique history. But people also develop **social identities** based on their nationality, ethnicity, religion, and social roles (Brewer, 1993; Hogg & Abrams, 1988; Tajfel & Turner, 1986). Social identities are important because they give people a feeling of place and position in the world. Without social identities, most people would feel like loose marbles rolling around in an unconnected universe. The

---

social identity The part of a person's self-concept that is based on his or her identification with a nation, culture, or ethnic group or with gender or other roles in society.

458 ◆ Part V   *The Sociocultural Perspective*

social identity that comes from belonging to a distinctive group satisfies two important motives: the individual's need for inclusion in a larger collective, and the individual's need to feel differentiated from others (Brewer, Manzi, & Shaw, 1993).

In modern societies, many social identities are possible. People face the dilemma of balancing an **ethnic identity,** a close identification with their own racial, religious, or ethnic group, with **acculturation,** identifying with and feeling part of the dominant culture (Cross, 1971; Helms, 1990; Spencer & Dornbusch, 1990). Research suggests that ethnic-identity formation and acculturation are separate processes. Some people learn to alternate easily between their culture of origin and the majority culture, slipping into the customs and language of each, as circumstances dictate. They are comfortable and competent in both cultures, just as bilingual people are in two languages, and they do not feel that they must choose one culture over another (LaFromboise, Coleman, & Gerton, 1993). Others, however, struggle to find a balance between their culture of origin and the dominant culture of the society.

For any individual, four outcomes are possible, depending on whether ethnic identity is strong or weak, and whether identification with the larger culture is strong or weak (Berry, 1994; Phinney, 1990). People who are truly *bicultural* have strong ties both to their ethnicity and to the larger culture: They say, "I am proud of my own ethnic heritage, but I identify just as much with my country." People who choose *assimilation* have weak feelings of ethnicity but a strong sense of acculturation: They might say, for example, "I'm an American, period." People who are *ethnic separatists* have a strong sense of ethnic identity but weak feelings of acculturation: They might say, "My ethnicity comes first; if I join the mainstream, I'm betraying my origins." And some people feel *marginal,* connected to neither their ethnicity nor the dominant culture: They may say, "I'm an individual and don't identify with any group" or "I don't belong anywhere."

		Ethnic Identity Is	
		Strong	**Weak**
Acculturation Is	**Strong**	Bicultural	Assimilated
	Weak	Separatist	Marginal

Some of the conflicts between cultural groups in North America, as well as within these groups, arise because people have different ideas about the relative benefits of acculturation versus ethnic identity and about how their different identities should be balanced. That is why ethnic labels have great symbolic and emotional significance. For example, *Hispanic* is a label used by the U.S. government to include all Spanish-

---

ethnic identity Having a close identification with one's own racial, religious, or ethnic group.
acculturation The process by which members of groups that are minorities in a given society come to identify with and feel part of the mainstream culture.

speaking groups. But many "Hispanics" dislike the term, pointing out that Spaniards, Cubans, Mexican-Americans (Chicanos), Latin Americans (Latinos), and Puerto Ricans differ in their culture and history, and therefore in their ethnic identity (Vasquez & Barón, 1988). Other Hispanics, however, dislike the term *Latino.* The 1992 Latino National Political Survey, a large random-sample survey, found that most Latinos don't think of themselves as such, preferring national-origin labels such as Mexican-American or just American (de la Garza et al., 1992). Likewise, Koreans, Japanese, Chinese, and Vietnamese are Asian, but many individuals in these groups resent being lumped into a single category. The Hopi, Navajo, Cheyenne, Lakota Sioux, Ojibwa, Iroquois, and hundreds of other groups are all considered Native American, but there are many cultural differences among them. For that matter, not all white Americans are WASPs—white Anglo-Saxon Protestants. Not all want to be called Anglos, which refers to a British heritage, or European-American, as if all European countries, from Greece to Norway, were the same.

Some groups are rejecting names that were imposed on them by the majority culture and insist instead on a name that reflects their own cultural identity. This is why the Eskimos are now called the Inuit, their own name. In the early 1970s, William Cross (1971) analyzed "The Negro-to-Black conversion experience," arguing that this change was critical for the psychology of black liberation. A decade later, Halford Fairchild (1985) analyzed the significance of labels that are based on skin color ("black"), race ("Negro"), or national origin ("Afro-American"), for each term has different historical and emotional connotations. Only a few years later, *African-American* became a popular term to identify people of African descent living in the Americas; those who like the term argue that it is analogous to Polish-American or Italian-American.

But not all members of each ethnic group agree on a group label, which creates confusion and sometimes hypersensitivity. Some—blacks?—feel no special kinship to Africa; the social critic Henry Louis Gates, Jr., called his autobiography *Colored People,* the term he prefers, and the writer Stanley Crouch prefers *Negro.* The American Indian Movement and the National Congress of American Indians continue to use the term *American Indian* even though the "correct" term is supposed to be *Native American* (Trimble & Medicine, 1993). The debate over group names is likely to continue, and the names are likely to keep changing, as ethnic groups in North America struggle to define their place in a medley of cultures.

What Do You Know?

A. Provide the term that describes each of the following:

1. Cultures whose members pay close attention to nonverbal signs and often don't spell things out directly.
2. Cultures whose members do things one at a time and consider time a precious commodity.
3. Cultures whose members regard the "self" as a collection of stable personality traits.

B. Which of the terms in the preceding question apply to the majority culture in the United States and Canada?

C. Frank, an African-American college student, finds himself caught between two philosophies on his campus. One holds that blacks should shed their identity as victims of racism and move toward full integration into American culture. The other favors Afrocentric education, holding that blacks should immerse themselves in the history, values, and contributions of African culture. Frank is caught between his _____ and _____.

ANSWERS:

A. **1.** high context   **2.** monochronic   **3.** individual-centered   **B.** Terms 2 and 3 apply to the majority culture.   **C.** ethnic identity, acculturation

Mental Abilities

What does it mean to be smart? Years ago, in a study of the Kpelle tribe in Africa (Scribner, 1977), researchers gave an unschooled farmer this reasoning problem, a standard example of a Western syllogism: "All Kpelle men are rice farmers. Mr. Smith is not a rice farmer. Is he a Kpelle man?" The farmer insisted that the information provided did not allow a conclusion:

> *Kpelle man:* I don't know the man in person. I have not laid eyes on the man himself.
>
> *Researcher:* Just think about the statement.
>
> *Kpelle man:* If I know him in person, I can answer that question, but since I do not know him in person I cannot answer that question.

The interviewer concluded that because the Kpelle farmer was accustomed to drawing on personal knowledge alone to reach conclusions, he could not approach the task analytically. Yet in the exchange with the researcher, the man showed that he *could* reason deductively:

> *premise*   If I do not know a person, I cannot draw any conclusions about that person.
>
> *premise*   I do not know Mr. Smith.
>
> *conclusion*   Therefore I cannot draw any conclusions about Mr. Smith.

The answer that the Kpelle farmer gave was perfectly smart in *his* culture's terms; it just was not what his interviewer expected. Cross-cultural research has found that most people everywhere are able to learn to reason deductively, but the areas in which they apply deductive reasoning will depend on their experiences and needs. It is the same with all areas of intelligence. Children in Zambia get a lot of experience making models out of wire and sticks, but they don't get the chance to do much drawing, as children in industrialized cultures do. If you measure these children's visual skills and spatial intelligence, you will find differences between the two cultures; the reason is that the children have had different experiences in modeling and making things (Serpell, 1994).

All aspects of cognition—reasoning, memory, and problem solving—occur in a social and cultural context. Even the very meaning of "intelligence" is determined by culture. Certain human capacities are universal, but cultures differ in which of those capacities they celebrate and foster and which they weed out as being unnecessary. Cross-cultural studies have supported Jean Piaget's theory, discussed in Chapter 9, of the hierarchical sequence of cognitive stages. Children everywhere are able to progress from the sensorimotor stage to the preoperational stage, and on to concrete operations and formal operations such as deductive reasoning. But cultural differences may occur in the *rate* of development of these stages, because cultures differ in which cognitive skills are needed and nurtured in their members (Rogoff & Chavajay, 1995).

Pierre Dasen (1994), who studied with Piaget, spent years testing Piaget's theory in different cultural contexts: among the Aborigines in Australia, the Inuit in Canada, the Ebri and the Baoulé in the Ivory Coast, and the Kikuyu in Kenya. Dasen found that traditional nomadic hunting peoples, such as the Inuit and the Aborigines, do not quantify things and do not need to. The Aborigines have number words only up to five; after that, all quantities are described as "many." In such cultures, the cognitive ability to understand the conservation of quantity or number (e.g., that an amount of water remains the same whether it is in a tall, narrow glass or a short, fat one) develops late, if at all. But nomadic hunting tribes rely on their spatial orientation—knowing where water holes and successful hunting routes are—and so spatial abilities develop rapidly. In contrast, children who live in settled agricultural communities, such as the Baoulé, develop rapidly in the domain of quantification and much more slowly in spatial reasoning.

Cross-cultural findings also shed light on why cultures and ethnic groups may differ, on the average, in their academic performance. (The biological perspective, as we saw in Chapter 3, can account for some of the individual variation in mental abilities within a group, but not for average differences between groups.) One factor influencing these differences is what people in a culture believe about the origins of intelligence and the reasons for achievement.

For more than a decade, Harold Stevenson and his colleagues (1990a, 1990b) have been studying attitudes toward achievement in Japan, China, and the United States. The researchers began by comparing large samples of first- and fifth-grade children, their parents, and their teachers in Minneapolis, Sendai (Japan), and Taipei (Taiwan). In another project, they compared children from 20 schools in Chicago and 11 schools in Beijing. In 1990, Stevenson, along with Chuansheng Chen and Shin-Ying Lee (1993), revisited the original schools to collect new data on fifth-graders, and they also retested many of the children who had been in first grade in the 1980 study and who were in the eleventh grade in 1990.

In 1980, the Asian children far outperformed the American children on a broad battery of mathematical tests. On computations and word problems, there was virtually no overlap between schools, with the lowest-scoring Beijing schools doing better than the highest-scoring Chicago schools. In 1990, the gap between the Asian and American children had grown even greater. Only 4 percent of the Chinese children and 10 percent of the Japanese children had scores as low as those of the *average* American child.

These differences could not be accounted for by educational resources: The Chinese had worse facilities and larger classes than the Americans. On the average, the American children's parents were far better off financially and better educated than the parents of the Chinese children. Nor could the test differences be accounted for by differences in the children's fondness for math: 85 percent of the Chinese kids said they liked math, but so did almost 75 percent of the American children. Nor did it have anything to do with intellectual ability in general, because the American children were just as knowledgeable and capable as the Asian children on tests of general information.

But the Asians and Americans were worlds apart, so to speak, in their attitudes, expectations, and efforts:

✦ American parents, teachers, and children were far and away more likely than Asians to believe that mathematical ability is innate. They thought that if you "have it," you don't have to work hard, and if you don't have it, there's no point in trying. When Japanese teachers were asked to choose the most important factor in mathematical performance, 93 percent chose "studying hard"—compared with only 26 percent of the American teachers. Students picked up these attitudes: 72 percent of the Japanese but only 27 percent of the American eleventh-graders thought that studying hard was the key to success in math.

✦ American parents had far lower standards for their children's performance. They said they would be satisfied with scores barely above average on a 100-point test; most felt that their children were doing fine in math and that the schools were doing a good or excellent job. In contrast, the Chinese and Japanese parents said they would be happy only with very high scores, and most were not highly satisfied with their children's schools or even with their children's excellent performance.

✦ American students had more stressful, conflicting demands on their time than their Asian counterparts. Chinese and Japanese students were expected to devote themselves to their studies, but American students were expected to be "well-rounded"—to have after-school jobs (74 percent of them did, compared with only 21 percent of the Asians), to have dates and an active social life (85 percent vs. 37 percent), and to have time for sports and other activities. Contrary to the stereotype of the stressed and overworked Japanese student, it was the American students who were most likely to report that school was a source of stress and anxiety (Crystal et al., 1994). The Japanese eleventh-graders actually had the lowest incidence of stress, depression, insomnia, aggression, and physical symptoms.

✦American students did not value education as much as Asian students did, and the Americans were more complacent with their mediocre work. When asked what they would wish for if a wizard could give them anything they wanted, more than 60 percent of the Chinese fifth-graders named something related to their education. Can you guess what the American children wanted? A majority said money or possessions.

These studies suggest that attitudes of teachers and parents toward achievement account for a big chunk of the cultural differences in test scores. Cultural research has also shown how specific interactions between parent and child affect performance on cognitive tests. For example, anthropologist Shirley Brice Heath (1989), who studied an African-American community in a southern city in the United States, notes that traditional black communities have a rich linguistic tradition that emphasizes verbal wit, nuances of meaning, striking metaphors, rapid-fire dialogue, and unexpected analogies. In this tradition, adults ask children many questions, but only *real* questions, to which the adults do not know the answers. Adults expect youngsters to *show* what they know rather than *tell* what they know. Therefore the black parents in Heath's study were less likely than white parents to ask their children "what," "where," "when," and "who" questions—the sorts of questions found on standardized tests and in schoolbooks ("What's this story about?" "Who is this?"). Many black parents preferred to ask analogy questions ("What's that like?") and story-starter questions ("Did you hear about . . .").

Schools, says Heath, do not take advantage of black children's strengths. Instead, they train children to give the "right" answers, and they treat literacy as a set of mechanistic operations. Teachers in the community used Heath's information to modify their teaching strategies. They encouraged their black pupils to ask "school-type" questions, but they also incorporated analogy and story-starter questions into their lessons. Soon the black children, who had previously been uncomfortable and quiet, became eager, confident participants.

Parents and teachers are not the only powerful environmental influences on children's academic ability; so are peers. In a large-scale study of 15,000 students at nine different American high schools, researchers sought reasons for the average difference in school performance of Asian-Americans, African-Americans, Latinos, and whites (Steinberg, Dornbusch, & Brown, 1992). Asian-American students, who had the highest grades on the average, reported having the highest level of peer support for academic achievement. They studied together in groups, cheered one another on, and praised one another's success. But many African-American students regarded academic success as a sign of selling out to the white establishment. High-achieving black students often said they had few black friends for this reason; they felt they had to choose between doing well in school and being popular with their peers. This dilemma affects students of any ethnicity or gender whose peer group thinks that academic success is only for nerds and sellouts (Arroyo & Zigler, 1995). And it can be emotionally difficult: As a series of studies with hundreds of high-school students found, among African-Americans, academic achievement is often correlated with high feelings of self-efficacy, but also with feelings of anxiety and depression (Arroyo & Zigler, 1995).

According to sociologist Signithia Fordham (1991), who studied black adolescents in six private high schools in New Jersey, many of these teenagers felt a sharp conflict between ethnic identity and acculturation. Academic success, they believe, requires "acting white," which in turn means pretending to be "raceless." Lowering one's ambitions to be in harmony with one's peers is a way to maintain the good feelings and sense of connection that come with having a strong social identity and group solidarity.

As Fordham and John Ogbu (1986) have argued, this is not an irrational strategy. The lower grades and aspirations of some minority groups, they maintain, are a rational response to the belief that effort is not going to pay off in the white professional world. (As we saw in the previous chapter, when people believe that their opportunities are limited, they scale down their ambitions.) Ogbu (1993) argues that "voluntary" minorities—groups that came to North America willingly, such as the Chinese, Punjabi, or South Americans—strongly endorse academic success as a way to get ahead. But "involuntary" minorities—groups that originally became part of the United States through slavery or conquest, such as African-Americans, Mexican-Americans, and Native Americans and Hawaiians—develop what Ogbu calls an "oppositional" stance toward the dominant culture. They tend, he says, to be skeptical of achievement and mainstream goals, preferring to maintain group identity and separateness. (As you evaluate this argument, be careful not to stereotype: In fact, growing numbers of all of these "oppositional" groups are succeeding in the mainstream culture. From 1950 to 1990, for example, the black population doubled, but the number of blacks holding white-collar jobs and entering middle-class occupations jumped 920 percent [Edsall & Edsall, 1991].)

"Intelligence," then, cannot be evaluated apart from the cultural context in which it occurs. Any child will seem to be unintelligent if the child must maneuver in a world that he or she knows little about or in a school system that does not capitalize on what the child already knows. Any adult will seem to be unintelligent if he or she develops skills that are not valued by the larger society, even if those skills are necessary for survival in his or her community. In the sociocultural perspective, intelligence must always be evaluated in a person's social context.

An appreciation of the rules of culture expands our understanding of human behavior. As we saw in this section, culture affects your sense of time; whether you give priority to other people's needs or to appointments and schedules; how you process information and communicate meaning; what nonverbal gestures you use and even whether you pay much attention to nonverbal signs; what notions about the self you hold and what value you place on relationships; what social identities matter to you, and whether you try to balance an ethnic identity with a national identity; and which cognitive abilities you value and acquire.

WHAT DO YOU KNOW?

A researcher studying ethnic differences in children's mental abilities focuses on one group's lower performance in school.

1. What factors might cultural psychologists investigate to explain this difference?
2. Can you think of a research question that might lead to a different view of these children's intellectual competence?

ANSWERS:

1. Some factors include each culture's values and attitudes toward academic success; the specific interactions between parents and children; the expectations that parents and teachers have for children's mental abilities; the relevance in the larger culture of the abilities being tested; and whether a child's peers support or discourage academic achievement.   **2.** One possible alternative is this: What mental skills and abilities have these children developed that help them do well in their own communities and in the world outside of school?

THE ORIGINS OF CULTURE

When most people read about the customs of other cultures, they are inclined to say, "Oh, boy, I like the attitudes of the Gorks but I hate the habits of the Dorks." But a culture's practices cannot easily be exported elsewhere, like cheese, or surgically removed, like a tumor. The reason is that a culture's attitudes and practices are deeply embedded in its history, environment, economy, and survival needs.

To explain the origins of cultural customs, researchers working from a sociocultural perspective study a culture's political system and its economy, and how that economy is affected by geography, natural resources, and even the weather. They find out who controls and distributes the resources, and how safe a society is from interlopers. They study the kinds of work that people do. They observe whether there is environmental pressure on a group to produce more children or to have fewer of them.

To illustrate this approach, we will take a look at how sociocultural researchers account for the origins of gender roles and why those roles often vary so much across cultures. Two stories demonstrate what we mean.

Scenario 1. A young wife leaves her house one morning to draw water from the local well as her husband watches from the porch. On her way back from the well, a male stranger stops her and asks for some water. She gives him a cupful and then invites him home to dinner. He accepts. The husband, wife, and guest have a pleasant meal together. The husband, in a gesture of hospitality, invites the guest to spend the night—with his wife. The guest accepts. In the morning, the husband leaves early to bring home breakfast. When he returns, he finds his wife again in bed with the visitor.

The question: At what point in this story does the husband feel angry?

The answer: It depends on his culture (Hupka, 1981, 1991). A North American husband would feel rather angry at a wife who had an extramarital affair, and a wife would feel rather angry at being offered to a guest as if she were a lamb chop. But these reactions are not universal. A Pawnee husband of the nineteenth century would be enraged at any man who dared ask his wife even for water. An Ammassalik Inuit husband finds it perfectly honorable to offer his wife to a stranger, but only once. He would be angry to find his wife and the guest having a second encounter. A Toda husband in turn-of-the-century India would not be angry at all, because the Toda allowed both husband and wife to take lovers. Both spouses might feel angry, though, if one of them had a *sneaky* affair, without announcing it publicly.

> *Scenario 2.* A young boy notices, at an early age, that he is not like other boys. He prefers playing with girls. He is attracted to the work that adult women do, such as cooking and sewing. He often dreams at night of being a girl, and he even likes to put on the clothes of girls. As the boy enters adolescence, people begin to whisper that he's "different," that he seems feminine in his movements, posture, and language. One day the boy can hide his secret feelings no longer and reveals them to his parents.

The question: How do they respond?

The answer: It depends on their culture. In the United States today, many parents would react with tears, anger, or guilt. They might haul their son off to a psychiatrist, who would diagnose him as having a "gender identity disorder" and begin intensive treatment (American Psychiatric Association, 1994). But these reactions are not universal. Until the late 1800s, in a number of Plains Indians and western American Indian tribes, parents and other elders reacted with sympathy and understanding when a young man wanted to live the life of a woman. A man in this role (whom whites called a *berdache*) was often given an honored status as a shaman, a person with the power to cure illness and act as an intermediary between the natural and spiritual worlds, and he was permitted to dress as and perform the duties of a woman. In some tribes, he was even permitted to marry another man (Williams, 1986).

In the Sambian society of Papua New Guinea, parents would react still differently (Herdt, 1984). In Sambia, all adolescent boys are *required* to engage in oral sex with older males as part of their initiation into manhood. Sambians believe that a boy cannot mature physically or emotionally unless he ingests another man's semen over a period of several years. However, Sambian parents would react with shock and disbelief if a son said he wanted to live as a woman. Every man and woman in Sambian society marries someone of the other sex and performs the work assigned to his or her own sex.

These diverse reactions support the social-learning view, discussed in Chapter 7, that although anatomical *sex* is universal and unchangeable (unless extraordinary surgical procedures are used), *gender*—which encompasses all the duties, rights, and behaviors a culture considers appropriate for males and females—is learned, or *socially constructed*. As we saw in Chapter 2, **social constructionism** is the view that there are no

---

social constructionism The view that there are no universal truths about human nature because people construct reality differently, depending on their culture, the historical moment, and their degree of power within their society.

Throughout history, a person's anatomical sex and the culturally assigned duties of the person's gender have not always corresponded. Some men have chosen to wear the clothes and play the roles of women, as in the tradition of the Native American berdache. *In the photo on the left, taken about 1885, We-wha, a Zuni Indian man, wears the traditional earrings, jewelry, and dress of a woman. Likewise, some women have worn the clothes and played the roles of men, as did the eighteenth-century pirate Mary Read (right).*

universal truths about human nature because people construct reality differently depending on their culture, the historical moment, and power arrangements within their society. In contrast, sociobiologists and evolutionary psychologists believe that sex heavily influences gender—that is, the biological fact of being male or female constrains the fundamental tasks and gender roles that men and women will play. By comparing different cultures around the world, cross-cultural psychologists hope to identify which aspects of gender roles are universally male or female as well as those that are culturally specific.

Gender and Culture: Themes and Variations

First, let's consider the commonalities. In general, men have had, and continue to have, more status and more power than women, especially in public affairs. Men have fought the wars and, on the average, are more aggressive and violent than women. If a society's economy includes hunting large game, traveling a long way from home, or making weapons, men typically handle these activities. Women have had the primary responsibility for cooking, cleaning, and taking care of children. Corresponding with this division of tasks, in many cultures around the world masculinity is regarded as something that boys must achieve through strenuous effort. Males must pass physical tests, endure pain, confront danger, and separate themselves psychologically and even physically from their mothers and the world of women. Sometimes they have to prove their self-reliance and courage in harsh initiation rites. Femininity, in contrast, tends to be associated with responsibility, obedience, and child care, and it is seen as something that develops without any special intervention from others.

Those are the common themes. Now for some variations:

✦ The status of women worldwide is not uniformly low (di Leonardo, 1991); it is highest in Scandinavian countries and lowest in Bangladesh, with tremendous variation in between. Women's status has been assessed by measures of economic security, educational opportunities, access to birth control and medical care, degree of self-determination, participation in public and political life, power to make decisions in the family, and physical safety. In some places, women are completely under the rule of men. Women in Saudi Arabia are not allowed to drive a car; many girls in India submit to arranged marriages as early as age 9. Yet elsewhere, as in Europe and North America, women are attaining greater power, education, influence, and independence. In this century, women have been elected heads of state in Israel, India, Norway, England, Iceland, Pakistan, Nicaragua, Bangladesh, Poland, Turkey. . . .

✦ The content of what is considered "men's work" and "women's work" varies from culture to culture. In some places, dentistry and teaching are men's work; in others, they are women's work. In many cultures women do the shopping and marketing, but in others marketing is men's work.

✦ In many cultures women are considered the "emotional" sex and are permitted to express their emotions more freely than men (Shields, 1991). But in cultures throughout the Middle East and South America, men are expected to be as emotionally expressive as women, or even more so, whereas many Asian cultures expect both sexes to control their emotions (Buck & Teng, 1987). In a large-scale international study, Israeli and Italian women were more likely than men to express sadness, but British, Spanish, Swiss, and German women were less likely to express sadness than were their male counterparts (Wallbott, Ricci-Bitti, & Bänninger-Huber, 1986).

✦ Cultures differ in the degree of contact that is permitted between the sexes. In many farm communities and in most modern occupations in North America and Europe, men and women work together. At the other end of the continuum, some Middle Eastern societies endorse *purdah,* the custom of veiling women and secluding them from all male eyes except those of their relatives.

✦ In some cultures, particularly those of East Asia, Southeast Asia, and Muslim societies, female chastity is highly prized. Women are expected to suppress all sexual feeling and behavior until marriage, and premarital or extramarital sex is cause for the woman's ostracism from the community or even her death. Yet in other cultures, such as those of Polynesia, Scandinavia, and northern Europe, female chastity is considered unimportant (Buss et al., 1990). Women are expected to have sex before marriage, and even extramarital sex is not necessarily cause for alarm.

✦ In some cultures men and women regard each other as opposite in nature, ability, and personality, a view that reflects their separate domains. In other cultures, such as those of the Ifaluk, the Tahitians, and people who live on Sudest Island near New Guinea, men and women do not regard each other as opposites or even as being very different (Lepowsky, 1994; Lutz, 1988). When Robert Levy (1973) lived in Tahiti, he found that Tahitian men were no more aggressive than women, nor were women gentler or more nurturant than men. To Tahitians, gender is no big deal.

Gender and Culture: Explaining the Differences

Cultural researchers argue that biological differences cannot account for the wide variation in gender roles around the world. They have examined instead two other fundamental factors: *production* (matters pertaining to the economy and to the creation of food, clothing, and shelter) and *reproduction* (matters pertaining to the bearing, raising, and nurturing of children).

One important finding is that rigid concepts of manhood tend to exist wherever there is a great deal of competition for resources—which is to say, in most places (Gilmore, 1990). For the human species, life has usually been harsh. Consider a tribe trying to survive in the wilds of a South American forest; or in the dry and unforgiving landscape of the desert; or in an icy arctic terrain that imposes limits on the number of people who can survive by fishing. When conditions such as these exist, men are the sex that is taught to hunt for large game, compete with one another for work, and fight off enemies. (This division of labor may originally have occurred because of men's relatively greater upper-body muscular strength and the fact that they do not become pregnant or nurse children.) Men are socialized to face confrontation. They are toughened up and pushed to take risks, even with their lives.

How do you get men to wage war and risk death, go off on long treks for food, and be willing to get bloodied defending the homestead? Far from being natural to men, some cultural researchers argue, aggressiveness has to be constantly rewarded. To persuade men to wage war and risk death, societies have to give them something; and the something is prestige and power—and women (Harris, 1974). That, in turn, means you have to raise obedient women; if the king is going to offer his daughter in marriage to the bravest warrior, she has to agree to be handed over. In contrast, in societies such as Tahiti and Sudest Island, where resources are abundant and there are no serious hazards or enemies to worry about, men don't feel they have to prove themselves or set themselves apart from women (Lepowsky, 1994).

A culture's economy and social structure also help account for the variations in the degree of aggression required and expected of men. In a fascinating analysis of the rates of violence in regional cultures of the United States, Richard Nisbett (1993) set out to explain why the American South, and some western regions of the country originally settled by southerners, have much higher rates of white homicide than the rest of the country. Southerners are more likely to endorse the use of violence for protection (recall the reactions to the homeowner's shooting of the Japanese exchange student) and as the proper response to perceived insults. "Violence has been associated with the South since the time of the American Revolution," begins an essay in the *Encyclopedia of Southern*

In most cultures, men are required to do dangerous, life-threatening work . . . but it's not always easy to get all of them to do it.

Reprinted with special permission of King Features Syndicate, Inc.

Culture, and it then devotes 39 pages to bloodcurdling accounts of feuds, duels, lynchings, violent sports, and murder.

Nisbett ruled out explanations based on poverty. Although poverty is associated with violence, "southernness" remains a predictor of homicide even when one controls for regional differences in poverty. Nisbett also ruled out explanations based on racial tensions; the counties with the smallest black populations have the highest white homicide rates. And he ruled out the southern tradition of slavery as an explanation; regions of the South that had the highest concentrations of slaves in the past have the lowest homicide rates today.

Nisbett argues that the South "is heir to a culture, deriving ultimately from economic determinants, in which violence is a natural and integral part." The New England and middle Atlantic states were settled by Puritans, Quakers, and Dutch and German farmers and artisans who had an advanced agricultural economy. For them, the best policy was one of cooperation for the common good. In contrast, the South was settled largely by immigrants from Scotland and Ireland, whose economies were based on herding and hunting, activities that continued to provide their economic base in America.

Why should herding, as opposed to farming, make such a difference in rates of violence? People who depend economically on their herds are extremely vulnerable; their livelihoods can be lost in an instant by the theft of their animals. To reduce the likelihood of theft, says Nisbett, herders "cultivate a posture of extreme vigilance toward any act that might be perceived as threatening in any way, and respond with sufficient force to frighten the offender and the community into recognizing that they are not to be trifled with." This is why cattle rustling and horse thievery were capital crimes in the Old West, and why Mediterranean and Middle Eastern herding cultures, as well as those of the southern United States, place a high value on male aggressiveness. When Nisbett examined agricultural practices within the South, he found that homicide rates were more than twice as high in the hills and dry plains regions (where herding occurs) than in the farming regions. As you can see, male biology does not automatically dictate aggressive behavior. Aggressiveness occurs primarily when it is useful for protecting a society's economic interests.

In terms of the kinds of gender roles they promote, cultures fall along a continuum from traditional to modern (egalitarian). In a cross-cultural study of 100 men and women from each of 14 countries in North and South America, Europe, and Asia, Deborah Best and John Williams (1993) asked people to fill out an inventory concerning ideal role relationships between women and men. Sample items included, "The husband should be regarded as the legal representative of the family group in all matters of law" (a traditional attitude) and "A woman should have exactly the same freedom of action as a man" (a modern attitude). Best and Williams found that gender-role ideologies are significantly related to a culture's social and economic development. As countries become industrialized and urban, their gender roles also become more modern. Why might this be so?

One answer is that industrialization eliminates the traditional reasons for a sexual division of labor. Most jobs in industrial nations, including military jobs, now involve service skills and brainwork that both sexes can do—a situation that has never existed before in human history. And another profound change has also occurred in this century for the first time: Reproduction has been revolutionized. Although women in many countries still lack access to safe and affordable contraceptives, it is now technologically possible for women to limit reliably the number of children they will have and to plan when to have them. Along with these changes, ideas about the "natural" qualities of men and women are being transformed. It is no longer news that a woman can be a Supreme Court justice or a miner, can walk in space or run a country. And it is no longer news that many men, whose own fathers would no more have diapered a baby than jumped into a vat of boiling oil, now want to be fully involved as fathers (Gerson, 1993).

What cross-cultural studies show, then, is that many of our gender arrangements, and the qualities associated with being male and female, are affected by economic, ecological, and other practical conditions. These conditions have a strong influence in determining whether men are expected to be fierce or gentle, and whether women are expected to be passive or ambitious. The cross-cultural perspective reminds us also that no matter how entrenched our own cultural habits and attitudes are, they change depending on the kind of work we do, technological advances, and the needs of society.

WHAT DO YOU KNOW?

Will your gender affect your answers to these questions?

1. Which of the following is most common in cultures around the world? (a) Women do the weaving, marketing, and teaching; (b) men have more status and power in public affairs than women do; (c) men and women are physically separated while working.
2. What two general factors do cultural researchers emphasize in explaining variations in gender roles around the world?
3. Nisbett's analysis of regional differences in violence showed that an important factor in predicting male aggressiveness is (a) how people earn their livings, (b) racial tensions, (c) poverty, (d) male biology.

ANSWERS:

1. b   2. production and reproduction   3. a

CROSS-CULTURAL RELATIONS

By now, you should be persuaded that cultures differ in countless ways and that a culture's customs do not arise for some arbitrary or foolish reason. But it has probably also been difficult for you to turn off your mental moral evaluator, the little voice that says, "Boy, a culture that does *that* must really be dumb." That little voice, which everyone hears to one degree or another, is the echo of **ethnocentrism,** the belief that one's own culture or ethnic group is superior to all others.

Ethnocentrism appears to be universal, and it probably aids survival by making people feel attached to their own group and willing to work on the group's behalf. But does the fact that people feel good about their own culture or nationality mean that prejudice toward other groups is inevitable? Can't people say, "Well, I'm really happy being an Agfloyp, and I love our customs, but I also am grateful to the people who invented jazz, small cars, chicken soup, movies, paper, the tango, democracy, penicillin, . . ."?

Ethnocentrism and Stereotypes

Ethnocentrism rests on a basic social identity: Us. As soon as people have created a category called "us," however, they invariably perceive everybody else as "not-us." The experiment at Robbers Cave (described in the previous chapter) showed how easy it is to activate *us–them thinking* when any two groups perceive themselves to be in competition. Although competition is sufficient to stimulate ethnocentrism, however, it isn't necessary. Just being a member of an in-group will do it.

Ethnocentric thinking is especially common during war, of course, when enemies regard each other as inhuman and deserving of destruction. "We" are good, noble, and human; "they," the enemy, are bad, stupid, and beastly. But you can see everyday examples of ethnocentric thinking at a football game, during an election, or in discussions of controversial issues. In fact, ethnocentrism can be manufactured in a minute in a laboratory, as Henri Tajfel and his colleagues (1971) first demonstrated in a classic experiment with British schoolboys. Tajfel showed the boys slides with varying numbers of dots on them and asked the boys to guess how many dots there were. The boys were arbitrarily told they were "overestimators" or "underestimators" and were then asked to work on another task. In this phase, they had the chance to allocate points to other boys who were known to be overestimators or underestimators. The researchers had created in-group favoritism: Although each boy worked alone in a private cubicle, almost every single one assigned far more points to other boys he thought were like him, an overestimator or an underestimator. As the boys emerged from their rooms, they were asked, "Which were you?"—and the answer received a mix of cheers and boos.

---

ethnocentrism The belief that one's own ethnic group, nation, or religion is superior to all others.

Even the collective pronouns that apply to *us* and *them* are powerful emotional signals. In one experiment, which students believed was testing their verbal skills, nonsense syllables such as *xeh, yof, laj,* or *wuh* were randomly paired with an in-group word (*us, we,* or *ours*), an out-group word (*them, they,* or *theirs*), or, for a control measure, another pronoun (such as *he, hers,* or *yours*). The students then had to rate the nonsense syllables on how pleasant or unpleasant they were. Why, you might ask, would anyone have an emotional reaction to the syllable *yof*? Yet, in fact, students liked the nonsense syllables significantly more when they had been paired with in-group words. Not one student guessed why; none was aware of how the words had been paired (Perdue et al., 1990).

Us–them thinking both creates and reflects stereotyping. A *stereotype* is a summary impression of a group of people in which a person believes that all members of that group share a common trait or traits. Stereotypes are among the cognitive schemas by which we map the world. They may be negative ("Artists are crazy"), positive ("My school produces the best athletes"), or neutral. There are stereotypes of people who drive Volkswagens or BMWs, of men who wear earrings and women who wear business suits, of engineering students and art students, of feminists and fraternities.

The fact that everyone occasionally thinks in stereotypes is itself neither good nor bad. Stereotypes help us process new information and retrieve old memories. They allow us to organize experience, make sense of the differences among individuals and groups, and predict how people will behave. They are, as some psychologists have called them, useful "tools in the mental toolbox"—energy-saving devices that allow us to make efficient decisions (Macrae, Milne, & Bodenhausen, 1994). For example, as one study found, people remember the qualities associated with stereotypes such as "prude" or "politician" better than they remember a list of specific traits ("reserved"; "extroverted"). The researchers concluded that "Categorization by stereotype provides a virtually instantaneous, detailed, and memorable portrait of an individual" (Andersen, Klatzky, & Murray, 1990).

Although stereotypes do help us put the world together, they also lead to three distortions of reality (Judd et al., 1995). First, *stereotypes accentuate differences between groups.* They emphasize the ways in which groups are different and overlook the common features. So the stereotyped group may seem odd, unfamiliar, or dangerous— "not like us." Second, *stereotypes produce selective perception.* People tend to see only what fits the stereotype and to reject any perceptions that do not fit. Third, *stereotypes underestimate differences within other groups.* People realize that their own groups are made up of all kinds of individuals. But stereotypes create the impression that all members of other groups are the same. One rude French waiter means that all French people are rude; one Greek thief means that all Greeks are thieves. But if someone in their own group is rude or steals, most people draw no such conclusions. This cognitive habit starts early. Social psychologist Marilynn Brewer (1993) reports that her daughter returned from kindergarten one day with the observation that "Boys are crybabies." The child's evidence was that she had seen two boys crying on their first day away from home. Brewer asked whether there hadn't been little girls who cried also. Oh yes, said her daughter. "But," she insisted, "only some girls cry; I didn't cry."

Stereotypes are not always entirely wrong. Many have a grain of truth, capturing with some accuracy something about the group (Allport, 1954/1979). The problems occur when people assume that the grain of truth is the whole seashore. For example, the stereotype that many American whites have about blacks is based on the troubling statistics that are in the news, such as the number of young black men who are in prison. But, as we noted earlier, there has also been a striking expansion of blacks into the middle class and into integrated occupations and communities. Many whites, however, have not assimilated these positive statistics into their racial stereotypes. For their part, many blacks have negative stereotypes about whites, whom they often see as unvarying in their attributes and prejudicial attitudes (Judd et al., 1995).

When people like a group, their stereotype of the group's behavior tends to be positive. When they dislike a group, their stereotype of the same behavior tends to be negative (Peabody, 1985). For example, if you like a woman who is careful with money, you might call her *thrifty*, but if you dislike her, you might call her *stingy*. Likewise, someone who is friendly toward strangers could be *trusting* or *gullible*; someone who enjoys spending time with the relatives could be *family-loving* or *clannish*.

Positive and negative sterotypes, in turn, depend on the cultural norms of the observer. People from different cultures will evaluate the same event differently (Taylor & Porter, 1994). Is coming late to class good, bad, or indifferent? Is it good or bad to argue with your parents about grades? Chinese students in Hong Kong, where communalism and respect for one's elders are highly valued, and students in Australia, where individualism is highly valued, give entirely different interpretations of these two events (Forgas & Bond, 1985). It is a small step from different interpretations to negative stereotypes: "Australians are selfish and disrespectful of adults"; "The Chinese are mindless slaves of authority." And it is a small step from negative stereotyping to prejudice.

Prejudice

A *prejudice* is an unreasonable negative feeling toward a category of people or a cultural practice. Prejudice consists of a negative stereotype of a group and a strong emotional discomfort with, dislike of, or outright hatred toward its members. Feelings of prejudice violate the spirit of critical thinking and the scientific method because they resist rational argument and evidence. In his classic book *The Nature of Prejudice*, social psychologist Gordon Allport (1954/1979) described the responses characteristic of a prejudiced person when confronted with evidence contradicting his or her beliefs:

Mr. X: The trouble with Jews is that they only take care of their own group.

Mr. Y: But the record of the Community Chest campaign shows that they give more generously, in proportion to their numbers, to the general charities of the community, than do non-Jews.

Mr. X: That shows they are always trying to buy favor and intrude into Christian affairs. They think of nothing but money; that is why there are so many Jewish bankers.

> *Mr. Y:*   But a recent study shows that the percentage of Jews in the banking business is negligible, far smaller than the percentage of non-Jews.

> *Mr. X:*   That's just it; they don't go in for respectable business; they are only in the movie business or run night clubs.

Notice that Mr. X doesn't respond to Mr. Y's evidence; he just moves along to another reason for his dislike of Jews. That is the nature of prejudice. Elliot Aronson (1995) gives another example: Suppose Mr. Y tried to persuade you to eat boiled insects. "Ugh," you might say, "they are so ugly." "But so are lobsters," he says, "and lots of people love lobsters." "Well, insects have no food value," you say. "Actually, they are a good source of protein," he answers. He might try other arguments, but the fact is that you have a food prejudice against eating insects, a reaction that does not exist in all cultures.

The Sources of Prejudice.   As we will see in Chapter 15, psychodynamic psychologists hold that much of the emotional heat in prejudice stems from unconscious mechanisms. Prejudice, they say, allows a person to ward off feelings of inadequacy, doubt, and fear by projecting them onto the target group and using it as a *scapegoat.* Social-learning and cognitive psychologists emphasize another psychological source of prejudice: low self-esteem. As research on samples from many nations has repeatedly confirmed, people are able to puff up their own low feelings of self-worth by disliking or hating other groups (Islam & Hewstone, 1993; Stephan et al., 1994; Tajfel & Turner, 1986).

In a demonstration of the link between low self-esteem and prejudice, 60 students participated in what they believed were two separate studies (Fein & Spencer, 1993). In the first, they got positive or negative feedback about their performance on a test of "social perceptiveness" and verbal skills. In the second, they were asked to evaluate the résumé of a woman who had applied for a job as personnel manager. All the subjects were shown the same résumé and photograph of the candidate, but half were told her name was Julie Goldberg and that she did volunteer work for a Jewish organization, and half were told her name was Maria D'Agostino and that she volunteered at a Catholic organization. The researchers found that the students who were feeling good about their test scores did not evaluate the "Jewish" woman differently from the "Italian" woman. But those who had received a blow to their self-esteem evaluated the woman they believed to be Jewish more harshly than the Italian candidate. Their denigration of her, in turn, had the effect of raising their own self-esteem.

Social and cultural psychologists do not deny the importance of such psychological functions of prejudice. However, they have identified some social and economic factors that also contribute to the persistence of prejudice:

1. **SOCIALIZATION.** Many prejudices are passed along from parents to children, in messages that say "We don't associate with people like that," sometimes without either generation having ever met the object of their dislike. Advertising, entertainment shows, and news reports also perpetuate derogatory images and stereotypes of groups such as old people, women, gay men and lesbians, fat people, disabled people, and ethnic minorities.

2. **SOCIAL BENEFITS.** Prejudices often bring support from others who share them—and the threat of losing that support if one abandons the prejudice. The pressures to conform make it difficult for most people to break away from the prejudices of their friends, families, and associates.

3. **ECONOMIC BENEFITS AND JUSTIFICATION OF DISCRIMINATION.** Many studies have found that prejudice rises when groups are in direct competition for jobs. In the nineteenth century, when Chinese immigrants were working in the gold mines, they were described by the local whites as being depraved and vicious, blood-thirsty and inhuman. Just a decade later, when the Chinese began working on the transcontinental railroad across the United States—doing difficult and dangerous jobs that few white men wanted—prejudice against them declined. They were considered hardworking, industrious, and law-abiding. But after the railroad was finished, jobs dwindled. The Chinese had to compete with Civil War veterans for scarce jobs, and white attitudes toward the Chinese changed again. Chinese workers were considered criminal, crafty, conniving, and stupid (Aronson, 1995). Thus prejudice served to justify the whites' treatment of the Chinese, as it serves to justify any majority group's ill treatment of a minority (Gaines & Reed, 1995). In a series of experiments in Bangladesh, Muslims (who are the majority there) and Hindus (a minority) both revealed strong in-group favoritism, but only the Muslims also denigrated the other group (Islam & Hewstone, 1993).

Years ago, an important study demonstrated the link between economic conditions and scapegoating in America. Using data from 14 states in the South, the researchers found a strong negative correlation between the number of black lynchings and the economic value of cotton; that is, the poorer the economic conditions for whites, the greater the number of lynchings of blacks (Hovland & Sears, 1940). These data were later reanalyzed to assess other possible explanations, but the correlation remained (Hepworth & West, 1988). Another research project used many different measures of economic threat and social insecurity (such as the unemployment rate, the rate of serious crimes, the number of work stoppages, and personal income levels) and of prejudice (the number of anti-Semitic incidents, activities by the Ku Klux Klan, and attitudes toward other groups) (Doty, Peterson, & Winter, 1991). Again, the researchers found that during times of high social and economic threat, prejudice increases significantly.

The Varieties of Prejudice.   One problem in studying prejudice is that not all prejudiced people are prejudiced in the same way or to the same extent. Gordon Allport (1954/1979) astutely observed that "defeated intellectually, prejudice lingers emotionally." That is, a person might want to lose a prejudice against a certain group yet still feel uncomfortable with members of the group. Should we put this person in the same category as one who is outspokenly bigoted or who actively discriminates against others by virtue of their gender, culture, sexual orientation, or skin color? Do good intentions count? What if a person is ignorant of another culture and mindlessly blurts out a remark that reflects that ignorance ("Gee, I was always told that Jews had little horns on their heads")? Does that count as prejudice or merely as ignorance?

Studies that define prejudice according to people's expressed attitudes find that prejudice is declining: White attitudes toward integration have become steadily more favorable, and beliefs that blacks are inferior to whites have markedly declined (Devine, 1995). Similarly, men's endorsement of gender equality has steadily increased; the number of men expressing prejudice toward women executives, for example, declined from 41 percent in 1965 to only 5 percent in 1985 (Tougas et al., 1995).

On the other hand, many people hold remnants of emotional prejudices that they acquired in childhood but that, as adults, they are consciously trying to eradicate. According to Patricia Devine, people who are actively trying to break their "prejudice habit" should not be accused of being bigots. In her research, she finds that such people are caught between what they know they *should* do when they meet a target of their old prejudice and what they fear they *would* do. Highly prejudiced people feel little guilt or conflict about their biases, and so they feel no conflict between "should" and "would." Less prejudiced whites and heterosexuals may feel uncomfortable when they are with blacks or gays, but they also feel guilty about having these feelings and struggle to overcome them (Devine et al., 1991). Research such as Devine's suggests that individuals might feel uncomfortable with one another as a result of unfamiliarity rather than prejudice. Or the discomfort could reflect an honest effort to put old prejudices aside; as Devine (1995) emphasizes, reducing prejudice is a *process,* not an "all or none event." It doesn't happen overnight.

A similar argument holds that the main problem dividing blacks and whites is not prejudice but differing cultural values. Surveys find that many white Americans place a high value on equality but also on individualism and self-reliance (Katz & Hass, 1988). Their support of equality leads many whites to feel sympathy toward blacks because of the disadvantages and discrimination that they know blacks have suffered. But the values of individualism and self-reliance lead many whites to accuse blacks of not taking enough responsibility for solving their problems. Many whites wish blacks would just "get on with it." Most African-Americans, however, place their highest value on equality and justice. They argue that their lower status and income are not a result of a failure of self-reliance but of the systematic injustice they have suffered at the hands of whites. As reactions to the acquittal of O. J. Simpson and to other events have shown, the gap in perceptions of racism and injustice in America is growing, and it confirms to many African-Americans that white Americans just "don't get it."

Other social scientists believe that racial animosity and sexism are undiminished. Overt attitudes, they say, are not an accurate measure of these prejudices, because people know they should not admit these feelings (Tougas et al., 1995). These observers maintain that prejudice toward blacks, for example, lurks behind a mask of *symbolic racism,* in which whites focus not on dislike of black individuals but on racial issues such as "reverse discrimination," "hard-core criminals," or "welfare abuse." In their view, these issues have become code words for the continuing animosity that many whites have for African-Americans.

The way to measure racism, according to this argument, is by using unobtrusive measures rather than direct attitude questionnaires. You might observe how people behave when they are with a possible object of prejudice; do they sit farther away than they normally would, or fail to smile and make eye contact as they would with others? You might observe how quickly people come up with positive or negative associations to stimulus pictures, for instance of black versus white faces—a possible measure of unconscious prejudice (Fazio et al., 1995). You might observe how people who say they are unprejudiced behave when they are emotionally upset (Jones, 1991). In one such experiment, in which students administered shock to confederates in an apparent study of biofeedback, whites initially showed *less* aggression toward blacks than toward whites. But as soon as the whites were angered by overhearing derogatory remarks about themselves, they showed *more* aggression toward blacks than toward whites (Rogers & Prentice-Dunn, 1981). This finding implies that whites may be willing to control their negative feelings toward blacks (or, if you recall the "Julie Goldberg" study, toward Jews or other targets of prejudice) under normal conditions, but as soon as they are angry, stressed, or provoked, their real prejudice reveals itself.

As if these complexities of prejudice were not enough, there is another. Peter Glick and Susan Fiske (1996) argue that sexism is "a special case of prejudice" that is often marked by "a deep ambivalence, rather than a uniform antipathy, toward women." Using a questionnaire they call the Ambivalent Sexism Inventory, which has been administered to more than 2,000 individuals of both sexes, they have identified two kinds of sexism that are empirically distinct. The first is *hostile sexism,* which involves strongly negative feelings about women, such as anger, hatred, and contempt; this kind of sexism is comparable to any other negative prejudice toward an entire group. The second is *benevolent sexism,* which involves positive feelings about women, along with paternalistic and stereotyped attitudes toward them—a prejudice that says "I like women, as long as they stay in their proper place."

As you can see, it has not been easy to define and study racism and other forms of prejudice. How does covert discomfort differ from explicit hostility? Can a woman hold sexist attitudes toward men, or should sexism refer only to prejudice and discrimination against women? Is an African-American who dislikes all whites a racist, or is racism an attribute only of institutions and of whites with power? Because people differ in their premises, such as the definitions of *racist* and *sexist,* and because they differ in their values, such as equality or self-reliance, their conclusions about prejudice will also differ.

WHAT DO YOU KNOW?

A. Identify which concept—ethnocentrism, stereotyping, or prejudice—is illustrated by each of the following three statements.

1. Juan believes that all Anglos are uptight and cold, and he won't listen to any evidence that contradicts his belief.
2. John knows and likes the Mexican minority in his town but he privately believes that Anglo culture is superior to all others.

3. Jane believes that Honda owners are thrifty and practical. June believes that Honda owners are stingy and dull.

B. A 1994 Louis Harris survey found that large percentages of blacks, Asian-Americans, and Latinos hold negative stereotypes of one another and resent other minorities almost as much as they resent whites. What are some of the reasons that people who have themselves been victims of stereotyping and prejudice would hold the same attitudes toward others?

ANSWERS:

A. 1. prejudice 2. ethnocentrism 3. stereotypes B. low self-esteem; socialization by parents and the larger society; peer pressure from friends who share these prejudices; and economic competition for jobs and resources

CAN CULTURES GET ALONG?

Sometimes the possibility of harmonious relations between cultures looks bleak indeed. All over the world, ancient animosities erupt in bloody battles, and new wars emerge even where groups had been living together companionably. In the cultural cauldron of the United States, hate crimes and ethnic tensions are on the increase. When cultures with different customs, values, and nonverbal languages collide, misunderstandings are no joke; they can be fatal. In Stockton, California, a driver used a hand signal to alert a car behind him at a stoplight that his headlights were off. The driver of the second car, taking this gesture as a sign of disrespect, shot at the first car, killing a passenger.

Cultural psychology, which has identified the continuing reasons for international and multicultural conflict, also gives us hope for reducing such conflict. The knowledge of how cultures differ, even in the smallest rules of time management and eye contact, benefits everyone who has to deal with another culture—which, on this shrinking planet, is all of us: neighbor, tourist, business executive, or diplomat. In the sociocultural view, conflict and aggression are not inherent in human biology, but rather in our circumstances. Therefore, as circumstances change, so does the need for violence. Indeed, throughout history, societies have changed from being warlike to being peaceful, and vice versa. The Swedes were once one of the most warlike nations on earth, but today they are among the most pacifistic and egalitarian (Groebel & Hinde, 1989).

Research from the sociocultural perspective can perhaps guide us between two unrealistic goals for cross-cultural relations on this small planet. At one extreme, some people would persuade or force every other group and religion to become just like them. At the other extreme, some people dream of all cultures living together in perfect harmony, respecting their differences. According to the sociocultural perspective, we would do better to recognize that conflicts will always occur—because of economic inequities and because of cultural misunderstandings—and then turn our attention to finding nonviolent ways of resolving them.

◆ ◆ ◆

Summary

1. *Culture* is (a) a program of shared rules that govern the behavior of members of a community or society, and (b) a set of values, beliefs, and attitudes shared by most members of that community. The study of culture is challenging because of difficulties in devising good methods and getting samples from many societies in order to make valid cultural comparisons; the difficulty of interpreting results when the same custom may have different meanings and functions across cultures; the risk of stereotyping; the common tendency to *reify* "culture" as an explanation without identifying the mechanisms or aspects of culture that influence behavior; and the political sensitivity of many findings.

2. Some signals of *body language* seem to be universal, but most, such as *conversational distance* and notions of when a smile is appropriate, are specific to particular cultures. This fact creates many possibilities for misunderstanding and offense. In *high-context cultures,* people pay close attention to nonverbal signs; they assume a shared knowledge and history, so things need not be spelled out. In *low-context cultures,* people pay more attention to words than to nonverbal language; they assume no shared knowledge and history, so everything must be explained and stated directly.

3. *Monochronic cultures* organize time into linear segments in which people do one thing at a time, and they value promptness. *Polychronic cultures* organize time along parallel lines; people do many things at once, and the demands of friends and family supersede those of the appointment book. A culture's way of organizing time stems from its economic system, social organization, political history, and ecology.

4. *Individual-centered cultures* define the "self" as a collection of personality traits; *collectivist* or *group-centered cultures* see the "self" as embedded in a community. The way that people define the self affects many aspects of individual psychology, including people's personalities, emotions, and motives, as well as how they perceive their need for relationships and how quickly they make friends. In collectivist cultures, the strongest human bond is usually not between husband and wife but between parent and child, and child rearing is communal.

5. People develop *social identities* based on their nationality, ethnicity, religion, and social roles. One important social identity is an *ethnic identity.* In multiethnic societies, many people face the problem of balancing ethnic identity with *acculturation.* Depending on whether ethnic identity and identification with the larger culture are strong or weak, a person may become *bicultural*; choose *assimilation*; become an *ethnic separatist*; or feel *marginal.* Ethnic labels have great symbolic and emotional significance, which is why they are so politically volatile.

6. All aspects of cognition and mental abilities are influenced by culture. For example, cultural differences occur in the pacing of the stages described by Piaget, because cultures differ in terms of which cognitive skills are needed and nurtured in their members. Beliefs about the origins of mental abilities, parental standards, and attitudes about the value of education help account for average group differences in academic performance, such as those between the Japanese and the Americans. Specific parent–child interactions may also explain some cultural dif-

ferences in cognitive test scores. A teenager's peer culture and beliefs about the chances of success affect the desire to achieve and help account for ethnic differences in academic performance.

7. In the cultural view, a culture's attitudes and practices are embedded in its history, environment, economy, and survival needs and thus are *socially constructed.* For example, although some gender differences appear to be universal, there are many variations in women's status, the work that men and women do, the degree of male–female contact, the value placed on female chastity, and the salience of gender differences. Factors pertaining to *production* (the economy and ecology) and *reproduction* (availability of birth control and the need for many or few children) help explain these variations.

8. Economic and social factors are also involved in the variations in male aggressiveness and in the status of women. High rates of male violence and white homicide in the American South and West are related to a history of reliance on herding rather than on farming. As countries become industrialized and urban, their gender roles also become more egalitarian; access to reliable birth control and the growth of jobs involving service skills and brainwork are eliminating the traditional reasons for a sexual division of labor.

9. *Ethnocentrism,* the belief that one's own group or nation is superior to all others, promotes us–them thinking. *Stereotypes* help people process new information, retrieve old memories, organize experience, make sense of the differences among individuals and groups, and predict how others will behave. But stereotypes distort reality in three ways: (1) They overemphasize differences between groups; (2) they underestimate the differences within groups; and (3) they produce selective perception. The values and rules of culture determine how people interpret the same event. When they like a group, their stereotypes of the group's behavior are positive; when they dislike a group, their stereotypes of the same behavior are often negative.

10. A *prejudice* is an unreasonable negative feeling toward a category of people or a cultural practice. Prejudice has several psychological functions, such as reducing anxiety by allowing people to feel superior and bolstering their self-esteem. But prejudice also has social and financial functions. People acquire prejudices through childhood socialization, the social support they receive, and the economic benefits they gain as a result. During times of economic insecurity, prejudice rises significantly.

11. Prejudice occurs in many varieties and degrees. This fact leads to debates about definitions of racism, sexism, and other forms of prejudice. Blacks and whites often disagree in their definitions of racism and on the question of whether racism is declining or has merely taken new forms, such as *symbolic racism.* Sexism, too, takes different forms. *Hostile sexism* involves dislike of and contempt for women, whereas *benevolent sexism* involves the attitude, "I like women, as long as they stay in their place."

12. Cultural psychologists have identified many reasons for cultural conflicts and also offer solutions for reducing them. In the sociocultural view, conflict and aggression are not inherent in human biology, but in our circumstances. Therefore, as circumstances change, so does the need for conflict and aggression.

Key Terms

culture *446*

cultural psychologists *446*

cross-cultural psychologists *446*

reification *450*

body language *451*

conversational distance *452*

high-context and low-context cultures *453*

monochronic and polychronic cultures *454*

individual-centered and collectivist (group-centered) cultures *456*

personal identity *456*

social identity *457*

ethnic identity *458*

acculturation *458*

bicultural identity *458*

assimilation *458*

ethnic separatism *458*

marginal identity *458*

sex versus gender *466*

social constructionism *466*

production *469*

reproduction *469*

ethnocentrism *472*

us–them thinking *472*

stereotype *473*

prejudice *474*

symbolic racism *477*

hostile and benevolent sexism *478*

CHAPTER 14

Evaluating the Sociocultural Perspective

The social psychologist Roger Brown (1986), who was born and bred in Indiana, went to a Big 10 university in the Midwest. There he encountered a young woman from New York, who seemed to him to have "the most extraordinarily original personality." But after he had met half a dozen other young women from New York, he realized that the personality he thought was unique was in fact "99 percent New York generic." In turn, he admits, the young women were learning that he was "99 percent Indiana standard."

Roger Brown had discovered the importance of culture—the cultures of New York and Indiana. In this respect, his story is a metaphor for what has happened to the whole discipline of psychology, because the sociocultural perspective is transforming the way psychologists think and do research. Indeed, it is safe to say that it is causing as much of an upheaval as the cognitive revolution did in the 1960s and 1970s, when behaviorism was challenged by the rediscovery of the mind.

CONTRIBUTIONS OF THIS PERSPECTIVE

The sociocultural perspective has made revolutionary contributions to the field of psychology in several ways:

1 PLACING THE INDIVIDUAL IN SOCIAL CONTEXT. Until recently, psychology tended to be a discipline that focused on the individual apart from any context—that is, without considering the person's generation (age), immediate situation, or contemporary historical circumstances (Gergen, 1973; Unger, 1990). The assumption was that it was possible to find laws of behavior that applied to all human beings everywhere. The sociocultural perspective, however, causes us to question the assumption that there are many, or even any, such laws. When researchers study individuals without regard for social context, their findings, far from being universal, are often only narrowly applicable. For example, as we saw in Chapter 12, many differences that seem to characterize men and women, such as "women's intuition" or habits of nonverbal communication, turn out to be artifacts of the situation they are in, such as which person is the leader and which one has greater power and authority.

Likewise, psychologists used to devise theories of adult development without considering how their samples might be affected by the moment in history in which the research was done. When psychologists first began to follow people's lives from childhood to adulthood, in the 1950s and 1960s, they found that most middle-class people's lives were consistent and predictable (Kagan & Moss, 1962). In the 1970s, popular books drew on some of this research to describe the supposedly inevitable "passages" of adult life. However, they were describing a life sequence that turned out to be true only for some people at a particular time and place. Today, because of changes in the economy and in social and gender roles, adult development in North America is marked by inconsistency. Most people no longer have one job or career for their whole lives. The timing and length of marriage are no longer predictable, and neither is parenthood: Some women have their first baby at age 15 and others have their first baby at age 45. All these changes mean that theories of adult development have had to be reconsidered, and the idea of universal stages or passages of development has been scrapped.

2 EMPHASIZING THE IMPORTANCE OF CULTURE IN EVERY DOMAIN OF PSYCHOLOGICAL RESEARCH. No topic in psychology has been unaffected by the growing awareness of the influence of culture on human behavior (Berry et al., 1992; Lonner & Malpass, 1994; Rogoff & Chavajay, 1995). For instance, in Western psychology, a supposed milestone of infant development occurs when babies are four to five months old and sleep eight uninterrupted hours at night. This is a major development for parents, too! But it occurs only in cultures in which babies sleep in their own cribs, apart from their parents. In the many cultures in which the infant sleeps with the mother and nurses on demand throughout the night, such as the Kipsigis of rural Kenya, no such milestone occurs (Super & Harkness, 1994).

Just as research now emphasizes the historical and social context of adult development, so it recognizes the importance of cultural context. For example, *adolescence* is the period of development between puberty, the age at which a person becomes capable of sexual reproduction, and adulthood. In some cultures, the time span between puberty and adulthood is only a few months; a sexually mature boy or girl is expected to soon marry and to start performing adult tasks. In modern Western societies, however, teenagers are not considered emotionally mature enough to be full-fledged adults with all the rights, responsibilities, and roles of adulthood. In psychology, the "turmoil theory" of adolescent development holds that anguish and rebellion are necessary and inevitable, the means by which teenagers separate themselves psychologically from their parents and form their own identities (Blos, 1962). The theory assumes that a child who maintains a close bond with the parents is immature; this is said to be especially true of young men. But cross-cultural research has found that separation is an issue primarily in *societies that value male independence.* Most other cultures place a high value on continued love and connection between child and parent (Apter, 1990).

Certainly many Western adolescents have a difficult time as they experiment with relationships, develop their social identities, and choose their values and goals. But because of cultural research, psychologists now recognize that the experience of adolescence is inextricably linked to cultural practices and beliefs, including the belief that separation is psychologically inevitable and healthy. Once North American researchers could see beyond the cultural assumption that separation is the main theme of adolescence, they found that attachment to parents is neither rare nor an indication of a young person's immaturity or dependence. For most adolescents in Western societies, quarrels with parents don't signify a rift, but a change from one-sided parental authority to a more reciprocal, adult relationship (Laursen & Collins, 1994).

3 MAKING PSYCHOLOGY MORE SCIENTIFIC, MORE ENCOMPASSING, AND MORE RELEVANT TO SOCIAL LIFE. The sociocultural perspective poses many challenges for psychologists because cross-cultural and cross-situational studies are difficult and costly to do. Yet its findings continually remind us that when we overlook this perspective, our ability to explain and predict behavior, let alone resolve misunderstandings and conflicts, is seriously diminished.

For example, when monochronic and polychronic people try to do business with one another, they often make unintentional mistakes if they ignore the powerful influence of culture. Consider the plight of a French salesman who had worked for a company that was bought by Americans. When the new American manager ordered him to step up his sales within the next three months, the employee quit in a huff, taking his customers with him. Why? In polychronic France, it takes years to develop customers; in family-owned businesses, relationships with customers may span generations. The monochronic American wanted instant results, as Americans do, but the French salesman knew that this was impossible and quit. The American view was, "He wasn't up to the job; he's lazy and disloyal, so he stole my customers." The French view was, "There is no point in explaining anything to a person who is so stupid as to think you can acquire loyal customers in three months" (in Tavris, 1987).

The sociocultural perspective helps us understand not only that people differ, however, but also that we share common needs and experiences. Cross-cultural studies have identified human commonalities, such as the universal need for attachment and love; shared emotions such as happiness, grief, and fear; the enjoyment of humor and music; and the experience of conflict and anger. As Pierre Dasen (1994) has written, "Universality and cultural diversity are not opposites, but are complementary aspects of all human behavior and development."

MISUSES AND MISINTERPRETATIONS OF THIS PERSPECTIVE

Despite these contributions, the sociocultural perspective also raises some concerns because of the potential for misinterpreting and misusing its findings.

1 SOCIOCULTURAL REDUCTIONISM. Reducing human behavior to the single factor of culture or society is no improvement over biological reductionism, behavioral reductionism, or cognitive reductionism. Any one-factor explanation can lead to an abdication of individual responsibility, which is why "The system made me do it" or "My culture made me do it" is no more valid than "My hormones made me do it" or "My upbringing made me do it." This perspective teaches us to appreciate the power of circumstances, situations, roles, and working conditions in influencing behavior, but we should not forget that there is an individual person rattling around in there. The writer Jane O'Reilly (1980) said that she shifted from taking 100 percent responsibility for everything that happened to her to blaming "the system" 100 percent. "Nowadays," she said, "I divide the blame more equitably: half for me and half for societal arrangements." We think most sociocultural researchers would agree with that assessment.

Some people reduce behavior to culture in a literal way, speaking as if there were "culture genes" that make people behave a certain way, just as biological genes cause eye color. The concepts of *culture* and *role* are extremely useful, but the processes they represent are not static. These terms describe customs and conventions that can and do change, not permanent states.

2 STEREOTYPING. A sociocultural emphasis can cause people to exaggerate differences between groups and overlook variations within them. During a dreary Boston winter, Roger Brown (1986) went to the Bahamas for a vacation. To his surprise, he found the people he met there unfriendly and rude, and he decided that the reason was that Bahamians "had to accommodate to spoiled, critical foreigners. It would be enough to turn anyone unfriendly." He tried out his hypothesis on a cab driver. The cab driver looked at Brown in amazement, smiled cheerfully, and told him that Bahamians don't mind tourists, just *unsmiling* tourists. And then Brown realized what had been going on. "Not tourists generally, but this tourist, myself, was the cause," he wrote. "Confronted with my unrelaxed wintry Boston face, they had assumed I had no interest in them and had responded non-committally, inexpressively. I had created the Bahamian national character. Everywhere I took my face it sprang into being. So I began smiling a lot, and the Bahamians changed their national character. In fact, they lost any national character and differentiated into individuals."

Stereotyping can affect everyone, including researchers. When she was doing fieldwork with Bedouin women, anthropologist Lila Abu-Lughod (1992) found considerable divergence among them. She warned that the scientist who strives for general descriptions of a culture "risks smoothing over contradictions, conflicts of interest, doubts and arguments, not to mention changing motivations and historical circumstances." Smoothing over contradictions within groups is the essence of stereotyping, and we need to resist the temptation to do so.

For example, consider the common assumption that women are more dependent than men on relationships. Note right away that such a statement fails to specify *which* women and men. Everybody? All ages? All ethnicities? All through life? Really? In her well-known studies, Carol Gilligan (1982) concluded that men are more likely than women to regard attachment as a source of danger and threat, whereas women are more likely to regard attachment as a source of safety and intimacy. Describing one study, she wrote, "The men in the class, considered as a group, projected more violence into situations of personal affiliation than they did into impersonal situations of achievement." "*The* men" implies that all or most of them responded this way, but in fact she was referring to only 25 percent of a group of 88 college males. That was a higher percentage of males than females, but not even close to a majority. Subsequent studies also failed to confirm Gilligan's intuitively appealing idea (Benton et al., 1983; Cochran & Peplau, 1985).

When we stereotype groups, our expectations and beliefs affect what we perceive about them (Geis, 1993). In the case of gender, for example, the belief that men are aggressive and women are nurturant has caused many people to overlook examples of male nurturance and female aggression. When anthropologist David Gilmore (1990) examined how cultures around the world define manhood, he expected to find masculinity equated with selfishness and hardness. But by resisting this stereotype, he was able to see that masculinity frequently entails selfless generosity and sacrifice. Men nurture their families and society, he observed, by "bringing home food for both child and mother . . . and by dying if necessary in faraway places to provide a safe haven for their people."

Conversely, the fact that men are more likely than women to behave aggressively does not mean that all men, or even most men, are aggressive. Nor does it mean that all women, or even most women, are unaggressive. Many women behave aggressively by saying cruel and hurtful things; by having arguments in which they slap, kick, or bite their partners, or throw objects; by abusing and humiliating their children; by having vengeful attitudes toward their perceived enemies; and by supporting and participating in war, in whatever ways their societies have permitted (Campbell, 1993; Elshtain, 1987; Gelles & Straus, 1988).

From the sociocultural perspective, the moral is that we can study and talk about average differences between groups, but we should do so without implying that the groups are as different as chocolate and cheese—or, as one book title grandiosely asserts, that *Men Are from Mars, Women Are from Venus. That's* stereotyping.

3 **EXTREME CULTURAL RELATIVISM.** Cultural psychologists have described problems with both "absolutist" and "relativist" attitudes toward cultural differences (Adamopolouos & Lonner, 1994). The *absolutist* assumptions of traditional psychology hold that there are universal truths and a common human nature; *relativists* conclude that every culture differs from every other and therefore can be judged only on its own terms. Extreme relativists take a nonjudgmental view of all cultural practices, even those that cause suffering and death, or that violate what many others regard as universal human rights.

But perhaps there is a route between extreme relativism and extreme absolutism. It is possible, after all, to study how economic conditions lead to the rise of hate groups without having to feel neutral about skinheads and neo-Nazis. Researchers in the sociocultural perspective try to find out why certain cultural practices have survived and what their adaptive consequences might be. This does *not* necessarily mean that any custom that survives must therefore be right and good.

For example, in more than 25 countries throughout Africa, the Middle East, and Indonesia, girls are subjected to genital mutilation. Performed on an estimated 2 million female children a year, ranging in age from infancy to adolescence, the operation takes one of three forms: in *circumcision,* part of the clitoris is removed; in *excision,* the entire clitoris and all or part of the vaginal lips (labia) are removed; and in *infibulation,* the clitoris and the inner and outer labia are removed, and the sides of the vaginal opening are stitched together, leaving only a small hole for urination and menstruation. These operations, usually done without anesthesia or even an antiseptic, are excruciatingly painful and hazardous; some girls bleed to death. Most women who have undergone excision or infibulation develop lifelong medical problems, and an estimated 20 percent die in childbirth (Bardach, 1993).

People in cultures that practice female genital mutilation believe that it will ensure a girl's chastity at marriage and her fidelity afterward. Most Westerners, and many members of these cultures as well, find this practice barbaric, which is why they call it genital mutilation (Burstyn, 1995; Walker & Parmar, 1995). This cultural conflict is not just an intellectual matter in countries such as France, England, and the United States, which have growing numbers of immigrants who subject their daughters to the surgery. The result is a clash between the law of the majority that forbids the practice and the immigrants' desire to continue their tradition.

The sociocultural perspective reminds us that most cultural customs are embedded in the larger structure of society, which is why efforts to outlaw entrenched customs often fail. Female genital mutilation works something like a marriage contract, guaranteeing a woman a place in society (Paige & Paige, 1981). Outsiders who want to barge in and make the custom illegal, ignoring the system of kinship and economic arrangements that support the practice, might actually condemn countless women to even more hardship—because, unmarried, they would have no family to support them. African women who are working to eliminate female genital mutilation know this (Burstyn, 1995). They know that although passing laws to prohibit the practice are an essential first step, the custom will not cease without other changes that raise the status and security of women.

The sociocultural perspective does not require us to abandon the concern for human rights; cultural psychologists can study the reasons for female genital mutilation while also wanting to see the practice eradicated. But this perspective alerts us to the dangers of climbing up on an ethnocentric high horse, galloping off in the certainty that our own ways are always right and normal and everyone else's are wrong. Writer Alice Walker, who with Pratibha Parmar (1995) wrote a haunting condemnation of female genital mutilation, pointed out in a television interview that plenty of American women mutilate themselves with breast implants, plastic surgery, and liposuction to fit their culture's standards of beauty. How would we like it, she said, if outsiders pressured the U.S. government to make plastic surgery for cosmetic purposes illegal? Or consider this: Among the developed nations of the world, only the United States continues to execute criminals in increasing numbers. To other nations, the death penalty is barbaric, a violation of human rights. But Americans who favor the death penalty would counter that it's their cultural custom, and no one has the right to interfere.

The sociocultural perspective, therefore, urges us to avoid the pitfalls of both extreme absolutism and extreme relativism. It teaches us to find stronger criteria than emotional reasoning ("I hate that custom") by which to decide when to let other cultures alone, when and how to try to influence them, and even—imagine this!—when we would be wise to let them influence us.

4 HEIGHTENED ETHNOCENTRISM. It is both ironic and tragic that the sociocultural perspective, which has done so much to make people aware of the dangers of ethnocentrism, is sometimes misused to foster it. The perspective was never meant to be perverted into ethnic, societal, and gender separatism, in which people celebrate only their own group and regard other cultures or the other gender as inherently inferior— or so hopelessly different that there's no point in trying to get along with them.

As groups that were once excluded from psychological research and theory have become aware of the injustice of this omission, they have done much to remedy matters. But some psychologists and social critics are concerned about tendencies to replace old biases with new ones (Appiah, 1994; Crawford & Marecek, 1989; Gates, 1992; R. Hughes, 1993; Yoder & Kahn, 1993). Thus, some women want to replace the view that women are the deficient sex with the view that women are the better, more peace-loving sex that will save the world (Eisler, 1987); some African-Americans support the belief that Africans are the "sun people" who have a "humanistic, spiritualistic value system," whereas Europeans are the "ice people" who are "egoistic, individualistic, and exploitative" (see Traub, 1993).

Assertions of superiority, however, are no more accurate than assertions of inferiority—and assertions, in any case, must be based on evidence. For example, it is understandable that many African-Americans would regard slavery as an invention of European whites, because white Europeans and Americans were responsible for slavery in the United States. In fact, however, the ancient Romans, Aztecs, and Egyptians all had slaves—people they conquered, of whatever skin color. So did Muslim Arabs for many centuries, and so did some Native American tribes (Davis, 1984; Oliver, 1992). Indeed, as Robert Hughes (1993) writes, "The *African* slave trade as such, the black traffic, was a Muslim invention, developed by Arab traders with the enthusiastic collaboration of black African ones, institutionalized with the most unrelenting brutality centuries before the white man appeared on the African continent, and continuing long after the slave market in North America was finally crushed."

Does this information detract one whit from the moral condemnation of American slavery? Not at all. But it does give us more insight into the long nightmare of slavery in history and confirms what the sociocultural perspective would predict: That no cultural or ethnic group has always and everywhere been superior to every other in its dealings with the rest of humanity. This is because all of us are subject to the behavioral processes that the sociocultural perspective has identified, from obedience to ethnocentrism. As Kwame Appiah (1994), a professor of Afro-American studies who is himself from Ghana, writes, "Cruelty and kindness are not Western prerogatives, any more than intelligence and creativity. . . . The proper response to Eurocentrism is surely not a reactive Afrocentrism, but a new understanding that humanizes all of us by learning to think beyond race."

Research from the sociocultural perspective has been applied to many domains of life: to managing cultural diversity in schools and the workplace; to international relations and diplomacy; to improving people's mental and physical health; to improving the effectiveness of psychotherapy; and to reducing conflict between groups. We turn now to three applications of the sociocultural perspective that illustrate both its promise and the difficulty of applying it to our complex world.

What Do You Know?

1. Name three contributions of the sociocultural perspective and four potential misuses of it.

2. When a chief of the Miranhas was asked why his people practiced cannibalism, he said, "It is all a matter of habit. When I have killed an enemy it is better to eat him than let him go to waste" (Askenasy, 1994). Colin and Carin are arguing about the Miranhas' custom. "If that's their tradition, there's nothing wrong with it," says Colin. "They are barbaric and stupid," says Carin. In what ways are Colin and Carin misinterpreting cultural findings, and what other approach might they take toward understanding cannibalism?

Answers:

1. Contributions include placing the individual in social context; emphasizing the importance of culture in every domain of research; and making psychology as a field more scientific, encompassing, and relevant. Misuses include sociocultural reductionism; stereotyping; extreme cultural relativism; and heightened ethnocentrism.   2. Colin is being extremely relativistic and Carin is being ethnocentric. A more useful middle course might be to ask how this custom evolved, what purpose it served, and the different functions it might have had in different cultures, from religious ritual to survival. (Taking this approach doesn't mean that Colin and Carin have to become cannibals!)

Issue 1: IQ Testing

Understanding how culture defines and shapes intelligence has had enormous implications, as you might expect, for educational policy and for the industry of intelligence testing. The sociocultural perspective has led researchers to confront two important issues: First, is it possible to design a test of intelligence that applies to everyone across all cultures? Second, if there are many kinds of intelligence (as we saw in the evaluation of the cognitive perspective), then is it wrong to use a test that accurately measures only the kind of intelligence valued by the dominant culture?

Intelligence tests developed between World War I and the 1960s favored city children over rural ones, middle-class children over poor ones, and white children over minority children. One item, for example, asked whether the *Emperor Concerto* was written by Beethoven, Mozart, Bach, Brahms, or Mahler. (The answer is Beethoven.) Another item asked, "What should you do if you find a 3-year-old lost on the street?" The correct answer was to call the police. But that response might not look attractive to a child living in the inner city, or to a farm child living where there are no police nearby and no streets, either.

"You can't build a hut, you don't know how to find edible
roots and you know nothing about predicting the
weather. In other words, you do *terribly* on our IQ test."

In the 1960s, criticism of the cultural bias in IQ tests and of the political uses of
tests to stigmatize children mounted. Some test-makers responded by trying to construct tests that were *culture-free*. Such tests were usually nonverbal (although, as you'll
recall from Chapter 13, nonverbal gestures are affected by culture too!). Yet culture
continued to affect test scores in unexpected ways. In one case, children who had emigrated from Arab countries to Israel were asked to show which detail was missing from
a picture of a face with no mouth (Ortar, 1963). The children, who were not used to
thinking of a drawing of a head as a complete picture, said that the *body* was missing!

Psychologists then tried to design tests that were *culture-fair*. Their aim was not to
eliminate the influence of culture but to find items that incorporate knowledge and
skills common to many cultures. But this approach, too, has limitations that prevent it
from eliminating group differences in test performance. Cultural values affect a person's attitude toward taking tests, comfort in the settings required for testing, motivation, rapport with the test-giver, competitiveness, and experience in solving problems
independently rather than with others (Anastasi, 1988; López, 1995). Moreover, cultures differ in the problem-solving strategies they emphasize. Children and adults in
Western families typically learn to classify things by category; they will say that an
apple and a peach are similar because both are fruits, and a saw and a rake are similar
because both are tools. But people in many other cultures, particularly if they are
unschooled, classify objects according to their function. For example, they will associate a hoe with a potato because a hoe is used to dig up a potato (Rogoff & Chavajay,
1995). Similarly, children who are not trained in Western middle-class ways of sorting
things may say that an apple and a peach are similar because they taste good. We think
that's a charming and imaginative answer, but test-givers interpret it as being a less
intelligent response (Miller-Jones, 1989). That is why culture-fair tests do not always
eliminate differences in group performance.

In theory, it should be possible to establish norms that are not based on white urban children, by throwing out items on which such children get higher scores than others. This strategy was actually used years ago to eliminate sex differences in IQ. On early tests, girls scored higher than boys at every age (Samelson, 1979). No one was willing to conclude that males were intellectually inferior, so in the 1937 revision of the Stanford-Binet test, one of the most commonly used IQ tests, items that showed sex differences were deleted. Poof! No sex differences.

But few people seem willing to do the same thing for cultural differences, and the reason reveals a dilemma at the heart of intelligence testing. Intelligence tests put some groups of children at a disadvantage, yet they also measure knowledge and skills useful in the classroom and are therefore good predictors of success in school. By identifying the persistent effects of culture and of social context on IQ scores, sociocultural researchers raised some thorny problems for educators and parents about the applications of the IQ test. Should tests fit what children know, or should children be helped to do well on existing tests? Or both? How can educators accept cultural differences and, at the same time, require students to demonstrate mastery of the skills that will help them succeed in school and in the larger society?

The research discussed in Chapter 13, on ethnic identity and acculturation, may help account for the conflict within some ethnic groups regarding these questions. Members of those groups who are highly assimilated, and who want their children to succeed in mainstream society, value the IQ test as a predictor of their children's ability to do well in the educational system. Those who have strong ethnic identities, however, want the system to accommodate their children, who may have different strengths and skills than those of middle-class white children.

These arguments divide researchers, too. Anne Anastasi (1988), a testing specialist, contended that concealing the effects of cultural disadvantage by rejecting tests is "equivalent to breaking a thermometer because it registers a body temperature of 101." Instead, she argues, special help should be given to any child who needs it. Others believe that conventional intelligence tests do more harm than good. Sociologist Jane Mercer (1988) tried for years to get testers to understand that children can be *ignorant* of information required by IQ tests without being *stupid,* but she finally gave up, deciding instead to try to "kill the IQ test."

Both arguments have much to commend them (López, 1995). Although sociocultural findings alone cannot resolve this issue, they have influenced researchers to abandon the "deficit model" of intelligence testing and to recognize that two groups can be different without one of them being deficient (recall the study on page 463, of black children whose verbal strengths were overlooked in school). The resolution of the IQ debate may ultimately depend on whether test-users can learn to use intelligence tests more intelligently—by keeping a person's background in mind, interpreting the results cautiously, and using the results to benefit individual children. But the sociocultural perspective reminds us that no psychological test exists in a cultural vacuum, and its use will depend on the culture's politics, prejudices, racial and gender ideologies, and educational goals.

In this respect, the story of the birth of the IQ test is instructive. In 1904, the French Ministry of Education asked psychologist Alfred Binet to design a test that would identify individual children who were slow learners and who would therefore benefit from remedial work. Binet wanted an impartial test so that children would not be subjected to the biases of teachers toward poor children. But when Binet's test crossed the Atlantic to the United States, his original intentions were lost at sea. Americans assumed that IQ tests revealed some permanent, inherited trait, and they used the test not to bring slow learners up to the average but to track people according to "natural" ability. One ironic lesson of a sociocultural analysis is that the IQ controversy might never have occurred if the United States had imported Binet's cultural values along with his test of intelligence.

WHAT DO YOU KNOW?

1. *True or false:* Culture-fair tests have eliminated group differences that show up on traditional IQ tests.
2. When Alfred Binet designed the first IQ test, his goal was to (a) label and categorize children, (b) identify children who could benefit from individualized remedial programs, (c) study intellectual differences among ethnic groups.
3. From the sociocultural view, what is the "dilemma at the heart of IQ testing"?

ANSWERS:

1. false 2. b 3. How can educators accept the existence of cultural differences that put some children at a disadvantage on IQ tests, and at the same time require students to demonstrate mastery of the skills they need for success in school and in the larger society, skills measured by standard IQ tests?

ISSUE 2: SOCIAL AND CULTURAL FACTORS IN PSYCHOTHERAPY

Several approaches to psychotherapy have evolved from the sociocultural perspective, both its social and its cultural halves. These approaches treat every individual as embedded, first, in a social context (family, friends, other relationships) and, second, in a cultural context (Szapocznik & Kurtines, 1993). Efforts to isolate and "therapize" a person without consideration of his or her sociocultural context are, in this view, doomed.

Let's start with an approach that emphasizes the social context of therapy. In the view of *family therapists,* most individual problems do not originate in the individual but in the person's social setting and relationships. It is important to try to work with the whole family together because every family member affects every other; each member has his or her own perceptions about the others, which may be entirely wrong; and family members are usually unaware of how they influence one another.

By observing the entire family (or, in the case of couples, both partners), the therapist hopes to discover the family's imbalances in power and communication (Luepnitz, 1988; Minuchin, 1984; Satir, 1983).

Even when it is not possible to work with the whole family, some therapists will treat individuals by taking a *family-systems* perspective (Bowen, 1978; Carter & McGoldrick, 1988). Clients learn that if they change in any way, in the course of getting rid of their problem or unhappiness, their families will usually protest noisily. Family members will send explicit and subtle messages that read, "Change back!" The family-systems view recognizes that if one family member changes, the others must change, too: If I won't tango with you, you can't tango with me. The family-systems approach makes people aware of how enmeshed they are in relationships and why change is therefore difficult. It's more than a matter of sheer willpower.

From the cultural side of the sociocultural perspective, researchers have demonstrated the importance to successful therapy of understanding cultural factors, which include everything from body language to beliefs (Betancourt & López, 1993). They have even identified cultural influences on definitions of "normal" and "abnormal" behavior. Some standards of normality are shared by most cultures, such as wearing at least some clothes and not committing murder. But many acts are normal in one culture and abnormal in another: Seeing visions might be a sign of schizophrenia in a twentieth-century farmer, but a sign of healthy religious fervor in a thirteenth-century monk. In Europe and most of North America, people who have hallucinations of a deceased loved one are thought to be abnormal. (Actually, this experience is not uncommon during bereavement; it is just that grieving spouses don't talk about it much because they fear being considered crazy.) In other cultures, such as those of the Chinese and the Hopi, hallucinations are regarded as normal expressions of grief and therefore are more prevalent and acceptable (Bentall, 1990).

Cultural research shows that therapists must be careful not to transform a cultural norm into a pathological problem. Latino and Asian clients, for example, are likely to react to a formal interview with a therapist with relative passivity, deference, and inhibited silence, but these reactions are in no way signs of emotional disorder. Latinos may respond to catastrophic stress with an *ataque de nervios,* a nervous attack of screaming, crying, fainting, and agitation. It is a culturally determined response, but an uninformed clinician might label it as a sign of pathology. Similarly, *susto,* or "loss of the soul," is a syndrome common in Latin American cultures as a response to extreme grief or fright; the person believes that his or her soul has departed along with that of the deceased relative. A psychiatrist unfamiliar with this culturally determined response might conclude that the sufferer was delusional or psychotic.

As a result of the growing understanding of the importance of culture, the American Psychiatric Association (1994) now recommends that all therapists take a patient's cultural background into consideration in diagnosis and treatment. For example, one New York psychiatrist, originally from Peru, treated a woman suffering from *susto* by "prescribing" a tradition important in her culture: a mourning ritual to help her assimilate the loss of her uncle. This wake "was quite powerful for her," the psychiatrist told *The New York Times* (December 5, 1995). "She didn't need any antidepressants, and within a few meetings, including two with her family, her symptoms lifted and she was back participating fully in life once again." And other psychologists, working with Puerto Rican children in the United States, have developed *cuento* ("folktale") therapy, which draws on traditional Puerto Rican folktales to model desirable behavior and attitudes. Puerto Rican children in this program feel less anxious and adapt to their new neighborhoods more quickly than control groups that receive either no treatments or traditional psychotherapeutic ones (Rogler et al., 1987).

When the therapist and client are from different cultures or ethnic groups, misunderstandings between them—whether a result of ignorance, dissimilar values and customs, or racism or prejudice on either side—make therapy more difficult. For example, some white therapists misread their black clients' body language. They regard lack of eye contact and frequent glancing around as the client's attempt to "size up what can be ripped off," instead of as signs of discomfort and an effort to get oriented (Brodsky, 1982). For their part, African-American clients often misunderstand or distrust the white therapist's demand for self-disclosure. Experience makes them reluctant to reveal feelings that a white person is likely to misunderstand or reject (Boyd-Franklin, 1989).

Cultural patterns can also set limits on how much a person can change. Monica McGoldrick and John Pearce (1982), Irish-American clinicians who edited a book on therapy with ethnic Americans of all kinds, describe problems typical of Irish-American families. These problems arise from Irish history and religious beliefs and are deeply ingrained. "In general, the therapist cannot expect the family to turn into a physically affectionate, emotionally intimate group, or to enjoy being in therapy very much," they observe. "The notion of Original Sin—that you are guilty before you are born—leaves them with a heavy sense of burden. Someone not sensitized to these issues may see this as pathological. It is not. But it is also not likely to change and the therapist should help the family tolerate this inner guilt rather than try to get rid of it."

Being aware of cultural differences, we emphasize again, doesn't mean stereotyping. The therapist must not assume that all clients from a particular culture are alike or tailor the therapy to fit some abstract notion of cultural rules (Sue, 1991). Some Asians, after all, do have problems with excessive shyness, some Latinos do have emotional disorders, and some Irish don't feel the burden of guilt! It definitely does not mean that a person will do poorly in therapy unless the therapist and client are matched according to ethnicity (Howard, 1991). It does mean that therapists must do what is necessary to ensure that the client will find the therapist to be trustworthy and effective, and clients must be aware of their prejudices, too.

The sociocultural perspective also helps us place the entire issue of psychotherapy in context. In his book *The Shrinking of America*, Bernie Zilbergeld (1983), a psychotherapist himself, argued that American psychotherapy, while often very helpful, promotes three myths that increase dissatisfaction: (1) That people should always be happy and competent, and if they aren't, they need fixing; (2) that almost any change is possible; and (3) that change is relatively easy. These notions reflect the Western stance toward reality, in which people try to influence existing circumstances by changing other people, events, or circumstances. If you don't like something, change it, fix it, or fight it.

In contrast, Eastern cultures have a less optimistic view of change; they are more tolerant of events they regard as being outside of human control. Their members are more likely to accommodate to reality by learning to live with a problem or acting in spite of it (Weisz, Rothbaum, & Blackburn, 1984). A Japanese psychologist offered some examples of Japanese proverbs that teach the benefits of yielding to the inevitable (Azuma, 1984): *To lose is to win* (giving in, to protect the harmony of a relationship, demonstrates the superior traits of generosity and self-control); *Willow trees do not get broken by piled up snow* (no matter how many problems come your way, flexibility will allow you to survive them); and *The true tolerance is to tolerate the intolerable* (some situations that seem unbearable are facts of life that no amount of protest will change). Perhaps you can imagine how long "to lose is to win" would survive on an American football field, or how long most Americans would be prepared to tolerate the intolerable!

Some Western psychotherapists have been borrowing ideas from the Japanese, attempting to teach greater self-acceptance instead of constant self-improvement (Reynolds, 1987). In the Japanese practice of Morita therapy, for example, clients are taught how to live with their most troubling emotions, instead of trying to eradicate them. The point is not that one cultural approach is better or healthier than the other, but rather that both have their place. A "fighting back" strategy encourages self-expression, independent thinking, and protest for change; but the price may be chronic anger, isolation, self-absorption, and unrealistic goals. A "live with it" strategy leads to acceptance of the inevitable and greater serenity; but the price may be self-denial, stagnation, and unnecessary acceptance of misery.

By alerting us to the influence of the external conditions and circumstances of our lives, to the forces that promote change or keep us stuck in unsatisfying routines or relationships, the sociocultural perspective helps us critically evaluate popular ideas about therapy and change in adult life. Few people, in this view, are immune to the influence of their families, working conditions, society, or culture. This perspective tells us to beware of books or programs that promise to "liberate the self," as if the self existed apart from a social and cultural world of obligations, pleasures, and possibilities.

Issue 3: Reducing Prejudice

How can prejudice and conflict between groups be reduced? One of the most common answers depends on changing individuals: In this view, if people have the right education, develop more self-esteem, or have a religious or spiritual conversion, their prejudices will fade. But the sociocultural perspective shows all too clearly that solutions to prejudice that focus on the individual have not been terribly successful. On the contrary, research finds repeatedly that formerly unprejudiced people can, under conditions of economic competition or the inflamed nationalism of wartime, become enraged haters of their new enemies. In addition, as we saw in Chapter 12, because of conformity, explicit group pressure, obedience, and social roles, people who themselves lack prejudiced feelings may nevertheless behave in discriminatory and prejudiced ways.

Researchers in the sociocultural perspective have therefore tended to investigate social and cultural approaches to reducing prejudice and conflict. One early theory, the *contact hypothesis,* held that the best solution is to bring members of both sides together and let them get acquainted; in this way, they will discover their shared humanity. Another was to focus on changing discriminatory laws; once prejudiced behavior is illegal, in this view, people's hearts and minds will follow. And a third approach held that groups in conflict need to put aside their individual interests and work together for a common goal—the lesson of the Eagles and the Rattlers (see Chapter 12), applied to adults.

The contact hypothesis had a moment of glory during the 1950s and 1960s. In some settings, such as integrated housing projects, contact between blacks and whites did reduce hostility (Deutsch & Collins, 1951; Wilner, Walkley, & Cook, 1955). However, as is apparent at most big-city high schools today, desegregation and opportunities to socialize are often unsuccessful (Stephan, 1985). In many integrated schools, ethnic groups form cliques and gangs, fighting other groups and defending their own ways.

As for the legal approach, changes in the law have been essential in achieving justice and in changing some prejudiced attitudes. Integration of public facilities in the American South would never have occurred if civil rights advocates had waited around for segregationists to have a change of heart. Women would never have gotten the right to vote, attend college, or become physicians without persistent challenges to the laws that permitted discrimination. But laws do not necessarily change attitudes if all they do is produce unequal contact between two former antagonists or if economic competition for jobs continues. Even with legal reforms, de facto segregation of schools and neighborhoods is still the rule in the United States.

Finally, although cooperative strategies are unquestionably beneficial to people of all ages, they, too, are not always enough to reduce hostility between groups. Years ago, Elliot Aronson and his colleagues (1978) learned this lesson when they tried to apply the research on cooperation to reducing ethnic conflict among white, Chicano, and black children in elementary schools. Aronson's team designed a "jigsaw method" to build cooperation. Classes were divided into groups of six students of mixed ethnicity, and every group worked together on a shared task that was broken up like a jigsaw puzzle. Each child needed the contributions of the others to put the assignment together. The cooperative students, in comparison to classmates in regular classes, did show greater self-esteem, liked their classmates better, and improved their grades . . . but only slightly. The differences were statistically significant, but so small as to be socially insignificant. In this case, children were in the jigsaw classroom only three times a week, for a 45-minute class period. That was not much time to overturn entrenched habits and conflicting customs outside the classroom.

Increasingly, members of majority groups and minority groups are called on to work together in school, business, sports, and other institutions. If simple contact, legal changes, and cooperation do not in and of themselves hold the answer, how can these groups learn to get along better? Social and cultural psychology offers some suggestions for answering this question. First, the research in this perspective reminds us, as we saw in Chapter 13, that reducing prejudice is a process that happens over time; prejudice isn't something people "have" and then "get rid of" overnight. As Patricia Devine (1995) has argued, it is important to reward people who are making the effort to change their biases, rather than condemning them for not being perfect. In fostering better relationships between cultural groups, she says, it is essential to distinguish between truly prejudiced people who lack any motivation to change, and people who are simply unfamiliar with members of another group.

Devine and her colleagues note that the usual approach to improving majority–minority relations has been to focus on changing the attitudes of the majority. The attitudes and reactions of the minority (gay men and lesbians, blacks, women, disabled people, whomever) were almost invisible in early research (Devine, Evett, & Vasquez-Suson, 1996). Today, researchers find that improving relations between minority and majority group members depends on understanding the *interaction* of all participants, identifying the expectations and concerns of both sides, and heading off potential cultural misunderstandings before they escalate.

For example, Devine and her colleagues describe the following common interaction sequence:

✦ Some majority group members are highly motivated to work with minorities without prejudice, but they are uncertain about their ability to do so. So they become self-conscious and anxious about doing the wrong thing. As a result of this anxiety, they behave awkwardly; they maintain too great a conversational distance, blurt out dumb remarks, and avoid eye contact with the minority members.

Doubts and anxieties felt by some majority group members.

✦ The minority group members, based on their own history with and expectation of prejudice, interpret the majority members' behavior not as evidence of anxiety, but of hostility. Having made this interpretation, the minority members may respond with withdrawal, aloofness, or hostility.

✦ The majority members, not understanding that their own behavior has been interpreted as evidence of hostility or prejudice, regard the minority members' behavior as unreasonable or mysterious; so they reciprocate the hostility or withdraw.

✦ This behavior confirms the minority members' suspicions about the majority's true feelings and prejudices.

In this way, write Devine and her associates (1996), "*Perceived* hostility is transformed into *actual* hostility on the part of both interactants. . . . a cycle of spiraling mistrust of the other can be established." Whenever people find themselves in situations that make them feel clumsy, anxious, or uncomfortable, they retreat from further contact with each other.

By understanding the cycle, people can learn to break it. Well-intentioned majority members can become aware of the discrepancy between their egalitarian beliefs and their actual behavior. They can learn to reduce their discomfort with people unlike themselves, and to acquire the skills that will lessen their anxiety. But breaking the cycle of distrust and hostility, Devine and her colleagues argue, is "not simply a 'majority group problem.'" Minorities must become part of the solution, too—for example, by recognizing their possible biases in seeing the majority members' behavior only in a negative light. As a colleague of ours who works in race relations once said, "It is really a watershed event in your life when you realize that the other side isn't entirely evil, but mostly just dumb."

Doubts and anxieties felt by some minority group members.

But what happens when both sides really do bear enormous animosity toward each other, for historical, economic, or political reasons? Sociocultural researchers have identified the *external* conditions necessary to reduce prejudice and conflict (Amir, 1994; Fisher, 1994; Rubin, 1994; Stephan & Brigham, 1985; Stephan & Stephan, 1992). The zinger is that for any of them to be effective, you have to have all of them:

1. BOTH SIDES MUST COOPERATE, WORKING TOGETHER FOR A COMMON GOAL, an enterprise that reduces us–them thinking and creates an encompassing social identity. Both sides must work together in finding solutions to their problems, in a spirit of collaboration and joint problem solving. If one side tries to bully and dominate the other, if one side passively capitulates or withdraws, or if both sides compete to see who will win, the conflict will continue (Rubin, 1994).

2. BOTH SIDES MUST HAVE EQUAL STATUS AND EQUAL ECONOMIC STANDING. If one side has more power or greater economic opportunity, prejudice can continue. Thus, putting blacks and whites in the same situation won't necessarily reduce conflict if the whites have all the decision-making authority and higher status. Indeed, in such cases, white stereotypes about blacks tend to be reinforced rather than weakened (Amir, 1994). But when blacks have equal or higher status, white attitudes typically change in a much more favorable direction.

3. BOTH SIDES MUST BELIEVE THAT THEY HAVE THE MORAL, LEGAL, AND ECONOMIC SUPPORT OF AUTHORITIES, such as teachers, employers, the judicial system, government officials, and the police. In other words, the larger culture must support the goal of equality in its laws and in the actions of its officials.

4. BOTH SIDES MUST HAVE OPPORTUNITIES TO WORK AND SOCIALIZE TOGETHER, FORMALLY AND INFORMALLY, if they are ever going to get used to one another's food, music, customs, attitudes, and everyday preferences (Fisher, 1994).

Perhaps one reason that cultural conflicts have been so persistent around the world is that these four sociocultural conditions are rarely met all at the same time.

WHAT DO YOU KNOW?

1. What are the four conditions necessary for the reduction of conflict and prejudice between two groups?
2. Millicent has had a spiritual conversion and now believes that prejudice against other groups is wrong. But when her sorority votes to reject an applicant who is Iranian, she goes along. In the sociocultural view, why has she done this? (a) Her conversion wasn't deep enough. (b) Her prejudice fulfills certain psychological needs. (c) The influence of group pressure is often stronger than an individual's personal preferences. (d) She hasn't had enough contact with Iranians.

ANSWERS:

1. Both sides must cooperate for a common goal; have equal status and power; have the moral, legal, and economic support of authorities; and have opportunities to socialize formally and informally. 2. c

In spite of the challenges of applying research to complex problems, the sociocultural perspective is making a difference in hundreds of ways, large and small. Because of research on the ways in which organizational structure affects workers' motivation, companies are experimenting with new forms of teamwork and incentive pay. Because of research on cross-cultural differences in nonverbal language, communication, and notions of time, some businesses are hiring cultural advisers to help them make the best use of their own employees' diversity and do better business with other countries. Because of research on the way that gender stereotypes limit girls' aspirations, teachers are being trained to identify their biases and to be sensitive to the subtle ways in which they treat the sexes differently.

And maybe, maybe, research on bystander intervention will someday mean fewer Kitty Genoveses and Rodney Kings, fewer people murdered or beaten while bystanders look on. Already, the California agency that sets standards for police officers has established a training program that will encourage officers to intervene when their colleagues are using too much force. The man hired to design the program is Ervin Staub, whose family was saved from the Nazis in 1944—by concerned bystanders.

Perhaps the most important contribution of the sociocultural perspective is the understanding that although cultures differ, no one of them has all the right answers; the understanding that although cultures differ, we are all subject to the same fundamental needs and social forces. Yet we must not forget the remarkable capacity of human beings to wriggle out of the confines of role and culture and, with impressive leaps of imagination and empathy, bridge the chasms of difference. Individuals are able to do this even when war has created animosities and ethnocentric self-justifications that might be expected to last forever.

And so we will end with a story of how one man finally put his animosities toward another culture to rest. People do not need to forget what has happened to them, he reasoned, but they can begin to forgive; and for that, they need to break out of their habitual pattern of stereotyping the enemy. They need to see their enemies as human beings and recognize the common humanity beneath their cultural differences.

Many years after the Vietnam War, veteran William Broyles, Jr., traveled to Vietnam to try to resolve his feelings about the horrors he had seen there. In a PBS documentary called "Faces of the Enemy," he explained that he wanted to meet his former enemies "as people, not abstractions." In a small village that had been a Marine base camp, he met a woman who had been with the Viet Cong. As they talked, Broyles realized that her husband had been killed at exactly the time that he and his men had been patrolling. "My men and I might have killed your husband," he said. She looked at him steadily and replied, "But that was during the war. The war is over now. Life goes on." Broyles said this about his healing visit to Vietnam:

> I used to have nightmares. Since I've been back from that trip, I haven't had any. Maybe that sounds too personal to support any larger conclusions, but it tells me that to end a war you have to return to the same personal relationships you would have had with people before it. You do make peace. Nothing is constant in history.

✦ ✦ ✦

Summary

1. The sociocultural perspective challenges the traditional assumption that the goal of psychology should be to find laws of behavior that apply to all human beings everywhere, regardless of their history, circumstance, or culture. This perspective has made three important contributions to psychology: placing the individual in a social context; making psychologists aware of the importance of culture in every domain of psychology; and making psychology more scientific, more encompassing, and more socially relevant.

2. One misinterpretation of the sociocultural perspective is *sociocultural reductionism,* the tendency to reduce the complexities of human behavior to the single factor of culture or society. Other misuses of this perspective include stereotyping—exaggerating differences between groups and overlooking variation within them; taking an entirely relativist, nonjudgmental view of all cultural practices, even when such practices cause suffering and violate what most people regard as universal human rights; and using cultural findings to foster greater ethnocentrism and ethnic, societal, and gender separatism.

3. The way that a culture defines "intelligence" has implications for educational policy and the industry of intelligence testing. The sociocultural perspective has inspired researchers to try to design *culture-free* and *culture-fair* intelligence tests, but the results have been disappointing. This perspective raises another important issue: whether a test that predicts school success but measures only the kind of intelligence valued by the dominant culture should be used in schools. The sociocultural perspective has influenced researchers to abandon the "deficit model" of intelligence testing, and to recognize that cultural groups can be different without one of them being deficient.

4. Several approaches to psychotherapy have evolved from the sociocultural perspective. The social side of the perspective has influenced *family therapists,* who view problems as originating in the person's social setting and relationships and who treat the whole family, and therapists who take a *family-systems* approach, even when treating individual clients. The cultural side has identified cultural influences on definitions of normality and abnormality, and on therapeutic diagnosis and treatment. It has raised awareness of the potential for misunderstandings between therapist and client because of cultural differences. It has also shown how cultural ideas about control, change, and the nature of reality can affect the practice of psychotherapy.

5. Sociocultural research has generated many efforts to reduce prejudice and conflict between groups. Approaches that focus on individual change or increased contact have not been very successful. Changes in the law have been essential in achieving justice and in changing some prejudices, but laws do not change attitudes if all they do is produce unequal contact between two former antagonists or if economic competition for jobs continues. Cooperative learning is unquestionably beneficial to students of all ages, but it is not enough to reduce prejudice and hostility between groups.

6. In groups where members of majority and minority groups work together, it is important for all participants to assess each other's behavior accurately and to avoid inferring prejudice or hostility when none is intended. Otherwise, a negative cycle can ensue, in which perceived hostility becomes actual hostility. Prejudice and conflict decrease when people from different cultural groups work together for a common goal; have equal status and equal economic standing; have the moral, legal, and economic support of authorities; and have opportunities to work and socialize together, formally and informally.

7. Perhaps the most important contribution of the sociocultural perspective is the understanding that groups and cultures differ, but that no one of them has all the right answers; and that in a fundamental way, all human beings are subject to the same needs and social forces.

Key Terms

sociocultural reductionism *485*

cultural absolutism versus relativism *487*

culture-free and culture-fair tests *491*

family therapy *493*

family-systems approach *494*

the contact hypothesis *497*

the "jigsaw method" *497*

PART VI

THE
PSYCHODYNAMIC
PERSPECTIVE

I magine this scene: Three hundred strangers in a room are told to pair up and ask their partner a single question, "What do you want?" When psychiatrist Irvin Yalom (1989) conducts this exercise, he is always stunned by the reaction it unleashes:

Often, within minutes, the room rocks with emotion. Men and women . . . are stirred to their depths. They call out to those who are forever lost—dead or absent parents, spouses, children, friends: "I want to see you again." "I want your love." "I want to know you're proud of me." "I want you to know I love you and how sorry I am I never told you." "I want you back—I am so lonely." "I want the childhood I never had." "I want to be healthy—to be young again." "I want to be loved, to be respected." "I want my life to mean something." "I want to accomplish something." "I want to matter, to be important, to be remembered."

"So much wanting," writes Yalom. "So much longing. And so much pain, so close to the surface, only minutes deep."

The psychodynamic perspective in psychology holds that other perspectives—biological, learning, cognitive, and sociocultural—cannot begin to account for the emotional pain and longing that are "only minutes deep" in human experience. To understand the full mystery of human behavior, this view holds, we must understand the inner life: the unconscious conflicts hidden from awareness that nonetheless drive our actions; the anxieties about death and loss that we try to suppress; the insecurities and fears originating in childhood that we re-experience in adulthood; and the symbols and themes that invade our uniquely human imaginations.

In Chapter 1 we described the psychodynamic perspective as the thumb on the hand of psychology—connected to the other fingers, yet set apart from them. Now you'll see why.

CHAPTER 15

The Inner Life

$\mathcal{R}$obert Hobson (1985), a psychodynamic therapist, spent many weeks trying to communicate with Stephen, a troubled 15-year-old boy who refused to speak or to look at him. One day, in frustration, Hobson took an envelope and drew a squiggly line. Then Hobson invited Stephen to add to the picture. Stephen drew a ship, thereby turning Hobson's meaningless line into a tidal wave:

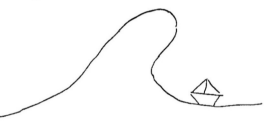

Was Stephen, Hobson wondered, afraid of being emotionally "drowned"? Hobson next drew a landing pier, representing safety. Stephen was not interested in safety. On his boat, he put a person waving goodbye:

Hobson, suspecting that Stephen's problem might stem from emotional separation from his mother, drew a woman waving goodbye from the landing pier. Ignoring the figure of the woman, Stephen added a creature caught in the wave, and spoke for the first time: "A flying fish." Hobson added an octopus in the water:

Stephen, shoulders drooping in sadness, marked up the entire sketch with lines, adding, "It's raining." Hobson, hoping to convey optimism, drew the sun, adding rays that conflicted with the rain:

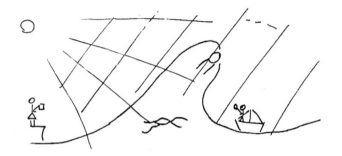

Stephen paused and looked at Hobson intently for the first time. He drew large arcs embracing the whole illustration. "A rainbow," said Stephen. He smiled.

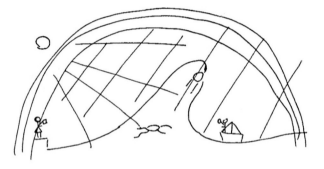

Biological, behavioral, cognitive, and sociocultural psychologists would have trouble accounting for this touching emotional exchange. The interaction between Stephen and his therapist is almost entirely nonverbal, yet it is filled with meaningful symbols and deeply felt emotion. To a psychodynamic psychologist, the other perspectives offer only the most superficial ways of understanding, let alone reaching, a boy like Stephen—or any of the rest of us.

More than any other psychological perspective, the psychodynamic approach to human behavior is embedded in popular culture, particularly in people's ways of talking and thinking about their problems and everyday actions. A man apologizes for "displacing" his frustrations at work onto his family. A woman suspects that she is "repressing" a childhood trauma. An alcoholic reveals that he is no longer "in denial" about his dependence on drinking. A newspaper columnist advises readers to vent their anger or risk becoming physically ill. A wife speculates about the unconscious reasons that might have caused her husband to lapse into depression. A teacher informs a divorcing couple that their eight-year-old child, formerly well behaved, is "regressing" to immature behavior on the playground. A husband tells his wife that her headaches and allergies are "psychosomatic." And everyone ponders the hidden meanings of dreams.

All of this language—about displacing, repressing, denying, venting, and regressing; about the unconscious; about the significance of dreams—derives from the first psychodynamic theory of personality, Sigmund Freud's theory of **psychoanalysis.** Today there are many others, differing in various ways from classical psychoanalysis and from one another. But they generally share five elements:

1. An emphasis on unconscious **intrapsychic** dynamics, the movement of psychic forces within the mind.
2. An assumption that adult behavior and ongoing problems are determined primarily by experiences in early childhood.
3. A belief that psychological development occurs in fixed stages, during which predictable mental events occur, and certain unconscious issues or crises must be resolved.
4. A focus on fantasies and the symbolic meaning of events as the unconscious mind perceives them—a person's *psychic reality*—as the main motivators of behavior.
5. A reliance on subjective rather than objective methods of getting at the truth of a person's life—for example, through analysis of dreams, myths, folklore, symbols, and, most of all, the revelations uncovered in therapy.

In this chapter, we will introduce you to classical Freudian theory, to the variations of Freud's theory offered by some of his dissenting colleagues during his lifetime, and to contemporary psychodynamic approaches that have added new rooms and levels to the original Freudian edifice. In the evaluation chapter that follows we will discuss why the psychodynamic perspective has been in such conflict with other psychological perspectives, and whether it is possible to find common ground among them.

FREUD AND PSYCHOANALYSIS

No one disputes the worldwide influence of Sigmund Freud (1856–1939). But there is plenty of dispute about the lasting significance of his work, reflected in three current attitudes toward Freud and his ideas. The first, held by Freud himself and by his most devoted followers to this day, is that Freud was one of the geniuses of history, an intellectual revolutionary like Copernicus, Darwin, and Newton; with minor exceptions, his theory is correct, universal, and timeless. The second view, probably the most common among psychiatrists and clinical psychologists today, is that Freud was a great thinker and that many of his ideas have lasting value, but some are dated, and others are plain wrong. The third view, held by many scientists and by psychologists in other perspectives, is that Freud was a fraud—a poor scientist and even an unethical therapist (Crews, 1995). The British scientist and Nobel laureate Peter Medawar (1982) called psychoanalysis a dinosaur in the history of ideas, doomed to extinction. For good measure, he added that it is "the most stupendous intellectual confidence trick of the twentieth century."

---

psychoanalysis A theory of personality and a method of psychotherapy developed by Sigmund Freud; it emphasizes unconscious motives and conflicts.
intrapsychic Within the mind (psyche) or self.

In order to understand the kind of theory that could produce such passionately different reactions, let us enter the world of Freud—a realm beneath our daily thoughts and conscious actions. Freud believed that the most important impulses and motives affecting behavior are sexual and aggressive. Because these primitive urges are threatening, we push them out of consciousness, deep into our unconscious minds. Yet they make themselves known in hundreds of ways: in dreams, apparent accidents, jokes, myths, art, and fantasy. Freud (1905a) wrote, "No mortal can keep a secret. If the lips are silent, he chatters with his fingertips; betrayal oozes out of him at every pore." A slip of the tongue was no random flub to Freud. The British member of Parliament who referred to the "honourable member from Hell" when he meant to say "Hull," said Freud (1920/1960), was revealing his true, unconscious appraisal of his colleague.

To chart the byways of the unconscious, Freud developed the theory and method of psychoanalysis. As he listened to his patients unburden themselves in therapy, revealing their random associations and dreams, he formulated a sweeping theory of the structure and dynamics of personality.

The Structure of Personality

According to Freud, the personality is made up of three major systems: the *id,* the *ego,* and the *superego.* Although each system has its own functions and elements, human behavior is nearly always a result of the interaction among them (Freud, 1905b, 1920/1960, 1923/1962).

The **id,** which is present at birth, is the reservoir of all psychological energies and inherited instincts. The id is unconcerned with objective reality and is unaffected by the environment, culture, or learning. The id operates according to the **pleasure principle,** seeking to reduce tension, avoid pain, and obtain pleasure.

The id contains what Freud considered to be two competing groups of instincts: the life, or sexual, instincts (fueled by psychic energy called the **libido**) and the death, or aggressive, instincts. You may remember from Chapter 1 that Freud relied on the nineteenth-century idea of the dynamics of energy: Within any system, he thought, including the human psyche, energy can be shifted or transformed, but the total amount of energy remains the same. As instinctive energy builds up in the id, like steam in a teapot, the result is an uncomfortable state of tension. The id may discharge this tension in the form of reflex actions, physical symptoms, or wishful thinking— uncensored mental images and unbidden thoughts.

The **ego,** the second system to emerge, is a referee between the needs of instinct and the demands of society. It obeys the **reality principle,** putting a rein on the id's

---

id In psychoanalysis, the part of the mind containing sexual and aggressive impulses; from the Latin for "it."
pleasure principle The principle guiding the operation of the id as it seeks to reduce tension, avoid pain, and enhance pleasure.
libido In psychoanalysis, the psychic energy that fuels the sexual instincts of the id.
ego In psychoanalysis, the part of the mind that represents reason, good sense, and rational self-control; it mediates between id and superego.
reality principle The principle guiding the operation of the ego as it seeks to find socially acceptable outlets for instinctual energies.

desire for pleasure until a suitable outlet can be found. The ego, said Freud, represents "reason and good sense." Freud (1923/1962) described the relationship between ego and id this way: "In relation to the id, [the ego] is like a man on horseback, who has to hold in check the superior strength of the horse; . . . Often a rider, if he is not to be parted from his horse, is obliged to guide it where it wants to go; so in the same way the ego constantly carries into action the wishes of the id as if they were its own."

The **superego,** the last system of personality to develop, represents the voice of morality, the rules of parents and society, the power of authority. The superego consists of the *ego ideal,* those moral and social standards you come to believe are right, and the *conscience,* the inner voice that says you did something wrong. The superego sits in judgment on the activities of the id, handing out good feelings (pride, satisfaction) when you do something well and handing out unpleasant feelings (guilt, shame) when you break the rules.

An old joke summarizes the roles of the id, ego, and superego this way: The id says, "I want, and I want it now"; the superego says, "You can't have it; it's bad for you"; and the ego, the rational mediator, says, "Well, maybe you can have some of it—later." According to Freud, the healthy personality must keep all three systems in balance. Someone who is too controlled by the id is governed by impulse and selfish desires. Someone who is too controlled by the superego is rigid, moralistic, and bossy. Someone who has a weak ego is unable to balance personal needs and wishes with social duties and realistic limitations.

If a person feels anxious or threatened when the wishes of the id conflict with the demands of conscience and social rules, the ego has certain weapons at its command to relieve the tension. These weapons, called **defense mechanisms,** have two characteristics: They deny or distort reality, and they operate unconsciously. According to Freud, ego defenses are necessary to protect us from uncomfortable conflict and anxiety; they become unhealthy only when they cause emotional problems and self-defeating behavior. Freud described 17 defense mechanisms; later, other psychoanalysts expanded and modified his list. Following are some of the primary defenses identified both by Freud's daughter Anna Freud (1946), who became an eminent psychoanalyst herself, and by most contemporary psychodynamic psychologists (Horowitz, 1988; Vaillant, 1992):

1. **REPRESSION** occurs when a threatening idea, memory, or emotion is blocked from becoming conscious. A woman who had a frightening experience in childhood that she cannot remember, for example, is said to be repressing her memory of it. Repression doesn't mean that you consciously bite your tongue rather than reveal a guilty secret. It refers to the mind's effort to keep a lid on unacceptable feelings and thoughts in the unconscious, so that you aren't even aware of them. In the psychodynamic view, people who say they never remember their dreams or they have never had a sexual fantasy are likely to be repressing.

---

superego In psychoanalysis, the part of the mind that represents conscience, morality, and social standards.
defense mechanisms Strategies used by the ego to prevent unconscious anxiety from reaching consciousness.

Drawing by Joe Mirachi; © 1985 The New Yorker Magazine, Inc.

"I'm sorry, I'm not speaking to anyone tonight.
My defense mechanisms seem to be out of order."

2. **PROJECTION** occurs when one's own unacceptable or threatening feelings are repressed and then attributed to someone else. A boy who dislikes his father, for instance, may feel anxious about disliking someone he depends on. So he may project his feelings onto his father, concluding that "he hates me." A person who is embarrassed about having sexual feelings toward members of a different ethnic group may project this discomfort onto them, saying, "Those people are dirty-minded and oversexed."

One of the most familiar targets of projection is the *scapegoat,* a powerless person or group that is blamed for a problem by individuals who feel insecure or threatened. (For the ancient Hebrews, a scapegoat was literally a goat. During the days of repentance at the start of the new year, a religious leader would place his hands on the head of a goat as he recited the sins of the community. The goat was then allowed to escape into the wilds, symbolically taking the people's sins with it.) You can see examples of scapegoating in many contexts. Some families make one weak child the scapegoat for their emotional conflicts. Some nations make an ethnic or religious minority the scapegoat for their economic difficulties, as the early Romans did with the Christians, as the Nazis did with the Jews, and as the Serbs and Croats have done with the Bosnian Muslims.

3. **REACTION FORMATION** occurs when a feeling that produces unconscious anxiety is transformed into its opposite in consciousness. A woman who is afraid to admit to herself that she doesn't love her husband may cling to the belief that she does love him. A person who is aroused by erotic images may angrily assert that pornography is disgusting. How does such a transformed emotion differ from a true emotion? Usually in reaction formation, the professed feeling is excessive: The person "protests too much" and is extravagant and compulsive about demonstrating it. ("Love him? Of course I love him! I *never* have any bad thoughts about him! He's perfect!")

4. **REGRESSION** occurs when a person reverts to a previous phase of psychic development. As we will see, Freud believed that personality develops in a series of stages from birth to maturity. Each new step, however, produces a certain amount of frustration and anxiety. If these become too great, normal development may be halted, and the child may remain *fixated* at the current stage; for instance, he or she may fail to outgrow clinging dependence. People may also regress to an earlier stage if they suffer a traumatic experience in a later one. An eight-year-old boy who is anxious about his parents' divorce may regress to earlier habits of thumb sucking or clinging. Adults may reveal "partial fixations" that they never outgrew, such as biting their nails, or they may regress to immature behavior when they are under pressure—for example, by having a temper tantrum if they don't get their way.

5. **DENIAL** occurs when people simply refuse to admit that something unpleasant is happening or that they are experiencing a "forbidden" emotion. Some people deny that they are angry; alcoholics may deny that they depend on liquor. In the psychodynamic view, people who assert that they *never, ever* have negative feelings or never feel disgusted by anything are revealing denial, for these are universal emotions. Denial protects the illusion of invulnerability—"It will never happen to me"—which is why people often behave in self-destructive and risky ways. When a woman ignores a lump in her breast, when a man having a heart attack says "It's only indigestion," when a diabetic fails to take needed medication, they are all showing denial.

6. **DISPLACEMENT** occurs when people direct their emotions (especially anger) toward things, animals, or other people that are not the real object of their feelings. People use displacement when they perceive the real target as being too threatening to confront directly. A boy who is forbidden to express anger at his father, for example, may "take it out" on his toys or his younger sister.

   Freud believed that the aggressive and sexual instincts of the id, if blocked from direct expression, would be displaced onto a substitute. Thus aggressive impulses might be displaced in sports competition instead of directly expressed in war; sexual impulses might be displaced in the creation of passionate poetry and literature. When displacement serves a higher cultural or socially useful purpose, as in the creation of art or inventions, it is called *sublimation*. Freud himself thought that for the sake of civilization and survival, sexual and aggressive energies could and should be displaced or sublimated into socially appropriate and constructive forms.

7. **ACTING OUT** consists of impulsive actions in which the person fails to consider the consequences of his or her behavior. A girl who suddenly starts behaving aggressively on the schoolyard might be acting out her anger over her parents' divorce; a teenager who commits delinquent acts might be acting out his frustration and loneliness.

8. **HUMOR** is a way of defending against fear, awareness of aging and death, sexual or aggressive impulses, or (in men) anxiety about sexual performance, which is why so many jokes are about these themes.

According to Freud, these defense mechanisms (summarized in Table 15.1 along with Freud's model of the mind) protect the ego from anxiety and allow the person to cope with the demands of the real world. Different personalities emerge because people differ in the defenses they use, in how rigid their defenses are, and in whether their defenses lead to healthy or disturbed functioning (Bernstein & Warner, 1993; Vaillant, 1992). Unhealthy efforts to defend against anxiety may produce a *neurosis*, characterized by self-punishing behavior (such as drinking too much), emotional symptoms (such as excessive anxiety), or physical symptoms (such as stomachaches). Freud thus promoted the idea that many physical problems have a psychological, "neurotic" cause.

In sum, psychoanalytic theory is based on the idea that every human being, throughout life, is always in a state of conflict, trying to balance internal conflicts between the id and superego, and external conflicts between one's wishes and the demands of the environment. Freud was fully aware of the ways in which culture, custom, and law shape human behavior and desires. Indeed, he wrote sympathetically and poignantly of the psychological impact on women of the sexual sublimation that society requires of them (Freud, 1908), and in his great book *Civilization and Its Discontents* (1930), he examined the inevitable tensions between individual desires and the needs of society. At the same time, Freud believed that the unconscious was primary and universal. Cultures come and go, societies and their laws differ and change, but the unconscious goes on forever. Out of the internal battle between the forces of order and anarchy, said Freud, civilization emerges. "Where id is," he wrote (1933), "there must ego come to be."

TABLE 15.1 ✦ Summary of Freud's Model of the Mind

Id	Ego	Superego
Location of the aggressive and sexual instincts	Relies on the reality principle to mediate between desires of the id and the demands of the superego	Location of conscience and the ego ideal
Follows the pleasure principle	Uses defense mechanisms to protect against unconscious anxiety, including repression projection reaction formation regression denial displacement and sublimation acting out humor	

WHAT DO YOU KNOW?

A. People who have antisocial personality disorder have little or no guilt when they hurt others; they are concerned only with their own pleasure. A Freudian would say that such people are ruled by their _____ and have too little _____.

B. Which Freudian concepts do these events suggest?
    1. A celibate priest writes poetry about sexual passion.
    2. A man who is angry at his boss shouts at his kids for making noise.
    3. A woman who has been physically assaulted by her husband for years assures her friends that she adores him and thinks he is perfect.
    4. A racist justifies segregation by saying that black men are only interested in sex with white women.
    5. A nine-year-old boy who moves to a new city starts having tantrums.
    6. A man ignores obvious signs that his lover is unfaithful.

C. A psychoanalyst and a social-learning theorist are arguing about the displacement of aggression in sports. What positions are they likely to take, and what kind of evidence would you need to decide who is right?

ANSWERS:

A. id, superego   **B.** 1. sublimation 2. displacement 3. reaction formation 4. projection 5. regression 6. denial   **C.** The Freudian would assume that levels of anger and aggression would decrease for participants and observers of aggressive sports, because their violent instincts are being displaced. The social-learning theorist would argue that people are likely to imitate aggressive behavior, especially that of sports heroes who are role models, and that playing aggressively increases anger because it gets reinforced. One way to test these notions is to measure people's level of anger and aggressive behavior before and after they watch or participate in aggressive sports, in contrast to nonaggressive sports. Another way is cross-cultural, finding out whether nations that encourage aggressive sports have fewer wars (the Freudian view) or more wars (the social-learning view) than nations that promote nonaggressive sports. (These studies have actually been done, and they strongly favor the social-learning explanation.)

The Development of Personality

Freud maintained that personality develops during childhood in a fixed series of five stages. He called these stages *psychosexual* because he believed that psychological development depends on the changing expression of sexual energy in different parts of the body as the child matures.

1. **THE ORAL STAGE** marks the first 12 to 18 months of life. Babies take in the world, as well as their nourishment, through their mouths; so the mouth, said Freud, is the focus of sensation at this stage. People who remain fixated at the oral stage may, as adults, seek constant oral gratification in such activities as smoking, drinking, or overeating.

2. **The anal stage,** at about age two to three, marks the start of ego development, as the child becomes aware of the self and of the demands of reality. The major issue at this stage, said Freud, is control of bodily wastes, a lesson in self-control that the child learns during toilet training. People who remain fixated at this stage, he thought, become "anal retentive," holding everything in, obsessive about neatness and cleanliness. Or they become just the opposite, "anal expulsive," that is, messy and disorganized.

3. **The Oedipal (or phallic) stage** lasts roughly from age three to six. Now sexual sensation is located in the penis, for boys, and in the clitoris, for girls. During this stage, said Freud, the child unconsciously wishes to possess the parent of the other sex and to get rid of the parent of the same sex. Children at this age often announce proudly that "I'm going to marry Daddy (or Mommy) when I grow up" and reject the same-sex "rival." Freud (1924a, 1924b) labeled this phenomenon the **Oedipus complex,** after the Greek legend of King Oedipus, who unwittingly killed his father and married his mother.

   Boys and girls, Freud believed, go through the Oedipal stage differently. Boys at this stage are discovering the pleasure and pride of having a penis. When they see a naked female for the first time, they are horrified. Their unconscious exclaims (in effect), "Her penis has been cut off! Who could have done this to her? Why, it must have been her powerful father. And if he could do it to her, my father could do it to me!" This **castration anxiety,** said Freud, causes the boy to repress his desire for his mother, accept the authority of his father, and identify with him.* Identification is the process by which boys take in, as their own, the father's standards of conscience and morality. The superego has emerged.

   Freud admitted that he didn't quite know what to make of females, who, lacking the penis, obviously couldn't go through the same steps. He speculated that a girl, upon discovering male anatomy, would panic that she had only a puny clitoris instead of a stately penis. She would conclude, said Freud, that she already *had* been castrated. As Freud (1924b) described it, "When she makes a comparison with a playfellow of the other sex, she perceives that she has 'come off badly' and she feels this is a wrong done to her and a ground for inferiority." As a result, girls don't have the motivating fear of castration anxiety that boys do to enable them to give up their Oedipal feelings. Girls have only a lingering sense of "penis envy," which lasts until they grow up and have children. "Her Oedipus complex culminates in a desire, which is long retained, to receive a baby from her father as a gift—to bear him a child," wrote Freud (1924b). "The two wishes—to possess a

---

Oedipus complex In psychoanalysis, a conflict in which a child desires the parent of the other sex and views the same-sex parent as a rival; the key issue in the phallic stage of development.
castration anxiety In psychoanalysis, the boy's unconscious fear of castration by the powerful father that motivates the resolution of the Oedipus complex.

*Freud used the term castration to mean loss of the penis, but in modern medical terms, it means removal of the testes.

penis and a child—remain strongly cathected [emotionally linked] in the uncon-scious and help to prepare the female creature for her later sex role." The neurotic female, in contrast, resolves penis envy by trying to be like men, perhaps by having a career. In either case, Freud concluded, women do not develop the strong moral superegos that men do.

One of Freud's most famous assertions was "Anatomy is destiny" (a phrase he borrowed from Napoleon). Freud did not mean that biology dictates the kind of person we will become or even that our gender roles are fixed and predetermined by our genes. On the contrary, he was ahead of his time in showing that masculin-ity and femininity are overlapping concepts, not polar opposites: "In human beings pure masculinity or femininity is not to be found in a psychological or a biological sense," he wrote (1905b). "Every individual on the contrary displays a mixture of the character traits belonging to his own and to the opposite sex." By "anatomy is destiny," he meant that gender development begins with children's *unconscious* reactions to anatomical differences. As long as women lack the penis, Freud believed, there will always be a certain amount of unconscious envy, fear, and suspicion between the sexes. That is the destiny that anatomy confers on us.

By age five or six, when the Oedipus complex is resolved, the child's personal-ity patterns are formed. Unconscious conflicts with parents, unresolved fixations and guilts, and attitudes toward the same and the other sex, said Freud, will con-tinue to replay themselves throughout life.

4. **THE LATENCY STAGE** lasts from the end of the phallic stage to puberty. The child settles down, goes to school, makes friends, develops self-confidence, and learns the social rules for appropriate behavior. The mental experiences that occurred in the pre-Oedipal and Oedipal phases, Freud said, are now repressed, which is why all children succumb to what he called *infantile amnesia*—the inability to remem-ber anything from the first few years of life. (Modern cognitive views of childhood amnesia were discussed in Chapter 10.)

5. **THE GENITAL STAGE** begins at puberty and marks the beginning of what Freud con-sidered mature adult sexuality. Sexual energy is now located in the genitals and eventually is directed toward sexual intercourse. Not everyone reaches this mature stage, said Freud. The defense mechanisms of the ego and the displacement of instinctual energy may prevent some people from reaching mature genital sexuality.

The "Talking Cure"

The greatest influence of psychoanalytic theory was on the practice of psychotherapy, which one patient of Freud's called the "talking cure" (Sulloway, 1992). Freud believed that intensive probing of the past and of the mind would produce *insight*—the patient's moment of truth, the awareness of the reason for his or her symptoms and anguish. With insight and emotional release, said Freud, the symptoms would disap-pear. Today, Freud's original method has evolved into many different forms, but the goal of insight unites them.

In classical psychoanalysis, the client lies on a couch, facing away from the analyst. The patient is told to use **free association** to say whatever comes to mind. For example, by free-associating to his dreams, his fantasies about work, and his early memories, a college student might gain the insight that he procrastinates as a way of expressing anger toward his parents. He might realize that he is angry because they insist that he study for a career he dislikes. Ideally, he will come to this insight by himself. If the analyst suggests it, the patient might feel too defensive about displeasing his parents to accept it.

The second major process in psychoanalysis is **transference,** the patient's transfer (displacement) of emotional elements of his or her inner life—usually feelings about the parents—outward onto the analyst. Have you ever found yourself responding to a new acquaintance with unusually quick affection or dislike, and later realized it was because the person reminded you of a loved or loathed relative? That's a version of transference. In psychoanalysis, the transference might involve images of important people in the patient's past; or it might involve aspects of the patient's own personality that he or she cannot accept. A woman who failed to resolve her Oedipal love for her father might seem to fall in love with the analyst. A man who is unconsciously angry at his mother for rejecting him might now become furious with his analyst for going on vacation. Through the analysis of transference, Freud believed, patients can resolve their problems.

Freudian psychoanalysis established two key assumptions that still guide psychodynamic therapists today: first, that conscious memories and perceptions are not as important in affecting behavior as unconscious dynamics such as defense mechanisms; and second, that what actually happened in a person's past is not as important as that person's "psychic reality"—how the unconscious has interpreted the experience. Unlike cognitive and behavioral therapists, who treat conscious problems that a person wishes to fix, psychodynamic therapists assume that the person doesn't know what the problem is. He or she may come to therapy complaining of unhappiness, family conflict, or self-defeating habits, but the analyst will seek the unconscious processes beneath these symptoms. As psychodynamic therapist Robert Fancher (1995) observes, "The greatest legacy of psychoanalysis is its highly developed art of listening for what is not being said, for self-deception that is being perpetrated, and for the wishes and terrors that patients cannot own honestly."

Now, perhaps you can imagine why these ideas were not exactly received with yawns. Sexual feelings in infants and children! Repressed longings in the most respectable adults! Unconscious meanings in dreams! Penis envy! Sexual sublimation! This was hot stuff, and before too long psychoanalysis had captured the public imagination in Europe and America (Hornstein, 1992).

---

free association In psychoanalytic therapy, a method of uncovering unconscious conflicts by saying freely whatever comes to mind.

transference In psychoanalysis, a critical step in which the patient transfers unconscious emotions or reactions, such as emotional responses to his or her parents, onto the therapist.

To his supporters, Freud was a brilliant explorer of the mind, the man who discovered and charted the mysterious pathways of the unconscious and revealed those pathways through the techniques of psychoanalysis. They regard him as a man who bravely battled public censure and ridicule in his unwavering pursuit of scientific truth (Gay, 1988). Yet to his critics, Freud was not so much an innovator as a clever packager and marketer of other people's ideas. They regard him as an egotistical self-promoter who actually manufactured a myth that he was a poor, misunderstood genius in order to gain sympathy and credibility (Crews, 1995; Sulloway, 1992).

Moreover, new scholarship on Freud, based on previously unpublished papers, has seriously, perhaps fatally, wounded Freud's claim that he was an impartial scientist who simply reported what his patients told him and deduced his theories from those accounts. Freud's own writings reveal that he often formulated his theories and then pressed his patients to accept them (Esterson, 1993; Powell & Boer, 1994; Webster, 1995). Early in his career, for example, Freud believed that traumatic early experiences, usually of sexual molestation, caused adult neuroses. When patients fail to report a traumatic memory, Freud wrote, "We must not believe what they say, we must always assume, and tell them, too, that they have kept something back because they thought it unimportant or found it distressing. We must insist on this, we must . . . represent ourselves as infallible, till at last we are really told something" (Breuer & Freud, 1895, cited in Powell & Boer, 1994).

A few years later, however, Freud made a critical shift of emphasis: He decided that his patients were reporting *fantasies* of sexual molestation rather than real events, and that all children fantasize about having sexual relations with the parent of the other sex. It is their unconscious guilt about wanting sex with the parent, not the actual experience of sexual abuse, that causes most adult emotional problems. With this turnaround, the cornerstone of psychoanalytic theory, the Oedipus complex, was established. But now Freud began to press his patients into accepting this revised theory, and he put greater weight on discovering their supposed sexual fantasies than on considering the effects of their actual sexual experiences (Powell & Boer, 1995).

A particularly chilling example is the famous case of "Dora," whose real name was Ida Bauer (Lakoff & Coyne, 1993). Eighteen-year-old Dora had been spurning the explicit sexual advances made by her father's friend, "Herr K," since she was 14 years old and she finally complained to her father. But her father wanted her to accept Herr K's overtures, perhaps because he himself was having an affair with Herr K's wife; so he sent her off to Freud, who attempted to "cure" Dora of her "hysterical" refusal to have sex with Herr K. Freud tried to convince Dora that it was not the ugly situation involving her father and his friend that was distressing her, but her own repressed desires for sex. "I should without question consider a person hysterical," Freud (1905a) wrote, "in whom an occasion for sexual excitement elicited feelings that were preponderantly or exclusively unpleasurable." Dora angrily left treatment after three months, and Freud was unable to accept her "obstinate" refusals to believe his analysis of her symptoms. If only Herr K had learned, said Freud, "that the slap Dora gave him by no means signified a final 'No' on her part," and if he had resolved "to press his suit with a passion which left room for no doubts, the result might very well have been a triumph of the girl's affection for him over all her internal difficulties."

Sigmund Freud was thus a man of contradictions—a mix of vision and blindness, sensitivity and stubbornness. In his provocative ideas, his approach to therapy, and his own complicated personality, Freud left a powerful legacy to psychology. And it was one that others began to tinker with immediately.

WHAT DO YOU KNOW?

Find out whether Freudian terms have registered in the conscious part of your mind by giving the term that a psychoanalyst might use to describe each of the following situations.

1. A toddler puts every new toy he encounters into his mouth.
2. A four-year-old girl wants to snuggle on Daddy's lap but refuses to kiss her mother.
3. A man in therapy reports everything that comes to mind when he thinks about a dream.
4. A woman believes she is deeply in love with her analyst.

ANSWERS:

1. oral stage 2. Oedipus complex 3. free association 4. transference

---

EARLY DISSENTERS

"Few theories in science," observed Frank Sulloway, a historian of science, "have spawned a following that can compare with the psychoanalytic movement in its cult-like manifestations, in its militancy, and in the aura of religion that has permeated it." Even the movement's own adherents recognized the religious zeal they brought to their "conversion." One said that he accepted psychoanalysis "as a revealed religion," and another follower wrote that he became "the apostle of Freud who was my Christ!" (quoted in Sulloway, 1992). Heretics within this new religion—those who questioned Freud's arguments—were dealt with by excommunication and banishment (Crews, 1995; Kerr, 1993). Many of them went on to formulate their own theories and schools.

Karen Horney

As you might expect, many of Freud's female colleagues were not happy with his notion that penis envy is the major motivation in women. Karen Horney (HORN-eye) (1885–1952) was one of the first psychoanalysts to challenge Freud's notions of penis envy and female inferiority (Horney, 1926/1973). She argued that it is both insulting philosophy and bad science to claim, as Freud did, that half the human race is dissatisfied with its anatomy. When women feel inferior to men, she said, we should look for explanations in the "actual social subordination of women" and their second-class status. As she had been 1 of only 58 women at a university with 2,350 students, she knew what she was talking about (Quinn, 1987). She worried that Freudian theory would justify continued discrimination against women by making it seem that female inferiority was in their nature and not in the conditions of their lives.

Horney went on to chastise her male colleagues for their one-sided point of view. "If we try to free our minds from this masculine mode of thought," she wrote (1926/1973), "nearly all the problems of feminine psychology take on a different appearance." The first thing we notice, she said, is a woman's "indisputable and by no means negligible physiological superiority." In fact, said Horney, if anyone has an envy problem, it is men. Men have "womb envy": They envy the female ability to bear and nurse children. Men glorify their own genitals, she said, because they are unable to give birth themselves and because they unconsciously fear women's sexual power over them. Horney agreed with Freud that males suffer from castration anxiety. But whereas Freud thought the reason was the little boy's unconscious fear that his father could castrate him, Horney (1967) thought the reason was the adult man's unconscious fear that his own female lover could castrate him. The "anatomical–psychological" origin of men's dread and fear of women, she wrote, "lies in the fact that during intercourse the male has to entrust his genitals to the female body, that he presents her with his semen and interprets this as a surrender of vital strength to the woman."

Horney (1945) also took issue with Freud's emphasis on sexual and aggressive motivations, his notion of genetically based instincts, and his view that inner conflicts are inevitable. For her the driving force in personality was **basic anxiety,** the feeling of being isolated and helpless in a hostile world. Because people are dependent on one another, she believed, they often end up in a state of anxious conflict when others don't treat them well. Insecure, anxious children develop personality patterns that help them cope with their feelings of isolation and helplessness. They may become aggressive as a way of protecting what little security they do have, not because they have an "aggressive drive." Alternatively, they may become overly submissive, or they may become selfish and self-pitying as a way of gaining attention or sympathy.

In general, said Horney, people can relate to one another in one of three ways: They can move toward others, seeking love, support, and cooperation; they can move away from others, trying to be independent and self-sufficient; or they can move against others, being competitive, critical, and domineering. Ideally, she said, the healthy personality balances all three orientations. But some people become locked into only one mode: too weak-willed and self-denying, afraid to offend anyone; too independent, afraid to admit dependency; or too hostile, afraid to express affection.

Although Freud tended to emphasize the constraining and repressive nature of the superego, Horney (1950) believed that healthy people are guided by an *ideal self*—an image of what they would like to be, around which they organize aspirations and actions. Contemporary researchers have expanded this idea to include a whole domain of *possible selves:* images of what you believe you could become and would like to become (Markus & Nurius, 1986). They have found support for Horney's view that

---

basic anxiety To Karen Horney, the feeling of being isolated and helpless in a hostile world; it is the motivating emotion in social relations.

the way we envision our ideal and possible selves affects our motivations, dreams, plans, and self-esteem.

Alfred Adler

Alfred Adler (1870–1937) had a more positive view of the human condition than Freud did, disagreeing with Freud's emphasis on the unconscious aggressive and sexual instincts of the id. To Freud, human beings are victims of unconscious forces; to Adler, people are directors of their own destinies. To Freud, creativity was a side effect of sublimation; to Adler, creativity was a central capacity of the species. To Freud, social cooperation was a grudging sacrifice of the id; to Adler, it was the essence of human life. In 1911, Adler was banished by Freud from the Vienna Psychoanalytic Society, and he and his followers formed their own organization.

Adler (1927/1959) argued that people have a *drive for superiority*, which is not the desire to dominate others but the desire for self-improvement, spurred by an "upward drive" for perfection. This impulse, said Adler, stems from the natural feelings of inferiority that all of us have, first as children, when we are weak and powerless as compared with adults, and then later, when we have to recognize limitations on our abilities. But some individuals, he wrote, develop an **inferiority complex** because they are raised by parents who fail to encourage their abilities. Unable to accept their natural limitations, they try to mask them by pretending to be strong and capable. Instead of coping with real problems in life, people with inferiority complexes become overly concerned with protecting their self-esteem.

Unlike Freud but like Horney, Adler emphasized the individual's need for others. A key concept in Adler's theory of personality was that of *social interest*, empathy and concern for others (Adler, 1938/1964). Social interest reflects the ability to be unselfish, to be sympathetic, to cooperate, and to feel connected to other people and to the world. It has a cognitive component (the ability to understand others, to see the connectedness of humanity and the world), an emotional component (the ability to feel empathy and attachment), and a behavioral component (the willingness to cooperate with others for the common welfare). Although social interest is the opposite of selfishness, it is harmonious with self-interest. Adler believed that people who are involved with others are better able to cope with problems, have higher self-esteem, and are psychologically stronger than people who are self-involved (Ansbacher, 1968).

Adler's ideas about the importance of social interest have been supported in modern research and psychotherapy. One large study used two measures of social interest: a scale of moral values and an index of cooperation in love, work, and friendship. People who were high in social interest, compared with others, had fewer stressful experiences and were better able to cope with the stressful episodes they did have. Among people low in social interest, stress was more likely to be associated with anxiety,

---

inferiority complex To Alfred Adler, an inability to accept one's natural limitations; it occurs when the need for self-improvement is blocked or inhibited.

depression, and hostility (Crandall, 1984). Social interest seems to mitigate the effects of stress, and it helps people recover from trauma. Julius Segal (1986)—a psychologist who worked with Holocaust survivors, prisoners of war, hostages, refugees, and other survivors of catastrophe—found that a key element in recovery is compassion, healing through helping. People gain strength, he said, by giving it to others.

Why is social interest so healthy? The ability to look outside of oneself, to be concerned with others, leads to solving problems instead of blaming others. Such an ability helps people reappraise a conflict, by trying to see it as others do instead of taking it personally. Because of its elements of forgiveness, tolerance, and connectedness, social interest helps people live with situations that are facts of life.

Adler (1935) further maintained that the real essence of human personality is the *creative self.* In this view, each person actively creates his or her own personality from the raw material of heredity and experience. The resulting personality structure is expressed in a unique *style of life,* which emerges from a combination of biological factors and the individual's conscious and unconscious motives, history, and goals (Ansbacher & Ansbacher, 1964). Whereas Freud held that personality development pretty much stops after the resolution of the Oedipal complex, Adler was one of the first psychologists to emphasize growth and change over the entire life span. He recognized the social factors that influence us throughout life, while maintaining that people have the ability to shape their own futures.

Carl Jung

Like Adler, Carl Jung (1875–1961) was originally one of Freud's closest friends; in fact, Jung accompanied Freud on his only visit to the United States. But Jung began to differ with Freud on the nature of the unconscious, and by 1914 Jung, too, had left Freud's inner circle.

Although Jung shared with Freud a fascination with the darker side of the personality, he also emphasized the positive, forward-moving strengths of the ego. For Jung, people are motivated not only by past conflicts, as Freud thought, but also by their goals and by the desire to fulfill themselves. In addition to the individual's personal unconscious, Jung (1967) believed, there is a **collective unconscious,** containing the universal memories and history of humankind. From his study of myths, folklore, and art in cultures all over the world, Jung was impressed by common, repeated images, which he called **archetypes.** An archetype can be a picture, such as the "magic circle," called a *mandala* in Eastern religions, which symbolizes the unity of life. It can be a mythical figure, such as the Hero, the Nurturing Mother, the Powerful Father, or the Wicked Witch. A different kind of archetype is the *shadow,* which reflects the prehistoric fear of wild animals and represents the animal side of human nature. In the late

---

collective unconscious To Carl Jung, the universal memories and experiences of humankind, represented in the symbols, stories, and images (archetypes) that occur across all cultures.
archetypes To Carl Jung, the universal, symbolic images that appear in myths, dreams, art, folklore, and other expressions of the collective unconscious.

1940s, Joseph Campbell (1949/1968) gathered supporting evidence that certain arche-types—such as the Hero, the Evil Beast, and the Earth Mother—appear in virtually every society.

Jung distinguished the conscious self from the constellation of unconscious arche-types. According to Jung, the *persona* is the public personality, the aspects of yourself that you reveal to others, the role that society expects you to play. The *anima* is (for men) the unconscious subpersonality. Jung defined anima in different ways through-out his work. Sometimes, he used it to mean "soul." Sometimes, he used it to refer to "all those common human qualities which the conscious attitude lacks. The tyrant tor-mented by bad dreams, gloomy forbodings, and inner fears is a typical figure. . . . Thus his anima contains all those fallible human qualities his persona lacks. If the persona is intellectual, the anima will quite certainly be sentimental." And sometimes he used it to mean the feminine quality within a man, the man's other side that he projects onto women and nature. Later, he added the corresponding archetype of the *animus,* the masculine quality within a woman.

Like Freud, Jung had a rather disdainful view of women, whom he regarded as being more emotional and less intellectual than men, better suited to relationships than to thinking: "In men, Eros, the function of relationship, is usually less developed than Logos," he said. "In women, on the other hand, Eros is an expression of their true nature, while their Logos is often only a regrettable accident." But also like Freud, Jung recognized that "masculine" and "feminine" qualities are to be found in both sexes. Problems can arise, Jung said, if a person tries to repress the internal archetype of the Other—that is, if a man totally denies his softer, "feminine" side or if a woman denies her "masculine" aspects. People also create problems in relationships when they expect a partner to behave like the ideal archetypal man or woman, instead of a real human being who has both sides. In his essay "Marriage as a Psychological Relationship," writ-ten originally in 1925, Jung (1967) argued that committed heterosexual relationships are opportunities for development, a way to confront the otherness of someone who sees the world through the filter of a different gender while recognizing in ourselves the archetypes we normally try to suppress. Therefore, he said, we must make an effort to stop projecting archetypes acquired in childhood, such as the Terrible Mother or the Hero, onto the partner.

Lately there has been a resurgence of interest in Jung's theory of archetypes. Jungians have applied archetype theory to explaining differences between women and men (especially in such popular books as *Iron John* and *Women Who Run with Wolves*), and to explaining recurring images in the films, books, and comics of popular culture—such as the endless versions of Dracula, the "shadow" monster (Iaccino, 1994). Modern Jungian analysts use the concept of archetypes to help clients in therapy understand some of the sources of their apparently irrational behavior. For example, a woman may overreact to her husband's mild criticism because his words trigger her "Terrible Father" archetype. "She does not see," says Jungian analyst Polly Young-Eisendrath (1993), "that her overwhelming fear comes from her own subjective state and originates in her early dependence on a caregiver who was sadistic and attacking."

Other Jungians, drawing on the cognitive concepts of *schema* and *narrative,* are interested in how universal images and stories affect the way people see their own lives. When Dan McAdams (1988) asked 50 people to tell their life stories in a two-hour session, he found that they tended to report a common archetype, a mythic character, at the heart of their life narratives. For example, many individuals told stories that could be symbolized by the myth of the Greek god Dionysus, the pleasure seeker who escapes responsibility. Archetypes, says McAdams, represent "the main characters in the life stories we construct as our identities."

LATER DESCENDANTS

Most contemporary psychodynamic psychologists regard Freud's theory as a blueprint of the personality, but this has not stopped them from tinkering with the blueprint, quibbling over some of its details, debating which elements are the most important, and eliminating some features while adding others. Some have expanded Freud's approach to include psychological development throughout life. Others have replaced Freud's "drive model" of personality, which portrays the individual as driven or motivated by aggressive and sexual instincts, with a relational model, which emphasizes the influence of other people. Still others have developed models of the personality that focus on inherent dilemmas of existence; they depart from other psychodynamic approaches in emphasizing conscious human choice and free will.

Erikson's Psychosocial Theory

Freud believed that personality development is completed by age five or six, when the Oedipal complex is resolved. A fuller theory of adult development, stretching from birth to death, was proposed by psychoanalyst Erik H. Erikson (1902–1994). Erikson (1950/1963, 1987) argued that everyone passes through eight developmental stages on the way to wisdom and maturity. Erikson called his theory *psychosocial,* instead of "psychosexual" as Freud had, because he believed that people are propelled by many kinds of psychological and social forces, not just by sexual motives. Each stage, said Erikson, is the result of a combination of biological drives and societal demands. At each one, there is a "crisis" that must be resolved for healthy development to proceed:

1. TRUST VERSUS MISTRUST is the crisis of the baby's first year. A baby depends on others for food, comfort, cuddling, and warmth. If these needs are not met, the child may never develop the essential trust necessary to get along in the world, especially in relationships.

2. AUTONOMY (INDEPENDENCE) VERSUS SHAME AND DOUBT is the crisis of the second stage, as the baby becomes a toddler. The young child is learning to "stand on his own feet," said Erikson, and must do so without feeling ashamed of his or her behavior or too doubtful of his or her growing abilities.

3. INITIATIVE VERSUS GUILT emerges as a crisis when the child starts acquiring new physical and mental skills, setting goals, and enjoying newfound talents, but at the same time must learn to control impulses and energies. The danger lies in developing too strong a sense of guilt over his or her fantasies, newfound power, and childish instincts.

4. COMPETENCE VERSUS INFERIORITY is the crisis of the school-age years, when the child is learning, said Erikson, "to be a worker and potential provider." The child now starts making things, using tools, and acquiring the skills for adult life. Children who fail these lessons of mastery and competence, Erikson argued, risk feeling inadequate and inferior.

5. IDENTITY VERSUS ROLE CONFUSION is the crisis that emerges at puberty. In the adolescent years, teenagers must decide what they are going to make of their lives, professionally and personally. Those who resolve this crisis successfully come out of this stage with a strong identity, ready to plan for the future. Others sink into confusion, unable to make decisions. The term *identity crisis* describes what Erikson considered to be the major conflict of adolescence.

6. INTIMACY VERSUS ISOLATION is the crisis of young adulthood. Once people have developed a clear self-identity, they must learn to share themselves with another and to make commitments. No matter how successful a person is at work, said Erikson, he or she is not developmentally complete if intimacy is lacking.

7. GENERATIVITY VERSUS STAGNATION is typically the major concern of people in their middle years. Will they sink into complacency and selfishness, or will they experience generativity, the pleasure of creativity and renewal? Parenthood is the most common means for the successful resolution of this stage, but people can be productive, creative, and nurturant in other ways, in their work or their relationships with the younger generation.

8. EGO INTEGRITY VERSUS DESPAIR is the final crisis of life. As they age, people strive to reach the ultimate goal—wisdom, spiritual tranquility, an acceptance of one's life and one's role in the larger scheme of things. Just as the healthy child will not fear life, said Erikson, the healthy adult will not fear death.

Erikson recognized that cultural and economic factors affect these developmental stages. Some societies, for example, make the transition from one stage to another relatively easy. If you know you are going to be a farmer like your mother and father and you have no alternative, then moving from adolescence into young adulthood is not a very painful or passionate step (unless you hate farming). If you have many choices, however, as adolescents in urban societies often do, the transition can become prolonged. Some people put off making choices indefinitely and never resolve their "identity crisis." Similarly, cultures that place a high premium on independence and individualism will make it difficult for many of their members to resolve Erikson's sixth crisis, that of intimacy versus isolation.

Erikson was correct in observing that in Western societies, adolescence and the college years are a time of confusion about identity and aspirations (Adams et al., 1985; Marcia, 1976). However, modern research in adult development suggests that his lockstep sequence of stages is far from universal. An "identity crisis" is not limited to adolescence. A man who has worked in one job all his adult life, and then is laid off and must find an entirely new career, may have an identity crisis too. Similarly, competence is not mastered once and for all in childhood. People learn new skills and lose old ones throughout their lives, and their sense of competence rises and falls accordingly. In addition, Erikson omitted women from his original work, and when they were later studied, they were often doing things out of order. Some women, for example, entered the stage of "generativity" by having families before they faced the matter of professional "identity" (Helson & McCabe, 1993). For these reasons, modern theories of adult development emphasize the transitions and milestones that mark adult life in all its variation, instead of a rigid developmental sequence that applies to everyone (Baltes, 1983; Schlossberg, 1984).

Despite the problems with his theory, Erikson, like Adler before him, showed that development is never finished; it is an ongoing process, and the unconscious crises or issues of one stage may be reawakened during another. Erikson was also the first psychodynamic theorist to look at changes in the functioning of the ego throughout the life cycle. Erikson made his most important contributions, however, by considering the individual in the context of family and society, and by identifying the essential concerns of adulthood: identity, competence, love and nurturance, and the ability to enjoy life and accept death.

The Object-Relations School

In the late 1950s, John Bowlby (1958), a British psychoanalyst, contested the Freudian view that an infant's attachment to the mother could be explained solely in terms of her ability to gratify the baby's oral needs. Bowlby had found that infants who were deprived of normal contact with parents and other adults suffered catastrophically, and he argued for the primacy of attachment needs—for social stimulation, warmth, and contact. Bowlby's work influenced other psychoanalysts to acknowledge the fundamentally *social* nature of human development. Although the need for social contact now seems obvious, this change in emphasis was a significant departure from the classical Freudian view, for Freud essentially regarded the baby as if it were an independent little organism ruled by its own instinctive desires.

Today, an emphasis on relationships as the foundation of unconscious dynamics and psychological development is associated most closely with the **object-relations school,** developed in Great Britain by Melanie Klein, W. Ronald Fairbairn, and D. W. Winnicott (Hughes, 1989). In contrast to Freud's emphasis on the Oedipal period, object-relations theory holds that the first two years of life are the most critical for development of the inner core of personality. Freud emphasized the child's fear of the father; object-relations analysts emphasize the child's need for the powerful mother,

---

object-relations school A psychodynamic approach that emphasizes the importance of the infant's first two years of life and the baby's formative relationships.

who is usually the baby's main caregiver during the first critical years. Freud's theory was based on the dynamics of inner drives and impulses; object-relations theory holds that the basic human drive is not impulse gratification but the need to be in relationships (Horner, 1991; Hughes, 1989; Kernberg, 1976).

The reason for the clunky word *object* in object-relations theory (instead of the warmer word *human* or even *parent*) is that the infant's attachment isn't only to a real person, in this view, but also to the infant's evolving perception of the person. The child "takes in" or *introjects* a representation of the mother—someone who is kind or fierce, protective or rejecting—that is not literally the same as the woman herself. A "representation" is a complex cognitive schema that is constructed by the child. Object relations reflect the numerous representations of the self and others, and the psychodynamic interplay among them (Horner, 1991).

In Freudian theory, the central dynamic tension is the displacement of psychic energy—sexual and aggressive drives in particular—onto other people. Other people are relevant only insofar as they gratify our drives or block them. But to object-relations theorists, other people are important as *sources of attachment.* Therefore the central dynamic tension, the key issue in life, is the constantly changing balance between independence and connection to others. This balance requires constant adjustment to separations and losses, from small ones that occur during quarrels and spats, to moderate ones such as leaving home for the first time, to major ones such as divorce or death. In object-relations theory, the way we react to these separations as adults is largely determined by our experiences in the first two years of life (and some analysts would say in the first months of life). The relationship with the first caregiver, usually the mother, forms a model for all later ones.

Other people, of course, can never treat us perfectly. Even the most loving and attentive mother will occasionally fail to be perfectly attuned to her infant. Thus infants learn virtually right away that Mom will occasionally let them down. As two object-relations therapists put it,

> During this early process of development, the infant is internalizing the unacknowledged distressing experience and attempting to change it. But alas, this attempt fails. The inner world is always interacting with the outside world, with real people. The internal construction of object relations is thus modified by these actual experiences. The unsatisfying experiences that occur in relation to mother then find their expressions in a particular reflection of her in the infant's inner world. Mother becomes a disappointing person who has to be split in two: the known and longed-for giving mother and the known and deeply disappointing mother. (Eichenbaum & Orbach, 1983)

This concept of **splitting** is important in object-relations theory (Kernberg, 1976; Ogden, 1989). It means the separating of opposites—good and bad, right and wrong,

---

splitting In object-relations theory, the division of qualities into their opposites, as in the Good Mother versus the Bad Mother; it reflects an inability to understand that people are made up of good and bad qualities.

weak and strong, pleasure and pain. Infants cannot comprehend that all of these opposites can be mixed together in one person, so "Mom" is split into two versions: The Terrific Mother and the Terrible Mother. Then, between the ages of about one and a half and three, they begin to accept ambivalent feelings about themselves and others (Young-Eisendrath, 1993). They understand that the "good" mother who comforts them is the same as the "bad" mother who went away for a weekend. By adulthood, healthy individuals can recognize and accept ambivalence. People who grow up with overwhelming pain and rejection, however, never seem able to understand that every relationship is a mix of good and bad, pleasure and unhappiness. They resort to the childish defense mechanism of splitting: The minute a partner reveals a normal human flaw, he or she becomes a completely terrible person who must be rejected. Even emotionally healthy adults, when threatened or overwhelmed, succumb to splitting. Object-relations people would regard the kind of "us–them" stereotyping that occurs during group conflict and war, which we discussed in Chapter 13, as an example of splitting. Few people can acknowledge the good qualities of their worst enemies.

Healthy adults understand that within any individual, good and bad qualities coexist, as revealed in M. C. Escher's dazzling optical illusion of heaven and hell. (Can you find all the angels and goblins?) But according to object-relations theorists, some people resort to the defense mechanism of "splitting": They see other people as being either totally angelic or totally demonic.

The object-relations school also departs from classical Freudian theory on the nature of male and female psychological development. Whereas Freud thought that female development was the problem, many proponents of the object-relations school regard male development as the problem (Chodorow, 1978; Dinnerstein, 1976; Sagan, 1988; Winnicott, 1957/1990). In their view, children of both sexes identify first with the mother. Girls, who are the same sex as the mother, do not need to separate from her; the mother treats a daughter as an extension of herself. But boys, if they are to develop a male identity, must break away from the mother; the mother encourages a son to be independent and separate. To some object-relations theorists, this process is inevitable because women are biologically suited to be the primary caregivers and nurturers. But others, such as Nancy Chodorow (1978), believe that the process is culturally determined, and that if men played a greater role in the nurturing of infants and small children, the sex difference in the need for separation from the mother would fade.

In either case, in the object-relations view, male identity is more precarious and insecure than female identity, because it is based on not being like women. Men develop more rigid *ego boundaries* between themselves and other people, whereas women's boundaries are more permeable. Later in life, the typical psychological problem for women is how to increase their autonomy and independence, so they can assert their own abilities and not be used as doormats in their close relationships. In contrast, the typical problem for men is how to develop attachment (Gilligan, 1982). In object-relations theory, the reason that men fear intimacy and disdain "women's qualities" such as softness and nurturance is that they fear losing their masculinity. As D. W. Winnicott (1957/1990) wrote, "Traced to its root in the history of each individual, this fear of *women* turns out to be a fear of recognizing the fact of dependence."

In object-relations theory, men's distance from and fear of women even affect their moral development. In Freud's theory, as you may recall, a boy's superego and moral conscience emerge after the Oedipal phase and develop because of his identification with the father's authority; girls, lacking this clear-cut resolution of the Oedipal conflict, develop a more limited moral capacity. But to some object-relations analysts, the real origin of moral values lies in the infant's relationship to the mother, long before the emergence of the superego, and it is men who have the limited moral capacity. Because men must defend themselves so thoroughly against the memory of the nurturing pre-Oedipal mother, in this view, and because they learn to regard women as a threat to their masculinity, they feel emotionally bound to disparage the moral virtues associated with females: nurturance, pity, compassion, love, and conscience (Sagan, 1988).

In the 1970s, Heinz Kohut (1971, 1977) modified object-relations theory in an approach called **self psychology.** According to Kohut, the most important human drive is the individual's need to develop a *cohesive sense of self* and to protect *self-esteem.* Like proponents of the object-relations school, self psychologists disagree with

---

self psychology A psychodynamic theory that emphasizes the importance of having a cohesive sense of self and self-esteem throughout life.

Freud that sex and aggression are basic human drives. People may use sex to enhance their self-esteem or to defend against threats to it, they would say, but sex itself is not the central motivator. And like object-relations psychologists, self psychologists believe that psychological development occurs throughout life in relations with other people.

Kohut used the metaphor of the parent as a *mirror:* The parent is not only an ideal object, onto whom the child projects desires and needs, but also a mirroring object, who confirms the child's sense of competence and self-esteem. In healthy development, said Kohut, the parents' words and nonverbal responses confirm for the child that he or she is unique and loved. The child looks into the "mirror" of the parents' affections and sees there a loved and worthy person. This is the beginning of self-esteem—the feeling that we are worthy individuals who do not need constant reassurance from others. However, when parents respond to a child's behavior by humiliating and shaming the child, by withdrawing love, or by treating the child as an unwanted or unworthy creature, the child will experience a severe wound to the self and self-esteem. He or she will later be vulnerable to every rejection, overreact to every criticism, and require all adult partners and friends to provide an "approving mirror." (Do you hear echoes of Alfred Adler?)

In Kohut's view, all children start out idealizing their parent or parents, and then they learn, as everyone eventually must, that a parent is imperfect and only human. With this knowledge, children become aware of their own power and competence, the basis of self-mastery and self-confidence. The third ingredient of a healthy, cohesive self (along with self-esteem and self-confidence) is the need to be like others, to have a sense of fitting into one's community. Throughout life, we continue to rely on other people to provide mirrors of our worthiness and to provide community and connection.

WHAT DO YOU KNOW?

You've read about many different theories and theorists by now. Can you match each idea (right) with the school or analyst who proposed it (left)?

1.	Sigmund Freud	a.	collective unconscious
2.	Karen Horney	b.	inferiority complex
3.	Erik Erikson	c.	womb envy
4.	Carl Jung	d.	Oedipus complex
5.	object-relations	e.	identity crisis
6.	Alfred Adler	f.	archetype
		g.	introjection of mother
		h.	superego
		i.	psychosocial stages
		j.	splitting
		k.	basic anxiety

ANSWERS:

1.d,h 2.c,k 3.e,i 4.a,f 5.g,j 6.b

HUMANISTIC AND EXISTENTIAL PSYCHOLOGY

As we have seen, psychodynamic psychologists seek the unconscious motivations that they believe are the keys to personality and behavior, which is why we called this chapter "The Inner Life." An offshoot of this perspective also emphasizes the inner life—not by emphasizing unconscious motives, however, but by concentrating on a person's own sense of self that exists beneath the external masks we present to the world. This approach, sometimes called **phenomenology,** does not seek to predict behavior or to uncover hidden motivations. It focuses on the person's subjective interpretation of what is happening right now.

Psychologists who adopt this view—humanists and existentialists—differ from traditional psychodynamic schools by focusing on the qualities that separate us from other animals: freedom of choice and free will. We include these schools with the psychodynamic perspective because they share a reliance on subjective methods, the therapeutic goals of insight and helping people find meaning in their experiences, and the emphasis on a person's psychic reality.

As we noted in Chapter 1, **humanistic psychology** was launched as a movement within psychology in the early 1960s. Its chief leaders—Abraham Maslow (1908–1970), Rollo May (1909–1994), and Carl Rogers (1902–1987)—rejected the psychoanalytic emphasis on hostility, biological instincts, and unconscious conflicts. The trouble with psychology, said Maslow (1971), was that it had forgotten that human nature includes some good things, such as joy, laughter, love, happiness, and *peak experiences,* rare moments of rapture caused by the attainment of excellence or the drive toward higher values. The qualities that Maslow thought most important to understand were those of what he called the *self-actualized person,* the person who strives for a life that is meaningful, challenging, and satisfying.

Carl Rogers, like Freud, derived many of his ideas from observing his clients in therapy. As a clinician, Rogers (1951, 1961) was interested not only in why some people cannot function well, but also in what he called the "fully functioning" individual. Rogers's theory of personality is based on the relationship between the *self* (your conscious view of yourself, the qualities that make up "I" or "me") and the *organism* (the sum of all of your experiences, including unconscious feelings, perceptions, and wishes). This experience is known only to you, through your own frame of reference. How you behave

---

phenomenology The study of events and situations as individuals experience them; in personality, the study of an individual's qualities from the person's own point of view.
humanistic psychology An approach to psychology that emphasizes personal growth and the achievement of human potential rather than the scientific understanding, prediction, and control of behavior.

depends on your own subjective reality, Rogers said, not on the external reality around you. Fully functioning people show a *congruence,* or harmony, between self and organism. Such people are trusting, warm, and open. They aren't defensive or intolerant. Their beliefs about themselves are realistic. When the self and the organism are in conflict, however, the person is said to be in a state of incongruence.

To become fully functioning people, Rogers maintained, we all need **unconditional positive regard,** love and support for the people we are, without strings (conditions) attached. This doesn't mean that Winifred should be allowed to kick her brother when she is angry with him or that Wilbur may throw his dinner out the window because he doesn't like pot roast. In these cases, a parent can correct the child's behavior without withdrawing love from the child. The child can learn that the behavior, not the child, is what is bad. "House rules are 'no violence,' Winifred," is a very different message from "You are a horrible person, Winifred."

Unfortunately, Rogers observed, many children are raised with *conditional* positive regard. The condition is "I'll love you if you behave well, and I won't love you if you behave badly." Adults often treat each other this way, too. People treated with conditional regard begin to suppress or deny feelings or actions that they believe are unacceptable to those they love. The result, said Rogers, is incongruence, the sensation of being "out of touch with your feelings," of not being true to your "real self." The suppression of feelings and parts of oneself produces low self-regard, defensiveness, and bitterness.

Not all humanists have been optimistic about human nature. Rollo May emphasized some of the fundamentally difficult and tragic aspects of the human condition, including loneliness, anxiety, and alienation. In books such as *The Meaning of Anxiety, Existential Psychology,* and *Love and Will,* May brought to American psychology elements of the European philosophy of *existentialism.* This doctrine holds that human beings have free will and freedom of choice, which confers on us responsibility for our actions. Such freedom, and its burden of responsibility, carries a price in anxiety and despair, which is why so many people try to escape from freedom into narrow certainties and blame others for their misfortunes. May, who was influenced by Alfred Adler, popularized the humanistic idea of "self-realization," arguing that people can choose to make the best of themselves because of such inner resources as love and courage. But his writings also were a major influence on the development of **existential psychology.**

Existential psychologists emphasize the universal struggle to find meaning in life, to live by moral standards, and to come to an understanding of suffering and death (Becker, 1971, 1973; Yalom, 1980). In the existential view, cognitive and behavioral approaches to moral development leave out the essence of what morality means. "We are ethical beings embedded in a web of human responsibility and care," says Brian Vandenberg (1993), "not simply individuals who can turn our logical gaze, when asked, to the problems of human relations." The path of moral development involves the challenge

---

unconditional positive regard To Carl Rogers, love or support given to another person, with no conditions attached.

existential psychology An approach to psychology that emphasizes free will and responsibility for one's actions, and the importance of struggling with the anxieties of existence such as the need to find meaning in life and to accept suffering and death.

of deciding what is right and then living with the burden of uncertainty about those choices. Vandenberg (1993) argues that recognition of the dilemmas of existence are almost entirely missing from mainstream psychology. The primary concerns of later life "include coming to terms with the meaning of our life, with suffering and dying," he writes. "But these issues are nearly ignored. In contrast, much attention is given to topics such as changes in cognitive abilities. These topics are certainly of critical importance, but they are just not enough."

According to Irvin Yalom (1989), the primal conflicts and concerns of life do not stem, as Freud thought, from repressed instinctual desires or traumatic childhood experiences. Rather, he argues, anxiety emerges from a person's efforts, conscious and unconscious, to cope with the harsh realities of life, "the 'givens' of existence." Those "givens" are "the inevitability of death for each of us and those we love; the freedom to make our lives as we will; our ultimate aloneness; and, finally, the absence of any obvious meaning or sense to life. However grim these givens may seem, they contain the seeds of wisdom and redemption." Perhaps the most remarkable example of a man able to find seeds of wisdom in a barren landscape was Victor Frankl (1955), who developed a form of existential therapy after surviving a Nazi concentration camp. In that pit of horror, he observed, some people maintained their dignity and sanity because they were able to find meaning in the experience, shattering though it was.

Existential and humanistic psychologists depart from other psychodynamic theorists in maintaining that our lives are not inevitably determined by our parents, our pasts, or our present circumstances; we have the power to choose our own destinies, even when fate delivers us into tragedy. They hope to add richness and depth to the study of psychology by acknowledging the importance of meaning, suffering, and narrative in how people construct their experiences and make decisions about their lives.

What Do You Know?

A. 1. According to Carl Rogers, a man who loves his wife only when she is looking her best is giving her (a) *conditional* or (b) *unconditional* positive regard.
    2. The humanist who described the importance of having peak experiences was (a) Rollo May, (b) Abraham Maslow, (c) Carl Rogers.

B. An existential psychologist and a psychoanalyst are arguing about human nature. What different assumptions are they likely to bring to their discussion?

Answers:

A. 1. a 2. b **B.** *Some possibilities:* The psychoanalyst may assume that people are inherently selfish and destructive; that "free will" is an illusion because we are all governed by unconscious processes stemming from early relations with our parents; that anxiety can be traced to early trauma; and that the most important motives in human behavior are sex and aggression. In contrast, the existentialist is likely to assume that people are inherently capable of wisdom and change because all human beings have free will and responsibility for their actions; and that the most important motives in human behavior are the struggles to find meaning in life, to cope with loneliness and alienation, and to accept loss and death.

THE PSYCHODYNAMIC PARADOX

Reflect for a moment on some conflicting views you have encountered in this chapter:

✦ Freud thought that because women lack the prized penis, they fear and envy men and therefore come to accept their inferior status. Horney thought that because men lack the wonderful womb, they fear and envy women and must therefore force women into an inferior status.

✦ Freud considered the Oedipal phase the most important; object-relations theorists think the first two years are the most important; and Adler, Erikson, and Kohut believed that development continues all through life.

✦ Freud assumed that sex and aggression are the driving forces in human development; Horney assumed that the most important motive is anxiety; self psychologists assume that it is the need for self-esteem and the cohesion of the self; existentialists assume that it is the need for meaning.

✦ Freud thought that women have the greater problem in psychic development and end up morally deficient; many object-relations adherents think that men have the greater problem in psychic development and end up morally deficient.

✦ As Freud observed his patients and the flow of events in history, he saw conflict, destructive drives, selfishness, lust, and dread. Other analysts and humanists, also observing their patients and the flow of events in history, have seen cooperation, creativity, altruism, love, and hope.

Of course, psychologists within every perspective disagree about certain concepts and assumptions; disagreement is not the problem. The difference between other psychologists and psychodynamic theorists, however, is that the latter rely almost entirely on inference and subjective interpretation to draw their conclusions—about what a baby feels or desires, about whether or why men and women unconsciously envy and fear each other, and about the central motivation of human behavior. Most psychodynamic assumptions are untestable by the usual methods of psychological research. And that is ultimately the most interesting and exasperating aspect of psychodynamic interpretations: How is one supposed to evaluate them? Which interpretation has more merit? Should we endorse one theorist over another on the basis of intuitive "rightness," or in some other way?

And yet, the psychodynamic perspective stands alone in trying to describe personality and behavior in a coherent framework. Biological research accounts for certain human qualities and limitations, trait by trait; learning principles account for some acquired habits and expectations, piece by piece; cognitive research focuses on thoughts and beliefs, one by one; and sociocultural research identifies the influential elements of our social worlds, situation by situation. But psychodynamic psychologists are the only ones who attempt to put all of these components together in terms of each person's lived experience. It's one thing to say that you do or don't have self-esteem; psychodynamic theories try to explain how self-esteem "gets inside you" via your parents. It's one thing to say that the mind is designed for cognitive consistency; the psychodynamic perspective tries to explain why people bring so much heat and passion—indeed, *defensiveness*—to protecting their beliefs.

For example, only the psychodynamic perspective confronts the depths of emotional loathing and panic that often characterize prejudice, as in public discussions in America about gay rights. Freud (1961) believed that homosexuality was "no vice, no degradation" but "a variation of the sexual function." Indeed, said Freud, everyone has at least an unconscious attraction to members of the same sex, although awareness of this "latent homosexuality" is highly threatening to most people. So Freud would not have been surprised to read a letter we saw recently in a magazine, written in response to an article about homosexuality on campus:

> [Homosexuality] ranks as an odious sex crime on the level of bestiality, rape and incest. It is a behavior that is a perversion of nature, and it is a sin that is repugnant to man and to society. It is the activity that is responsible for the degradation and the mutilation of human lives and beautiful people. By publishing articles not only condoning this aberration, but brazenly, shamelessly and audaciously promoting it, you . . . undermine the very core and foundation of this great educational institution so that it will ultimately crumble and be destroyed.

Why is the man who wrote this letter so emotional, so overwrought? Psychodynamic theorists would say that something is going on in his unconscious that involves far more than an objective appraisal of homosexuality—something that is impeding his ability to reason objectively about the issue. They would point out that it is possible for heterosexuals to be uncomfortable about homosexuality without sharing the letter writer's wholesale condemnation of homosexuals or the *ferocity* and irrationality he brings to the discussion. Psychodynamic theorists would bring different metaphors to their analysis: A Freudian might say that the man is repressing his own homosexual impulses; a Jungian might speak of his inability to accept the Other into his persona; an object-relations analyst might suspect that he had difficulty separating from his mother and defining his own masculinity. But they are all on a similar track in addressing the unconscious fears, needs, and hostility that are motivating this man's attitudes.

And so the psychodynamic perspective leaves us with a paradox: Many of its ideas and analyses are intuitively appealing; yet, as scientists in psychology and other fields have repeatedly shown, intuition is not a secure ground to stand on. When put to objective test, many psychodynamic intuitions, like those of researchers in other perspectives, have turned out to be dead wrong. Perhaps the sex researcher Havelock Ellis said it best. In 1910, Ellis was called on to write a review of one of Freud's early works. "Even when Freud selects a very thin thread" in tying together his theories, Ellis concluded, "he seldom fails to string pearls on it, and these have their value whether the thread snaps or not." In the next chapter, we turn to an examination of the weak points in the psychodynamic thread, and to the beauty of the pearls.

✦ ✦ ✦

Summary

1. The psychodynamic perspective holds that the key to understanding human behavior is the inner, unconscious life. The first psychodynamic theory of personality was Sigmund Freud's theory of *psychoanalysis.* Today there are many others that differ from classical psychoanalysis and from one another, but they generally share five elements: an emphasis on unconscious *intrapsychic* dynamics; an assumption that adult behavior and problems are determined primarily by experiences in early childhood; a belief that psychological development occurs in fixed stages; a focus on fantasies and the symbolic meaning of events as the main motivators of behavior; and a reliance on subjective rather than objective methods of getting at the truth of a person's life.

2. Freud believed that the most important motives affecting behavior are sexual and aggressive. According to Freud, the personality consists of the *id* (the source of unconscious instincts), which follows the *pleasure principle;* the *ego* (the source of reason), which obeys the *reality principle;* and the *superego* (the source of conscience and the ego ideal). The healthy personality must keep all three systems in balance.

3. The ego, in Freud's view, uses unconscious *defense mechanisms* to ward off the anxiety and tension that occur when the wishes of the id conflict with the demands of conscience and social rules. These mechanisms include repression, projection, reaction formation, regression, denial, displacement and sublimation, acting out, and humor. Different personalities emerge because people differ in the defenses they use, in how rigid their defenses are, and in whether their defenses lead to healthy or disturbed functioning. Unhealthy efforts to defend against anxiety may produce a *neurosis.*

4. Freud believed that personality develops in a series of *psychosexual stages:* oral, anal, phallic (Oedipal), latency, and genital. During the phallic stage, Freud believed, the Oedipus complex occurs, in which the child desires the parent of the other sex and feels rivalry with the same-sex parent. When the complex is resolved, the child identifies with the same-sex parent. Freud thought that boys and girls resolve the Oedipal stage differently and that girls are left with a lingering sense of "penis envy." Women, Freud said, do not develop the strong moral superegos that men do.

5. The greatest influence of Freud's theory was on the practice of psychotherapy. Two important elements in psychoanalytic therapy are *free association* and *transference.*

6. Freud's conclusions and techniques came from the analyses he conducted with relatively few patients. New studies suggest, however, that Freud often formulated his theories and then pressed his patients to accept and confirm them. For example, when he believed that childhood sexual abuse caused neurosis, he encouraged his patients to "remember" experiences of childhood abuse; when he decided that children only fantasize about sexual abuse, he put greater weight on discovering their supposed sexual fantasies than on considering the effects of their actual experiences.

7. Freudian psychoanalysis established two key assumptions that still guide psycho-dynamic therapists: that conscious memories and beliefs are not as important in affecting behavior as unconscious dynamics are; and that what actually happened in a person's past is not as important as that person's psychic reality.

8. Many early dissenters within psychoanalysis went on to formulate their own psy-chodynamic theories and schools. Karen Horney believed that *basic anxiety* was the central human motive. She emphasized social relationships rather than bio-logical instincts, and she challenged Freud's ideas about female inferiority and penis envy. She believed that healthy people are guided by an *ideal self.*

9. Alfred Adler argued that people have a need for self-improvement—a drive for superiority—that stems from the natural feelings of inferiority that everyone has, beginning in childhood. Some individuals develop an *inferiority complex,* becom-ing overly concerned with protecting their self-esteem. Adler's ideas about the importance of *social interest* in psychological functioning have been supported by modern research. In Adler's view, each person actively creates his or her own per-sonality from the raw material of heredity and experience (the *creative self*).

10. Carl Jung believed that people are motivated not only by past conflicts but also by their future goals and by the desire to fulfill themselves. He argued that people share a *collective unconscious* that contains universal human memories and *arche-types,* such as the *shadow,* the *anima,* and the *animus.*

11. Erik Erikson proposed a *psychosocial theory* of development, which holds that life consists of eight stages, each characterized by a particular psychological crisis: trust versus mistrust; autonomy versus shame and doubt; initiative versus guilt; competence versus inferiority; identity versus role confusion; intimacy versus iso-lation; generativity versus stagnation; and ego integrity versus despair. Erikson's sequence of stages is not universal, and contemporary theories of adult develop-ment emphasize the transitions and milestones that mark adult life instead of a rigid developmental sequence. But Erikson made important contributions by considering the individual in the context of society and by identifying the con-cerns of adulthood.

12. The *object-relations school* puts relationships at the center of psychological devel-opment. This approach differs from classical Freudian theory in emphasizing the importance of the first two years of life, rather than the Oedipal phase; the infant's relationships to important figures, especially the mother, rather than sexual needs and drives; and the problem in male development of breaking away from the mother. The central dynamic tension in life, in this view, is the constantly chang-ing balance between independence and connection to others, with men typically needing to develop attachment and women typically needing to increase their autonomy. According to some object-relations theorists, men's distance from and fear of women causes them to disparage the moral virtues associated with females, such as nurturance and compassion.

13. In *self psychology,* the most important human drive is the individual's need both to develop a cohesive sense of self and to protect self-esteem. Heinz Kohut used the

metaphor of the parent as a *mirror* to explain why people grow up to differ in self-esteem, self-confidence, and a sense of fitting in with others.

14. Humanistic and existential psychologists take a *phenomenological* approach to personality, focusing on the person's sense of self, perceptions of the world, and free will to change. *Humanistic psychologists* emphasize human potential and the strengths of human nature, such as Abraham Maslow's concepts of *peak experiences* and *self-actualization*. Carl Rogers stressed the importance of *unconditional positive regard* in creating a "fully functioning" person. Rollo May was another important humanistic psychologist who helped bring existentialism to American psychology. *Existential psychologists* emphasize the inherent dilemmas of the human condition, including loneliness and anxiety; the search for meaning and moral standards in life; and the quest to understand suffering and death. They depart from other psychodynamic theorists in maintaining that people are not determined by their parents, pasts, or unconscious drives but by their power to choose their own destinies.

15. Psychodynamic theorists rely almost entirely on inference and subjective interpretation to draw their conclusions, and most psychodynamic assumptions are untestable by the usual methods of psychological research. But this perspective stands alone in trying to describe personality and behavior in a coherent framework and in terms of each person's lived, subjective experiences.

Key Terms

psychoanalysis *509*

intrapsychic *509*

psychic reality *509*

id *510*

pleasure principle *510*

libido *510*

death (aggressive) instincts *510*

ego *510*

reality principle *510*

superego *511*

ego ideal *511*

defense mechanisms *511*

   repression *511*

   projection *512*

   reaction formation *512*

   regression *513*

   fixation *513*

denial *513*

displacement *513*

sublimation *513*

acting out *513*

humor *513*

neurosis *514*

psychosexual stages *515*

oral stage *515*

anal stage *516*

phallic stage *516*

   Oedipus complex *516*

   castration anxiety *516*

   penis envy *516*

latency stage *517*

infantile (childhood) amnesia *517*

genital stage *517*

free association *518*

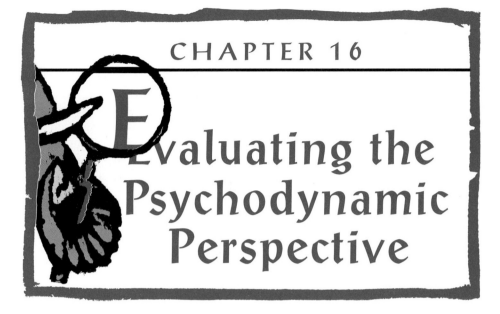

CHAPTER 16

Evaluating the Psychodynamic Perspective

*T*hroughout this century, the psychodynamic perspective and scientific psychology—the kind represented by the previous four perspectives in this book—have been at war, fighting over fundamental assumptions about the meaning of science and truth. What is science? How do we know what is true? What kind of evidence is required to support a hypothesis?

As far as the early psychoanalysts were concerned, "science" had nothing to do with controlled experiments, interviews, statistics, or counting the frequency of some behavior. According to Gail Hornstein (1992), "Constructing a science of the mind could mean only one thing—finding some way to peer through the watery murk of consciousness to the subaquean reality that lay beyond. The efforts of [research] psychologists, with their bulky equipment and piles of charts and graphs, seemed superficial and largely irrelevant to this goal." Psychoanalysts rejected all this paraphernalia and relied solely on their own interpretations of individuals they saw in therapy, of myths and literature, and of people's behavior in everyday life.

But to research psychologists, the idea that analysts could claim to be doing science while chucking out the cardinal rules of the scientific method—replicable findings, publicly verifiable data, objective confirmation of evidence, and the concerted effort to control prejudices and any other possible sources of bias—was enough to make them break out in hives. When psychoanalysis first became popular in the United States in the 1920s, many scientific psychologists regarded it as a popular craze, something on a par with mind reading or phrenology, that would blow over. John Watson called it "voodooism." "Psychoanalysis attempts to creep in wearing the uniform of science," wrote another critic at the time, "and to strangle it from the inside" (quoted in Hornstein, 1992).

These two opposite notions of what science meant, and how a psychologist could discover the "truth" of a person's life, put the psychodynamic perspective and empirical psychology on a collision course. "Psychoanalysis is a pseudoscience, with which we have been associated too long," complains Hans Eysenck (1993), representing the view of many researchers. "The Freudian empire has been found wanting in every detail, including truthful accounts of its origins, its effectiveness, and its theoretical cogency. If we do not make it clear that modern scientific psychology has nothing to do with Freudian psychoanalysis, we will forever be tarred with the same brush." But to those in the psychodynamic tradition, their perspective alone captures the inner life that eludes behavioral observations and questionnaires. Nancy Chodorow (1992), explaining why she fell "intellectually in love" with psychoanalysis, says, "I have learned from psychoanalysis that we cannot measure human life solely in socially determinist terms. In the integration of their conscious and unconscious lives, in the quality of their primary emotional relationships with others, as in social organization and politics, people can help to create for themselves a more meaningful life."

CONTRIBUTIONS OF THIS PERSPECTIVE

Psychodynamic psychologists argue that scientific psychology, in contrast to their own approach, misses the essence and intensity of people's mental lives. In aiming to pin down small pieces of the personality, they add, scientific psychologists fail to see the whole person. As for their methods, psychodynamic psychologists observe that the fact that they don't use traditional methods doesn't mean that they have none at all. Let's look more closely, then, at this perspective's contributions.

1 A WILLINGNESS TO ADDRESS "BIG PICTURE" QUESTIONS. Psychologists in the psychodynamic perspective are not only willing but eager to take on large, important concerns in human life that are often difficult to study empirically. As we saw in the last chapter, they have speculated about the reasons for universal symbols and images, folktales and myths. They have theorized about the consequences of the unique human awareness of mortality and the need to find meaning in life. They have grappled with the irrational energy that people often bring to matters of sexuality and gender, trying to explain why so many women and men regard one another as exotic, mysterious creatures—the "Other."

2 AN IMAGINATIVE USE OF QUALITATIVE INFORMATION. Psychodynamic theorists are willing to look everywhere for evidence, creatively drawing on cultural rituals, literature, fairy tales, jokes, or any other source of information they find useful. Such an approach, they argue, allows them to explore questions that are difficult and perhaps impossible to study by the usual methods of scientific psychology. Consider the common, apparently worldwide, fascination with horror stories and fairy tales about ghosts and evil witches. Specific psychodynamic explanations of these phenomena vary, but they share a view that such stories both reflect and exorcise unconscious anxieties about danger and death. These explanations are appealing because they make sense of behavior that seems irrational.

For example, why do so many people like going to movies in order to be scared out of their wits? In his cultural history of modern horror movies, David Skal (1993) uses psychodynamic concepts to argue that the themes in these films reflect uncon-scious anxieties caused by specific economic and social conditions. The ultimate appeal of all fictitious monsters, says Skal, is that they allow audiences to displace their anxieties (about the economy, about strangers, about death) and also to transcend them. Horror movies were born after the unprecedented slaughter of soldiers and civilians in World War I, with *The Cabinet of Dr. Caligari* and *Nosferatu*. In the 1920s, the prevalence of mutilated and maimed war veterans prompted an outpouring of films with disfigured heroes, such as *The Phantom of the Opera* and *The Hunchback of Notre Dame*. During the Great Depression of the 1930s, films such as *Frankenstein* and *Dracula* captured the national anxiety and despair about the economy. After World War II, horror movies took a new shape, reflecting people's fears of the atomic bomb and the new enemy, communists. The popular horror films of this era were about giant, mutated monsters (*Godzilla*) or about invasions of aliens (*Invasion of the Body Snatchers*). In the 1960s and 1970s, horror films featured monstrous babies and unnat-ural births—this time, Skal believes, reflecting national insecurities about the sexual revolution and changing gender roles. (And what are horror movies about in the 1990s? Computers run amok, the control and destruction of lives through the Inter-net—reflecting, perhaps, our current anxiety about the direction this technology is taking us.)

Notice the difference between this analysis and that, say, of the social-learning approach. A learning theorist would say that people should worry about violent hor-ror films because they model behavior that children might imitate and because they desensitize viewers to cruelty. Psychodynamic theorists would reply that we have about as much chance of getting rid of horror films and stories as we do of actually killing the Devil or Dracula. Because these creatures serve our unconscious needs, they will always return in one form or another.

3 AN EMPHASIS ON SELF-KNOWLEDGE, ESPECIALLY THE FACTORS BELOW CONSCIOUS AWARENESS THAT INFLUENCE OUR BEHAVIOR. On a more personal level, perhaps the most important contribution of the psychodynamic perspective lies in showing us that because of unconscious patterns and needs, individuals are often the last to know the reasons for their own behavior. Explanations based on unconscious dynamics try to account for the unpredictability of the ways that people react to one another; the unwanted negative moods that seem to arrive for no reason; and the emotional over-reactions to innocent remarks. To illustrate this point, psychoanalyst Mardi Horowitz (1988) describes the reactions of a man he treated, whom he calls Tom. One day when Tom was under a lot of pressure at work, he got a call from his father telling him that his mother had died suddenly. Tom's reaction was to laugh harshly and say "Damn it!" in a bitter tone. His father, startled and hurt, hung up, and Tom went home to get ready to fly across the country for the funeral. He felt dull and unresponsive as he packed his clothes, and his five-year-old daughter tried to joke with him. Tom sudden-ly snarled angrily at her. When she fled the room in tears, he was overcome by remorse and began to cry.

"It is not surprising that Tom cried," observes Horowitz, "but *when* he cried was—as also were his laughter and abrupt anger at the unexpected news of his mother's death, and his explosive rage at his beloved daughter. More important, these reactions were inappropriate, distressing to others, and followed by his own remorse." In the psychodynamic view, many unconscious mechanisms caused Tom's inappropriate reactions: denial of the reality of his mother's death; projection of his anger at fate onto his father, who was only the messenger of bad news; and regression to feeling like a "needy child" himself, which prevented him from being able to respond maturely to his daughter's demands for attention.

A contribution of the object-relations school, in particular, has been to show how unconscious expectations and habits, established in early relations with important family members, reproduce themselves in adult relationships. "Experiences with our mother, father, siblings, and others form powerful impressions, like engravings on some inner wall of our psyche, which become the standards against which all other relationships are measured," write Barry Dym and Michael Glenn (1993). They observe that a boy who learns that he can trust his mother with his secrets and worries will, as an adult, continue to trust women. But a boy whose mother changes the subject every time he confesses a problem, or who tells him that "real boys" don't have silly worries, may feel betrayed and inadequate; later in life, he is likely to be reluctant to share his confidences with women.

Of course, the learning and cognitive perspectives also recognize the importance of learned patterns in affecting adult behavior, but the psychodynamic perspective emphasizes their *unconscious* aspects. Imagine a woman who finds, much to her own puzzlement, that she keeps sabotaging close relationships. An object-relations analyst would suspect that she had suffered repeated losses of, or separations from, one or both parents, experiencing these losses as personal rejections and thus growing up to expect further rejections. The reason she sabotages her current relationships, according to object-relations theory, is that she is projecting her image of a rejecting parent onto her friends and lovers, inducing them to fulfill her expectation. Dym and Glenn (1993) put it this way: "If, for example, I cast the image of a rejecting person onto you and then act as if you were indeed rejecting me, you might pull away, be critical, or otherwise treat me rejectingly. The closer your actions mirror my projections, the more my beliefs about who you are are confirmed." Again, this process is mostly unconscious.

MISUSES AND LIMITATIONS
OF THIS PERSPECTIVE

The contributions of psychodynamic theorists have been important to the study of psychology. Critics, however, are concerned about one common misuse of the psychodynamic perspective and about several inherent limitations in it.

Every perspective in psychology, as we have seen throughout this book, suffers from the risk of reductionism, and the psychodynamic perspective is no exception. Psychodynamic psychologists tend to emphasize a person's psychic reality over the actual circumstances of the person's life. However, psychic reality isn't everything; it is a mistake to reduce all behavior to unconscious processes and thereby overlook the importance of biology, conscious thoughts, experiences, culture, and circumstance. Yet psychoanalysts and some other psychodynamic therapists often regard a patient's conflicts with children, financial problems, job stresses, or relationships with family not as potential *sources of distress* but solely as *results of unconscious dynamics* (Fancher, 1995).

The practice of explaining a person's behavior entirely in terms of intrapsychic dynamics was not invented by psychoanalysts. In the early years of the nineteenth century, a physician named Samuel Cartwright argued that many slaves were suffering from the mental illness of "drapetomania," an uncontrollable urge to escape from slavery. "Symptoms" included being disobedient, talking back, refusing to work, and fighting back when beaten (Landrine, 1988). Thus doctors could assure slave owners that a mental illness, not the intolerable condition of slavery, made slaves seek freedom. Today drapetomania sounds irrational and cruel, but it reflects a way of thinking that still occurs: attributing a person's behavior to internal, unconscious dynamics and failing to consider external circumstances.

Psychodynamic reductionism is often apparent in literary psychobiographies, in which an author (who may or may not be a psychologist) relies on psychodynamic ideas to explain the behavior of some famous person. You get arguments such as "Adolf Hitler hated his mother and had sexual insecurities, so he caused World War II"; never mind the historical, cultural, and economic events that created him and allowed him to attain power.

At least a biography can't hurt anyone, except perhaps the reputation of its subject. But other examples of psychodynamic reductionism have had disastrous, even fatal, results—such as when people with brain tumors or diseases have been diagnosed entirely in terms of unconscious dynamics, and the real cause of their illness has been left untreated (Thornton, 1984). In spite of the fact that most North American psychoanalysts were psychiatrists (and therefore trained as medical doctors), they committed this error throughout this century. They maintained that autism, rheumatoid arthritis, ulcers, migraines, and other physical disorders were caused by neurotic personality patterns, unconscious anger, suppressed hatred of parents, and other such factors. This error still occurs. In California in 1995, a psychiatrist was convicted of malpractice because he failed to diagnose a patient who was suffering from myasthenia gravis, a progressive but treatable muscle disease. For *12 years,* she got steadily worse, until she couldn't even lift her hand to brush her teeth. The reason, he said, was her "repressed rage" at her parents.

With any diagnosis of physical symptoms or emotional problems, therefore, it is essential to avoid reductionism. Many possibilities should be considered, and the evidence for each should be reviewed, before drawing conclusions.

But the psychodynamic perspective itself also contains several inherent weaknesses that set it apart from empirical psychology:

1 Violating the principle of falsifiability. As we saw in Chapter 2, a theory that is impossible to disconfirm in principle is not a scientific theory. Many psychodynamic ideas about unconscious motivations are, in fact, impossible either to

confirm or disprove. If your experience seems to support these ideas, it is taken as evidence of their correctness; but if you doubt their veracity, you must be "revealing defensiveness" or have "faulty observational skills." (A favorite accusation is that you are "in denial.") This way of responding to criticism started with Freud (1924a), who once remarked, "One hears of analysts who boast that, though they have worked for dozens of years, they have never found a sign of the existence of a castration complex. We must bow our heads in recognition of . . . [this] piece of virtuosity in the art of overlooking and mistaking." So if analysts see castration anxiety in their patients, Freud was right; and if they fail to see it, they are "overlooking it"—and Freud was still right. This is neither scientific nor fair reasoning!

This is why arguing with some psychodynamic theorists can be exasperating: If you agree with them, fine; but if you don't agree and you offer counterevidence, there must be something wrong with *you.* As we will see later in this evaluation, cognitive scientists have raised serious doubts about some claims of recovered memories of childhood incest, citing research on the reconstructive nature of memory. According to one psychodynamic therapist who runs a Center for Abuse Recovery, these criticisms are signs of "displaced rage" at therapists for bringing the issue of abuse to public attention (quoted in Wylie, 1993). She and others think that anyone who raises any doubts about recovered memories is either in denial about the reality of sexual abuse or part of an anti-child backlash. This way of thinking means that only one analysis of the phenomenon can even be considered—theirs.

The inherent subjectivity of psychodynamic explanations and the fact that they often violate the principle of falsifiability may be why this perspective, more than any other, is full of names: Freud, Horney, Adler, Jung, Erikson, Klein, Winnicott, Kohut, Rogers. . . . When theories cannot be disconfirmed, their appeal depends more on the popularity and charisma of their proponents than on the accuracy of their content. Researchers in other perspectives call themselves "neuropsychologists," "cognitive scientists," "social-learning theorists," "cross-cultural psychologists," and the like; even most radical behaviorists no longer call themselves "Skinnerians." But psychodynamic psychologists go around calling themselves "Kleinians," "Freudians," "Jungians," and so forth. Their critics believe that this allegiance to individuals is one of the perspective's problems. Robert Fancher (1995), who was trained as a psychoanalyst but has become disenchanted with many aspects of the profession, observes that because psychoanalysis lacks scientifically reliable methods by which differences of opinion can be resolved, it "is always ripe for schism"—for people breaking away from established doctrine to form their own schools. But "To be a member of a new 'school' of psychoanalytic thought," says Fancher, "is only to prefer, for whatever non-scientific reason, the orthodoxy of that imaginative enclave."

2 DRAWING UNIVERSAL PRINCIPLES FROM THE EXPERIENCES OF A FEW, ATYPICAL PATIENTS. Freud and most of his followers generalized from a very few individuals, often patients in therapy, to all human beings. Of course, the problem of overgeneralizing from small samples occurs in other perspectives, too, and insights about human behavior may certainly be obtained from observations of limited numbers of people. Jean Piaget, for one, originally developed his theories of cognitive development from

closely observing a very small sample: his own three children. The problem occurs when the observer fails to confirm these observations by studying other samples, incorrectly inferring that what applies to one group applies to all.

For instance, if a gay man goes into therapy with emotional problems, a therapist cannot logically conclude that all gay men have emotional problems; gay men who are not in therapy would have to be studied. Indeed, when such research was finally done, it disproved the once-common belief among psychoanalysts that homosexuality is a mental disorder or that gay men and lesbians are more emotionally disturbed than heterosexuals (Hooker, 1957; Kurdek, 1987). Similarly, Freud did not seek to confirm his ideas about penis envy by actually observing or talking to young children. However, researchers find that many children of *both* sexes envy one another. In a study of 65 preschool-age boys and girls, Linda Linday (1994) found that 45 percent of the girls had fantasized about having a penis or being male in other ways, and 44 percent of the boys had fantasized about being pregnant.

Many psychodynamic psychologists, like psychologists in other perspectives, are becoming aware of the relevance of culture to their theories; they recognize the error of generalizing from a few people in one culture and historical moment to everyone across time and place. But traditional psychoanalysts still tend to ignore the importance of culture and elevate this oversight into something of a virtue. As psychoanalyst Stephen Mitchell (1993) says, members of his profession "see themselves as dealing with universal, timeless dimensions of human experience, currents that run deeper than the surface ripples of cultural change and intellectual or social fashion." As the sociocultural perspective shows, however, culture is not a "surface ripple"; it exerts a profound influence on every aspect of human behavior.

3 BASING THEORIES OF DEVELOPMENT ON THE RETROSPECTIVE ACCOUNTS AND FALLIBLE MEMORIES OF PATIENTS. Most psychodynamic theorists have not observed random samples of children at different ages, as modern cognitive and child psychologists do, to construct their theories of development. Instead they have worked backward, creating theories based on themes in adults' recollections. From Freud to present-day psychoanalysts, nearly all have concluded that children develop according to a series of fixed psychological stages, at which key "issues" or "crises" occur. The seeds of adult pathology are said to be planted when a child has a traumatic experience, becomes fixated at a specific stage, and then carries the unresolved emotional problem into the next stage. The corollary is that adults must look backward to their childhoods to find the origins of their current emotional problems.

Analysis of memories can be a useful and illuminating way to achieve insights about a person's life; in fact, it is the only way we can think about our own lives because none of us can be our own control group! But as we saw in Chapter 10, memory is often inaccurate, influenced as much by what is going on in a person's *current* life as by what *actually* happened. If you are currently not getting along with your mother, you may remember all the times in your childhood she seemed to treat you unkindly, and forget the counterexamples of her kindness.

Retrospective analysis has another problem: It creates an *illusion of causality* between events. We assume that if A came before B, then A must have caused B. For example, if your mother spent three months in the hospital when you were five and today you are having trouble in school, an object-relations analyst might draw a connection between the two facts. Perhaps these events really are connected, but a lot of other things in your present circumstances might be causing your difficulties. Yet looking backward to derive theories of forward development is the error that Freud and many of his followers committed.

Because looking backward at our lives creates, as Freud (1920/1963) himself acknowledged, "the impression of an inevitable sequence of events," *retrospective* studies, in which people tell interviewers or therapists about their pasts, often find what seem to be consistent patterns of development. But *longitudinal* studies, in which people are followed from childhood to adulthood, often do not. On the contrary, such research finds that psychological development is far more gradual and fluctuating than traditional psychoanalytic theories maintain. Child development consists of day-to-day incremental changes, not precipitous stages. Psychodynamic themes such as orality, dependence, autonomy, and trust are issues that are important all through life, although they take different forms (Stern, 1985). Similarly, there is no latency stage during which children lack sexual feelings. Some children discover the pleasure of genital self-stimulation as infants or toddlers, and the percentage of children who masturbate steadily increases during the years before puberty (Wade & Cirese, 1991).

4 **RELYING ON SUBJECTIVE METHODS THAT ARE OFTEN UNVALIDATED AND UNRELIABLE.** Some psychologists have used psychodynamic concepts to design tests of personality and unconscious motivation. Many clinicians today rely on **projective tests,** which are based on the psychodynamic assumption that when people are asked to make up a story about a neutral picture or statement, they will project their own unconscious feelings and beliefs onto it. Perhaps the most famous projective test is the **Thematic Apperception Test (TAT),** developed by Henry Murray and Christiana Morgan in the 1930s. The TAT consists of a set of ambiguous pictures. Subjects are asked to speculate about what is happening: What are the characters thinking and feeling? What will happen next?

When validated empirically, the TAT can be a useful research method. Long ago, David McClelland and his associates (1953), experimental psychologists trained in the methods of research design and statistical inference, used the TAT to study the unconscious aspects of what they called the **achievement motive.** A person's behavior, said McClelland (1961), is influenced by many things, but the strength of the internal motive to achieve is best captured in the fantasies one tells. "In fantasy anything is at least symbolically possible," he explained. "A person may rise to great heights, sink to

---

projective tests Psychological tests used to infer a person's motives, conflicts, and unconscious dynamics on the basis of the person's interpretations of ambiguous or unstructured stimuli.

Thematic Apperception Test (TAT) A projective personality test that asks respondents to interpret a series of drawings showing ambiguous scenes of people.

achievement motive A learned motive to meet personal standards of success and excellence in a chosen area.

great depths, kill his grandmother, or take off for the South Sea Islands on a pogo stick."

Needless to say, people with high achievement motivation do not fantasize about taking off for the South Seas or sinking to great depths. Their fantasies are about working hard, becoming rich and famous, and clobbering the opposition with their wit and brilliance. Such fantasies predict behavior: High scorers are more likely than low scorers to start their own business, set high personal standards, and prefer to work with capable colleagues who can help them succeed rather than with co-workers who are merely friendly (McClelland, 1987). By using representative selections from a nation's popular literature as if they were a giant TAT and scoring them for images of achievement, McClelland (1961) and others have even been able to measure the level of achievement motivation in entire societies. They have been able to validate this use of the TAT by showing that test scores predict the number of patents issued, businesses started, indicators of productivity, and other economic measures of success.

However, most projective tests are not used for research purposes, but rather to diagnose personality problems and emotional disorders on an individual basis. The test is administered to an individual patient by a psychologist, and the psychologist alone interprets the responses. When used this way, projective tests have repeatedly been shown to be unreliable, because different clinicians often interpret the same test differently. The clinicians themselves may be "projecting" when they decide what a specific response means (Dawes, 1994).

Such problems are apparent in the **Rorschach Inkblot Test,** which was devised by Swiss psychiatrist Hermann Rorschach in 1921. It consists of ten cards with symmetrical abstract patterns, originally formed by spilling ink on paper and folding the paper in half. The test-taker reports what he or she sees in the inkblots, and clinicians interpret the answers according to the symbolic meanings emphasized by psychodynamic theories.

Although the Rorschach is enormously popular among clinicians, efforts to confirm its reliability and validity have failed. As early as 1959, Lee Cronbach, one of the world's leading experts on testing, observed that "The test has repeatedly failed as a prediction of practical criteria"; and another testing expert, Raymond McCall, concluded, "Though tens of thousands of Rorschach tests have been administered . . . and while many relationships to personality dynamics and behavior have been hypothesized, the vast majority of these relationships *have never been validated empirically,* despite the appearance of more than 2000 publications about the test" (emphasis in original; quoted in Dawes, 1994). In recent years, a different scoring method for the Rorschach, called the Comprehensive System, has become widely used (Exner, 1993). But a recent critical examination found significant problems with this method too: Clinicians often still disagree with one another on what a particular response means;

Rorschach Inkblot Test A projective personality test that requires respondents to interpret abstract, symmetrical inkblots.

many of the scores are of questionable validity (i.e., they don't measure what they claim to measure, such as "dependency"); and most claims of the system's success come from Rorschach workshops where clinicians are taught how to use the new method, which is not an impartial way of assessing its reliability or validity (Wood, Nezworski, & Stejskal, 1996).

Yet many clinicians love the Rorschach and swear by its accuracy in helping them understand their clients. They maintain that projective techniques are a rich source of information because test-takers cannot fake or lie as easily as on objective tests. The tests can help a clinician to establish rapport with a client and encourage a person to open up about anxieties, conflicts, and problems. And projective tests may help clinicians determine when someone is defensively attempting to hide worries or mental problems (Shedler, Mayman, & Manis, 1993).

The real problem seems to occur when clinicians rely *exclusively* on projective tests and are overconfident about what they reveal. Here is a true story told to us by a colleague, who is both a clinical psychologist and a researcher (James Wood, personal communication):

> A mother kept contacting Child Protection Services (CPS), alleging that her ex-husband was sexually molesting their four-year-old son during parental visitations. However, when the boy was interviewed, his statements were ambiguous. Wondering if the mother might be deranged in making this accusation, CPS arranged for her to be evaluated by a psychologist. The psychologist, solely on the basis of the woman's replies to the Rorschach Inkblot Test, concluded that the mother's allegations against the father were the result of "distortions," exacerbated by depression and an inability to handle stress, and that she probably persisted in the allegations because of greater sensitivity to her own needs than those of her child.
>
> CPS thus refused to investigate the mother's later charges. About a year afterward, the child was brought to an emergency room immediately following visitation with his father. He said his father had molested him that day, and sperm was found in his rectum.

And so we come back to the theme that most divides psychodynamic psychologists and scientific psychologists: the failure of many psychodynamic assumptions to survive the scrutiny of scientific methods—and the disagreement as to whether that failure matters. Indeed, the divergent attitudes of the two sides toward the role of research has contributed to a situation now often called the *scientist–practitioner gap.* Many psychodynamic practitioners (therapists and others who work in the mental-health field) argue that psychotherapy is an art, not a science, and research is irrelevant to what they do. Most believe that clinical experience is more valuable and accurate than the methods of traditional research, and that laboratory and survey studies capture only a small and shriveled image of the real person. They wish that academic psychologists would pay more attention to *clinical* evidence and observations in the research they do (Edelson, 1994). A survey of 400 clinical psychologists found that the great majority paid little attention to empirical research at all, stating that they gained their most useful information from "clinical work with clients" (Elliott & Morrow-Bradley, 1994).

For their part, scientific psychologists argue that when therapists fail to keep up with empirical findings in the field—not only about beneficial or potentially harmful techniques in therapy, but also about basic psychological topics relevant to therapy, such as memory, hypnosis, and normal child development—their clients may pay the price. Frederick Crews (1995), a scholar and social critic, has observed that "Incorrect but widely dispersed ideas about the mind inevitably end by causing social damage. Thanks to the once imposing prestige of psychoanalysis, people harboring diseases or genetic conditions have deferred effective treatment while scouring their infantile past for the sources of their troubles. Parents have agonized about having caused their children's homosexuality. Women have accepted a view of themselves as inherently envious, passive, and amoral."

Because the assumptions of the psychodynamic approach are so ingrained in popular culture, we will devote the rest of this evaluation to the scientist–practitioner gap: first, as it affects the assessment of psychodynamic therapy in contrast to other therapies; second, as it affects two divisive and socially important clinical issues—multiple personality disorder and recovered memories of sexual abuse. In the conclusion, we will consider some contemporary efforts, on both sides, to narrow the gap between them.

What Do You Know?

1. Name three contributions of the psychodynamic perspective and four of its limitations.
2. Name one clinical benefit of projective tests and one scientific limitation.

Answers:

1. Contributions include a willingness to look at "big picture" topics; an imaginative use of qualitative information, such as folktales and cultural symbols; an emphasis on self-knowledge and unconscious motives. Limitations include violating the principle of falsifiability; drawing universal principles from atypical individuals in therapy; basing theories on retrospective accounts and fallible memories rather than on longitudinal studies; and relying on subjective methods that are often unvalidated and unreliable. 2. One benefit is helping the clinician to establish rapport with a client and tell when the client seems defensive and anxious. A major limitation is that many projective tests are unreliable (i.e., clinicians show low agreement with one another on interpreting people's answers) and invalid (i.e., the tests don't measure what they claim to measure).

Issue 1: Assessing Psychotherapy

Freud was the father of the "talking cure," and when it comes to psychotherapy, psychodynamic approaches (although not classical psychoanalysis itself) are still the most widespread. All of them share an emphasis on defenses and transference, and on working through emotional conflicts that originated in childhood. In recent years, however, as competing schools of therapy have emerged, arguments about the effectiveness of these therapies have grown noisier. Do they "work"? And do they work any better than the other kinds of therapy described in previous perspectives?

Of course, whether therapy is "successful" depends on how success is defined. For researchers and most clinicians, success means the elimination of the symptoms or suffering that brought the person to therapy to begin with. But many psychodynamic psychotherapists believe that "feeling better" is a good enough measure of success. Some don't even attempt "cures"; the goal, they say, is not change but understanding. In addition, many patients themselves will say that *any* therapy or self-improvement program they go through has been successful, even if their problems or symptoms remain unchanged, because of the justification-of-effort phenomenon (see Chapter 9): People are motivated to justify the time, effort, and money they invest in a program.

Nevertheless, *claims* of effectiveness do not substitute for *demonstrations* of effectiveness, especially because psychotherapy can be costly and time-consuming for clients. Economic pressures and the rise of managed-care health programs are forcing psychotherapists of all persuasions to produce clear guidelines for which therapies are most effective, which therapies are best for which disorders, and which therapies are ineffective or potentially harmful (Barlow, 1994; Chambless, 1995; Orlinsky, 1994). To develop these guidelines, clinical researchers conduct *controlled clinical trials,* in which patients with a given problem or disorder are randomly assigned to one or more treatment groups or to a control group. To date, hundreds of evaluation studies have been designed to test the effectiveness of different kinds of therapy, counseling, and self-help groups. Although much remains to be learned, here are the overall results, which contain some good news and some bad news for therapists:

1. PSYCHOTHERAPY IS BETTER THAN DOING NOTHING AT ALL. People who receive almost any professional treatment improve more than people who do not get help (Lambert & Bergin, 1994; Lipsey & Wilson, 1993; Maling & Howard, 1994; Robinson, Berman, & Neimeyer, 1990; Smith, Glass, & Miller, 1980; Weisz et al., 1995).

2. THE PEOPLE WHO DO THE BEST IN PSYCHOTHERAPY HAVE TREATABLE PROBLEMS AND ARE MOTIVATED TO IMPROVE. Emotional disorders, self-defeating habits, and problems coping with life crises are more successfully treated by psychotherapy than are long-standing personality problems and psychotic disorders. The people who make best use of therapy tend to have more adaptive levels of mental and behavioral functioning to begin with, are prepared for treatment, and are ready to change (Orlinsky & Howard, 1994; Strupp, 1982).

3. FOR MANY COMMON MILD DISORDERS AND EVERYDAY PROBLEMS, PARAPROFESSIONALS MAY BE AS EFFECTIVE AS PROFESSIONAL THERAPISTS. Numerous meta-analyses of studies of therapist effectiveness find there is no difference in overall success rates between professional therapists and paraprofessionals—that is, people without graduate training in any mental-health field (Christensen & Jacobson, 1994; Dawes, 1994; Smith, Glass, & Miller, 1980; Strupp, 1982; Weisz et al., 1987, 1995). A meta-analysis of 150 psychotherapy studies with children and adolescents, for example, found no overall difference in effectiveness between profes-

sional therapists, graduate-student therapists, and paraprofessional therapists (Weisz et al., 1995).

4. **IN A SIGNIFICANT MINORITY OF CASES, PSYCHOTHERAPY IS HARMFUL BECAUSE OF THE THERAPIST'S INCOMPETENCE, BIAS AGAINST THE CLIENT, OR UNETHICAL BEHAVIOR** (Brodsky, 1982; Garnets et al., 1991; Lambert & Bergin, 1994; López, 1989; McHugh, 1993b; Pope & Bouhoutsos, 1986). Individual therapists can do great harm by behaving unethically or prejudicially. Some psychologists are concerned that therapeutic malpractice may be increasing because of the recent surge in the number of poorly trained therapists who use unvalidated methods (such as "facilitated communication," which we discussed in Chapter 2).

What about psychoanalysis and other forms of psychodynamic psychotherapy? These "depth" therapies are as helpful as any other kind in helping people cope with general problems. However, they have been shown to be significantly *less* effective than cognitive and cognitive-behavior therapy for a very wide array of specific disorders, particularly major depression; anxiety, fears, and panic; eating disorders; health problems such as coping with chronic pain; behavior problems such as procrastination and other bad habits; and family conflicts (Chambless, 1995). Psychodynamic therapies are best suited to people who are introspective, who are not seriously disturbed, who want to explore their pasts, and who are intellectually drawn to the metaphors of psychodynamic approaches.

In the classical analytic view, the longer the therapy goes on, the more successful it will be. The rationale is that people need time to uncover all their sources of resistance to the analysis, to work through their transference to the therapist, and to break through their unconscious defenses. In orthodox psychoanalysis, the client usually meets with the analyst three to five times a week, often for many years. A meta-analysis of longitudinal studies, however, found that about half of all clients obtain the maximum benefits of therapy within 8 to 11 sessions, and another one-fourth benefit from treatment lasting up to a year (Kopta et al., 1994).

Of course, people who have serious, chronic mental disorders such as schizophrenia or autism often require continued therapeutic care, sometimes for their entire lives. But for people who have one or another of the common emotional problems of life, short-term treatment is usually all that is necessary. Recognizing this, and responding also to the increasing cost of long-term psychotherapy, many psychoanalysts have modified their approach. In *time-limited analysis,* therapy consists of 15, 20, or 25 sessions (Sifneos, 1992; Strupp & Binder, 1984). This is the average number of sessions offered by almost all other therapies, too.

Some problems, and some clients, are immune to any single kind of therapy but respond to combined methods. People who have continuing, difficult problems, such as living with chronic pain or coping with a disturbed family member, often are best helped by a combination approach that might include cognitive-behavioral, family-systems, and psychodynamic methods. In practice, most psychotherapists are *eclectic,* borrowing a method from here, an idea from there, and avoiding strong allegiances to narrow theories or schools of thought (Lambert & Bergin, 1994). This flexibility suits their own styles and enables them to treat many different clients with whatever meth-

"I UTILIZE THE BEST FROM FREUD, THE BEST FROM JUNG AND THE BEST FROM MY UNCLE MARTY, A VERY SMART FELLOW."

Successful therapists are flexible in their methods.

ods are appropriate and effective. In a survey of 800 therapists trained in clinical psychology, marriage and family therapy, social work, or psychiatry, 68 percent said they were eclectic in orientation, drawing on psychodynamic, cognitive-behavioral, humanistic, and family-systems techniques as necessary (Jensen, Bergin, & Greaves, 1990).

Ultimately, therapy is a relationship, and like any relationship its success depends on how well the therapist and client work together—whether they form an effective bond called the **therapeutic alliance.** Qualities of both client and therapist are important in establishing this bond. For example, an important predictor of successful therapy is the client's cooperativeness and positive feelings during the therapy session. Hostile, negative individuals are more resistant to treatment and less likely to benefit from it (Orlinsky & Howard, 1994). The personality of the therapist is also important to the success of any therapy, particularly the qualities that Carl Rogers praised: empathy, warmth, genuineness, and imagination. Successful therapists tend to be empathic and actively invested in the interaction with the client—as opposed to being an "impartial," detached observer in the manner of Freud (Orlinsky & Howard, 1994). These qualities are not limited to professional psychologists, which may be one reason for the finding that paraprofessionals are often as effective as trained psychologists in treating most everyday problems.

Because of research, we now understand some of the limitations and achievements of psychodynamic psychotherapy—indeed, of all forms of therapy. It cannot transform you into someone you're not. It cannot cure you overnight. It cannot provide a life without problems. Moreover, researchers have shown that for most problems, short-term therapy is sufficient, and long-term psychoanalysis offers no unique benefits over other therapies.

---

therapeutic alliance The bond of confidence and mutual understanding established between therapist and client, which allows them to work together to solve the client's problems.

Nevertheless, psychodynamic psychotherapists are probably right when they say that some aspects of therapy are unmeasurable, that psychotherapy will never yield its soul to the scrutiny of empirical methods. Further, as the existentialists point out, all forms of psychotherapy share the elusive function of helping clients explore the great questions of life—freedom, free will, alienation from oneself and others, loneliness, and death—and find the courage, morale, and hope to confront them (Frank, 1985; Yalom, 1989). Psychotherapy can help people get "unstuck" from self-defeating patterns and make constructive decisions. It can get them through bad times when no one seems to care or understand. It helps people confront the origins of their pain and suffering and move forward with greater confidence. These achievements cannot easily be captured by statistics.

In this respect, perhaps the best comment about psychodynamic therapy was offered long ago by "Anna O." (Bertha Pappenheim), who was treated by Freud's colleague Josef Breuer and was one of the cases in their 1895 book *Studies on Hysteria*. "Psychoanalysis," she remarked years after her (unsuccessful) treatment, "is in the hand of the physician what the confessional is in the hand of the Catholic clergyman; it depends upon the person applying it and the [specific] application whether it is a good instrument or a double-edged sword" (quoted in Sulloway, 1992). Her observation is just as true today.

WHAT DO YOU KNOW?

1. Summarize the four major conclusions of psychotherapy-evaluation research.
2. On a talk show, Dr. Blitznik announces a fabulous program: Chocolate Immersion Therapy. "People who spend one day a week doing nothing but eating chocolate are soon cured of eating disorders, depression, drug abuse, and poor study habits," says Dr. Blitznik. What should you find out about C.I.T. before signing up?

ANSWERS:

1. Overall, any kind of psychotherapy is more beneficial than getting no help; the people who do best in therapy have treatable problems and are motivated to improve; for everyday problems, paraprofessionals are as effective as professional therapists; and in some cases, therapy can be harmful because of the therapist's incompetence, bias, or unethical behavior. *2. Some questions to ask:* Has Dr. Blitznik shown that people who go through C.I.T. do better than those in a control group who have had no therapy or have had a different therapy? How were the subjects selected? How was success defined? Has the research been replicated by others? (And would Broccoli Immersion Therapy work as well?)

ISSUE 2: THE MYSTERY OF MULTIPLE PERSONALITY DISORDER

Stress or shock can make any of us feel temporarily *dissociated*—that is, cut off from ourselves, feeling strange, dazed, or "unreal." In the psychodynamic view, if shock is too severe, people cope by relying on two unconscious mechanisms: They may repress the memory of the upsetting experience, sending it into the unconscious; or they may have a "dissociated" reaction, in which consciousness, behavior, and identity are split or altered. We will take up the debate about repression in the next section.

According to some psychiatrists and clinical psychologists, the most extreme form of dissociation is a mental illness called **multiple personality disorder** (MPD), which involves the appearance, within one person, of two or more distinct identities, sometimes called "alters." (In the diagnostic manual of the American Psychiatric Association [1994], MPD is now officially called **dissociative identity disorder,** but for convenience, we will retain the term still commonly used by clinicians.) In this disorder, each identity appears to have its own memories, preferences, handwriting, and even medical problems. In a case study of one person with four identities, for example, the researcher concluded that it was "as if four different people had been tested" (Larmore et al., 1977). Cases of MPD are extremely dramatic: Those portrayed in the films *The Three Faces of Eve* and *Sybil* fascinated audiences for years, and so do the legal cases that make the news: A woman charges a man with rape, claiming that only one of her personalities consented to have sex with him while another objected; a man commits murder and claims that his "other personality" did it.

MPD provides a classic example of the scientist–practitioner gap, with the two sides tending to hold *totally incompatible* views of what it is and what causes it. Many practitioners, especially those in the psychodynamic tradition, are convinced that it is a real disorder, common but often underdiagnosed. Many scientists and clinical researchers, and a majority of psychiatrists themselves, are skeptical: They think that most cases are generated by therapists who believe in it, in unwitting collusion with vulnerable and suggestible patients, and that if it exists at all it is extremely rare. Before 1980, fewer than 200 cases of MPD had ever been diagnosed anywhere in the world. Since 1980, more than 30,000 cases have been reported, virtually all of them in the United States and Canada (Nathan, 1994). Does this mean that the disorder is being better identified, and that it is a uniquely North American problem at that, or does it mean that it is being overdiagnosed by those North American clinicians who are looking for it?

Those in the MPD-is-real camp believe that the disorder originates in childhood, as a means of coping with unspeakable, ongoing traumas such as torture (Herman, 1992; Kluft, 1993). In this view, the trauma produces a mental "splitting" or dissociation; one personality emerges to handle everyday experiences, and another emerges to cope with the bad ones. MPD patients are frequently described as having lived for years with several personalities of which they were unaware, until hypnosis and other techniques in therapy revealed them. Clinicians who endorse MPD argue that diagnoses can be made more accurately now because the physiological changes that occur within each personality cannot be faked.

---

multiple personality disorder (dissociative identity disorder) A controversial disorder marked by the appearance within one person of two or more distinct personalities, each with its own name and traits.

The Three Faces of Eve—*both the book and the film starring Joanne Woodward (pictured here in an ad campaign)—aroused the public's fascination with "multiple personality disorder." Although MPD was once extremely rare, thousands of cases have been reported since 1980. Controversy exists about whether this increase is a result of better diagnosis or the result of unwitting therapist influence and sensational stories in the media.*

Those who are skeptical about MPD, however, have shown that most of the research used to support the diagnosis is seriously flawed. A review of the claims that MPD patients have different physiological patterns associated with each "personality" found that most of the studies are anecdotal, have many methodological problems, and have failed to be replicated (Brown, 1994). Most important, research in this area has been marred by that familiar research mistake, the *missing control group*. When one research team corrected this flaw by comparing the EEG activity of two MPD patients with that of a normal person who merely role-played different personalities, they found EEG differences between "personalities" to be *greater* in the normal person (Coons et al., 1982). Other studies comparing MPD patients with control subjects who are merely role-playing have not found any reliable differences (Miller & Triggiano, 1992). Because normal people can create EEG changes by changing their moods, energy levels, and concentration, brain-wave activity cannot be used to verify the existence of MPD.

Clinicians and researchers who are doubtful about this diagnosis point out that cases of MPD seem to turn up only in patients who go to therapists who believe in it and are looking for it (McHugh, 1993a; Merskey, 1992, 1994; Piper, 1994; Spanos,

1996). They fear that clinicians who are convinced of the widespread existence of MPD may actually be creating the disorder in their patients through the power of suggestion. For example, one leading proponent of MPD, Frank Putnam (1989), wrote, "The therapist who wishes to 'elicit alter personalities' should ask gentle questions about whether or not the patient has ever felt like more than one person, searching for another part, and ultimately asking, 'Do you ever feel as if you are not alone, as if there is someone else or some other part watching you?'" (In fact, almost everyone has this feeling on occasion.) And here is the way another psychologist questioned the "Hillside Strangler," Kenneth Bianchi, a man who killed more than a dozen young women:

> I've talked a bit to Ken, but I think that perhaps there might be another part of Ken that I haven't talked to, another part that maybe feels somewhat differently from the part that I've talked to. . . . And I would like that other part to come to talk to me . . . Part, would you please come to communicate with me? (Quoted in Holmes, 1994)

Notice that the psychologist repeatedly asked Bianchi to produce another "part" of himself and even addressed the "part" directly. Before long, Bianchi was maintaining that the murders were really committed by another personality called "Steve Walker." Did the psychologist in this case *permit* another personality to reveal itself or did he actively *create* such a personality by planting the suggestion that one existed?

Proponents of the view that MPD is real and widespread often seem unaware of the difference. One of the best-known advocates of the MPD diagnosis, Richard Kluft (1987), maintains that efforts designed to determine the presence of MPD—that is, to get the patient to reveal a dissociated personality—may require "between 2 ½ and 4 hours of continuous interviewing. Interviewees must be prevented from taking breaks to regain composure, averting their faces to avoid self-revelation, etc. In one recent case of singular difficulty, the first sign of dissociation was noted in the 6th hour, and a definitive spontaneous switching of personalities occurred in the 8th hour." After eight hours of "continuous interviewing" without a single break, how many of us wouldn't do what the interviewer wanted?

An alternative, *sociocognitive* explanation of multiple personality disorder is that it is an extreme form of a normal human process: the ability we all have to present different aspects of our personalities to others (Piper, 1994; Spanos, 1996). In this view, the diagnosis of MPD provides a way for some troubled people to understand and legitimize their problems—or to account for embarrassing, regretted, or even criminal behavior that they commit ("My other personality did it"). In turn, therapists who believe in MPD reward such patients by paying attention to their various "symptoms" and "personalities," thus further influencing the patients to reorganize their memories and make them consistent with the diagnosis.

Canadian psychiatrist Harold Merskey (1992) reviewed several famous cases of MPD, including those of Eve and Sybil, and was unable to find a single case in which a patient developed MPD without being influenced by the therapist's suggestions or reports about the disorder in books and the media. For example, Sybil's psychiatrist, Cornelia Wilbur, first diagnosed Sybil as being schizophrenic, but later encouraged her to produce multiple personalities and memories of having endured severe sexual abuse in childhood (reports that were never corroborated). (Some investigators think that this change of diagnosis was part of a marketing strategy for the psychiatrist's book [Nathan, 1994].) Herbert Spiegel, another psychiatrist who later interviewed Sybil, reported, "Well, she said, when I'm with Dr. Wilbur, she wants me to be that person [another personality named Flora]. And I said, well, if you want, you can, but you don't have to if you don't want to. So, with me, she didn't have to be these personalities" (quoted in Merskey, 1994). And she wasn't.

Psychiatrist Paul McHugh (1993c) concludes that the solution to the growing number of MPD cases is simple: Close the MPD-treatment centers in hospitals. "Ignore the alters," he advises therapists. "Stop talking to them, taking notes on them, and discussing them in staff conferences. Pay attention to real present problems and conflicts rather than fantasy. If these simple, familiar rules are followed, multiple personalities will soon wither away and psychotherapy can begin."

Of course, the fact that MPD is a controversial diagnosis with little empirical evidence to support it does not mean that no legitimate cases exist (Holmes, 1994). It does mean that caution is warranted, especially because diagnoses of MPD have implications regarding responsibility for criminal acts. In the case of the Hillside Strangler, a determined and skeptical prosecutor discovered that Bianchi had read numerous psychology textbooks on MPD and had modeled "Steve" on a student he knew! When another psychologist purposely misled Bianchi by telling him that "real" multiple personalities come in packages of at least three, Bianchi suddenly produced a third personality. Bianchi was convicted of murder and sentenced to life in prison. But Paul Miskamen, who battered his wife to death, convinced psychiatrists and a jury that the man who killed his wife was a separate personality named Jack Kelly. Judged insane, Miskamen was committed to a mental hospital and released after 14 months.

WHAT DO YOU KNOW?

According to his psychiatrist, Frank suffers from multiple personality disorder and has 38 distinct "alters." The psychiatrist has published several articles on the case, opened an MPD clinic, and appeared on television and in court cases as an expert on the phenomenon. As a critical thinker, what questions might you want to ask about Frank's disorder? What alternative explanations—from this chapter or from research in previous perspectives—might you suggest for his behavior?

ANSWERS:

Some possibilities: You might ask when and how Frank's other personalities first appeared—before he entered therapy or during it. What did he enter treatment for? Did he have a history of other mental illness? As for alternative explanations, behaviorists would observe that Frank is being rewarded with attention, and his therapist is being rewarded too, with fame and prestige. Social psychologists would argue that the patient might be responding to subtle or even direct pressures to conform to the psychiatrist's expectations and diagnosis. And a sociocognitive explanation is that the diagnosis appeals to Frank because it offers a clear and dramatic answer to his psychological problems.

ISSUE 3: THE MYSTERY OF RECOVERED MEMORIES

In 1989, a 28-year-old woman named Eileen Franklin Lipsker was playing with her young daughter when suddenly, she later said, a shocking memory blazed through her consciousness. Her daughter reminded her of a close childhood friend, a girl named Susan Nason, who had been murdered at the age of eight. The case had never been solved, but in that horrible moment, Eileen remembered who had killed Susan because she remembered being there: It was her own father, George Franklin. Eileen Lipsker had always been aware that her father was an alcoholic who unpredictably beat his children. A few months after her memory of the Nason murder, she also began remembering that her father had committed incest with her, starting when she was three years old.

Eileen Franklin Lipsker's recovered memories eventually resulted in the conviction of her father for murder in the first degree. This verdict polarized her family (her siblings do not believe her and have severed relations with her), the public, the legal establishment, and psychologists. One psychologist who testified on her behalf is convinced that her recovered memories are true (Terr, 1994). An attorney who investigated the story came to the opposite conclusion, arguing that Lipsker is a disturbed woman who indeed had a terrible father, but that there is no persuasive evidence that he committed murder (MacLean, 1993).

Many other claims of recovered memories of sexual abuse have since been reported all over the country, along with lawsuits against alleged perpetrators. In a typical case, a woman sues her father for hundreds of thousands of dollars, claiming that he had sexually abused her for many years but that she had completely repressed the memories until she entered therapy. In 1995, for example, in a small courtroom in New Hampshire, Laura B. sued her father, Joel Hungerford, claiming that he had molested her from the ages of 5 to 23, including raping her just days before her wedding. She had no memories of these events, she said, until she entered therapy (Loftus, 1995). (We'll tell you what happened to this case and the Franklin case later.)

A controversy is raging about whether such accusations should be believed, and whether they provide sufficient evidence, in the absence of other corroboration, to convict alleged perpetrators. To better assess the controversy, it is helpful to envision a fourfold table (Nash, 1994):

	Sexually Abused as a Child?	
	Yes	No
Remembers Abuse? Yes	A: Was abused, true memory	B: No abuse, false memory
No	C: Was abused, no memory	D: No abuse, no memory

In the present discussion, we will not be talking about group A, the people who were abused in childhood and have no trouble remembering it; for most of them, the problem is not being able to *forget* the abuse. The argument has to do with how many people who recover memories in therapy fall into group B (false or induced memories) and how many people fall into group C ("repressed" memories). For that matter, psychologists are arguing about what is really going on with group C: whether they have "repressed" their memories, temporarily forgotten the experience because other events were more significant in their lives, or failed to encode the memory in the first place.

As with the issue of children's eyewitness testimony (discussed in Chapter 11), much is at stake in this matter: finding justice and safety for children who are molested or raped, while also protecting adults from false charges that can destroy their lives. Understandably, emotions run high among professionals and the public. On one side (let's call them the *recovered-memory school*), some psychologists believe that virtually all memories recovered in therapy should be taken seriously. In their view, false memories occur, but they are rare, compared with the many valid ones. This side fears that people who raise doubts about recovered memories are betraying children and supporting pedophiles (Herman & Harvey, 1993). On the other side (let's call them the *pseudomemory school*), some psychologists feel that many false memories of abuse are being manufactured by naïve, unscrupulous, or uninformed therapists. They know that many cases of abuse occur, but they also believe that there is a rising tide of spurious accusations (Loftus & Ketcham, 1994).

There are researchers on the recovered-memory side, and psychiatrists and clinical psychologists on the pseudomemory side, but in general, mental-health practitioners are overrepresented in the first group and research psychologists in the second. Indeed, the quarrel over recovered memories of sexual abuse is one of the most dramatic outcomes of the scientist–practitioner gap that anyone could imagine. The polarization between the two schools of thought results in part from their respective beliefs about key *psychodynamic* assumptions that scientific research has either disputed or been unable to validate (Lindsay & Read, 1995).

1. MEMORY AND REPRESSION. In the psychodynamic view, forgetting—whether it takes the form of infantile (childhood) amnesia or amnesia for later traumatic events—occurs because of repression. In psychodynamic terms, repression has three elements (Holmes, 1990): It is the selective forgetting of information that causes the individual pain; it is not under voluntary control; and the repressed material is not lost, but stored in the brain, and can be retrieved when the anxiety associated with the memory is removed.

   The research on memory, as we saw in Chapter 10, disputes the psychodynamic view that all forgetting of early memories is motivated by anxiety. On the contrary, the evidence indicates that infantile amnesia is a normal result of physiological and cognitive immaturity, which means that claims of memories of events that happened "in the crib" should certainly be regarded as doubtful. Further, memories are not stored in an uncontaminated state for years; all memories, even of shocking experiences, are subject to distortion and error.

The research on repression, however, is much more ambiguous. For one thing, it is extremely difficult to define what repression is and how you would know it if you saw it. Studies by experimentalists typically involve the blocking out (literally "not seeing") of threatening or taboo words in a list presented rapidly; the recall of uncompleted tasks; or the recall of pleasant versus unpleasant experiences (Holmes, 1990). These methods hardly touch the actual kinds of traumatic experiences that people would be likely to repress. But studies by clinicians who are trying to demonstrate repression are no better; they typically get results that could be interpreted as simple forgetting, normal infantile amnesia, or intentionally refusing to think about upsetting experiences. Both sides agree that people can have traumatic experiences that they don't think about, sometimes for years, until a cue in the current environment reminds them (see Chapter 10). But are such examples of delayed recall the same as "repression"?

This question is difficult to answer because you have to ask people whether they remember a time in their lives when they could not remember something that happened to them! In one survey of 280 women and 225 men, ages 18 to 75, who responded to a mailed questionnaire, over 80 percent of those who had suffered a trauma (such as childhood sexual abuse, rape, military combat, or witnessing the murder of a loved one) said they had continuously remembered the event. But about 20 percent said that there had been a period of temporary amnesia for the entire experience, until an event triggered the memory (Elliott, 1995). Was that repression or intentionally trying not to think about the experience? In another study, therapists were told to ask their clients—450 adults, mostly white women, who had reported sexual abuse—this question: "During the period of time between when the first forced sexual experience happened and your 18th birthday, was there ever a time when you could not remember the forced sexual experience?" (Briere & Conte, 1993). Of this group, 59 percent said yes, there had been such a time. Is that large number evidence of repression or of the influence of the therapist?

Longitudinal studies might help answer this question, but they too have problems. In a widely reported study of 100 African-American women who as children had been treated in a hospital for sexual abuse (at the time, they ranged in age from 10 months to 12 years), 38 percent did not remember or did not choose to report the specific incident in an interview 17 years later (Williams, 1994). Had they "repressed" the memory? This explanation is questionable for several reasons. First, the majority of the woman *did* report other experiences of sexual abuse. Second, because abuse was defined as everything from fondling to intercourse, some of these experiences may have been less traumatic that others and were therefore forgotten rather than actively "repressed." Third, that 38 percent included women who were abused as infants as well as those abused as older children; normal infantile amnesia would account for the failure to recall very early experiences. Finally, some of the women might simply have been reluctant to reveal the experience in question to an unfamiliar interviewer.

The pseudomemory school agrees that people can and do forget *details* of experiences they found traumatic at the time, but they doubt that people routinely forget the fact that they experienced the trauma *at all*. Veterans of war may forget horrible details of battle, but they do not forget that they were in a war; to memory researchers, therefore, claims that a person repressed repeated acts of incest over many years are highly improbable. Moreover, to the pseudomemory school, the clinical argument—"I know repression when I see it"—carries little validity. David Holmes (1990), who is both a clinician and an academic researcher, describes a conference on repression at which he was the only skeptic. One psychoanalyst brought along videotapes that supposedly illustrated the use of repression by a client in psychotherapy. The trouble was that none of the conference members could agree on whether, or even if, repression was occurring. "This is a serious blow to the clinical evidence," reported Holmes dryly.

Perhaps a combination of better experimental and clinical research will eventually provide an understanding of how repression, if it exists, differs from normal forgetting, and when and why it occurs.

2. **THE INFLUENCE OF THE THERAPIST.** In any therapeutic exchange, the client will be influenced by the therapist's explanation of his or her problems and by the questions the therapist asks. That is why the person has gone to the therapist in the first place—for understanding and explanation of troubles that seem mysterious. The problem occurs when some therapists so zealously believe in certain ideas that, consciously or unconsciously, they induce the client to produce the symptoms they are looking for (McHugh, 1993b; Merskey, 1994; Spanos et al., 1991). This risk is increased when a therapist uses hypnosis, sodium amytal (a barbiturate misleadingly called "truth serum"), guided imagery, and similar techniques to try to "uncover" memories. These methods are highly unreliable. For example, as we saw in Chapter 10, hypnosis sometimes allows people to retrieve accurate memories, but it is just as likely to lead people to create erroneous ones.

Unfortunately, studies of random samples of mental-health professionals now suggest that a significant minority of American therapists—between a fourth and a third—use hypnosis and other suggestive techniques to try to retrieve their patients' memories—although just as many *disapprove* of these techniques (Poole et al., 1995) (see Table 16.1 on the following page). Many of the users are unaware of the research on hypnosis. When Michael Yapko (1994), a clinical psychologist who uses hypnosis in his own practice (though not to recover memories), surveyed 869 members of the American Association of Marriage and Family Therapists, he discovered that more than half mistakenly believed that "Hypnosis can be used to recover memories from as far back as birth." A third agreed that "The mind is like a computer, accurately recording events that actually occurred." And a fourth of them agreed that "Someone['s] feeling certain about a memory means the memory is likely to be correct." Finally, Yapko reports, many "had little or no formal knowledge of the role and power of suggestion in therapy." (About a third of his sample had Ph.D.s and the rest M.A.s, but academic degrees made only a marginal difference in their beliefs.)

The recovered-memory school counters that although therapists do influence their clients in a general sense, it is just about impossible to implant a memory of

TABLE 16.1 ✦ Percentage of American Clinical Psychologists Who Approve and Disapprove of Various Memory-Recovery Techniques to Help Clients Remember Childhood Sexual Abuse[a]

TECHNIQUE	PERCENTAGE OF THERAPISTS USING TECHNIQUE	PERCENTAGE OF THERAPISTS DISAPPROVING OF TECHNIQUE
Hypnosis	31	30
Age regression	18	34
Dream interpretation	41	27
Guided imagery related to abuse situations	29	33
Interpreting physical symptoms	36	24

[a]*Note:* Percentages averaged for two samples of licensed clinicians, most with advanced degrees, listed in the National Register of Health Service Providers in Psychology.

Source: From Poole et al., 1995.

something as horrible as childhood incest. Patients are not just passive vessels awaiting the wisdom of the therapist; as Freud himself explained, they often resist fiercely the interpretations of the therapist. For these reasons, many clinicians say, laboratory studies of artificially generated pseudomemories do not apply to cases of traumatic memories (Herman & Harvey, 1993; Terr, 1994; Wylie, 1993).

But some studies of real-life incidents have provided evidence that even traumatic pseudomemories can be induced by suggestion. In one, schoolchildren were asked for their recollections of an actual sniper who had terrorized their schoolyard. Many of the children who were not at the school during the shooting, including some who were on vacation at the time, reported "memories" of hearing shots, seeing someone lying on the ground, and other details they could not possibly have seen. Apparently, they had been influenced by the accounts of the children who had been there (Pynoos & Nader, 1989).

Several researchers have systematically demonstrated how traumatic memories can be implanted in some people. Elizabeth Loftus and her associates asked 24 individuals, ages 18 to 53, to recall several events (Loftus, 1995; Loftus & Pickrell, 1995). Three of the events were true, having been supplied to the researchers by close relatives of the subjects. But one was a false event—being lost in a shopping mall, store, or other public place when the subject was about 5 years old. (The researchers confirmed with relatives that this event did not happen.) Only 7 of the 24 "remembered" the false event, but they did so with often vivid details. One young man, Chris, correctly claimed at first to have no memory of the experience, but two days later, he spontaneously recalled how frightened he had been. On day 5, he "remembered" the store and the man who found him. Two weeks later, he had even more details: "An old man, I think he was wearing blue flannel, came up to me. . . . He was kind of old and bald on top. . . . He had a ring of gray hair . . . and he had glasses." Even when Chris was told that his newly acquired memory was false, he had trouble letting go of it. He remembered it all so clearly, he said; how he cried, and how scared he was, and how worried and angry his mother was.

In a similar series of studies, Ira Hyman and his colleagues (1995) were able to implant false memories of highly distinctive events, such as being hospitalized overnight for a high fever or being at a wedding and accidentally spilling a punch bowl on the parents of the bride. Subjects were then interviewed several times about these events (similar to the repetitive questions that might occur in therapy over time). Very few people "recalled" the false events during the first interview, but more than one fourth did by the third interview. One person who correctly had no memory of the wedding accident later said, "It was an outdoor wedding and I think we were running around and knocked something over like the punch bowl or something and, um, made a big mess and of course got yelled at for it."

Notice that most of the people in these studies were *not* induced to believe something that didn't happen, but 20 to 25 percent *were* induced to believe these pseudomemories. "Examples of such confidently held and richly detailed false memories do not prove, of course, that all recovered memories of abuse are false," says Loftus (1993). "But they do demonstrate a mechanism by which false memories can be created by suggestion."

3. **THE EMPHASIS ON PSYCHIC REALITY.** Because of their adherence to the importance of unconscious processes, many psychodynamic therapists are not terribly concerned about verifying a patient's perceptions and memories. They argue that what really happened, even if you could find it out, is less relevant than the patient's beliefs about his or her memories. Consider a woman who feels that her mother was neglectful and that her father was aloof and unkind. It isn't relevant that the mother didn't mean to be neglectful, but her job demanded it; or that the father was aloof because he believed that men should be emotionally controlled. The woman knows what she feels, and that's the issue. Psychotherapist David Calof (1993) says, "I do not encourage clients to seek external validation, from me or anyone else; it's much more important that they decide for themselves what their memories mean."

The pseudomemory school replies that the stories people tell about their lives and the explanations they choose for their behavior are critically important. This is why cognitive therapists emphasize the importance of trying to find evidence to confirm or disprove beliefs about one's parents or anyone else. Although the absence of corroborating evidence for a memory may not make much difference in everyday matters, such evidence becomes critical when the memories lead to accusations of criminal behavior, such as rape, incest, or murder. Psychiatrist Paul McHugh has treated victims of abuse (who have always remembered it) and people who he believes have been induced to have pseudomemories of abuse. To distinguish these two groups, McHugh (1993a) maintains, "a scrupulous search for corroborating evidence must be launched on every occasion. To treat for repressed memories without any effort at external validation is malpractice pure and simple."

4. **THE AFTERMATH OF ABUSE.** The recovered-memory school accepts the psychodynamic assumption that sexual abuse in childhood inevitably causes long-term trauma and predictable symptoms. Surprisingly, empirical research disputes this claim. Like any other trauma—being orphaned, having alcoholic parents, surviving war—sexual abuse has many possible long-term outcomes, depending on what else happens to the child and on the support the child gets from adults. Some children develop long-lasting problems, but many others recover. In an important review of 45 longitudinal studies that investigated the emotional consequences for children who had been sexually abused, researchers found that although these children grew up to have more symptoms than nonabused children, one-third of them had no symptoms (Kendall-Tackett, Williams, & Finkelhor, 1993). The researchers concluded that "No one symptom characterized a majority of sexually abused children. . . . The findings suggest the absence of any specific syndrome in children who have been sexually abused and no single traumatizing process."

Other longitudinal studies also find discontinuities between childhood and adulthood. With adequate love and support, children can survive even extraordinary hardships and traumas, including homelessness, deprivation, abuse, and war (Cowen et al., 1990; Garmezy, 1991; Kaufman & Zigler, 1987; Thomas & Chess, 1984; Tillman, Nash, & Lerner, 1994; Werner, 1989; Wyatt & Mickey, 1987). As Daniel Stern (1985), a psychiatrist who has examined psychodynamic assumptions about child development in the light of empirical evidence, concluded, "Psychological insults and trauma at a specific age or stage should result in predictably specific types of clinical problems later on. No such evidence exists."

As a result of the efforts of research psychologists, more people are becoming cautious in evaluating claims of recovered memories. In 1993, Laura Pasley became the first woman to win a settlement from her therapist for "creating false memories," and since then hundreds of malpractice lawsuits have been filed against professionals on the same grounds. In Ohio, an appeals court upheld a malpractice award to a woman whose psychiatrist had injected her with sodium amytal more than 140 times to help her uncover memories of abuse; in Minnesota, a jury convicted another psychiatrist who used drugs, hypnosis, and coercion to induce false memories in her patient. And in a landmark ruling in the New Hampshire case we mentioned at the beginning of this section, the judge wrote that Laura B.'s recovered memories would not be admissible evidence because "The phenomenon of memory repression, and the process of therapy used in these cases to recover the memories, have not gained general acceptance in the field of psychology; *and are not scientifically reliable*" (*State of New Hampshire* v. *Joel Hungerford*, May 23, 1995).

Most dramatically, the case that launched the recovered-memory issue in the first place, Eileen Franklin Lipsker's accusation of her father, has fallen apart. In 1995, George Franklin's conviction was reversed on the grounds that Eileen's testimony could have been based on information she read in the newspapers rather than on her memories (this fact had not been presented to the jury); and in 1996, the prosecutors decided they had no evidence on which to base a retrial. In the interim, Eileen had "remembered" her father murdering two other girls, but an investigation of this claim completely exonerated him.

Research by clinicians and experimenters continues to shed light on the complex issues involved in recovered memories of sexual abuse. But of course, no research can tell us for sure about any *individual* case of recovered memory. How, then, should a person evaluate such claims? We think the answer lies somewhere between "believe all of them" and "believe none of them" and depends on the specific evidence in each case. Following are some indications that skepticism is warranted and that a person may be having pseudomemories as a result of therapist influence:

◆ The person claims that, thanks to therapy, he or she now clearly remembers being molested in the first year or two of life.

◆ Over time, the memories of abuse become more and more bizarre—for instance, that every member of the family was also a perpetrator, or that the abuse continued day and night for 15 years without ever being remembered and without anyone else in the household noticing.

◆ The therapist's diagnosis of sexual abuse was made during the first or second session, based on problems a client could have for many reasons (e.g., depression, low self-esteem, or an eating disorder). One therapist told a television interviewer that incest is "so common that I'll tell you that within 10 minutes, I can spot it as a person walks in the door, often before they even realize it"—a claim that is patently ludicrous (quoted in Dawes, 1994).

◆ The therapist resorted to hypnosis, drugs, guided imagery, trance induction, or other pseudoscientific techniques to "help" a patient recall unremembered abuse.

In contrast, did the recollection of the abuse or other trauma occur spontaneously, as part of a discussion of other issues occurring in the therapy? Did the person show other symptoms of trauma after the abuse originally occurred, such as nightmares and disturbed behavior? Is it possible to find corroborating evidence from school or medical records or the recollections of other family members? In one case, a man in therapy began to recall details of a sexually humiliating incident that happened when he was 10 years old in his older cousin's house—a group of slightly older boys held him down and ejaculated on him (Nash, 1994). He decided to contact the cousin, who reluctantly admitted that the event had indeed happened; he had always been sorry and embarrassed that he had not been able to stop it. In such cases, the therapist is helping the client to remember these experiences rather than inducing them.

WHAT DO YOU KNOW?

If you were on the jury in a case of recovered memories of childhood sexual abuse, what information would you want to have in evaluating the accuser's testimony about his or her memories?

ANSWERS:

You would want to know, among other things, how and when the accuser recovered those memories—during therapy, or in some other context? Did the therapist use hypnosis, drugs, or other suggestive measures to encourage the client's recall? Was there any corroborating evidence for the memories, such as school or medical records? Were the recovered memories stable, or did contradictory details and additional accusations keep emerging?

The controversy about repressed memories shows how important it is to chip away at the wall between scientific psychology and psychodynamic psychology, and lots of people are now taking a swing at it. Increasingly, psychodynamic psychologists are using empirical methods and research findings from other perspectives to formulate and refine their theories. They draw on cognitive findings on schemas, narratives, consciousness, and infant mental abilities (Horowitz, 1988; Schafer, 1992; Stern, 1985); social-learning and sociocultural findings on gender roles and the impact of culture (Young-Eisendrath, 1993); findings on nonconscious processes in emotion (Murphy, Monahan, & Zajonc, 1995); and biological findings on the hereditary aspects of personality traits and the physiology of emotions (Plutchik, 1988).

For their part, some research psychologists have stopped trying to keep the psychoanalytic wolf from the door. Across the other perspectives of psychology, researchers are studying many ideas spawned by psychodynamic theories. Many, as we have seen in previous chapters, are investigating unconscious processes. Some are incorporating psychodynamic principles of transference and object-relations theory into cognitive psychology (Westen, 1991). Some have developed empirical tests of defense mechanisms, studying the ways in which defenses protect self-esteem and reduce anxiety (Plutchik et al., 1988), although others prefer to emphasize the positive, adaptive aspects of defenses, which they call "coping strategies" (Taylor, 1995). Other empirical researchers are investigating psychodynamic notions of the ego ideal, the inner world of fantasy, and the ideal self (Markus & Nurius, 1986; Ogilvie, 1987). Jerome Singer (1984) called the inner life, the sense of continuity that we carry with us, the *private personality*. In this concept, he subsumes the psychodynamic idea that the essence of personality is more than the sum of a person's biology, learned behaviors, or immediate perceptions.

In the final analysis—so to speak—there may be no resolution of many of the fundamental tensions between the psychodynamic perspective and the empirical branches of psychology. The people who work in this perspective do so for the framework of meaning it provides, knowing that many of its tenets will never be confirmed through scientific methods. In the coming years, it will be interesting to see what happens to this perspective in relation to the rest of psychology. Will it continue on a separate, parallel track? Will it break off from the discipline entirely and become allied with literary criticism and the humanities? Will it turn out to be, as Peter Medawar (1982) predicted, a dinosaur in the history of ideas? Or will its best concepts become woven into scientific psychology, forming a seamless vision of human behavior?

✦ ✦ ✦

Summary

1. To most research psychologists in the other four perspectives of psychology, the psychodynamic perspective is unscientific. But psychodynamically minded people reply that this perspective alone captures the inner life that eludes questionnaires

and behavioral observations and describes the whole person in all of his or her emotional complexity.

2. The main contributions of the psychodynamic perspective are a willingness to raise "big picture" questions; an imaginative use of qualitative information, such as analysis of movies, folktales, and cultural symbols; and the emphasis on self-knowledge, especially of our unconscious motives. The object-relations school in particular has shown how unconscious expectations and patterns established early in life with important family members can reproduce themselves in adult relationships.

3. As with all perspectives, one misuse of this perspective is reductionism—in this case, the tendency to overemphasize a person's psychic reality and ignore biological and cultural factors and the actual circumstances of the person's life.

4. Critics have identified four practices that they believe are inherent limitations of the psychodynamic perspective: (1) violating the principle of falsifiability; (2) drawing universal principles from the experiences of few, atypical patients in a particular culture; (3) basing theories of development on the retrospective accounts and fallible memories of patients, which may create an *illusion of causality* and which has often led to conclusions that are not supported by longitudinal research; and (4) relying on subjective methods that are often unvalidated and unreliable. *Projective tests,* such as the *Thematic Apperception Test* (TAT), can be useful as research tools, as seen in the study of *achievement motivation.* But when used for clinical diagnosis, projective tests such as the *Rorschach Inkblot Test* tend to be unreliable because clinicians do not agree with one another on how to interpret them.

5. Many psychodynamic psychologists believe that empirical research is irrelevant to the practice of psychotherapy, a stance that has helped create the "scientist–practitioner gap."

6. One result of the scientist–practitioner gap is the debate over the effectiveness of psychodynamic therapy. Overall, *controlled clinical studies* find that psychotherapy of any kind is better than doing nothing at all; that the people who do best are those who have the least serious problems and who are motivated to improve; that for many common mild disorders and everyday problems, paraprofessionals may be as effective as professional therapists; and that in some circumstances, people can be harmed by the therapist's unethical practices, bias, or incompetence.

7. In comparison to other therapies, psychodynamic therapies are significantly less effective for many problems and are best suited to people who are introspective and who seek understanding rather than change. For most problems, short-term treatment is usually sufficient, and cognitive and cognitive-behavior therapies are empirically the most effective. Some problems respond best to combined treatments; in any case, most therapists are *eclectic,* using many different methods. Successful therapy depends on a good *therapeutic alliance* between the client and therapist, involving the client's cooperation and optimism and the therapist's empathy

and active participation. Psychodynamic psychotherapists are probably right, however, when they say that some aspects of therapy are unmeasurable.

8. The debate over *multiple personality disorder* (MPD), officially called *dissociative identity disorder,* provides a classic illustration of the scientist–practitioner gap. In MPD, two or more distinct personalities and identities are said to appear within one person. However, there is considerable controversy about the validity and nature of this disorder. Some clinicians think that it is fairly common but is often undiagnosed, and that it originates in childhood trauma; other clinicians and many researchers prefer a *sociocognitive* explanation, arguing that most cases of MPD are manufactured in unwitting collusion between therapists who believe in the disorder and suggestible patients who find it an appealing explanation for their problems.

9. The debate over recovered memories of sexual abuse is another outcome of the scientist–practitioner gap. The *recovered-memory school* and the *pseudomemory school* disagree about the nature of memory and repression, and the role that repression plays (if any) in forgetting; the probability that a therapist, by using leading questions, hypnosis, and other techniques, can induce a client to produce the memories the therapist is looking for; the importance of a patient's psychic reality versus a patient's verification of her or his memories; and whether certain symptoms inevitably follow childhood abuse. Skepticism about a recovered memory is warranted when the memory is said to be of an event very early in life; when particular recollections of events become more and more improbable; when the therapist has made an immediate diagnosis; or when the therapist has used hypnosis or other questionable techniques to elicit the memory. In contrast, when the experience was associated with other signs of trauma, the memory occurred spontaneously, and there is corroborating evidence, the memory is more likely to be accurate.

10. Increasingly, psychodynamic psychologists are using empirical research methods and drawing on findings from other perspectives to formulate their theories. For their part, some research psychologists are studying issues raised by psychodynamic theories, such as the nature of defenses and unconscious processes. But the relationship between the psychodynamic perspective and the rest of psychology remains uneasy and uncertain.

Key Terms

psychodynamic reductionism *545*

illusion of causality *547*

projective test *548*

Thematic Apperception Test (TAT) *548*

achievement motive *548*

Rorschach Inkblot Test *549*

scientist–practitioner gap *550*

controlled clinical trials *552*

time-limited psychoanalysis *553*

eclectic approaches to therapy *553*

therapeutic alliance *554*

dissociation *555*

multiple personality disorder (MPD)
   (dissociative identity disorder) *556*

sociocognitive explanation (of MPD)
   558

recovered memories *560*

"recovered-memory school" *561*

"pseudomemory school" *561*

psychic reality *565*

PART VII

PUTTING THE PERSPECTIVES TOGETHER

A friend of ours attended a conference in which psychologists were discussing the case of a troubled girl. The girl was disruptive and belligerent, and this behavior made her mother angry. The father, who worked long hours, came home tired most nights and didn't want to deal with the situation.

The first psychologist thought the problem was that the child was temperamentally difficult from birth—a biological matter that could be treated with drugs. The second psychologist thought the problem was that the child had learned to behave inappropriately and aggressively in order to get the attention of her father; this pattern could be treated with behavior therapy. The third psychologist thought the problem was the mother, who was misinterpreting her daughter's behavior as an intentional effort to provoke her; the mother could be helped with cognitive therapy. The fourth psychologist saw the situation as stemming from traditional gender roles within this family's culture (the "absent" father, the "overprotective" mother) and the role of each individual in a family network; all of them would benefit from family therapy. The fifth psychologist thought that the problem was the child's unresolved Oedipal feelings, the mother's displacement of affectional needs for her husband onto the child, and the father's unconscious anxieties about being a father; the child and the parents could be helped with psychodynamic therapy.

Like the blind men and the elephant in the poem that began this book, each of these psychologists "was partly in the right, and all of them were wrong." Fortunately for this family, the psychologists on the child's case decided on a team approach. Instead of blaming the child, the mother, or the father for causing the problem, they treated it as an interaction of many different factors. The child learned to control her outbursts; the father faced the fears and unspoken reasons in his own past for avoiding his wife and daughter; the mother, feeling undervalued as a homemaker, took steps to develop her own interests. As each individual changed, so did the family.

We don't want to imply that the contributions of all five psychological perspectives carry equal weight in explaining every human problem or experience. As we have seen, some problems, such as autism, are due to biology; some issues, such as concepts of time, are primarily cultural; and some behaviors, such as a child's whining, are learned. But most topics can be best understood with a "team approach." In this final chapter, we will consider what psychologists from each of the perspectives can contribute to understanding common human experiences, and what we might learn, in an ideal world, by studying the whole elephant.

CHAPTER 17

The Whole Elephant

*E*very society on earth has discovered the joy of music. Why is this so, when music does not have any obvious survival value? Where does musical genius come from? Why are there so many differences in the kinds of music that people like, and why are these differences related to the social class, culture, ethnicity, and age group they belong to?

Music consists of three basic elements: *pitch* (melody); *rhythm* (sounds grouped according to a prescribed system); and *timbre* (the qualities of a tone that make a C-sharp sound different, say, on a tuba than on a guitar). From these building blocks, human beings have created rock and roll, rap, sonatas, blues, folk songs, chants, symphonies, jazz, opera, . . . the variations are endless. Where there are human beings, there is music.

One researcher, Howard Gardner (1983), has brought findings from diverse perspectives to the study of what he calls "musical intelligence." His ability to weave together research on the brain, on culture, on perception and other cognitive processes, and on the role of learning is a model of the kind of multiperspective approach we have been advocating, so we want to give you a brief look at how he went about it.*

Gardner first distinguishes the qualities that might be responsible for musical *genius* from the "core musical abilities" that everyone shares, to one degree or another. Biographies of musical prodigies suggest that musical genius is in part heritable. Mozart played the harpsichord at three and he wrote his first composition before he was seven; and, as Gardner notes, other brilliant composers have described how natural creating music always felt to them—Wagner said he composed like a cow producing milk, and Saint-Saëns compared the process to an apple tree producing apples. But different forms of musical genius might have different origins. A child who can sing a complete aria from an opera after hearing it only once, for example, might be an *idiot savant* (someone who has severe intellectual impairments yet has one stunning ability—in this case, the ability to imitate flawlessly any musical piece).

As Gardner shows, even those of us who are not musical geniuses are born with an ability to recognize and appreciate the basic structure of music, which suggests that it

---

*Gardner has nothing to say about the psychodynamic approach, whose contributions he believes are more literary and philosophical than scientific (Gardner, 1992).

is a biologically based phenomenon. Babies sing as well as babble, and before long, they are imitating tones sung by others. Infants only two months old can match the pitch, loudness, and melodic line of their mother's songs, and at four months they can match the rhythmic structure of a song as well.

Biological researchers have found that the mechanisms by which pitch is apprehended and stored are different from the mechanisms that process other sounds, particularly those of language. Studies of people whose brains have been damaged by stroke or other trauma also confirm that music and language are localized in different places in the brain: linguistic abilities are located almost exclusively in the left hemisphere, musical abilities in the right hemisphere. This means that people can suffer impaired verbal ability but retain their musical ability, and vice versa. Recently, researchers have made great advances in identifying brain differences among musicians, nonmusicians, and musical geniuses. For example, the left hands of string musicians, especially those who began training before age 12, are represented by larger brain areas than are the left hands of nonmusicians—suggesting that musical experience such as years of practice in childhood can affect the brain (Elbert et al., 1995). On the other hand (so to speak), some musical skills, such as perfect pitch—the ability to identify a note just by hearing it—appear very early in life and seem to be innate. In musicians with perfect pitch, a region in the left hemisphere that processes sounds is relatively larger than it is in nonmusicians or musicians without perfect pitch (Schlaug et al., 1995).

Of course, all babies are born into specific cultures, and cultures differ in which of the fundamental components of music they emphasize—pitch, rhythm, or timbre. In most Asian societies, pitch gets the musical emphasis: music consists of small quarter-tone intervals without great rhythmic variation. In sub-Saharan Africa, in contrast, rhythmic patterns of dazzling complexity are the main musical form. Cultures also differ widely in their attitudes and expectations about musical ability. In the United States, many people seem to think you're either born with musical ability or you're not, so most children fail to develop their musical abilities after they leave elementary school, unless they are exceptionally gifted. But the Anang of Nigeria believe that everyone is capable of making music. Infants only a week old are introduced to music and dancing by their mothers, and fathers make drums for their children as soon as the babies can pound them. At age two, children join groups where they learn to sing, dance, and play instruments. By age five, Anang children can sing hundreds of songs, play several percussion instruments, and dance complicated steps. In Japan, China, and Hungary, children are expected to become proficient in singing and, if possible, also playing an instrument.

Between the contributions of biology and culture, Gardner writes, are those of cognition and learning. By school age, most children have developed a cognitive schema of what a song should be like, and they can imitate the tunes they commonly hear. Culture imposes these schemas when children are very young, which is why it is often hard for people to respond emotionally to songs outside their cultural experience. And learning affects all aspects of musical intelligence. Even children born with musical potential in a culture that values musical ability need something more if they are to succeed as musicians. As behavioral and social-learning research predicts, they need motivation, persistence, drive, social support, rewards and encouragement, and great teachers and role models.

In sum, Gardner shows, all of these lines of research are necessary if we are to understand the incredible emotional power of music on all of us—and the incredible musical abilities of some of us. Of course, most psychologists don't analyze a particular problem or topic from many different points of view because they are busy doing the kind of research they were trained to do, working on the specific questions that most interest them. A cross-cultural psychologist studying the musical attitudes of the Anang, for example, is unlikely to also be studying areas of the brain associated with music recognition. In the next section, therefore, we want to give you an extended example of the different ways that psychologists in each of the five perspectives might approach another universal and complex phenomenon: drug use and drug abuse.

DRUG USE AND ABUSE

Most adults, everywhere in the world, have taken a **psychoactive drug,** a substance that alters perception, mood, thinking, memory, or behavior. Around the world and throughout history, the most commonly used psychoactive drugs have been tobacco, alcohol, marijuana, opium, cocaine, peyote—and let's not forget coffee. The reasons for taking such drugs vary: to alter consciousness, as part of a religious ritual, for recreation, or for psychological escape. But human beings are not the only species that enjoys the occasional experience of altering normal states of mind or chemically changing moods. Many animals, too, like to get "high." Baboons ingest tobacco, elephants love the alcohol in fermented fruit, and reindeer and rabbits seek out intoxicating mushrooms (R. Siegel, 1989).

Most drugs can be classified as *stimulants, depressants, opiates,* or *psychedelics,* depending on their effects on the central nervous system and their impact on behavior and mood. (See Chapter 5 for an extended discussion of the drugs used in treating mental and emotional disorders.)

1. **STIMULANTS,** such as cocaine, amphetamines ("uppers"), nicotine, and caffeine, speed up activity in the central nervous system. In moderate amounts, they tend to produce feelings of excitement, confidence, and well-being or euphoria. In large amounts, they make a person anxious, jittery, and hyperalert. In very large doses, they may cause convulsions, heart failure, and death.

   Amphetamines are synthetic drugs usually taken in pill form. Cocaine ("coke") is a natural drug, derived from the leaves of the coca plant. Rural workers in Bolivia and Peru chew coca leaf every day, without apparent ill effects. In the United States, the drug is usually inhaled ("snorted") or injected, or it's smoked in

---

psychoactive drug   A drug capable of influencing perception, mood, cognition, or behavior.

the highly refined form known as "crack." These methods give the drug a more immediate, powerful, and dangerous effect. Amphetamines and cocaine make users feel peppy but do not actually increase energy reserves. Fatigue, irritability, and depression may occur when the effects of these drugs wear off.

2. **DEPRESSANTS,** such as alcohol, tranquilizers, and barbiturates, slow down activity in the central nervous system. Also known as *sedatives,* they usually make a person feel calm or drowsy, and they may reduce anxiety, guilt, tension, and inhibitions. In large amounts, they may produce insensitivity to pain and other sensations. Like stimulants, in very large doses, they can cause convulsions and death.

    People are often surprised to learn that alcohol is a central nervous system depressant. In small amounts, alcohol has some of the effects of a stimulant, because it suppresses activity in parts of the brain that normally inhibit such behaviors as loud laughter and clowning around. Like barbiturates and opiates, alcohol can be used as an anesthetic; if you drink enough, you will eventually pass out. Extremely large amounts of alcohol can kill, by inhibiting the nerve cells in the brain centers that control breathing and heartbeat.

3. **OPIATES** include opium, derived from the opium poppy; morphine, a derivative of opium; heroin, a derivative of morphine; and synthetic drugs, such as methadone. All these drugs relieve pain, mimicking the action of endorphins, and most have a powerful effect on the emotions. When injected, they may produce a sudden feeling of euphoria, called a "rush." There may be a decrease in anxiety and a decrease in motivation, although the effects vary.

4. **PSYCHEDELIC DRUGS** alter consciousness by disrupting the normal perception of time and space, as well as normal thought processes. Sometimes psychedelics produce hallucinations. Some, such as lysergic acid diethylamide (LSD), are made in the laboratory. Others, such as mescaline (from the peyote cactus) and psilocybin (from certain mushrooms), are natural substances. Emotional reactions to psychedelics vary from person to person, and from one time to another for any individual. A "trip" may be mildly pleasant or unpleasant, a mystical revelation or a nightmare.

Marijuana ("pot," "grass," "weed") is probably the most widely used illicit drug in the United States. Some researchers classify it as a mild psychedelic, but others feel that its chemical makeup and its psychological effects place it outside the major classifications. The active ingredient in marijuana is tetrahydrocannabinol (THC), derived from the hemp plant, *Cannabis sativa.* In some respects, THC appears to be a mild stimulant, increasing heart rate and making tastes, sounds, and colors seem more intense. But users often report mild euphoria and relaxation, or even sleepiness. Time often seems to go by slowly.

Although most people around the world use psychoactive drugs moderately and for short-lived effects, some people overuse them. The consequences of drug misuse for society are costly in terms of loss of productive work, high rates of violence and crime, and family disruption. The consequences for individuals and their families are tragic: unhappiness, illness, and the increased likelihood of early death due to accident or disease. For such reasons, many people are deeply concerned about drug abuse.

They hear the word *drugs* and conjure up images of homelessness, crime, domestic violence, gang wars, and crack and heroin addicts whose lives have been devastated by their drug dependence.

Unfortunately, concern over these very real and terrible social problems has made it difficult to discuss the issue of drugs dispassionately and to evaluate research calmly. At one extreme, some people cannot accept evidence that their favorite drug—such as coffee, tobacco, alcohol, or marijuana—might have harmful effects. At the other extreme, some people cannot accept the evidence that their most hated drug—such as alcohol, morphine, or the coca leaf—might not be dangerous in all forms or amounts, and might even have beneficial effects. In thinking about drugs, extremists on both sides often make two errors: They fail to distinguish the effects of moderate use from those of excessive use; and they assume that all legal drugs are relatively harmless but that all illegal drugs are equally dangerous (or equally beneficial).

In fact, research finds that with most drugs, there is a big difference between light or moderate use and heavy or excessive use. (However, even moderate amounts of drugs that are taken in extremely potent or concentrated form, such as crack cocaine, can be harmful.) In a longitudinal study that followed a large sample of children from preschool through age 18, adolescents who had experimented moderately with alcohol and marijuana were actually the best adjusted in the sample; there were no detrimental effects of moderate use. Those who had never experimented with any drug were the most anxious, emotionally constricted, and lacking in social skills. But the teenagers who *abused* drugs were the most maladjusted, alienated, and impulsive (Shedler & Block, 1990). Heavy use of alcohol or illicit drugs interfered with nearly every aspect of a teenager's life, from relationships to schoolwork (Scheier, Newcomb, & Bentler, 1990).

The clinical definition of *substance abuse* is "a maladaptive pattern of substance use leading to clinically significant impairment or distress" (American Psychiatric Association, 1994). Symptoms of such impairment include the failure to fulfill role obligations at work, home, or school (the person cannot hold a job, care for children, or complete coursework because of excessive drug use); use of the drug in hazardous situations (e.g., while driving a car or operating machinery); recurrent arrests for drug use; and persistent conflicts that are either caused by the drug or about the use of the drug.

Moderate use of most drugs, however, does not have these effects. Indeed, moderate social drinking—up to three glasses of wine or a couple of drinks of liquor a day—has a variety of health benefits for men, notably a significant reduction in the risk of heart attacks and strokes and increased longevity, compared to men who don't drink at all (Casswell, 1993; Gaziano & Hennekens, 1995; Gronbaek et al., 1995; Klatsky, 1994). Among women, however, similar levels of alcohol consumption produce an increased risk of breast cancer, which complicates the balance of risks and benefits. Studies suggest that women should drink less than men to benefit from reduced risk of heart attack and increased longevity—no more than a drink or two a day—because women are typically smaller, and their bodies metabolize alcohol differently (Fuchs et al., 1995).

Whenever these results are reported in the media, American health professionals always worry that people will use them as an excuse to drink too much; we hope you won't. Heavy drinking in the United States is second only to smoking as a cause of cancer deaths and overall mortality, perhaps because heavy drinkers are more likely to wreck their livers—and their cars. Even occasional heavy drinking can be detrimental to health and to abstract reasoning. In short, a Saturday night binge is more dangerous than a daily drink.

In all societies, there are legal drugs that are considered "good" and illegal drugs that are considered "bad," but this distinction is usually drawn without any medical or biological basis (Gould, 1990; Weil, 1972/1986). As a result, some odd situations have occurred:

- ◆ In the United States, methadone is a legal but tightly regulated substitute for heroin, yet both drugs are opiates. As Stephen Jay Gould (1990) observed, to say that methadone blocks the craving for heroin is like saying that "a Coke blocks the craving for a Pepsi."

- ◆ Opiates were legal in America until 1914; members of the Women's Christian Temperance Union, who campaigned against alcohol, saw nothing wrong in drinking laudanum (tincture of opium).

- ◆ Nicotine, which is legal, is as addictive as heroin and cocaine, which are illegal; tobacco use contributes to more than 400,000 deaths in the United States every

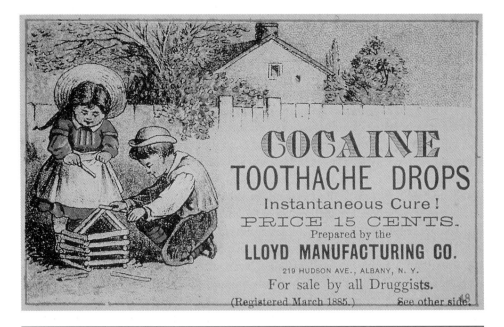

Before its sale was banned in the 1920s, cocaine was widely touted as a cure for everything from toothaches to timidity. The drug found its way into teas, tonics, throat lozenges, and even soft drinks (including, briefly, Coca-Cola). However, as cocaine use became associated with criminality and as concerns about abuse grew, public opinion turned against it.

year, about 20 times the number of deaths from all other forms of drug use combined (McGinnis & Foege, 1993).

◆Some people think of illicit drugs as being "unnatural," but mescaline, psilocybin, and cocaine, which are illegal, are made from natural products (the peyote cactus, a species of mushroom, and the coca leaf), just as wine and whiskey are.

The line between legal and illegal drugs is therefore an arbitrary one, drawn for social, economic, and cultural reasons. But once drawn, the line comes to be regarded as inevitable and obvious. And once a drug is declared illegal, many people assume that it is deadly, even though some illegal drugs are less dangerous than legal ones.

For example, when used occasionally and in moderation, marijuana is less harmful than cigarettes or alcohol—unless, of course, it is mixed with other, more hazardous drugs. Over time, smoking mild marijuana can cause lung damage, but the risk is not as severe as that of smoking tobacco (Wu et al., 1988). It's true that much of the marijuana now available on the street has far greater concentrations of THC than it did a generation ago, but advocates point out that users have adjusted to this change by smoking less of the drug—just as a person might choose to drink one potent martini instead of two less potent vodka tonics (Danish, 1994).

In their book *Marihuana, the Forbidden Medicine*, Lester Grinspoon and James Bakalar (1993) reviewed the many studies done over the past decades suggesting that marijuana may have medical benefits: It reduces the nausea and vomiting that often accompany chemotherapy treatment for cancer and AIDS; it reduces the physical tremors, loss of appetite, and other symptoms caused by multiple sclerosis; it helps reduce the frequency of seizures in some epileptic patients; and it alleviates the retinal swelling caused by glaucoma. Critics reply that most of these claims have not been validated to their satisfaction, but apparently the medical benefits of marijuana are known to many physicians. In a survey of 1,035 cancer specialists, half said that they would prescribe marijuana if it were legal, and 44 percent had already recommended its illegal use to their patients (Doblin & Kleiman, 1991).

In 1990, an advisory panel of scientists for the state of California recommended legalizing the cultivation of marijuana for personal use, after concluding that the drug causes less individual and social damage than alcohol and cigarettes; but the state attorney general's office refused to print their recommendations. And when former Surgeon General Joycelyn Elders suggested, in late 1993, that perhaps it would be worth studying the possibility of legalizing the drugs that many addicts commit theft or murder to get, her suggestion was met with waves of outrage.

Obviously, then, there are many emotional issues surrounding drugs and drug policies. Some people are committed to the eradication of all illegal drugs; some wish to legalize narcotics for medical use and marijuana for recreational use but also wish to ban tobacco; some think that all drugs should be decriminalized; and some think that all drugs should be decriminalized but that people should avoid them anyway on moral, religious, or medical grounds. Andrew Weil, a physician who has been a vocal critic of the war on drugs, nevertheless strongly encourages people "to satisfy their [psychological] needs without using drugs at all" (Goldstein, 1980). To formulate your own opinions on these issues, consider what psychologists have learned about why some people are able to use drugs moderately, while others become addicted.

The Biological Perspective

The biological perspective has contributed to our understanding of the physiology of drug effects and the possible biological contributions to addiction. Psychoactive drugs work primarily by acting on brain neurotransmitters, the substances that enable messages to pass from one nerve cell to another. Some cause more or fewer neurotransmitter molecules to be released at a synapse. Others prevent the reabsorption ("reuptake") of a neurotransmitter after its release. Still others block the effects of a neurotransmitter on a receiving nerve cell. For example, cocaine increases the amount of norepinephrine and dopamine in the brain by blocking the reabsorption of these substances. The result is overstimulation of certain brain circuits and a brief euphoric "high." Then, when the drug wears off, a depletion of dopamine may cause the user to "crash" and become sleepy and depressed.

The use of some psychoactive drugs, such as heroin and tranquilizers, can lead to **tolerance:** As time goes by, more and more of the drug is needed to get the same effect. When habitual heavy users stop taking a drug (whether it causes tolerance or not), they may suffer **withdrawal symptoms,** such as nausea, abdominal cramps, muscle spasms, depression, and sleep problems, depending on the drug. Tolerance and withdrawal are often assumed to be purely physiological matters, but as we will see, learning also plays a role.

Biological views of addiction are based on the *disease model,* which holds that addiction is a biochemical process. This model is most often invoked to explain alcoholism. Before the disease model came into prominence, many people believed that alcoholism was a sin, caused by lack of willpower and moral judgment. But in 1960, in a book called *The Disease Concept of Alcoholism,* E. M. Jellinek argued that alcoholism is a medical disorder, caused by a biological vulnerability that is not the person's fault. This theory transformed the public's view of alcoholism.

Because having biological relatives who are alcoholic contributes to a person's risk of becoming alcoholic, proponents of the disease model believe that alcoholism involves an inherited predisposition. Researchers in the biological perspective are trying to identify the key genes or biological anomalies that might be involved in alcoholism, or at least in some kinds of alcoholism (Blum, 1991; Kendler et al., 1992; Polich, Pollock, & Bloom, 1994). A more severe kind of alcoholism, for example, is implicated in antisocial behavior, impulsivity, violent criminality, and other mental illness (Bohman et al., 1987; McGue, Pickens, & Svikis, 1992). Lowered activity of the enzyme MAOB (monoamine oxidase-B) in the platelets and other tissues of these alcoholics, as compared with nonalcoholics, is the most replicated biological finding in genetic research in alcoholism. It is not a direct cause of addiction but may reflect an underlying physiological problem leading to severe alcoholism and other psychiatric problems (Devor et al., 1994).

---

tolerance The increasing resistance to a drug's effects with continued use; as tolerance develops, larger doses are required to produce effects once brought on by smaller ones.

withdrawal symptoms Physical and psychological symptoms that occur when someone who is addicted to a drug stops taking it.

As with so many other disorders, however, one study's positive results are often contradicted by another study's negative ones. Several studies have found that a specific gene, which affects the function of key dopamine receptors on brain cells, is more likely to be present in the DNA of alcoholics than in that of nonalcoholics (Noble et al., 1991). Dopamine helps regulate pleasure-seeking actions, so researchers suspect that this gene might help explain why alcoholics drink. However, other studies, using different measurements, have found no difference between alcoholics and controls in the presence of this gene (Bolos et al., 1990; Gelernter et al., 1991). Similarly, some researchers, comparing alcoholism rates among identical and fraternal twins, conclude that genetic factors play a part in alcoholism in women (Kendler et al., 1992), but other studies find evidence of genetic factors only in men (McGue, Pickens, & Svikis, 1992).

At present, then, we cannot conclude that a single gene causes alcoholism in any direct way. It is possible that several genes in combination may affect the response to alcohol, the compulsive use of alcohol (or other mood-altering drugs), or the progression of alcohol-related diseases such as cirrhosis of the liver. It is possible that genes contribute to temperament or to personality traits that predispose some people to become alcoholics. And it is possible that genes affect how the liver metabolizes alcohol. But it also possible that genes have little to do with alcoholism, and that alcoholism results, basically, from alcohol! Heavy drinking alters brain function, reduces the level of painkilling endorphins, produces nerve damage, shrinks the cerebral cortex, and wrecks the liver. In the view of some researchers, these changes then create biological dependence, an inability to metabolize alcohol, and psychological problems.

Although they disagree about the causes of alcoholism and other addictions, researchers in the biological tradition do agree that these are medical problems. Thus they seek medical solutions, such as the development of a nonaddictive drug that will break an addict's craving. One research team has developed an artificial enzyme that seeks out and binds to the cocaine molecule, making it inert; the enzyme would presumably destroy most cocaine in the bloodstream before it reaches the brain (Landry et al., 1993). But psychologists in other perspectives think that this effort is probably doomed because addiction is primarily a psychological matter. They believe that there is no point in trying to find a perfect drug that has no addictive qualities; instead, they look at the human qualities that make a drug seem perfect.

The Learning Perspective

People often talk as if the effects of drugs were automatic, the inevitable result of the drug's chemistry ("I couldn't help what I said; the booze made me do it"). But reactions to a psychoactive drug involve more than the drug's chemical properties. When people take an opiate such as heroin or morphine recreationally, for example, they usually get high. Yet when people take opiates in order to relieve chronic and incapacitating pain, the narcotics do *not* make them high or addicted; they just remove the pain (Portenoy, 1994). In a study of 100 hospital patients who had been given strong doses of narcotics, 99 had no withdrawal symptoms upon leaving the hospital; they left the pain behind them, along with the drug (Zinberg, 1974). And in a study of 10,000 burn patients who received narcotics as part of their hospital care, *not one* became an addict (Perry & Heidrich, 1982). Thus the biochemistry of drugs cannot be the whole story.

To researchers in the learning perspective, the disease model of addiction, popular though it is, has other flaws as well. Television "addicts" compulsively watch TV the way that drug addicts compulsively use drugs—to relieve loneliness, sadness, or anger (Jacobvitz, 1990); what "disease" are they catching? "Exercise addicts" have a compulsion to exercise that goes far beyond a desire to be healthy, and they even suffer withdrawal symptoms when prevented from exercising (Chan & Grossman, 1988). Conversely, not all drug addicts go through physiological withdrawal symptoms when they stop taking the drug. On the contrary, many people who are addicted to alcohol, cigarettes, tranquilizers, or painkillers are able to stop taking these drugs, without help and with no withdrawal symptoms (Lee & Hart, 1985; Prochaska, Norcross, & DiClemente, 1994). If addiction were exclusively a physiological process, how could this be?

Trying any drug for the first time is often a neutral or unpleasant experience, but reactions change once a person has become familiar with the drug's effects. This fact suggests that people have to learn what a drug is like and how to respond to it. In his controversial book *Heavy Drinking: The Myth of Alcoholism as a Disease,* Herbert Fingarette (1988) argued that alcoholism is a result of physical, personal, and social factors. It is neither a sin nor a disease but "a central activity of the individual's way of life." People learn how to drink, how to react to drink, and when to drink; heavy or problem drinkers learn that alcohol helps them escape or avoid their problems. When people no longer need to drink or use other drugs as the "central activity" of their lives, most of them are able to stop.

Researchers in the learning perspective have also applied principles of classical conditioning to understanding certain aspects of drug addiction (Poulos & Cappell, 1991; Siegel, 1990; Siegel & Sdao-Jarvie, 1986). In their view, a drug's effect is the unconditioned stimulus for a *compensatory* bodily response, a response that opposes the drug's effect in order to restore a normal biological state. For example, when morphine causes numbness to pain, the body attempts to compensate by becoming increasingly sensitive to pain. Environmental cues that are paired with the drug's effect, such as needles or a particular location, may then become conditioned stimuli for this compensatory response:

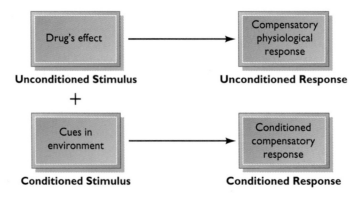

This analysis can explain why tolerance to drugs often develops in people who have episodes of acute pain (in contrast to those who have chronic pain, which is mediated by different neurological pathways in the brain). In the presence of environmental cues associated with drug taking, a compensatory response occurs, so more of the drug is needed to produce the usual effects. On the other hand, a drug dose that would ordinarily be safe, given an addict's tolerance level, may be lethal when the drug is used in novel circumstances, because the usual conditioned compensatory response doesn't occur. The result may be sudden and seemingly inexplicable death.

Experiments with both animals and human beings, using a wide variety of drugs, support this theory. In one study, male college students drank large amounts of beer at the same place on each of four consecutive days. On the fifth day, some of the students downed their beers at a new place. Students who remained at the original location scored higher on tests of intellectual and perceptual–motor skills, apparently because their bodies had learned to moderate the effects of alcohol in the presence of familiar cues (Lightfoot, 1980). In another study, researchers gave rats a strong dose of heroin. Some of the rats were already experienced with the drug. In inexperienced rats, the injection was almost always fatal, but in experienced ones, the outcome depended on the setting: Two-thirds of the rats that were injected while in a strange environment died, as compared with only a third of those who remained in a familiar place (Siegel et al., 1982).

The importance of environmental cues may help explain why in-hospital drug-treatment programs often fail: When people return to the neighborhoods where they used to take drugs, conditioned stimuli elicit the usual compensatory responses. In the absence of the drug, such responses are now experienced as a return of unpleasant withdrawal symptoms, and a craving for the drug again develops (Siegel, 1990). The implication is that people who want to overcome drug dependence either must relocate to a new environment or must receive treatment that systematically exposes them to familiar features of their usual environment until their conditioned physiological responses to these cues are extinguished.

Learning theories of drug abuse also focus on the *reasons* that people drink. For example, many people drink in order to regulate their emotions. Some drink to reduce negative feelings when they are anxious, depressed, or tense ("coping" drinkers); others to increase positive feelings when they are tired, bored, or stressed ("enhancement" drinkers) (Cooper et al., 1995). Some drink for no reason other than to be sociable or to conform to the group they are with. In this view, drinking has several *psychologically distinct* functions. To understand why some people abuse alcohol, therefore, you would need to know what function drinking serves for them. Coping drinkers have significantly more drinking problems than do enhancement drinkers.

As you can imagine, the differences between the disease and learning models of addictions are profound, and so are their practical consequences. In the disease model, an addict is always an addict; the only cure is abstinence or a substitute drug such as methadone. In the learning model, the person has learned to become an addict, perhaps as a way of avoiding problems or pain; the cure is to change the person's behavioral patterns and the environment that rewards drug use. Stanton Peele and his associates (1991) have contrasted some of the underlying assumptions of the biological and learning models of addiction:

Disease Model	Learning Model
Addiction is genetic, biological.	Addiction is a way of coping.
A person is always an addict.	A person can grow beyond the need for alcohol or other drugs.
An addict must abstain from the drug forever.	Most problem drinkers can learn to drink in moderation.
A person is either addicted or not.	The degree of addiction will vary, depending on the situation.
Therapy focuses on the addiction.	Therapy focuses on a person's problems and environment.
An addict needs the same treatment and group support forever.	Treatment or group support lasts only as long as the person abuses the drug.
A person must accept his or her identity as an addict.	A person focuses on problems, not on permanent labels.

The differences between the disease and the learning models of addiction become apparent in the heated debate over controlled drinking: whether it is possible for former alcoholics to drink moderately without showing signs of dependence and intoxication and without causing harm to themselves or others. To those who hold the disease model, there is no such thing as a "former" alcoholic and controlled drinking is impossible; once an addict has even a single drink, he or she cannot stop. Daniel Flavin, medical and scientific director of the National Council on Alcoholism and Drug Dependence, observes that "In general, it's not a good idea under any circumstances to encourage an alcoholic to moderate [his or her drinking], or the heavy drinker whose natural history would be to go on to alcoholism. How do you tease those people out?" (quoted in Foderaro, 1995). He and others believe that problem drinkers who learn to cut back to social-drinking levels were never true alcoholics in the first place.

To those who hold a learning model, however, controlled drinking is possible; once a person no longer needs to become drunk, he or she can learn to drink socially and in moderation. Across North America, alternatives to the total-abstinence program of Alcoholics Anonymous have emerged, such as Moderation Management and DrinkWise. As Frederick Rotgers, director of research at the Center of Alcohol Studies at Rutgers University, says, "Unfortunately, in this country, for many, many years even to talk about people with a drinking problem simply cutting down has been anathema . . . it is heresy. Among pragmatic people who are reading the scientific literature, it's no longer heresy" (quoted in Foderaro, 1995).

How can we assess these two positions critically? The first step is to avoid either–or thinking. Because alcoholism and problem drinking occur for many and varied reasons, neither model offers the only solution. Many alcoholics, perhaps most, simply cannot learn to drink moderately, especially if they have had drinking problems for many years (Vaillant, 1995). On the other hand, although Alcoholics Anonymous (AA) has unquestionably saved many lives, it doesn't work for everyone. According to its own surveys, one-third to one-half of those who join AA drop out, and some of these dropouts benefit from programs that teach moderate drinking and how to keep drinking under control (Peele & Brodsky, 1991; Rosenberg, 1993).

In a major review of the factors that predict whether an addict or problem drinker will be able to learn to control excessive drinking, Harold Rosenberg (1993) found that the most important predictors were these: previous severity of dependence on the drug; social stability (not having a criminal record, having a stable work history, being married); and beliefs about the necessity of abstinence. Alcoholics who believe that one drink will set them off—those who accept the alcoholics' creed, "first drink, then drunk"—are in fact more likely to behave that way, as compared with those who believe that controlled drinking is possible. Ironically, then, the course that alcoholism takes may reflect, in part, a person's belief in the disease model or the learning model. As we will see next, beliefs and expectations can influence how people respond to drugs of any kind.

The Cognitive Perspective

Researchers in the cognitive perspective have found that responses to psychoactive drugs depend considerably on your *mental set:* that is, your expectations about the drug's effects, your reasons for taking it, and whether you want to justify some behavior by being "under the influence." Some people drink to become more sociable, friendly, or seductive; others drink in order to have an excuse for verbal abusiveness or physical violence. Opiate addicts use drugs to escape from the real world; people living with chronic pain use the same drugs in order to function in the real world.

According to the cognitive perspective, then, people's reactions to a drug will vary, depending on how they have learned to interpret its effects. Most Americans start their day with a cup of coffee because it increases alertness. But when coffee was first introduced in Europe in the sixteenth century, there were protests against it. Women said it suppressed their husbands' sexual performance and made men inconsiderate, and maybe it did! In the nineteenth century, Americans regarded marijuana as a mild sedative with no mind-altering properties. They didn't expect it to give them a high, and it didn't; it merely put them to sleep (Weil, 1972/1986).

Thinking even affects responses to drinking. During the 1980s, several studies identified a "think–drink" effect by comparing people who were actually drinking liquor (vodka and tonic) with those who *thought* they were drinking liquor but were actually getting only tonic and lime juice. (Vodka has a subtle taste, and most people cannot tell the real and the phony drinks apart.) Men behaved more belligerently when they thought they were drinking vodka than when they thought they were drinking plain tonic water, regardless of the actual content of the drinks. Both sexes reported feeling sexually aroused when they thought they were drinking vodka, whether they actually got vodka or not (Abrams & Wilson, 1983; Marlatt & Rohsenow, 1980). Other research finds that people's expectations about alcohol, which develop in childhood, affect when and how much they drink, and this is true of both social drinkers and alcoholics (Goldman et al., 1991). Children and adolescents have acquired expectations about alcohol long before they ever try it, so their expectations about alcohol's effects aren't simply derived from their own physical reactions (Goldman et al., 1991; Miller, Smith, & Goldman, 1990). Rather, their expectations come from their observations of whether and how their parents and other adults use alcohol, how these adults react to it, whether they see drinking being rewarded, and so forth.

Because so many crimes of violence are committed when the participants have been drinking and because so many marital quarrels accompany drinking, alcohol is often assumed to "release" anger and aggression. A meta-analysis of experimental studies found that alcohol does in fact increase the likelihood of aggressive behavior, but not on its own: People must also be aware that they are consuming liquor (Bushman, 1993). According to cognitive scientists, therefore, the real source of aggression is not in the alcohol but in the mind of the drinker. About half of all men arrested for assaulting their wives claim to have been drinking at the time. Yet research finds that most of these men do not have enough alcohol in their bloodstream to qualify as legally intoxicated, and most have not been drinking immediately prior to being violent (Gelles & Straus, 1988). This finding suggests that alcohol did not make the men violent, but rather that *their use of alcohol provided an excuse to behave violently.* Indeed, the link between alcohol and aggression disappears when people believe they will be held responsible for their actions while drunk (Critchlow, 1983).

None of this means that alcohol and other drugs are merely placebos; drugs do have physiological effects, many of them quite powerful. Smoking cigarettes is seriously hazardous to your health no matter how cool you think they are or what you expect them to do for you. However, the cognitive perspective shows that people's expectations and beliefs play a role in all psychological drug reactions, including those to coffee and cigarettes. It reminds us that between a drug's physical effects and its behavioral consequences are mental processes: expectations of what the drug will feel like, beliefs about the excuses it will provide, memories of the highs or lows it can generate, and the purposes for taking the drug in the first place. These expectations and beliefs, in turn, are shaped by the culture in which a person lives.

The Sociocultural Perspective

Sociocultural researchers have identified the many external conditions in a person's situation, environment, and culture that affect drug use and abuse. Peer pressure, for example, is one reason for drug use; if all your friends smoke, you are more likely to smoke, too. Another important influence on a person's response to a drug is the *envi-*

ronmental setting. Setting is the reason that a person can have one glass of wine at home alone and feel sleepy but have three glasses of wine at a party and feel full of pep. It is the reason that a person might feel happy drinking with good friends but fearful and nervous drinking with strangers. In one study of reactions to alcohol, researchers found that most of the drinkers became depressed, angry, confused, and unfriendly. Then it dawned on them that anyone might become depressed, angry, confused, and unfriendly if asked to drink bourbon at 9:00 A.M. in a bleak hospital room, which was the setting for the experiment (Warren & Raynes, 1972).

In longitudinal research that followed three groups of men for more than 40 years, George Vaillant and his colleagues found, to their surprise, that many people went through a period of heavy drinking—even serious problem drinking—but eventually healed themselves. For them, heavy drinking was not a progressive downward spiral to skid row. They became moderate, social drinkers as their environments changed (Vaillant, 1983, 1995). (Vaillant doesn't think true alcoholics can do this, however.) Perhaps you know people who drank heavily in school but stopped when they got a job, or people who drank heavily in one social circle but not when they moved to a new city and made new friends. New environments can even break heroin addiction. During the war in Vietnam, nearly 30 percent of the soldiers were taking heroin in doses far stronger than those available on the streets of American cities, and experts predicted a drug-withdrawal disaster among the returning veterans. It never materialized. More than 90 percent of the men simply gave the drug up, without withdrawal pain, when they came home to new circumstances (Robins, Davis, & Goodwin, 1974).

Researchers in the sociocultural perspective account for these results, and for patterns and rates of alcoholism and other forms of drug dependence, by looking at factors in culture and society. Cultural practices, such as family drinking or saloon drinking, and social policies, such as those regarding moderation or abstinence, affect addiction rates dramatically. In colonial America, the average person drank two to three times the amount of liquor that is consumed today, yet alcoholism was not the serious social problem it is now. Drinking was a universally accepted social activity. Families drank and ate together. Alcohol was believed to produce pleasant feelings and relaxation. Indeed, the Puritan minister Cotton Mather called liquor "the good creature of God." If a person committed a crime or became violent while drunk, the colonials did not conclude that liquor was to blame. Rather, they believed that it was the person's own tendencies that led to drunkenness *and* crime (Critchlow, 1986). But between 1790 and 1830, when the American frontier was expanding, drinking came to symbolize masculine independence, toughness, and violence. The saloon became the place for drinking away from home, and alcoholism rates shot up. The temperance movement, which followed, argued that drinking inevitably led to drunkenness, and drunkenness to crime. The solution it proposed, and implemented, was national abstinence during the Prohibition years (1920–1933).

Study after study has found that alcoholism is much more likely to occur in societies that forbid children to drink but condone drunkenness in adults (as in Ireland) than in societies that teach children how to drink responsibly but disapprove of adult drunkenness (as in Italy, France, and Greece) (Fingarette, 1988). An Italian friend of ours, who doesn't like the taste of wine, refused wine at family gatherings when he was growing up. His father was terribly worried by this refusal; he feared that if his son did not learn to drink socially, the boy would eventually become a drunk. As research shows, the father's concern was justified in general, although not for his son in particular. In cultures with low rates of alcoholism, adults demonstrate correct drinking habits to their children, gradually introducing them to alcohol in safe family settings. These lessons are maintained by adult customs. Alcohol is not used as a rite of passage into adulthood, nor is it associated with masculinity and power (Peele, 1989). Drinking is considered neither a virtue nor a sin. Drunkenness is not considered charming, comical, or manly; it's considered stupid and obnoxious.*

As such cultural patterns might predict, policies of total abstinence tend to *increase* rates of alcoholism rather than to reduce them. When people don't learn how to drink moderately, they are more likely to drink irresponsibly and in binges (unless they are committed to a religion that forbids all drugs). In the United States, Prohibition actually created higher rates of alcoholism. Sociologist Joan McCord (1989) found that men who were teenagers at the time of Prohibition were far and away more likely to become serious problem drinkers in adulthood than were older men, who had learned how to drink alcohol before it became illegal. Similarly, the Inuit of British Columbia were forbidden alcohol until 1951; after that, they were permitted to drink only in licensed bars. As a result, many Inuit would drink as much as they could while in a bar. It was a policy virtually guaranteed to create drunkenness.

The sociocultural perspective draws our attention to the importance of understanding the context in which drug use occurs: the role of the immediate environment and peer groups, public policy and attitudes, and cultural values and customs.

The Psychodynamic Perspective

Psychologists in the psychodynamic perspective try to identify the internal, unconscious reasons that some people come to abuse alcohol or other drugs—for example, to compensate for parental rejection, to try to escape feelings of anguish or loss, or to hide other psychological problems such as the need for intimacy (Liebeskind, 1991). In the study of adolescents mentioned earlier, those who were maladjusted and who had personal problems were the ones most likely to abuse drugs (Shedler & Block, 1990). The best-adjusted students were able to use drugs in moderation possibly *because* they were well adjusted.

Psychodynamic psychologists also seek other unconscious reasons a person may have for escaping into drugs. "We all have, deep inside, feelings of sexuality, aggression, desperation, terror, anxiety, guilt, frustration, and, at times, a sense of helplessness and hopelessness," writes analyst Mitchell May (1991). Addicts try to stave off awareness of these feelings by retreating into drugs. Drugs have other psychological effects, too, that

---

*European students often tell us how puzzled they are by the drinking habits of their American classmates. One young man from Switzerland, where drinking wine with meals is considered normal and desirable, said, "But students here drink to get *drunk!* What is the pleasure in that?"

have short-term benefits. As psychiatrist Arthur Liebeskind (1991) observes, "Drugs tone down rage, make the individual feel less hungry, less lustful, less afraid, less disorganized, less psychotic. Drugs also facilitate role playing and deception, and take the edge off any vestige of conscience that one hurt someone else." Perhaps most of all, he adds, drugs compensate for low self-esteem: "With ten bucks for crack, one can feel like a million bucks, on top of the world, the greatest talker, lover, wheeler and dealer, intellect, or friend imaginable." Of course, the high self-esteem lasts only as long as the chemical high.

The strongest contribution of the psychodynamic perspective to the understanding of drug abuse may lie in its description of people who already have become addicted. Many of the terms and concepts of psychodynamic psychologists, particularly those having to do with defense mechanisms, are commonly applied in the treatment of addicts. For example, in therapy, most alcoholics and addicts rely on the defense mechanisms of *denial* ("I'm not an addict"; "I can stop any time"); *projection* of blame ("I drink because my family is out to get me"; "It's their fault for not treating me right"); and *rationalization* ("I need to drink to relieve stress"). These defenses characterize addicts of all kinds and prevent them from recognizing that their abuse is harmful to themselves and to those around them.

In summary, the five psychological perspectives show that drug abuse and addiction reflect an interaction of physiology *and* psychology, person *and* culture. They occur when an individual who is vulnerable to abusing drugs—because of psychological pain, troubling experiences, and perhaps a genetic susceptibility—finds a culture and environment that support drug abuse, and when the abuse is positively reinforced.

> ◆The biological perspective shows that drug abuse is more likely to occur when a drug is taken in its most potent and distilled form (e.g., crack cocaine), and when a person has a biological vulnerability to certain drugs.

> ◆The learning perspective shows that drug abuse is more likely to occur when people learn (or when laws or customs encourage them) to take a drug in binges rather than in moderation, and when they learn that drugs can be used to justify behavior that would not otherwise be socially tolerated.

> ◆The cognitive perspective shows that addiction is more likely to occur among people who believe that the drug is stronger than they are—that is, who believe that they are addicted and will always be addicted—and who expect that drugs will solve their problems or excuse their actions.

> ◆The sociocultural perspective shows that drug abuse is more likely to occur when the drug becomes a permanent part of a person's life instead of an occasional experience; when "everyone" in one's peer group drinks heavily or uses other drugs; and when social and cultural customs encourage binges or abstinence rather than moderation.

> ◆The psychodynamic perspective shows that drug abuse is more likely to occur when people come to rely on a drug as a way of coping with problems, relieving pain, or avoiding conflict; and when it provides a sense of power, control, and self-esteem that the individual lacks without it.

By knowing what each psychological perspective contributes to the understanding of drug use and abuse, people can think more critically about their own drug use and can evaluate social policies about drugs. The evidence suggests that for numerous individual reasons, some small percentage of people will come to abuse any drug, legal or illegal, just as they might abuse exercise, chocolate, or television watching; the reason for their addiction lies in them, not in the drug or in the activity. Further, given the wide prevalence of moderate drug use, social policies designed to prohibit a popular drug, promote complete abstinence, or eradicate addiction entirely seem destined to fail.

Moreover, policies that prohibit the medicinal use of marijuana and narcotics— even for patients who are undergoing cancer treatment, suffering from debilitating diseases, or living with constant, excruciating pain—seem irrational and harsh. For this reason, a panel of researchers commissioned by the Agency for Health Care Policy and Research, after reviewing more than 9,600 studies, has issued new federal guidelines for pain management. Noting that cancer pain is "frequently undertreated in both adults and children" because doctors unrealistically fear that patients will become addicted, the panel recommends the use of morphine and other opiates when other painkillers fail (Jacox, Carr, & Payne, 1994).

The findings from the five perspectives suggest that instead of asking how we can eradicate all drug use, we would do better to ask these questions: How can we create mental sets and environmental settings that permit the harmless recreational use of some drugs and the medicinal use of others? How can we discourage the sets, settings, and cultural attitudes that foster drug abuse and its deadly consequences?

What Do You Know?

If you are not yet addicted to studying, try these questions:

1. Cognitive studies suggest that alcohol (a) releases repressed anger, (b) stimulates aggressive behavior, (c) makes most men violent, (d) may provide an excuse for violent behavior.
2. Which cultural practice is associated with *low* rates of alcoholism? (a) drinking in family or group settings, (b) infrequent but binge drinking, (c) drinking as a rite of passage, (d) regarding alcohol as a sinful drink
3. What seems to be the most reasonable conclusion about the role of genes in alcoholism? (a) Without a key gene, a person cannot become alcoholic; (b) the presence of a key gene or genes will almost always cause a person to become alcoholic; (c) genes may work in combination to increase a person's vulnerability to some kinds of alcoholism.
4. For a century, people have been searching for a magic drug that can be used recreationally but is not addictive. Heroin, cocaine, barbiturates, methadone, and tranquilizers were all, at first, thought to be nonaddictive. But in each case, some people became addicted and abuse of the drug became a social problem. Based on what you've read, what are some possible reasons for the failure to find a mood-altering but nonaddictive drug?

ANSWERS:

1. d   2. a   3. c   4. Perhaps some people are biologically vulnerable to addiction to any mind-altering drug. Perhaps the psychological need for addiction exists in the individual and not in the chemical properties of the drug. Perhaps the chemistry of the drug is less important than the cultural practices that encourage drug abuse among some groups. If so, there will never be a recreational drug with no addictive properties.

REFLECTIONS ON PSYCHOLOGY

As we have seen in the preceding chapters and in our extended discussion of drugs, no single perspective in psychology has a monopoly on insights into human behavior. This means that in trying to solve a personal problem, understand the puzzling behavior of a friend, or choose the wisest position on a matter of social policy, we would do well to expand our vistas—to try to see the whole elephant from different angles:

◆ **BIOLOGICAL FACTORS.** If you are having a problem, you might start with questions such as these: What is going on in your body? Do you have a physical condition that might be affecting your behavior? Do you have a temperamental tendency to be easily aroused or to be calm? Are drugs altering your ability to make decisions or behave as you would like? Might an irregular schedule be impairing your efficiency?

◆ **LEARNING FACTORS.** As you further analyze the situation, you would want to ask, What are the contingencies and consequences governing your behavior and that of others? What rewards are maintaining your behavior? Of the many messages being aimed at you by television, books, parents, and teachers, which have the greatest influence? Who are the people you most admire and wish to emulate?

◆ **COGNITIVE FACTORS.** To solve your problem, you would need to ask yourself how you are framing the situation you are in. Are your explanations of what is causing the problem reasonable? Have you tested them? Are you wallowing in negative thoughts? Do you attribute your successes to luck but take all the blame for your failures—or vice versa? Do you assume the worst about others? Do you make external attributions or internal ones? Are you responding to other people's behavior in a mindless way?

◆ **SOCIOCULTURAL FACTORS.** Everyone conforms, to one extent or another, to the expectations and demands of others. Who are the people who affect your attitudes and behavior? Do your friends and relatives support or hinder you in achieving your goals? Which situations make you feel ambitious, confident, or content, and which ones make you feel helpless, pessimistic, or angry? Would you be different if the situation changed? How do your ethnicity and nationality affect your beliefs, values, roles, and behavior? What gender roles do they specify for you in close relationships?

◆**PSYCHODYNAMIC FACTORS.** If you find that you are repeating self-defeating patterns, expectations, and emotional reactions that you acquired in childhood, you might want to consider unconscious motivations. Do other people "push your buttons" for reasons you cannot explain? Are you displacing feelings about your parents onto your friends or intimates? Are you carrying around "unfinished business" from childhood losses and hurts?

It may seem daunting to keep all these factors in mind. But once you get into the habit of seeing a situation from many points of view, relying on any one approach will feel as if you are wearing blinders. Cultivating the ability to see the world and your own part in it from different perspectives will also make you wary of anyone who offers single-answer solutions. And it will inoculate you against pop-psych ideas that are unsupported by evidence.

As we noted at the beginning of this book, psychobabble is pervasive in our society, and sometimes the worst culprits are psychologists and psychotherapists (Dawes, 1994; Yapko, 1994). Because clinical judgment is a subjective process, therapists who testify in criminal trials, custody battles, and hearings on child abuse often contradict one another (Faust & Ziskin, 1988). In deciding whether to accept or reject the judgment of any "expert," therefore, critical thinkers begin by examining the evidence for a person's assertions. We hope you will never be like a juror who voted to convict a young woman of sexually abusing children at the North Carolina Little Rascals Day Care Center. "There was no really good evidence," the juror said. "It was the therapists' notes that convinced me she was guilty" (*Frontline*, July 22, 1993; quoted in Dawes, 1994). When assertions are based only on clinical judgment, as we saw in the evaluation of the psychodynamic perspective, it is wise to seek other, confirming information.

Researchers, too, can fall victim to psychobabble. Just as pop psychology can lead people to accept popular ideas that lack evidence, so it can lead people to reject evidence that contradicts popular ideas. For example, several years ago, the state of California created a Task Force on the Social Importance of Self-esteem, a committee that included many social scientists. The task force's guiding assumption was that low self-esteem is a major cause of violence, low school achievement, teenage pregnancy, child abuse, welfare dependency, drug abuse, and many other ills. If self-esteem could be raised, they reasoned, these problems would decline (Smelser, Vasconcellos, & Mecca, 1989).

Unfortunately, after reviewing virtually every study done on the relationship of self-esteem to anything—and there are thousands of them—the task force found absolutely no support for any of what it called its "intuitively correct" ideas! Did the committee then conclude that its intuitions were wrong, and that public money should be spent on programs that actually do improve children's school performance or reduce violence? Not at all: "Policy interventions to reduce child abuse [and other problems] that involve increasing self-esteem," the report asserts, "should be encouraged and should include interventions at the individual, family, group, community, and societal levels." Robyn Dawes (1994) argues that the task force did perform a valuable public service, but not the one it intended. It demonstrated, he said, that "the Holy Grail of pop psychology"—the belief that high self-esteem is the ticket to happiness, and low self-esteem is the cause of social problems—"is nothing more than a mirage."

"The uncertainty of knowledge and its application in the mental health area," writes Dawes (1994), "means that *responsible professionals should practice with a cautious, open, and questioning attitude.*" In our view, this is wise advice for everyone—for researchers in each of the psychological perspectives, as well as for consumers of psychological information and services. "A cautious, open, and questioning attitude" is, of course, the hallmark of critical thinking. Psychobabble, in contrast, asks us to accept mindlessly its offer of quick interpretations, instant cures, and simple answers.

Serious psychology, real psychology, offers a challenge that is more difficult yet ultimately more gratifying than pop psychology; for it recognizes that daily hassles, difficult decisions, conflicts, and occasional tragedies are what force us to grow, and to grow up. The study of psychology will never eliminate emotional crises, the pain of loss, or anger at injustice; but it can illuminate some pathways out of the blind alleys and dark corners that, as human beings, we all will encounter on the journey of life. As we have seen throughout this book, empirical findings from each of the perspectives in psychology have made enormous contributions to understanding human behavior, to analyzing social problems, and to alleviating emotional distress. At its superficial worst, psychology narrows our vision, offering quick fixes and solutions. At its complex best, psychology expands our vision, contributing to a rich understanding of the human spirit and its capacity for self-delusion and self-awareness, cowardice and compassion, hatred and love.

Drawing by Lorenz; © 1989 The New Yorker Magazine, Inc.

"I still don't have all the answers,
but I'm beginning to ask the right questions."

✦　✦　✦

Summary

1. Many topics in psychology, such as the universal appeal of music and the rarer phenomenon of musical genius, can be best understood by integrating findings across several perspectives, although most researchers themselves work within one perspective on the particular topic of interest to them.

2. Understanding the use and misuse of *psychoactive drugs* requires a multiperspective approach. Most psychoactive drugs can be classified as *stimulants, depressants, opiates,* or *psychedelics,* depending on their effects on the central nervous system and their impact on behavior and mood; marijuana falls outside these categories.

3. Concern over the terrible problems caused by the misuse of drugs has made dispassionate discussion and evaluation of drug-related issues difficult. Extremists who are pro- or anti-drug often fail to distinguish the effects of moderate use from those of excessive use; they wrongly assume that legal drugs are relatively harmless and that all illegal drugs are equally dangerous or equally beneficial. In reality, with most psychoactive drugs, there is a big difference between light or moderate use and heavy or excessive use. The social labeling of some drugs as good and others as bad often has no medical or biological basis.

4. The biological perspective shows how drugs affect neurotransmitters in the brain. Biological views of addiction are based on the *disease model,* which holds that addiction is a biochemical process and that alcoholism involves inherited predispositions. At present, we cannot conclude that a single gene causes alcoholism in any direct way. Biological researchers are seeking medical solutions for addiction.

5. The learning perspective shows that the effects of a particular drug are not automatic; often, people have to learn what a drug is like and how to respond to it. Classical conditioning may help account for *tolerance* and *withdrawal:* a compensatory physiological response to the drug may become a conditioned response to environmental cues, so that more and more of the drug is needed to produce its usual effects. When the drug is used in novel circumstances, the usual compensatory response does not occur. In the learning view, the cure for drug addiction is to change the person's behavioral patterns and the environment that rewards drug use. The disease model and the learning model make many different predictions—for example, about whether controlled drinking by former alcoholics is possible.

6. Research in the cognitive perspective shows that responses to psychoactive drugs depend considerably on one's *mental set,* expectations, purposes, and beliefs, as well as how one has learned to interpret the drug's effects. The reason that some people are more likely to behave aggressively when they have been drinking lies not in the alcohol but in the mind of the drinker; the link between alcohol and aggression fades considerably when people believe they will be held responsible for their actions while drunk.

7. Sociocultural researchers have shown how a person's situation, environment, and culture can affect drug use and abuse, including peer pressure and *environmental setting.* New environments can break a pattern of addiction. Cultural practices

affect rates of alcoholism and other addictions: Cultures that have low rates of alcoholism are those in which children learn to drink moderately, adults drink in a family context with meals, and adult drunkenness is not considered manly or otherwise desirable. Alcoholism rates increase in cultures that foster binge drinking in bars, in which drinking is separated from meals, and in which drunkenness is approved. National policies of total abstinence tend to increase rates of alcoholism rather than reduce them.

8. Psychologists in the psychodynamic perspective try to identify the unconscious reasons that some people abuse alcohol or other drugs. The strongest contribution of psychodynamic approaches may be their description of the defense mechanisms used by addicts.

9. In sum, the five psychological perspectives show that drug abuse and addiction reflect an interaction of physiology and psychology, person and culture. Knowing what each psychological perspective contributes can help people think more critically about their own drug use and evaluate social policies about drugs.

10. In trying to solve personal problems, understand the puzzling behavior of a friend, or choose the wisest position on a matter of social policy, people do best when they consider evidence from all five perspectives in psychology. Developing the habit of approaching problems from different perspectives guards against the temptations of psychobabble and ultimately offers a more useful and satisfying vision of human behavior and the human spirit.

Key Terms

psychoactive drug *577*

stimulants *577*

depressants *578*

opiates *578*

psychedelics *578*

marijuana *578*

tolerance *582*

withdrawal symptoms *582*

disease model of addiction *582*

compensatory response *584*

learning model of addiction *586*

mental set *587*

"think–drink" effect *587*

environmental setting *589*

Glossary

accommodation   In Piaget's theory, the process of modifying existing cognitive structures in response to experience and new information.

acculturation   The process by which members of groups that are minorities in a given society come to identify with and feel part of the mainstream culture.

achievement motive   A learned motive to meet personal standards of success and excellence in a chosen area.

activation–synthesis theory   The theory that dreaming results from the cortical synthesis and interpretation of neural signals triggered by activity in the lower part of the brain.

adrenal hormones   Hormones produced by the adrenal glands that are involved in emotion and stress; they include cortisol, epinephrine, and norepinephrine.

agoraphobia   A set of phobias (irrational fears) involving the basic fear of being away from a safe place or person.

algorithm   A problem-solving strategy guaranteed to produce a solution even if the user does not know how it works.

alpha waves   Relatively large, slow brain waves characteristic of relaxed wakefulness.

amygdala   A brain structure involved in the arousal and regulation of emotion and the initial emotional response to sensory information.

anterograde amnesia   The inability to form lasting memories for new events and facts.

antidepressant drugs   A category of drugs that are used primarily in the treatment of mood disorders, especially depression and anxiety.

antipsychotic drugs   Major tranquilizers used primarily in the treatment of schizophrenia and other psychotic disorders.

antisocial personality disorder   A disorder characterized by antisocial behavior such as lying, stealing, manipulating others, and sometimes violence; a lack of social emotions (guilt, shame, and empathy); and impulsivity. (Sometimes called *psychopathy* or *sociopathy*.)

applied psychology   The study of psychological issues that have direct practical significance; also, the application of psychological findings.

archetypes   To Carl Jung, the universal, symbolic images that appear in myths, dreams, art, folklore, and other expressions of the collective unconscious.

assimilation   In Piaget's theory, the process of absorbing new information into existing cognitive structures.

attribution theory   The theory that people are motivated to explain their own and other people's behaviors by attributing causes of those behaviors either to a situation or to a disposition.

autonomic nervous system   The subdivision of the peripheral nervous system that regulates the internal organs and glands.

availability heuristic   The tendency to judge the probability of a type of event by how easy it is to think of examples or instances.

axon   A neuron's extending fiber that conducts impulses away from the cell body and transmits them to other neurons.

basic anxiety   To Karen Horney, the feeling of being isolated and helpless in a hostile world; it is the motivating emotion in social relations.

basic psychology The study of psychological issues in order to seek knowledge for its own sake rather than for its practical application.

behavioral genetics An interdisciplinary field of study concerned with the genetic bases of behavior and personality.

behaviorism An approach to psychology that emphasizes the study of observable behavior and the role of the environment as a determinant of behavior.

behavior modification The application of conditioning techniques to teach new responses or to reduce or eliminate maladaptive or problematic behavior.

biological perspective An approach to behavior that emphasizes bodily events and changes associated with actions, feelings, and thoughts.

biological rhythm A periodic, more or less regular fluctuation in a biological system; it may or may not have psychological implications.

bipolar disorder A mood disorder in which depression alternates with mania.

brain stem The part of the brain at the top of the spinal cord; it is responsible for automatic functions such as heartbeat and respiration.

case study A detailed description of a particular individual being studied or treated.

castration anxiety In psychoanalysis, the boy's unconscious fear of castration by the powerful father that motivates the resolution of the Oedipus complex.

cell body The part of the neuron that keeps it alive and determines whether it will fire.

central nervous system (CNS) The portion of the nervous system consisting of the brain and spinal cord.

cerebellum A brain structure that regulates movement and balance and is involved in the learning of certain kinds of simple responses.

cerebral cortex A collection of several thin layers of cells covering the cerebrum; it is largely responsible for higher mental functions; *cortex* is Latin for "bark" or "rind."

cerebral hemispheres The two halves of the cerebrum.

cerebrum The largest brain structure, consisting of the upper part of the brain; it is in charge of most sensory, motor, and cognitive processes; from the Latin for "brain."

childhood (infantile) amnesia The inability to remember events and experiences that occurred during the first two or three years of life.

chromosomes Rod-shaped structures within every body cell that carry the genes.

chunk A meaningful unit of information; it may be composed of smaller units.

circadian rhythm A biological rhythm that recurs approximately every 24 hours.

classical conditioning The process by which a previously neutral stimulus acquires the capacity to elicit a response through association with a stimulus that already elicits a similar or related response; also called *Pavlovian* or *respondent conditioning.*

cognitive dissonance A state of tension that occurs when a person simultaneously holds two cognitions that are psychologically inconsistent, or when a person's belief is incongruent with his or her behavior.

cognitive ethology The study of cognitive processes in nonhuman animals.

cognitive map A mental representation of the environment.

cognitive perspective An approach to behavior that emphasizes mental processes in perception, memory, language, problem solving, and other areas of behavior.

cognitive schema An integrated mental network of knowledge, beliefs, and expectations concerning a particular topic or aspect of the world.

collective unconscious To Carl Jung, the universal memories and experiences of humankind, represented in the symbols, stories, and images (archetypes) that occur across all cultures.

concept A mental category that groups objects, relations, activities, abstractions, or qualities having common properties.

conditioned response (CR) The classical-conditioning term for a response that is elicited by a conditioned stimulus; occurs after the conditioned stimulus is associated with an unconditioned stimulus.

conditioned stimulus (CS)   The classical-conditioning term for an initially neutral stimulus that comes to elicit a conditioned response after being associated with an unconditioned stimulus.

conditioning   A basic kind of learning that involves associations between environmental stimuli and the organism's responses.

confirmation bias   The tendency to look for or to pay attention only to information that confirms one's beliefs.

conservation   The understanding that the physical properties of objects—such as the number of items in a cluster or the amount of liquid in a glass—can remain the same even when their form or appearance changes.

continuous reinforcement   A reinforcement schedule in which a particular response is always reinforced.

control condition   In an experiment, a comparison condition in which subjects are not exposed to the same treatment or manipulation of the independent variable as in the experimental condition.

convergent thinking   Thinking aimed at finding a single correct answer to a problem.

corpus callosum   The bundle of nerve fibers connecting the two cerebral hemispheres.

correlation   A measure of how strongly two variables are related to one another; it is expressed statistically by the *coefficient of correlation,* which can range in value from −1.00 to +1.00.

correlational study   A descriptive study that looks for a consistent relationship between two phenomena.

counterconditioning   In classical conditioning, the process of pairing a conditioned stimulus with a stimulus that elicits a response that is incompatible with an unwanted conditioned response.

critical thinking   The ability and willingness to assess claims and make objective judgments on the basis of well-supported reasons, to resist claims that have no supporting evidence, and to be creative and constructive in explaining events.

cross-sectional study   A study in which subjects of different ages are compared at a given time.

cue-dependent forgetting   The inability to retrieve information stored in memory because of insufficient cues for recall.

culture   A program of shared rules that govern the behavior of members of a community or society, and a set of values, beliefs, and attitudes shared by most members of that community.

decay theory   The theory that information in memory eventually disappears if it is not accessed; it applies more to short-term than to long-term memory.

declarative memories   Memories of facts, rules, concepts, and events ("knowing that"); they include semantic and episodic memories.

deductive reasoning   A form of reasoning in which a conclusion follows necessarily from certain premises; if the premises are true, the conclusion must be true.

deep processing   In the encoding of information, the processing of meaning rather than of simply the physical or sensory features of a stimulus.

defense mechanisms   Strategies used by the ego to prevent unconscious anxiety from reaching consciousness.

deindividuation   In groups or crowds, the loss of awareness of one's own individuality and the abdication of mindful action.

delta waves   Slow, regular brain waves characteristic of Stage 3 and Stage 4 sleep.

dendrites   A neuron's branches that receive information from other neurons and transmit it to the cell body.

dependent variable   A variable that an experimenter predicts will be affected by manipulations of the independent variable.

descriptive methods   Methods that yield descriptions of behavior but not necessarily causal explanations.

descriptive statistics   Statistics that organize and summarize research data.

dialectical reasoning   A process in which opposing facts or ideas are weighed and compared, with a view to determining the best solution or to resolving differences.

diffusion of responsibility   In organized or anonymous groups, the tendency of members to avoid taking responsibility for actions or decisions, assuming that others will do so.

discriminative stimulus   A stimulus that signals when a particular response is likely to be followed by a certain type of consequence.

dissociative identity disorder   *See* multiple personality disorder.

divergent thinking   Mental exploration of unconventional alternatives in solving problems; it tends to enhance creativity.

DNA (deoxyribonucleic acid)   The chromosomal molecule that transfers genetic characteristics by way of coded instructions for the structure of proteins.

double-blind study   An experiment in which neither the subjects nor the individuals running the study know which subjects are in the control group(s) and which are in the experimental group(s) until after the results are tallied.

ego   In psychoanalysis, the part of the mind that represents reason, good sense, and rational self-control; it mediates between id and superego.

egocentric thinking   Seeing the world from only one's own point of view; the inability to take another person's perspective.

elaborative rehearsal   Association of new information with other knowledge and analysis of the new information to make it memorable.

electroencephalogram (EEG)   A recording of neural activity detected by electrodes.

empirical   Relying on or derived from observation, experimentation, or measurement.

encoding   The conversion of information into a form that can be stored in and retrieved from memory.

endocrine glands   Internal organs that produce and release hormones into the bloodstream.

endorphins   Chemical substances in the nervous system that are similar in structure and action to opiates; they are involved in pain reduction, pleasure, and memory, and are known technically as *endogenous opioid peptides*.

entrapment   A gradual process in which individuals escalate their commitment to a course of action to justify their investment of time, money, or effort.

episodic memories   Memories for personally experienced events and the contexts in which they occurred.

ethnic identity   Having a close identification with one's own racial, religious, or ethnic group.

ethnocentrism   The belief that one's own ethnic group, nation, or religion is superior to all others.

evolution   A change in gene frequencies within a population over many generations; a mechanism by which genetically influenced characteristics of a population change.

evolutionary psychology   A field of psychology emphasizing evolutionary mechanisms that may help explain human commonalities in cognition, development, emotion, social practices, and other areas of behavior.

existential psychology   An approach to psychology that emphasizes free will and responsibility for one's actions, and the importance of struggling with the anxieties of existence such as the need to find meaning in life and to accept suffering and death.

experiment   A controlled test of a hypothesis in which the researcher manipulates one variable to discover its effect on another.

experimenter effects   Unintended changes in subjects' behavior due to cues inadvertently given by the experimenter.

explicit memory   Conscious, intentional recollection of an event or of an item of information.

extinction   The weakening and eventual disappearance of a learned response. In classical conditioning, it occurs when the conditioned stimulus is no longer paired with the unconditioned stimulus. In operant conditioning, it occurs when a response is no longer followed by a reinforcer.

extrinsic reinforcers   Reinforcers that are not inherently related to the activity being reinforced, such as money, prizes, and praise.

factor analysis   A statistical method for analyzing the intercorrelations among different measures or test scores; clusters of measures or scores that are highly correlated are assumed to measure the same underlying trait, ability, or aptitude (factor).

flashbulb memory   A vivid, detailed recollection of a significant or startling event, or the circumstances in which a person learned of such an event.

fraternal (dizygotic) twins   Twins that develop from two separate eggs fertilized by different sperm; they are no more alike genetically than are any other pair of siblings.

free association   In psychoanalytic therapy, a method of uncovering unconscious conflicts by saying freely whatever comes to mind.

functionalism   An early psychological approach that stressed the function or purpose of behavior and consciousness.

fundamental attribution error   The tendency, in explaining other people's behavior, to overestimate personality factors and to underestimate the influence of the situation.

gender identity   The fundamental sense of being male or female, regardless of whether one conforms to the rules of sex typing.

gender schema   A cognitive schema (mental network) of knowledge, beliefs, metaphors, and expectations about what it means to be male or female.

gender socialization (sex typing)   The process by which children learn the behaviors, attitudes, and expectations associated with being masculine or feminine in their culture.

genes   The functional units of heredity; they are composed of DNA and specify the structure of proteins.

genome   The full set of genes in each cell of an organism (with the exception of sperm and egg cells).

glial cells   Cells that hold neurons in place, insulate neurons, and provide neurons with nutrients.

groupthink   In close-knit groups, the tendency for all members to think alike for the sake of harmony and conformity and to suppress dissent.

heritability   A statistical estimate of the proportion of the total variance in some trait within a group that is attributable to genetic differences among individuals within the group.

heuristic   A rule of thumb that suggests a course of action or guides problem solving but does not guarantee an optimal solution.

high-context cultures   Cultures in which people pay close attention to nonverbal forms of communication and assume a shared context—a common history and set of attitudes—for their interactions.

higher-order conditioning   In classical conditioning, a procedure in which a neutral stimulus becomes a conditioned stimulus through association with an already established conditioned stimulus.

hindsight bias   The tendency to overestimate one's ability to have predicted an event, once the outcome is known; the "I knew it all along" phenomenon.

hippocampus   A brain structure involved in the storage of new information in memory.

hormones   Chemical substances, secreted by organs called glands, that affect the functioning of other organs.

humanistic psychology   An approach to psychology that emphasizes personal growth and the achievement of human potential rather than the scientific understanding, prediction, and control of behavior.

hypothalamus   A brain structure involved in emotions and drives vital to survival, such as fear, hunger, thirst, and reproduction; it regulates the autonomic nervous system.

hypothesis   A statement that attempts to predict or account for a set of phenomena; scientific hypotheses specify relationships among events or variables and are supported or disconfirmed by empirical investigation.

id   In psychoanalysis, the part of the mind containing sexual and aggressive impulses; from the Latin for "it."

identical (monozygotic) twins Twins that develop when a fertilized egg divides into two parts that become separate embryos.

implicit memory Unconscious retention in memory, as evidenced by the effect of a previous experience or previously encountered information on current thoughts or actions.

independent variable A variable that an experimenter manipulates.

induction A method of correcting a child's behavior in which the parent appeals to the child's own abilities, sense of responsibility, and feelings for others.

inductive reasoning A form of reasoning in which the premises provide support for a certain conclusion, but it is still possible for the conclusion to be false.

infantile amnesia *See* childhood amnesia.

inferential statistics Statistical tests that allow researchers to assess how likely it is that their results occurred merely by chance.

inferiority complex To Alfred Adler, an inability to accept one's natural limitations; it occurs when the need for self-improvement is blocked or inhibited.

insight A form of learning that occurs in problem solving and appears to involve the (often sudden) understanding of how elements of a situation are related or can be reorganized to achieve a solution.

instinctive drift The tendency of an organism to revert to an instinctive behavior over time; it can interfere with learning.

intelligence quotient (IQ) A measure of intelligence originally computed by dividing a person's mental age by his or her chronological age and multiplying the result by 100; it is now derived from norms provided for standardized intelligence tests.

intermittent (partial) schedule of reinforcement A reinforcement schedule in which a particular response is sometimes but not always reinforced.

intrapsychic Within the mind (psyche) or self.

intrinsic reinforcers Reinforcers that are inherently related to the activity being reinforced, such as enjoyment of the task and the satisfaction of accomplishment.

language A system that combines meaningless elements such as sounds or gestures into structured utterances that convey meaning.

latent learning A form of learning that is not immediately expressed in an overt response; it occurs without obvious reinforcement.

lateralization Specialization of the two cerebral hemispheres for particular psychological operations.

learning (mastery) goals Motivational goals that emphasize the intrinsic satisfaction of increasing one's competence and skills.

libido In psychoanalysis, the psychic energy that fuels the sexual instincts of the id.

limbic system A group of brain areas involved in emotional reactions and motivated behavior.

linkage studies Studies that look for patterns of inheritance of genetic markers in large families in which a particular condition is common; the markers consist of DNA segments that vary considerably among individuals and that have known locations on the chromosomes.

locus of control A general expectation about whether the results of one's actions are under one's own control (*internal* locus) or beyond one's control (*external* locus).

longitudinal study A study in which subjects are followed and periodically reassessed over a period of time.

long-term memory (LTM) In the three-box model of memory, the memory system involved in the long-term storage of information.

long-term potentiation A long-lasting increase in the strength of synaptic responsiveness, thought to be a biological mechanism of memory.

low-context cultures Cultures in which people do not take a shared context for granted and instead emphasize direct verbal communication.

maintenance rehearsal Rote repetition of material in order to maintain its availability in memory.

major depression A mood disorder involving disturbances in emotion (excessive sadness); behavior (loss of interest in one's usual activities); cognition (distorted thoughts of hopelessness and low self-esteem); and body function (fatigue and loss of appetite).

medulla A structure in the brain stem responsible for certain automatic functions, such as breathing and heart rate.

melatonin A hormone secreted by the pineal gland that is involved in the regulation of daily (circadian) biological rhythms.

mental set A tendency to solve problems using procedures that worked before on similar problems.

meta-analysis A statistical procedure for combining and analyzing data from many studies; it determines how much of the variance in scores across all studies can be explained by a particular variable.

metacognition The knowledge or awareness of one's own cognitive processes.

metamemory The ability to monitor and be aware of one's own retention of information.

"minor" tranquilizers Depressants commonly but often inappropriately prescribed for patients who complain of unhappiness or worry; they are the least effective drugs for treating emotional disorders.

mnemonics Strategies and tricks for improving memory, such as the use of a verse or a formula.

monochronic cultures Cultures in which time is organized sequentially; schedules and deadlines are valued over people.

motivated forgetting Forgetting that occurs because of a desire to eliminate awareness of painful, embarrassing, or otherwise unpleasant experiences.

motivation An inferred process within a person or animal that causes that individual to move toward a goal.

MRI (magnetic resonance imaging) A method for studying body and brain tissue by using magnetic fields and special radio receivers.

multiple personality disorder (dissociative identity disorder) A controversial disorder marked by the appearance within one person of two or more distinct personalities, each with its own name and traits.

myelin sheath A fatty insulation that may surround the axon of a nerve cell; many axons have such insulation.

natural selection The evolutionary process in which individuals with genetically influenced traits that are adaptive in a particular environment tend to survive and to reproduce in greater numbers than do other individuals not possessing such traits; as a result, these traits become more common in the population over time.

negative correlation An association between increases in one variable and decreases in another.

negative reinforcement A reinforcement procedure in which a response is followed by the removal, delay, or decrease in intensity of an unpleasant stimulus; as a result, the response becomes stronger or more likely to occur.

nerve A bundle of nerve fibers (axons and sometimes dendrites) in the peripheral nervous system.

neuromodulators Chemical substances in the nervous system that increase or decrease the action of specific neurotransmitters.

neuron A cell that conducts electrochemical signals; the basic unit of the nervous system. Also called a *nerve cell*.

neuropsychology The field of psychology concerned with the neural and biochemical bases of behavior and mental processes.

neurotransmitter A chemical substance that is released by a transmitting neuron at the synapse and that alters the activity of a receiving neuron.

nonconscious processes Mental processes occurring outside of and not available to conscious awareness.

norms Generally accepted procedures and rules. In test construction, established standards of performance for a test. In society, conventions that regulate human life, including explicit laws and implicit cultural standards.

object permanence The understanding, which develops in the first year of life, that an object continues to exist even when you can't see it or touch it.

object-relations school A psychodynamic approach that emphasizes the importance of the infant's first two years of life and the baby's formative relationships.

observational learning A learning process in which an individual learns new responses by observing the behavior of another (a model) rather than through direct experience; in behaviorism, it is called *vicarious conditioning.*

observational study A study in which the researcher carefully and systematically observes and records behavior without interfering with the behavior; it may involve either naturalistic observation or laboratory observation.

obsessive–compulsive disorder An anxiety disorder in which a person feels trapped in repetitive, persistent thoughts (obsessions) and repetitive, ritualized behaviors (compulsions) designed to reduce anxiety.

Oedipus complex In psychoanalysis, a conflict in which a child desires the parent of the other sex and views the same-sex parent as a rival; the key issue in the phallic stage of development.

operant conditioning The process by which a response becomes more or less likely to occur, depending on its consequences.

operational definition A precise definition of a term in a hypothesis, which specifies the operations for observing and measuring the process or phenomenon being defined.

operations In Piaget's theory, mental actions that are cognitively reversible.

panic attack A brief feeling of intense fear and impending doom or death, accompanied by intense physiological symptoms such as rapid breathing and pulse, and dizziness.

parallel distributed processing (PDP) An alternative to the information-processing model of memory, in which knowledge is represented not as propositions or images but as connections among thousands of interacting processing units, distributed in a vast network and all operating in parallel.

parasympathetic nervous system The subdivision of the autonomic nervous system that operates during relaxed states and that conserves energy.

perception The process by which the brain organizes and interprets sensory information.

performance goals Motivational goals that emphasize external rewards, such as doing well, being judged highly, and avoiding criticism.

peripheral nervous system (PNS) All portions of the nervous system outside the brain and spinal cord; it includes sensory and motor nerves.

PET (positron-emission tomography) scan A method for analyzing biochemical activity in the brain, using injections of a glucose-like substance containing a radioactive element.

phenomenology The study of events and situations as individuals experience them; in personality, the study of an individual's qualities from the person's own point of view.

pituitary gland A small endocrine gland at the base of the brain that releases many hormones and regulates other endocrine glands.

placebo An inactive substance or fake treatment used as a control in an experiment or given by a medical practitioner to a patient.

pleasure principle The principle guiding the operation of the id as it seeks to reduce tension, avoid pain, and enhance pleasure.

polychronic cultures Cultures in which time is organized horizontally; people tend to do several things at once and value relationships over schedules.

pons A structure in the brain stem involved in, among other things, sleeping, waking, and dreaming.

positive correlation An association between increases in one variable and increases in another.

positive reinforcement A reinforcement procedure in which a response is followed by the presentation of, or increase in intensity of, a reinforcing stimulus; as a result, the response becomes stronger or more likely to occur.

power assertion A method of correcting a child's behavior in which the parent uses punishment and authority.

primary punisher A stimulus that is inherently punishing; an example is electric shock.

primary reinforcer A stimulus that is inherently reinforcing, typically satisfying a physiological need; an example is food.

priming A method for measuring implicit memory in which a person reads or listens to information and is later tested to see whether the information is "activated" on another type of task.

principle of falsifiability The principle that a scientific theory must make predictions that are specific enough to expose the theory to the possibility of disconfirmation; that is, the theory must predict not only what will happen, but also what will not happen.

proactive interference Forgetting that occurs when previously stored material interferes with the ability to remember similar, more recently learned material.

procedural memories Memories for the performance of actions or skills ("knowing how").

projective tests Psychological tests used to infer a person's motives, conflicts, and unconscious dynamics on the basis of the person's interpretations of ambiguous or unstructured stimuli.

proposition A unit of meaning that is made up of concepts and expresses a unitary idea.

psychiatry The medical specialty concerned with mental disorders, maladjustment, and abnormal behavior.

psychoactive drug A drug capable of influencing perception, mood, cognition, or behavior.

psychoanalysis A theory of personality and a method of psychotherapy developed by Sigmund Freud; it emphasizes unconscious motives and conflicts.

psychodynamic perspective A psychological approach, originating with Freud's theory of psychoanalysis, that emphasizes unconscious energy dynamics within the individual, such as inner forces, conflicts, or the movement of instinctual energy.

psychological tests Procedures used to measure and evaluate personality traits, emotional states, aptitudes, interests, abilities, and values.

psychology The scientific study of behavior and mental processes and how they are affected by an organism's physical state, mental state, and external environment.

psychosis An extreme mental disturbance involving distorted perceptions and irrational behavior; it may have psychological or physiological causes.

punishment The process by which a stimulus or event weakens the response that it follows, reducing the probability of the response.

random assignment A procedure for assigning people to experimental and control groups in which each individual has the same probability as any other of being assigned to a given group.

rapid eye movement (REM) sleep Sleep periods characterized by eye movements, loss of muscle tone, and dreaming.

reality principle The principle guiding the operation of the ego as it seeks to find socially acceptable outlets for instinctual energies.

recall The ability to retrieve and reproduce from memory previously encountered material.

recognition The ability to identify previously encountered material.

reinforcement The process by which a stimulus or event strengthens the response that it follows, increasing the probability of the response.

relearning method A method for measuring retention that compares the time required to relearn material with the time required for the initial learning of the material.

reliability In test construction, the consistency, from one time and place to another, of scores derived from a test.

representative sample A sample that matches the population in question on important characteristics, such as age and sex.

reticular activating system (RAS) A dense network of neurons found in the core of the brain stem; it arouses the cortex and screens incoming information.

retroactive interference Forgetting that occurs when recently learned material interferes with the ability to remember similar material stored previously.

retrograde amnesia Loss of the ability to remember events or experiences that occurred before some particular point in time.

role A given social position that is governed by a set of norms for proper behavior.

Rorschach Inkblot Test A projective personality test that asks respondents to interpret abstract, symmetrical inkblots.

sample A group of subjects selected from a population for study in order to estimate characteristics of the population.

schizophrenia A mental disorder or group of disorders marked by some or all of these symptoms: delusions, hallucinations, disorganized and incoherent speech, severe emotional abnormalities, inappropriate behavior, and withdrawal into an inner world.

secondary punisher A stimulus that has acquired punishing properties through association with other punishers.

secondary reinforcer A stimulus that has acquired reinforcing properties through association with other reinforcers.

self-efficacy The belief that one is capable of producing, through one's own efforts, desired results, such as mastering new skills and reaching goals.

self-fulfilling prophecy An expectation that comes true because of the tendency of the person holding it to act in ways that confirm it.

self psychology A psychodynamic theory that emphasizes the importance of having a cohesive sense of self and self-esteem throughout life.

self-serving bias The tendency, in explaining one's own behavior, to take credit for one's good actions and to rationalize one's mistakes.

semantic memories Memories of general knowledge, including facts, rules, concepts, and propositions.

sensation The detection or direct experience of physical energy in the external or internal environment due to stimulation of receptors in the sense organs.

sensory memory A memory system that momentarily preserves extremely accurate images of sensory information.

serial-position effect The tendency for recall of the first and last items on a list to surpass recall of items in the middle of the list.

set point According to one theory, the genetically influenced weight range for an individual, thought to be maintained by a biological mechanism that regulates food intake, fat reserves, and metabolism.

sex hormones Hormones that regulate the development and functioning of reproductive and sex organs and that stimulate the development of male and female sexual characteristics; they include androgens (such as testosterone), estrogens, and progesterone.

shaping An operant conditioning procedure in which successive approximations of a desired response are reinforced; it is used when the desired response has a low probability of occurring spontaneously.

short-term memory (STM) In the three-box model of memory, a limited-capacity memory system involved in the retention of information for brief periods; it is also used to hold information retrieved from long-term memory for temporary use.

single-blind study An experiment in which subjects do not know whether they are in an experimental or a control group.

social constructionism The view that there are no universal truths about human nature because people construct reality differently, depending on their culture, the historical moment, and the power arrangements within their society.

social identity The part of a person's self-concept that is based on his or her identification with a nation, culture, or ethnic group, or with gender or other roles in society.

social-learning theories Theories of learning that typically emphasize a person's reciprocal interaction with the environment and that focus on observational learning, cognitive processes, and motivational beliefs.

sociobiology An interdisciplinary field of study that emphasizes evolutionary explanations of social behavior in animals, including human beings.

sociocultural perspective An approach to behavior that emphasizes social and cultural influences.

somatic nervous system The subdivision of the peripheral nervous system that connects to sensory receptors and skeletal muscles; sometimes called the *skeletal nervous system.*

splitting In object-relations theory, the division of qualities into their opposites, as in the Good Mother versus the Bad Mother; it reflects an inability to understand that people are made up of good and bad qualities.

spontaneous recovery The reappearance of a learned response after its apparent extinction.

standardize In test construction, to develop uniform procedures for giving and scoring a test.

state-dependent memory The tendency to remember something when one is in the same physical or mental state as during the original learning or experience.

statistically significant A term used to refer to a result that is extremely unlikely to have occurred by chance.

stimulus control Control over the occurrence of a response by a discriminative stimulus.

stimulus discrimination The tendency to respond differently to two or more similar stimuli. In classical conditioning, it occurs when a stimulus similar to the conditioned stimulus fails to evoke the conditioned response. In operant conditioning, it occurs when an organism learns to make a response in the presence of one stimulus but not in the presence of other, similar stimuli that differ from it on some dimension.

stimulus generalization After conditioning, the tendency to respond to a stimulus that resembles one involved in the original conditioning. In classical conditioning, it occurs when a stimulus that resembles the conditioned stimulus elicits the conditioned response. In operant conditioning, it occurs when a response that has been reinforced (or punished) in the presence of one stimulus occurs (or is suppressed) in the presence of other, similar stimuli.

subconscious processes Mental processes occurring outside of conscious awareness but accessible to consciousness when necessary.

successive approximations In the operant-conditioning procedure of shaping, behaviors that are ordered in terms of increasing similarity or closeness to the desired response.

superego In psychoanalysis, the part of the mind that represents conscience, morality, and social standards.

surveys Questionnaires and interviews that ask people directly about their experiences, attitudes, or opinions.

sympathetic nervous system The subdivision of the autonomic nervous system that mobilizes bodily resources and increases the output of energy during emotion and stress.

synapse The site where transmission of a nerve impulse from one nerve cell to another occurs; it includes the axon terminal, the synaptic cleft, and receptor sites in the membrane of the receiving cell.

tacit knowledge Strategies for success that are not explicitly taught but instead must be inferred.

temperaments Characteristic styles of responding to the environment, which are present in infancy and are assumed to be innate.

thalamus The brain structure that relays sensory messages to the cerebral cortex.

Thematic Apperception Test (TAT) A projective personality test that asks respondents to interpret a series of drawings showing ambiguous scenes of people.

theory An organized system of assumptions and principles that purports to explain a specified set of phenomena and their interrelationships.

theory of mind A theory about how one's own mind and other people's minds work and how people are affected by their beliefs and feelings.

therapeutic alliance The bond of confidence and mutual understanding established between therapist and client, which allows them to work together to solve the client's problems.

token economy A behavior-modification technique in which secondary reinforcers called *tokens,* which can be collected and exchanged for primary or other secondary reinforcers, are used to shape behavior.

tolerance The increasing resistance to a drug's effects with continued use; as tolerance develops, larger doses are required to produce effects once brought on by smaller ones.

trait A descriptive characteristic of an individual, assumed to be stable across situations and time.

transference In psychoanalysis, a critical step in which the patient transfers unconscious emotions or reactions, such as emotional responses to his or her parents, onto the therapist.

unconditional positive regard To Carl Rogers, love or support given to another person, with no conditions attached.

unconditioned response (UR) The classical-conditioning term for a reflexive response elicited by a stimulus in the absence of learning.

unconditioned stimulus (US) The classical-conditioning term for a stimulus that elicits a reflexive response in the absence of learning.

validity The ability of a test to measure what it was designed to measure.

validity effect The tendency of people to believe that a statement is true or valid simply because it has been repeated many times.

variables Characteristics of behavior or experience that can be measured or described by a numeric scale; variables are manipulated and assessed in scientific studies.

variance A measure of the dispersion of scores around the mean.

volunteer bias A shortcoming of findings derived from a sample of volunteers instead of a representative sample.

withdrawal symptoms Physical and psychological symptoms that occur when someone who is addicted to a drug stops taking it.

Bibliography

Abel, Gene G.; Mittelman, Mary; Becker, Judith V.; Rathner, Jerry; et al. (1988). Predicting child molesters' response to treatment. Conference of the New York Academy of Sciences: Human sexual aggression: Current perspectives. *Annals of the New York Academy of Sciences, 528,* 223–234.

Abrams, David B., & Wilson, G. Terence (1983). Alcohol, sexual arousal, and self-control. *Journal of Personality and Social Psychology, 45,* 188–198.

Abu-Lughod, Lila (1992). *Writing women's worlds: Bedouin stories.* Berkeley: University of California Press.

Adamopoulos, John, & Lonner, Walter J. (1994). Absolutism, relativism, and universalism in the study of human behavior. In W. J. Lonner & R. S. Malpass (eds.), *Psychology and culture.* Needham Heights, MA: Allyn & Bacon.

Adams, Gerald R.; Ryan, John H.; Hoffman, Joseph J.; Dobson, William R.; & Nielsen, Elwin C. (1985). Ego identity status, conformity behavior, and personality in late adolescence. *Journal of Personality and Social Psychology, 47,* 1091–1104.

Adams, James L. (1986). *Conceptual blockbusting: A guide to better ideas* (3rd ed.). Boston: Addison-Wesley.

Adams, M. J. (1990). *Learning to read: Thinking and learning about print.* Cambridge, MA: MIT Press.

Ader, Robert, & Cohen, Nicholas (1993). Psychoneuroimmunology: Conditioning and stress. *Annual Review of Psychology, 44,* 53–85.

Adler, Alfred (1927/1959). *Understanding human nature.* New York: Premier.

Adler, Alfred (1935). The fundamental views of individual psychology. *International Journal of Individual Psychology, 1,* 5–8.

Adler, Alfred (1938/1964). *Social interest: A challenge to mankind.* New York: Capricorn.

Affleck, Glenn; Tennen, Howard; Croog, Sydney; & Levine, Sol (1987). Causal attribution, perceived control, and recovery from a heart attack. *Journal of Social and Clinical Psychology, 5,* 339–355.

Ainsworth, Mary D. S. (1973). The development of infant–mother attachment. In B. M. Caldwell & H. N. Ricciuti (eds.), *Review of child development research* (Vol. 3). Chicago: University of Chicago Press.

Ainsworth, Mary D. S. (1979). Infant–mother attachment. *American Psychologist, 34,* 932–937.

Ainsworth, Mary D. S.; Blehar, Mary L.; Waters, Everett; & Wall, Sally (1978). *Patterns of attachment.* Hillsdale, NJ: Erlbaum.

Alagna, Sheryle W., & Hamilton, Jean A. (1986). Science in the service of mythology: The psychopathologizing of menstruation. Paper presented at the annual meeting of the American Psychological Association, Washington, DC.

Aldag, Ramon J., & Fuller, Sally R. (1993). Beyond fiasco: A reappraisal of the groupthink phenomenon and a new model of group decision processes. *Psychological Bulletin, 113,* 533–552.

Aldhouse, Peter (1992). The promise and pitfalls of molecular genetics. *Science, 257,* 164–165.

Allison, David B.; Heshka, Stanley; Neale, Michael C.; Lykken, David T.; et al. (1994). A genetic analysis of relative weight among 4,020 twin pairs, with an emphasis on sex effects. *Health Psychology, 13,* 362–365.

Allport, Gordon W. (1954/1979). *The nature of prejudice.* Reading, MA: Addison-Wesley.

Alpert, Bené; Field, Tiffany; Goldstein, Sheri; & Perry, Susan (1990). Aerobics enhances cardiovascular fitness and agility in preschoolers. *Health Psychology, 9,* 48–56.

Amabile, Teresa M. (1983). *The social psychology of creativity.* New York: Springer-Verlag.

American Psychiatric Association (1994). *The diagnostic and statistical manual of mental disorders* (4th ed.). Washington, DC: Author.

American Psychological Association (1984). *Survey of the use of animals in behavioral research at U.S. universities.* Washington, DC: Author.

Amir, Yehuda (1994). The contact hypothesis in intergroup relations. In W. J. Lonner & R. Malpass (eds.), *Psychology and culture.* Needham Heights, MA: Allyn & Bacon.

Anastasi, Anne (1988). *Psychological testing* (6th ed.). New York: Macmillan.

Andersen, Barbara L.; Kiecolt-Glaser, Janice K.; & Glaser, Ronald (1994). A biobehavioral model of cancer stress and disease course. *American Psychologist, 49,* 389–404.

Andersen, Susan M.; Klatzky, Roberta L.; & Murray, John (1990). Traits and social stereotypes: Efficiency differences in social information processing. *Journal of Personality and Social Psychology, 59,* 192–201.

Anderson, James A., & Rosenfeld, Edward (eds.) (1988). *Neurocomputing: Foundations of research.* Cambridge, MA: MIT Press.

Anderson, John R. (1990). *The adaptive nature of thought.* Hillsdale, NJ: Erlbaum.

Anderson, John R., & Bower, Gordon H. (1973). *Human associative memory.* Washington, DC: Winston.

Andreasen, Nancy C.; Arndt, Stephan; Swayze, Victor, II; Cizadlo, Ted; et al. (1994). Thalamic abnormalities in schizophrenia visualized through magnetic resonance image averaging. *Science, 266,* 294–298.

Ansbacher, Heinz (1968). The concept of social interest. *Journal of Individual Psychology, 24,* 131–149.

Ansbacher, Heinz, & Ansbacher, Rowena (eds.) (1964). *The individual psychology of Alfred Adler.* New York: Harper Torchbooks.

Antrobus, John (1991). Dreaming: Cognitive processes during cortical activation and high afferent thresholds. *Psychological Review, 98,* 96–121.

APA Commission on Violence and Youth (1993). *Violence and youth: Psychology's response.* Washington, DC: American Psychological Association.

Appiah, Kwame A. (1994). Beyond race: Fallacies of reactive Afrocentrism. *Skeptic, 2*(4), 104–107.

Apter, Terri (1990). *Altered loves: Mothers and daughters during adolescence.* New York: St. Martin's Press.

Archer, J., & Lloyd, B. (1982). *Sex and gender.* Cambridge, England: Cambridge University Press.

Arendt, Hannah (1963). *Eichmann in Jerusalem: A report on the banality of evil.* New York: Viking.

Arendt, Josephine; Aldhous, Margaret; & Wright, John (1988, April 2). Synchronization of a disturbed sleep–wake cycle in a blind man by melatonin treatment. *Lancet, 1*(8588), 772–773.

Arkes, Hal R. (1991). Some practical judgment/decision making research. Paper presented at the annual meeting of the American Psychological Association, Boston.

Arkes, Hal R.; Boehm, Lawrence E.; & Xu, Gang (1991). The determinants of judged validity. *Journal of Experimental Social Psychology, 27,* 576–605.

Arkes, Hal R.; Faust, David; Guilmette, Thomas J.; & Hart, Kathleen (1988). Eliminating the hindsight bias. *Journal of Applied Psychology, 73,* 305–307.

Aronson, Elliot (1995). *The social animal* (7th ed.). New York: Freeman.

Aronson, Elliot, & Mills, Judson (1959). The effect of severity of initiation on liking for a group. *Journal of Abnormal and Social Psychology, 59,* 177–181.

Aronson, Elliot; Stephan, Cookie; Sikes, Jev; Blaney, Nancy; & Snapp, Matthew (1978). *The jigsaw classroom.* Beverly Hills, CA: Sage.

Aronson, Elliot; Wilson, Timothy D.; & Akert, Robin M. (1994). *Social psychology: The heart and the mind.* New York: HarperCollins.

Arroyo, Carmen G., & Zigler, Edward (1995). Racial identity, academic achievement, and the psychological well-being of economically disadvantaged adolescents.

Journal of Personality and Social Psychology, 69, 903–914.

Asch, Solomon E. (1952). *Social psychology.* Englewood Cliffs, NJ: Prentice-Hall.

Asch, Solomon E. (1965). Effects of group pressure upon the modification and distortion of judgments. In H. Proshansky & B. Seidenberg (eds.), *Basic studies in social psychology.* New York: Holt, Rinehart and Winston.

Aserinsky, Eugene, & Kleitman, Nathaniel (1955). Two types of ocular motility occurring in sleep. *Journal of Applied Physiology, 8,* 1–10.

Ashton, P. T., & Webb, R. B. (1986). *Making a difference: Teachers' sense of efficacy and student achievement.* White Plains, NY: Longman.

Askenasy, Hans (1994). *Cannibalism: From sacrifice to survival.* Amherst, New York: Prometheus.

Astington, J. W., & Gopnik, Alison (1991). Theoretical explanations of children's understanding of the mind. In G. E. Butterworth, P. L. Harris, A. M. Leslie, & H. M. Wellman (eds.), *Perspectives on the child's theory of mind.* New York: Oxford University Press.

Atkinson, Richard C., & Shiffrin, Richard M. (1968). Human memory: A proposed system and its control processes. In K. W. Spence & J. T. Spence (eds.), *The psychology of learning and motivation. Vol. 2: Advances in research and theory.* New York: Academic Press.

Atkinson, Richard C., & Shiffrin, Richard M. (1971, August). The control of short-term memory. *Scientific American, 225*(2), 82–90.

Azrin, Nathan H., & Foxx, Richard M. (1974). *Toilet training in less than a day.* New York: Simon & Schuster.

Azuma, Hiroshi (1984). Secondary control as a heterogeneous category. *American Psychologist, 39,* 970–971.

Bahrick, Harry P. (1984). Semantic memory content in permastore: Fifty years of memory for Spanish learned in school. *Journal of Experimental Psychology: General, 113,* 1–29.

Bahrick, Harry P.; Bahrick, Phyllis O.; & Wittlinger, Roy P. (1975). Fifty years of memory for names and faces: A cross-sectional approach. *Journal of Experimental Psychology: General, 104,* 54–75.

Bailey, J. Michael (1993, March 25). Science and the fear of knowledge. *Chicago Tribune,* opinion page.

Bailey, J. Michael, & Benishay, Deana S. (1993). Familial aggregation of female sexual orientation. *American Journal of Psychiatry, 150,* 272–277.

Bailey, J. Michael; Bobrow, David; Wolfe, Marilyn; & Mikach, Sarah (1995). Sexual orientation of adult sons of gay fathers. *Developmental Psychology, 31,* 124–129.

Bailey, J. Michael; Gaulin, Steven; Agyei, Yvonne; & Gladue, Brian A. (1994). Effects of gender and sexual orientation on evolutionarily relevant aspects of human mating psychology. *Journal of Personality and Social Psychology, 66,* 1081–1093.

Bailey, J. Michael, & Pillard, Richard C. (1991). A genetic study of male sexual orientation. *Archives of General Psychiatry, 48,* 1089–1096.

Bailey, J. Michael; Pillard, Richard C.; Neale, Michael C.; & Agyei, Yvonne (1993). Heritable factors influence sexual orientation in women. *Archives of General Psychology, 50,* 217–223.

Baillargeon, Renée (1991). Reasoning about the height and location of a hidden object in 4.5- and 6.5-month-old infants. *Cognition, 38,* 13–42.

Baillargeon, Renée (1994). How do infants learn about the physical world? *Current Directions in Psychological Science, 5,* 133–140.

Baker, Robert A. (1992). *Hidden memories: Voices and visions from within.* Buffalo, NY: Prometheus.

Baltes, Paul B. (1983). Life-span developmental psychology: Observations on history and theory revisited. In R. M. Lerner (ed.), *Developmental psychology: Historical and philosophical perspectives.* Hillsdale, NJ: Erlbaum.

Baltes, Paul B.; Dittmann-Kohli, Freya; & Dixon, Roger A. (1984). New perspectives on the development of intelligence in adulthood: Toward a dual-process conception and a model of selective optimization with compensation. In P. B. Baltes & O. G. Brim, Jr. (eds.), *Life-span development and behavior* (Vol. 6). New York: Academic Press.

Bandura, Albert (1986). *Social foundations of thought and action: A social cognitive theory.* Englewood Cliffs, NJ: Prentice-Hall.

Bandura, Albert (1990). Self-regulation of motivation through goal systems. In R. A. Dienstbier (ed.), *Nebraska Symposium on Motivation* (Vol. 38). Lincoln: University of Nebraska Press.

Bandura, Albert (1991). Social cognitive theory of moral thought and action. In W. M. Kurtines & J. L. Gewirtz (eds.), *Handbook of moral behavior and development: Vol. 1. Theory.* Hillsdale, NJ: Erlbaum.

Bandura, Albert (1994). Self-efficacy. In *Encyclopedia of human behavior* (Vol. 4). Orlando, FL: Academic Press.

Bandura, Albert; Ross, Dorothea; & Ross, Sheila A. (1963). Vicarious reinforcement and imitative learning. *Journal of Abnormal and Social Psychology, 67,* 601–607.

Banks, Martin S. (in collaboration with Philip Salapatek) (1984). Infant visual perception. In P. Mussen (series ed.), M. M. Haith & J. J. Campos (vol. eds.), *Handbook of child psychology: Vol. II. Infancy and developmental psychobiology* (4th ed.). New York: Wiley.

Bardach, Ann Louise (1993, August). Tearing the veil. *Vanity Fair,* 123–127, 154–158.

Barinaga, Marcia (1992). Challenging the "no new neurons" dogma. *Science, 255,* 1646.

Barkow, Jerome H.; Cosmides, Leda; & Tooby, John (eds.) (1992). *The adapted mind: Evolutionary psychology and the generation of culture.* New York: Oxford University Press.

Barlow, David H. (1994). Empirically validated psychological procedures. Paper presented at the annual meeting of the American Psychological Association, Los Angeles.

Baron, Miron; Risch, Neil; Hamburger, Rahel; Mandel, Batsheva; et al. (1987, March 19). Genetic linkage between X-chromosome markers and bipolar affective illness. *Nature, 326,* 289–292.

Bartlett, Frederic C. (1932). *Remembering.* Cambridge, England: Cambridge University Press.

Barton, Scott (1994). Chaos, self-organization, and psychology. *American Psychologist, 49,* 5–14.

Batson, C. Daniel (1990). How social an animal? The human capacity for caring. *American Psychologist, 45,* 336–346.

Bauer, Patricia J., & Dow, Gina Annunziato (1994). Episodic memory in 16- and 20-month-old children: Specifics are generalized but not forgotten. *Developmental Psychology, 30,* 403–417.

Bauer, Patricia J., & Fivush, Robyn (1992). Constructing event representations: Building on a foundation of variation and enabling relations. *Cognitive Development, 7,* 381–401.

Bauer, Patricia J., & Hertsgaard, Louise A. (1993). Increasing steps in recall of events: Factors facilitating immediate and long-term memory in 13.5- and 16.5-month-old children. *Child Development, 64,* 1204–1223.

Baum, William M. (1994). *Understanding behaviorism: Science, behavior, and culture.* New York: Harper-Collins.

Baumrind, Diana (1966). Effects of authoritative parental control on child behavior. *Child Development, 37,* 887–907.

Baumrind, Diana (1971). Current patterns of parental authority. *Developmental Psychology Monograph, 4* (1, Part 2).

Baumrind, Diana (1973). The development of instrumental competence through socialization. In A. D. Pick (ed.), *Minnesota Symposium on Child Psychology* (Vol. 7). Minneapolis: University of Minnesota Press.

Baumrind, Diana (1989). Rearing competent children. In W. Damon (ed.), *Child development today and tomorrow.* San Francisco: Jossey-Bass.

Baumrind, Diana (1991). Parenting styles and adolescent development. In R. Lerner, A. C. Petersen, & J. Brooks-Gunn (eds.), *The encyclopedia of adolescence.* New York: Garland.

Baumrind, Diana (1995). Commentary on sexual orientation: Research and social policy implications. *Developmental Psychology, 31,* 130–136.

Bechtel, William, & Abrahamsen, Adele (1990). *Connectionism and the mind: An introduction to parallel processing in networks.* Cambridge, MA: Basil Blackwell.

Beck, Aaron T. (1976). *Cognitive therapy and the emotional disorders.* New York: International Universities Press.

Beck, Aaron T. (1991). Cognitive therapy: A 30-year retrospective. *American Psychologist, 46,* 368–375.

Becker, Ernest (1971). *The birth and death of meaning* (2nd ed.). New York: Free Press.

Becker, Ernest (1973). *The denial of death.* New York: Free Press.

Bee, Helen (1997). *The developing child* (8th ed.). New York: Longman.

Beebe, B.; Gerstman, L.; Carson, B.; et al. (1982). Rhythmic communication in the mother–infant dyad. In M. Davis (ed.), *Interaction rhythms: Periodicity in communicative behavior.* New York: Human Sciences Press.

Bekenstein, Jonathan W., & Lothman, Eric W. (1993). Dormancy of inhibitory interneurons in a model of temporal lobe epilepsy. *Science, 259,* 97–100.

Bell, Alan P.; Weinberg, Martin S.; & Hammersmith, Sue K. (1981). *Sexual preference: Its development in men and women.* Bloomington: Indiana University Press.

Bellugi, Ursula; Bihrle, Amy; Neville, Helen; Doherty, Sally; & Jernigan, Terry L. (1992). Language, cognition, and brain organization in a neurodevelopmental disorder. In M. Gunnar & C. Nelson (eds.), *Developmental behavioral neuroscience: The Minnesota Symposia on Child Psychology.* Hillsdale, NJ: Erlbaum.

Bem, Sandra L. (1985). Androgyny and gender schema theory: A conceptual and empirical integration. In T. B. Sonderegger (ed.), *Nebraska Symposium on Motivation: Vol. 32. Psychology and gender, 1984.* Lincoln: University of Nebraska Press.

Benbow, Camilla P., & Stanley, Julian C. (1983). Sex differences in mathematical reasoning: More facts. *Science, 222,* 1029–1031.

Benedek, E. P., & Schetky, D. H. (1987). Problems in validating allegations of sexual abuse: Parts 1 and 2. Factors affecting perception and recall of events. *Journal of the American Academy of Child and Adolescent Psychiatry, 26,* 915–922.

Benjamin, J.; Li, L.; Patterson, C.; et al. (1996). Population and familial association between the D4 dopamine receptor gene and measures of novelty seeking. *Nature Genetics, 12,* 81–84.

Bentall, R. P. (1990). The illusion of reality: A review and integration of psychological research on hallucinations. *Psychological Bulletin, 107,* 82–95.

Benton, Cynthia; Hernandez, Anthony; Schmidt, Adeny; Schmitz, Mary; et al. (1983). Is hostility linked with affiliation among males and with achievement among females? A critique of Pollak and Gilligan. *Journal of Personality and Social Psychology, 45,* 1167–1171.

Bereiter, Carl, & Bird, Marlene (1985). Use of thinking aloud in identification and teaching of reading comprehension strategies. *Cognition and Instruction, 2,* 131–156.

Berenbaum, Sheri A., & Hines, Melissa (1992). Early androgens are related to childhood sex-typed toy preferences. *Psychological Science, 3,* 203–206.

Bernieri, Frank J.; Davis, Janet M.; Rosenthal, Robert; & Knee, C. Raymond (1994). Interactional synchrony and rapport: Measuring synchrony in displays devoid of sound and facial affect. *Personality and Social Psychology Bulletin, 20,* 303–311.

Bernstein, Anne E., & Warner, Gloria M. (1993). *An introduction to contemporary psychoanalysis.* New York: Jason Aronson.

Bernstein, Ilene L. (1985). Learning food aversions in the progression of cancer and treatment. *Annals of the New York Academy of Sciences, 443,* 365–380.

Berry, John W. (1994). Acculturative stress. In W. J. Lonner & R. S. Malpass (eds.), *Psychology and culture.* Needham Heights, MA: Allyn & Bacon.

Berry, John W.; Poortinga, Ype; Segall, Marshall H.; & Dasen, Pierre R. (1992). *Cross-cultural psychology: Research and applications.* Cambridge, England: Cambridge University Press.

Besalel-Azrin, V.; Azrin, N. H.; & Armstrong, P. M. (1977). The student-oriented classroom: A method of improving student conduct and satisfaction. *Behavior Therapy, 8,* 193–204.

Best, Deborah L., & Williams, John E. (1993). Cross-cultural viewpoint. In A. E. Beall & R. J. Sternberg (eds.), *The psychology of gender.* New York: Guilford Press.

Betancourt, Hector, & López, Steven R. (1993). The study of culture, ethnicity, and race in American psychology. *American Psychologist, 48,* 629–637.

Bettelheim, Bruno (1967). *The empty fortress.* New York: Free Press.

Bevan, William (1991). Contemporary psychology: A tour inside the onion. *American Psychologist, 46,* 475–483.

Birdwhistell, Ray L. (1970). *Kinesics and context: Essays on body motion communication.* Philadelphia: University of Pennsylvania Press.

Bjork, Daniel W. (1993). *B. F. Skinner: A life.* New York: Basic Books.

Black, Donald W.; Wesner, Robert; Bowers, Wayne; & Gabel, Janelle (1993). A comparison of fluvoxamine, cognitive therapy, and placebo in the treatment of panic disorder. *Archives of General Psychiatry, 50,* 44–50.

Blakemore, Colin, & Cooper, Grahame F. (1970). Development of the brain depends on the visual environment. *Nature, 228,* 477–478.

Blass, Thomas (1993). What we now know about obedience: Distillations from 30 years of research on the Milgram paradigm. Paper presented at the annual meeting of the American Psychological Association, Toronto.

Bliss, T. V., & Collingridge, G. L. (1993). A synaptic model of memory: Long-term potentiation in the hippocampus. *Nature, 361*(6407), 31–39.

Block, Jeanne (1971). *Lives through time.* Berkeley, CA: Bancroft.

Bloom, Lois M. (1970). *Language development: Form and function in emerging grammars.* Cambridge, MA: MIT Press.

Blos, Peter (1962). *On adolescence.* New York: Free Press.

Blum, Kenneth, with James E. Payne (1991). *Alcohol and the addictive brain.* New York: Free Press/Science News Press.

Boehm, Lawrence E. (1994). The validity effect: A search for mediating variables. *Personality and Social Psychology Bulletin, 20,* 285–293.

Boesch, Cristophe (1991). Teaching among wild chimpanzees. *Animal Behavior, 41,* 530–532.

Boggiano, Ann K.; Shields, Ann; Barrett, Marty; Kellam, Teddy; et al. (1992). Helplessness deficits in students: The role of motivational orientation. *Motivation and Emotion, 16,* 271–296.

Bohannon, John N. (1988). Flashbulb memories for the space shuttle disaster: A tale of two theories. *Cognition, 29,* 179–196.

Bohannon, John N., & Stanowicz, Laura (1988). The issue of negative evidence: Adult responses to children's language errors. *Developmental Psychology, 24,* 684–689.

Bohannon, John N., & Symons, Victoria (1988). Conversational conditions of children's imitation. Paper presented at the biennial Conference on Human Development, Charleston, South Carolina.

Bohman, Michael; Cloninger, R.; Sigvardsson, S.; & von Knorring, Anne-Liis (1987). The genetics of alcoholisms and related disorders. *Journal of Psychiatric Research, 21,* 447–452.

Bolos, Annabel M.; Dean, M.; Lucas-Derse, S.; Ramsburg, M.; et al. (1990, December 26). Population and pedigree studies reveal a lack of association between the dopamine D2 receptor gene and alcoholism. *Journal of the American Medical Association, 264,* 3156–3160.

Bond, Rod, & Smith, Peter B. (1996). Culture and conformity: A meta-analysis of studies using Asch's (1952b, 1956) line judgment task. *Psychological Bulletin, 119,* 111–137.

Bothwell, R. K., Deffenbacher, K. A., & Brigham, J. C. (1987). Correlation of eyewitness accuracy and confidence: Optimality hypothesis revised. *Journal of Applied Psychology, 72,* 691–698.

Bouchard, Claude; Tremblay, A.; Despres, J. P.; Nadeau, A.; et al. (1990, May 24). The response to long-term overfeeding in identical twins. *New England Journal of Medicine, 322,* 1477–1482.

Bouchard, Thomas J., Jr. (1984). Twins reared together and apart: What they tell us about human diversity. In S. W. Fox (ed.), *Individuality and determinism.* New York: Plenum.

Bouchard, Thomas J., Jr. (1995). Nature's twice-told tale: Identical twins reared apart—what they tell us about human individuality. Paper presented at the annual meeting of the Western Psychological Association, Los Angeles.

Bouchard, Thomas J., Jr. (1996). IQ similarity in twins reared apart: Findings and responses to critics. In R. J. Sternberg & E. Grigorenko (eds.), *Intelligence: Heredity and environment.* New York: Cambridge University Press.

Bouchard, Thomas J., Jr. (in press). The genetics of personality. In K. Blum & E. P. Noble (eds.), *Handbook of psychoneurogenetics.* Boca Raton FL: CRC Press.

Bouchard, Thomas J., Jr.; Lykken, David T.; McGue, Matthew; Segal, Nancy L.; et al. (1990). Sources of human psychological differences: The Minnesota Study of Twins Reared Apart. *Science, 250,* 223–228.

Bouchard, Thomas J., Jr.; Lykken, David T.; McGue, Matthew; Segal, Nancy L.; et al. (1991). "Sources of human psychological differences: The Minnesota Study of Twins Reared Apart": Response. *Science, 252,* 191–192.

Bousfield, W. A. (1953). The occurrence of clustering in the recall of randomly arranged associates. *Journal of General Psychology, 49,* 229–240.

Bowen, Murray (1978). *Family therapy in clinical practice.* New York: Jason Aronson.

Bower, Gordon H., & Clark, M. C. (1969). Narrative stories as mediators of serial learning. *Psychonomic Science, 14,* 181–182.

Bowers, Kenneth S.; Regehr, Glenn; Balthazard, Claude; & Parker, Kevin (1990). Intuition in the context of discovery. *Cognitive Psychology, 22,* 72–110.

Bowlby, John (1958). The nature of the child's tie to his mother. *International Journal of Psycho-Analysis, 39,* 350–373.

Bowlby, John (1969). *Attachment and loss. Vol. I: Attachment.* New York: Basic Books.

Bowlby, John (1973). *Attachment and loss. Vol. II: Separation.* New York: Basic Books.

Bowlby, John (1988). *A secure base: Parent–child attachment and healthy human development.* New York: Basic Books.

Boyd-Franklin, Nancy (1989). *Black families in therapy: A multisystems approach.* New York: Guilford Press.

Boysen, Sarah T., & Berntson, Gary G. (1989). Numerical competence in a chimpanzee *(Pan troglodytes).* *Journal of Comparative Psychology, 103,* 23–31.

Bracha, H. Stefan; Torrey, E. Fuller; Bigelow, Llewellyn B.; Lohr, James B.; & Linington, Beverly B. (1991). Subtle signs of prenatal maldevelopment of the hand ectoderm in schizophrenia: A preliminary monozygotic twin study. *Biological Psychiatry, 30,* 719–725.

Bradley, Robert H., & Caldwell, Bettye M. (1984). 174 children: A study of the relationship between home environment and cognitive development during the first 5 years. In Allen W. Gottfried (ed.), *Home environment and early cognitive development: Longitudinal research.* Orlando, FL: Academic Press.

Bradley, R. H.; Caldwell, B. M.; Rock, S. L.; et al. (1989). Home environment and cognitive development in the first 3 years of life: A collaborative study involving six sites and three ethnic groups in North America. *Developmental Psychology, 25,* 217–235.

Brainerd, C. J.; Reyna, V. F.; & Brandse, E. (1995). Are children's false memories more persistent than their true memories? *Psychological Science, 6,* 359–364.

Breggin, Peter R. (1991). *Toxic psychiatry.* New York: St. Martin's Press.

Brehm, Sharon S. (1992). *Intimate relationships* (2nd ed.). New York: McGraw-Hill.

Breland, Keller, & Breland, Marian (1961). The mis-behavior of organisms. *American Psychologist, 16,* 681–684.

Bretherton, Inge, & Beeghly, Marjorie (1982). Talking about internal states: The acquisition of an explicit theory of mind. *Developmental Psychology, 18,* 906–921.

Breuer, Josef, & Freud, Sigmund (1895). *Studies on hysteria.* In J. Strachey (ed.), *The standard edition of the complete psychological works of Sigmund Freud* (Vol. 2). London: Hogarth Press.

Brewer, Marilynn B. (1993). Social identity, distinctiveness, and in-group homogeneity. *Social Cognition, 11,* 150–164.

Brewer, Marilynn B.; Manzi, Jorge M.; & Shaw, John S. (1993). In-group identification as a function of depersonalization, distinctiveness, and status. *Psychological Science, 4,* 88–92.

Briere, John, & Conte, Jon R. (1993). Self-reported amnesia for abuse in adults molested as children. *Journal of Traumatic Stress, 6,* 21–31.

Brigham, John C., & Malpass, Roy S. (1985, Fall). The role of experience and contact in the recognition of faces of own- and other-race persons. *Journal of Social Issues, 41,* 139–155.

Brockner, Joel, & Rubin, Jeffrey Z. (1985). *Entrapment in escalating conflicts: A social psychological analysis.* New York: Springer-Verlag.

Brodie-Scott, Cheryl, & Hobbs, Stephen H. (1992). Biological rhythms and publication practices: A follow-up survey, 1987–1991. Paper presented at the Southeastern Psychological Association, Knoxville, Tennessee.

Brodsky, Annette M. (1982). Sex, race, and class issues in psychotherapy research. In J. H. Harvey & M. M. Parks (eds.), *Psychotherapy research and behavior change: Vol. 1. The APA Master Lecture Series.* Washington, DC: American Psychological Association.

Brown, Alan S. (1991). A review of the tip-of-the-tongue experience. *Psychological Bulletin, 109,* 204–223.

Brown, Jonathon D. (1991). Staying fit and staying well. *Journal of Personality and Social Psychology, 60,* 555–561.

Brown, Jonathon D., & Smart, S. April (1991). The self and social conduct: Linking self-representations to prosocial behavior. *Journal of Personality and Social Psychology, 60,* 368–375.

Brown, Laura S. (1986). Diagnosis and the Zeitgeist: The politics of masochism in the DSM-III-R. Paper presented at the annual meeting of the American Psychological Association, Washington, DC.

Brown, Paul (1994). Toward a psychobiological study of dissociation. In S. J. Lynn & J. Rhue (eds.), *Dissociation: Clinical, theoretical and research perspectives.* New York: Guilford Press.

Brown, Robert, & Middlefell, Robert (1989). Fifty-five years of cocaine dependence [letter]. *British Journal of Addiction, 84,* 946.

Brown, Roger (1986). *Social psychology* (2nd ed.). New York: Free Press.

Brown, Roger; Cazden, Courtney; & Bellugi, Ursula (1969). The child's grammar from I to III. In J. P. Hill (ed.), *Minnesota Symposium on Child Psychology* (Vol. 2). Minneapolis: University of Minnesota Press.

Brown, Roger, & Fraser, C. (1964). The acquisition of syntax. In U. Bellugi & R. Brown (eds.), The acquisition of language. *Monographs of the Society for Research in Child Development, 29* (Serial No. 92), 43–79.

Brown, Roger, & Hanlon, C. (1970). Derivational complexity and order of acquisition in child speech. In J. R. Hayes (ed.), *Cognition and the development of language.* New York: Wiley.

Brown, Roger, & Kulik, James (1977). Flashbulb memories. *Cognition, 5,* 73–99.

Brown, Roger, & McNeill, David (1966). The "tip of the tongue" phenomenon. *Journal of Verbal Learning and Verbal Behavior, 5,* 325–337.

Brownell, Kelly D., & Rodin, Judith (1994). The dieting maelstrom: Is it possible and advisable to lose weight? *American Psychologist, 49,* 781–791.

Bruck, Maggie; Ceci, Stephen J.; Francoeur, Emmett; & Renick, Ashley (1995). Anatomically detailed dolls do not facilitate preschoolers' reports of a pediatric examination involving genital touching. *Journal of Experimental Psychology: Applied, 1,* 95–105.

Brunner, H. G.; Nelen, M. R.; & van Zandvoort, P. (1993). X-linked borderline mental retardation with prominent behavioral disturbance: Phenotype, genetic localization, and evidence for disturbed monoamine metabolism. *American Journal of Human Genetics, 52,* 1032–1039.

Buck, Ross (1984). *The communication of emotion.* New York: Guilford Press.

Buck, Ross, & Teng, Wan-Cheng (1987). Spontaneous emotional communication and social biofeedback: A cross-cultural study of emotional expression and communication in Chinese and Taiwanese students. Paper presented at the annual meeting of the American Psychological Association, New York.

Burke, Deborah M.; Burnett, Gayle; & Levenstein, Peggy (1978). Menstrual symptoms: New data from a double-blind study. Paper presented at the annual meeting of the Western Psychological Association, San Francisco.

Burke, Deborah M.; MacKay, Donald G.; Worthley, Joanna S.; & Wade, Elizabeth (1991). On the tip of the tongue: What causes word finding failures in young and older adults? *Journal of Memory and Language, 30,* 237–246.

Burstyn, Linda (1995, October). Female circumcision comes to America. *The Atlantic Monthly,* 28–35.

Bushman, Brad J. (1993). Human aggression while under the influence of alcohol and other drugs: An integrative research review. *Psychological Science, 2,* 148–152.

Bushman, Brad J. (1995). Moderating role of trait aggressiveness in the effects of violent media on aggression. *Journal of Personality and Social Psychology, 69,* 950–960.

Buss, David M. (1994). *The evolution of desire: Strategies of human mating.* New York: Basic Books.

Buss, David M. (1995). Evolutionary psychology: A new paradigm for psychological science. *Psychological Inquiry, 6,* 1–30.

Buss, David M. (1996). Sexual conflict: Can evolutionary and feminist perspectives converge? In D. M. Buss & N. Malamuth (eds.), *Sex, power, conflict: Evolutionary and feminist perspectives.* New York: Oxford University Press.

Buss, David M.; Abbott, M.; Angleitner, Alois; et al. (1990). International preferences in selecting mates: A study of 37 cultures. *Journal of Cross-Cultural Psychology, 21,* 5–47.

Bussey, Kay, & Bandura, Albert (1992). Self-regulatory mechanisms governing gender development. *Child Development, 63,* 1236–1250.

Bussey, Kay, & Maughan, Betty (1982). Gender differences in moral reasoning. *Journal of Personality and Social Psychology, 42,* 701–706.

Butler, S.; Chalder, T.; Ron, M.; Wessely, S.; et al. (1991). Cognitive behaviour therapy in chronic fatigue syndrome. *Journal of Neurology, Neurosurgery & Psychiatry, 54,* 153–158.

Buunk, Bram; Angleitner, Alois; Oubaid, V.; & Buss, David M. (1996). Sex differences in jealousy in evolutionary and cultural perspective: Tests from the Netherlands, Germany, and the United States. *Psychological Science,* forthcoming.

Byne, William (1993). Sexual orientation and brain structure: Adding up the evidence. Paper presented at the annual meeting of the International Academy of Sex Research, Pacific Grove, California.

Cabezas, A.; Tam, T. M.; Lowe, B. M.; Wong, A.; & Turner, K. (1989). Empirical study of barriers to upward mobility of Asian Americans in the San Francisco Bay area. In G. Nomura (ed.), *Frontiers of Asian American studies.* Pullman: Washington State University Press.

Cahill, Larry; Prins, Bruce; Weber, Michael; & McGaugh, James L. (1994). b-Adrenergic activation and memory for emotional events. *Nature, 371,* 702–704.

Cain, Kathleen M., & Dweck, Carol S. (1995, January). The relation between motivational patterns and achievement cognitions through the elementary school years. *Merrill-Palmer Quarterly, 41,* 25–52.

Calof, David (1993, September/October). Facing the truth about false memory. *The Family Therapy Networker, 17,* 38–45.

Camel, J. F.; Withers, G. S.; & Greenough, William T. (1986). Persistence of visual cortex dendritic alterations induced by postweaning exposure to a "super-enriched" environment in rats. *Behavioral Neuroscience, 100,* 810–813.

Camera, Wayne J., & Schneider, Dianne L. (1994). Integrity tests: Facts and unresolved issues. *American Psychologist, 49,* 112–119.

Campbell, Anne (1993). *Men, women, and aggression.* New York: Basic Books.

Campbell, Frances A., & Ramey, Craig T. (1994). Effects of early intervention on intellectual and academic achievement: A follow-up study of children from low-income families. *Child Development, 65,* 684–698.

Campbell, Frances A., & Ramey, Craig T. (1995). Cognitive and school outcomes for high risk students at middle adolescence: Positive effects of early intervention. *American Educational Research Journal, 32,* 743–772.

Campbell, Jennifer; Trapnell, Paul D.; Heine, Steven J.; Katz, Ilana M.; et al. (1996). Self-concept clarity: Measurement, personality correlates, and cultural boundaries. *Journal of Personality and Social Psychology, 70,* 141–156.

Campbell, Joseph (1949/1968). *The hero with 1,000 faces* (2nd ed.). Princeton, NJ: Princeton University Press.

Campos, Joseph J.; Barrett, Karen C.; Lamb, Michael E.; Goldsmith, H. Hill; & Stenberg, Craig (1984). Socioemotional development. In P. H. Mussen (series ed.), M. M. Haith & J. J. Campos (vol. eds.), *Handbook of child psychology: Vol. 2. Infancy and developmental psychobiology* (4th ed.). New York: Wiley.

Caplan, Paula J. (1995). *They say you're crazy.* Reading, MA: Addison-Wesley.

Caramazza, Alfonso, & Hillis, Argye E. (1991, February 28). Lexical organization of nouns and verbs in the brain. *Nature, 349,* 788–790.

Carli, Linda L. (1990). Gender, language, and influence. *Journal of Personality and Social Psychology, 59,* 941–951.

Carpenter, William T., Jr.; Sadier, John H.; et al. (1983). The therapeutic efficacy of hemodialysis in schizophrenia. *New England Journal of Medicine, 308*(12), 669–675.

Carr, Edward G., & Durand, V. Mark (1985). Reducing behavior problems through functional communication training. *Journal of Applied Behavior Analysis, 18,* 111–126.

Carr, Edward G., & McDowell, Jack J. (1980). Social control of self-injurious behavior of organic etiology. *Behavior Therapy, 11,* 402–409.

Carroll, Kathleen M.; Rounsaville, Bruce J.; & Nich, Charla (1994). Blind man's bluff: Effectiveness and significance of psychotherapy and pharmacotherapy blinding procedures in a clinical trial. *Journal of Consulting and Clinical Psychology, 62,* 276–280.

Carter, Betty, & McGoldrick, Monica (eds.) (1988). *The changing family life cycle: A framework for family therapy* (2nd ed.). New York: Gardner Press.

Carver, Charles S.; Ironson, G.; Wynings, C.; Greenwood, D.; et al. (1993). Coping with Andrew: How coping responses relate to experience of loss and symptoms of poor adjustment. Paper presented at the annual meeting of the American Psychological Association, Toronto.

Carver, Charles S.; Scheier, Michael F.; & Weintraub, Jagdish K. (1989). Assessing coping strategies: A theoretically based approach. *Journal of Personality and Social Psychology, 56,* 267–283.

Cassel, W. S., & Bjorklund, D. F. (1992). Age differences and suggestibility of eyewitnesses. Symposium paper presented at the annual meeting of the Conference on Human Development, Atlanta.

Casswell, Sally (1993). Public discourse on the benefits of moderation: Implications for alcohol policy development. *Addiction, 88,* 459–465.

Cattell, Raymond B. (1965). *The scientific analysis of personality.* Baltimore: Penguin.

Cattell, Raymond B. (1973). *Personality and mood by questionnaire.* San Francisco: Jossey-Bass.

Ceci, Stephen J. (1994). Cognitive and social factors in children's testimony. In B. Sales & G. Vandenbos (eds.), *Psychology in litigation and legislation.* Washington, DC: American Psychological Association.

Ceci, Stephen J., & Bruck, Maggie (1993). Suggestibility of the child witness: A historical review and synthesis. *Psychological Bulletin, 113,* 403–439.

Ceci, Stephen J., & Bruck, Maggie (1995). *Jeopardy in the courtroom: A scientific analysis of children's testimony.* Washington, DC: American Psychological Association.

Celis, William, III (1993, August 1). Down from the self-esteem high. *New York Times,* Education Section.

Cermak, Laird S., & Craik, Fergus I. M. (eds.) (1979). *Levels of processing in human memory.* Hillsdale, NJ: Erlbaum.

Chambless, Dianne L. (1995). Training in and dissemination of empirically validated psychological treatments: Report and recommendations. *The Clinical Psychologist, 48,* 3–24.

Chan, Connie S., & Grossman, Hildreth Y. (1988). Psychological effects of running loss on consistent runners. *Perceptual & Motor Skills, 66,* 875–883.

Chance, June E., & Goldstein, Alvin G. (1995). The other-race effect in eyewitness identification. In S. L. Sporer, G. Koehnken, & R. S. Malpass (eds.), *Psychological issues in eyewitness identification.* Hillsdale, NJ: Erlbaum.

Chance, Paul (1988, October). Knock wood. *Psychology Today,* 68–69.

Chance, Paul (1989, November). The other 90%. *Psychology Today,* 20–21.

Chance, Paul (1992, November). The rewards of learning. *Phi Delta Kappan, 74,* 200–207.

Chance, Paul (1994). *Learning and behavior* (3rd ed.). Belmont, CA: Wadsworth.

Chen, S. C. (1937). Social modification of the activity of ants in nest-building. *Physiological Zoology, 10,* 420–436.

Cheney, Dorothy L., & Seyfarth, Robert M. (1985). Vervet monkey alarm calls: Manipulation through shared information? *Behavior, 94,* 150–166.

Cheney, Dorothy L., & Seyfarth, Robert M. (1990). *How monkeys see the world: Inside the mind of another species.* Chicago: University of Chicago Press.

Chipuer, Heather M.; Rovine, Michael J.; & Plomin, Robert (1990). LISREL modeling: Genetic and environmental influences on IQ revisited. *Intelligence, 14,* 11–29.

Chodorow, Nancy (1978). *The reproduction of mothering.* Berkeley: University of California Press.

Chodorow, Nancy (1992). *Feminism and psychoanalytic theory.* New Haven, CT: Yale University Press.

Chomsky, Noam (1957). *Syntactic structures.* The Hague, Netherlands: Mouton.

Chomsky, Noam (1980). Initial states and steady states. In M. Piatelli-Palmerini (ed.), *Language and learning: The debate between Jean Piaget and Noam Chomsky.* Cambridge, MA: Harvard University Press.

Chrisler, Joan C.; Johnston, Ingrid K; Champagne, Nicole M.; & Preston, Kathleen E. (1994). Menstrual joy: The construct and its consequences. *Psychology of Women Quarterly, 18,* 375–387.

Christensen, Andrew, & Jacobson, Neil S. (1994). Who (or what) can do psychotherapy: The status and challenge of nonprofessional therapies. *Psychological Science, 5,* 8–14.

Chua, Streamson C., Jr.; Chung, Wendy K.; Wu-Peng, S. Sharon; et al. (1996). Phenotypes of mouse *diabetes* and rat *fatty* due to mutations in the OB (leptin) receptor. *Science, 271,* 994–996.

Cialdini, Robert B. (1993). *Influence: The psychology of persuasion.* New York: Quill.

Clark, Margaret S.; Milberg, Sandra; & Erber, Ralph (1987). Arousal state dependent memory: Evidence and some implications for understanding social judgments and social behavior. In K. Fiedler & J. P. Forgas (eds.), *Affect, cognition and social behavior.* Toronto: Hogrefe.

Clarke-Stewart, K. Alison; Thompson, W.; & Lepore, S. (1989). Manipulating children's interpretations through interrogation. Paper presented at the biennial meeting of the Society for Research on Child Development, Kansas City, Missouri.

Clarke-Stewart, K. Alison; VanderStoep, Laima P.; & Killian, Grant A. (1979). Analyses and replication of mother–child relations at two years of age. *Child Development, 50,* 777–793.

Cloninger, C. Robert; Svrakic, Dragan M.; & Przybeck, Thomas R. (1993). A psychobiological model of temperament and character. *Archives of General Psychiatry, 50,* 975–990.

Clopton, Nancy A., & Sorell, Gwendolyn T. (1993). Gender differences in moral reasoning: Stable or situational? *Psychology of Women Quarterly, 17,* 85–101.

Cochran, Susan D., & Peplau, Letitia Anne (1985). Value orientations in heterosexual relationships. *Psychology of Women Quarterly, 9,* 477–488.

Cohn, Lawrence D. (1991). Sex differences in the course of personality development: A meta-analysis. *Psychological Bulletin, 109,* 252–266.

Colby, Anne; Kohlberg, Lawrence; Gibbs, J.; & Lieberman, M. (1983). A longitudinal study of moral judgment. *Monographs of the Society for Research in Child Development, 48* (1–2, Serial No. 200).

Cole, Michael (1984). The world beyond our borders: What might our students need to know about it? *American Psychologist, 39,* 998–1005.

Cole, Michael (1990). Cultural psychology: A once and future discipline? In J. J. Berman (ed.), *Cross-cultural perspectives: Nebraska Symposium on Motivation, 1989.* Lincoln: University of Nebraska Press.

Cole, Michael, & Cole, Sheila R. (1993). *The development of children* (2nd ed.). New York: W. H. Freeman.

Collins, Allan M., & Loftus, Elizabeth F. (1975). A spreading-activation theory of semantic processing. *Psychological Review, 82,* 407–428.

Collins, Barry (1993). Using person perception methodologies to uncover the meanings of the Milgram obedience paradigm. Paper presented at the annual meeting of the American Psychological Association, Toronto.

Collins, Bud (1981, August 30). Rivals at Flushing Meadows. *The New York Times Magazine,* 71.

Comstock, George; Chaffee, Steven; Katzman, Natan; McCombs, Maxwell; & Roberts, Donald (1978). *Television and human behavior.* New York: Columbia University Press.

Condon, William (1982). Cultural microrhythms. In M. Davis (ed.), *Interaction rhythms: Periodicity in communicative behavior.* New York: Human Sciences Press.

Considine, R. V.; Sinha, M. K.; Heiman, M. L.; et al. (1996). Serum immunoreactive-leptin concentrations in normal-weight and obese humans. *New England Journal of Medicine, 334,* 292–295.

Conway, Martin A.; Anderson, Stephen J.; Larsen, Steen F.; Donnelly, C. M.; et al. (1994). The formation of flashbulb memories. *Memory and Cognition, 22,* 326–343.

Conway, Michael, & Ross, Michael (1984). Getting what you want by revising what you had. *Journal of Personality and Social Psychology, 47,* 738–748.

Coons, Philip M.; Milstein, Victor; & Marley, Carma (1982). EEG studies of two multiple personalities and a control. *Archives of General Psychiatry, 39,* 823–825.

Cooper, M. Lynne; Frone, Michael R.; Russell, Marcia; & Mudar, Pamela (1995). Drinking to regulate positive and negative emotions: A motivational model of alcohol use. *Journal of Personality and Social Psychology, 69,* 990–1005.

Copi, Irving M., & Burgess-Jackson, Keith (1992). *Informal logic* (2nd ed.). New York: Macmillan.

Corder, E. H.; Saunders, A. M.; Strittmatter, W. J.; et al. (1993). Gene dose of apolipoprotein E type 4 allele and the risk of Alzheimer's disease in late onset families. *Science, 261,* 921–923.

Corkin, Suzanne (1984). Lasting consequences of bilateral medial temporal lobectomy: Clinical course and experimental findings in H. M. *Seminars in Neurology, 4,* 249–259.

Cornell-Bell, A. H.; Finkbeiner, S. M.; Cooper, M. S.; & Smith, S. J. (1990). Glutamate induces calcium waves in cultured astrocytes: Long-range glial signaling. *Science, 247,* 470–473.

Cose, Ellis (1994). *The rage of a privileged class.* New York: HarperCollins.

Cosmides, Leda; Tooby, John; & Barkow, Jerome H. (1992) Introduction: Evolutionary psychology and conceptual integration. In J. H. Barkow, L. Cosmides, & J. Tooby (eds.), *The adapted mind: Evolutionary psychology and the generation of culture.* New York: Oxford University Press.

Costa, Paul T., Jr., & McCrae, Robert R. (1994). "Set like plaster"? Evidence for the stability of adult personality. In R. Heatherton & J. Weinberger (eds.), *Can personality change?* Washington, DC: American Psychological Association.

Cowen, Emory L.; Wyman, Peter A.; Work, William C.; & Parker, Gayle R. (1990). The Rochester Child Resilience Project (RCRP): Overview and summary of first year findings. *Development and Psychopathology, 2,* 193–212.

Craik, Fergus I. M., & Tulving, Endel (1975). Depth of processing and the retention of words in episodic memory. *Journal of Experimental Psychology: General, 104,* 268–294.

Crain, Stephen (1991). Language acquisition in the absence of experience. *Behavioral & Brain Sciences, 14,* 597–650.

Crandall, James E. (1984). Social interest as a moderator of life stress. *Journal of Personality and Social Psychology, 47,* 164–174.

Crawford, Mary, & Marecek, Jeanne (1989). Psychology constructs the female: 1968–1988. *Psychology of Women Quarterly, 13,* 147–165.

Crews, Frederick, and his critics (1995). *The memory wars: Freud's legacy in dispute.* New York: New York Review of Books.

Critchlow, Barbara (1983). Blaming the booze: The attribution of responsibility for drunken behavior. *Personality and Social Psychology Bulletin, 9,* 451–474.

Critchlow, Barbara (1986). The powers of John Barleycorn: Beliefs about the effects of alcohol on social behavior. *American Psychologist, 41,* 751–764.

Crocker, Jennifer, & Major, Brenda (1989). Social stigma and self-esteem: The self-protective properties of stigma. *Psychological Review, 96,* 608–630.

Crook, John H. (1987). The nature of conscious awareness. In C. Blakemore & S. Greenfield (eds.), *Mindwaves: Thoughts on intelligence, identity, and consciousness.* Oxford: Basil Blackwell.

Cross, A. J. (1990). Serotonin in Alzheimer-type dementia and other dementing illnesses. *Annals of the New York Academy of Science, 600,* 405–415.

Cross, William E. (1971). The Negro-to-Black conversion experience: Toward a psychology of Black liberation. *Black World, 20,* 13–27.

Crystal, David S.; Chen, Chuansheng; Fuligni, Andrew J.; Stevenson, Harold W.; et al. (1994). Psychological maladjustment and academic achievement: A cross-cultural study of Japanese, Chinese, and

American high school students. *Child Development, 65,* 738–753.

Crystal, Jonathon D., & Shettleworth, Sara J. (1994). Spatial list learning in black-capped chickadees. *Animal Learning and Behavior, 22,* 77–83.

Cubelli, Roberto (1991, September 19). A selective deficit for writing vowels in acquired dysgraphia. *Nature, 353,* 209–210.

Curtiss, Susan (1977). *Genie: A psycholinguistic study of a modern-day "wild child."* New York: Academic Press.

Curtiss, Susan (1982). Developmental dissociations of language and cognition. In L. Obler & D. Fein (eds.), *Exceptional language and linguistics.* New York: Academic Press.

Dabbs, James M., Jr., & Morris, Robin (1990). Testosterone, social class, and antisocial behavior in a sample of 4,462 men. *Psychological Science, 1,* 209–211.

Dahlstrom, W. Grant (1993). Tests: Small samples, large consequences. *American Psychologist, 48,* 393–399.

Daly, Martin, & Wilson, Margo (1983). *Sex, evolution, and behavior* (2nd ed.). Belmont, CA: Wadsworth.

Damasio, Antonio R. (1990). Category-related recognition defects as a clue to the neural substrates of knowledge. *Trends in Neurosciences, 13,* 95–98.

Damasio, Antonio R. (1994). *Descartes' error: Emotion, reason, and the human brain.* New York: Grosset/Putnam.

Damasio, Hanna; Grabowski, Thomas; Frank, Randall; Galaburda, Albert M.; & Damasio, Antonio R. (1994). The return of Phineas Gage: Clues about the brain from the skull of a famous patient. *Science, 264,* 1102–1105.

Danish, Paul (1994, February 13). Legalizing marijuana would allow regulation of its potency. *New York Times,* letters page.

Darley, John M. (1993). Research on morality: Possible approaches, actual approaches [review of *Handbook of moral behavior and development*]. *Psychological Science, 4,* 353–357.

Darling, Nancy, & Steinberg, Laurence (1993). Parenting style as context: An integrative model. *Psychological Bulletin, 113,* 487–496.

Darwin, Charles (1859). *On the origin of species.* [A facsimile of the first edition, edited by Ernst Mayer, 1964.] Cambridge, MA: Harvard University Press.

Darwin, Charles (1872/1965). *The expression of the emotions in man and animals.* Chicago: University of Chicago Press.

Darwin, Charles (1874). *The descent of man and selection in relation to sex* (2nd ed.). New York: Hurst.

Dasen, Pierre R. (1994). Culture and cognitive development from a Piagetian perspective. In W. J. Lonner & R. S. Malpass (eds.), *Psychology and culture.* Needham Heights, MA: Allyn & Bacon.

Davidson, Richard J.; Ekman, Paul; Saron, Clifford D.; Senulis, Joseph A.; & Friesen, Wallace V. (1990). Approach-withdrawal and cerebral asymmetry: I. Emotional expression and brain physiology. *Journal of Personality and Social Psychology, 58,* 330–341.

Davis, David B. (1984). *Slavery and human progress.* New York: Oxford University Press.

Davis, Joel (1984). *Endorphins: New waves in brain chemistry.* Garden City, NY: Dial Press.

Dawes, Robyn M. (1994). *House of cards: Psychology and psychotherapy built on myth.* New York: Free Press.

Dawson, Neal V.; Arkes, Hal R.; Siciliano, C.; et al. (1988). Hindsight bias: An impediment to accurate probability estimation in clinicopathologic conferences. *Medical Decision Making, 8*(4), 259–264.

Dean, Geoffrey (1986–1987, Winter). Does astrology need to be true? Part I: A look at the real thing. *The Skeptical Inquirer, 11,* 166–184.

Dean, Geoffrey (1987, Spring). Does astrology need to be true? Part II: The answer is no. *The Skeptical Inquirer, 11,* 257–273.

Deaux, Kay (1985). Sex and gender. *Annual Review of Psychology, 36,* 49–81.

Deaux, Kay, & Major, Brenda (1987). Putting gender into context: An interactive model of gender-related behavior. *Psychological Review, 94,* 369–389.

Deaux, Kay, & Major, Brenda (1990). A social-psychological model of gender. In D. L. Rhode (ed.), *Theoretical perspectives on sexual difference.* New Haven, CT: Yale University Press.

de Bono, Edward (1971). *The dog exercising machine.* New York: Touchstone.

de Bono, Edward (1985). *de Bono's thinking course.* New York: Facts on File.

Deci, Edward L., & Ryan, Richard M. (1987). The support of autonomy and the control of behavior. *Journal of Personality and Social Psychology, 53,* 1024–1037.

de Lacoste-Utamsing, Christine, & Holloway, Ralph L. (1982). Sexual dimorphism in the human corpus callosum. *Science, 216,* 1431–1432.

de la Garza, Rodolfo O.; DeSipio, Luis; Garcia, F. Chris; Garcia, John; & Falcon, Angelo (1992). *Latino voices: Mexican, Puerto Rican, & Cuban perspectives on American politics.* Boulder, CO: Westview.

DeLoache, Judy S. (1987, December 11). Rapid change in the symbolic functioning of very young children. *Science, 238,* 1556–1557.

DeLoache, Judy S. (1995). The early development of symbolic understanding: Implications for children's testimony. Paper presented at the annual meeting of the American Psychological Association, New York.

Dement, William (1955). Dream recall and eye movements during sleep in schizophrenics and normals. *Journal of Nervous and Mental Disease, 122,* 263–269.

Dement, William (1978). *Some must watch while some must sleep.* New York: W. W. Norton.

Dement, William (1992). *The sleepwatchers.* Stanford, CA: Stanford Alumni Association.

Dement, William, & Kleitman, Nathaniel (1957). The relation of eye movements during sleep to dream activity: An objective method for the study of dreaming. *Journal of Experimental Psychology, 53,* 339–346.

DeMyer, Marian K. (1975). Research in infantile autism: A strategy and its results. *Biological Psychiatry, 10,* 433–452.

Denmark, Florence; Russo, Nancy F.; Frieze, Irene H.; & Sechzer, Jeri A. (1988). Guidelines for avoiding sexism in psychological research. *American Psychologist, 43,* 582–585.

Dennett, Daniel C. (1991). *Consciousness explained.* Boston: Little, Brown.

de Rivera, Joseph (1989). Comparing experiences across cultures: Shame and guilt in America and Japan. *Hiroshima Forum for Psychology, 14,* 13–20.

Deutsch, Morton (1949). An experimental study of the effects of cooperation and competition among group processes. *Human Relations, 2,* 199–231.

Deutsch, Morton (1980). Fifty years of conflict. In L. Festinger (ed.), *Retrospections on social psychology.* New York: Oxford University Press.

Deutsch, Morton, & Collins, Mary Ellen (1951). *Interracial housing: A psychological evaluation of a social experiment.* Minneapolis: University of Minnesota Press.

Devine, Patricia G. (1995). Breaking the prejudice habit: Progress and prospects. Award address paper presented at the annual meeting of the American Psychological Association, New York.

Devine, Patricia G.; Evett, Sophia R.; & Vasquez-Suson, Kristin A. (1996). Exploring the interpersonal dynamics of intergroup contact. In R. M. Sorrentino & E. T. Higgins (eds.), *Handbook of motivation and cognition: Vol. 3. The interpersonal context.* New York: Guilford Press.

Devine, Patricia G.; Monteith, Margo J.; Zuwerink, Julia R.; & Elliot, Andrew J. (1991). Prejudice with and without compunction. *Journal of Personality and Social Psychology, 60,* 817–830.

Devolder, Patricia A., & Pressley, Michael (1989). Metamemory across the adult lifespan. *Canadian Psychology, 30,* 578–587.

Devor, E. J.; Abell, C. W.; Hoffman, P. L.; Tabakoff, B.; & Cloninger, C. R. (1994). Platelet MAO activity in type I and type II alcoholism. *Annals of the New York Academy of Sciences, 708,* 119–128.

Diamond, Jared (1994, November). Race without color. *Discover,* 82–89.

Diamond, Marian C. (1993). An optimistic view of the aging brain. *Generations, 17,* 31–33.

Dickinson, Alyce M. (1989). The detrimental effects of extrinsic reinforcement on "intrinsic motivation." *The Behavior Analyst, 12,* 1–15.

DiFranza, Joseph R.; Winters, Thomas H.; Goldberg, Robert J.; Cirillo, Leonard; et al. (1986). The relationship of smoking to motor vehicle accidents and traffic violations. *New York State Journal of Medicine, 86,* 464–467.

Digman, John M. (1990). Personality structure: Emergence of the five-factor model. In M. R. Rosenzweig &

L. W. Porter (eds.), *Annual Review of Psychology.* Palo Alto, CA: Annual Reviews.

di Leonardo, Micaela (1987). The female world of cards and holidays: Women, families, and the work of kinship. *Signs, 12,* 1–20.

di Leonardo, Micaela (1991). Introduction. In M. di Leonardo (ed.), *Gender at the crossroads of knowledge.* Berkeley: University of California Press.

Dinges, David F.; Whitehouse, Wayne G.; Orne, Emily C.; Powell, John W.; et al. (1992). Evaluating hypnotic memory enhancement (hypermnesia and reminiscence) using multitrial forced recall. *Journal of Experimental Psychology: Learning, Memory, and Cognition, 18,* 1139–1147.

Dinnerstein, Dorothy (1976). *The mermaid and the Minotaur: Sexual arrangements and human malaise.* New York: Harper & Row.

Dinsmoor, James A. (1992). Setting the record straight: The social views of B. F. Skinner. *American Psychologist, 47,* 1454–1463.

Doblin, R., & Kleiman, M. A. R. (1991). Marihuana as anti-emetic medicine: A survey of oncologists' attitudes and experiences. *Journal of Clinical Oncology, 9,* 1275–1280.

Doi, L. T. (1973). *The anatomy of dependence.* Tokyo: Kodansha International.

Dollard, John, & Miller, Neal E. (1950). *Personality and psychotherapy: An analysis in terms of learning, thinking, and culture.* New York: McGraw-Hill.

Doty, Richard M.; Peterson, Bill E.; & Winter, David G. (1991). Threat and authoritarianism in the United States, 1978–1987. *Journal of Personality and Social Psychology, 61,* 629–640.

Dovidio, John F.; Allen, Judith L.; & Schroeder, David A. (1990). Specificity of empathy-induced helping: Evidence for altruistic motivation. *Journal of Personality and Social Psychology, 59,* 249–260.

Druckman, Daniel, & Swets, John A. (eds.) (1988). *Enhancing human performance: Issues, theories, and techniques.* Washington, DC: National Academy Press.

Dunford, Franklyn; Huizinga, David; & Elliott, Delbert S. (1990). The role of arrest in domestic assault: The Omaha police experiment. *Criminology, 28,* 183–206.

du Verglas, Gabrielle; Banks, Steven R.; & Guyer, Kenneth E. (1988). Clinical effects of fenfluramine on children with autism: A review of the research. *Journal of Autism and Developmental Disorders, 18,* 297–308.

Dweck, Carol S. (1990). Toward a theory of goals: Their role in motivation and personality. In R. A. Dienstbier (ed.), *Nebraska Symposium on Motivation* (Vol. 38). Lincoln: University of Nebraska Press.

Dweck, Carol S. (1992). The study of goals in psychology [Commentary to feature review]. *Psychological Science, 3,* 165–167.

Dym, Barry, & Glenn, Michael L. (1993). *Couples: Exploring and understanding the cycles of intimate relationships.* New York: HarperCollins.

Eagly, Alice H. (1987). *Sex differences in social behavior: A social-role interpretation.* Hillsdale, NJ: Erlbaum.

Eagly, Alice H., & Carli, Linda L. (1981). Sex of researchers and sex-typed communications as determinants of sex differences in influencibility: A meta-analysis of social influence studies. *Psychological Bulletin, 90,* 1–20.

Eagly, Alice H.; Makhijani, M. G.; & Klonsky, B. G. (1990). Gender and the evaluation of leaders: A meta-analysis. *Psychological Bulletin, 111,* 3–22.

Eagly, Alice H., & Wood, Wendy (1991). Explaining sex differences in social behavior: A meta-analytic perspective. *Personality and Social Psychology Bulletin, 17,* 306–315.

Ebbinghaus, Hermann M. (1885/1913). *Memory: A contribution to experimental psychology* (H. A. Ruger & C. E. Bussenius, trans.). New York: Teachers College, Columbia University.

Eberlin, Michael; McConnachie, Gene; Ibel, Stuart; & Volpe, Lisa (1993). Facilitated communication: A failure to replicate the phenomenon. *Journal of Autism and Developmental Disorders, 23,* 507–530.

Ebstein, R. P.; Novick, O.; Umansky, R.; et al. (1996). Dopamine D4 receptor (D4DR) exon III polymorphism associated with the human personality trait of novelty seeking. *Nature Genetics, 12,* 78–80.

Eccles, Jacquelynne S. (1993). Parents and gender-role socialization during the middle childhood and adolescent years. In S. Oskamp & M. Costanzo (eds.), *The Claremont Symposium on Applied Social Psychology: Gender issues in contemporary society.* Newbury Park, CA: Sage.

Eccles, Jacquelynne S.; Jacobs, Janis E.; & Harold, Rena D. (1990). Gender role stereotypes, expectancy effects, and parents' socialization of gender differences. *Journal of Social Issues, 46,* 183–201.

Eckensberger, Lutz H. (1994). Moral development and its measurement across cultures. In W. J. Lonner & R. Malpass (eds.), *Psychology and culture.* Needham Heights, MA: Allyn & Bacon.

Edelson, Marshall (1994). Can psychotherapy research answer this psychotherapist's questions? In P. F. Talley, H. H. Strupp, & S. F. Butler (eds.), *Psychotherapy research and practice: Bridging the gap.* New York: Basic Books.

Edsall, Thomas B., & Edsall, Mary D. (1991). *Chain reaction: The impact of race, rights, and taxes on American politics.* New York: W. W. Norton.

Edwards, Carolyn P. (1987). Culture and the construction of moral values. In J. Kagan & S. Lamb (eds.), *The emergence of morality in young children.* Chicago: University of Chicago Press.

Egeland, Janice A.; Gerhard, Daniela; Pauls, David; Sussex, James; et al. (1987, February 26). Bipolar affective disorders linked to DNA markers on chromosome 11. *Nature, 325,* 783–787.

Eich, Eric (1995). Searching for mood dependent memory. *Psychological Science, 6,* 67–75.

Eichenbaum, Luise, & Orbach, Susie (1983). *Understanding women: A feminist psychoanalytic approach.* New York: Basic Books.

Eisenberger, Robert, & Selbst, Michael (1994). Does reward increase or decrease creativity? *Journal of Personality and Social Psychology, 66,* 1116–1127.

Eisler, Riane (1987). *The chalice and the blade.* San Francisco: HarperCollins.

Ekman, Paul (1994). Strong evidence for universals in facial expressions: A reply to Russell's mistaken critique. *Psychological Bulletin, 115,* 268–287.

Ekman, Paul; Friesen, Wallace V.; O'Sullivan, Maureen; et al. (1987). Universals and cultural differences in the judgements of facial expression of emotion. *Journal of Personality and Social Psychology, 53,* 712–717.

Ekman, Paul, & Heider, Karl G. (1988). The universality of a contempt expression: A replication. *Motivation and Emotion, 12,* 303–308.

Elbert, Thomas; Pantev, Christo; Wienbruch, Christian; Rockstroh, Brigitte; & Taub, Edward (1995, October 13). Increased cortical representation of the fingers of the left hand in string players. *Science, 270,* 305–307.

Elliott, Diana M. (1995). Delayed recall of traumatic events: Correlates and clinical implications. Paper presented at the annual meeting of the American Psychological Association, New York.

Elliott, Robert, & Morrow-Bradley, Cheryl (1994). Developing a working marriage between psychotherapists and psychotherapy researchers: Identifying shared purposes. In P. F. Talley, H. H. Strupp, & S. F. Butler (eds.), *Psychotherapy research and practice: Bridging the gap.* New York: Basic Books.

Ellis, Albert (1993). Changing rational-emotive therapy (RET) to rational emotive behavior therapy (REBT). *Behavior Therapist, 16,* 257–258.

Elshtain, Jean B. (1987). *Women and war.* New York: Basic Books.

Emmorey, Karen; Kosslyn, Stephen M.; & Bellugi, Ursula (1993). Visual imagery and visual-spatial language: Enhanced imagery abilities in deaf and hearing ASL signers. *Cognition, 46,* 139–181.

Englander-Golden, Paula; Whitmore, Mary R.; & Dienstbier, Richard A. (1978). Menstrual cycle as focus of study and self-reports of moods and behavior. *Motivation and Emotion, 2,* 75–86.

Ennis, Robert H. (1986). A taxonomy of critical thinking dispositions and abilities. In J. B. Baron & R. J. Sternberg (eds.), *Teaching thinking skills.* New York: W. H. Freeman.

Epstein, Robert (1990). Generativity theory and creativity. In M. A. Runco & R. S. Albert (eds.), *Theories of creativity.* Newbury Park, CA: Sage.

Epstein, Robert; Kirshnit, C. E.; Lanza, R. P.; & Rubin, L. C. (1984, March 1). "Insight" in the pigeon: Antecedents and determinants of an intelligent performance. *Nature, 308,* 61–62.

Erikson, Erik H. (1950/1963). *Childhood and society* (2nd ed.). New York: W. W. Norton.

Erikson, Erik H. (1987). *A way of looking at things: Selected papers from 1930 to 1980* (Stephen Schlein, ed.). New York: W. W. Norton.

Eron, Leonard D. (1980). Prescription for reduction of aggression. *American Psychologist, 35,* 244–252.

Eron, Leonard D. (1982). Parent-child interaction, television violence, and aggression of children. *American Psychologist, 37,* 197–211.

Eron, Leonard D. (1995). Media violence: How it affects kids and what can be done about it. Invited address presented at the annual meeting of the American Psychological Association, New York.

Eron, Leonard D., & Huesmann, L. Rowell (1987). Television as a source of maltreatment of children. *School Psychology Review, 16,* 195–202.

Ervin-Tripp, Susan (1964). Imitation and structural change in children's language. In E. H. Lenneberg (ed.), *New directions in the study of language.* Cambridge, MA: MIT Press.

Esterson, Allen (1993). *Seductive mirage: An exploration of the work of Sigmund Freud.* New York: Open Court.

Evans, Christopher (1984). *Landscapes of the night* (edited and completed by Peter Evans). New York: Viking.

Exner, John E. (1993). *The Rorschach: A comprehensive system. Vol. 1: Basic foundations* (3rd ed.). New York: Wiley.

Eyferth, Klaus (1961). [The performance of different groups of the children of occupation forces on the Hamburg-Wechsler Intelligence Test for Children.] *Archiv für die Gesamte Psychologie, 113,* 222–241.

Eysenck, Hans J. (1990). The prediction of death from cancer by means of personality/stress questionnaire: Too good to be true? *Perceptual and Motor Skills, 71,* 216–218.

Eysenck, Hans J. (1993, August). Psychoanalysis: Pseudo-science [letter to the editor]. *Monitor, 4,* 68.

Eysenck, Hans J. (1994). The "Big Five" or "Giant 3"? Criteria for a paradigm. In C. F. Halverson, G. A. Kohnstamm, & R. P. Martin (eds.), *The developing structure of temperament and personality from infancy to adulthood.* Hillsdale, NJ: Erlbaum.

Fabes, Richard A.; Eisenberg, Nancy; Karbon, Mariss; Bernzweig, Jane; et al. (1994). Socialization of children's vicarious emotional responding and prosocial behavior: Relations with mothers' perceptions of children's emotional reactivity. *Developmental Psychology, 30,* 44–55.

Fagot, Beverly I. (1984). Teacher and peer reactions to boys' and girls' play styles. *Sex Roles, 11,* 691–702.

Fagot, Beverly I. (1985). Beyond the reinforcement principle: Another step toward understanding sex role development. *Developmental Psychology, 2,* 1097–1104.

Fagot, Beverly I. (1993, June). Gender role development in early childhood: Environmental input, internal construction. Invited address presented at the annual meeting of the International Academy of Sex Research, Monterey, California.

Fagot, Beverly I.; Hagan, R.; Leinbach, Mary D.; & Kronsberg, S. (1985). Differential reactions to assertive and communicative acts of toddler boys and girls. *Child Development, 56,* 1499–1505.

Fagot, Beverly I., & Leinbach, Mary D. (1993). Gender-role development in young children: From discrimination to labeling. *Developmental Review, 13,* 205–224.

Fairchild, Halford H. (1985). Black, Negro, or Afro-American? The differences are crucial! *Journal of Black Studies, 16,* 47–55.

Falk, Ruma, & Greenbaum, Charles W. (1995). Significance tests die hard: The amazing persistence of a probabilistic misconception. *Theory and Psychology, 5*(1), 75–98.

Fancher, Robert T. (1995). *Cultures of healing.* New York: W. H. Freeman.

Faraone, Stephen V.; Kremen, William S.; & Tsuang, Ming T. (1990). Genetic transmission of major affective disorders: Quantitative models and linkage analyses. *Psychological Bulletin, 108,* 109–127.

Faust, David, & Ziskin, Jay (1988, July 1). The expert witness in psychology and psychiatry. *Science, 241,* 31–35.

Fausto-Sterling, Anne (1985). *Myths of gender: Biological theories about women and men.* New York: Basic Books.

Fazio, Russell H.; Jackson, Joni R.; Dunton, Bridget C.; & Williams, Carol J. (1995). Variability in automatic activation as an unobtrusive measure of racial attitudes: A bona fide pipeline? *Journal of Personality and Social Psychology, 69,* 1013–1027.

Feather, N. T. (1966). Effects of prior success and failure on expectations of success and subsequent performance. *Journal of Personality and Social Psychology, 3,* 287–298.

Feeney, Dennis M. (1987). Human rights and animal welfare. *American Psychologist, 42,* 593–599.

Fein, Steven, & Spencer, Steven J. (1993). Self-esteem and stereotype-based downward social comparison. Paper presented at the annual meeting of the American Psychological Association, Toronto.

Feingold, Alan (1988). Cognitive gender differences are disappearing. *American Psychologist, 43,* 95–103.

Fernald, L. D. (1984). *The Hans legacy: A story of science.* Hillsdale, NJ: Erlbaum.

Feshbach, Norma; Feshbach, Seymour; Fauvre, Mary; & Ballard-Campbell, Michael (1983). *Learning to care: A curriculum for affective and social development.* Glenview, IL: Scott, Foresman.

Festinger, Leon (1957). *A theory of cognitive dissonance.* Evanston, IL: Row, Peterson.

Festinger, Leon (1980). Looking backward. In L. Festinger (ed.), *Retrospections on social psychology.* New York: Oxford University Press.

Festinger, Leon, & Carlsmith, J. Merrill (1959). Cognitive consequences of forced compliance. *Journal of Abnormal and Social Psychology, 58,* 203–210.

Festinger, Leon; Pepitone, Albert; & Newcomb, Theodore (1952). Some consequences of deindividuation in a group. *Journal of Abnormal and Social Psychology, 47,* 382–389.

Festinger, Leon; Riecken, Henry W.; & Schachter, Stanley (1956). *When prophecy fails.* Minneapolis: University of Minnesota Press.

Field, Tiffany (1989, Summer). Individual and maturational differences in infant expressivity. *New Directions for Child Development, 44,* 9–23.

Field, Tiffany; Cohen, Debra; Garcia, Robert; & Greenberg, Reena (1984). Mother-stranger face discrimination by the newborn. *Infant Behavior and Development, 7,* 19–25.

Fincham, Frank D., & Bradbury, Thomas N. (1993). Marital satisfaction, depression, and attributions: A longitudinal analysis. *Journal of Personality and Social Psychology, 64,* 442–452.

Fingarette, Herbert (1988). *Heavy drinking: The myth of alcoholism as a disease.* Berkeley: University of California Press.

Fiore, Edith (1989). *Encounters: A psychologist reveals case studies of abduction by extraterrestrials.* New York: Bantam.

Fischhoff, Baruch (1975). Hindsight is not equal to foresight: The effect of outcome knowledge on judgment under uncertainty. *Journal of Experimental Psychology: Human Perception and Performance, 1,* 288–299.

Fisher, Ronald J. (1994). Generic principles for resolving intergroup conflict. *Journal of Social Issues, 50,* 47–66.

Fisher, Ronald P., & Geiselman, R. Edward (1992). *Memory-enhancing techniques for investigative interviewing: The cognitive interview.* New York: C. C. Thomas.

Fisher, Seymour, & Greenberg, Roger P. (eds.) (1989). *A critical appraisal of biological treatments for psychological distress: Comparisons with psychotherapy and placebo.* Hillsdale, NJ: Erlbaum.

Fisher, Seymour, & Greenberg, Roger P. (1993). How sound is the double-blind design for evaluating psychotropic drugs? *The Journal of Nervous and Mental Disease, 181,* 345–350.

Fiske, Susan T. (1993). Controlling other people: The impact of power on stereotyping. *American Psychologist, 48,* 621–628.

Fitzgerald, Joseph M. (1988). Vivid memories and the reminiscence phenomenon: The role of a self narrative. *Human Development, 31,* 261–273.

Fivush, Robyn (1993). Developmental perspectives on autobiographical recall. In G. S. Goodman & B. L. Bottoms (eds.), *Child victims, child witnesses: Understanding and improving testimony.* New York: Guilford Press.

Fivush, Robyn, & Hamond, Nina R. (1991). Autobiographical memory across the school years: Toward reconceptualizing childhood amnesia. In R. Fivush & J. A. Hudson (eds.), *Knowing and remembering in young children.* New York: Cambridge University Press.

Flavell, John H. (1993). Young children's understanding of thinking and consciousness. *Current Directions in Psychological Science, 2,* 40–43.

Flavell, John H.; Green, F. L.; & Flavell, E. R. (1990). Developmental changes in young children's knowledge about the mind. *Cognitive Development, 5,* 1–27.

Foa, Edna, & Emmelkamp, Paul (eds.) (1983). *Failures in behavior therapy.* New York: Wiley.

Foderaro, Lisa W. (1995, May 28). Can problem drinkers really just cut back? *The New York Times,* National section, 15.

Fogelman, Eva (1994). *Conscience and courage: Rescuers of Jews during the Holocaust.* New York: Anchor Books.

Fordham, Signithia (1991, Spring). Racelessness in private schools: Should we deconstruct the racial and cultural identity of African-American adolescents? *Teachers College Record, 92,* 470–484.

Fordham, Signithia, & Ogbu, John (1986). Black students' school success: Coping with the burden of "acting White." *Urban Review, 18,* 176–206.

Forgas, Joseph, & Bond, Michael H. (1985). Cultural influences on the perception of interaction episodes. *Personality and Social Psychology Bulletin, 11,* 75–88.

Forsyth, G. Alfred; Arpey, Stacie H.; & Stratton-Hess, Caroline L. (1992). Correcting errors in the interpretation of research. Poster session paper presented at the annual meeting of the American Psychological Association, Washington, DC.

Fouts, Roger S.; Fouts, Deborah H.; & Van Cantfort, Thomas E. (1989). The infant Loulis learns signs from cross-fostered chimpanzees. In R. A. Gardner, B. T. Gardner, & T. E. Van Cantfort (eds.), *Teaching sign language to chimpanzees.* New York: State University of New York Press.

Fouts, Roger S., & Rigby, Randall L. (1977). Manchimpanzee communication. In T. A. Seboek (ed.), *How animals communicate.* Bloomington: University of Indiana Press.

Fox, Nathan A., & Davidson, Richard J. (1988). Patterns of brain electrical activity during facial signs of emotion in 10-month-old infants. *Developmental Psychology, 24,* 230–236.

Fox, Ronald E. (1994). Training professional psychologists for the twenty-first century. *American Psychologist, 49,* 200–206.

Frank, Jerome D. (1985). Therapeutic components shared by all psychotherapies. In M. J. Mahony & A. Freeman (eds.), *Cognition and psychotherapy.* New York: Plenum.

Frankl, Victor E. (1955). *The doctor and the soul: An introduction to logotherapy.* New York: Knopf.

Frederich, R. C.; Hamann, A.; Anderson, S.; et al. (1995). Leptin levels reflect body lipid content in mice: evidence for diet-induced resistance to leptin action. *Nature Medicine, 1,* 1311–1314.

Freed, C. R.; Breeze, R. E.; Rosenberg, N. L.; & Schneck, S. A. (1993). Embryonic dopamine cell implants as a treatment for the second phase of Parkinson's disease. Replacing failed nerve terminals. *Advances in Neurology, 60,* 721–728.

Freedman, Jonathan L. (1988). Television violence and aggression: What the evidence shows. In S. Oskamp (ed.), *Applied social psychology annual: Vol. 8. Television as a social issue.* Newbury Park, CA: Sage.

Freeman, Ellen; Rickels, Karl; Sondheimer, S. J.; & Polansky, M. (1990). Ineffectiveness of progesterone suppository treatment for premenstrual syndrome. *Journal of the American Medical Association, 264,* 349–353.

Freud, Anna (1946). *The ego and the mechanisms of defence.* New York: International Universities Press.

Freud, Sigmund (1900/1953). *The interpretation of dreams.* In J. Strachey (ed. and trans.), *The standard edition of the complete psychological works of Sigmund Freud* (Vols. 4 and 5). London: Hogarth Press.

Freud, Sigmund (1905a). Fragment of an analysis of a case of hysteria. In J. Strachey (ed. and trans.), *The standard edition of the complete psychological works of Sigmund Freud* (Vol. 7). London: Hogarth Press and the Institute of Psycho-Analysis (1964 edition).

Freud, Sigmund (1905b). Three essays on the theory of sexuality. In Strachey, *Standard edition* (Vol. 7).

Freud, Sigmund (1908). Civilized sexual morality and modern nervousness. In Strachey, *Standard edition* (Vol. 9).

Freud, Sigmund (1920/1960). *A general introduction to psychoanalysis* (Joan Riviere, trans.). New York: Washington Square Press.

Freud, Sigmund (1920/1963). The psychogenesis of a case of homosexuality in a woman. In S. Freud, *Sexuality and the psychology of love.* New York: Collier Books.

Freud, Sigmund (1923/1962). *The ego and the id* (Joan Riviere, trans.). New York: W. W. Norton.

Freud, Sigmund (1924a). The dissolution of the Oedipus complex. In Strachey, *Standard edition* (Vol. 19).

Freud, Sigmund (1924b). Some psychical consequences of the anatomical distinction between the sexes. In Strachey, *Standard edition* (Vol. 19).

Freud, Sigmund (1930/1962). *Civilization and its discontents* (J. Strachey, ed. and trans.). New York: W. W. Norton.

Freud, Sigmund (1933). Femininity. In Strachey, *Standard edition* (Vol. 22).

Freud, Sigmund (1961). *Letters of Sigmund Freud, 1873–1939* (E. L. Freud, ed.). London: Hogarth Press.

Friedman, William; Robinson, Amy; & Friedman, Britt (1987). Sex differences in moral judgments? A test of Gilligan's theory. *Psychology of Women Quarterly, 11,* 37–46.

Frijda, Nico H. (1988). The laws of emotion. *American Psychologist, 43,* 349–358.

Fuchs, C. S.; Stampfer, M. J.; Colditz, G. A.; Giovannucci, E. L.; et al. (1995, May 11). Alcohol consumption and mortality among women. *New England Journal of Medicine, 332,* 1245–1250.

Funder, David C., & Colvin, C. Randall (1991). Explorations in behavioral consistency: Properties of persons, situations, and behaviors. *Journal of Personality and Social Psychology, 60,* 773–794.

Gaertner, Samuel L.; Mann, Jeffrey A.; Dovidio, John F.; Murrell, Audrey J.; & Pomare, Marina (1990). How does cooperation reduce intergroup bias? *Journal of Personality and Social Psychology, 59,* 692–704.

Gaines, Stanley O., Jr., & Reed, Edward S. (1995). Prejudice: From Allport to DuBois. *American Psychologist, 50,* 96–103.

Galanter, Marc (1989). *Cults: Faith, healing, and coercion.* New York: Oxford University Press.

Gale, Anthony (ed.) (1988). *The polygraph test: Lies, truth, and science.* London: Sage.

Ganaway, George K. (1991). Alternative hypotheses regarding satanic ritual abuse memories. Paper presented at the annual meeting of the American Psychological Association, San Francisco.

Garcia, John, & Koelling, Robert A. (1966). Relation of cue to consequence in avoidance learning. *Psychonomic Science, 4,* 23–124.

Gardner, Howard (1983). *Frames of mind: The theory of multiple intelligences.* New York: Basic Books.

Gardner, Howard (1985). *The mind's new science: A history of the cognitive revolution.* New York: Basic Books.

Gardner, Howard (1992). Scientific psychology: Should we bury it or praise it? *New Ideas in Psychology, 10,* 179–190.

Gardner, Howard (1993). *Multiple intelligences: The theory in practice.* New York: Basic Books.

Gardner, R. Allen, & Gardner, Beatrice T. (1969). Teaching sign language to a chimpanzee. *Science, 165,* 664–672.

Garmezy, Norman (1991). Resilience and vulnerability to adverse developmental outcomes associated with poverty. *American Behavioral Scientist, 34,* 416–430.

Garnets, Linda; Hancock, Kristin A.; Cochran, Susan D.; Goodchilds, Jacqueline; & Peplau, Letitia A. (1991). Issues in psychotherapy with lesbians and gay men: A survey of psychologists. *American Psychologist, 46,* 964–972.

Garnets, Linda, & Kimmel, Douglas C. (eds.) (1993). *Psychological perspectives on lesbian and gay male experiences.* New York: Columbia University Press.

Gates, Henry Louis (1992, July 20). Black demagogues and pseudo-scholars. *New York Times,* opinion page.

Gay, Peter (1988). *Freud: A life for our time.* New York: W. W. Norton.

Gaziano, J. Michael, & Hennekens, Charles (1995, July 1). Royal colleges' advice on alcohol consumption [editorial]. *British Medical Journal, 311,* 3–4.

Gazzaniga, Michael S. (1967). The split brain in man. *Scientific American, 217*(2), 24–29.

Gazzaniga, Michael S. (1983). Right hemisphere language following brain bisection: A 20-year perspective. *American Psychologist, 38,* 525–537.

Gazzaniga, Michael S. (1985). *The social brain: Discovering the networks of the mind.* New York: Basic Books.

Gazzaniga, Michael S. (1988). *Mind matters.* Boston: Houghton Mifflin.

Geis, Florence L. (1993). Self-fulfilling prophecies: A social psychological view of gender. In A. E. Beall & R. J. Sternberg (eds.), *The psychology of gender.* New York: Guilford Press.

Gelernter, Joel; O'Malley, S.; Risch, N.; Kranzler, H. R.; et al. (1991, October 2). No association between an allele at the D2 dopamine receptor gene (DRD2) and alcoholism. *Journal of the American Medical Association, 266,* 1801–1807.

Geller, E. Scott, & Lehman, Galen R. (1988). Drinking-driving intervention strategies: A person-situation-behavior framework. In M. D. Laurence, J. R. Snortum, & F. E. Zimring (eds.), *The social control of drinking and driving.* Chicago: University of Chicago Press.

Gelles, Richard J., & Straus, Murray A. (1988). *Intimate violence: The causes and consequences of abuse in the American family.* New York: Touchstone.

Gerbner, George (1988). Telling stories in the information age. In B. D. Ruben (ed.), *Information and behavior* (Vol. 2). New Brunswick, NJ: Transaction Books.

Gergen, Kenneth J. (1973). Social psychology as history. *Journal of Personality and Social Psychology, 26,* 309–320.

Gergen, Kenneth J. (1985). The social constructionist movement in modern psychology. *American Psychologist, 40,* 266–274.

Gergen, Kenneth J. (1994). Exploring the postmodern: Perils or potentials? *American Psychologist, 49,* 412–416.

Gergen, Mary M. (1992). Life stories: Pieces of a dream. In G. Rosenwald & R. Ochberg (eds.), *Storied lives.* New Haven, CT: Yale University Press.

Gerson, Kathleen (1993). *No man's land: Men's changing commitments to family and work.* New York: Basic Books.

Gewirtz, Jacob L. (1991). An analysis of infant social learning. Paper presented at the annual meeting of the American Psychological Association, San Francisco.

Gewirtz, Jacob L., & Peláez-Nogueras, Martha (1991a). The attachment metaphor and the conditioning of infant separation protests. In J. L. Gewirtz & W. M. Kurtines (eds.), *Intersections with attachment.* Hillsdale, NJ: Erlbaum.

Gewirtz, Jacob L., & Peláez-Nogueras, Martha (1991b). Infants' separation difficulties and distress due to misplaced maternal contingencies. In T. Field, P. McCabe, & N. Schneiderman, *Stress and coping in infancy and childhood.* Hillsdale, NJ: Erlbaum.

Gibbons, Frederick X.; McGovern, Paul G.; & Lando, Harry A. (1991). Relapse and risk perception among members of a smoking cessation clinic. *Health Psychology, 10,* 42–45.

Gibson, Eleanor J. (1994). Has psychology a future? *Psychological Science, 5,* 69–76.

Gibson, Eleanor, & Walk, Richard (1960). The "visual cliff." *Scientific American, 202,* 80–92.

Gilbert, Daniel T.; Pelham, Brett W.; & Krull, Douglas S. (1988). On cognitive busyness: When person perceivers meet persons perceived. *Journal of Personality and Social Psychology, 54,* 733–739.

Gillham, Jane E.; Reivich, Karen J.; Jaycox, Lisa H.; & Seligman, Martin E. P. (1995). Prevention of depressive symptoms in schoolchildren: Two-year follow-up. *Psychological Science, 6,* 343–351.

Gilligan, Carol (1982). *In a different voice.* Cambridge, MA: Harvard University Press.

Gilligan, Carol, & Wiggins, Grant (1987). The origins of morality in early childhood relationships. In J. Kagan & S. Lamb (eds.), *The emergence of morality in young children.* Chicago: University of Chicago Press.

Gillin, J. Christian; Sitaram, N.; Janowsky, D.; et al. (1985). Cholinergic mechanisms in REM sleep. In A. Wauquier, J. M. Gaillard, J. M. Monti, & M. Radulovacki (eds.), *Sleep: Neurotransmitters and neuromodulators.* New York: Raven Press.

Gilmore, David D. (1990). *Manhood in the making: Cultural concepts of masculinity.* New Haven, CT: Yale University Press.

Giordano, Magda; Ford, Lisa M.; Shipley, Michael T.; et al. (1990). Neural grafts and pharmacological intervention in a model of Huntington's disease. *Brain Research Bulletin, 25,* 453–465.

Gise, Leslie H. (ed.) (1988). *The premenstrual syndromes.* New York: Churchill Livingstone.

Gladue, Brian A. (1994). The biopsychology of sexual orientation. *Current Directions in Psychological Science, 3,* 150–154.

Glanzer, Murray, & Cunitz, Anita R. (1966). Two storage mechanisms in free recall. *Journal of Verbal Learning and Verbal Behavior, 5,* 351–360.

Glazer, Myron P., & Glazer, Penina M. (1990). *The whistleblowers: Exposing corruption in government and industry.* New York: Basic Books.

Glick, Peter, & Fiske, Susan T. (1996). The ambivalent sexism inventory: Differentiating hostile and benevolent sexism. *Journal of Personality and Social Psychology, 70,* 491–512.

Goddard, Henry H. (1917). Mental tests and the immigrant. *Journal of Delinquency, 2,* 243–277.

Gold, Paul E. (1987). Sweet memories. *American Scientist, 75,* 151–155.

Goldberg, Lewis R. (1990). An alternative "description of personality": The big-five factor structure. *Journal of Personality and Social Psychology, 59,* 1216–1229.

Goldberg, Lewis R. (1993). The structure of phenotypic personality traits. *American Psychologist, 48,* 26–34.

Goldman, Alan (1994, Winter). The centrality of "Ningensei" to Japanese negotiating and interpersonal relationships: Implications for U.S.-Japanese communication. *International Journal of Intercultural Relations, 18,* 29–54.

Goldman, Mark S.; Brown, Sandra A.; Christiansen, Bruce A.; & Smith, Gregory T. (1991). Alcoholism and memory: Broadening the scope of alcohol-expectancy research. *Psychological Bulletin, 110,* 137–146.

Goldstein, Richard (1980, September 30). Getting real about getting high: An interview with Andrew Weil, M.D. *The Village Voice.*

Goleman, Daniel (1995). *Emotional intelligence.* New York: Bantam.

Golub, Sharon (1992). *Periods: From menarche to menopause.* Newbury Park, CA: Sage.

Goodman, Gail S.; Qin, Jianjian; Bottoms, Bette L.; & Shaver, Phillip R. (1995). Characteristics and sources of allegations of ritualistic child abuse. Final report to the National Center on Child Abuse and Neglect, Washington, DC. [Executive summary and complete report available from NCCAN, 1-800-394-3366.]

Goodman, Gail S.; Rudy, L.; Bottoms, B.; & Aman, C. (1990). Children's concerns and memory: Issues of ecological validity in the study of children's eyewitness testimony. In R. Fivush & J. Hudson (eds.), *Knowing and remembering in young children.* New York: Cambridge University Press.

Goodman, Gail S.; Wilson, M. E.; Hazan, C.; & Reed, R. S. (1989). Children's testimony nearly four years after an event. Paper presented at the annual meeting of the Eastern Psychological Association, Boston.

Gopnik, Myrna (1991). Familial aggregation of a developmental language disorder. *Cognition, 39,* 1–50.

Gopnik, Myrna (1994). Prologue. (Special issue: Linguistic aspects of familial language impairment) In J. Matthews (ed.), *McGill working papers in linguistics,* Vol. 10 (1&2). Montreal, Quebec: McGill University.

Gore, P. M., & Rotter, Julian B. (1963). A personality correlate of social action. *Journal of Personality, 31,* 58–64.

Goren, C. C.; Sarty, J.; & Wu, P. Y. (1975). Visual following and pattern discrimination of face-like stimuli by newborn infants. *Pediatrics, 56,* 544–549.

Gorn, Gerald J. (1982). The effects of music in advertising on choice behavior: A classical conditioning approach. *Journal of Marketing, 46,* 94–101.

Gottesman, Irving I. (1994). Perils and pleasures of genetic psychopathology. Distinguished Scientist Award address presented at the annual meeting of the American Psychological Association, Los Angeles.

Gottfried, Adele Eskeles; Fleming, James S.; & Gottfried, Allen W. (1994). Role of parental motivational practices in children's academic intrinsic motivation and achievement. *Journal of Educational Psychology, 86,* 104–113.

Gould, James L., & Gould, Carol G. (1995). *The animal mind.* San Francisco: W. H. Freeman.

Gould, Stephen Jay (1981). *The mismeasure of man.* New York: W. W. Norton.

Gould, Stephen Jay (1987). *An urchin in the storm.* New York: W. W. Norton.

Gould, Stephen Jay (1990, April). The war on (some) drugs. *Harper's,* 24.

Gould, Stephen Jay (1994, November 28). Curveball. [Review of *The Bell Curve,* by Richard J. Herrnstein and Charles Murray.] *The New Yorker,* 139–149.

Gould, Stephen Jay, & Eldredge, Niles (1977). Punctuated equilibria: The tempo and mode of evolution reconsidered. *Paleobiology, 3,* 115–151.

Graf, Peter, & Schacter, Daniel A. (1985). Implicit and explicit memory for new associations in normal and amnesic subjects. *Journal of Experimental Psychology: Learning, Memory, and Cognition, 11,* 501–518.

Graham, Jill W. (1986). Principled organizational dissent: A theoretical essay. *Research in Organizational Behavior, 8,* 1–52.

Greene, Robert L. (1986). Sources of recency effects in free recall. *Psychological Bulletin, 99,* 221–228.

Greenfield, Patricia, & Beagles-Roos, Jessica (1988). Radio vs. television: Their cognitive impact on children of different socioeconomic and ethnic groups. *Journal of Communication, 38,* 71–92.

Greenough, William T. (1991). The animal rights assertions: A researcher's perspective. *Psychological Science Agenda* (American Psychological Association), 4(3), 10–12.

Greenough, William T., & Anderson, Brenda J. (1991). Cerebellar synaptic plasticity: Relation to learning vs. neural activity. *Annals of the New York Academy of Sciences, 627,* 231–247.

Greenough, William T., & Black, James E. (1992). Induction of brain structure by experience: Substrates for cognitive development. In M. Gunnar & C. A. Nelson (eds.), *Behavioral developmental neuroscience: Vol. 24. Minnesota Symposia on Child Psychology.* Hillsdale, NJ: Erlbaum.

Gregor, Anne (1993, June 1). Getting to root of cultural gaffes. *Los Angeles Times,* D3, D10.

Greven, Philip (1991). *Spare the child: The religious roots of punishment and the psychological impact of physical abuse.* New York: Knopf.

Gribbin, Kathy; Schaie, K. Warner; & Parham, Iris A. (1980). Complexity of life style and maintenance of intellectual abilities. *Journal of Social Issues, 36*(2), 47–61.

Griffin, Donald R. (1992). *Animal minds.* Chicago: University of Chicago Press.

Griffith, James E., & Villavicencio, Sandra (1985). Relationships among acculturation, sociodemographic characteristics and social supports in Mexican American adults. *Hispanic Journal of Behavioral Sciences, 7,* 75–92.

Grinspoon, Lester, & Bakalar, James B. (1993). *Marihuana, the forbidden medicine.* New Haven, CT: Yale University Press.

Groebel, Jo, & Hinde, Robert (eds.) (1989). The Seville statement on violence. In *Aggression and war: Their biological and social bases.* Cambridge, England: Cambridge University Press.

Gronbaek, M.; Deis, A.; Sorensen, T. I.; Becker, U.; Schnohr, P.; & Jensen, G. (1995, May 6). Mortality associated with moderate intakes of wine, beer, or spirits. *British Medical Journal, 310,* 1165–1169.

Gross, Martin (1978). *The psychological society.* New York: Random House.

Gross, Paul R., & Levitt, Norman (1994). *Higher superstition: The academic left and its quarrels with science.* Baltimore: Johns Hopkins University Press.

Grusec, Joan E., & Goodnow, Jacqueline J. (1994). Impact of parental discipline methods on child's internalization of values: A reconceptualization of current points of view. *Developmental Psychology, 30,* 4–19.

Grusec, Joan E.; Saas-Kortsaak, P.; & Simutis, Z. M. (1978). The role of example and moral exhortation in the training of altruism. *Child Development, 49,* 920–923.

Guba, Egon G. (1990). The alternative paradigm dialog. In E. G. Guba (ed.), *The paradigm dialog.* Newbury Park, CA: Sage.

Gudykunst, W. B., & Ting-Toomey, S. (1988). *Culture and interpersonal communication.* Newbury Park, CA: Sage.

Guilford, J. P. (1950). Creativity. *American Psychologist, 5,* 444–454.

Gutheil, Thomas G. (1993). The psychology of pharmacology. In M. Schacter (ed.), *Psychotherapy and medication.* Worthvale, NJ: Jason Aronson.

Haber, Ralph N. (1970, May). How we remember what we see. *Scientific American, 222,* 104–112.

Hackett, Gail; Betz, Nancy E.; Casas, J. Manuel; & Rocha-Singh, Indra A. (1992). Gender, ethnicity, and social cognitive factors predicting the academic achievement of students in engineering. *Journal of Counseling Psychology, 39,* 527–538.

Haier, Richard J.; Siegel, Benjamin V., Jr.; MacLachlan, Andrew; Soderling, Eric; et al. (1992). Regional glucose metabolic changes after learning a complex visuospatial/motor task: A positron emission tomographic study. *Brain Research, 570,* 134–143.

Haier, Richard J.; Siegel, Benjamin V., Jr.; Nuechterlein, Keith H.; Hazlett, Erin; et al. (1988). Cortical glucose metabolic rate correlates of abstract reasoning and attention studied with positron emission tomography. *Intelligence, 12,* 199–217.

Halaas, Jeffrey L.; Gajiwala, Ketan S.; Maffei, Margherita; et al. (1995). Weight-reducing effects of the plasma protein encoded by the obese gene. *Science, 269,* 543–546.

Hall, Edward T. (1959). *The silent language.* Garden City, NY: Doubleday.

Hall, Edward T. (1976). *Beyond culture.* New York: Anchor.

Hall, Edward T. (1983). *The dance of life: The other dimension of time.* Garden City, NY: Anchor Press.

Hall, Edward T., & Hall, Mildred R. (1990). *Understanding cultural differences.* Yarmouth, ME: Intercultural Press.

Halpern, Diane (1995). The disappearance of cognitive gender differences: What you see depends on where you look. *American Psychologist, 44,* 1156–1157.

Halpern, Diane (1995). *Thought and knowledge: An introduction to critical thinking* (3rd ed.). Hillsdale, NJ: Erlbaum.

Hamer, Dean H.; Hu, Stella; Magnuson, Victoria L.; et al. (1993). A linkage between DNA markers on the X chromosome and male sexual orientation. *Science, 261,* 321–327.

Haney, Craig; Banks, Curtis; & Zimbardo, Philip (1973). Interpersonal dynamics in a simulated prison. *International Journal of Criminology and Penology, 1,* 69–97.

Hanna, Elizabeth, & Meltzoff, Andrew N. (1993). Peer imitation by toddlers in laboratory, home, and daycare contexts: Implications for social learning and memory. *Developmental Psychology, 29,* 701–710.

Hanson, F. Allan (1993). *Testing testing: Social consequences of the examined life.* Berkeley: University of California Press.

Hare, Robert D. (1965). Temporal gradient of fear arousal in psychopaths. *Journal of Abnormal Psychology, 70,* 442–445.

Hare, Robert D. (1993). *Without conscience: The disturbing world of the psychopaths among us.* New York: Pocket Books.

Hare-Mustin, Rachel T. (1991). Sex, lies, and headaches: The problem is power. In T. J. Goodrich (ed.), *Women and power: Perspectives for therapy.* New York: W. W. Norton.

Hare-Mustin, Rachel T., & Marecek, Jeanne (1990). Gender and the meaning of difference: Postmodernism and psychology. In R. Hare-Mustin & J. Marecek (eds.), *Psychology and the construction of gender.* New Haven, CT: Yale University Press.

Haritos-Fatouros, Mika (1988). The official torturer: A learning model for obedience to the authority of violence. *Journal of Applied Social Psychology, 18,* 1107–1120.

Harkins, Stephen G., & Szymanski, Kate (1989). Social loafing and group evaluation. *Journal of Personality and Social Psychology, 56,* 934–941.

Harlow, Harry F. (1958). The nature of love. *American Psychologist, 13,* 673–685.

Harlow, Harry F., & Harlow, Margaret K. (1966). Learning to love. *American Scientist, 54,* 244–272.

Harlow, Harry F.; Harlow, Margaret K.; & Meyer, D. R. (1950). Learning motivated by a manipulation drive. *Journal of Experimental Psychology, 40,* 228–234.

Harmon-Jones, Eddie; Brehm, Jack W.; Greenberg, Jeff; Simon, Linda; & Nelson, David E. (1996). Evidence that the production of aversive consequences is not necessary to create cognitive dissonance. *Journal of Personality and Social Psychology, 70,* 5–16.

Harris, Marvin (1974). *Cows, pigs, wars, and witches: The riddles of culture.* New York: Simon & Schuster.

Harris, Marvin (1985). *Good to eat: Riddles of food and culture.* New York: Simon & Schuster.

Harris, P.; Brown, E.; Marriott, C.; Whittall, S.; & Harmer, S. (1991). Monsters, ghosts and witches: Testing the limits of the fantasy-reality distinction in young children. *British Journal of Developmental Psychology, 9,* 105–123.

Hart, John, Jr.; Berndt, Rita S.; & Caramazza, Alfonso (1985, August 1). Category-specific naming deficit following cerebral infarction. *Nature, 316,* 339–340.

Harter, Susan, & Jackson, Bradley K. (1992). Trait vs. nontrait conceptualizations of intrinsic/extrinsic motivational orientation. *Motivation and Emotion, 16,* 209–230.

Hasher, Lynn, & Zacks, Rose T. (1984). Automatic processing of fundamental information: The case of frequency of occurrence. *American Psychologist, 39,* 1372–1388.

Hatfield, Elaine, & Rapson, Richard L. (1993). *Love, sex, and intimacy.* New York: HarperCollins.

Hawkins, Scott A., & Hastie, Reid (1990). Hindsight: Biased judgments of past events after the outcomes are known. *Psychological Bulletin, 107,* 311–327.

Heath, Shirley B. (1989). Oral and literate traditions among Black Americans living in poverty. *American Psychologist, 44,* 367–373.

Heinrichs, R. Walter (1993). Schizophrenia and the brain: Conditions for a neuropsychology of madness. *American Psychologist, 48,* 221–233.

Helms, Janet E. (1990). *Black and White racial identity theory, research, and practice.* Westport, CT: Greenwood Press.

Helson, Ravenna, & McCabe, Laurel (1993). The social clock project in middle age. In B. F. Turner & L. E. Troll (eds.), *Women growing older.* Newbury Park, CA: Sage.

Helson, Ravenna; Roberts, Brent; & Agronick, Gail (1995). Enduringness and change in creative personality and the prediction of occupational creativity. *Journal of Personality and Social Psychology, 6,* 1173–1183.

Hepworth, Joseph T., & West, Stephen G. (1988). Lynchings and the economy: A time-series reanalysis of Hovland and Sears (1940). *Journal of Personality and Social Psychology, 55,* 239–247.

Herdt, Gilbert (1984). *Ritualized homosexuality in Melanesia.* Berkeley: University of California Press.

Herman, John H. (1992). Transmutative and reproductive properties of dreams: Evidence for cortical modulation of brainstem generators. In J. Antrobus & M. Bertini (eds.), *The neuropsychology of dreaming.* Hillsdale, NJ: Erlbaum.

Herman, Judith L. (1992). *Trauma and recovery.* New York: Basic Books.

Herman, Judith L., & Harvey, Mary R. (1993, April). The false memory debate: Social science or social backlash? *The Harvard Mental Health Letter, 9,* 4–6.

Herman, Louis M. (1987). Receptive competencies of language-trained animals. In J. S. Rosenblatt, C. Beer, M. C. Busnel, & P. J. B. Slater (eds.), *Advances in the study of behavior* (Vol. 17). Petaluma, CA: Academic Press.

Herman, Louis M.; Kuczaj, Stan A.; & Holder, Mark D. (1993). Responses to anomalous gestural sequences by a language-trained dolphin: Evidence for processing of semantic relations and syntactic information. *Journal of Experimental Psychology: General, 122,* 184–194.

Heron, Woodburn (1957). The pathology of boredom. *Scientific American, 196*(1), 52–56.

Herrnstein, Richard J., & Murray, Charles (1994). *The bell curve: Intelligence and class structure in American life.* New York: Free Press.

Hershberger, Scott L.; Lykken, David T.; & McGue, Matt (1995). A twin registry study of male and female sexual orientation. Paper presented at the annual meeting of the American Psychological Association, New York.

Hicks, Robert D. (1991). The police model of satanism crime. In J. T. Richardson, J. Best, & D. G. Bromley (eds.), *The satanism scare.* New York: Aldine de Gruyter.

Higley, J. D.; Hasert, M. L.; Suomi, S. J.; & Linnoila, M. (1991). A nonhuman primate model of alcohol abuse: Effects of early experience, personality, and stress on alcohol consumption. *Proceedings of the National Academy of Science, 88,* 7261–7265.

Hilts, Philip J. (1995). *Memory's ghost: The strange tale of Mr. M. and the nature of memory.* New York: Simon & Schuster.

Hirsch, Helmut V. B., & Spinelli, D. N. (1970). Visual experience modifies distribution of horizontally and vertically oriented receptive fields in cats. *Science, 168,* 869–871.

Hirschel, J. David; Hutchinson, Ira W., III; Dean, Charles; et al. (1990). *Charlotte spouse assault replication project: Final report.* Washington, DC: National Institute of Justice.

Hirst, William; Neisser, Ulric; & Spelke, Elizabeth (1978, January). Divided attention. *Human Nature, 1,* 54–61.

Hite, Shere (1987). *Women and love: A cultural revolution in progress.* New York: Knopf.

Hobson, J. Allan (1988). *The dreaming brain.* New York: Basic Books.

Hobson, J. Allan (1990). Activation, input source, and modulation: A neurocognitive model of the state of the brain-mind. In R. R. Bootzin, J. F. Kihlstrom, & D. L. Schacter (eds.), *Sleep and cognition.* Washington, DC: American Psychological Association.

Hobson, J. Allan, & McCarley, Robert W. (1977). The brain as a dream state generator: An activation-synthesis hypothesis of the dream process. *American Journal of Psychiatry, 134,* 1335–1348.

Hobson, Robert F. (1985). *Forms of feeling: The heart of psychotherapy.* London: Tavistock.

Hoffman, Martin L. (1977). Empathy, its development and prosocial implications. In C. B. Keasey (ed.), *Nebraska Symposium on Motivation* (Vol. 25). Lincoln: University of Nebraska Press.

Hoffman, Martin L. (1987). The contribution of empathy to justice and moral judgment. In N. Eisenberg & J. Strayer (eds.), *Empathy and its development.* New York: Cambridge University Press.

Hoffman, Martin L. (1989). Empathy, social cognition, and moral action. In W. Kurtines & J. Gewirtz (eds.), *Moral behavior and development: Vol. 1. Advances in theory, research, and application.* Hillsdale, NJ: Erlbaum.

Hoffman, Martin L. (1994). Discipline and internalization. *Developmental Psychology, 30,* 26–28.

Hoffman, Martin L., & Saltzstein, Herbert (1967). Parent discipline and the child's moral development. *Journal of Personality and Social Psychology, 5,* 45–57.

Hofstede, Geert, & Bond, Michael H. (1988). The Confucius connection: From cultural roots to economic growth. *Organizational Dynamics,* 5–21.

Hogg, Michael A., & Abrams, Dominic (1988). *Social identifications: A social psychology of intergroup relations and group processes.* New York: Routledge.

Holmes, David S. (1990). The evidence for repression: An examination of sixty years of research. In J. L. Singer (ed.), *Repression and dissociation.* Chicago: University of Chicago Press.

Holmes, David S. (1994). *Abnormal psychology* (2nd ed.). New York: HarperCollins.

Holt, Jim (1994, October 19). Anti-social science? *New York Times,* op-ed page.

Hooker, Evelyn (1957). The adjustment of the male overt homosexual. *Journal of Projective Techniques, 21,* 18–31.

Hooven, Carole; Gottman, John M.; & Katz, Lynn F. (1995). Parental meta-emotion structure predicts family and child outcomes. *Cognition and Emotion, 9,* 229–269.

Hopkins, Bill L. (1987). Comments on the future of applied behavior analysis. *Journal of Applied Behavior Analysis, 20,* 339–346.

Hoptman, Matthew J., & Davidson, Richard J. (1994). How and why do the two cerebral hemispheres interact? *Psychological Bulletin, 116,* 195–219.

Horn, G., & Hinde, R. A. (eds.) (1970). *Short-term changes in neural activity and behaviour.* New York: Cambridge University Press.

Horne, J. A. (1988). Sleep loss and "divergent" thinking ability. *Sleep, 11,* 528–536.

Horner, Althea J. (1991). *Psychoanalytic object relations therapy.* New York: Jason Aronson.

Horner, Matina (1972). Toward an understanding of achievement-related conflicts in women. *Journal of Social Issues, 28,* 157–176.

Horney, Karen (1926/1973). The flight from womanhood. Reprinted in J. B. Miller (ed.), *Psychoanalysis and women.* New York: Brunner/Mazel.

Horney, Karen (1945). *Our inner conflicts.* New York: W. W. Norton.

Horney, Karen (1950). *Neurosis and human growth.* New York: W. W. Norton.

Horney, Karen (1967). *Feminine psychology.* New York: W. W. Norton.

Hornstein, Gail (1992). The return of the repressed: Psychology's problematic relations with psychoanalysis, 1909–1960. *American Psychologist, 47,* 254–263.

Horowitz, Mardi J. (1988). *Introduction to psychodynamics: A new synthesis.* New York: Basic Books.

Hovland, Carl I., & Sears, Robert R. (1940). Minor studies of aggression: Correlation of lynchings with economic indices. *Journal of Psychology, 9,* 301–310.

Howard, George S. (1991). Culture tales: A narrative approach to thinking, cross-cultural psychology, and psychotherapy. *American Psychologist, 46,* 187–197.

Howe, Mark L., & Courage, Mary L. (1993). On resolving the enigma of infantile amnesia. *Psychological Bulletin, 113,* 305–326.

Howe, Mark L.; Courage, Mary L.; & Peterson, Carole (1994). How can I remember when "I" wasn't there? Long-term retention of traumatic experiences and emergence of the cognitive self. (Special issue: The recovered memory/false memory debate.) *Consciousness and Cognition, 3,* 327–355.

Hrdy, Sarah B. (1988). Empathy, polyandry, and the myth of the coy female. In R. Bleier (ed.), *Feminist approaches to science.* New York: Pergamon.

Hrdy, Sarah B. (1994). What do women want? In T. A. Bass (ed.), *Reinventing the future: Conversations with the world's leading scientists.* Reading, MA: Addison-Wesley.

Hu, S.; Pattatucci, A. M.; Patterson C; et al. (1995). Linkage between sexual orientation and chromosome Xq28 in males but not in females. *Nature Genetics, 11,* 248–256.

Hubbard, Ruth (1990). *The politics of women's biology.* New Brunswick, NJ: Rutgers University Press.

Hubbard, Ruth, & Wald, Elijah (1993). *Exploding the gene myth.* Boston: Beacon Press.

Hubel, D. H., & Wiesel, T. N. (1962). Receptive fields, binocular interaction and functional architecture in the cat's visual cortex. *Journal of Physiology* (London), *160,* 106–154.

Hubel, D. H., & Wiesel, T. N. (1968). Receptive fields and functional architecture of monkey striate cortex. *Journal of Physiology* (London), *195,* 215–243.

Huesmann, L. Rowell; Eron, Leonard; Lefkowitz, Monroe M.; & Walder, Leopold (1984). The stability of aggression over time and generations. *Developmental Psychology, 20,* 1120–1134.

Hughes, Judith M. (1989). *Reshaping the psychoanalytic domain: The work of Melanie Klein, W. R. D. Fairbairn, & D. W. Winnicott.* Berkeley: University of California Press.

Hughes, Robert (1993). *The culture of complaint: The fraying of America.* New York: Oxford University Press.

Hunt, Morton M. (1993). *The story of psychology.* New York: Doubleday.

Huntington's Disease Collaborative Research Group (1993). A novel gene containing a trinucleotide repeat that is expanded and unstable on Huntington's disease chromosomes. *Cell, 72,* 971–983.

Hupka, Ralph B. (1981). Cultural determinants of jealousy. *Alternative Lifestyles, 4,* 310–356.

Hupka, Ralph B. (1991). The motive for the arousal of romantic jealousy: Its cultural origin. In P. Salovey (ed.), *The psychology of jealousy and envy.* New York: Guilford Press.

Huston, Aletha, & Wright, John C. (1995). Effects of educational TV viewing of lower-income preschoolers on academic skills, school readiness, and school adjustment 1 to 3 years later. Report to Children's Television Workshop from the Center for Research on the Influences of Television on Children, University of Kansas, Lawrence.

Hyde, Janet S. (1981). How large are cognitive gender differences? A meta-analysis using w^2 and d. *American Psychologist, 36,* 892–901.

Hyde, Janet S. (1984). How large are gender differences in aggression? A developmental meta-analysis. *Developmental Psychology, 20,* 722–736.

Hyde, Janet S.; Fennema, Elizabeth; & Lamon, Susan J. (1990). Gender differences in mathematics performance: A meta-analysis. *Psychological Bulletin, 107,* 139–155.

Hyde, Janet S., & Linn, Marcia C. (1988). Gender differences in verbal ability: A meta-analysis. *Psychological Bulletin, 104,* 53–69.

Hyman, Ira E.; Husband, Troy H.; & Billings, F. James (1995). False memories of childhood experiences. *Applied Cognitive Psychology, 9,* 181–197.

Hyman, Irwin A. (1994). Is spanking child abuse? Conceptualizations, research and policy implications. Paper presented at the annual meeting of the American Psychological Association, Los Angeles.

Hyman, Ray (1994). Anomaly or artifact? Comments on Bem and Honorton. *Psychological Bulletin, 115,* 25–27.

Iaccino, James F. (1994). *Psychological reflections on cinematic terror: Jungian archetypes in horror films.* Westport, CT: Praeger/Greenwood.

Inglehart, Ronald (1990). *Culture shift in advanced industrial society.* Princeton, NJ: Princeton University Press.

Irons, Edward D., & Moore, Gilbert W. (1985). *Black managers: The case of the banking industry.* New York: Praeger/Greenwood.

Islam, Mir Rabiul, & Hewstone, Miles (1993). Intergroup attributions and affective consequences in majority and minority groups. *Journal of Personality and Social Psychology, 64,* 936–950.

Izard, Carroll E. (1994a). Four systems for emotion activation: Cognitive and noncognitive processes. *Psychological Review, 100,* 68–90.

Izard, Carroll E. (1994b). Innate and universal facial expressions: Evidence from developmental and cross-cultural research. *Psychological Bulletin, 115,* 288–299.

Jacklin, Carol N., & Reynolds, Chandra (1993). Gender and childhood socialization. In A. E. Beall & R. J. Sternberg (eds.), *The psychology of gender.* New York: Guilford Press.

Jacobs, Janis E., & Eccles, Jacquelynne S. (1985). Gender differences in math ability: The impact of media reports on parents. *Educational Researcher, 14,* 20–25.

Jacobsen, Teresa; Edelstein, Wolfgang; & Hofmann, Volker (1994). A longitudinal study of the relation between representations of attachment in childhood and cognitive functioning in childhood and adolescence. *Developmental Psychology, 30,* 112–124.

Jacobson, John W., & Mulick, James A. (1994). Facilitated communication: Better education through applied ideology. *Journal of Behavioral Education, 4,* 93–105.

Jacobvitz, Robin N. S. (1990). Defining and measuring TV addiction. Paper presented at the annual meeting of the American Psychological Association, Boston.

Jacox, Ada; Carr, D. B.; & Payne, Richard (1994, March 3). New clinical-practice guidelines for the management of pain in patients with cancer. *New England Journal of Medicine, 330,* 651–655.

James, William (1890/1950). *Principles of psychology* (Vol. 1). New York: Dover.

Janis, Irving L. (1982). *Groupthink: Psychological studies of policy decisions and fiascoes* (2nd ed.). Boston: Houghton Mifflin.

Janis, Irving L. (1989). *Crucial decisions: Leadership in policymaking and crisis management.* New York: Free Press.

Janis, Irving L.; Kaye, Donald; & Kirschner, Paul (1965). Facilitating effects of "eating-while-reading" on responsiveness to persuasive communications. *Journal of Personality and Social Psychology, 1,* 181–186.

Jellinek, E. M. (1960). *The disease concept of alcoholism.* New Haven, CT: Hillhouse Press.

Jenkins, Sharon Rae (1994). Need for power and women's careers over 14 years: Structural power, job satisfaction, and motive change. *Journal of Personality and Social Psychology, 66,* 155–165.

Jensen, Arthur R. (1969). How much can we boost IQ and scholastic achievement? *Harvard Educational Review, 39,* 1–123.

Jensen, Arthur R. (1981). *Straight talk about mental tests.* New York: Free Press.

Jensen, J. P.; Bergin, Allen E.; & Greaves, D. W. (1990). The meaning of eclecticism: New survey and analysis of components. *Professional Psychology: Research and Practice, 21,* 124–130.

John, E. R.; Tang, Y.; Brill, A. B.; Young, R.; & Ono, K. (1986). Double-labeled metabolic maps of memory. *Science, 233,* 1167–1175.

Johnson, Kent R., & Layng, T. Joe (1992). Breaking the structuralist barrier: Literacy and numeracy with fluency. *American Psychologist, 47,* 1475–1490.

Johnson, Marcia K. (1995). The relation between memory and reality. Paper presented at the annual meeting of the American Psychological Association, New York.

Johnson, Mark H.; Dziurawiec, Suzanne; Ellis, Hadyn; & Morton, John (1991). Newborns' preferential tracking of face-like stimuli and its subsequent decline. *Cognition, 40,* 1–19.

Johnson, Robert, & Downing, Leslie (1979). Deindividuation and valence of cues: Effects of prosocial and antisocial behavior. *Journal of Personality and Social Psychology, 37,* 1532–1538.

Johnson-Laird, Philip N. (1988). *The computer and the mind: An introduction to cognitive science.* Cambridge, MA: Harvard University Press.

Jones, James M. (1991). Psychological models of race: What have they been and what should they be? In J. D. Goodchilds (ed.), *Psychological perspectives on human diversity in America.* Washington, DC: American Psychological Association.

Jones, Mary Cover (1924). A laboratory study of fear: The case of Peter. *Pedagogical Seminary, 31,* 308–315.

Jones, Russell A. (1977). *Self-fulfilling prophecies.* Hillsdale, NJ: Erlbaum.

Jones, Steve (1994). *The language of genes.* New York: Anchor.

Judd, Charles M.; Park, Bernadette; Ryan, Carey S.; Brauer, Markus; & Kraus, Susan (1995). Stereotypes and ethnocentrism: Diverging interethnic perceptions of African American and White American youth. *Journal of Personality and Social Psychology, 69,* 460–481.

Jung, Carl (1967). *Collected works.* Princeton, NJ: Princeton University Press.

Kagan, Jerome (1984). *The nature of the child.* New York: Basic Books.

Kagan, Jerome (1989). *Unstable ideas: Temperament, cognition, and self.* Cambridge, MA: Harvard University Press.

Kagan, Jerome (1993). The meanings of morality. *Psychological Science, 4,* 353, 357–360.

Kagan, Jerome (1994). *Galen's prophecy: Temperament in human nature.* New York: Basic Books.

Kagan, Jerome, & Lamb, Sharon (eds.) (1987). *The emergence of morality in young children.* Chicago: University of Chicago Press.

Kagan, Jerome, & Moss, Howard (1962). *Birth to maturity.* New York: Wiley.

Kagan, Jerome, & Snidman, Nancy (1991). Infant predictors of inhibited and uninhibited profiles. *Psychological Science, 2,* 40–44.

Kagan, Jerome; Snidman, Nancy; Julia-Sellers, Martha; & Johnson, Maureen O. (1991). Temperament and allergic symptoms. *Psychosomatic Medicine, 53,* 332–340.

Kahneman, Daniel, & Treisman, Anne (1984). Changing views of attention and automaticity. In R. Parasuraman, D. R. Davies, & J. Beatty (eds.), *Varieties of attention.* New York: Academic Press.

Kameda, Tatsuya, & Sugimori, Shinkichi (1993). Psychological entrapment in group decision making: An assigned decision rule and a groupthink phenomenon. *Journal of Personality and Social Psychology, 65,* 282–292.

Kamin, Allen; Houston, Susan E.; Axton, Ted R.; & Hall, Rosalie (1995). Self-efficacy and race car driver performance: A field investigation. Paper presented at the annual meeting of the American Psychological Association, New York.

Kandel, Eric R., & Schwartz, James H. (1982). Molecular biology of learning: Modulation of transmitter release. *Science, 218,* 433–443.

Kane, John M. (1987). Treatment of schizophrenia. *Schizophrenia Bulletin, 13,* 133–156.

Kanter, Rosabeth Moss (1977/1993). *Men and women of the corporation.* New York: Basic Books.

Kantor, J. R. (1982). *Cultural psychology.* Chicago: Principia Press.

Kaplan, Meg S.; Morales, Miguel; & Becker, Judith V. (1993). The impact of verbal satiation of adolescent sex offenders: A preliminary report. *Journal of Child Sexual Abuse, 2,* 81–88.

Kaplan, Stephen L.; Randolph, Stephen W.; & Lemli, James M. (1991). Treatment outcomes in the reduction of fear: A meta-analysis. Paper presented at the annual meeting of the American Psychological Association, San Francisco.

Karasek, Robert, & Theorell, Tores (1990). *Healthy work: Stress, productivity, and the reconstruction of working life.* New York: Basic Books.

Karau, Steven J., & Williams, Kipling D. (1993). Social loafing: A meta-analytic review and theoretical integration. *Journal of Personality and Social Psychology, 65,* 681–706.

Karney, Benjamin R.; Bradbury, Thomas N.; Fincham, Frank D.; & Sullivan, Kieran T. (1994). The role of negative affectivity in the association between attributions and marital satisfaction. *Journal of Personality and Social Psychology, 66,* 413–424.

Karon, Bertram P. (1994). Psychotherapy: The appropriate treatment of schizophrenia. Paper presented at the annual meeting of the American Psychological Association, Los Angeles.

Kashima, Yoshihisa; Yamaguchi, Susumu; Kim, Uichol; Choi, Sang-Chin; et al. (1995). Culture, gender, and self: A perspective from individualism-collectivism research. *Journal of Personality and Social Psychology, 69,* 925–937.

Katz, Irwin, & Hass, R. Glen (1988). Racial ambivalence and American value conflict: Correlational and priming studies of dual cognitive structures. *Journal of Personality and Social Psychology, 55,* 893–905.

Katz, Jonathan Ned (1995). *The invention of heterosexuality.* New York: Dutton.

Katz, Lilian G. (1993, Summer). All about me. *American Educator, 17*(2), 18–23.

Katz, Phyllis A., & Ksansnak, Keith R. (1994). Developmental aspects of gender role flexibility and traditionality in middle childhood and adolescence. *Developmental Psychology, 30,* 272–282.

Kaufman, Joan, & Zigler, Edward (1987). Do abused children become abusive parents? *American Journal of Orthopsychiatry, 57,* 186–192.

Kaye, Kenneth (1977). Toward the origin of dialogue. In H. R. Schaffer (ed.), *Studies in mother-infant interaction.* New York: Academic Press.

Keane, M. M.; Gabrieli, J. D. E.; & Corkin, S. (1987). Multiple relations between fact-learning and priming in global amnesia. *Society for Neuroscience Abstracts, 13,* 1454.

Keating, Caroline F. (1994). World without words: Messages from face and body. In W. J. Lonner & R. Malpass (eds.), *Psychology and culture.* Needham Heights, MA: Allyn & Bacon.

Keirstead, Susan A.; Rasminsky, Michael; Fukuda, Y.; et al. (1989). Electrophysiologic responses in hamster superior colliculus evoked by regenerating retinal axons. *Science, 246,* 255–257.

Kelman, Herbert C., & Hamilton, V. Lee (1989). *Crimes of obedience: Toward a social psychology of authority and responsibility.* New Haven, CT: Yale University Press.

Kelsoe, John R.; Ginns, Edward I.; Egeland, Janice A.; Gerhard, Daniela S.; et al. (1989). Re-evaluation of the linkage relationship between chromosome 11p loci and the gene for bipolar affective disorder in the Old Order Amish. *Nature, 342,* 238–243.

Kendall-Tackett, Kathleen A.; Williams, Linda Meyer; & Finkelhor, David (1993). Impact of sexual abuse on children: A review and synthesis of recent empirical studies. *Psychological Bulletin, 113,* 164–180.

Kendler, K. S.; Heath, A. C.; Neale, M. C.; Kessler, R. C.; & Eaves, L. J. (1992, October 14). A population-based twin study of alcoholism in women. *Journal of the American Medical Association, 268,* 1877–1882.

Keneally, Thomas (1982/1993). *Schindler's list.* New York: Simon & Schuster.

Kenrick, Douglas T., & Trost, Melanie R. (1993). The evolutionary perspective. In A. E. Beall & R. J. Sternberg (eds.), *The psychology of gender.* New York: Guilford Press.

Kernberg, Otto F. (1976). *Object relations theory and clinical practice.* New York: Jason Aronson.

Kerr, John (1993). *A most dangerous method: The story of Jung, Freud, and Sabina Spielrein.* New York: Knopf.

Kesner, Raymond P.; Chiba, Andrea A.; & Jackson-Smith, Pamela (1994). Rats do show primacy and recency effects in memory for lists of spatial locations: A reply to Gaffan. *Animal Learning and Behavior, 22,* 214–218.

Kesner, Raymond P.; Measom, Michael O.; Forsman, Shawn L.; & Holbrook, Terry H. (1984). Serial-position curves in rats: Order memory for episodic spatial events. *Animal Learning and Behavior, 12,* 378–382.

Kihlstrom, John F. (1994). Hypnosis, delayed recall, and the principles of memory. *International Journal of Clinical and Experimental Hypnosis, 40,* 337–345.

Kihlstrom, John F. (1995). From a subject's point of view: The experiment as conversation and collaboration between investigator and subject. Invited address presented at the seventh annual meeting of the American Psychological Society, New York.

Kihlstrom, John F., & Harackiewicz, Judith M. (1982). The earliest recollection: A new survey. *Journal of Personality, 50,* 134–148.

Kihlstrom, John F.; Schacter, Daniel L.; Cork, Randall C.; Hurt, Catherine A.; and Behr, Steven E. (1990). Implicit and explicit memory following surgical anesthesia. *Psychological Science, 1,* 303–306.

Kimble, Gregory A. (1993). A modest proposal for a minor revolution in the language of psychology. *Psychological Science, 4,* 253–255.

Kimble, Gregory A. (1994). A frame of reference for psychology. *American Psychologist, 49,* 510–519.

Kimble, Gregory A. (1996). *Psychology: The hope of a science.* Cambridge, MA: MIT Press.

King, Patricia M., & Kitchener, Karen S. (1994). *Developing reflective judgment: Understanding and promoting intellectual growth and critical thinking in adolescents and adults.* San Francisco: Jossey-Bass.

Kinsbourne, Marcel (1982). Hemispheric specialization and the growth of human understanding. *American Psychologist, 37,* 411–420.

Kipnis, David, & Schmidt, Stuart (1985, April). The language of persuasion. *Psychology Today, 19*(4), 40–46.

Kirschenbaum, B.; Nedergaard, M.; Preuss, A.; et al. (1994). In vitro neuronal production and differentiation by precursor cells derived from the adult human forebrain. *Cerebral Cortex, 4,* 576–589.

Kitchener, Karen S., & King, Patricia M. (1990). The Reflective Judgment Model: Ten years of research. In M. L. Commons (ed.), *Models and methods in the study of adolescent and adult thought: Vol. 2. Adult development.* Westport, CT: Greenwood Press.

Kitchener, Karen S.; Lynch, Cindy L.; Fischer, Kurt W.; & Wood, Phillip K. (1993). Developmental range of reflective judgment: The effect of contextual support and practice on developmental stage. *Developmental Psychology, 29,* 893–906.

Kitzinger, Celia, & Wilkinson, Sue (1995). Transitions from heterosexuality to lesbianism: The discursive production of lesbian identities. *Developmental Psychology, 31,* 95–104.

Klatsky, Arthur L. (1994). Epidemiology of coronary heart disease-influence of alcohol. *Alcohol: Clinical and Experimental Research, 18,* 88–96.

Kleinmuntz, Benjamin, & Szucko, Julian J. (1984, March 29). A field study of the fallibility of polygraph lie detection. *Nature, 308,* 449–450.

Klima, Edward S., & Bellugi, Ursula (1966). Syntactic regularities in the speech of children. In J. Lyons & R. J. Wales (eds.), *Psycholinguistics papers.* Edinburgh, Scotland: Edinburgh University Press.

Kluft, Richard P. (1987). The simulation and dissimulation of multiple personality disorder. *American Journal of Clinical Hypnosis, 30,* 104–118.

Kluft, Richard P. (1993). Multiple personality disorders. In D. Spiegel (ed.), *Dissociative disorders: A clinical review.* Lutherville, MD: Sidran.

Knight, George P.; Johnson, Lora G.; Carlo, Gustavo; & Eisenberg, Nancy (1994). A multiplicative model of the dispositional antecedents of a prosocial behavior: Predicting more of the people more of the time. *Journal of Personality and Social Psychology, 66,* 178–183.

Koch, Sigmund (1992). "Psychology" or "The psychological studies"? *American Psychologist, 48,* 902–904.

Koegel, Robert L.; Schreibman, Laura; O'Neill, Robert E.; & Burke, John C. (1983). The personality and family-interaction characteristics of parents of autistic children. *Journal of Consulting and Clinical Psychology, 51,* 683–692.

Koeske, Randi D. (1987). Premenstrual emotionality: Is biology destiny? In M. R. Walsh (ed.), *The psychology of women: Ongoing debates.* New Haven, CT: Yale University Press.

Kohlberg, Lawrence (1964). Development of moral character and moral ideology. In M. Hoffman & L. W. Hoffman (eds.), *Review of child development research.* New York: Russell Sage Foundation.

Kohlberg, Lawrence (1966). A cognitive-developmental analysis of children's sex-role concepts and attitudes. In E. E. Maccoby (ed.), *The development of sex differences.* Stanford, CA: Stanford University Press.

Kohlberg, Lawrence (1976). Moral stages and moralization: The cognitive-developmental approach. In T. Lickona (ed.), *Moral development and behavior.* New York: Holt, Rinehart and Winston.

Kohlberg, Lawrence (1984). *Essays on moral development, Vol. 2. The psychology of moral development: The nature and validity of moral stages.* San Francisco: Harper & Row.

Köhler, Wolfgang (1925). *The mentality of apes.* New York: Harcourt, Brace.

Kohn, Alfie (1992). *No contest: The case against competition* (rev. ed.). Boston: Houghton Mifflin.

Kohn, Alfie (1993). *Punished by rewards.* Boston: Houghton Mifflin.

Kohn, Melvin, & Schooler, Carmi (1983). *Work and personality: An inquiry into the impact of social stratification.* Norwood, NJ: Ablex.

Kohut, Heinz (1971). *The analysis of the self.* New York: International Universities Press.

Kohut, Heinz (1977). *The restoration of the self.* New York: International Universities Press.

Kolbert, Elizabeth (1995, June 5). Public opinion polls swerve with the turns of a phrase. *The New York Times,* A1.

Koocher, Gerald P.; Goodman, Gail S.; White, C. Sue; Friedrich, William N.; et al. (1995). Psychological science and the use of anatomically detailed dolls in child sexual-abuse assessments. *Psychological Bulletin, 118,* 199–222.

Kopta, Stephen M.; Howard, Kenneth I.; Lowry, Jenny L.; & Beutler, Larry E. (1994). Patterns of symptomatic recovery in psychotherapy. *Journal of Consulting and Clinical Psychology, 62,* 1009–1016.

Kosslyn, Stephen M. (1980). *Image and mind.* Cambridge, MA: Harvard University Press.

Kosslyn, Stephen M.; Margolis, Jonathan A.; Barrett, Anna M.; Goldknopf, Emily J.; et al. (1990a). Age differences in imagery abilities. *Child Development, 61,* 995–1010.

Kosslyn, Stephen M.; Seger, Carol; Pani, John R.; & Hillger, Lynn A. (1990b). When is imagery used in everyday life? A diary study. *Journal of Mental Imagery, 14,* 131–152.

Kraemer, G. W.; Ebert, M. H.; Lake, C. R.; & McKinney, W. T. (1984). Hypersensitivity to d-amphetamine several years after early social deprivation in rhesus monkeys. *Psychopharmacology, 82,* 266–271.

Kramer, Peter (1993). *Listening to Prozac.* New York: Viking.

Kroll, Barry M. (1992). *Teaching hearts and minds: College students reflect on the Vietnam War in literature.* Carbondale: Southern Illinois University Press.

Krupa, David J.; Thompson, Judith K.; & Thompson, Richard F. (1993). Localization of a memory trace in the mammalian brain. *Science, 260,* 989–991.

Kuczmarski, R. J.; Flegal, K. M; Campbell, S. M.; & Johnson, C. L. (1994). Increasing prevalence of overweight among U.S. adults: The National Health and Nutrition Examination Surveys, 1960 to 1991. *Journal of the American Medical Association, 272,* 205–211.

Kuhn, Deanna; Weinstock, Michael; & Flaton, Robin (1994). How well do jurors reason? Competence dimensions of individual variation in a juror reasoning task. *Psychological Science, 5,* 289–296.

Kunda, Ziva (1990). The case for motivated reasoning. *Psychological Bulletin, 108,* 480–498.

Kurdek, L. A. (1987). Sex role self schema and psychological adjustment in coupled homosexual and heterosexual men and women. *Sex Roles, 17,* 549–562.

Kurtines, William M., & Gewirtz, Jacob L. (eds.) (1991). *Handbook of moral behavior and development* (Vols. 1–3). Hillsdale, NJ: Erlbaum.

Lader, Malcolm (1989). Benzodiazepine dependence. (Special issue: Psychiatry and the addictions.) *International Review of Psychiatry, 1,* 149–156.

Lader, Malcolm, & Morton, Sally (1991). Benzodiazepine problems. *British Journal of Addiction, 86,* 823–828.

LaFromboise, Teresa; Coleman, Hardin L. K.; & Gerton, Jennifer (1993). Psychological impact of biculturalism: Evidence and theory. *Psychological Bulletin, 114,* 395–412.

Lakoff, Robin T. (1990). *Talking power.* New York: Basic Books.

Lakoff, Robin T., & Coyne, James C. (1993). *Father knows best: The use and abuse of power in Freud's case of "Dora."* New York: Teachers College Press.

Lambert, Michael J., & Bergin, Allen E. (1994). The effectiveness of psychotherapy. In A. E. Bergin & S. L. Garfield (eds.), *Handbook of psychotherapy and behavior change* (4th ed.). New York: Wiley.

Landrine, Hope (1988). Revising the framework of abnormal psychology. In P. Bronstein & K. Quina (eds.), *Teaching a psychology of people.* Washington, DC: American Psychological Association.

Landry, D. W.; Zhao, K.; Yang, G. X.; Glickman, M.; & Georgiadis, T. M. (1993, March 26). Antibody-catalyzed degradation of cocaine. *Science, 259,* 1899–1901.

Lane, Charles (1994, December 1). The tainted sources of "The Bell Curve." *New York Review of Books,* 14–18.

Langer, Ellen J. (1989). *Mindfulness.* Reading, MA: Addison-Wesley.

Langer, Ellen J.; Blank, Arthur; & Chanowitz, Benzion (1978). The mindlessness of ostensibly thoughtful action: The role of placebic information in interpersonal interaction. *Journal of Personality and Social Psychology, 36,* 635–642.

Langer, Ellen J., & Piper, Alison I. (1988). Television from a mindful/mindless perspective. In S. Oskamp (ed.), *Applied social psychology annual: Vol. 8. Television as a social issue.* Newbury Park, CA: Sage.

Larmore, Kim; Ludwig, Arnold M.; & Cain, Rolene L. (1977). Multiple personality: An objective case study. *British Journal of Psychiatry, 131,* 35–40.

Lashley, Karl S. (1950). In search of the engram. In *Symposium of the Society for Experimental Biology* (Vol. 4). New York: Cambridge University Press.

Latané, Bibb, & Darley, John (1976). Help in a crisis: Bystander response to an emergency. In J. Thibaut, J. Spence, & R. Carlson (eds.), *Contemporary topics in social psychology.* Morristown, NJ: General Learning Press.

Latané, Bibb; Williams, Kipling; & Harkins, Stephen (1979). Many hands make light the work: The causes and consequences of social loafing. *Journal of Personality and Social Psychology, 37,* 822–832.

Laumann, Edward O.; Gagnon, John H.; Michael, Robert T.; & Michaels, Stuart (1994). *The social organization of sexuality.* Chicago: University of Chicago Press.

Laursen, Brett, & Collins, W. Andrew (1994). Interpersonal conflict during adolescence. *Psychological Bulletin, 115,* 197–209.

Lazarus, Arnold A. (1990). If this be research. . . . *American Psychologist, 58,* 670–671.

Lazarus, Richard S. (1991). Cognition and motivation in emotion. *American Psychologist, 46,* 352–367.

LeDoux, Joseph E. (1989). Cognitive-emotional interactions in the brain. *Cognition and Emotion, 3,* 267–289.

Lee, Jerry W., & Hart, Richard (1985). Techniques used by individuals who quit smoking on their own. Paper presented at the annual meeting of the American Psychological Association, Los Angeles.

Lent, James R. (1968, June). Mimosa cottage: Experiment in hope. *Psychology Today,* 51–58.

Lepowsky, Maria (1994). *Fruit of the motherland: Gender in an egalitarian society.* New York: Columbia University Press.

Lepper, Mark R.; Greene, David; & Nisbett, Richard E. (1973). Undermining children's intrinsic interest with extrinsic rewards. *Journal of Personality and Social Psychology, 28,* 129–137.

LeVay, Simon (1991). A difference in hypothalamic structure between heterosexual and homosexual men. *Science, 253,* 1034–1037.

Levenson, Leah (1983). *With wooden sword: A portrait of Francis Sheehy-Skeffington, militant pacifist.* Boston: Northeastern University Press.

Levenson, Robert W. (1992). Autonomic nervous system differences among emotions. *Psychological Science, 3,* 23–27.

Leventhal, Howard (1970). Findings and theory in the study of fear communications. In L. Berkowitz (ed.), *Advances in experimental social psychology* (Vol. 5). New York: Academic Press.

Levine, Daniel S. (1990). *Introduction to cognitive and neural modeling.* Hillsdale, NJ: Erlbaum.

Levine, Joseph, & Suzuki, David (1993). *The secret of life: Redesigning the living world.* Boston: WBGH Educational Foundation.

Levine, Robert V.; Martinez, Todd S.; Brase, Gary; & Sorenson, Kerry (1994). Helping in 36 U.S. cities. *Journal of Personality and Social Psychology, 67,* 69–82.

Levinthal, Charles F. (1988). *Messengers of paradise: Opiates and the brain.* New York: Anchor.

Levy, Jerre (1985, May). Right brain, left brain: Fact and fiction. *Psychology Today,* 38–39, 42–44.

Levy, Jerre; Trevarthen, Colwyn; & Sperry, Roger W. (1972). Perception of bilateral chimeric figures following hemispheric deconnection. *Brain, 95,* 61–78.

Levy, Robert I. (1973). *Tahitians: Mind and experience in the Society Islands.* Chicago: University of Chicago Press.

Levy-Lahad, Ephrat; Wasco, Wilma; Poorkaj, Parvoneh; et al. (1995a). Candidate gene for the chromosome 1 familial Alzheimer's disease locus. *Science, 269,* 973–977.

Levy-Lahad, Ephrat; Wijsman, Ellen M.; Nemens, Ellen; et al. (1995b). A familial Alzheimer's disease locus on chromosome 1. *Science, 269,* 970–973.

Lewis, Marc D. (1993). Early socioemotional predictors of cognitive competency at 4 years. *Developmental Psychology, 29,* 1036–1045.

Lewis, Michael (1992). *Shame: The exposed self.* New York: Free Press.

Lewontin, Richard C. (1970). Race and intelligence. *Bulletin of the Atomic Scientists, 26*(3), 2–8.

Lewontin, Richard C. (1982). *Human diversity.* New York: Scientific American Library.

Lewontin, Richard C. (1993). *Biology as ideology: The doctrine of DNA.* New York: HarperPerennial.

Lewontin, Richard C.; Rose, Steven; & Kamin, Leon J. (1984). *Not in our genes: Biology, ideology, and human nature.* New York: Pantheon.

Lewy, Alfred J.; Ahmed, Saeeduddin; Jackson, Jeanne L.; & Sack, Robert L. (1992). Melatonin shifts human circadian rhythms according to a phase-response curve. *Chronobiology International, 9,* 380–392.

Libet, Benjamin (1985). Unconscious cerebral initiative and the role of conscious will in voluntary action. *Behavioral and Brain Sciences, 8,* 529–566.

Lichtenstein, Sarah; Slovic, Paul; Fischhoff, Baruch; Layman, Mark; & Combs, Barbara (1978). Judged frequency of lethal events. *Journal of Experimental Psychology: Human Learning and Memory, 4,* 551–578.

Lickona, Thomas (1983). *Raising good children.* New York: Bantam.

Liebeskind, Arthur S. (1991). Chemical dependency and the denial of the need for intimacy. In A. Smaldino (ed.), *Psychoanalytic approaches to addiction.* New York: Brunner/Mazel.

Lifton, Robert J. (1986). *The Nazi doctors: Medical killing and the psychology of genocide.* New York: Basic Books.

Lightdale, Jenifer R., & Prentice, Deborah A. (1994). Rethinking sex differences in aggression: Aggressive behavior in the absence of social roles. *Personality and Social Psychology Bulletin, 20,* 34–44.

Lightfoot, Lynn O. (1980). Behavioral tolerance to low doses of alcohol in social drinkers. Unpublished doctoral dissertation, University of Waterloo, Waterloo, Ontario.

Linday, Linda A. (1994). Maternal reports of pregnancy, genital, and related fantasies in preschool and kindergarten children. *Journal of the American Academy of Child and Adolescent Psychiatry, 33,* 416–423.

Lindsay, D. Stephen, & Read, J. Don (1995). "Memory work" and recovered memories of childhood sexual abuse: Scientific evidence and public, professional, and personal issues. *Psychology, Public Policy, and the Law, 1,* 846–908.

Lindvall, O.; Sawle, G.; Widner, H.; et al. (1994). Evidence for long-term survival and function of dopaminergic grafts in progressive Parkinson's disease. *Annals of Neurology, 35,* 172–180.

Linton, Marigold (1978). Real-world memory after six years: An in vivo study of very long-term memory. In M. M. Gruneberg, P. E. Morris, & R. N. Sykes (eds.), *Practical aspects of memory.* London: Academic Press.

Lips, Hilary M. (1991). *Women, men, and power.* Mountain View, CA: Mayfield.

Lipsey, Mark W., & Wilson, David B. (1993). The efficacy of psychological, educational, and behavioral treatment: Confirmation from meta-analysis. *American Psychologist, 48,* 1181–1209.

Lipstadt, Deborah E. (1993). *Denying the Holocaust: The growing assault on truth and memory.* New York: Free Press.

Lipstadt, Deborah E. (1994, Spring). Denying the Holocaust: The fragility of memory. *Brandeis Review,* 30–33.

Lissner, L.; Odell, P. M.; D'Agostino, R. B.; Stokes, J., III; et al. (1991, June 27). Variability of body weight and health outcomes in the Framingham population. *New England Journal of Medicine, 324* (26), 1839–1844.

Lochman, John E. (1992). Cognitive-behavioral intervention with aggressive boys: Three-year followup and preventive effects. *Journal of Consulting and Clinical Psychology, 60,* 426–432.

Locke, Edwin A., & Latham, Gary P. (1990). Work motivation and satisfaction: Light at the end of the tunnel. *Psychological Science, 1,* 240–246.

Loehlin, John C. (1988). Partitioning environmental and genetic contributions to behavioral development. Invited address presented at the annual meeting of the American Psychological Association, Atlanta.

Loehlin, John C. (1992). *Genes and environment in personality development.* Newbury Park CA: Sage.

Loehlin, John C.,; Horn, J. M.; & Willerman, L. (1996). Heredity, environment, and IQ in the Texas adoption study. In R. J. Sternberg & E. Grigorenko (eds.), *Intelligence: Heredity and environment.* New York: Cambridge University Press.

Loftus, Elizabeth F. (1980). *Memory.* Reading, MA: Addison-Wesley.

Loftus, Elizabeth F. (1993). The reality of repressed memories. *American Psychologist, 48,* 518–537.

Loftus, Elizabeth F. (1995). Memories of childhood trauma or traumas of childhood memory. Paper presented at the annual meeting of the American Psychological Association, New York.

Loftus, Elizabeth F., & Greene, Edith (1980). Warning: Even memory for faces may be contagious. *Law and Human Behavior, 4,* 323–334.

Loftus, Elizabeth F., & Ketcham, Katherine (1994). *The myth of repressed memory.* New York: St. Martin's Press.

Loftus, Elizabeth F.; Miller, David G.; & Burns, Helen J. (1978). Semantic integration of verbal information into a visual memory. *Journal of Experimental Psychology: Human Learning and Memory, 4,* 19–31.

Loftus, Elizabeth F., & Palmer, John C. (1974). Reconstruction of automobile destruction: An example of the interaction between language and memory. *Journal of Verbal Learning and Verbal Behavior, 13,* 585–589.

Loftus, Elizabeth F., & Pickrell, Jacqueline E. (1995). The formation of false memories. (Special issue on false memories.) *Psychiatric Annals, 25,* 720–725.

Loftus, Elizabeth E., & Zanni, Guido (1975). Eyewitness testimony: The influence of the wording of a question. *Bulletin of the Psychonomic Society, 5,* 86–88.

Loftus, Geoffrey R. (1993). A picture is worth a thousand p values: On the irrelevance of hypothesis testing in the microcomputer age. *Behavior Research Methods, Instruments & Computers, 25,* 150–156.

Lonner, Walter J. (1995). Culture and human diversity. In E. Trickett, R. Watts, & D. Birman (eds.), *Human diversity: Perspectives on people in context.* San Francisco: Jossey-Bass.

Lonner, Walter J., & Malpass, Roy S. (1994). When psychology and culture meet: An introduction to cross-cultural psychology. In W. J. Lonner & R. S. Malpass (eds.), *Psychology and culture.* Needham Heights, MA: Allyn & Bacon.

López, Steven R. (1989). Patient variable biases in clinical judgment: Conceptual overview and methodological considerations. *Psychological Bulletin, 106,* 184–203.

López, Steven R. (1995). Testing ethnic minority children. In B. B. Wolman (ed.), *The encyclopedia of psychology, psychiatry, and psychoanalysis.* New York: Henry Holt.

Lott, Bernice, & Maluso, Diane (1993). The social learning of gender. In A. E. Beall & R. J. Sternberg (eds.), *The psychology of gender.* New York: Guilford Press.

Lovaas, O. Ivar (1977). *The autistic child: Language development through behavior modification.* New York: Halsted Press.

Lovaas, O. Ivar; Schreibman, Laura; & Koegel, Robert L. (1974). A behavior modification approach to the treatment of autistic children. *Journal of Autism and Childhood Schizophrenia, 4,* 111–129.

Luce, Gay Gaer, & Segal, Julius (1966). *Current research on sleep and dreams.* Bethesda, MD: U.S. Department of Health, Education, and Welfare.

Luengo, M. A.; Carrillo-de-la-Peña, M. T.; Otero, J. M.; & Romero, E. (1994). A short-term longitudinal study of impulsivity and antisocial behavior. *Journal of Personality and Social Psychology, 66,* 542–548.

Luepnitz, Deborah A. (1988). *The family interpreted: Feminist theory in clinical practice.* New York: Basic Books.

Lugaresi, Elio; Medori, R.; Montagna, P.; et al. (1986, October 16). Fatal familial insomnia and dysautonomia with selective degeneration of thalamic nuclei. *New England Journal of Medicine, 315,* 997–1003.

Luria, Alexander R. (1968). *The mind of a mnemonist* (L. Soltaroff, trans.). New York: Basic Books.

Luria, Alexander R. (1980). *Higher cortical functions in man* (2nd rev. ed.). New York: Basic Books.

Lutz, Catherine (1988). *Unnatural emotions.* Chicago: University of Chicago Press.

Lykken, David T. (1981). *A tremor in the blood: Uses and abuses of the lie detector.* New York: McGraw-Hill.

Lytton, Hugh, & Romney, David M. (1991). Parents' differential socialization of boys and girls: A meta-analysis. *Psychological Bulletin, 109,* 267–296.

Maccoby, Eleanor E. (1990). Gender and relationships: A developmental account. *American Psychologist, 45,* 513–520.

Maccoby, Eleanor E., & Martin, John A. (1983). Socialization in the context of the family: Parent-child interaction. In E. M. Hetherington (ed.), *Handbook of child psychology: Vol. 20. Socialization, personality, and social development.* Orlando, FL: Academic Press.

MacKavey, William R.; Malley, Janet E.; & Stewart, Abigail, J. (1991). Remembering autobiographically consequential experiences: Content analysis of psychologists' accounts of their lives. *Psychology and Aging, 6,* 50–59.

MacKinnon, Donald W. (1968). Selecting students with creative potential. In P. Heist (ed.), *The creative college student: An unmet challenge.* San Francisco: Jossey-Bass.

MacLean, Harry N. (1993). *Once upon a time: A true story of memory, murder, and the law.* New York: Harper-Collins.

Macrae, C. Neil; Milne, Alan B.; & Bodenhausen, Galen V. (1994). Stereotypes as energy-saving devices: A peek inside the cognitive toolbox. *Journal of Personality and Social Psychology, 66,* 37–47.

Madigan, Carol O., & Elwood, Ann (1984). *Brainstorms and thunderbolts.* New York: Macmillan.

Maffei, M.; Halaas, J.; Ravussin, E.; et al. (1995). Leptin levels in human and rodent: Measurement of plasma leptin and ob RNA in obese and weight-reduced subjects. *Nature Medicine, 1,* 1155–1161.

Malamuth, Neil, & Dean, Karol (1990). Attraction to sexual aggression. In A. Parrot & L. Bechhofer (eds.), *Acquaintance rape: The hidden crime.* Newark, NJ: Wiley.

Maling, Michael S., & Howard, Kenneth I. (1994). From research to practice to research to. . . . In P. F. Talley, H. H. Strupp, & S. F. Butler (eds.), *Psychotherapy research and practice: Bridging the gap.* New York: Basic Books.

Manning, Carol A.; Hall, J. L.; & Gold, Paul E. (1990). Glucose effects on memory and other neuropsychological tests in elderly humans. *Psychological Science, 1,* 307–311.

Manning, Carol A.; Ragozzino, Michael E.; & Gold, Paul E. (1993). Glucose enhancement of memory in patients with probable senile dementia of the Alzheimer's type. *Neurobiology of Aging, 14,* 523–528.

Marcia, James E. (1976). Identity six years later: A follow-up study. *Journal of Youth and Adolescence, 5,* 145–160.

Marcus, Gary F.; Pinker, Steven; Ullman, Michael; Hollander, Michelle; et al. (1992). Overregularization in language acquisition. *Monographs of the Society for Research in Child Development, 57* (Serial No. 228), 1–182.

Markus, Hazel R., & Kitayama, Shinobu (1991). Culture and the self: Implications for cognition, emotion, and motivation. *Psychological Review, 98,* 224–253.

Markus, Hazel R., & Nurius, Paula (1986). Possible selves. *American Psychologist, 41,* 954–969.

Marlatt, G. Alan, & Rohsenow, Damaris J. (1980). Cognitive processes in alcohol use: Expectancy and the balanced placebo design. In N. K. Mello (ed.), *Advances in substance abuse* (Vol. 1). Greenwich, CT: JAI Press.

Marshall, Grant N. (1991). A multidimensional analysis of internal health locus of control beliefs: Separating the wheat from the chaff? *Journal of Personality and Social Psychology, 61*, 483–491.

Marshall, Grant N.; Wortman, Camille B.; Vickers, Ross R., Jr.; Kusulas, Jeffrey W.; & Hervig, Linda K. (1994). The five-factor model of personality as a framework for personality-health research. *Journal of Personality and Social Psychology, 67*, 278–286.

Maslow, Abraham H. (1971). *The farther reaches of human nature.* New York: Viking.

Matthews, John (ed.). (1994). Special issue: Linguistic aspects of familial language impairment. *McGill working papers in linguistics*, Vol. 10 [1&2]. Montreal, Quebec: McGill University.

Mawhinney, T. C. (1990). Decreasing intrinsic "motivation" with extrinsic rewards: Easier said than done. *Journal of Organizational Behavior Management, 11*, 175–191.

May, Mitchell (1991). Observations on countertransference, addiction, and treatability. In A. Smaldino (ed.), *Psychoanalytic approaches to addiction.* New York: Brunner/Mazel.

Mayer, John D.; McCormick, Laura J.; & Strong, Sara E. (1995). Mood-congruent memory and natural mood: New evidence. *Personality and Social Psychology Bulletin, 21*, 736–746.

Mayer, John D., & Salovey, Peter (1993). The intelligence of emotional intelligence. *Intelligence, 17*, 433–442.

McAdams, Dan P. (1988). *Power, intimacy, and the life story: Personological inquiries into identity.* New York: Guilford Press.

McClearn, Gerald E. (1993). Behavioral genetics: The last century and the next. In R. Plomin & G. E. McClearn (eds.), *Nature, nurture, and psychology.* Washington, DC: American Psychological Association.

McClelland, David C. (1961). *The achieving society.* New York: Free Press.

McClelland, David C. (1987). Characteristics of successful entrepreneurs. *Journal of Creative Behavior, 3*, 219–233.

McClelland, David C.; Atkinson, John W.; Clark, Russell A.; & Lowell, Edgar L. (1953). *The achievement motive.* New York: Appleton-Century-Crofts.

McClelland, James L. (1994). The organization of memory: A parallel distributed processing perspective. *Revue Neurologique, 150*, 570–579.

McCloskey, Michael, & Cohen, Neal J. (1989). Catastrophic interference in connectionist networks: The sequential learning problem. *The Psychology of Learning and Motivation, 24*, 109–165.

McCloskey, Michael; Wible, Cynthia G.; & Cohen, Neal J. (1988). Is there a special flashbulb-memory mechanism? *Journal of Experimental Psychology: General, 117*, 171–181.

McConnell, James V. (1962). Memory transfer through cannibalism in planarians. *Journal of Neuropsychiatry, 3* (Monograph Supplement 1).

McCord, Joan (1989). Another time, another drug. Paper presented at the conference, Vulnerability to the Transition from Drug Use to Abuse and Dependence, Rockville, Maryland.

McCord, Joan (1990). Crime in moral and social contexts. *Criminology, 28*, 1–26.

McCord, Joan (1991). Questioning the value of punishment. *Social Problems, 38*, 167–179.

McCrae, Robert R. (1987). Creativity, divergent thinking, and openness to experience. *Journal of Personality and Social Psychology, 52*, 1258–1265.

McCrae, Robert R., & Costa, Paul T., Jr. (1988). Do parental influences matter? A reply to Halverson. *Journal of Personality, 56*, 445–449.

McDonough, Laraine, & Mandler, Jean M. (1994). Very long-term recall in infancy. *Memory, 2*, 339–352.

McFarlane, Jessica; Martin, Carol L.; & Williams, Tannis M. (1988). Mood fluctuations: Women versus men and menstrual versus other cycles. *Psychology of Women Quarterly, 12*, 201–223.

McGaugh, James L. (1990). Significance and remembrance: The role of neuromodulatory systems. *Psychological Science, 1*, 15–25.

McGinnis, Michael, & Foege, William (1993, November 10). Actual causes of death in the United States. *Journal of the American Medical Association, 270*, 2207–2212.

McGlynn, Susan M. (1990). Behavioral approaches to neuropsychological rehabilitation. *Psychological Bulletin, 108*, 420–441.

McGoldrick, Monica, & Pearce, John K. (1982). Family therapy with Irish Americans. In M. McGoldrick, J. K. Pearce, & J. Giordano (eds.), *Ethnicity and family therapy.* New York: Guilford Press.

McGrath, Ellen; Keita, Gwendolyn P.; Strickland, Bonnie; & Russo, Nancy F. (eds.) (1990). *Women and depression: Risk factors and treatment issues.* Washington, DC: American Psychological Association.

McGue, Matt; Bouchard, Thomas J., Jr.; Iacono, William G.; & Lykken, David T. (1993). Behavioral genetics of cognitive ability: A life-span perspective. In R. Plomin & G. E. McLearn (eds.), *Nature, nurture, and psychology.* Washington, DC: American Psychological Association.

McGue, Matt, & Lykken, David T. (1992). Genetic influence on risk of divorce. *Psychological Science, 3*, 368–373.

McGue, Matt; Pickens, Roy W.; & Svikis, Dace S. (1992). Sex and age effects on the inheritance of alcohol problems: A twin study. *Journal of Abnormal Psychology, 101*, 3–17.

McGuinness, Diane (1993). Sex differences in cognitive style: Implications for math performance and achievement. In L. A. Penner, G. M. Batsche, & H. Knoff (eds.), *The challenge in mathematics and science education: Psychology's response*. Washington, DC: American Psychological Association.

McHugh, Paul R. (1993a). History and the pitfalls of practice. Unpublished paper, Johns Hopkins University.

McHugh, Paul R. (1993b, December). Psychotherapy awry. *American Scholar*, 17–30.

McHugh, Paul R. (1993c, September). Multiple personality disorder. *The Harvard Mental Health Letter*, 10, 4–6.

McKee, Richard D., & Squire, Larry R. (1992). Equivalent forgetting rates in long-term memory for diencephalic and medical temporal lobe amnesia. *Journal of Neuroscience*, 12, 3765–3772.

McKee, Richard D., & Squire, Larry R. (1993). On the development of declarative memory. *Journal of Experimental Psychology: Learning, Memory, and Cognition*, 19, 397–404.

McLeod, Beverly (1985, March). Real work for real pay. *Psychology Today*, 42–44, 46, 48–50.

McNally, Richard J. (1994). *Panic disorder: A critical analysis*. New York: Guilford Press.

McNeill, David (1966). Developmental psycholinguistics. In F. L. Smith & G. A. Miller (eds.), *The genesis of language: A psycholinguistic approach*. Cambridge, MA: MIT Press.

Mealey, Linda (1996). Evolutionary psychology: The search for evolved mental mechanisms underlying complex human behavior. In J. P. Hurd (ed.), *Investigating the Biological Foundations of Human Morality* (Vol. 37). Lewiston, NY: Edwin Mellen Press.

Medawar, Peter B. (1979). *Advice to a young scientist*. New York: Harper & Row.

Medawar, Peter B. (1982). *Pluto's republic*. Oxford: Oxford University Press.

Mednick, Martha T. (1989). On the politics of psychological constructs: Stop the bandwagon, I want to get off. *American Psychologist*, 44, 1118–1123.

Mednick, Sarnoff A. (1962). The associative basis of the creative process. *Psychological Review*, 69, 220–232.

Mednick, Sarnoff A.; Huttunen, Matti O.; & Machón, Ricardo (1994). Prenatal influenza infections and adult schizophrenia. *Schizophrenia Bulletin*, 20, 263–267.

Meichenbaum, Donald (1975). Self-instruction methods. In F. H. Kanfer & A. P. Goldstein (eds.), *Helping people change*. Elmsford, NY: Pergamon Press.

Meltzer, Herbert Y. (1987). Biological studies in schizophrenia. *Schizophrenia Bulletin*, 13, 77–111.

Meltzoff, Andrew N., & Gopnik, Alison (1993). The role of imitation in understanding persons and developing a theory of mind. In S. Baron-Cohen, H. Tager-Flusberg, & D. Cohen (eds.), *Understanding other minds*. New York: Oxford University Press.

Melzack, Ronald (1973). *The puzzle of pain*. New York: Basic Books.

Mercer, Jane (1988, May 18). Racial differences in intelligence: Fact or artifact? Talk given at San Bernardino Valley College, San Bernardino, California.

Mershon, Bryan, & Gorsuch, Richard L. (1988). Number of factors in the personality sphere: Does increase in factors increase predictability of real-life criteria? *Journal of Personality and Social Psychology*, 55, 675–680.

Merskey, Harold (1992). The manufacture of personalities: The production of MPD. *British Journal of Psychiatry*, 160, 327–340.

Merskey, Harold (1994). The artifactual nature of multiple personality disorder. *Dissociation*, VII, 173–175.

Meyer-Bahlburg, Heino F. L.; Ehrhardt, Anke A.; Rosen, Laura R.; Gruen, Rhoda S.; Veridiano, Norma P.; Vann, Felix H.; & Neuwalder, Herbert F. (1995). Prenatal estrogens and the development of homosexual orientation. *Developmental Psychology*, 31, 12–21.

Meyerowitz, Beth E., & Chaiken, Shelley (1987). The effect of message framing on breast self-examination attitudes, intentions, and behavior. *Journal of Personality and Social Psychology*, 52, 500–510.

Michaels, J. W.; Bloommel, J. M.; Brocato, R. M.; Linkous, R. A.; & Rowe, J. S. (1982). Social facilitation and inhibition in a natural setting. *Replications in Social Psychology*, 2, 21–24.

Milavsky, J. Ronald (1988). Television and aggression once again. In S. Oskamp (ed.), *Applied social psychology annual: Vol. 8. Television as a social issue*. Newbury Park, CA: Sage.

Milgram, Stanley (1963). Behavioral study of obedience. *Journal of Abnormal and Social Psychology*, 67, 371–378.

Milgram, Stanley (1974). *Obedience to authority: An experimental view*. New York: Harper & Row.

Miller, George A. (1956). The magical number seven, plus or minus two: Some limits on our capacity for processing information. *Psychological Review*, 63, 81–97.

Miller, Joan G. (1984). Culture and the development of everyday social explanation. *Journal of Personality and Social Psychology*, 46, 961–978.

Miller, Jonathan (1983). *States of mind*. New York: Pantheon.

Miller, Neal E. (1978). Biofeedback and visceral learning. *Annual Review of Psychology*, 29, 421–452.

Miller, Neal E. (1985). The value of behavioral research on animals. *American Psychologist*, 40, 423–440.

Miller, Paris M.; Smith, Gregory T.; & Goldman, Mark S. (1990). Emergence of alcohol expectancies in childhood: A possible critical period. *Journal of Studies on Alcohol*, 51, 343–349.

Miller, Richard L.; Brickman, Philip; & Bolen, Diana (1975). Attribution versus persuasion as a means for modifying behavior. *Journal of Personality and Social Psychology*, 31, 430–441.

Miller, Scott D., & Triggiano, Patrick J. (1992). The psychophysiological investigation of multiple personality disorder: Review and update. *American Journal of Clinical Hypnosis*, 35, 47–61.

Miller-Jones, Dalton (1989). Culture and testing. *American Psychologist, 44*, 360–366.

Milner, Brenda (1970). Memory and the temporal regions of the brain. In K. H. Pribram & D. E. Broadbent (eds.), *Biology of memory*. New York: Academic Press.

Minuchin, Salvador (1984). *Family kaleidoscope*. Cambridge, MA: Harvard University Press.

Mischel, Walter (1966). A social-learning view of sex differences in behavior. In E. E. Maccoby (ed.), *The development of sex differences*. Stanford, CA: Stanford University Press.

Mischel, Walter (1973). Toward a cognitive social learning reconceptualization of personality. *Psychological Review, 80*, 252–253.

Mischel, Walter (1984). Convergences and challenges in the search for consistency. *American Psychologist, 39*, 351–364.

Mischel, Walter (1990). Personality dispositions revisited and revised: A view after three decades. In L. A. Pervin (ed.), *Handbook of personality: Theory and research*. New York: Guilford Press.

Mistry, Jayanthi, & Rogoff, Barbara (1994). Remembering in cultural context. In W. J. Lonner & R. Malpass (eds.), *Psychology and culture*. Needham Heights, MA: Allyn & Bacon.

Mitchell, D. E. (1980). The influence of early visual experience on visual perception. In C. S. Harris (ed.), *Visual coding and adaptability*. Hillsdale, NJ: Erlbaum.

Mitchell, Stephen A. (1993). *Hope and dread in psychoanalysis*. New York: Basic Books.

Mithers, Carol L. (1994). *Reasonable insanity: A true story of the seventies*. Reading, MA: Addison-Wesley.

Moffitt, Terrie E. (1993). Adolescence-limited and life-course-persistent antisocial behavior: A developmental taxonomy. *Psychological Review, 100*, 674–701.

Moore, Timothy E. (1995). Subliminal self-help auditory tapes: An empirical test of perceptual consequences. *Canadian Journal of Behavioural Science, 27*, 9–20.

Morris, Michael W., & Peng, Kaiping (1994). Culture and cause: American and Chinese attributions for social and physical events. *Journal of Personality and Social Psychology, 67*, 949–971.

Morrison, Ann M., & Von Glinow, Mary Ann (1990). Women and minorities in management. *American Psychologist, 45*, 200–208.

Moscovici, Serge (1985). Social influence and conformity. In G. Lindzey & E. Aronson (eds.), *Handbook of social psychology* (Vol. 2, 3rd ed.). New York: Random House.

Moston, S. (1987). The suggestibility of children in interview studies. *First Language, 2*, 67–78.

Mulick, James (1994, November/December). The non-science of facilitated communication. *Science Agenda* (APA newsletter), 8–9.

Murphy, Sean (ed.) (1993). *Astrocytes: Pharmacology and function*. San Diego, CA: Academic Press.

Murphy, Sheila T.; Monahan, Jennifer L.; & Zajonc, R. B. (1995). Additivity of nonconscious affect: Combined effects of priming and exposure. *Journal of Personality and Social Psychology, 69*, 589–602.

Murphy, Sheila T., & Zajonc, R. B. (1993). Affect, cognition, and awareness: Affective priming with optimal and suboptimal stimulus exposures. *Journal of Personality and Social Psychology, 64*, 723–739.

Myers, David G. (1980). *The inflated self*. New York: Seabury.

Myers, Ronald E., & Sperry, R. W. (1953). Interocular transfer of a visual form discrimination habit in cats after section of the optic chiasm and corpus callosum. *Anatomical Record, 115*, 351–352.

Nadel, Lynn, & Zola-Morgan, Stuart (1984). Infantile amnesia: A neurobiological perspective. In M. Moscovitch (ed.), *Infantile memory: Its relation to normal and pathological memory in humans and other animals*. New York: Plenum.

Nash, Michael R. (1987). What, if anything, is regressed about hypnotic age regression? A review of the empirical literature. *Psychological Bulletin, 102*, 42–52.

Nash, Michael R. (1994). Memory distortion and sexual trauma: The problem of false negatives and false positives. *International Journal of Clinical and Experimental Hypnosis, 42*, 346–362.

Nash, Michael R., & Nadon, R. (1996). The scientific status of hypnosis in the courts. In D. Faigman, D. Kaye, M. Saks, & J. Sanders (eds.), *The West companion to scientific evidence*. St. Paul, MN: West Publishing.

Nathan, Debbie (1994, Fall). Dividing to conquer? Women, men, and the making of multiple personality disorder. *Social Text, 40*, 77–114.

Nedergaard, Maiken (1994). Direct signaling from astrocytes to neurons in cultures of mammalian brain cells. *Science, 263*, 1768–1771.

Needleman, Herbert L.; Riess, Julie A.; Tobin, Michael J.; et al. (1996). Bone lead levels and delinquent behavior. *Journal of the American Medical Association, 275*, 363–369.

Needleman, Herbert L.; Schell, Alan; Bellinger, David; Leviton, Alan; et al. (1990). The long-term effects of exposure to low doses of lead in childhood: An 11-year follow-up report. *New England Journal of Medicine, 322*, 83–88.

Neisser, Ulric, & Harsch, Nicole (1992). Phantom flashbulbs: False recollections of hearing the news about *Challenger*. In E. Winograd & U. Neisser (eds.), *Affect and accuracy in recall: Studies of "flashbulb memories."* New York: Cambridge University Press.

Neisser, Ulric; Winograd, Eugene; & Weldon, Mary Sue (1991). Remembering the earthquake: "What I experienced" vs. "How I heard the news." Paper presented at the annual meeting of the Psychonomic Society, San Francisco.

Nelson, Thomas O., & Dunlosky, John (1991). When people's judgments of learning (JOLs) are extremely accurate at predicting subsequent recall: The "delayed JOL effect." *Psychological Science, 2,* 267–270.

Nelson, Thomas O., & Leonesio, R. Jacob (1988). Allocation of self-paced study time and the "labor in vain effect." *Journal of Experimental Psychology: Learning, Memory, and Cognition, 14,* 676–686.

Newman, Eric A., & Hartline, Peter H. (1982). The infrared "vision" of snakes. *Scientific American, 246*(3), 116–127.

Newman, Leonard S., & Baumeister, Roy F. (1994). "Who would wish for the trauma?" Explaining UFO abductions. Paper presented at the annual meeting of the American Psychological Association, Los Angeles.

Niemi, G.; Katz, R. S.; & Newman, D. (1980). Reconstructing past partisanship: The failure of party identification recall questions. *American Journal of Political Science, 24,* 633–651.

Nigg, Joel T., & Goldsmith, H. Hill (1994). Genetics of personality disorders: Perspectives from personality and psychopathology research. *Psychological Bulletin, 115,* 346–380.

Nisbett, Richard E. (1988, October 6). Testimony on behalf of the American Psychological Association before the U.S. House of Representatives Committee on Armed Services, *Congressional Record.*

Nisbett, Richard E. (1993). Violence and U.S. regional culture. *American Psychologist, 48,* 441–449.

Nisbett, Richard E., & Ross, Lee (1980). *Human inference: Strategies and shortcomings of social judgment.* Englewood Cliffs, NJ: Prentice-Hall.

Noble, Ernest P.; Blum, Kenneth; Ritchie, T.; Montgomery, A.; & Sheridan, P. J. (1991). Allelic association of the D2 dopamine receptor gene with receptor-binding characteristics in alcoholism. *Archives of General Psychiatry, 48,* 648–654.

Noelle-Neumann, Elisabeth (1984). *The spiral of silence.* Chicago: University of Chicago Press.

Oatley, Keith (1993). *Best laid schemes: The psychology of emotions.* New York: Cambridge University Press.

Ofshe, Richard J., & Watters, Ethan (1994). *Making monsters: False memory, psychotherapy, and sexual hysteria.* New York: Scribner.

Ogbu, John U. (1993). Differences in cultural frame of reference. *International Journal of Behavioral Development, 16,* 483–506.

Ogden, Jenni A., & Corkin, Suzanne (1991). Memories of H. M. In W. C. Abraham, M. C. Corballis, & K. G. White (eds.), *Memory mechanisms: A tribute to G. V. Goddard.* Hillsdale, NJ: Erlbaum.

Ogden, Thomas H. (1989). *The primitive edge of experience.* New York: Jason Aronson.

Ogilvie, D. M. (1987). The undesired self: A neglected variable in personality research. *Journal of Personality and Social Psychology, 52,* 379–385.

Olds, James (1975). Mapping the mind onto the brain. In F. G. Worden, J. P. Swazy, & G. Adelman (eds.), *The neurosciences: Paths of discovery.* Cambridge, MA: Colonial Press.

Olds, James, & Milner, Peter (1954). Positive reinforcement produced by electrical stimulation of septal area and other regions of the rat brain. *Journal of Comparative and Physiological Psychology, 47,* 419–429.

Oliner, Samuel P., & Oliner, Pearl M. (1988). *The altruistic personality: Rescuers of Jews in Nazi Europe.* New York: Free Press.

Oliver, Roland (1992). *The African experience.* New York: HarperCollins.

O'Reilly, Jane (1980). *The girl I left behind.* New York: Macmillan.

Orlinsky, David E. (1994). Research-based knowledge as the emergent foundation for clinical practice in psychotherapy. In P. F. Talley, H. H. Strupp, & S. F. Butler (eds.), *Psychotherapy research and practice: Bridging the gap.* New York: Basic Books.

Orlinsky, David E., & Howard, Kenneth I. (1994). Unity and diversity among psychotherapies: A comparative perspective. In B. Bongar & L. E. Beutler (eds.), *Foundations of psychotherapy: Theory, research, and practice.* New York: Oxford University Press.

Ortar, G. (1963). Is a verbal test cross-cultural? *Scripts Hierosolymitana* (Hebrew University, Jerusalem), *13,* 219–235.

Ortony, Andrew; Clore, Gerald L.; & Collins, Allan (1988). *The cognitive structure of emotions.* Cambridge, England: Cambridge University Press.

Oskamp, Stuart (ed.) (1988). *Television as a social issue.* Newbury Park, CA: Sage.

Ozer, Elizabeth M., & Bandura, Albert (1990). Mechanisms governing empowerment effects: A self-efficacy analysis. *Journal of Personality and Social Psychology, 58,* 472–486.

Paige, Karen E., & Paige, Jeffery M. (1981). *The politics of reproductive ritual.* Berkeley: University of California Press.

Palmer, Stephen; Schreiber, Charles; & Fox, Craig (1991). Remembering the earthquake: "Flashbulb" memory for experienced vs. reported events. Paper presented at the annual meeting of the Psychonomic Society, San Francisco.

Panksepp, J.; Herman, B. H.; Vilberg, T.; Bishop, P.; & DeEskinazi, F. G. (1980). Endogenous opioids and social behavior. *Neuroscience and Biobehavioral Reviews, 4,* 473–487.

Park, Denise C.; Smith, Anderson D.; & Cavanaugh, John C. (1990). Metamemories of memory researchers. *Memory and Cognition, 18,* 321–327.

Parks, Randolph W.; Loewenstein, David A.; Dodrill, Kathryn L.; Barker, William W.; et al. (1988). Cerebral metabolic effects of a verbal fluency test: A PET scan study. *Journal of Clinical and Experimental Neuropsychology, 10,* 565–575.

Parlee, Mary Brown (1982). Changes in moods and activation levels during the menstrual cycle in experimentally naive subjects. *Psychology of Women Quarterly, 7,* 119–131.

Patterson, Charlotte J. (1992). Children of lesbian and gay parents. *Child Development, 63,* 1025–1042.

Patterson, Charlotte J. (1995). Sexual orientation and human development: An overview. *Developmental Psychology, 31,* 3–11.

Patterson, Francine, & Linden, Eugene (1981). *The education of Koko.* New York: Holt, Rinehart and Winston.

Patterson, Gerald R. (1994). Developmental perspectives on violence. Invited address presented at the annual meeting of the American Psychological Association, Los Angeles.

Patterson, Gerald R.; DeBaryshe, Barbara D.; & Ramsey, Elizabeth (1989). A developmental perspective on antisocial behavior. *American Psychologist, 44,* 329–335.

Patterson, Gerald R.; Reid, John; & Dishion, Thomas (1992). *Antisocial boys.* Eugene, OR: Castalia.

Paul, Richard W. (1984, September). Critical thinking: Fundamental to education for a free society. *Educational Leadership,* 4–14.

Paulus, Paul B., & Dzindolet, Mary T. (1993). Social influence processes in group brainstorming. *Journal of Personality and Social Psychology, 64,* 575–586.

Peabody, Dean (1985). *National characteristics.* Cambridge, England: Cambridge University Press.

Pedersen, Nancy L.; Plomin, Robert; McClearn, G. E.; & Friberg, Lars (1988). Neuroticism, extraversion, and related traits in adult twins reared apart and reared together. *Journal of Personality and Social Psychology, 55,* 950–957.

Peele, Stanton (1989). *Diseasing of America: Addiction treatment out of control.* Lexington, MA: Lexington Books.

Peele, Stanton, & Brodsky, Archie, with Mary Arnold (1991). *The truth about addiction and recovery.* New York: Simon & Schuster.

Pellegrini, Anthony D., & Galda, Lee (1993). Ten years after: A reexamination of symbolic play and literacy research. *Reading Research Quarterly, 28,* 163–175.

Penfield, Wilder, & Perot, Phanor (1963). The brain's record of auditory and visual experience: A final summary and discussion. *Brain, 86,* 595–696.

Pennisi, Elizabeth (1994, January). A molecular whodunit. *Science News, 145,* 8–11.

Peplau, Letitia A., & Conrad, Eva (1989). Beyond nonsexist research: The perils of feminist methods in psychology. *Psychology of Women Quarterly, 13,* 379–400.

Peplau, Letitia A., & Gordon, Steven L. (1985). Women and men in love: Gender differences in close heterosexual relationships. In V. O'Leary, R. Unger, & B. Wallston (eds.), *Women, gender, and social psychology.* Hillsdale, NJ: Erlbaum.

Pepperberg, Irene M. (1990). Cognition in an African gray parrot (*Psittacus erithacus*): Further evidence for comprehension of categories and labels. *Journal of Comparative Psychology, 104,* 41–52.

Pepperberg, Irene M. (1994). Numerical competence in an African gray parrot (*Psittacus erithacus*). *Journal of Comparative Psychology, 108,* 36–44.

Perdue, Charles W.; Dovidio, John F.; Gurtman, Michael B.; & Tyler, Richard B. (1990). Us and them: Social categorization and the process of intergroup bias. *Journal of Personality and Social Psychology, 59,* 475–486.

Perloff, Robert (1992, Summer). "Where ignorance is bliss, 'tis folly to be wise." *The General Psychologist Newsletter, 28,* 34.

Perry, David G.; Perry, Louise C.; & Rasmussen, Paul (1986). Cognitive social learning mediators of aggression. *Child Development, 57,* 700–711.

Perry, Samuel W., & Heidrich, George (1982). Management of pain during debridement: A survey of U.S. burn units. *Pain, 13,* 267–280.

Pert, Candace B., & Snyder, Solomon H. (1973). Opiate receptor: Demonstration in nervous tissue. *Science, 179,* 1011–1014.

Peters, Douglas P. (1991). Confrontational stress and children's testimony. Paper presented at the biennial meeting of the Society for Research in Child Development, Seattle.

Peterson, Lloyd R., & Peterson, Margaret J. (1959). Short-term retention of individual verbal items. *Journal of Experimental Psychology, 58,* 193–198.

Pfungst, Oskar (1911/1965). *Clever Hans (The horse of Mr. von Osten): A contribution to experimental animal and human psychology.* New York: Holt, Rinehart and Winston.

Phares, E. Jerry (1976). *Locus of control in personality.* Morristown, NJ: General Learning Press.

Phillips, D. P.; Ruth, T. E.; & Wagner, L. M. (1993, November 6). Psychology and survival. *Lancet, 342*(8880), 1142–1145.

Phinney, Jean S. (1990). Ethnic identity in adolescents and adults: Review of research. *Psychological Bulletin, 108,* 499–514.

Piaget, Jean (1929/1960). *The child's conception of the world.* Paterson, NJ: Littlefield, Adams.

Piaget, Jean (1951). *Plays, dreams, and imitation in childhood.* New York: W. W. Norton.

Piaget, Jean (1952). *The origins of intelligence in children.* New York: International Universities Press.

Piaget, Jean (1984). Piaget's theory. In P. Mussen (series ed.) & W. Kessen (vol. ed.), *Handbook of child psychology: Vol. 1. History, theory, and methods* (4th ed.). New York: Wiley.

Pickens, Jeffrey (1994). Perception of auditory-visual distance relations by 5-month-old infants. *Developmental Psychology, 30,* 537–544.

Pines, Maya (1983, September). The human difference. *Psychology Today,* 62–68.

Pinker, Steven (1994). *The language instinct: How the mind creates language.* New York: Morrow.

Pipe, Margaret-Ellen, & Goodman, Gail S. (1991). Elements of secrecy: Implications for children's testimony. *Behavioral Sciences and the Law, 9,* 33–41.

Piper, August, Jr. (1994). Multiple personality disorder. *British Journal of Psychiatry, 164,* 600–612.

Plomin, Robert (1988). The nature and nurture of cognitive abilities. In R. J. Sternberg (ed.), *Advances in the psychology of human intelligence* (Vol. 4). Hillsdale, NJ: Erlbaum.

Plomin, Robert (1989). Environment and genes: Determinants of behavior. *American Psychologist, 44,* 105–111.

Plomin, Robert; Corley, Robin; DeFries, J. C.; & Fulker, D. W. (1990). Individual differences in television viewing in early childhood: Nature as well as nurture. *Psychological Science, 1,* 371–377.

Plomin, Robert, & Daniels, D. (1987). Why are children in the same family so different from one another? *Behavioral and Brain Sciences, 10,* 1–16.

Plomin, Robert, & DeFries, John C. (1985). *Origins of individual differences in infancy: The Colorado Adoption Project.* New York: Academic Press.

Plous, Scott L. (1991). An attitude survey of animal rights activists. *Psychological Science, 2,* 194–196.

Plutchik, Robert (1987). Evolutionary bases of empathy. In N. Eisenberg & J. Strayer (eds.), *Empathy and its development.* New York: Cambridge University Press.

Plutchik, Robert (1988). The nature of emotions: Clinical implications. In M. Clynes & J. Panksepp (eds.), *Emotions and psychopathology.* New York: Plenum.

Plutchik, Robert; Conte, Hope R.; Karasu, Toksoz; & Buckley, Peter (1988, Fall/Winter). The measurement of psychodynamic variables. *Hillside Journal of Clinical Psychology, 10,* 132–147.

Polich, John; Pollock, Vicki E.; & Bloom, Floyd E. (1994). Meta-analysis of P300 amplitude from males at risk for alcoholism. *Psychological Bulletin, 115,* 55–73.

Poole, Debra A. (1995). Strolling fuzzy-trace theory through eyewitness testimony (or vice versa). *Learning and Individual Differences, 7,* 87–93.

Poole, Debra A.; Lindsay, D. Stephen; Memon, Amina; Bull, Ray (1995). Psychotherapy and the recovery of memories of childhood sexual abuse: U.S. and British practitioners' opinions, practices, and experiences. *Journal of Consulting and Clinical Psychology. 63,* 426–437.

Poole, Debra A., & White, Lawrence T. (1991). Effects of question repetition on the eyewitness testimony of children and adults. *Developmental Psychology, 27,* 975–986.

Pope, Kenneth, & Bouhoutsos, Jacqueline (1986). *Sexual intimacy between therapists and patients.* New York: Praeger.

Portenoy, Russell K. (1994). Opioid therapy for chronic nonmalignant pain: Current status. In H. L. Fields & J. C. Liebeskind (eds.), *Progress in pain research and management. Pharmacological approaches to the treatment of chronic pain: Vol. 1. New concepts and critical issues.* Seattle: International Association for the Study of Pain.

Posada, German; Lord, Chiyoko; & Waters, Everett (1995). Secure base behavior and children's misbehavior in three different contexts: Home, neighbors, and school. Paper presented at the annual meeting of the Society for Research in Child Development, Indianapolis.

Poulin-Dubois, Diane; Serbin, Lisa A.; Kenyon, Brenda; & Derbyshire, Alison (1994). Infants' intermodal knowledge about gender. *Developmental Psychology, 30,* 436–442.

Poulos, Constantine X., & Cappell, Howard (1991). Homeostatic theory of drug tolerance: A general model of physiological adaptation. *Psychological Review, 98,* 390–408.

Powell, Russell A., & Boer, Douglas P. (1994). Did Freud mislead patients to confabulate memories of abuse? *Psychological Reports, 74,* 1283–1298.

Powell, Russell A., & Boer, Douglas P. (1995). Did Freud misinterpret reported memories of sexual abuse as fantasies? *Psychological Reports, 77,* 563–570.

Pratkanis, Anthony, & Aronson, Elliot (1992). *Age of propaganda: The everyday use and abuse of persuasion.* New York: W. H. Freeman.

Premack, David, & Premack, Ann James (1983). *The mind of an ape.* New York: W. W. Norton.

Pribram, Karl H. (1971). *Languages of the brain: Experimental paradoxes and principles.* Englewood Cliffs, NJ: Prentice-Hall.

Pribram, Karl H. (1982). Localization and distribution of function in the brain. In J. Orbach (ed.), *Neuropsychology after Lashley.* Hillsdale, NJ: Erlbaum.

Prochaska, James O.; Norcross, John C.; & DiClemente, Carlo C. (1994). *Changing for good.* New York: Morrow.

Pulkkinen, Lea (1982). Self-control and continuity in childhood and delayed adolescence. In P. Baltes & O. Brim (eds.), *Life span development and behavior* (Vol. 4). New York: Academic Press.

Putnam, Frank (1989). *Diagnosis and treatment of multiple personality disorder.* New York: Guilford Press.

Pynoos, R. S., & Nader, K. (1989). Children's memory and proximity to violence. *Journal of the American Academy of Child and Adolescent Psychiatry, 28,* 236–241.

Quinn, Susan (1987). *A mind of her own: The life of Karen Horney.* New York: Summit Books.

Radetsky, Peter (1991, April). The brainiest cells alive. *Discover, 12,* 82–85, 88, 90.

Raine, Adrian; Brennan, Patricia; & Mednick, Sarnoff A. (1994). Birth complications combined with early maternal rejection at age one year predispose to violent crime at age 18 years. *Archives of General Psychiatry, 51,* 984–988.

Raine, Adrian; Buchsbaum, Monte S.; Stanley, Jill; et al. (1994). Selective reductions in prefrontal glucose metabolism in murderers. Paper presented at the annual meeting of the American Psychological Association, Los Angeles.

Randi, James (1982, March). The 1980 divining tests. *The Skeptic, 2–6.*

Ratcliff, Roger (1990). Connectionist models of recognition memory: Constraints imposed by learning and forgetting functions. *Psychological Review, 97,* 285–308.

Raz, Sarah, & Raz, Naftali (1990). Structural brain abnormalities in the major psychoses: A quantitative review of the evidence from computerized imaging. *Psychological Bulletin, 108,* 93–108.

Rechtschaffen, Allan; Gilliland, Marcia A.; Bergmann, Bernard M.; & Winter, Jacqueline B. (1983). Physiological correlates of prolonged sleep deprivation in rats. *Science, 221,* 182–184.

Reppert, Steven M.; Weaver, David R.; Rivkees, Scoff A.; & Stopa, Edward G. (1988). Putative melatonin receptors in a human biological clock. *Science, 242,* 78–81.

Rescorla, Robert A. (1968). Probability of shock in the presence and absence of CS in fear conditioning. *Journal of Comparative and Physiological Psychology, 66,* 1–5.

Rescorla, Robert A. (1988). Pavlovian conditioning: It's not what you think it is. *American Psychologist, 43,* 151–160.

Rescorla, Robert A., & Wagner, Allan R. (1972). A theory of Pavlovian conditioning: Variations in the effectiveness of reinforcement and nonreinforcement. In A. H. Black & W. F. Prokasy (eds.), *Classical conditioning II: Current research and theory.* New York: Appleton-Century-Crofts.

Restak, Richard (1983, October). Is free will a fraud? *Science Digest, 91*(10), 52–55.

Restak, Richard M. (1994). *The modular brain.* New York: Macmillan.

Reynolds, Brent A., & Weiss, Samuel (1992). Generation of neurons and astrocytes from isolated cells of the adult mammalian central nervous system. *Science, 255,* 1707–1710.

Reynolds, David K. (1987). *Water bears no scars: Japanese lifeways for personal growth.* New York: Morrow.

Rhoades, David F. (1985). Pheromonal communication between plants. In G. A. Cooper-Driver, T. Swain, & E. E. Conn (eds.), *Research advances in phytochemistry* (Vol. 19). New York: Plenum.

Rice, Mabel L. (1989). Children's language acquisition. *American Psychologist, 44,* 149–156.

Richards, Ruth L. (1991). Everyday creativity and the arts. Paper presented at the annual meeting of the American Psychological Association, San Francisco.

Richards, Ruth L.; Kinney, Dennis K.; Benet, Maria; & Merzel, Ann (1988). Everyday creativity: Characteristics of the Lifetime Creativity Scales and validation with three large samples. *Journal of Personality and Social Psychology, 54,* 476–485.

Richardson-Klavehn, Alan, & Bjork, Robert A. (1988). Measures of memory. *Annual Review of Psychology, 39,* 475–543.

Ristau, Carolyn A. (ed.) (1991). *Cognitive ethology: The minds of other animals.* Hillsdale, NJ: Erlbaum.

Robertson, John, & Fitzgerald, Louise F. (1990). The (mis)treatment of men: Effects of client gender role and life-style on diagnosis and attribution of pathology. *Journal of Counseling Psychology, 37,* 3–9.

Robins, Lee N.; Davis, Darlene H.; & Goodwin, Donald W. (1974). Drug use by U.S. Army enlisted men in Vietnam: A follow-up on their return home. *American Journal of Epidemiology, 99,* 235–249.

Robins, Lee N.; Tipp, Jayson; & Przybeck, Thomas R. (1991). Antisocial personality. In L. N. Robins & D. A. Regier (eds.), *Psychiatric disorders in America.* New York: Free Press.

Robinson, Leslie A.; Berman, Jeffrey S.; & Neimeyer, Robert A. (1990). Psychotherapy for the treatment of depression: A comprehensive review of controlled outcome research. *Psychological Bulletin, 108,* 30–49.

Rodin, Judith (1988). Control, health, and aging. Invited address presented at the annual meeting of the Society of Behavioral Medicine, Boston.

Rodin, Judith; Silberstein, Lisa R.; & Striegel-Moore, Ruth H. (1990). Vulnerability and resilience in the age of eating disorders: Risk and protective factors for bulimia. In J. E. Rolf et al. (eds.), *Risk and protective factors in the development of psychopathology.* Cambridge, England: Cambridge University Press.

Roediger, Henry L., III (1990). Implicit memory: Retention without remembering. *American Psychologist, 45,* 1043–1056.

Roediger, Henry L., & McDermott, Kathleen B. (1995). Creating false memories: Remembering words not presented in lists. *Journal of Experimental Psychology; Learning, Memory, and Cognition, 21,* 803–814.

Roehrs, Timothy; Timms, Victoria; Zsyghuizen-Doorenbos, Ardith; Buzenski, Raymond; et al. (1990). Polysomnographic, performance, and personality differences of sleepy and alert normals. *Sleep, 13,* 395–402.

Rogers, Carl (1951). *Client-centered therapy: Its current practice, implications, and theory.* Boston: Houghton Mifflin.

Rogers, Carl (1961). *On becoming a person.* Boston: Houghton Mifflin.

Rogers, Ronald W., & Prentice-Dunn, Steven (1981). Deindividuation and anger-mediated interracial aggression: Unmasking regressive racism. *Journal of Personality and Social Psychology, 41,* 63–73.

Rogler, Lloyd H.; Malgady, Robert G.; Costantino, Giuseppe; & Blumenthal, Rena (1987). What do culturally sensitive mental health services mean? The case of Hispanics. *American Psychologist, 42,* 565–570.

Rogoff, Barbara, & Chavajay, Pablo (1995). What's become of research on the cultural basis of cognitive development? *American Psychologist, 50,* 859–877.

Rosaldo, Renato (1989). *Culture and truth: The remaking of social analysis.* Boston: Beacon Press.

Rosen, B. R.; Aronen, H. J.; Kwong, K. K.; et al. (1993). Advances in clinical neuroimaging: Functional MR imaging techniques. *Radiographics, 13,* 889–896.

Rosen, R. D. (1977). *Psychobabble.* New York: Atheneum.

Rosenberg, Harold (1993). Prediction of controlled drinking by alcoholics and problem drinkers. *Psychological Bulletin, 113,* 129–139.

Rosenthal, Robert (1966). *Experimenter effects in behavioral research.* New York: Appleton-Century-Crofts.

Rosenzweig, Mark R. (1984). Experience, memory, and the brain. *American Psychologist, 39,* 365–376.

Ross, Hildy S., & Lollis, Susan P. (1987). Communication within infant social games. *Developmental Psychology, 23,* 241–248.

Ross, Michael (1989). Relation of implicit theories to the construction of personal histories. *Psychological Review, 96,* 341–357.

Rotter, Julian B. (1966). Generalized expectancies for internal versus external control of reinforcement. *Psychological Monographs, 80* (Whole no. 609, 1–28).

Rotter, Julian B. (1982). *The development and applications of social learning theory: Selected papers.* New York: Praeger.

Rotter, Julian B. (1990). Internal versus external control of reinforcement: A case history of a variable. *American Psychologist, 45,* 489–493.

Roueché, Berton (1984, June 4). Annals of medicine: The hoof-beats of a zebra. *The New Yorker,* 71–86.

Rowe, Walter F. (1993, Winter). Psychic detectives: A critical examination. *Skeptical Inquirer, 17,* 159–165.

Rubin, Jeffrey Z. (1994). Models of conflict management. *Journal of Social Issues, 50,* 33–45.

Ruggiero, Vincent R. (1988). *Teaching thinking across the curriculum.* New York: Harper & Row.

Ruggiero, Vincent R. (1991). *The art of thinking: A guide to critical and creative thought* (3rd ed.). New York: HarperCollins.

Rumbaugh, Duane M. (1977). *Language learning by a chimpanzee: The Lana project.* New York: Academic Press.

Rumbaugh, Duane M.; Savage-Rumbaugh, E. Sue; & Pate, James L. (1988). Addendum to "Summation in the chimpanzee *(Pan troglodytes).*" *Journal of Experimental Psychology: Animal Behavior Processes, 14,* 118–120.

Rumelhart, David E., & McClelland, James L. (1987). Learning the past tenses of English verbs: Implicit rules or parallel distributed processing. In B. MacWhinney (ed.), *Mechanisms of language acquisition.* Hillsdale, NJ: Erlbaum.

Rumelhart, David E.; McClelland, James L.; & the PDP Research Group (1986). *Parallel distributed processing: Explorations in the microstructure of cognition* (Vols. 1 and 2). Cambridge, MA: MIT Press.

Rushton, J. Philippe (1993). Cyril Burt: Victim of the scientific hoax of the century. Paper presented at the annual meeting of the American Psychological Association, Toronto, Canada.

Russell, Michael; Peeke, Harman V. S.; et al. (1984). Learned histamine release. *Science, 225,* 733–734.

Ryle, Gilbert (1949). *The concept of mind.* London: Hutchinson.

Rymer, Russ (1993). *Genie: An abused child's flight from silence.* New York: HarperCollins.

Sabini, John, & Silver, Maury (1985, Winter). Critical thinking and obedience to authority. *National Forum (Phi Beta Kappa Journal),* 13–17.

Sacks, Oliver (1985). *The man who mistook his wife for a hat and other clinical tales.* New York: Simon & Schuster.

Sacks, Oliver (1993, May 10). To see and not see. *The New Yorker,* 59–66, 68–73.

Sadri, Golnaz, & Robertson, Ivan T. (1993). Self-efficacy and work-related behaviour: A review and meta-analysis. *Applied Psychology: An International Review, 42,* 139–152.

Sagan, Eli (1988). *Freud, women, and morality: The psychology of good and evil.* New York: Basic Books.

Sahley, Christie L.; Rudy, Jerry W.; & Gelperin, Alan (1981). An analysis of associative learning in a terrestrial mollusk: 1. Higher-order conditioning, blocking, and a transient US preexposure effect. *Journal of Comparative Physiology, 144,* 1–8.

Saltz, Bruce L.; Woerner, M. G.; Kane, J. M.; Lieberman, J. A.; et al. (1991, November 6). Prospective study of tardive dyskinesia incidence in the elderly. *Journal of the American Medical Association, 266*(17), 2402–2406.

Salzinger, Kurt (1990). A behavioral analysis of human error. Paper presented at the annual meeting of the American Psychological Association, Boston.

Samelson, Franz (1979). Putting psychology on the map: Ideology and intelligence testing. In A. R. Buss (ed.), *Psychology in social context.* New York: Irvington.

Sanberg, Paul R.; Koutouzis, Ted K.; Freeman, Thomas B.; et al. (1993). Behavioral effects of fetal neural transplants: Relevance to Huntington's disease. *Brain Research Bulletin, 32,* 493–496.

Sank, Zachary B., & Strickland, Bonnie (1973). Some attitudes and behavioral correlates of a belief in militant or moderate social action. *Journal of Social Psychology, 90,* 337–338.

Sapolsky, Robert M. (1987, July). The case of the falling nightwatchmen. *Discover, 8,* 42–45.

Sarbin, Theodore R. (1986). The narrative as a root metaphor for psychology. In T. R. Sarbin (ed.), *Narrative psychology: The storied nature of human conduct.* New York: Praeger.

Satir, Virginia (1983). *Conjoint family therapy* (3rd ed.). Palo Alto, CA: Science and Behavior Books.

Saucier, Gerard (1994). Separating description and evaluation in the structure of personality attributes. *Journal of Personality and Social Psychology, 66,* 141–154.

Savage-Rumbaugh, E. Sue (1986). *Ape language: From conditioned response to symbol.* New York: Columbia University Press.

Savage-Rumbaugh, Sue, & Lewin, Roger (1994). *Kanzi: The ape at the brink of the human mind.* New York: Wiley.

Savage-Rumbaugh, Sue; Shanker, Stuart; & Taylor, Talbot (1996). *Apes, language and the human mind.* New York: Oxford University Press.

Saxe, Leonard (1991). Lying: Thoughts of an applied psychologist. *American Psychologist, 46,* 409–415.

Saywitz, Karen; Goodman, Gail S.; Nicholas, Elissa; & Moan, Susan (1991). Children's memory for genital exam: Implications for child sexual abuse. *Journal of Consulting and Clinical Psychology, 59,* 682–691.

Scarnati, James T.; Kent, William; & MacKenzie, William (1993). Peer coaching and cooperative learning: One room school concept. *Journal of Instructional Psychology, 20,* 65–71.

Scarr, Sandra (1993). Biological and cultural diversity: The legacy of Darwin for development. *Child Development, 64,* 1333–1353.

Scarr, Sandra; Pakstis, Andrew J.; Katz, Soloman H.; & Barker, William B. (1977). Absence of a relationship between degree of white ancestry and intellectual skill in a black population. *Human Genetics, 39,* 69–86.

Scarr, Sandra, & Weinberg, Richard A. (1977). Intellectual similarities within families of both adopted and biological children. *Intelligence, 1,* 170–191.

Scarr, Sandra, & Weinberg, Robert A. (1994). Educational and occupational achievement of brothers and sisters in adoptive and biologically related families. *Behavioral Genetics, 24,* 301–325.

Schachter, Stanley, & Singer, Jerome E. (1962). Cognitive, social, and physiological determinants of emotional state. *Psychological Review, 69,* 379–399.

Schacter, Daniel L. (1990). Memory. In M. I. Posner (ed.), *Foundations of cognitive science.* Cambridge, MA: MIT Press.

Schacter, Daniel L.; Chiu, C.-Y. Peter; & Ochsner, Kevin N. (1993). Implicit memory: A selective review. *Annual Review of Neuroscience, 16,* 159–182.

Schacter, Daniel L., & Moscovitch, Morris (1984). Infants, amnesics, and dissociable memory systems. In M. Moscovitch (ed.), *Infant memory.* New York: Plenum.

Schafer, Roy (1992). *Retelling a life: Narration and dialogue in psychoanalysis.* New York: Basic Books.

Schaie, K. Warner (1984). Midlife influences upon intellectual functioning in old age. *International Journal of Behavioral Development, 7,* 463–478.

Schaie, K. Warner (1993). The Seattle Longitudinal Studies of adult intelligence. *Current Directions in Psychological Science, 2,* 171–175.

Schaie, K. Warner, & Willis, Sherry L. (1986). Can decline in adult intellectual functioning be reversed? *Developmental Psychology, 22,* 223–232.

Schank, Roger, with Peter Childers (1988). *The creative attitude.* New York: Macmillan.

Schatzman, M.; Worsley, A.; & Fenwick, P. (1988). Correspondence during lucid dreams between dreamed and actual events. In J. Gackenbach & S. LaBerge (eds.), *Conscious mind, sleeping brain.* New York: Plenum.

Scheier, Lawrence M.; Newcomb, Michael D.; & Bentler, Peter M. (1990). Influences of drug use on mental health: An 8-year study. Paper presented at the annual meeting of the American Psychological Association, Boston.

Schein, Edgar; Schneier, Inge; & Barker, Curtis H. (1961). *Coercive persuasion.* New York: W. W. Norton.

Schlaug, Gottfried; Jäncke, Lutz; Huang, Yanxiong; & Steinmetz, Helmuth (1995, February 3). In vivo evidence of structural brain asymmetry in musicians. *Science, 267,* 699–701.

Schlossberg, Nancy K. (1984). Exploring the adult years. In A. M. Rogers & C. J. Scheirer (eds.), *The G. Stanley Hall Lecture Series* (Vol. 4). Washington, DC: American Psychological Association.

Schmidt, Peter J.; Nieman, Lynnette K.; Grover, Gay N.; Muller, Kari L.; et al. (1991). Lack of effect of induced menses on symptoms in women with premenstrual syndrome. *New England Journal of Medicine, 324,* 1174–1179.

Schneider, Allen M., & Tarshis, Barry (1986). *An introduction to physiological psychology* (3rd ed.). New York: Random House.

Schnell, Lisa, & Schwab, Martin E. (1990, January 18). Axonal regeneration in the rat spinal cord produced by an antibody against myelin-associated neurite growth inhibitors. *Nature, 343,* 269–272.

Schulkin, Jay (1994). Melancholic depression and the hormones of adversity: A role for the amygdala. *Current Directions in Psychological Science, 3,* 41–44.

Schulman, Michael (1991). *The passionate mind: Bringing up an intelligent and creative child.* New York: Free Press.

Schulman, Michael, & Mekler, Eva (1994). *Bringing up a caring child* (rev. ed.). New York: Doubleday.

Schuman, Howard, & Scott, Jacqueline (1989). Generations and collective memories. *American Journal of Sociology, 54,* 359–381.

Schwartz, Barry, & Reilly, Martha (1985). Long-term retention of a complex operant in pigeons. *Journal of Experimental Psychology: Animal Behavior Processes, 11,* 337–355.

Schwartz, Jeffery; Stoessel, Paula W.; Baxter, Lewis R.; Martin, Karron M.; & Phelps, Michael E. (1996). Systematic changes in cerebral glucose metabolic rate after successful behavior modification treatment of obsessive-compulsive disorder. *Archives of General Psychiatry, 53,* 109–113.

Scofield, Michael (1993, June 6). About men: Off the ladder. *New York Times Magazine,* 22.

Scribner, Sylvia (1977). Modes of thinking and ways of speaking: Culture and logic reconsidered. In P. N. Johnson-Laird & P. C. Wason (eds.), *Thinking: Readings in cognitive science.* Cambridge, England: Cambridge University Press.

Segal, Julius (1986). *Winning life's toughest battles.* New York: McGraw-Hill.

Seidenberg, Mark S., & Petitto, Laura A. (1979). Signing behavior in apes: A critical review. *Cognition, 7,* 177–215.

Seif, Ellie (1979, June). A young mother's story. *Redbook,* 165–167.

Seligman, Martin E. P. (1975). *Helplessness: On depression, development, and death*. San Francisco: W. H. Freeman.

Seligman, Martin E. P. (1991). *Learned optimism*. New York: Knopf.

Seligman, Martin E. P., & Hager, Joanne L. (1972, August). Biological boundaries of learning: The sauce-béarnaise syndrome. *Psychology Today*, 59–61, 84–87.

Sem-Jacobsen, C. W. (1959). Effects of electrical stimulation on the human brain. *Electroencephalography and Clinical Neurophysiology, 11*, 379.

Serbin, Lisa A.; Powlishta, Kimberly K.; & Gulko, Judith (1993). The development of sex typing in middle childhood. *Monographs of the Society for Research in Child Development, 58*(2, Serial No. 232), v-74.

Serpell, Robert (1994). The cultural construction of intelligence. In W. J. Lonner & R. S. Malpass (eds.), *Psychology and culture*. Needham Heights, MA: Allyn & Bacon.

Shatz, Marilyn, & Gelman, Rochel (1973). The development of communication skills: Modifications in the speech of young children as a function of the listener. *Monographs of the Society for Research in Child Development, 38*.

Shaver, Phillip R. (1994). Attachment and care giving in adult romantic relationships. Paper presented at the annual meeting of the American Psychological Association, Los Angeles.

Shaywitz, Bennett A.; Shaywitz, Sally E.; Pugh, Kenneth R.; et al. (1995). Sex differences in the functional organization of the brain for language. *Nature, 373*, 607–609.

Shedler, Jonathan, & Block, Jack (1990). Adolescent drug use and psychological health. *American Psychologist, 45*, 612–630.

Shedler, Jonathan; Mayman, Martin; & Manis, Melvin (1993). The illusion of mental health. *American Psychologist, 48*, 1117–1131.

Sheehan, Neil (1988). *A bright shining lie: John Paul Vann and America in Vietnam*. New York: Random House.

Shepard, Roger N. (1967). Recognition memory for words, sentences and pictures. *Journal of Verbal Learning and Verbal Behavior, 6*, 156–163.

Shepard, Roger N., & Metzler, Jacqueline (1971). Mental rotation of three-dimensional objects. *Science, 171*, 701–703.

Sherif, Carolyn Wood (1979). Bias in psychology. In J. Sherman & E. T. Beck (eds.), *The prism of sex*. Madison: University of Wisconsin Press.

Sherif, Muzafer (1958). Superordinate goals in the reduction of intergroup conflicts. *American Journal of Sociology, 63*, 349–356.

Sherif, Muzafer; Harvey, O. J.; White, B. J.; Hood, William; & Sherif, Carolyn (1961). *Intergroup conflict and cooperation: The Robbers Cave experiment*. Norman: University of Oklahoma Institute of Intergroup Relations.

Sherman, Bonnie R., & Kunda, Ziva (1989). Motivated evaluation of scientific evidence. Paper presented at the annual meeting of the American Psychological Society, Arlington, Virginia.

Sherman, Lawrence W. (1992). *Policing domestic violence*. New York: Free Press.

Sherman, Lawrence W., & Berk, Richard A. (1984). The specific deterrent effects of arrest for domestic assault. *American Sociological Review, 49*, 261–271.

Sherman, Lawrence W.; Schmidt, Janell D.; Rogan, Dennis P.; et al. (1991). From initial deterrence to long-term escalation: Short-custody arrest for poverty ghetto domestic violence. *Criminology, 29*, 821–849.

Shermer, Michael (1997). *Why people believe weird things: Pseudoscience, superstitions, and other confusions of our age*. New York: W. H. Freeman.

Sherrington, R.; Rogaev, E. I.; Liang, Y.; et al. (1995). Cloning of a gene bearing missense mutations in early-onset familial Alzheimer's disease. *Nature, 375*, 754–760.

Shields, Stephanie A. (1991). Gender in the psychology of emotion: A selective research review. In K. T. Strongman (ed.), *International review of studies on emotion* (Vol. 1). New York: Wiley.

Shuchman, Miriam, & Wilkes, Michael S. (1990, October 7). Dramatic progress against depression. *The New York Times Magazine*, pt. 2: *The Good Health Magazine*, 12, 30ff.

Shweder, Richard A. (1990). Cultural psychology—What is it? In J. W. Stigler, R. A. Shweder, & G. Herdt (eds.), *Cultural psychology: The Chicago Symposia on Human Development*. Cambridge, England: Cambridge University Press.

Shweder, Richard A.; Mahapatra, Manamohan; & Miller, Joan G. (1990). Culture and moral development. In J. W. Stigler, R. A. Shweder, & G. Herdt (eds.), *Cultural psychology: Essays on comparative human development*. Cambridge, England: Cambridge University Press.

Siegel, Ronald K. (1989). *Intoxication: Life in pursuit of artificial paradise*. New York: Dutton.

Siegel, Shepard (1990). Classical conditioning and opiate tolerance and withdrawal. In D. J. K. Balfour (ed.), *Psychotropic drugs of abuse*. New York: Pergamon.

Siegel, Shepard; Hinson, Riley E.; Krank, Marvin D.; & McCully, Jane (1982). Heroin "overdose" death: Contribution of drug-associated environmental cues. *Science, 216*, 436–437.

Siegel, Shepard, & Sdao-Jarvie, Katherine (1986). Attenuation of ethanol tolerance by a novel stimulus. *Psychopharmacology, 88*, 258–261.

Siegler, Robert (1996). *Emerging minds: The process of change in children's thinking*. New York: Oxford University Press.

Sifneos, Peter E. (1992). *Short-term anxiety-provoking psychotherapy*. New York: Basic Books.

Sigman, M.; Neumann, C.; Carter, E.; et al. (1988). Home interactions and the development of Embu toddlers in Kenya. *Child Development, 59*, 1251–1261.

Silverstein, Brett, & Perlick, Deborah (1995). *The cost of competence.* New York: Oxford University Press.

Simon, Herbert A. (1973). The structure of ill-structured problems. *Artificial Intelligence, 4,* 181–202.

Sims, Ethan A. (1974). Studies in human hyperphagia. In G. Bray & J. Bethune (eds.), *Treatment and management of obesity.* New York: Harper & Row.

Singer, Jerome L. (1984). The private personality. *Personality and Social Psychology Bulletin, 10,* 7–30.

Singer, Jerome L., & Singer, Dorothy G. (1988). Some hazards of growing up in a television environment: Children's aggression and restlessness. In S. Oskamp (ed.), *Applied social psychology annual: Vol. 8. Television as a social issue.* Newbury Park, CA: Sage.

Singer, Margaret T.; Temerlin, Maurice K.; & Langone, Michael D. (1990). Psychotherapy cults. *Cultic Studies Journal, 7,* 101–125.

Skal, David J. (1993). *The monster show: A cultural history of horror.* New York: W. W. Norton.

Skeptic (1994). Roper Poll highly exaggerated says Gallup [Skeptical News column]. *Skeptic, 2*(4), 24.

Skinner, B. F. (1938). *The behavior of organisms: An experimental analysis.* New York: Appleton-Century-Crofts.

Skinner, B. F. (1948). Superstition in the pigeon. *Journal of Experimental Psychology, 38,* 168–172.

Skinner, B. F. (1948/1976). *Walden two.* New York: Macmillan.

Skinner, B. F. (1956). A case history in the scientific method. *American Psychologist, 11,* 221–233.

Skinner, B. F. (1968). *The technology of teaching.* New York: Appleton-Century-Crofts.

Skinner, B. F. (1972). The operational analysis of psychological terms. In B. F. Skinner, *Cumulative record* (3rd ed.). New York: Appleton-Century-Crofts.

Skinner, B. F. (1978). *Reflections on behaviorism and society.* Englewood Cliffs, NJ: Prentice-Hall.

Skinner, B. F. (1983). *A matter of consequences.* New York: Knopf.

Skinner, B. F. (1987). What is wrong with daily life in the Western world? In B. F. Skinner, *Upon further reflection.* Englewood Cliffs, NJ: Prentice-Hall.

Skinner, B. F. (1990). Can psychology be a science of mind? *American Psychologist, 45,* 1206–1210.

Skinner, B. F., & Vaughan, Margaret (1984). *Enjoy old age.* New York: W. W. Norton.

Skinner, J. B.; Erskine, A.; Pearce, S. A.; Rubenstein, I.; et al. (1990). The evaluation of a cognitive behavioural treatment programme in outpatients with chronic pain. *Journal of Psychosomatic Research, 34,* 13–19.

Skreslet, Paula (1987, November 30). The prizes of first grade. *Newsweek,* 8.

Slade, Pauline (1984). Premenstrual emotional changes in normal women: Fact or fiction? *Journal of Psychosomatic Research, 28,* 1–7.

Slobin, Daniel I. (1970). Universals of grammatical development in children. In G. B. Flores d'Arcais & W. J. M. Levelt (eds.), *Advances in psycholinguistics.* Amsterdam, Netherlands: North-Holland.

Slobin, Daniel I. (ed.) (1985). *The cross-linguistic study of language acquisition* (Vols. 1 & 2). Hillsdale, NJ: Erlbaum.

Slobin, Daniel I. (ed.) (1991). *The cross-linguistic study of language acquisition* (Vol. 3). Hillsdale, NJ: Erlbaum.

Smelser, Neil J.; Vasconcellos, John; & Mecca, Andrew (eds.) (1989). *The social importance of self-esteem.* Berkeley: University of California Press.

Smith, James F., & Kida, Thomas (1991). Heuristics and biases: Expertise and task realism in auditing. *Psychological Bulletin, 109,* 472–489.

Smith, M. Brewster (1994). Selfhood at risk: Postmodern perils and the perils of postmodernism. *American Psychologist, 49,* 405–411.

Smith, Mary Lee; Glass, Gene; & Miller, Thomas I. (1980). *The benefits of psychotherapy.* Baltimore, MD: Johns Hopkins University Press.

Smith, N.; Tsimpli, I.-M.; & Ouhalla, J. (1993). Learning the impossible: The acquisition of possible and impossible languages by a polyglot savant. *Lingua, 91,* 279–347.

Smither, Robert D. (1994). *The psychology of work and human performance* (2nd ed.). New York: Harper-Collins.

Snodgrass, Sara E. (1985). Women's intuition: The effect of subordinate role on interpersonal sensitivity. *Journal of Personality and Social Psychology, 49,* 146–155.

Snodgrass, Sara E. (1992). Further effects of role versus gender on interpersonal sensitivity. *Journal of Personality and Social Psychology, 62,* 154–158.

Snow, Margaret E.; Jacklin, Carol N.; & Maccoby, Eleanor (1983). Sex-of-child differences in father-child interaction at one year of age. *Child Development, 54,* 227–232.

Sommer, Robert (1969). *Personal space: The behavioral basis of design.* Englewood Cliffs, NJ: Prentice-Hall.

Sorce, James F.; Emde, Robert N.; Campos, Joseph; & Klinnert, Mary D. (1985). Maternal emotional signaling: Its effect on the visual cliff behavior of 1-year-olds. *Developmental Psychology, 21,* 195–200.

Spanos, Nicholas P. (1996). *Multiple identities and false memories: A sociocognitive perspective.* Washington, DC: American Psychological Association.

Spanos, Nicholas P.; Burgess, Cheryl A.; & Burgess, Melissa F. (1994). Past-life identities, UFO abductions, and satanic ritual abuse: The social construction of memories. *International Journal of Clinical and Experimental Hypnosis, 42,* 433–446.

Spanos, Nicholas P.; DuBreuil, Susan C.; & Gabora, Natalie J. (1991). Four month follow-up of skill training induced enhancements in hypnotizability. *Contemporary Hypnosis, 8,* 25–32.

Spelke, Elizabeth S.; Breinlinger, Karen; Macomber, Janet; & Jacobson, Kristen (1992). Origins of knowledge. *Psychological Review, 99,* 605–632.

Speltz, Matthew L.; Greenberg, Mark T.; & Deklyen, Michelle (1990). Attachment in preschoolers with disruptive behavior: A comparison of clinic-referred and nonproblem children. *Development and Psychopathology, 2,* 31–46.

Spence, Janet T. (1985). Gender identity and its implications for concepts of masculinity and femininity. In T. Sonderegger (ed.), *Nebraska Symposium on Motivation.* Lincoln: University of Nebraska Press.

Spencer, M. B., & Dornbusch, Sanford M. (1990). Ethnicity. In S. S. Feldman & G. R. Elliott (eds.), *At the threshold: The developing adolescent.* Cambridge, MA: Harvard University Press.

Sperling, George (1960). The information available in brief visual presentations. *Psychological Monographs, 74*(498).

Sperry, Roger W. (1964). The great cerebral commissure. *Scientific American, 210*(1), 42–52.

Sperry, Roger W. (1982). Some effects of disconnecting the cerebral hemispheres. *Science, 217,* 1223–1226.

Spilich, George J.; June, Lorraine; & Renner, Judith (1992). Cigarette smoking and cognitive performance. *British Journal of Addiction, 87,* 113–126.

Sporer, Siegfried L.; Penrod, Steven; Read, Don; & Cutler, Brian (1995). Choosing, confidence, and accuracy: A meta-analysis of the confidence-accuracy relation in eyewitness identification studies. *Psychological Bulletin, 118,* 315–327.

Sprecher, Susan; Sullivan, Quintin; & Hatfield, Elaine (1994). Mate selection preferences: Gender differences examined in a national sample. *Journal of Personality and Social Psychology, 66,* 1074–1080.

Squire, Larry R. (1987). *Memory and the brain.* New York: Oxford University Press.

Squire, Larry R.; Ojemann, Jeffrey G.; Miezin, Francis M.; et al. (1992). Activation of the hippocampus in normal humans: A functional anatomical study of memory. *Proceedings of the National Academy of Science, 89,* 1837–1841.

Squire, Larry R., & Zola-Morgan, Stuart (1991). The medial temporal lobe memory system. *Science, 253,* 1380–1386.

Staats, Carolyn K., & Staats, Arthur W. (1957). Meaning established by classical conditioning. *Journal of Experimental Psychology, 54,* 74–80.

Stanovich, Keith (1996). *How to think straight about psychology* (4th ed.). New York: HarperCollins.

Staples, Brent (1994). *Parallel time.* New York: Pantheon.

State of New Hampshire v. *Joel Hungerford* (St. 94 45 7) & *State* v. *John Morahan* (St. 93 1734 6) Superior Court, Northern District of Hillsborough County, State of New Hampshire. Notice of Decision, May 23, 1995.

Staub, Ervin (1989). *The roots of evil: The origins of genocide and other group violence.* New York: Cambridge University Press.

Staub, Ervin (1990). The psychology and culture of torture and torturers. In P. Suedfeld (ed.), *Psychology and torture.* Washington, DC: Hemisphere.

Steele, Claude M. (1994, October 31). Bizarre black IQ claims abetted by media. *San Francisco Chronicle,* op-ed page.

Steinberg, Laurence; Dornbusch, Sanford M.; & Brown, B. Bradford (1992). Ethnic differences in adolescent achievement: An ecological perspective. *American Psychologist, 47,* 723–729.

Steiner, Robert A. (1989). *Don't get taken!* El Cerrito, CA: Wide-Awake Books.

Stenberg, Craig R., & Campos, Joseph (1990). The development of anger expressions in infancy. In N. Stein, B. Leventhal, & T. Trabasso (eds.), *Psychological and biological approaches to emotion.* Hillsdale, NJ: Erlbaum.

Stephan, K. M.; Fink, G. R.; Passingham, R. E.; et al. (1995). Functional anatomy of the mental representation of upper movements in healthy subjects. *Journal of Neurophysiology, 73,* 373–386.

Stephan, Walter (1985). Intergroup relations. In G. Lindzey & E. Aronson (eds.), *Handbook of social psychology* (Vol. 2). New York: Random House.

Stephan, Walter G.; Ageyev, Vladimir; Coates-Shrider, Lisa; Stephan, Cookie W.; & Abalakina, Marina (1994). On the relationship between stereotypes and prejudice: An international study. *Personality and Social Psychology Bulletin, 20,* 277–284.

Stephan, Walter, & Brigham, John C. (1985). Intergroup contact: Introduction. *Journal of Social Issues, 41*(3), 1–8.

Stephan, Walter G., & Stephan, Cookie (1992). Reducing intercultural anxiety through intercultural contact. *International Journal of Intercultural Relations, 16,* 96–106.

Stephens, Mitchell (1991, September 20). The death of reading. *Los Angeles Times Magazine,* 10, 12, 16, 42, 44.

Stern, Daniel (1985). *The interpersonal world of the infant.* New York: Basic Books.

Stern, Marilyn, & Karraker, Katherine H. (1989). Sex stereotyping of infants: A review of gender labeling studies. *Sex Roles, 20,* 501–522.

Sternberg, Robert J. (1986). *Intelligence applied: Understanding and increasing your intellectual skills.* San Diego: Harcourt Brace Jovanovich.

Sternberg, Robert J. (1988). *The triarchic mind: A new theory of human intelligence.* New York: Viking.

Sternberg, Robert J., & Kolligian, John, Jr. (eds.) (1990). *Competence considered.* New Haven, CT: Yale University Press.

Sternberg, Robert J.; Okagaki, Lynn; & Jackson, Alice S. (1990). Practical intelligence for success in school. *Educational Leadership, 48,* 35–39.

Sternberg, Robert J., & Wagner, Richard K. (1989). Individual differences in practical knowledge and its acquisition. In P. Ackerman, R. J. Sternberg, & R. Glaser (eds.), *Individual differences*. New York: W. H. Free-man.

Sternberg, Robert J.; Wagner, Richard K.; & Okagaki, Lynn (1993). Practical intelligence: The nature and role of tacit knowledge in work and at school. In H. Reese & J. Puckett (eds.), *Advances in lifespan development*. Hillsdale, NJ: Erlbaum.

Sternberg, Robert J.; Wagner, Richard K.; Williams, Wendy M.; & Horvath, Joseph A. (1995). Testing common sense. *American Psychologist, 50,* 912–927.

Stevenson, Harold W.; Chen, Chuansheng; & Lee, Shin-ying (1993, January 1). Mathematics achievement of Chinese, Japanese, and American children: Ten years later. *Science, 259,* 53–58.

Stevenson, Harold W.; Lee, Shin-ying; Chen, Chuansheng; Lummis, Max; et al. (1990a). Mathematics achievement in children in China and the United States. *Child Development, 61,* 1053–1066.

Stevenson, Harold W.; Lee, Shin-ying; Chen, Chuansheng; Stigler, James W.; et al. (1990b). Contexts of achievement: A study of American, Chinese, and Japanese children. *Monographs of the Society for Research in Child Development, 55*(1–2).

Stickler, Gunnar B.; Salter, Margery; Broughton, Daniel D.; & Alario, Anthony (1991). Parents' worries about children compared to actual risks. *Clinical Pediatrics, 30,* 522–528.

Stimpson, Catharine (1996, Winter). Women's studies and its discontents. *Dissent, 43,* 67–75.

Straus, Murray A. (1991). Discipline and deviance: Physical punishment of children and violence and other crime in adulthood. *Social Problems, 38*(2), 133–154.

Strickland, Bonnie R. (1965). The prediction of social action from a dimension of internal-external control. *Journal of Social Psychology, 66,* 353–358.

Strickland, Bonnie R. (1989). Internal-external control expectancies: From contingency to creativity. *American Psychologist, 44,* 1–12.

Strupp, Hans H. (1982). The outcome problem in psychotherapy: Contemporary perspectives. In J. H. Harvey & M. M. Parks (eds.), *Psychotherapy research and behavior change: Vol. 1. The APA Master Lecture Series.* Washington, DC: American Psychological Association.

Strupp, Hans H., & Binder, Jeffrey (1984). *Psychotherapy in a new key.* New York: Basic Books.

Stunkard, Albert J. (ed.) (1980). *Obesity.* Philadelphia: Saunders.

Sue, Stanley (1991). Ethnicity and culture in psychological research and practice. In J. Goodchilds (ed.), *Psychological perspectives on human diversity in America.* Washington, DC: American Psychological Association.

Suedfeld, Peter; Little, B. R.; Rank, A. D.; Rank, D. S.; & Ballard, E. (1986). Television and adults: Thinking, personality and attitudes. In T. M. Williams (ed.), *The impact of television: A natural experiment in three communities.* San Diego: Academic Press.

Sulloway, Frank J. (1992). *Freud, biologist of the mind: Beyond the psychoanalytic legend* (rev. ed.). Cambridge, MA: Harvard University Press.

Sundstrom, Eric; De Meuse, Kenneth P.; & Futrell, David (1990). Work teams: Applications and effectiveness. *American Psychologist, 45,* 120–133.

Suomi, Stephen J. (1987). Genetic and maternal contributions to individual differences in rhesus monkey biobehavioral development. In N. Krasnegor, E. Blass, M. Hofer, & W. Smotherman (eds.), *Perinatal development: A psychobiological perspective.* New York: Academic Press.

Suomi, Stephen J. (1989). Primate separation models of affective disorders. In J. Madden (ed.), *Adaptation, learning, and affect.* New York: Raven Press.

Suomi, Stephen J. (1991). Uptight and laid-back monkeys: Individual differences in the response to social challenges. In S. Branch, W. Hall, & J. E. Dooling (eds.), *Plasticity of development.* Cambridge, MA: MIT Press.

Super, Charles A., & Harkness, Sara (1994). The developmental niche. In W. J. Lonner & R. Malpass (eds.), *Psychology and culture.* Needham Heights, MA: Allyn & Bacon.

Sweat, Jane A., & Durm, Mark W. (1993, Winter). Psychics: Do police departments really use them? *Skeptical Inquirer, 17,* 148–158.

Swedo, Susan E., & Rapoport, Judith L. (1991). Trichotillomania [hair-pulling]. *Journal of Child Psychology and Psychiatry and Allied Disciplines, 32,* 401–409.

Symons, Donald (1979). *The evolution of human sexuality.* New York: Oxford University Press.

Szapocznik, Jose, & Kurtines, William M. (1993). Family psychology and cultural diversity. *American Psychologist, 48,* 400–407.

Taffel, Ronald (1990, September/October). The politics of mood. *Family Therapy Networker,* 49–53, 72.

Tajfel, Henri; Billig, M. G.; Bundy, R. P.; & Flament, C. (1971). Social categorization and intergroup behavior. *European Journal of Social Psychology, 1,* 149–178.

Tajfel, Henri, & Turner, John C. (1986). The social identity theory of intergroup behavior. In S. Worchel & W. G. Austin (eds.), *Psychology of intergroup relations.* Chicago: Nelson-Hall.

Tanur, Judith M. (ed.). (1992). *Questions about questions: Inquiries into the cognitive basis of surveys.* New York: Russell Sage Foundation.

Tartter, Vivien C. (1986). *Language processes.* New York: Holt, Rinehart and Winston.

Taub, David M. (1984). *Primate paternalism.* New York: Van Nostrand Reinhold.

Tavris, Carol (1987, January). How to succeed in business abroad. *Signature,* 86–87, 110–113.

Tavris, Carol (1989). *Anger: The misunderstood emotion* (rev. ed.). New York: Touchstone.

Tavris, Carol (1992). *The mismeasure of woman.* New York: Touchstone.

Taylor, Donald M., & Porter, Lana E. (1994). A multicultural view of stereotyping. In W. J. Lonner & R.

Malpass (eds.), *Psychology and culture.* Needham Heights, MA: Allyn & Bacon.

Taylor, Shelley E. (1995). *Health psychology* (3rd ed.). New York: McGraw-Hill.

Taylor, Shelley E.; Peplau, Letitia A.; & Sears, David O. (1997). *Social psychology* (9th ed.). Englewood Cliffs, NJ: Prentice-Hall.

Tellegen, Auke; Lykken, David T.; Bouchard, Thomas J., Jr.; et al. (1988). Personality similarity in twins reared apart and together. *Journal of Personality and Social Psychology, 54,* 1031–1039.

Terr, Lenore (1990). *Too scared to cry.* New York: Basic Books.

Terr, Lenore (1994). *Unchained memories: True stories of traumatic memories, lost and found.* New York: Basic Books.

Terrace, H. S. (1985). In the beginning was the "name." *American Psychologist, 40,* 1011–1028.

Thibodeau, Ruth, & Aronson, Elliot (1992). Taking a closer look: Reasserting the role of the self-concept in dissonance theory. *Personality and Social Psychology Bulletin, 18,* 591–602.

Thoma, Stephen J. (1986). Estimating gender differences in the comprehension and preference of moral issues. *Developmental Review, 6,* 165–180.

Thomas, Alexander, & Chess, Stella (1980). *The dynamics of psychological development.* New York: Brunner/Mazel.

Thomas, Alexander, & Chess, Stella (1982). Temperament and follow-up to adulthood. In R. Porter & G. M. Collins (eds.), *Temperamental differences in infants and young children.* London: Pitman.

Thomas, Alexander, & Chess, Stella (1984). Genesis and evolution of behavioral disorders: From infancy to early adult life. *American Journal of Psychiatry, 141,* 1–9.

Thompson, Richard F. (1986). The neurobiology of learning and memory. *Science, 233,* 941–947.

Thorndike, Edward L. (1898). Animal intelligence: An experimental study of the associative processes in animals. *Psychological Review Monograph Supplement, 2* (Whole No. 8).

Thorndike, Edward L. (1903). *Educational psychology.* New York: Columbia University Teachers College.

Thornhill, Randy (1980). Rape in *Panorpa* scorpionflies and a general rape hypothesis. *Animal Behavior, 28,* 52–59.

Thornton, E. M. (1984). *The Freudian fallacy: An alternative view of Freudian theory.* Garden City, NY: Dial.

Tillman, Jane G.; Nash, Michael R.; & Lerner, Paul M. (1994). Does trauma cause dissociative pathology? In S. Lynn & J. Rhue (eds.), *Dissociation: Clinical and theoretical perspectives.* New York: Guilford Press.

Tolman, Edward C. (1938). The determiners of behavior at a choice point. *Psychological Review, 45,* 1–35.

Tolman, Edward C. (1948). Cognitive maps in rats and men. *Psychological Review, 55,* 189–208.

Tolman, Edward C., & Honzik, Chase H. (1930). Introduction and removal of reward and maze performance

in rats. *University of California Publications in Psychology, 4,* 257–275.

Torrey, E. Fuller (1988). *Surviving schizophrenia* (rev. ed.). New York: Harper & Row.

Torrey, E. Fuller; Bowler, Ann E.; Taylor, Edward H.; & Gottesman, Irving I. (1994). *Schizophrenia and manic-depressive disorder.* New York: Basic Books.

Tougas, Francine; Brown, Rupert; Beaton, Ann M.; & Joly, Stéphane (1995). Neosexism: Plus ça change, plus c'est pareil. *Personality and Social Psychology Bulletin, 21,* 842–849.

Trafimow, David; Triandis, Harry C.; & Goto, Sharon G. (1991). Some tests of the distinction between the private self and the collective self. *Journal of Personality and Social Psychology, 60,* 649–655.

Tranel, Daniel, & Damasio, Antonio (1985). Knowledge without awareness: An autonomic index of facial recognition by prosopagnosics. *Science, 228,* 1453–1454.

Traub, James (1993, June 7). The hearts and minds of City College. *The New Yorker,* 42–53.

Triandis, Harry C. (1994). *Culture and social behavior.* New York: McGraw-Hill.

Triandis, Harry C. (1995). *Individualism and collectivism.* Boulder, CO: Westview.

Trimble, Joseph E., & Medicine, Beatrice (1993). Diversification of American Indians: Forming an indigenous perspective. In U. Kim & J. W. Berry (eds.), *Indigenous psychologies: Research and experience in cultural context.* Newbury Park, CA: Sage.

Trivers, Robert (1972). Parental investment and sexual selection. In B. Campbell (ed.), *Sexual selection and the descent of man.* New York: Aldine de Gruyter.

Tulving, Endel (1985). How many memory systems are there? *American Psychologist, 40,* 385–398.

Tversky, Amos, & Kahneman, Daniel (1981). The framing of decisions and the psychology of choice. *Science, 211,* 453–458.

Tversky, Amos, & Kahneman, Daniel (1986). Rational choice and the framing of decisions. *Journal of Business, 59,* S251–S278.

Tzischinsky, Orna; Pal, I.; Epstein, Rachel; Dagan, Y.; & Lavie, Peretz (1992). The importance of timing in melatonin administration in a blind man. *Journal of Pineal Research, 12,* 105–108.

Unger, Rhoda (1990). Imperfect reflections of reality: Psychology constructs gender. In R. T. Hare-Mustin & J. Marecek (eds.), *Making a difference: Psychology and the construction of gender.* New Haven, CT: Yale University Press.

Usher, JoNell A., & Neisser, Ulric (1993). Childhood amnesia and the beginnings of memory for four early life events. *Journal of Experimental Psychology: General, 122,* 155–165.

Vaillant, George E. (1983). *The natural history of alcoholism: Causes, patterns, and paths to recovery.* Cambridge, MA: Harvard University Press.

Vaillant, George E. (ed.) (1992). *Ego mechanisms of defense.* Washington, DC: American Psychiatric Press.

Vaillant, George E. (1995). *The natural history of alcoholism revisited.* Cambridge, MA: Harvard University Press.

Vaillant, George E., & Milofsky, Eva S. (1982). The etiology of alcoholism. *American Psychologist, 37,* 494–503.

Valkenburg, Patti M., & van der Voort, Tom H. A. (1994). Influence of TV on daydreaming and creative imagination: A review of research. *Psychological Bulletin, 116,* 316–339.

Van Cantfort, Thomas E., & Rimpau, James B. (1982). Sign language studies with children and chimpanzees. *Sign Language Studies, 34,* 15–72.

Vandenberg, Brian (1985). Beyond the ethology of play. In A. Gottfried & C. C. Brown (eds.), *Play interactions.* Lexington, MA: Lexington Books.

Vandenberg, Brian (1993). Existentialism and development. *American Psychologist, 48,* 296–297.

Van Lancker, Diana R., & Kempler, Daniel (1987). Comprehension of familiar phrases by left- but not by right-hemisphere damaged patients. *Brain and Language, 32,* 265–277.

Vasquez, Melba J. T., & Barón, Augustine, Jr. (1988). The psychology of the Chicano experience: A sample course structure. In P. Bronstein & K. Quina (eds.), *Teaching a psychology of people.* Washington, DC: American Psychological Association.

Vila, J., & Beech, H. R. (1980). Premenstrual symptomatology: An interaction hypothesis. *British Journal of Social and Clinical Psychology, 19,* 73–80.

Von Lang, Jochen, & Sibyll, Claus (eds.) (1984). *Eichmann interrogated: Transcripts from the archives of the Israeli police.* New York: Random House.

Voyer, Daniel; Voyer, Susan; & Bryden, M. P. (1995). Magnitude of sex differences in spatial abilities: A meta-analysis and consideration of critical variables. *Psychological Bulletin, 117,* 250–270.

Wadden, Thomas A.; Foster, G. D.; Letizia, K. A.; & Mullen, J. L. (1990, August 8). Long-term effects of dieting on resting metabolic rate in obese outpatients. *Journal of the American Medical Association, 264,* 707–711.

Wade, Carole, & Cirese, Sarah (1991). *Human sexuality* (2nd ed.). San Diego: Harcourt Brace Jovanovich.

Wagemaker, Herbert, Jr., & Cade, Robert (1978). Hemodialysis in chronic schizophrenic patients. *Southern Medical Journal, 71,* 1463–1465.

Wagenaar, Willem A. (1986). My memory: A study of autobiographical memory over six years. *Cognitive Psychology, 18,* 225–252.

Walker, Alice, & Parmar, Pratibha (1995). *Warrior marks: Female genital mutilation and the sexual binding of women.* Fort Worth, TX: Harcourt Brace.

Walker, Anne (1994). Mood and well-being in consecutive menstrual cycles: Methodological and theoretical implications. *Psychology of Women Quarterly, 18,* 271–290.

Walker, Lawrence J. (1989). A longitudinal study of moral reasoning. *Child Development, 60,* 157–166.

Walker, Lawrence J.; de Vries, Brian; & Trevethan, Shelley D. (1987). Moral stages and moral orientations in real-life and hypothetical dilemmas. *Child Development, 58,* 842–858.

Wallbott, Harald G.; Ricci-Bitti, Pio; & Bänninger-Huber, Eva (1986). Non-verbal reactions to emotional experiences. In K. R. Scherer, H. G. Wallbott, & A. B. Summerfield (eds.), *Experiencing emotion: A cross-cultural study.* Cambridge, England: Cambridge University Press.

Waller, Niels G.; Kojetin, Brian A.; Bouchard, Thomas J., Jr.; Lykken, David T.; & Tellegen, Auke (1990). Genetic and environmental influences on religious interests, attitudes, and values: A study of twins reared apart and together. *Psychological Science, 1,* 138–142.

Wang, Alvin Y.; Thomas, Margaret H.; & Ouellette, Judith A. (1992). The keyword mnemonic and retention of second-language vocabulary words. *Journal of Educational Psychology, 84,* 520–528.

Ward, L. Monique (1994). Preschoolers' awareness of associations between gender and societal status. Paper presented at the annual meeting of the American Psychological Association, Los Angeles.

Warren, Gayle H., & Raynes, Anthony E. (1972). Mood changes during three conditions of alcohol intake. *Quarterly Journal of Studies on Alcohol, 33,* 979–989.

Washburn, David A., & Rumbaugh, Duane M. (1991). Ordinal judgments of numerical symbols by macaques *(Macaca mulatta). Psychological Science, 2,* 190–193.

Waters, Everett; Merrick, Susan K.; Albersheim, Leah J.; & Treboux, Dominique (1995). Attachment security from infancy to early adulthood: A 20-year-longitudinal study. Paper presented at the annual meeting of the Society for Research in Child Development, Indianapolis.

Watson, John B. (1913). Psychology as the behaviorist views it. *Psychological Review, 20,* 158–177.

Watson, John B. (1925). *Behaviorism.* New York: W. W. Norton.

Watson, John B., & Rayner, Rosalie (1920). Conditioned emotional reactions. *Journal of Experimental Psychology, 3,* 1–14.

Webb, Wilse B., & Cartwright, Rosalind D. (1978). Sleep and dreams. In M. Rosenzweig & L. Porter (eds.), *Annual Review of Psychology, 29,* 223–252.

Webster, Richard (1995). *Why Freud was wrong.* New York: Basic Books.

Wegner, Daniel M. (1994). Ironic processes of mental control. *Psychological Review, 101,* 34–57.

Weil, Andrew T. (1972/1986). *The natural mind: A new way of looking at drugs and the higher consciousness.* Boston: Houghton Mifflin.

Weiner, Bernard (1986). *An attributional theory of motivation and emotion.* New York: Springer-Verlag.

Weiss, Bahr; Dodge, Kenneth A.; Bates, John E.; & Petitt, Gregory S. (1992). Some consequences of early harsh discipline: Child aggression and a maladaptive social information processing style. *Child Development, 63*, 1321–1335.

Weisz, John R.; Rothbaum, Fred M.; & Blackburn, Thomas C. (1984). Standing out and standing in: The psychology of control in America and Japan. *American Psychologist, 39*, 955–969.

Weisz, John R.; Weiss, Bahr; Alicke, Mark D.; & Klotz, M. L. (1987). Effectiveness of psychotherapy with children and adolescents: A meta-analysis for clinicians. *Journal of Consulting and Clinical Psychology, 55*, 542–549.

Weisz, John R.; Weiss, Bahr; Han, Susan S.; Granger, Douglas A.; & Morton, Todd (1995). Effects of psychotherapy with children and adolescents revisited: A meta-analysis of treatment outcome studies. *Psychological Bulletin, 117*, 450–468.

Wells, Gary L. (1993). What do we know about eyewitness identification? *American Psychologist, 48*, 553–571.

Wells, Gary L.; Luus, C.A. Elizabeth; & Windschitl, Paul D. (1994). Maximizing the utility of eyewitness identification evidence. *Current Directions in Psychological Science, 3*, 194–197.

Werner, Emmy E. (1989). High-risk children in young adulthood: A longitudinal study from birth to 32 years. *American Journal of Orthopsychiatry, 59*, 72–81.

Westen, Drew (1991). Social cognition and object relations. *Psychological Bulletin, 109*, 429–455.

Wheeler, Douglas L.; Jacobson, John W.; Paglieri, Raymond A.; & Schwartz, Allen A. (1993). An experimental assessment of facilitated communication. *Mental Retardation, 31*, 49–59.

Whisman, Mark A. (1993). Mediators and moderators of change in cognitive therapy of depression. *Psychological Bulletin, 114*, 248–265.

Whitam, Frederick L.; Diamond, Milton; & Martin, James (1993). Homosexual orientation in twins: A report on 61 pairs and 3 triplet sets. *Archives of Sexual Behavior, 22*, 187–206.

White, Robert W. (1959). Motivation reconsidered: The concept of competence. *Psychological Review, 66*, 297–333.

White, Sheldon H., & Pillemer, David B. (1979). Childhood amnesia and the development of a socially accessible memory system. In J. F. Kihlstrom & F. J. Evans (eds.), *Functional disorders of memory*. Hillsdale, NJ: Erlbaum.

Whitehurst, Grover J.; Arnold, David S.; Epstein, Jeffrey N.; Angell, Andrea L.; et al. (1994). A picture book reading intervention in day care and home for children from low-income families. *Developmental Psychology, 30*, 679–689.

Whitehurst, Grover J.; Falco, F. L.; Lonigan, C. J.; Fischel, J. E.; et al. (1988). Accelerating language development through picture book reading. *Developmental Psychology, 24*, 552–559.

Whiting, Beatrice B., & Edwards, Carolyn P. (1988). *Children of different worlds: The formation of social behavior*. Cambridge, MA: Harvard University Press.

Whiting, Beatrice B., & Whiting, John (1975). *Children of six cultures*. Cambridge, MA: Harvard University Press.

Whitney, Kristina; Sagrestano, Lynda M.; & Maslach, Christina (1994). Establishing the social impact of individuation. *Journal of Personality and Social Psychology, 66*, 1140–1153.

Widner, H.; Tetrud, J.; Rehncrona, S.; et al. (1993). Fifteen months' follow-up on bilateral embryonic mesencephalic grafts in two cases of severe MPTP-induced Parkinsonism. *Advances in Neurology, 60*, 729–733.

Widom, Cathy S. (1989). Does violence beget violence? A critical examination of the literature. *Psychological Bulletin, 106*, 3–28.

Williams, Kipling D., & Karau, Steven J. (1991). Social loafing and social compensation: The effects of expectations of co-worker performance. *Journal of Personality and Social Psychology, 61*, 570–581.

Williams, Linda M. (1994). Recall of childhood trauma: A prospective study of women's memories of child sexual abuse. *Journal of Consulting and Clinical Psychology, 62*, 1167–1176.

Williams, Walter (1986). *The spirit and the flesh: Sexual diversity in American Indian culture*. Boston: Beacon Press.

Williams, Wendy M.; Blythe, Tina; White, Noel; Li, Jin; et al. (1996). *Practical intelligence for school*. New York: HarperCollins.

Wilner, Daniel; Walkley, Rosabelle; & Cook, Stuart (1955). *Human relations in interracial housing*. Minneapolis: University of Minnesota Press.

Wilson, Edward O. (1975). *Sociobiology: The new synthesis*. Cambridge, MA: Belknap/Harvard University Press.

Wilson, Edward O. (1978). *On human nature*. Cambridge, MA: Harvard University Press.

Wilson, Edward O. (1994). *Naturalist*. Washington, DC: Island Press.

Wilson, G. Terence, & Fairburn, Christopher G. (1993). Cognitive treatments for eating disorders (Special section: Recent developments in cognitive and constructivist psychotherapies). *Journal of Consulting and Clinical Psychology, 61*, 261–269.

Windholz, George, & Lamal, P. A. (1985). Köhler's insight revisited. *Teaching of Psychology, 12*, 165–167.

Winnicott, D. W. (1957/1990). *Home is where we start from*. New York: W. W. Norton.

Witelson, Sandra F.; Glazer, I. I., & Kigar, D. L. (1994). Sex differences in numerical density of neurons in human auditory association cortex. *Society for Neuroscience Abstracts, 30* (Abstr. No. 582.12).

Woo, Elaine (1995, January 21). Teaching that goes beyond IQ. *Los Angeles Times*, A1, A22, A23.

Wood, James M.; Nezworski, Teresa; & Stejskal, William J. (1996). The comprehensive system for the Rorschach: A critical examination. *Psychological Science, 7*, 3–10.

Wood, Robert, & Bandura, Albert (1989). Impact of conceptions of ability on self-regulatory mechanisms and complex decision making. *Journal of Personality and Social Psychology, 56,* 407–415.

Wooley, Susan; Wooley, O. Wayne; & Dyrenforth, Susan (1979). Theoretical, practical, and social issues in behavioral treatments of obesity. *Journal of Applied Behavior Analysis, 12,* 3–25.

Wright, Daniel B. (1993). Recall of the Hillsborough disaster over time: Systematic biases of "flashbulb" memories. *Applied Cognitive Psychology, 7,* 129–138.

Wright, R. L. D. (1976). *Understanding statistics: An informal introduction for the behavioral sciences.* New York: Harcourt Brace Jovanovich.

Wu, Tzu-chin; Tashkin, Donald P.; Djahed, Behnam; & Rose, Jed E. (1988). Pulmonary hazards of smoking marijuana as compared with tobacco. *New England Journal of Medicine, 318,* 347–351.

Wurtman, Richard J. (1982). Nutrients that modify brain function. *Scientific American, 264*(4), 50–59.

Wyatt, Gail E., & Mickey, M. Ray (1987). Ameliorating the effects of child sexual abuse: An exploratory study of support by parents and others. *Journal of Interpersonal Violence, 2,* 403–414.

Wylie, Mary S. (1993, September/October). The shadow of a doubt. *The Family Therapy Networker, 17,* 18–29, 70, 73.

Yalom, Irvin D. (1980). *Existential psychotherapy.* New York: Basic Books.

Yalom, Irvin D. (1989). *Love's executioner and other tales of psychotherapy.* New York: Basic Books.

Yapko, Michael (1994). *Suggestions of abuse: True and false memories of childhood sexual trauma.* New York: Simon & Schuster.

Yee, Albert H.; Fairchild, Halford H.; Weizmann, Fredric; & Wyatt, Gail E. (1993). Addressing psychology's problems with race. *American Psychologist, 48,* 1132–1140.

Yoder, Janice D., & Kahn, Arnold S. (1993). Working toward an inclusive psychology of women. *American Psychologist, 48,* 846–850.

Young-Eisendrath, Polly (1993). *You're not what I expected: Learning to love the opposite sex.* New York: Morrow.

Zahn-Waxler, Carolyn; Radke-Yarrow, Marian; & King, Robert (1979). Child rearing and children's prosocial initiations toward victims of distress. *Child Development, 50,* 319–330.

Zajonc, Robert B. (1965). Social facilitation. *Science, 149,* 269–274.

Zajonc, Robert B. (1968). Attitudinal effects of mere exposure. *Journal of Personality and Social Psychology, 9, Monograph Supplement 2,* 1–27.

Zhang, Yiying; Proenca, Ricardo; Maffei, Margherita; et al. (1994). Positional cloning of the mouse obese gene and its human homologue. *Nature, 372*(6505), 425–432.

Zilbergeld, Bernie (1983). *The shrinking of America: Myths of psychological change.* Boston: Little, Brown.

Zimbardo, Philip G. (1970). The human choice: Individuation, reason, and order versus deindividuation, impulse, and chaos. In W. J. Arnold & D. Levine (eds.), *Nebraska Symposium on Motivation, 1969.* Lincoln: University of Nebraska Press.

Zimbardo, Philip G., & Leippe, M. R. (1991). *The psychology of attitude change and social influence.* New York: McGraw-Hill.

Zinberg, Norman (1974). The search for rational approaches to heroin use. In P. G. Bourne (ed.), *Addiction.* New York: Academic Press.

Zuckerman, Marvin (1990). Some dubious premises in research and theory on racial differences: Scientific, social, and ethical issues. *American Psychologist, 45,* 1297–1303.

Zuckerman, Marvin; Kuhlman, D. Michael; & Camac, Curt (1988). What lies beyond E and N? Factor analyses of scales believed to measure basic dimensions of personality. *Journal of Personality and Social Psychology, 54,* 96–107.

Zuckerman, Marvin; Kuhlman, D. Michael; Joireman, Jeffrey; Teta, Paul; & Kraft, Michael (1993). A comparison of three structural models for personality: The Big Three, the Big Five, and the Alternative Five. *Journal of Personality and Social Psychology, 65,* 757–768.

Credits

TEXT

pp. 321–323, From *Developing reflective judgment* by Patricia M. King and Karen S. Kitchener, 1994. Reprinted by permission of Jossey-Bass Publishers, Inc. / p. 348, From *Encounters: A psychologist reveals case studies of abductions by extraterrestrials* by Edith Fiore, 1989. Reprinted by permission of Doubleday, a division of Bantam Doubleday Dell Publishing Group, Inc. / p. 405, From "Suggestibility of the child witness: A historical review and synthesis" by Stephen J. Ceci and Maggie Bruck, from *Psychological Bulletin, 113,* pp. 403–439. Copyright © 1993 by the American Psychological Association. / p. 460, From "Modes of thinking and ways of speaking" by Sylvia Scribner, in *Thinking: Readings in cognitive science* edited by P. N. Johnson-Laird and P. C. Wason, 1977. Reprinted by permission of Cambridge University Press. / pp. 474–475 , From *The nature of prejudice* by Gordon W. Allport. Copyright © 1979 by Addison-Wesley Publishing Company, Inc. Reprinted by permission of the publisher.

ILLUSTRATIONS

Note: Unless otherwise acknowledged, all photographs are the property of Scott, Foresman and Company. Page abbreviations are as follows: (t) top, (c) center, (b) bottom, (r) right.

Page 10, Punch/Rothco / p. 28, The Metropolitan Museum of Art, Gift of Thomas F. Ryan, 1910 (11.173.9) / p. 31, M. P. Kahl/Photo Researchers / p. 36, *Bent Offerings* by Don Addis. By permission of Don Addis and Creators Syndicate. / p. 40, Alan Carey/Image Works / p. 52, Copyright © 1994, Los Angeles Times Syndicate. Reprinted with permission. / pp. 55 and 56 (Figs. 2.1 and 2.2), From *Understanding statistics: An informational introduction for the behavioral sciences* by R. L. D. Wright. Copyright © 1976 by Harcourt Brace & Company. Reproduced by permission of the publisher. / p. 71 (Fig. 2.4), "Opinion illustration," from *Discover* Magazine, July 1987. Reprinted by permission of Discover Magazine. / p. 86, Biophoto Associates/SS/Photo Researchers / p. 95, William Vandivert / p. 98 (Fig. 3.2), Harlow Primate Laboratory, University of Wisconsin / p. 105, David Young-Wolff/PhotoEdit / p. 109, Drawing by Chas. Addams/©1981 New Yorker Magazine, Inc. / p. 146(l) (Fig. 4.8), Brookhaven National Laboratory & New York University Medical Center / p. 146(r) (Fig. 4.8), Howard Sochurek / p. 184 (Fig. 5.1), Adapted from "Mood changes in men and women" by Jessica McFarlane, Carol Lynn Martin, and Tannis M. Williams, *Psychology of Women Quarterly, 12,* 1988. Reprinted by permission of Cambridge University Press / p. 193, Drawing by Lorenz/©1993 New Yorker Magazine, Inc. / p. 212, Reprinted with special permission of King Features Syndicate. / p. 223 (Fig. 6.4), Adapted from "Reinforcement schedules and behavior," from "Teaching machines" by B. F. Skinner, Scientific American, November 1961. Copyright © 1961 by Scientific American, Inc. All rights reserved. Reprinted with permission. / p. 225, Ira Wyman/Sygma / p. 231 (Fig. 6.5), From "Intrinsic motivation: How to turn play into

Author Index

Subject Index

Note: Page numbers in italics refer to illustrations.